Comprehensive
Clinical
Psychology

Comprehensive Clinical Psychology

Editors-in-Chief

Alan S. Bellack
The University of Maryland at Baltimore, MD, USA

Michel Hersen
Pacific University, Forest Grove, OR, USA

Volume 3

RESEARCH AND METHODS

Volume Editor

Nina R. Schooler
Hillside Hospital, Glen Oaks, NY, USA

1998

AN IMPRINT OF ELSEVIER SCIENCE

AMSTERDAM—LAUSANNE—NEW YORK—OXFORD—SHANNON—SINGAPORE—TOKYO

Elsevier Science Ltd., The Boulevard, Langford Lane, Kidlington, Oxford,
OX5 1GB, UK

First edition 1998

Library of Congress Cataloging-in-Publication Data
Comprehensive clinical psychology / editors-in-chief. Alan S. Bellack,
   Michel Hersen. —1st ed.
      p. cm.
      Includes indexes.
         Contents: v. 1. Foundations / volume editor, C. Eugene Walker —
      v. 2. Professional issues / volume editor, Arthur N. Wiens — v. 3.
      Research and Methods / volume editor, Nina R. Schooler — v. 4.
      Assessment / volume editor, Cecil R. Reynolds — v. 5. Children &
      adolescents / volume editor, Thomas Ollendick — v. 6. Adults / volume
      editor, Paul Salkovskis — v. 7. Clinical geropsychology / volume editor,
      Barry Edelstein — v. 8. Health psychology / volume editors, Derek W.
      Johnston and Marie Jonhston — v. 9. Applications in diverse
      populations / volume editor, Nirbhay N. Singh — v. 10. Sociocultural
      and individual differences / volume editor, Cynthia D. Belar — v. 11.
      Indexes.
         1. Clinical psychology. I. Bellack, Alan S. II. Hersen, Michel.
      [DNLM: 1. Psychology, Clinical. WM 105 C737 1998]
RC467.C597 1998
616.89--dc21
DNLM/DLC
for Library of Congress   97-50185
                                                                 CIP

British Library Cataloguing in Publication Data
A catalogue record for this book is available from the British Library.

ISBN 0-08-042707-3 (set : alk. paper)
ISBN 0-08-043142-9 (Volume 3)

Typeset by Bibliocraft, Dundee, UK.
Printed and bound in Great Britain by BPC Wheatons Ltd., Exeter, UK.

Contents

Introduction to *Comprehensive Clinical Psychology*

Co-Editors-in-Chief

Alan S. Bellack and Michel Hersen

Background

Clinical psychology is a relatively new field. While its roots can be traced back to at least the late nineteenth century, its evolution as a distinct academic discipline and profession dates only to the Second World War. The first 20 years of this postwar period saw steady, albeit nonspectacular, growth. Based substantially in the United States and Europe during this period, the study of clinical psychology developed as an alternative to medical school and psychiatry for many students interested in clinical service careers or the scientific study of human behavior. Postgraduate training was conducted exclusively in large university psychology departments within a strict scientist–practitioner model. The total number of Ph.D. candidates admitted to graduate school programs each year was relatively small; there were fewer than 50 accredited programs in the United States during much of this period, each admitting only 5–10 students. The number of new Ph.D.'s produced each year was substantially less, as many students failed to complete the rigorous scientific requirements of these elite programs. Career opportunities were similarly delimited, due in no small part to restraints on clinical practice imposed by psychiatrists and other physicians. The dominant form of psychotherapy was psychoanalysis, and psychologists were either excluded from psychoanalytic institutes or trained only as lay analysts who were proscribed from clinical practice. Few jurisdictions awarded licenses for independent practice, and psychologists generally were not reimbursed for their activities unless they worked under the direction of a physician. A sizable minority of clinical psychologists followed their mentors into university positions, teaching and conducting research. The majority, who were more interested in clinical service, opted for work in large psychiatric or Veterans Administration hospitals, where the modal activity was psychological testing; verbal psychotherapy was provided at the discretion of medical supervisors. A gradually increasing number of psychologists elected to be in private practice, where there was a greater professional autonomy. Medical hegemony over services for psychiatric disorders was even greater in Europe and Latin America.

The last 30 years has witnessed a massive change in the profession, stimulated by a number of scientific, clinical, and economic factors. Psychoanalysis gradually fell out of favor due to a dearth of data on its effectiveness and a desire for shorter term treatments that were not the primary purview of psychiatrists. First, client-centered therapy and then behavior therapy emerged as brief, highly effective alternatives. The former was entirely a product of clinical psychology, and was the intellectual and technical forebear of the current mandate for empirical evaluation of psychotherapies.

Carl Rogers, his colleagues, and students were the first to demonstrate the feasibility of careful, objective evaluation of the therapy process as well as outcome. While behavior therapy owes much of its legacy to psychiatrists such as Joseph Wolpe, it was substantially a product of academic psychologists searching for an approach with a strong scientific underpinning (in this case learning theory) that could be subjected to rigorous scientific scrutiny. Early behavior therapy emerged simultaneously in the UK and the US: in the UK psychologists such as Hans Eysenck based their work on Pavlov and classical conditioning, while in the US researchers were following Skinner and operant conditioning theories. The two schools merged with cognitive therapy, developed largely by Beck and Ellis through the 1960s, when the limitations of behavior therapy in isolation became apparent, particulary with depressed patients, and cognitive-behavior therapy is now widely practised.

Behavior therapy and cognitive-behavior therapy have not only proven themselves to be effective with a broad array of disorders, they have since been shown to be very successful alternatives to pharmacotherapy as well. Notably, behavior therapy was able to produce significant changes in populations that had previously been warehoused as untreatable, including people with physical and developmental disabilities and schizophrenia. Many of the most important contributions to the behavior therapies came from the UK, The Netherlands, South Africa, Australia, and Scandinavia, providing a tremendous stimulus for the development of clinical psychology globally. The availability of cost-effective, scientifically sound nonmedical treatments has decreased the medical monopoly of psychiatric/mental health services around the world and fostered the evolution of clinical psychology as a legally sanctioned helping profession, as well as a prestigious scientific discipline.

Scientific advances in our understanding of the brain and the role of psychosocial factors in physical health and illness have led to the development of two other rapidly growing subspecialties of clinical psychology: neuropsychology and health psychology. Novel assessment and treatment technologies in these two areas have created professional opportunities for clinical psychologists in medical schools, general medical hospitals, and other nonpsychiatric settings. Clinical psychologists can now be found conducting research and providing services in departments of neurology and neurosurgery, medicine, cardiac surgery, pediatrics, anesthesiology, oncology, and other medical specialty areas, as well as in the traditional psychiatric settings. They increasingly serve as directors of governmental agencies and service facilities. They comprise a large percentage of research grant recipients in the US, Canada, and the UK, and sit on prestigious government and foundation review boards. In fact the field has earned sufficient public recognition that it now has the somewhat dubious distinction of having clinical psychologists as lead characters on television shows and in cinema.

Stimulated, in part, by these exciting developments in scientific progress and clinical creativity, the field has grown geometrically in the past two decades. Psychology is now the second leading undergraduate major in the US and is increasingly popular elsewhere in the world as well. There are now more than 175 doctoral programs in the United States, each admitting many more students per annum than the 5–10 that has been typical of traditional scientist–practitioner Ph.D. programs over the past 25 years. Some of these schools have entering classes as large as 200 per year. Moreover, along with the professional school movement, which began in the 1970s, a new degree, the Psy.D. (or Doctorate in Psychology), is regularly being offered as an alternative to the Ph.D. Basically a professional rather than an academic degree, the Psy.D. is reflective of the local practitioner–scientist model rather than the scientist–practitioner.

Yet another trend in the field is the proliferation of master's level psychologists, specifically trained to carry out some of the more mundane functions formerly implemented by doctoral level psychologists. Indeed, each year in the United States alone 10 000 new master's level psychologists graduate from university programs. The financial and programmatic implication of such large numbers is obvious.

Statistics are not readily available about the size of the profession in all regions of the globe, but anecdotal evidence supports the hypothesis that the field is growing worldwide. As previously indicated, behavioral and cognitive-behavioral therapies owe a substantial debt to scientists and clinicians from Europe, Australia, and South Africa. There are now enough cognitive-behavior therapists to support national societies in most Western European countries, as well as Asia, Australia, and Latin America. Many of the most important developments in the psychosocial treatment of severe and persistent mental illness in the last decade have come from the United Kingdom, Australia, Switzerland, and Germany. Psychologists in Scandinavia, the United Kingdom, and the Netherlands have played a central role in the development of cognitive-behavioral treatments for anxiety and depression, and there have also been notable contributions from these regions to health psychology. As the hold of psychoanalytic therapies on psychiatric treatment in Europe continues its inevitable decline, there will be increasing opportunities for clinical psychologists to provide shorter term behavioral and cognitive-behavioral treatments. In addition, exciting developments are also emerging from Japan, China, and other countries in the Pacific rim. It seems likely that the global influence of regional approaches and thinking will lead to a more multicultural and universal psychology than has been the case in the past.

The scientific and clinical literatures have burgeoned along with the number of clinical psychologists in the world. This has been an era of rapid growth of knowledge and increasing specialization. General topics, such as psychological assessment, clinical child psychology, and psychotherapy, that used to merit only one or two graduate courses to establish expertise, have expanded and are subdivided to the extent that circumscribed specialty areas, such as neuropsychology, geropsychology, behavioral pediatrics, or cognitive-behavior therapy for depression can each require postdoctoral training. Consequently, hundreds of undergraduate, graduate, and professional level texts are published each year. Specialty journals abound. Where a few key generalist journals such as the *Journal of Consulting and Clinical Psychology* used to represent the entire field, each subdiscipline now has multiple journals, and there are both national journals (e.g., the *British Journal of Clinical Psychology*, the *British Journal of Health Psychology*, the *Australian Journal of Cognitive and Behavioral Therapy*) and journals representing specific populations or disorders (e.g., *Addictive Behaviors*, *Journal of Family Violence*, *Journal of Clinical Geropsychology*), or domains of practice (e.g., *Journal of Clinical Psychology in Medical Setting*). Specialization has made it difficult for professionals to keep abreast of developments within their immediate areas of expertise, and impossible for them to be conversant with the literature in other areas. Moreover, given the plethora of choices, it is also virtually impossible for either students or professionals to know where to find the most accurate, up-to-date information in most areas.

The combination of a large and increasing number of students and professionals, and rapidly growing scientific and clinical literature, makes this a particularly appropriate time for *Comprehensive Clinical Psychology*. This multivolume work encompasses the entire field, and represents a single source of information on the scientific status of clinical psychology and its subspecialties, on theory, and on clinical techniques. The work covers the history of the field, and current thinking about training, professional standards and practices, and sociocultural factors in mental health and illness.

Genesis of Comprehensive Clinical Psychology

Following preliminary conceptual discussions between Elsevier Science and Alan S. Bellack at several international conferences in 1994, Michel Hersen was asked to join as Co-Editor-in-Chief. The first official planning meeting for the project took place in June 1995. In addition to Elsevier Science staff, Alan S. Bellack and Michel Hersen invited Tom Ollendick, Nina Schooler, and Warren Tryon to serve as consultants. At that meeting, the philosophical and international scope of the project was agreed upon and established, with the scientific underpinnings of the field identified as the model. The objective here was to ensure that chapters reflect our core knowledge and that the material stand the test of time.

At that meeting, we also underscored that since clinical psychology was now an international discipline, the work should reflect contributions at the cross-cultural level, with chapters solicited from eminent psychologists worldwide. Although it was acknowledged that the United States was in the forefront of the field, the work could not simply represent the American perspective but to the extent possible would represent diversity at its best. Consistent with the international perspective, at the initial planning meeting, the importance of having an Honorary International Editorial Advisory Board comprised of international representatives was acknowledged, and the 10 specific volumes to comprise *Comprehensive Clinical Psychology* were identified. Preliminary outlines for each volume were developed and volumes editors were considered.

The international perspective was to be reflected at a tripartite level. First, diversity among editors and contributors for their respective volumes was selected as a goal. Second, chapters in each volume were designed to reflect diversity by providing the reader with worldwide examples, not simply the Anglo-Saxon view. Of course, where basic facts and principles were the same, there was no need to present regional diversity. Third, and related to the first two parts, the Honorary International Editorial Advisory Board provided us with an international perspective on overall organization and specifics for the individual volumes.

Between June and October 1995, Alan S. Bellack and Michel Hersen, in consultation with Elsevier Science, invited the ten volume editors to assume their positions, and a meeting of the Editors-in-Chief, the ten volume editors (C. Eugene Walker, Arthur N. Wiens, Nina R. Schooler, Cecil R. Reynolds, Thomas Ollendick, Paul Salkovskis, Barry Edelstein, Marie Johnston and Derek W. Johnston, Nirbhay N. Singh, and Cynthia D. Belar), and Elsevier Science staff was convened in October of that year. At that meeting, each of the volume editors presented his or her conception of the relevant volume, and the nature of coverage and particular contributors was discussed at length. Most of all the philosophical underpinnings of the work were stressed so as to insure intervolume consistency.

Subsequent to the October 1995 meeting, the enormous work to bring this project to fruition began, with potential authors invited to contribute, manuscripts reviewed, and then edited. Were it not for the wonders of electronic communication, a project of this scope would not have been possible, especially given the international aspects involved. A lengthy series of checks and balances was instituted to guarantee the quality and excellence of each contribution. The volume editor first approved each contributor's chapter outline, followed by editing and approval of the text. This process frequently required several revisions. The Co-Editor-in-Chief then reviewed each chapter for scope, level, and overlap, but only after the volume editor had first verified the accuracy of references cited. After the Co-Editor-in-Chief's labors, the manuscript was reviewed by Elsevier staff for format, writing style, reference checking, and other technical issues.

Aims and Scope

The final organization and contents of the work evolved over a series of discussions between the Editors-in-Chief, the volume editors, and Elsevier Science. It was comparatively easy to select the primary domains that needed to be covered: history, treatment, assessment, research, training, and professional issues. It was also comparatively easy to identify the first two-thirds, or so, of specific topics that required chapter-length coverage: treatment of the primary *DSM/ICD* disorders, basic research strategies, standard assessment techniques, etc. However, organizing the vast set of requisite topics into coherent volumes, determining which topics warranted independent chapters, and assigning page limits to individual chapters proved to be daunting. Two broad organizational themes immediately suggested themselves: a focus on core themes or techniques across populations vs. integrated coverage of populations. For example, the former would have entailed volumes on treatment modalities, such as behavior therapy, as they are applied to children and adults, while the latter would call for separate volumes on children and adults that covered diverse approaches. To complicate matters, some topics, such as Research Methods and Professional Issues, do not lend themselves to breakdown by population, and others, such as Behavioral Medicine, do not lend themselves to a breakdown by themes or techniques. Volume length was also an important factor, making some content-based solutions less practical than others. For example, we determined that treatment should receive more attention than assessment; a strict population-based solution would have led to separate short volumes on assessment of adults and children. Ultimately, we opted for an organizational structure that balanced practical considerations with our collective prediction about how the individual volumes would be used. While it was different earlier in the development of the field, we believe that the current trend is for people to be more organized around populations than techniques. Hence, more people are likely to pick up and cross-reference a single volume on children or the elderly than a volume on Behavior Therapy. Our strategy for identifying chapter length topics and associated page limits is more difficult to explain. Once again, we relied on our collective judgement, honed by negotiation. In rough order, priority was given to topics that had established empirical literatures, that were deemed to be "important," that had broad interest, and that were likely to be at least as important in the next decade. Page limits were determined substantially by estimates of the first two criteria. We began with an overall target for the entire work and minimums and maximums for volumes, and then worked backwards to divide up the allotted pages among the chapters designated for each volume. Given that no scheme will please everyone, we are confident that the organization of the work adequately reflects the field now and in the foreseeable future.

Under the careful aegis of the outstanding group of experts comprising the Honorary International Editorial Advisory Board, 10 leading international scholars were selected to edit the 10 specific volumes.

Volume 1 (Foundations), edited by C. Eugene Walker, provides a complete overview of the basic foundations of clinical psychology, with special emphasis on the relationship between clinical psychology and other fields of science. Beginning with a brief history of clinical psychology, as well as a look at its current scientific status, this informative volume covers such topics as the biological bases of clinical psychology, elucidating research in genetics, psychobiology, psychopharmacology, and the use of animal models in human mental health problems; clinical psychology in the behavioral sciences, including anthropology, epidemiology, sociology, and research psychology; and the major systems and theories that are used in clinical psychology. The volume also describes various techniques for library research and information retrieval in psychology.

Volume 2 (Professional Issues), edited by Arthur W. Wiens, focuses on the professional, legal, and ethical issues that are relevant to clinical psychology. The volume addresses the various educational and training programs available, such as doctoral study, internship training, and postdoctoral residency programs, and reviews the accreditation of these programs. Also highlighted are the various international government guidelines for registration, certification, and licensing, including a discussion of the advantages of specialty recognition and practice certificates. The volume concludes with a look at ethical and legal guidelines in the management of clinical psychology practices, national healthcare policies, and advocacy efforts for government support for practitioners.

Volume 3 (Research and Methods), edited by Nina R. Schooler, explores the function of research in clinical psychology. The volume begins with an in-depth look at research approaches, including the use of descriptive studies, single case designs, observational methods, and other methods of analysis. The volume goes on to explore a broad range of topics that have been the focus of research, such as test development and validation, personality assessment, clinical interventions, and service evaluations and outcomes. Finally, various statistical techniques are reviewed, including descriptive and inferential statistics, factor analysis, and sampling and generalizability.

Volume 4 (Assessment), edited by Cecil R. Reynolds, provides valuable information on the development and role of assessment in clinical practice, analyzing such topics as psychometrics; taxonomic, functional, and actuarial approaches to diagnosis; and specific instruments, techniques, and procedures. Chapters also review the range of assessment techniques and procedures used in clinical practice, with emphasis on intelligence, neuropsychological, personality, projective, computer-assisted, therapeutic, and forensic assessment. The volume concludes with a review of legal guidelines and regulations in the use of psychological testing.

Volume 5 (Children & Adolescents: Clinical Formulation & Treatment), edited by Thomas Ollendick, draws on the experience and research of leading scientists and clinicians from Australia, Canada, Israel, the United Kingdom, and the United States to present state-of-the-art information on all aspects of child psychology and psychiatry, with special attention given to the psychopathology, assessment, treatment, and prevention of childhood behavioral disorders. The volume highlights the developmental-contextual framework used in the clinical formulation of these disorders, as well as process and outcome issues in treatment. Various theoretical perspectives are also reviewed, including applied behavior analysis, family systems therapy, play therapy, and pharmacologic therapy. In the final section, all of the major childhood disorders found in the *DSM* and *ICD* are described, with information on their prevalence, etiology, assessment, and treatment. This section also analyzes the empirical status of the various therapies used for treatment of childhood disorders.

Volume 6 (Adults: Clinical Formulation & Treatment), edited by Paul Salkovskis, provides valuable insights into the basis of the psychological theories and interventions used for behavioral and emotional problems and reviews how to integrate clinical skills with these theories. Various treatment approaches are addressed, such as cognitive therapy, family therapy, and Humanistic/Rogerian/Gestalt approaches, as well as the issues related to treatments, including stress management, arousal reduction methods, suicidal behavior, and specific issues in working with groups. The final section details specific problem areas and disorders, ranging from such universally recognized problems as gambling and substance abuse to more specific disorders such as post-traumatic stress, depression, obsessive-compulsive, and the various phobias. Each chapter in the volume emphasizes approaches that have an empirical basis.

Volume 7 (Clinical Geropsychology), edited by Barry Edelstein, addresses the emerging field of clinical psychology in the aging population. The volume begins with a review of this area of research, presenting important epidemiological information. The volume then offers a detailed look at issues that range from analyzing physiological and cognitive aspects to cognitive changes and specific neurological disorders common among older adults. Specific topics covered include sexuality, bereavement, anxiety, substance abuse, and schizophrenia. Each chapter presents a summary of clinical research and its practical application. Voids in the knowledge base are also noted, along with recommendations for the direction of future investigations. The volume also addresses management problems, such as incontinence, wandering, and aggressive behavior, and reviews the various mental healthcare systems available in different countries.

Volume 8 (Health Psychology), edited by Derek W. Johnston and Marie Johnston, provides a comprehensive overview of the development and application of clinical health psychology. Beginning with a discussion of training, assessment, and measurement issues, this volume analyzes the key behaviors that either affect or are related to health. Topics covered include stress and disease, the experience of illness, and behavior that can affect the neuroendocrine, cardiovascular, and immune systems. The volume also provides a detailed analysis of specific clinical problems and their psychological aspects and interventions. These include cancer, diabetes, epilepsy, disfigurement, and smoking.

Volume 9 (Applications in Diverse Populations), edited by Nirbhay N. Singh, covers the broad spectrum of diverse issues that clinical psychologists typically face in their work. Four sections outline the various psychological aspects found in different populations, as well as methods for assessment, diagnostic information, and interventions useful with these different groups. Section I focuses on select child, adolescent, and adult populations, including those with developmental disorders, learning disabilities, and mental retardation. Section II is devoted to various types of families and their issues, including families of individuals with HIV or AIDS, families of alcoholics, and families of children with serious emotional disturbances. Section III covers victims of violence and abuse, including child sexual abuse. Section IV examines perpetrators of violence and abuse, including sex offenders and issues of domestic violence.

Volume 10 (Sociocultural and Individual Differences), edited by Cynthia D. Belar, covers cross-cultural psychopathology and interventions. Chapters examine such select topics as gender, sexual orientation, socioeconomic status, religions, and training for clinical psychologists. The volume also provides valuable insights into the use of clinical psychology in different parts of the world, as well as personality assessment across international settings.

Given the scope and detail of *Comprehensive Clinical Psychology*, Volume 11 is devoted to: (i) a Name Index, (ii) a Subject Index, (iii) a List of Contributors, and (iv) a list of the Contents of All Volumes. The Name Index is an accumulation of all the authors who are cited in text in the reference sections throughout the entire work. The Subject Index, consisting of more than 40 000 entries, is a consolidation of all the individual volume subject indexes. It is presented in word-by-word alphabetical sequence with a maximum of three levels of heading. Terminology in the index is based on standard internationally recognized sources. Cross-references are provided to assist the user to locate preferred terms and terms of related interest.

Acknowledgments

To produce a tome of this magnitude requires an enormous number of individuals with unique talents working in concert. To begin with, we applaud the herculean efforts of our driving force and friend at Elsevier Science, Barbara Barrett. We also gratefully acknowledge the efforts of two other publishing editors at Elsevier Science, Susan Hanscom and David Hoole, who provided guidance and encouragement along the way. We are particularly thankful for the exceptionally hard work of Angela Greenwell and her staff in Oxford, who made sure that all tasks were implemented reasonably on time and who orchestrated the day-to-day management of this huge undertaking. Next, we thank our eminent volume editors, who had the difficult job of soliciting, tracking, and editing manuscripts for their respective volumes. Similarly, we thank the Honorary International Editorial Advisory Board for their excellent input in developing the outline for the work and suggestions as to potential international contributors. Of course, we owe a great deal to the individual contributors who agreed to share their expertise with us in a timely fashion. Finally, we are most appreciative of our own editorial assistants, Sonia McQuarters and Burt G. Bolton, who repeatedly have provided us with the kind of support that makes all of this a possibility.

HONORARY INTERNATIONAL EDITORIAL ADVISORY BOARD

Preface

Why is there a volume in *Comprehensive Clinical Psychology* specifically titled *Research and Methods* when much of the material in the other volumes draws on the research base of the field? The Editors-in-Chief believe that the value of research to the field justifies the prominence of a volume that directly addresses research methodologies rather than allowing readers to recognize the importance of research by reading of its results in all the volumes of this series. Volume 3 builds on Volume 1, *Foundations*, which provides the linkage of clinical psychology to other fields in psychology and other behavioral sciences. The present volume addresses research methods and areas that are core to clinical psychology but also attempts to go beyond the traditional boundaries of the field by introducing methods and techniques that historically have not been core to the field. Clinical psychological research today utilizes a broad array of methods that have evolved from simple description and use of correlational approaches to complex experimental designs and statistical techniques.

Traditionally, training in research has had a prominent role in the education that clinical psychologists receive and represents the scientist–practitioner model of the field. That model was developed for the training of clinical psychologists but it can be extended to a view of the field. A basic tenet of the scientist–practitioner model is that the interaction between research and clinical practice serves to enhance the quality of practice and to generate research that addresses questions that are relevant to practice. Much of clinical practice is grounded in research findings and as a result, many established clinical conventions have their roots in research.

One goal of this volume is to examine the research base of clinical psychology and to provide the reader with a critical review and a framework for examining the research literature in a given area. Extensive citations should equip the reader to go beyond the chapters to the research literature. Although the volume is not intended to be a research primer, teachers and students may find it useful in a variety of courses. A further goal of this volume is to increase the familiarity of clinical psychologists with the wide range and scope of contemporary research methodologies. To serve this goal, a number of chapter authors do not have their primary focus in clinical psychology research but were chosen in the hope that their perspectives would further broaden the field.

The volume is divided into three complementary sections. The first section, Chapters 1–6, considers research strategies that have been applied in clinical psychology or that may be useful to the field. The second section, Chapters 7–11, reviews a number of specific content areas or themes within clinical psychology that have been important subjects of research attention. The third section, Chapters 12–15, addresses statistical methodology.

Chapter authors in the first section have been asked to address the kinds of questions to which particular methods are pertinent and to provide examples of studies that have used a given method appropriately and with profit. The basic premise of this section is that no one research methodology fits all research questions.

Chapter 1, *Observational Methods*, by Frank Floyd and colleagues considers the extension of the common human propensity to observe others into a formal research tool that can provide data about a wide range of problems that clinical psychology addresses. Among other topics, the authors contrast the advantages and disadvantages of observation in natural and laboratory environments, the development of coding schemes and issues in training observers and maintaining reliability. The authors pay particular attention to the many decisions that observational researchers make that can influence the outcome of their research and caution readers to be attentive to the consequences of such decisions.

In Chapter 2, *Single Case Experimental Designs: Clinical Research and Practice*, Steven Hayes and John Blackledge consider the wide variety of single case experimental designs (SCEDs) or time series studies. They identify the advantages and disadvantages of such designs and note that they came into wide use with the development and popularization of behavioral approaches in clinical treatment. They describe the wide range of variants of SCEDs and consider the circumstances under which each may be appropriate. They emphasize the fact that SCEDs represent a potentially important link between clinical practice and clinical science because the methods may be used by clinicians to inform clinical decision making at the same time as they generate scientifically valid data.

Chapter 3, *Group Comparisons: Randomized Designs,* by Nina Schooler reviews the classical experimental designs that have been used to study psychological treatments. She discusses the ethical requirements for such experiments. She provides detailed descriptions of a number of common experimental designs and uses examples of studies that have used these designs to clarify their strengths and weaknesses. She pays particular attention to the methodological requirements of studies that compare psychological and pharmacological treatments.

Chapter 4, *Multiple Group Comparisons: Quasi-experimental Designs,* by Hans-Christian Waldmann and Franz Petermann addresses the distinction between true or randomized experiments and "quasi"-experimental designs. The authors consider the critical elements in quasi-experimental designs. Lacking randomization as a control, other elements assume great importance such as pretests, definition of comparison groups and careful measurement of treatment effects.

In Chapter 5, *Epidemiological Methods,* William Eaton addresses the place of these methods in clinical psychology research. He reminds the reader that epidemiology focuses on populations, whereas clinical psychology more traditionally focuses on individual differences. Issues of sampling are considered. He describes a number of epidemiological methods and pays attention to the various sources of bias in such studies—contrasting these biases with those seen in psychological studies.

In Chapter 6, *Qualitative and Discourse Analysis,* Jonathan Potter addresses the revival of interest in qualitative analysis since the late 1980s and suggests that such methods offer interesting possibilities for understanding human behavior in clinical settings. He selects three prominent and modern qualitative methods for consideration. Grounded theory, participant observation, and the analysis of discourses are reviewed. They each represent a precise and distinctive methodology that has the ability to provide novel perspectives to clinical psychological problems. For example, all these methods can be applied to the transactions in therapeutic encounters.

Section II of the volume, Chapters 7–11, addresses a number of the research themes in clinical psychology. These are areas that are the focus of research. Each of these chapters provides a summary of the research base in a field, but equally importantly, the authors emphasize the challenges that are waiting for researchers to address—the questions that are unanswered and the methodological problems that need to be considered.

In Chapter 7, *Personality Assessment,* Thomas Widiger and Kimberly Saylor focus on the methods that have been used. Thus, they examine self-report inventories, semistructured interviews and projective techniques. They present examples of each methodology and address strengths and weaknesses and potential research opportunities. They emphasize the importance of the study of personality to the understanding of psychopathology and note that convergence of findings across methods of personality assessment is particularly compelling.

In Chapter 8, *Assessment of Psychopathology: Nosology and Etiology,* Nader Amir and Catherine Feuer discuss issues of classification in mental illness and identify measures that have been developed for clinical assessment. They focus on definitions of psychopathology and the problem that true co-occurrence of mental disorders represents for taxonomies of disorder. They review models of taxonomy including dimensional, categorical, and prototypic models and the advantages and disadvantages of each in advancing understanding the range of psychopathology. They point to a promising recent development which is the use of etiological factors in the diagnosis.

Chapter 9, *Intervention Research: Development and Manualization,* by John Clarkin addresses the role of treatment manuals in research on the efficacy and effectiveness of psychological interventions. He points to the important role of treatment manuals in providing a potential bridge between intervention research and practice and discusses the advantages and disadvantages of manualization. The chapter reviews the current standards against which treatment manuals may be evaluated and examines several treatment manuals in detail to illustrate the current state of the art in manualization of psychotherapies. He concludes by assessing the kinds of developments that may be anticipated in manual development and the role of such manuals in future research.

Chapter 10, *Internal and External Validity of Intervention Studies,* by Karla Moras reviews the seminal concepts of internal and external validity that have influenced the field of clinical psychology for the past 35 years. She analyzes methods for enhancing validity in terms of research design, research conduct and statistical approaches. She identifies the potential transformation of the field from viewing internal and external validity as goals that represent research "trade-offs" to a model that seeks to enhance both. Toward that goal she reviews recent studies that have attempted to blend efficacy and effectiveness research seeking high internal and external validity.

Chapter 11, *Mental Health Services Research,* by William Hargreaves and colleagues begins precisely where Chapter 10 finished. They provide a definition of mental health services research and define the contrast between efficacy and three specific types of effectiveness or services research: cost-outcome, service system, and policy. They offer a model of services research as a nested system of causal processes, provide definitions, and contrast the features of each type of research so that the distinctive contributions of each are highlighted. The potential causal paths between various domains of effects are noted and specific examples of each type of research are reviewed.

The final section of Volume 3 comprises four chapters that address statistical methods and approaches. Topics considered in this section have all been raised in the context of the earlier chapters in the volume. These chapters provide the reader with a detailed and critical evaluation. The scope of these chapters reflects the evolution of statistical methods from simple correlational approaches to increasingly sophisticated approaches that allow complex clinical questions to be addressed and answered.

Chapter 12, *Descriptive and Inferential Statistics*, by Andrew Leon begins by reminding the reader that clinical psychological research is conducted to understand individual differences and provides a review of methods for description—when the goal is simply to characterize the subjects studied; and for inference—when the goal is to generalize from the subjects studied to a broader population of subjects. The chapter moves logically from description to inference, always providing the rationale for particular statistical tests discussed, the hypothesis testing steps involved, and the implications of decisions. He concludes by emphasizing two important points: the value of description to insure adequate familiarity with the characteristics of a data set even if the ultimate goal of the research is inference; and the caution that statistical significance should be examined against the standard of clinical meaning or relevance.

The goal of Chapter 13, *Latent Variables, Factor Analysis, and Causal Modeling*, by Brian Everitt is to review methods for evaluation of multivariate data. The methods discussed are useful when more than a single variable is observed for each subject and the goal is to understand the relationships among the variables or to test hypotheses about how they are linked. The concept of latent variables is used to guide the discussion of exploratory factor analysis, confirmatory factor analysis, and the testing of causal models using structural equation modeling.

In Chapter 14, *The Shift From Significance Testing to Effect Size Estimation*, Michael Borenstein tackles the important question of clinical significance of findings. He presents in detail the argument raised in Chapter 12 that statistical significance defines whether or not there is an effect but does not address the question of the magnitude of a treatment effect. Methods for measuring effect size address the question directly. The chapter introduces the concept of statistical power and the logic of power analysis in the planning of a research study. It then goes on to consider ways in which statistical significance and p values can be misinterpreted and concludes with a discussion of effect size estimation in the planning and reporting of clinical research.

The final chapter, Chapter 15, *Meta-analytic Research Synthesis*, by Sharon Kramer and Robert Rosenthal addresses the important question of cumulative knowledge. Meta-analysis provides quantitative techniques for combining research studies that go beyond the traditional "review of the literature." As in Chapter 14, the concept of effect size is central to the logic of meta-analysis. Methods are described for carrying out meta-analyses to address a number of specific questions that require combing results from more than one study. Finally, the authors address the limitations of meta-analysis and suggest methods for addressing specific problems.

Thus, Volume 3 has addressed a range of research concerns ranging from study designs and research topics through statistical methods. Concluding with a chapter on meta-analysis sets the stage for the research cycle to resume. It can be argued that a meta-analysis of the relevant literature should be the necessary precondition for the next research study.

Contributors to Volume 3

Dr. N. Amir
Department of Psychology, University of Georgia, Athens, GA 30602-3013, USA

Professor D. H. Baucom
Department of Psychology, CB#3270, Davie Hall, University of North Carolina, Chapel Hill,
NC 27599-3270, USA

Dr. J. T. Blackledge
Department of Psychology, College of Arts and Science, University of Nevada, Reno,
NV 89557-0062, USA

Dr. M. Borenstein
Hillside Hospital, Glen Oaks, NY 11004, USA
1421 Hudson Road, Teaneck, NJ 07666, USA

Dr. R. A. Catalano
School of Public Health, 413 Warren Hall, University of California, Berkeley, CA 94720, USA

Dr. J. F. Clarkin
New York Hospital, Westchester Division, 21 Bloomingdale Road, White Plains, NY 10605, USA

Dr. B. J. Cuffel
Research & Evaluation, United Behavioral Health, 425 Market Street, 27th Floor, San Francisco,
CA 94105, USA

Dr. W. W. Eaton
Department of Mental Hygiene, School of Public Health, Johns Hopkins University, 624 North
Broadway, Baltimore, MD 21205, USA

Professor B. S. Everitt
Department of Biostatistics and Computing, Institute of Psychiatry, De Crespigny Park,
Denmark Hill, London, SE5 8AF, UK

Dr. C. A. Feuer
Center for Trauma Recovery, University of Missouri at St. Louis, 8001 Natural Bridge Road,
St. Louis, MO 63121, USA

Dr. F. J. Floyd
Department of Psychology, CB#3270, Davie Hall, University of North Carolina, Chapel Hill,
NC 27599-3270, USA

Dr. J. J. Godfrey
Department of Psychology, CB#3270, Davie Hall, University of North Carolina, Chapel Hill,
NC 27599-3270, USA

Dr. W. Hargreaves
Department of Psychiatry, San Francisco General Hospital, 1001 Potrero Avenue, Suite 2100,
San Francisco, CA 94110, USA
330 Laurel Way, Mill Valley, CA 94941-4046, USA

Professor S. C. Hayes
Department of Psychology, College of Arts and Science, University of Nevada, Reno,
NV 89557-0062, USA

Dr. T.-W. Hu
School of Public Health, 412 Warren Hall, University of California, Berkeley, CA 94720, USA

Dr. S. H. Kramer
Department of Psychology, Harvard University, William James Hall, 33 Kirkland Street,
Cambridge, MA 02138, USA

Professor A. C. Leon
Department of Psychiatry, Cornell University Medical College, Box 147, 525 East 68th Street,
New York City, NY 10021, USA

Professor K. Moras
Department of Psychiatry, Center for Psychotherapy Research, University of Pennsylvania Health
System, 3600 Market Street, 7th Floor, Philadelphia, PA 19104, USA

Dr. C. Palmer
Department of Psychology, CB#3270, Davie Hall, University of North Carolina, Chapel Hill,
NC 27599-3270, USA

Professor F. Petermann
Zentrum für Rehabilitationsforschung, Universität Bremen, Grazer Straße 6,
28359 Bremen, Germany

Professor J. A. Potter
Discourse and Rhetoric Group, Department of Social Sciences, Loughborough University,
Loughborough, Leicestershire, LE11 3TU, UK

Dr. R. Rosenthal
Department of Psychology, Harvard University, William James Hall, 33 Kirkland Street,
Cambridge, MA 02138, USA

Mr. K. I. Saylor
Department of Psychology, University of Kentucky, College of Arts and Sciences,
115 Kastle Hall, Lexington, KY 40506-0044, USA

Professor N. R. Schooler
Psychiatry Research, Hillside Hospital, Glen Oaks, NY 11004, USA

Dr. H.-C. Waldmann
Zentrum für Rehabilitationsforschung, Universität Bremen, Grazer Straße 6, 28359 Bremen,
Germany

Dr. T. A. Widiger
Department of Psychology, University of Kentucky, College of Arts and Sciences, 115 Kastle Hall,
Lexington, KY 40506-0044, USA

Volume Editors

Volume 1: Foundations
Professor C. Eugene Walker, *University of Oklahoma Health Sciences Center, Oklahoma City, OK, USA*

Volume 2: Professional Issues
Professor Arthur N. Wiens, *Oregon Health Sciences University, Portland, OR, USA*

Volume 3: Research and Methods
Professor Nina R. Schooler, *Hillside Hospital, Glen Oaks, NY, USA*

Volume 4: Assessment
Professor Cecil R. Reynolds, *Texas A&M University, College Station, TX, USA*

Volume 5: Children & Adolescents: Clinical Formulation & Treatment
Professor Thomas Ollendick, *Virginia Tech, Blacksburg, VA, USA*

Volume 6: Adults: Clinical Formulation & Treatment
Professor Paul Salkovskis, *University of Oxford, Warneford Hospital, UK*

Volume 7: Clinical Geropsychology
Professor Barry Edelstein, *West Virginia University, Morgantown, WV, USA*

Volume 8: Health Psychology
Professor Derek W. Johnston and Professor Marie Johnston, *University of St. Andrews, UK*

Volume 9: Applications in Diverse Populations
Dr Nirbhay N. Singh, *Virginia Commonwealth University, Richmond, VA, USA*

Volume 10: Sociocultural and Individual Differences
Professor Cynthia D. Belar, *University of Florida Health Sciences Center, Gainesville, FL, USA*

Volume 11: Indexes

3.01
Observational Methods

FRANK J. FLOYD, DONALD H. BAUCOM, JACOB J. GODFREY, and
CARLETON PALMER
University of North Carolina, Chapel Hill, NC, USA

3.01.1 INTRODUCTION

Behavioral observation is a commonplace practice in our daily lives. As social creatures and "informal scientists," we rely upon observations of behavior to understand current social experiences and predict future social events. In fact, direct observation of behavior is one of the most important strategies we use to process our social world. Thus, it is not surprising that the field of psychology also is drawn to behavioral observation as a research method for understanding human behavior. The current chapter will focus upon behavioral observation as a formal research tool. In this context, behavioral observation involves the systematic observation of specific domains of behavior such that the resulting descriptions of behavior are replicable. In order to accomplish this task, the ongoing stream of behavior must be coded or broken down into recordable units, and the criteria for the assignment of labels or for making evaluations must be objectified. These practices of specifying units of behavior and objectifying coding criteria are the key steps in translating informal behavioral observations into formal, scientific observations. As will be seen below, the challenge of employing behavioral observation in research settings involves the myriad of decisions that an investigator must make in this translation process from informal to formal observation.

3.01.2 HISTORICAL INFLUENCES ON BEHAVIORAL OBSERVATION

The development of behavioral observation methodology is attributable to two major sources, the science of human behavior and the clinical practice of behaviorally oriented interventions. The science of human behavior is often traced to Watson and his colleagues (e.g., Watson & Raynor, 1924), who developed sophisticated methods to observe the behavior of children. Several important features distinguish this approach from early research that also used the observation of human actions as data. Most notably, unlike earlier trait-based researchers who measured behavior to make inferences about internal causes (e.g., Binet, Galton), the behavior itself is the focus of study. The approach also emphasizes direct observation in naturalistic settings as opposed to contrived responses that are elicited under artificial, controlled conditions. The further development of this approach was greatly stimulated by Skinner's (e.g., Skinner, 1938) theories that emphasized a focus on overt observable behavior, and by research manuals (e.g., Sidman, 1960) that further developed the rationale and methods for conducting and interpreting research on directly observed behaviors (Johnston & Pennypacker, 1993).

The second historical influence, behaviorally oriented clinical practice, also emphasizes direct observation under naturalistic circumstances. This approach defines pathology in terms of maladaptive behavior and then focuses on how environmental factors control maladaptive responding. Thus, behaviorally oriented clinicians conduct functional analyses to determine the environmental events that elicit and maintain maladaptive as opposed to adaptive behaviors, and they focus on observable behavior change as the criterion for treatment success. The need for precision both in measuring the behavior of interest and in identifying relevant environmental events has produced a body of scholarship on behavioral assessment as a clinical tool (e.g., Haynes, 1978; Hersen & Bellack, 1998), of which systematic behavioral observation is generally considered the hallmark strategy.

Ironically, Haynes (1998) notes that despite the theoretical importance of direct observation of behavior as a central feature of the behavioral approach, most research and clinical practice from a behaviorally oriented perspective relies on indirect measures such as self-report questionnaires. This increased reliance upon indirect assessment stems in part from the recognition that demonstrating improvement in subjective well-being is important, in addition to showing changes in overt behavior (e.g., Jacobson, 1985). Also, there has been an increasing emphasis on cognitions and other internal, nonobservable experiences (e.g., fear, dysphoria) as relevant focuses for behavioral intervention. However, Haynes suspects that most researchers and clinicians fail to conduct direct observations of relevant behaviors because they believe that the difficulty associated with conducting naturalistic observations outweighs the expected benefits in terms of incremental validity of the assessment.

Accordingly, recent advances in observational methodology and technology tend to come from fields of study and practice in which the veracity of self-reports is particularly suspect. For example, researchers and clinicians working with people who have mental retardation have produced important contributions in theory and methodology (e.g., Sackett, 1979b) as well as observational technology (Tapp & Walden, 1993). Similarly, research on infants and young children continues to emphasize direct observation over other types of measures (e.g., parent or teacher report).

Another more recent source for advances in behavioral observation is the growth of the marital and family systems perspective in clinical research and practice. This perspective emphasizes interpersonal exchanges as both focuses of interest in their own right and as contexts for individual functioning. The theoretical justification for this emphasis stems from family clinicians (e.g., Haley, 1971; Minuchin, 1974) who argue that couples, parent–child dyads, siblings, and larger family units are interacting subsystems that may cause and maintain pathological responding for individuals. In behavioral terms, marital and family interactions elicit and maintain maladaptive responding (e.g., Patterson, 1982). Because individuals are often biased reporters who have a limited perspective on the operation of the family system, observation of family interactions by outside observers is necessary for understanding these family processes. Thus, research and clinical work on marriage (e.g., Gottman, 1979), parenting (Patterson, 1982), and larger family units (e.g., Barton & Alexander, 1981) paved the way for many advances in observational technology and statistical approaches to analyzing observational data (e.g., Bakeman & Gottman, 1997).

3.01.3 THE PROS AND CONS OF BEHAVIORAL OBSERVATION

Behavioral observation is a fundamental form of measurement in clinical research and practice. The function of observation is the conversion of an ongoing, complex array of behavioral events into a complete and accurate set of data that can influence scientific or clinical decisions (Hawkins, 1979; Johnston & Pennypacker, 1993). As a measurement tool, behavioral observation is systematic; it is guided by a predetermined set of categories and criteria, and it is conducted by reliable observers (Bakeman & Gottman, 1997). In many instances, behavioral observation is the most objective form of measurement of relevant behaviors in relevant contexts because it is the most direct approach. Indeed, observations provide the yardstick against which other, more indirect measures, such as self-reports or rating scales, are evaluated.

In addition to providing direct, objective measurements, behavioral observation has several other strengths as an assessment tool. Hartmann and Wood (1990) note that (i) observation is flexible in providing various forms of data, such as counts of individual behaviors, or records of sequences of events; (ii) the measurements are relatively simple and noninferential, so that they are readily obtained by nonprofessional observers; and (iii) observations have a wide range of applicability across populations, behaviors, and settings. For clinical purposes, behavioral observation produces specificity in identifying problem behaviors that are targets for intervention, and in identifying causal and maintaining variables. Thus, it supports an idiographic, functional-analytic approach in which assessment leads to specific treatment goals. Furthermore, when observation is conducted in relevant settings, the data are criterion-referenced, so that

treatment effects are likely to generalize to the natural environment.

Despite these strengths, behavioral observation also has several limitations. First, the "objectivity" of behavioral observation is far from absolute. Even when relatively simple forms of behavior are observed, the observational system imposes considerable structure on how behaviors are segmented and labeled which substantially affects the nature of the data that are obtained. Second, behavioral observation is expensive and labor-intensive as compared to self-reports. Third, observation cannot access inner experiences that are unobservable. Finally, observations provide only a limited snapshot of behavior under a specific set of circumstances, which often is not helpful for generalizing to other situations. Ironically, this latter limitation reveals how sensitivity to the effects of context on behavior is both a strength and limitation of this approach. Although behavioral observation is the method of choice for examining functional relationships that elicit and maintain actions in a particular context, such observations may have limited utility for predicting responses in different contexts or circumstances.

In designing a research study, an investigator has a variety of strategies available for gathering data, including self- and other-report measures, behavioral observation, and physiological indices, and must decide which and how many of these strategies are appropriate. Whereas behavioral observation may be more direct than self-report measures in many cases, observation is only a reasonable candidate if the investigator wishes to assess how an individual or group actually behaves in a given context. Understanding the different types of information that are obtained with each measurement strategy is critical when interpreting findings.

For example, in prevention studies to assist couples getting married, investigators often teach communication skills. Then, to assess whether the couples have learned these skills, they might employ behavioral observations of the couples' interactions, as well as obtaining self-report measures from the couples about their communication. In reviewing the findings across such investigations, an interesting pattern of results seems to have evolved. In most instances, investigators have been able to demonstrate that, based on behavioral observation, couples change the ways that they communicate with each other when asked to do so in a laboratory setting. However, on self-report measures, these same couples often report that their communication has not changed (Van Widenfelt, Baucom, & Gordon, 1997). How can we interpret these seemingly discrepant findings? Some investigators would argue that the behavioral observation findings are in some sense more meaningful because they reflect how the couple actually behaves. The self-report findings are more suspect because self-reports are subject to memory distortion, might reflect the couples' overall feelings about their marriages, and are impacted by response sets or test-taking attitudes. However, the results could be interpreted in other ways as well. Perhaps the couples' behavior in the laboratory does not reflect how they actually behave at home, and this discrepancy is demonstrated by the self-report data. Conversely, the behavioral observation in the laboratory might reflect ongoing behavior at home, but this behavior does not impact the couples' experience of their overall communication. That is, perhaps the intervention did not target, or the behavioral coding system did not capture, the critical elements of communication that impact the couples' subjective experience of how they communicate with each other.

When behavior is observed, the investigator must make a series of decisions that can significantly impact the results and interpretation of the findings. First, the investigator must decide what behavior to observe. This will include a consideration of (i) the setting in which the behavior will be observed, (ii) the length of time for observing the behavior on a given occasion, (iii) the number of occasions on which behavior will be observed, (iv) who will observe the behavior, and (v) the actual behavior that will be the focus of the investigation. After or while the data are gathered, it is coded according to some scheme or coding system. Thus, in evaluating a child's social behavior, the investigator must decide whether nonverbal facial cues will be coded, what verbal categories will be included in the coding system, whether the type of interaction such as play or classroom activities will be coded, and so forth. Once the behavior is coded, then the investigator must decide how to analyze the data. Often due to limited amounts of data or for conceptual reasons, specific codes are collapsed into larger codes; for example, many specific codes may be summarized as positive or negative behaviors. Finally, the investigator must decide how to analyze the data obtained from the observational coding scheme. Is the investigator interested in the frequency of various behaviors that were observed, or is the investigator focused upon the pattern of interaction and the interdependencies among various behaviors? These different questions of interest to the investigator will result in different data analytic strategies that will provide different information about the observed behavior.

3.01.4 OBTAINING OBSERVATIONS OF BEHAVIOR

The first challenge for an investigator who wishes to employ behavioral observation is deciding upon what behavior to observe, which actually involves a series of decisions. In almost all instances, the investigator is interested in drawing conclusions about a class of behaviors. However, the investigator can observe only a sample of that behavior while wishing to draw broader conclusions. For example, a family researcher might be interested in family interaction patterns and decide to observe a family while they interact around a dinner table; however, the investigator is interested in much more than dinner-time behavior. Similarly, a marital investigator might be interested in couples' communication fairly broadly, but observes their interaction for only 10 minutes in a laboratory setting. Or someone studying children's peer relationships might observe playground behavior at school but not in the neighborhood. In all of these instances, the investigator must be concerned with whether the sample of behavior is a representative or reasonable sample of the broader domain to which the investigator wishes to generalize.

3.01.4.1 Selection of a Setting for Observing Behavior

One major decision that the investigator must make is the setting for observing the behavior. A major distinction in this regard is whether the behavior is to be observed in a controlled or laboratory setting or in a more natural setting. Both strategies have their advantages and disadvantages. Laboratory settings have the asset of being more controlled, such that the behavior of various participants can be observed under more standard conditions. For example, a variety of parents and children can be brought into a laboratory setting and observed in the same setting with the same task. This standardized environment can be of help when interpreting the findings because it can help to exclude some alternative explanations of the findings based around differences among settings. For example, observing families in their home settings might be greatly impacted by whether there are interruptions from the outside, whether the home is excessively hot or cold, and so forth.

However, typically the investigator is interested in much more than laboratory behavior and wishes to draw conclusions about behavior in other settings in the natural environment. Not only are natural environments typically less controlled, but often the effort and expense involved in observing behavior in its natural environment is prohibitive. Therefore, in deciding which setting to employ in observing behavior, the investigator must address the question of the extent to which behavior observed in one setting is generalizable to other settings. Understandably, there is no general answer to this question, and it must be evaluated for the particular settings and participants of interest.

As an example of how this issue of generalizability of behavior across settings has been explored, Gottman (1979) evaluated couples' conversations both in a laboratory setting and at home. His findings indicated that although there is a tendency for couples to be more negative with each other at home than in a laboratory setting, along with more reciprocation of negative emotion at home, the couples generally demonstrated similar interaction patterns across settings. Even so, this finding applies only to the types of interaction that Gottman assessed with his particular sample, employing a given coding system. This issue of generalizability across settings from control/research settings to natural settings applies equally to generalizability within one of these domains, as is discussed later. For example, dinner-time behavior among family members in their own home might or might not reflect family interaction later in the evening when homework or bedtime activities are the focus of the family's discussion. Thus, even within a natural environment, behavior in one aspect of that setting might not reflect behavior in other aspects of the natural family environment. Consequently, the investigator should give a great deal of thought to the setting in which the behavior is observed in order to increase the likelihood that the resulting behavioral observations access the behavior of interest.

3.01.4.2 Selection of Live vs. Recorded Observation

The setting is altered by the experimenter when coders or recording devices are introduced into the environment. The decision to have coders present for the actual observation session, or instead to record the session for later coding, raises two major concerns. The first concern is the reactivity of live observation and recording equipment. Although research on this topic has a long history (e.g., Haynes & Horn, 1982; Kazdin, 1982), the findings are mixed and do not specifically address the relative effects on reactivity of having an observer present as opposed to using video or audio recording equipment. Much research shows that the presence of a live observer alters the behavior of subjects (Kazdin, 1982), and this reactivity may be greatest in intervention studies when the demands to display desired behaviors are relatively clear (e.g., Harris & Lahey, 1986). However, research on the reactivity of recording equipment is less certain. For example, studies using repeated sampling with recording equipment fail to detect habituation effects (e.g., Christensen & Hazzard, 1983; Pett, Wampold, Vaughn-Cole, & East, 1992), which suggests that the equipment does not evoke an initial orienting response. Further, studies that compare different recording methods show that relatively obtrusive as opposed to unobtrusive procedures produce few differences in the quality of most behaviors observed, although positivity may be increased somewhat (e.g., Carpenter & Merkel, 1988; Jacob, Tennenbaum, Seilhamer, Bargiel, & Sharon, 1994). Of course, it is possible that the mere presence of any type of recording equipment (or knowledge that it is present although unseen) may cause sustained changes in behavior similar to the effects of self-monitoring or participant observation (e.g., Jarrett & Nelson, 1984). Nevertheless, this set of studies suggests that using recording equipment with no observer present may be a relatively less reactive approach than live observation of behavior.

Another concern about live as opposed to recorded behavior is the accuracy of coded data. In general, we assume that video and audio recorded data help to improve coder accuracy because they provide the capacity to play back events repeatedly that are ambiguous or happen quickly. However, recorded data also may interfere with a coder's ability to attend selectively to salient behavior, particularly in a setting in which there is considerable background activity and noise. For example, Fagot and Hagen (1988) found that coders evaluating children in a preschool setting were less reliable and tended to miss relevant events when they coded from videotape as opposed to live observations. In part, the superiority of recorded observations depends on the ability to obtain excellent recordings. In many circumstances, audio recordings are particularly problematic because behavior is ambiguous without visual cues. When audio recordings are transcribed, some investigators also include live observers who make notes about nonverbal events that are added to the transcript.

3.01.4.3 Selection of a "Task" or Stimulus Conditions for Observing Behavior

Not only must investigators decide upon the physical setting for observing behavior, but the task or stimulus conditions within which the behavior is to be observed also must be decided. On many occasions, investigators ask the participants to engage in a specific task; on other occasions, the investigator merely decides to observe the participants' behavior in a given setting at a given time. If a particular task or interaction is structured by the investigator, then the effects of this particular task on the interaction must be considered. This is of less importance if the investigator is interested only in this particular type of interaction. For example, if an investigator is interested only in how a family would make weekend plans as a full family if asked to do so, then asking the full family to have such a discussion is relatively straightforward. However, the investigator might be interested in some more general question having to do with how the family makes decisions. If this is the issue of interest, then the investigator must carefully consider, and hopefully assess, the impact of this particular task involving planning a weekend. Deciding how to spend the weekend might or might not generalize to how the family makes decisions in other domains, such as how to divide household chores. Indeed, asking the family to sit and have a discussion resulting in weekend plans might not mirror how decisions are made in the family at all. Perhaps the parents make such decisions, or perhaps these decisions occur over the course of a number of informal interactions with different persons present at different times. More generally, when investigators structure particular types of interactions or ask the participants to engage in specific tasks, they must carefully consider whether the task or stimulus conditions that they have created mirror the ways in which the participants typically behave. Either the participants might behave differently when the task is different, or they might not typically engage in the task or situation that is constructed. The degree of concern raised by these issues is a function of the degree to which the investigator wishes to describe how the participants typically behave in their day-to-day lives.

How the task is selected also might impact the behavior. For example, Christensen and Heavey (1990) have described different interaction patterns among husbands and wives. This includes a well-known interaction pattern that they label "demand-withdraw," in which one partner presses for the discussion of a topic, and the other partner attempts to withdraw from the interaction. A number of investigations indicate that females are more likely to assume the "demand" role, and husbands are more likely to assume the "withdraw" role in marital interactions. However, Christensen and Heavey found

that husbands were more likely to engage in the demand role during problem-solving interactions when the husbands selected the topic of conversation, compared to interactions in which the wife selected the topic to discuss. Thus, factors that influence an individual's interest in a task or motivation to participate in the task might significantly influence the resulting behavior that is observed.

3.01.4.4 Selection of a Time Period for Observing Behavior

In making decisions about the representativeness of the behavior that is observed, the investigator must also be concerned with the degree to which the observed behavior is generalizable across time. Classical test theory indicates that longer "tests" are more reliable in the sense that, keeping all other factors constant, they generally include a more representative sample of behavior and thus are more stable across time. In terms of behavioral observation, this raises two questions. First, how long should behavior be observed on a given occasion; second, on how many different occasions should behavior be observed? Whereas the answers to these questions should be based upon empirical findings, often pragmatic and logistic issues influence investigators' decisions along these lines. For example, sending observers into persons' homes or into classrooms can be troublesome and intrusive; sending observers to Africa to follow the social interactions among baboons can prove to be a logistical nightmare. Consequently, the difficulty, intrusiveness, and expense of behavioral observation often are a limiting factor in deciding how long to observe behavior. Similarly, the amount of time required to employ certain coding systems limits the length of behavioral observation. For example, some coding systems might require 20 hours to code one hour of recorded behavioral interaction. Therefore if the investigator intends to employ such a coding system, he or she might limit the amount of observed behavior to short time periods.

In deciding how long to observe behavior during a given observation period, several factors come into play. First and most generally, a long enough time period is needed such that the findings are relatively stable and replicable on other occasions. In part this is related to the frequency or base rate with which the behaviors of interest occur. If the behavior of interest is a relatively infrequent behavior, then longer observation periods are needed to obtain a stable assessment of its occurrence. However, if a behavior occurs with a high degree of frequency, then shorter observation periods can suffice. Second, the length of the observation period is influenced by the "complexity" of the phenomenon under consideration. For example, the investigator might be interested in whether there are different stages or phases in a couple's conversation as they attempt to reach resolution to a problem; in this instance, it would be essential to observe the entire problem-solving interaction. Or the investigator might be interested in whether there are different stages or phases in how a child responds to a new setting with the mother present. Attachment theory has explored this question and has provided indications of how securely and insecurely attached children initially respond in such settings, how they venture forth into a room after an initial exposure, and how their interaction with their mothers changes across time in this setting (Ainsworth, Blehar, Waters, & Wall, 1978). Therefore, if the investigator hypothesizes or wishes to explore whether there are different stages or phases in the interaction, this necessitates following the interaction for a sufficient time period to allow for an examination of the different phases of interest.

Second, the investigator must decide on how many occasions to observe the behavior. A given observation period might be significantly influenced by the occurrence of a major event, or the interaction of participants being observed might proceed in a given manner based upon what happens early in the interaction. For example, if a child is taunted on the playground early during a recess period, the child might withdraw from the group, which will significantly impact the child's behavior for the duration of the observation period on the playground. If the child is not taunted the next day, then his or her interaction pattern might proceed quite differently. Consequently, the number of occasions on which to observe interaction will differ according to the variability in the behavior being observed. If the behavior of interest occurs in a relatively consistent manner across different occasions, then fewer occasions are necessary for obtaining a stable sample of behavior.

Whereas there are far too few empirical investigations that have been conducted to determine the number of observational sessions needed to obtain stable results, some such investigations do exist. For example, Wieder and Weiss (1980) explored how many observational sessions were needed in order to obtain a stable assessment of couples' interaction when employing the Marital Interaction Coding System (MICS; Weiss, 1986). Based on generalizability theory, they concluded that observing couples on a single occasion could provide meaningful information about the couple, but observations across two separate evenings provide more stable interactions patterns when coded by the MICS. Similarly, Haynes, Follingstad, and Sullivan (1979) found that across three evenings, there was high stability on only 5 of 10 selected coding categories of communication between spouses. Interestingly, in spite of these findings, no marital therapy outcome investigations have observed couples' interactions across two or more consecutive evenings.

As can be seen based on the above discussion, there are a number of questions that the investigator must address in deciding what behaviors to observe. The decisions that are made will certainly impact the investigator's findings. Yet before these findings are obtained, there are many more decisions for the investigator to make that will influence the results.

3.01.5 ADOPTING OR DEVELOPING A BEHAVIORAL CODING SYSTEM

Foremost among the additional decisions to be made is the choice of coding system to employ to classify the data that have been observed. In fact, in order to address the questions raised above regarding what behavior to assess, the investigator needs to know ahead of time what coding system he or she will employ. At times the behavior is coded live during the interaction, so the coding system must be known. Even if the observed behavior is to be coded later based on video recordings of the behavior, it is important to decide ahead of time what coding system will be employed. For example, some coding systems might be appropriate only in certain settings or with certain tasks. Similarly, some coding systems might break behavior into a number of fine-grained categories that occur on a somewhat infrequent basis, thus necessitating longer observational periods. Therefore, deciding what coding system to employ is a significant factor in developing a thoughtful study based on behavioral observation.

An initial consideration in selecting a coding system is whether to adopt an existing coding system or to develop a new one. Each approach has some obvious benefits and limitations, as well as other subtle impacts that may not be apparent to investigators until they are well into the task of coding the behavioral observations.

3.01.5.1 Adopting an Existing Coding System

In many cases, it may be possible to adopt a coding system that has been used previously in the same research area, or one that can be imported from another area where similar constructs were assessed. Adoption of an existing system has the great advantage of saving the time and energy required to develop a reliable, valid, and practical coding scheme. It also links research across laboratories, samples, and locations, and thus provides for ready synthesis of research findings from various studies.

The selection of a coding system is guided by both theoretical and practical considerations. The primary theoretical issue is whether the coding system assesses behaviors that address the constructs of interest to the investigator. All coding systems organize data into some set of categories or units for coding, and these categories are based on issues of importance to the person who developed the coding system; however, they might or might not coincide with another investigator's concerns or theoretical model. Before beginning a search for a coding system, it is essential that the investigator first review theory and research to clarify the nature of the behavioral phenomena under investigation.

Behavioral phenomena related to a construct under one situation may take on different characteristics in a new situation, thus making an existing system inappropriate. For example, Ammerman, Van Hasselt, and Hersen (1991) coded problem-solving interactions between children with visual impairments and their parents using the Marital Interaction Coding System, III (MICS III; Weiss, 1986), a well-validated system for assessing problem-solving interactions within marital dyads. The study detected no differences between groups of families with and without children with disabilities, possibly because the coding system was inappropriate for the family context. Whereas the MICS III evaluates warm and hostile exchanges that indeed were similar across the groups, it does not assess factors such as behavior management, instruction, or other socialization practices that are important aspects of parent–child exchanges that are responsive to children's disabilities (Floyd & Costigan, 1997). Thus, a behavioral coding system may be sensitive to relevant variables only for certain types of people, relationships, or circumstances.

In addition to the substantive content of the system, various coding systems differ in the ways that they "chunk" or segment behavior into coding units. This "chunking" of behavior has both theoretical and practical implications for investigators. From a theoretical perspective, the nature of the phenomena being assessed should influence how the stream of ongoing behavior is segmented (Floyd, 1989). More specifically, relatively small, elemental units of

analysis may be appropriate for evaluating discrete events that require little inference; however, larger units of behavior might be needed to capture more complex phenomena. Foster, Inderbitzen, and Nangle (1993) discuss a similar point regarding the selection of a coding system to evaluate the effectiveness of social skills training with children. They note that a frequent problem with interpreting the results of treatment outcome studies is that whereas the treatment teaches children specific social skills, such as offering to share a toy, the observational assessment evaluates only molar, or global codes, such as "positive interactions." From data such as these, it is impossible to know whether the behaviors that were trained actually were displayed during the assessment.

Alternatively, it also is important to question whether a complex phenomenon is accurately evaluated by merely summarizing elemental codes. For example, Jacob (1975) illustrates how power in interpersonal interactions may not be indicated by who speaks more frequently or wins more disagreements, but rather by the ability to prevail on the central, important conflicts. Evaluations such as these may require making judgments about relatively large units of behavior.

Choosing among systems with different units of observation also has practical implications. Microanalytic coding systems that parse behaviors into minute elements may be overly complex and labor-intensive for investigators who merely want to assess global levels of characteristics, such as positiveness, competence, anxiety, or irritability. In such cases, it may be more efficient to use a system that rates dimensions such as the intensity or quality of behavior exhibited over an extended period of time. On the other hand, small, elemental units of observation and analysis are useful for detecting situational influences on behavior and sequential patterns among minute events; larger, more integrative units are useful for understanding cross-situational consistency (Cairns & Green, 1979). Thus, findings based on larger units of observation may be more generalizable than microanalytic coding. Some investigators appear to assume that behavioral observation is synonymous with microanalytic coding; such assumptions can serve as a major impediment to the more widespread use of observational measures in research settings with limited resources. We encourage investigators to explore macroanalytical coding procedures as a practical and, in some cases, more informative alternative to microanalytic coding.

Every coding system incorporates an array of assumptions, biases, and procedural preferences that the originator used to guide coding decisions. These preferences are particularly relevant in decisions about how to handle ambiguous incidents. Many decision rules are not made explicit in published reports and coding manuals, so that it is difficult for investigators who did not participate in its development to apply an existing system accurately and in a way that is consistent with other research. Whenever possible, consultation with the originator is invaluable. Some originators of popular measures conduct periodic workshops to train new users (e.g., SASB, Humphrey & Benjamin 1989; SPAFF, Gottman, 1994). Most developers cannot be expected to provide ongoing consultation to support their system, but should be willing to share examples of coded data and advice about common problems.

3.01.5.2 Developing a New Coding System

New ideas focused on new constructs and employing new assumptions are the lifeblood of progress in the social sciences. Thus, there will always be a need to develop new coding schemes. Even when well-known constructs are studied, if observational procedures become highly standardized within a research area, the phenomenon of interest may become totally dependent on the existing measure. This situation can lead to replicated, well-established findings that are largely an artifact of a particular measurement procedure. The need to disentangle method variance from the phenomenon of interest is strong justification for the development of new coding systems.

Detailed instructions about developing coding systems are given in Bakeman & Gottman (1997) regarding interpersonal interaction, and by O'Neill, Horner, Albin, Storey, and Sprague (1990) regarding functional analysis of problem behaviors. The key steps in developing any coding system are summarized below.

3.01.5.2.1 Cataloging relevant behaviors

A useful initial step is to develop an exhaustive list of all relevant behaviors to be coded. In some cases, this may be accomplished by conducting initial observations and recording all relevant behaviors that occur. Animal researchers frequently use this procedure to develop an ethogram, which is a comprehensive list of all behaviors that are characteristic of a species. Several ethograms are published to describe the behavior repertoire of different animal species. However, because it is usually impossible to sample all possible behaviors for a species, investigators estimate the quality of

sample coverage with the theta statistic, calculated as 1 − (number of different behaviors seen/ total number of acts observed). As the value of theta approaches 1, the probability of encountering a new behavior approaches zero. That is, we assume that if new behaviors are not encountered with additional observations, the behavioral repertoire has been adequately sampled.

Of course, a strictly empirical approach such as this usually is not adequate for evaluating human behavior. As we noted at the beginning of the chapter, a stream of human behavior often can be classified according to an enormous variety of characteristics. In order to focus attention on a limited set of characteristics, the investigator should begin with a list of these characteristics and their manifestations as gleaned from previous research, experience, and theory. Pilot observations then can be directed toward refining this list by broadening some categories, tightening others to make finer distinctions between theoretically disparate behaviors, and adding new categories not suggested by previous research. For an excellent example of this process, see Jacob, Tennenbaum, Bargiel and Seilhamer's (1995) description of the development of their Home Interaction Scoring System.

One frequent concern while developing coding systems involves what to do with rare but theoretically important events. Rare events tend to decrease the reliability of coding systems; however, such rare events may be highly meaningful, and thus they cannot be excluded from a system without compromising validity and utility. It may be possible to collapse similar rare events into broader categories or to alter the observational situation in order to elicit these behaviors more consistently and reliably.

3.01.5.2.2 Selecting a unit of observation

An important component of identifying relevant behaviors is to determine the appropriate unit of observation. This involves the decision to evaluate behavioral states, events, or some combination of the two. In general, a state is any ongoing condition that persists over an extended period of time, whereas an event is a discrete action. States are usually measured with time-based indices such as duration or latency, whereas events are usually measured with frequency counts or sequential patterns. Both types of unit also can be rated for intensity. The distinction between states and events is blurred by the fact that the same behavior might be measured with both units, such as measuring both the duration of anxiety episodes or disruptive episodes in the classroom, as well as the frequency of the episodes. The type of unit is not always mandated by the content of the behavior and, once again, the decision about the appropriate unit for a particular purpose must be guided by theoretical, empirical, and practical considerations. At first glance, it may appear that recording onset and offset times for all behaviors is desirable so that information about duration and latency can always be retrieved. However, Bakeman and Gottman (1997) warn against "the tyranny of time" and propose that, even with sophisticated recording and analytical devices, the precise measurement of time adds substantial complexity to data recording and analysis, and can cause problems with reliability that outweigh the benefits of having these data.

The unit of observation also involves the sampling protocol. The two most common sampling protocols in clinical psychology research are event sampling, which involves noting each occurrence of events during the entire observation period, and time sampling or interval coding, which involves noting occurrences during selected time intervals. Most commonly, time sampling involves alternating periods of watching and recording, each lasting for several seconds. During the recording period, the coder usually records whether or not each possible code occurred during the preceding interval. This procedure is useful for live observations in which the coder must track a large number of behaviors, so that recording each event would interfere with accurate observation. The procedure assumes that recording periods are random, and will not distort the data. Several studies challenge this assumption and reveal that interval coding can distort the amount of behavior, sequential patterns, and observer agreement for both behavioral events (e.g., Mehm & Knutson, 1987) and behavioral states (e.g., Ary, 1984; Gardner & Griffin, 1989). However, other studies demonstrate that interval coding can accurately reflect actual behavior rates and durations (e.g., Klesges, Woolfrey, & Vollmer, 1985). A study by Mann, ten-Have, Plunkett, and Meisels (1991) on mother–infant interactions illustrates that the accuracy of data from interval sampling depends on how well the duration of the sampling interval matches with the duration of the behavior of interest. They found that the actual durations or frequencies of mother and infant behaviors, which tended to occur in relatively short episodes ("bouts"), were inaccurately assessed when the sampling interval was relatively long. Thus, before proceeding with a time-sampling/interval-coding approach, the investigator should test the time-sampled

data against actual rates or durations, and adjust the length of the recording interval to produce the most accurate data possible. See Altmann (1974) for an extensive review of sampling protocols, and Bakeman and Quera (1995) for considerations about how to design sampling protocols and record the data for data analysis purposes.

3.01.5.2.3 *Creating code categories*

Typically, code categories will be mutually exclusive and exhaustive Mutual exclusivity means that coding categories are discrete and homogeneous, and that each event can be classified into one and only one category. Exhaustiveness means that all manifestations of a construct are included in the system. In most cases, exhaustiveness can be achieved by including a category, such as "other" or "neutral," to label all behaviors that do not fit well into any other category. For example, a measure of parent–adolescent interaction by Robin and Foster (1989) includes a "talk" code to cover all behaviors that are not instances of other categories. In some cases, the investigator may believe that it is necessary to violate these guidelines. For example, another measure of parent–adolescent interaction, the Constraining and Enabling Coding System (Leaper et al., 1989), allows behaviors by parents to receive both "constraining" and "enabling" codes because the authors believe that these "mixed messages" may be highly relevant to adolescent functioning. In other cases, investigators only label certain subsets of behaviors (i.e., as in scan sampling where, for example, only instances of target children's aggressive behavior and provocations by peers are recorded). Both situations create difficulties for the analysis of sequences of events, although Bakeman and Quera (1995) provide some solutions for managing these types of data.

Often it is useful to organize codes into groups and, if appropriate, to arrange the groups into a hierarchical classification. This arrangement makes the codes easier to recall; in addition, this hierarchical arrangement can help to fashion a set of decision steps to employ in the coding process, both of which may improve observer reliability. For example, children's social behaviors might first be classified as initiations versus reactions, and initiations could be classified as prosocial versus antagonistic, followed by more specific categories of events within each of these general categories. The coders can then use this hierarchical arrangement to organize their decision process, so that once they decide that a particular action is an initiation, and it is prosocial, there is a relatively small number of "prosocial initiation" codes to choose among.

An alternative approach to forming a hierarchical organization is exemplified in the Structural Analysis of Social Behavior (SASB) system (Humphrey & Benjamin, 1989). This system uses a rating scale format as an aid to categorical coding. In this system, all code categories are classified within a circumplex defined by two dimensions: Interdependence and Affiliation. Coders receive extensive instruction in the theory underlying each dimension, and they learn to rate behaviors in terms of their degree of interdependence, represented on a vertical axis, and their degree of affiliation, represented on a horizontal axis. The axes intersect at their midpoints. The location on the circumplex defined by the coordinates of these dimensional ratings is the code for that act. Thus, for example, a behavior rated as + 5 for Interdependence (i.e., somewhat independent) and − 4 for Affiliation (i.e., somewhat disaffiliative) is assigned to the category "walling off and distancing."

3.01.5.2.4 Content validation of codes

A useful, though often neglected, step in coding system development is content validation of the codes. This might be accomplished by having "experts" or the actors themselves classify codes into relevant categories, then comparing these categories to the expected categories. For example, in order to evaluate a family coding system that classified family behaviors as aversive and nonaversive, Snyder (1983) had family members rate the aversiveness of concrete examples of behaviors classified by the coding system.

3.01.5.2.5 Developing a codebook

After codes are labeled, defined, and classified, the next step is to produce a codebook. In general, most experts recommend that the more thorough, precise, and clearly written the codebook, the better the chances of training new coders to produce reliable, valid data (e.g., Hartmann & Wood, 1990; Herbert & Attridge, 1975); however, other studies demonstrate that naive coders can at times produce valid codes (e.g., Prinz & Kent, 1978). The codebook should include a list of all codes, a descriptive definition for each code, and examples of behaviors that represent each code, along with examples that do not match the code. In order to assist with reliable coding, it is particularly important to include examples of differential decisions in borderline or ambiguous cases. The APA guidelines for educational and psychological tests (APA, 1985) lists several other types of information that would also be useful to include in codebooks, including information about the theoretical underpinnings for the measure, and data on reliability and validity from research to date. Herbert and Attridge (1975) propose that providing this type of information to coders may help to facilitate training and improve coder reliability.

3.01.6 TRAINING CODERS

Once a coding system has been adopted or developed, the next step is to train coders in its use. A preliminary step in conducting efficient and effective coder training is the selection of coders who will perform well. Unfortunately, there is little research on personal characteristics or abilities that predict good performance as a behavioral coder. Research on interpersonal communication indicates that, in some circumstances, women tend to be more accurate than men at decoding the meaning of interpersonal behaviors (e.g., Noller, 1980). However, this effect is hardly large enough to warrant the exclusion of male coders in studies of interpersonal behavior. To the extent that coder characteristics such as gender, age, education, or ethnicity may be associated with biases that could influence coding decisions, it may be important to ensure that coders are diverse on these characteristics in order to randomize these effects and improve the validity of the data.

Ironically, one characteristic that may be important to select *against* is prior experience or personal investment in the research area under consideration. The use of naive, uninvolved observers controls for biases caused by factors such as familiarity with the research hypotheses and prior expectations. We believe that in many instances naive observers also tend to provide more reliable codes. Extensive research on clinical decision making demonstrates that highly experienced judges tend to employ idiosyncratic and inconsistent decision criteria that can reduce both intraobserver consistency and interobserver agreement as compared to naive observers (e.g., Dawes, 1979). Our experiences bear this out. When coders have extensive previous training or experience in the domain of interest, they tend to have difficulty adhering strictly to the coding criteria outlined in the coding manual, particularly if their experiences involved a different theoretical perspective or set of assumptions than those that undergird the coding system.

Wilson (1982) wisely proposed that observer training should address two equally important goals: teaching the skills needed to perform the coding task, and motivating the coders to perform well. Teaching the skills usually involves a combination of didactic and experiential training sessions. A helpful first step is to explain the rationale and theory that underlie the coding system. In cases where the coding involves considerable judgment in the application of a theory or model, the coders might benefit from readings and instruction about the model. The coders should read and demonstrate a thorough working knowledge of the coding manual and should be tested on this material before proceeding. Practice with the coding system should begin with the presentation of examples of behaviors, followed by an explanation for the coding decisions. Initial examples should be relatively unambiguous representations of the coding categories or examples of the extremes of the rating scales. The coders should be required to practice the coding with feedback about their accuracy and discussion of the rationale for coding decisions. Of course, the practice materials should match the actual coding situation as closely as possible. Training sessions should be relatively frequent and relatively brief to enhance alertness. Training continues until the coders reach acceptable levels of agreement with preestablished criterion codes. Because accuracy can be expected to decrease once actual coding begins (e.g., Taplin & Reid, 1973), most investigators set a training criterion that is higher than the minimal acceptable criterion during actual coding. Typically, this criterion is 80–90% agreement.

The maintenance of the coders' motivation to perform well probably involves the same types of factors that enhance performance in any work setting, including clarity of the task, investment in the outcome, personal responsibility, monitoring of performance, and a fair reward structure. One typical procedure used by investigators is to develop a contract that specifies the tasks to be completed, the expectations, and the reward structure. Coder investment in the project might be enhanced by providing them with the opportunity to participate as a member of the scientific or clinical team, to the extent that this does not bias coding, or by group interactions that build solidarity and cohesion among the coding team. As described below, reliability should be monitored on an ongoing basis. An unfortunate feature of reliability monitoring is that there is a built-in punishment schedule for inadequate performance, such as having to recode sessions or completing additional training, but the rewards for good performance are less tangible. Investigators should be sensitive to the need to instigate a reward system in whatever way possible, including providing raises for a good

record, greater responsibility in the form of training and monitoring new coders, or public acknowledgment of good work.

3.01.7 RELIABILITY

In observational research, the reliability, or precision, of the measure is almost always evaluated with indices of interobserver agreement. Actually, according to psychometric theory, reliability concerns the extent to which coded data map onto "true scores," and thus, the reliability of coded data also relates to intraobserver consistency in applying the coding scheme (Bakeman & Gottman, 1997). However, because agreement between independent coders is a higher standard for judging precision, it is the focus of formal psychometric evaluations, and intraobserver consistency is addressed more informally through the implementation of training and monitoring procedures to prevent observer drift.

3.01.7.1 Enhancing Reliability

As noted throughout the previous sections, reliability can be enhanced in the way the codes are developed, in the procedures for training and monitoring the observers, and in the procedures for conducting the observations. Regarding code development, greater reliability can be expected when codes are clearly defined in operational terms, when categories are relatively elemental and overt as opposed to complex and inferential, and when coded behaviors occur at least moderately frequently. If some of these conditions cannot be met, coders likely will need relatively more training, practice, and experience in order to produce reliable data. Instructions that explicitly discourage or encourage specific expectancies about frequencies or patterns of codes either tend to reduce observer agreement or spuriously inflate it (Kazdin, 1977). Similar to guidelines for training sessions, frequent and relatively short observation sessions produce more reliable data than infrequent, longer observation sessions. In addition to booster sessions to reduce observer drift, periodically training new coders may help to reduce the biasing effects of prior experience on the data, and observations involving different subject groups or experimental conditions should be intermingled whenever possible to avoid systematic effects related to observer drift. Studies repeatedly demonstrate that coders are less reliable when they believe that their agreement is not being checked, although this effect may abate with increased experience (e.g., Serbin, Citron, &

Conner, 1978; Weinrott & Jones, 1984). Therefore, frequent, overt, and random assessments
of reliability should help to maintain coder
precision.

3.01.7.2 Evaluating Reliability

The appropriate procedure and calculations
for evaluating reliability depend on the purposes of the evaluation and the nature of the
inferences that will be drawn from the data.
Thus, there is no one way to evaluate reliability,
but rather an array of approaches that can be
followed. Helpful reviews of various procedures
and computational formulas are presented by
Bakeman and Gottman (1997), Hartmann
(1977, 1982), Jacob, Tennenbaum, and Krahn
(1987), Stine (1989), and Suen, Ary, and Covalt
(1990). Two important decisions include (i)
whether to compute exact agreement for specific
codes (point-by-point agreement) or aggregate
agreement for larger units, and (ii) whether and
how to correct for chance agreement. Below is a
summary of some of the more common
procedures, along with guidelines for selecting
among them.

For the purpose of training, monitoring, and
providing corrective feedback to coders, in most
cases it is useful to assess the most precise form
of point-by-piont agreement that is possible
with the coding system. For example, with event
recording, an observer's codes for each event are
compared with a set of criterion codes or those
of an independent coder. A contingency table
that cross-lists the two sets of codes and tallies
the frequencies of each pair of codes (i.e., a
"confusion matrix") is a useful method of
feedback for the coders. The total percent
agreement for all codes (# agreements/total #
events), and the percent agreement for specific
codes (# agreements/(#agreements + #disagree-
ments)) are summary scores that are easy to
understand. During coder training, we compute
these statistics beginning with the first practice
assignments because the rapid improvement
that usually occurs during the first few assignments can be highly rewarding and reinforcing
for new coders. The contingency table also can
display a pattern of disagreements that is
instructive, such as when two coders consistently give a different code to the same type of
behavior. Even when the actual observational
procedure involves a larger or less precise unit of
observation, such as in interval sampling, it may
be helpful to employ an event-based tracking
procedure during coder training in order to have
more precise information about when disagreements occur. In our experience, the identification of consistent disagreements is helpful when

follow-up instruction is used to clarify and
resolve the confusion about the coding criteria.
However, providing feedback about disagreements without instruction or resolution can
make coders feel more confused and uncertain
and can decrease reliability. Also, it usually is
not helpful to coders to correct their scores for
chance agreement, because corrected scores
may be highly variable depending on the range
of behaviors displayed in each session; thus they
present a confusing picture of absolute agreement. Finally, if agreement statistics are used to
identify unreliable coders in need of additional
training, it is important to base this decision on
multiple observation sessions, because occa-
sional unreliable sessions can be expected due to
the ambiguity in the target's behavior rather
than because of coder error.

For the purpose of determining the precision
of the measurement after coding has been
completed, the method of computing reliability
depends on the type of data that will be analyzed
(Hartmann, 1977). That is, the investigator
typically is interested in the reliability/precision
of the scores that are actually computed from
the data. Although it is common for investigators to report some form of point-by-point
agreement for individual codes, most data
analyses focus on aggregate indices such as
the frequency, relative frequency, or rates of
groups of behaviors. Thus, if several specific
codes are combined or aggregated into a
broader category of "positive behavior" for
data-analytic purposes, then reliability estimates should be performed at the level of
"positive behavior." We usually assume that
observer agreement for specific codes ensures
that aggregate scores are reliable; nonetheless, it
is useful to determine the actual level of
reliability for these aggregate codes. Furthermore, agreement at the specific code level is
usually an overly stringent requirement that can
unnecessarily prolong a study.

For the purpose of assessing the precision of
the measure, percent agreement statistics are
usually corrected for chance agreement between
coders by using Cohen's kappa statistic. This
statistic uses the information about agreements
and disagreements from the confusion matrix,
and evaluates the observed amount of agreement relative to the expected amount of
agreement due to chance because of the base
rates of the behaviors. The formula for kappa is:
kappa = [p(Observed agreement) − p(Expected
agreement)]/[1 − p(Expected agreement)], where
p(Observed agreement) is the percent agreement
for the two coders, and p(Expected agreement) is
the percent agreement expected by chance. The
probability of chance agreement is computed by
calculating the relative frequencies for each code

by each coder, obtaining the product of the two coders' relative frequency scores for each code, then summing these products. Usually, kappa is computed for each reliability session, and the mean and range across all reliability sessions are reported. One complication with the kappa statistic is that it can severely underrepresent observer agreement in sessions during which the subject displays a limited number of behaviors and/or some behaviors have exceptionally high base rates. This situation produces very large values for expected agreement, and thus can produce a very low score for kappa even when the proportion of observed agreement is very high. A potential solution in this situation is to use a sample-wise estimate of expected agreement derived from the base rates for the entire set of data (Bakeman & Gottman, 1997). Another complication is that point-by-point kappa may be overly stringent when, as frequently occurs, the actual scores used in the data analysis are aggregates (e.g., total frequency scores). Jacob et al. (1987) present a method for computing kappa for aggregate scores.

Often the measure of interest in the data analysis represents the data on an interval scale of measurement (e.g., relative frequency scores or average ratings). In this situation, the question of measurement precision concerns the relative positions of subjects on the interval scale rather than agreement between coders on individual coded behaviors. Coder agreement for interval data can be assessed with the correlation between the scores for pairs of coders; for example, the correlation between summary scores for a group of subjects, or the correlation between interval ratings within an observation session. Alternatively, the intraclass correlation is also appropriate for interval data. This approach is derived from the analysis of variance (Winer, 1971), and is the most commonly used application of generalizability theory for evaluating coder agreement. It assesses the proportion of variance in the scores that can be attributed to variation among subjects as opposed to variation among observers. An advantage of the approach is that when more than two coders are being evaluated, one score can reflect the level of agreement (i.e., proportion of variation attributed to differences among subjects) for the entire group of coders, rather than calculating individual correlations for all possible pairs of coders. Shrout and Fleiss (1979) outline the procedures for computing intraclass correlations under various assumptions about the data.

Alternative procedures for detecting agreement between coders may also be appropriate when the focus of study is the sequential

patterns in the behavioral stream. Bakeman and Gottman (1997) vividly illustrate how point-by-point agreement between coders can be sharply deflated when one coder occasionally inserts extra codes, although the agreement about the sequential pattern of the codes is very high. Wampold and Holloway (1983) make a similar case that agreement about individual codes may be too stringent a criterion for sequential data. Gottman (1980) recommends an approach similar to intraclass correlation in which the investigator demonstrates that the measures of sequential dependency (e.g., lag z-scores, see below) are consistent across observers.

3.01.8 ANALYZING DATA GATHERED THROUGH BEHAVIORAL OBSERVATION

Apart from the usual decisions that guide the design of data analysis, observational data present some unique challenges for investigators. These include questions about data reduction, dimensions and scales of measurement, and the identification of sequential patterns of behavior.

3.01.8.1 Data Reduction

Most observational studies produce a large amount of data for each subject, particularly when the coding scheme exhaustively labels all behaviors emitted by one or more subjects during an observational session. Even sessions lasting only 5–10 minutes can produce several hundred codes when behavior units are small. The challenge is to reduce these data to make them interpretable, without sacrificing the rich descriptive information in the coded data.

A first step is to group individual codes into broader categories. For the purposes of data analysis, the primary problem with many observational coding schemes is that they include behavioral events that rarely or never occur for many subjects, and thus produce highly skewed distributions of scores for the sample, resulting in missing cells in contingency tables for sequential analyses. Whenever possible, it is important to incorporate rare events into categories of events that occur with sufficient frequency to be used in subsequent analyses. In most cases, categories are specified on an *a priori* basis by investigators, using theory and rational analysis to determine how codes are grouped.

Another approach is to factor analyze individual codes to identify clusters of codes that share common variance. This approach is probably most appropriate when the investigator is interested in examining behavior styles, because the factor analysis identifies groups of behaviors that covary across subjects. That is, behaviors are grouped based on their co-occurrence within subjects, irrespective of their meaning or functional impact. For example, if different children in classrooms tend to misbehave in different ways, with some children spending much time out of their seats, others talking out of turn, and others being withdrawn and inattentive, a factor analysis would likely identify these three types of behaviors as three separate clusters. Kuller and Linsten (1992) used this method and identified social behaviors and individual concentration as separate clusters of behaviors by children in classrooms. An alternative approach is to group behaviors according to their functional impact. If all three types of behaviors disrupt the activities of other children in the classroom, they can be grouped into one functional category of disruptive behavior. For example, Schaap (1982) used lag sequential analysis of marital interactions to identify a set of behaviors that were most likely to elicit negative responses from a spouse. These specific behaviors could then be grouped together as negative eliciting behaviors.

3.01.8.1.1 Measurement of base rates of behavior

Base rates of behavior can be expressed in various scales of measurement. For example, the frequency of events can be expressed as raw frequency, relative frequency, rate per minute, or ratio scores (i.e., ratio of positive to negative behaviors). The selection of a scale of measurement is usually determined by factors such as the focus of the investigation, the precedent in the field of study, and psychometric properties of various scales of measurement (e.g., distributions of the scores, reliability of the index). Tryon (1991) argues that scores should also be expressed in "natural" scientific units in order to make measurements as comparable as possible across time, situations, or different investigations. A compelling point in this argument is that relativistic measurements such as standardized z-scores, which provide information about the position of the subject relative to other subjects in the same study, are highly "unnatural" units that vary as a function of who participates in the study. Instead, scores should be expressed in relation to some objective criterion that remains invariant across samples, so that a body of knowledge about the phenomenon of interest can more readily develop. For example, because raw frequency counts will depend on the duration of the

measurement period, relative frequency scores may be preferable because they are comparable across measurement situations. However, the comparability of relative frequency scores requires exhaustive coding of all behavior with the same set of codes. Thus, rate per minute scores may be preferable because they are less dependent on other characteristics of the coding scheme or measurement situation.

3.01.8.1.2 Measurement of sequential patterns of behavior

When events or states are coded exhaustively, it is possible to evaluate patterns of behavior for an individual or between individuals interacting with each other. The behaviors can occur concurrently (e.g., the co-occurrence of eyebrow arch and smile) or serially (e.g., reciprocal negative behaviors between spouses). Sequential patterns are usually derived from Bayesian statistics that relate the occurrence or nonoccurrence of an antecedent event or state with the occurrence or nonoccurrence of a consequent event or state. In lag-sequential analysis (e.g., Bakeman & Gottman, 1997; Sackett, 1979a), the investigator is concerned with the transitional probability of the antecedent/consequent sequence, which reveals the probability that the consequent occurs, given the antecedent event or state. The important question regarding sequential dependency is the extent to which this transitional probability exceeds (or is smaller than) the base rate for the consequent. If the consequent is more (or less) likely to occur in the presence of, or following, the antecedent than in other circumstances, then there is dependency between the antecedent and the consequent. If, for example, the probability that a mother smiles at her infant (consequent behavior) is greater after the infant smiles at her (antecedent behavior) than after other types of infant behaviors, then there is a sequential dependency in infant smile–mother smile exchanges.

Sequential dependency can be estimated with several statistics. One common metric is the lag sequential z-score developed by Sackett (1979a), and a modification developed by Allison and Liker (1982) that corrects for sampling error. This statistic compares the observed frequency of the antecedent/consequent sequence with the expected frequency of the sequence (based on the base rates for both events). More recently, Bakeman and colleagues (Bakeman & Gottman, 1997; Bakeman & Quera, 1995) recommended a slightly different formula derived from two-way contingency tables, which is the adjusted residual obtained in log-linear analysis. A convenient feature of this statistic is that because the scores are distributed as z, the statistical significance of sequential patterns is readily discerned (i.e., scores greater than $z = 1.96$). The statistic can be computed with standard statistical packages. Importantly, Bakeman and Quera (1995) also suggest statistical programs to compute these scores when codes in a sequence cannot repeat, such as when the coding system requires that new codes are assigned only when the behavior changes. Because a behavior can never follow itself, this situation produces "structural zeros" in the diagonal of the contingency table.

The z-statistic or adjusted residual is most useful for examining a sequential pattern in a single set of observations on an individual subject or a group of subjects. However, it is not recommended for use when separate sequential scores for each of multiple subjects are entered as data points into subsequent inferential analyses. The problem is that the size of adjusted residuals will vary (become larger) as a function of the number of observations that are made, even when the actual conditional probabilities remain constant. Thus, the z-scores are influenced by the base rates of behaviors, and can differ dramatically across subjects when response productivity differs. Wampold (1989) recommends a transformed kappa statistic as an alternative; however, this statistic requires selecting among three different computational formulas depending on the relative size of expected and actual probabilities. Other commonly used statistics are Yule's Q and phi. Bakeman and Casey (1995) provide computational formulas, discuss the conditions under which various statistics may be applicable, and suggest that investigators examine the distributions of scores for each statistic to determine which statistic provides the best distribution of scores for a particular set of data.

Investigators are commonly concerned about the amount of data needed to calculate sequential statistics. This issue is most relevant when the investigator is interested in studying sequences involving relatively rare events. Unfortunately, clinically relevant phenomena are often rare phenomena, so the problem is a common one in the field of clinical psychology. Bakeman and Gottman (1997) present a detailed analysis of this issue using guidelines employed in log-linear analysis of contingency tables. As a general rule of thumb, the investigator should obtain enough data so that each antecedent and consequent event in a contingency table occurs at least five times. In many cases, this criterion can be met by collapsing codes into more general categories. Another strategy is to conduct analyses using pooled observations on a group of subjects,

rather than calculating sequential statistics for individual subjects. For example, Gottman, Markman, and Notarius (1977) examined sequences of effective and ineffective problem solving in groups of distressed and nondistressed married couples. Although incidents of positive behaviors such as "validate" and negative behaviors such as "put-down" were rare in some couples, within the two groups they occurred with sufficient frequency to identify patterns of supportive interactions that were more typical of happily married couples, and patterns of hostile exchange that were more typical of spouses in distressed marriages.

3.01.8.2 Computer Technology for Recording and Coding Behavioral Observations

Since the late 1970s, computer technology has become increasingly available for use in recording and coding observational data. Whereas the use of devices and software requires extra initial costs in time and money, they may ultimately increase the efficiency of data collection, coding, and data management. If developers find a market for these devices, we can expect that their availability will become more widespread. Because specific products are likely to undergo rapid changes and development, a list of currently available products would be immediately out of date, and thus would be of little use. However, it is possible to illustrate the range of current options and some of the factors to consider in selecting equipment and software.

For most situations in which behavioral observation is used, the major function of automated systems is to record the observations and the codes reported by the human observer. Although Tryon (1991) catalogs many automated devices that actually measure "actions," most of these devices track physiological responses or simple, gross motor activity. To date, no automated system can code the types of complex events that are the focus of this chapter. The first systems designed for event recording were "dedicated devices" because their sole function was to aid in data collection. Data could be stored in a temporary system and then uploaded to a computer for analysis. These devices have been rapidly replaced by software systems that run on standard computers. The newest automated systems combine data entry and management functions with computer control of video playback devices.

One consideration in selecting a system is the number of codes the system can handle. For example, one software package, the Observational Data Acquisition Program (ODAP; Hetrick, Isenhart, Taylor & Sandman, 1991), allows for recording frequency and duration of up to 10 behaviors. Duration is recorded by depressing a key during the occurrence of a behavior. Taylor et al. (1991) used this system to measure six types of self-injurious behaviors. Although this system is easy to use, the major limitation is that only a circumscribed range of behavior can be evaluated with simple, one dimensional codes. In contrast, other systems allow the investigator to configure a data entry file to handle as many as 1000 codes, and the codes can be multifaceted. For example, the Observer system (Noldus, 1991) has the capacity to hold 1000 different codes which can be classified as occurring only under certain circumstances. The system prompts the coder to correct errors when codes that violate the classification structure are entered (e.g., the same behavior entered twice in systems where codes cannot repeat, or when a teacher code is assigned to a student). The Multiple Option Observation System for Experimental Studies (MOOSES; Tapp, Wehby, & Ellis, 1995) offers similar flexibility. In a study by Shores et al. (1993), MOOSES was used to record classroom interactions of children with behavior disorders. Codes were devised to indicate the actor, the behavior exhibited, and the recipient of the behavior. In addition, conditional variables such as the presence of a teacher or the grouping of students who were present were also recorded.

A second consideration is whether the system can interface with video playback devices. Several systems are available that link the computer with professional quality videotape players that include a computer interface port. A machine-readable time code is stamped on the videotape, and the computer reads the time code to track onset and offset times for events, duration for states, or to access specific intervals. The advantage of these systems over simple real-time recording devices is that the videotape can be stopped, reversed, and started repeatedly without needing to reset a timer. Examples are the Observer system (Noldus, 1991), Observation Coding System Toolset (OCS Tools; Triangle Research Collaborative, Inc, 1994), and Procoder (Tapp & Walden, 1993). These systems differ greatly in terms of the number and complexity of codes they can handle and the ability and ease of controlling the video player from the computer keyboard. More recently, packages are becoming available that use CD-ROM instead of videotape input (e.g., vPrism; Digital LAVA Inc., 1996). These systems provide easier access to specific sections of an observation session because of the digital access features of CD-ROM, and easier replay as compared to rewinding a video player. They may also allow for greater precision in labeling exact time segments. However, they require converting videotaped observations to compact disks, which is expensive when completed by companies that provide this service, and time-consuming when equipment is available for converting data in-house. Nevertheless, the reduced storage requirements for CDs as opposed to videotapes is an advantage.

A third consideration is the statistical analysis that a particular program may offer. Whereas some systems include software for calculating coder agreement, linking multiple channels (e.g., behavioral codes with heart rate data), and conducting sequential analyses, others output the data so that it can be imported into other programs for these purposes. Graphic presentation of data is also an option with some packages. In some cases, statistical programs are included as part of the basic system; in other instances, the statistical software is optional.

3.01.9 INTERPRETING DATA GATHERED THROUGH BEHAVIORAL OBSERVATION

As can be seen, there are a number of steps before investigators obtain findings based on behavioral observation. The final step for the investigator is interpreting these findings. Whereas this interpretive process is psychological in nature and dependent upon the specifics of the particular investigation, our own research on couples' relationships, marital therapy, and family development illustrates how a pattern of findings that include both behavioral observation and self-report measures can help to elucidate family/marital functioning.

Baucom and his colleagues have conducted several treatment outcome studies with maritally distressed couples from a cognitive-behavioral perspective. Cognitive-behavioral conceptualizations of marital distress have placed a major emphasis on the centrality of communication as essential for effective marital functioning. However, the pattern of findings across our investigations indicates that communications training might be neither necessary nor sufficient for affecting changes in marital functioning. In these investigations, couples' communication was assessed by the MICS III (Weiss, 1986) after the couples attempted to solve problems on areas of difficulty in their marriage in a laboratory setting. In the first study, all couples received some set of behavioral interventions to assist their marriages (Baucom, 1982). The difference among the treatment conditions involved whether the couples received communications training.

The findings indicated that couples in all of the active treatment conditions improved equally on communication and marital adjustment, suggesting that communications training was not the critical element in the treatment. In a subsequent investigation, Baucom, Sayers, and Sher (1990) provided maritally distressed couples with a variety of cognitive-behavioral interventions, but all couples received communications training. Again, the findings indicated that couples in all active treatment conditions improved equally on communication and marital adjustment. However, additional analyses indicated that changes in communication were not correlated with changes in marital adjustment; thus, communication training could not be interpreted as the critical ingredient that altered marital adjustment (Iverson & Baucom, 1990). This is not to say that communication is unimportant in marriage; a number of investigations indicates that it is (e.g., Gottman & Krokoff, 1989). However, the results from these investigations and others have led cognitive-behavioral investigators to develop more complex and multifaceted models of marital distress that include, but are not limited to, a communications skills deficit explanation (e.g., Karney & Bradbury, 1995). Thus, in this instance, the findings from investigations involving behavioral observation of communication with couples have led to theoretical changes in the conceptualization of marital adjustment.

Research by Floyd and colleagues investigates associations among subsystems within the families of children who have disabilities, and examines how family relationships predict adaptive functioning for the child and the other family members. All observations and data collection are conducted in the families' homes in order to maximize the likelihood that observed behaviors are relevant to daily functioning in the family. One set of reports (Floyd, Gilliom, & Costigan, in press; Floyd & Zmich, 1991) focuses on the hypothesis that the quality of the parents' marital functioning and their parenting alliance influence the quality of parenting experiences. In order to test the hypothesis, observational measures were combined with self-reports of both marital functioning and parenting experiences.

Similar to procedures commonly employed in studies of marital relationships, and as illustrated in the studies by Baucom and colleagues, the parents' marital problem-solving skills were assessed by having them discuss and attempt to resolve a significant area of disagreement in their relationship. This procedure linked the investigation to the large body of previous observational research on marriage and marital therapy. Also, because the focus of the study was to understand how the parents functioned as a marital dyad, the marital discussions were conducted in a room separate from the children. Other studies interested in how children witness marital conflict have used procedures where children are present either as observers or participants in the discussions (e.g., Cummings, 1987). In order to reduce reactive effects associated with the presence of a live observer, the couples were left alone together for 10 minutes to complete the discussion, and the discussions were videotaped for later coding.

Parenting experiences were evaluated in a separate family interaction session. The procedures for this session were adopted from the work of Patterson, Reid, and colleagues (Patterson, 1982; Patterson, Reid, & Dishion, 1992) with aggressive children and their families. These procedures had been used to identify how behavior management and control are disrupted, and lead to the escalation of negative exchanges in the families of aggressive children. Because children with mental retardation also present behavior management challenges for parents, the possibility of negative escalation was potentially relevant to these families. In order to make the interaction as naturalistic as possible, families were videotaped in the home while completing a task of their own choosing. All family members were present. However, it was also necessary to structure the session somewhat in order to ensure that the family members interacted together and that the videotapes were sufficiently clear so that the behaviors could be reliably coded. Thus, families were instructed to complete an activity together (e.g., baking cookies, working on a crafts project), to refrain from watching television or making or taking telephone calls, and to remain together in one or two rooms within range of the video camera. The families were observed for a total of 50 minutes, which, for coding purposes, was divided into 10 minute segments. During each segment, one family member was identified as the focus of coding, and only behaviors that occurred by the focus person and anyone interacting with that person were coded by the observer. This procedure allowed the camera operator to focus on subsets of family members rather than trying to keep all family members in view at all times.

The findings support the value of these observational methods. Most notably, whereas self-report measures of marital quality, the parenting alliance, and parenting experiences failed to distinguish families of children with mental retardation from a comparison group with typically developing children, both the marital interactions and the family interactions demonstrated greater marital negativity and more parent–child behavior management struggles for the MR group (Floyd & Zmich, 1991). Furthermore, negative marital interactions were predictive of negative parent–child exchanges. A subsequent longitudinal evaluation demonstrated that marital quality, including the quality of marital problem-solving interactions, predicts changes in negative parent–child exchanges over a two-year period, with couples who are most negative together showing increases in their negative exchanges with children over time (Floyd, Gilliom, & Costigan, in press).

3.01.10 CONCLUDING COMMENTS

As can be seen in the above discussion, behavioral observation provides an extremely rich source of information for investigators as they attempt to understand the complexities of human behavior and interaction. This richness presents many opportunities for investigators and many challenges as well. These challenges are incorporated in the myriad of decisions that the investigator must make in employing behavioral observation, and obviously the route that the investigator chooses greatly impacts the findings. Thus, the investigator incurs responsibility for understanding the impact of these decisions on the questions under investigation. Often in reporting the results of investigations employing behavioral observation, the method section of the report involving the application of coding systems and data analytic strategies is presented in a few short paragraphs. Consequently, most readers will have only a general level of understanding of how the coding system was employed and how that impacts the findings. Therefore, the investigator must thoroughly understand the coding process so that discussions of the findings accurately represent what is indicated by the data. When this is done in a thoughtful manner, we have the opportunity to use one of our most natural strategies, observing people's behavior, as a major way to advance the science of clinical psychology.

3.01.11 REFERENCES

Ainsworth, M. D., Blehar, M. C., Waters, E., & Wall, S. (1978). *Patterns of attachment: A psychological study of the strange situation.* Hillsdale, NJ: Erlbaum.
Allison, P. D., & Liker, J. K. (1982). Analyzing sequential categorical data on dyadic interaction: A comment on Gottman. *Psychological Bulletin, 91,* 393–403.
Altmann, J. (1974). Observational study of behavior: Sampling methods. *Behaviour, 49,* 227–265.
American Psychological Association (1985). *Standards for educational and psychological testing.* Washington, DC: Author.
Ammerman, R. T., Van Hasselt, V. B., & Hersen, M. (1991). Parent–child problem-solving in families of visually impaired youth. *Journal of Pediatric Psychology, 16,* 87–101.
Ary, D. (1984). Mathematical explanation of error in duration recording using partial interval, whole interval, and momentary time sampling. *Behavioral Assessment, 6,* 221–228.
Bakeman, R., & Casey, R. L. (1995). Analyzing family interaction: Taking time into account. *Journal of Family Psychology, 9,* 131–143.
Bakeman, R., & Gottman, J. M. (1997). *Observing interaction: An introduction to sequential analysis* (2nd ed.). New York: Cambridge University Press.
Bakeman, R., & Quera, V. (1995). Log-linear approaches to lag-sequential analysis when consecutive codes may and cannot repeat. *Psychological Bulletin, 118,* 272–284.
Barton, C. & Alexander, J. F. (1981). Functional family therapy. In A. S. Gurman & D. P. Kniskern (Eds.), *Handbook of family therapy* (pp. 403–443). New York: Brunner/Mazel.
Baucom, D. H. (1982). A comparison of behavioral contracting and problem-solving/communications training in behavioral marital therapy. *Behavior Therapy, 13,* 162–174.
Baucom, D. H., Sayers, S. L., & Sher, T. G. (1990). Supplementing behavioral marital therapy with cognitive restructuring and emotional expressiveness training: An outcome investigation. *Journal of Consulting and Clinical Psychology, 58,* 636–645.
Cairns, R. B., & Green, J. A. (1979). How to assess personality and social patterns: Observations or ratings? In R. B. Cairns (Ed.), *The analysis of social interactions: Methods, issues, and illustrations* (pp. 209–226). Hillsdale, NJ: Erlbaum.
Carpenter, L. J., & Merkel, W. T. (1988). The effects of three methods of observation on couples in interactional research. *American Journal of Family Therapy, 16,* 144–157.
Christensen, A., & Hazzard, A. (1983). Reactive effects during naturalistic observation of families. *Behavioral Assessment, 5,* 349–362.
Christensen, A., & Heavey, C. L. (1990). Gender and social structure in the demand/withdraw pattern of marital conflict. *Journal of Personality and Social Psychology, 59,* 73–81.
Cummings, E. M. (1987). Coping with background anger in early childhood. *Child Development, 58,* 976–984.
Dawes, R. M. (1979). The robust beauty of improper linear models in decision making. *American Psychologist, 34,* 571–582.
Digital LAVA Inc. (1996). 10850 Wilshire Blvd., Suite 1260, LA, CA 90024.
Fagot, B., & Hagan, R. (1988). Is what we see what we get? Comparisons of taped and live observations. *Behavioral Assessment, 10,* 367–374.
Floyd, F. J. (1989). Segmenting interactions: Coding units for assessing marital and family behaviors. *Behavioral Assessment, 11,* 13–29.
Floyd, F. J., & Costigan, C. L. (1997). Family interactions and family adaptation. In N. W. Bray (Ed.), *International review of research in mental retardation* (Vol. 20, pp. 47–74). New York: Academic Press.
Floyd, F. J., Gilliom, L. A., & Costigan, C. L. (in press). Marriage and the parenting alliance: Longitudinal prediction of change in parenting perceptions and behaviors. *Child Development.*
Floyd, F. J., & Zmich, D. E. (1991). Marriage and the parenting partnership: Perceptions and interactions of parents with mentally retarded and typically developing children. *Child Development, 62,* 1434–1448.

Foster, S. L., Inderbitzen, H. M., & Nangle, D. W. (1993). Assessing acceptance and social skills with peers in childhood. *Behavior Modification, 17,* 255–286.

Gardner, W., & Griffin, W. A. (1989). Methods for the analysis of parallel streams of continuously recorded social behaviors. *Psychological Bulletin, 105,* 446–455.

Gottman, J. M. (1979). *Marital interaction: Experimental investigations.* New York: Academic Press.

Gottman, J. M. (1980). Analyzing for sequential connection and assessing interobserver reliability for the sequential analysis of observational data. *Behavioral Assessment, 2,* 361–368.

Gottman, J. M. (1994). *What predicts divorce?* Hillsdale, NJ: Erlbaum.

Gottman, J. M., & Krokoff, L. J. (1989). Marital interaction and satisfaction: A longitudinal view. *Journal of Consulting & Clinical Psychology, 57*(1), 47–52.

Gottman, J. M., Markman, H., & Notarius, C. (1977). The topography of marital conflict: A sequential analysis of verbal and nonverbal behavior. *Journal of Marriage and the Family, 39,* 461–477.

Haley, J. (Ed.) (1971). *Changing families.* New York: Grune & Stratton.

Harris, F. C. & Lahey, B. B. (1986). Condition-related reactivity: The interaction of observation and intervention in increasing peer praising in preschool children. *Education and Treatment of Children, 9,* 221–231.

Hartmann, D. P. (1977). Considerations in the choice of interobserver reliability estimates. *Journal of Applied Behavior Analysis, 10,* 103–116.

Hartmann, D. P. (Ed.) (1982). *Using observers to study behavior.* San Francisco: Jossey-Bass.

Hartmann, D. P., & Wood, D. D. (1990). Observational methods. In A. S. Bellack, M. Hersen, & A. E. Kazdin (Eds.), *International handbook of behavior modification and therapy* (2nd ed., pp. 109–138). New York: Plenum.

Hawkins, R. P. (1979). The functions of assessment: Implications for selection and development of devices for assessing repertoires in clinical, educational, and other settings. *Journal of Behavioral Assessment, 12,* 501–516.

Haynes, S. N. (1978). *Principles of behavioral assessment.* New York: Gardner Press.

Haynes, S. N. (1998). The changing nature of behavioral assessment. In M. Hersen & A. S. Bellack (Eds.), *Behavioral assessment: A practical handbook* (4th ed., pp. 1–21). Boston: Allyn & Bacon.

Haynes, S. N., Follingstad, D. R., & Sullivan, J. C. (1979). Assessment of marital satisfaction and interaction. *Journal of Consulting and Clinical Psychology, 47,* 789–791.

Haynes, S. N., & Horn, W. F. (1982). Reactivity in behavioral observation: A review. *Behavioral Assessment, 4,* 369–385.

Herbert, J., & Attridge, C. (1975). A guide for developers and users of observational systems and manuals. *American Educational Research Journal, 12,* 1–20.

Hersen, N., & Bellack, A. S. (1998). *Behavioral assessment: A practical handbook* (4th ed.). Boston: Allyn & Bacon.

Hetrick, W. P., Isenhart, R. C., Taylor, D. V., & Sandman, C. A. (1991). ODAP: A stand-alone program for observational data acquisition. *Behavior, Research Methods, Instruments, and Computers, 23,* 66–71.

Humphrey, L. L., & Benjamin, L. S. (1989). *An observational coding system for use with structural analysis of social behavior: The training manual.* Unpublished manuscript, Northwestern University Medical School, Chicago.

Iverson, A., & Baucom, D. H. (1990). Behavioral marital therapy outcomes: Alternate interpretations of the data. *Behavior Therapy, 21*(1), 129–138.

Jacob, T. (1975). Family interaction in disturbed and normal families: A methodological and substantive review. *Psychological Bulletin, 82,* 33–65.

Jacob, T., Tennenbaum, D., Bargiel, K., & Seilhamer, R.

A. (1995). Family interaction in the home: Development of a new coding system. *Behavior Modification, 19,* 147–169.

Jacob, T., Tennenbaum, D. L., & Krahn, G. (1987). Factors influencing the reliability and validity of observation data. In T. Jacob (Ed.), *Family interaction and psychopathology: Theories, methods, and findings* (pp. 297–328). New York: Plenum.

Jacob, T., Tennenbaum, D., Seilhamer, R. A., Bargiel, K., & Sharon, T. (1994). Reactivity effects during naturalistic observation of distressed and nondistressed families. *Journal of Family Psychology, 8,* 354–363.

Jacobson, N. S. (1985). The role of observational measures in behavior therapy outcome research. *Behavioral Assessment, 7,* 297–308.

Jarrett, R. B., & Nelson, R. O. (1984). Reactivity and unreliability of husbands as participant observers. *Journal of Behavioral Assessment, 6,* 131–145.

Johnston, J. M., & Pennypacker, H. S. (1993). *Strategies and tactics of behavioral research* (2nd ed.). Hillsdale, NJ: Erlbaum.

Karney, B. R., & Bradbury, T. N. (1995). The longitudinal course of marital quality and stability: A review of theory, methods, and research. *Psychological Bulletin, 118*(1), 3–34

Kazdin, A. E. (1977). Artifact, bias and complexity of assessment: The ABC's of reliability. *Journal of Applied Behavior Analysis, 10,* 141–150.

Kazdin, A. E. (1982). Observer effects: Reactivity of direct observation. *New Directions for Methodology of Social and Behavioral Science, 14,* 5–19.

Klesges, R. C., Woolfrey, J., & Vollmer, J. (1985). An evaluation of the reliability of time sampling versus continuous observation data collection. *Journal of Behavior Therapy and Experimental Psychiatry, 16,* 303–307.

Kuller, R., & Linsten, C. (1992). Health and behavior of children in classrooms with and without windows. *Journal of Environmental Psychology, 12,* 305–317.

Leaper, C., Hauser, S., Kremen, A., Powers, S. I., Jacobson, A. M., Noam, G. G., Weiss-Perry, B., & Follansbee, D. (1989). Adolescent–parent interactions in relation to adolescents' gender and ego development pathway: A longitudinal study. *Journal of Early Adolescence, 9,* 335–361.

Mann, J., ten-Have, T., Plunkett, J. W., & Meisels, S. J. (1991). Time sampling: A methodological critique. *Child Development, 62,* 227–241.

Mehm, J. G., & Knutson, J. F. (1987). A comparison of event and interval strategies for observational data analysis and assessments of observer agreement. *Behavioral Assessment, 9,* 151–167.

Minuchin, S. (1974). *Families and family therapy.* Cambridge, MA: Harvard University Press.

Noldus, L. P. J. J. (1991). The Observer: A software system for collection and analysis of observational data. *Behavior Research Methods, Instruments, and Computers, 23,* 415–429.

Noller, P. (1980). Misunderstandings in marital communication: A study of couples' nonverbal communication. *Journal of Personality and Social Psychology, 39,* 1135–1148.

O'Neill, R. E., Horner, R. H., Albin, R. W., Storey, K., & Sprague, J. R. (1990). *Functional analysis of problem behavior: A practical assessment guide.* Sycamore, IL: Sycamore Publishing.

Patterson, G. R. (1982). *A social learning approach, Vol 3: Coercive family process.* Eugene, OR: Castalia Publishing Company.

Patterson, G. R., Reid, J. B., & Dishion, T. J. (1992). *Antisocial Boys.* Eugene, OR: Castalia.

Pett, M. A., Wampold, B. E., Vaughn-Cole, B., & East, T. D. (1992). Consistency of behaviors within a naturalistic setting: An examination of the impact of context and repeated observations on mother–child interactions. *Behavioral Assessment, 14,* 367–385.

Prinz, R. J., & Kent, R. N. (1978). Recording parent-adolescent interactions without the use of frequency or interval-by-interval coding. *Behavior Therapy, 9,* 602–604.

Robin, A. L., & Foster, S. L. (1989). *Negotiating parent-adolescent conflict: A behavioral-family systems approach.* New York: Guilford.

Sackett, G. P. (1979a). The lag sequential analysis of contingency and cyclicity in behavioral interaction research. In J. D. Osofsky (Ed.), *Handbook of infant development* (pp. 623–649). New York: Wiley.

Sackett, G. P. (Ed) (1979b). *Observing behavior. Vol. 2: Data collection and analysis methods.* Baltimore: University Park Press.

Schaap, C. (1982). *Communication and adjustment in marriage.* Lisse, Holland: Swetts & Zeitlinger.

Serbin, L. A., Citron, C., & Connor, J. M. (1978). Covert assessment of observer agreement: An application and extension. *Journal of Genetic Psychology, 133,* 155–161.

Shores, R. E., Jack, S. L., Gunter, P. L., Ellis, D. N., Debreire, T. J., & Wehby, J. H. (1993). Classsroom interactions of children with behavior disorders. *Journal of Emotional and Behavioral Disorders, 1,* 27–39.

Shrout, P. E., & Fleiss, J. L. (1979). Intraclass correlations: Uses in assessing rater reliability. *Psychological Bulletin, 86,* 420–428.

Sidman, M. (1960). *Tactics of scientific research: Evaluating experimental data in psychology.* New York: Basic Books.

Skinner, B. F. (1938). *The behavior of organisms.* New York: Appleton-Century-Crofts.

Snyder, J. (1983). Aversive social stimuli in the Family Interaction Coding System: A validation study. *Behavioral Assessment, 5,* 315–331.

Stine, W. W. (1939). Interobserver relational agreement. *Psychological Bulletin, 106,* 341–347.

Suen, H. K., Ary, D., & Covalt, W. (1990). A decision tree approach to selecting an appropriate observation reliability index. *Journal of Psychopathology and Behavioral Assessment, 12,* 359–363.

Taplin, P. S. & Reid, J. B. (1973). Effects of instructional set and experimenter influence on observer reliability. *Child Development, 44,* 547–554.

Tapp, J., & Walden, T. (1993). PROCORDER: A professional tape control, coding, and analysis system for behavioral research using videotape. *Behavior Research Methods, Instruments, and Computers, 25,* 53–56.

Tapp, J., Wehby, J., & Ellis, D. (1995). A multiple option observation system for experimental studies: MOOSES. *Behavior Research Methods, Instuments, and Computers, 27,* 25–31.

Taylor, D. V., Hetrick, W. P., Neri, C. L., Touchette, P., Barron, J. L., & Sandman, C. A. (1991). Effect of naltrexone upon self-injurious behavior, learning, and activity: A case study. *Pharmacology, Biochemistry, and Behavior, 40,* 79–82.

Triangle Research Collaborative, Inc. (1994). P. O. Box 12167, 100 Park, Suite 115, Research Triangle Park, NC 27709.

Tryon, W. W. (1991). *Activity measurement in psychology and medicine.* New York: Plenum.

Van Widenfelt, B., Baucom, D. H., & Gordon, K. C. (1997). *The Prevention and Relationship Enhancement Program: An empirical analysis.* Manuscript submitted for publication.

Wampold, B. E. (1989). Kappa as a measure of pattern in sequential data. *Quality and Quantity, 23,* 171–187.

Wampold, B. E., & Holloway, E. L. (1983). A note on interobserver reliability for sequential data. *Journal of Behavioral Assessment, 5,* 217–225.

Watson, J. B., & Raynor, R. (1920). Conditioned emotional reactions. *Journal of Experimental Psychology, 3,* 1–12.

Weinrott, M. R. & Jones, R. R. (1984). Overt versus covert assessment of observer reliability. *Child Development, 5,* 1125–1137.

Weiss, R. L. (1986). *MICS-III manual.* Unpublished manuscript, Oregon Marital Studies Program, University of Oregon, Eugene.

Wieder, G. B., & Weiss, R. L. (1980). Generalizability theory and the coding of marital interactions. *Journal of Consulting and Clinical Psychology, 48,* 469–477.

Wilson, F. R. (1982). Systematic rater training model: An aid to counselors in collecting observational data. *Measurement and Evaluation in Guidance, 14,* 187–194.

Winer, B. J. (1971). *Statistical principles in experimental design* (2nd ed.). New York: McGraw-Hill.

3.02
Single Case Experimental Designs: Clinical Research and Practice

STEVEN C. HAYES and JOHN T. BLACKLEDGE
University of Nevada, Reno, NV, USA

3.02.1 INTRODUCTION

The purpose of clinical research from the point of view of the consumer of research knowledge can be stated succinctly: "What treatment, by whom, is most effective for this individual with that specific problem under which set of circumstances, and how does it come about?" (Paul, 1969, p. 44). This question has always been of relevance to practicing clinical psychologists in the fee-for-service environment, but it is also of increasing relevance in the era of managed care. Mental health delivery systems cannot succeed, either in the world of public opinion or in the world of fiscal reality, without finding a way to deliver services that are both effective and efficient (Cummings, Cummings, & Johnson, 1997; Cummings, Pollack, & Cummings, 1996). In order to do that, Paul's clinical question above must be answered for the varieties of clients demanding and receiving services.

There is another way to say this. Clinical research must have external validity (must apply to the settings and clients of the research consumer), not merely internal validity (an unambiguous relationship between a dependent and independent variable). In group comparison research, external validity flows in principle from internal validity. In a classic group comparison design, researchers hope to randomly sample from a known population, randomly assign to a treatment and control group, and collect before and after measures on all. If these methodological requirements have been met, the results should apply to other random samples from that same population. In the practical world of clinical research, however, we do not have access to the entire population of interest (say, all panic disordered clients). We cannot randomly sample from this population because clients nonrandomly refuse to participate. We cannot randomly assign because clients nonrandomly drop out. And even if all this were not true, we never apply clinical research to other random samples from the same population—rather, a clinician treats the person who (nonrandomly) walked through the door.

External validity thus must be earned—whether in group comparison or single-case research—in a piecemeal inductive fashion by demonstrating that particular treatments work with particular clients with particular problems. In group comparison research, this is usually done by showing that treatments work in highly homogeneous groups of clients. By replicating effects across many such homogenous groups, external validity can be demonstrated in group research. Efforts to show broad external validity in a single group comparison experiment are

usually extremely difficult. Blocking or stratifying samples on even a few factors in a single study can lead to huge designs that cannot be mounted without millions of dollars of research funds. One compromise is to use diagnostic categories as a way of establishing homogeneity; however, large and unexplained between-subject variation invariably results because the current diagnostic system is based on loose collections of signs and symptoms rather than functional processes.

An alternative approach is to build this knowledge base about treatment response from the ground up, person by person. In this approach, clinical replication across myriad clients provides the evidence that a treatment effect holds for a population and that it is moderated by specific subject, therapist, or setting variables. That is the approach of single case experimental designs (SCEDs) or what has also been termed "time-series designs." The former term is more popular but falsely suggests that the number of subjects is necessarily few in this approach. The latter correctly points to the source of the analysis but it is not very popular. Both terms will be used.

The purpose of this chapter is to show how single case designs are used in a research and practice environment, to provide an introduction to the various types of designs, and to explore the advantages of this research approach in the modern world of health care delivery.

3.02.1.1 Brief History of Single Case Experimental Designs

The origin of SCEDs in clinical psychology can be traced back to the beginnings of the scientist–practitioner model. Two years before at the first Boulder Conference, Thorne (1947) advocated the use of such designs as a practical way for clinicians to incorporate empirical science into their everyday interactions with clients, a goal concurrently explicated by Shakow et al. (1947). The type of experimental designs proposed by Thorne were a very significant improvement over the traditional case study because continual data collection over a series of phase changes were required, allowing more objective, data-driven decisions to be made. These designs were an adaptation of those previously used by experimental psychologists (Ferster & Skinner, 1957) working with animals.

Single case designs became considerably more popular with the popularization of behavioral approaches in the 1960s. For example, Baer, Wolf, and Risley (1968) described a number of these designs in an early issue of the *Journal of Applied Behavior Analysis*. Hersen and Barlow's groundbreaking text (1976) in turn brought these designs into the mainstream of behavior therapy.

Probably the biggest factors inhibiting the use of SCEDs by many clinicians has been a bias against ideographic research. Yet many methodological leaders of the field have been quite accepting of such an approach. For example, Cronbach (1975) advocated careful observation of individual clinical cases using SCED controls, maintaining that the use of such design tools allows a level of detail in observation and hypothesis testing not available in traditional group designs. Many others (Campbell, 1957; Koan & McGuire, 1973; Snow, 1974) have agreed, adding that tightly controlled, fixed condition, group experimentation is often not well-suited to a science of vastly differing humans with often vastly differing needs. Cone (1986) noted that ideographic, single-subject research is particularly well-suited for detecting point-to-point behavioral changes occurring in response to environmental variables, including psychological treatment.

3.02.1.2 Utility of Single-subject Designs

A clinician carefully conducting an appropriate single-subject design for a client could both circumvent the above difficulties and obtain scientifically useful results. Often no subject pool larger than one is needed to conduct a single-subject design (although it is necessary that the results of many such analysis be considered before any general conclusions can be made about a treatment's efficacy). Single-subject experiments are extremely flexible. For example, if a client is not responding as hoped to a treatment, components can be added or subtracted or an altogether new treatment can be implemented, without necessarily damaging the validity of conclusions drawn from the experiment. Essentially, the only limitation on the usefulness of single-subject designs in research and clinical practice is the flexibility of the researcher. If use of a planned design does not allow an adequate interpretation of emerging data, then the design can be altered at that point.

Perhaps more importantly, a properly used single-subject design can be extremely useful in facilitating responsible assessment and treatment. A clinician conducting a single-subject experiment is forced to pay close attention to repeated assessments of client behavior that provide invaluable information about target behaviors and treatment efficacy. With the continuous feedback that single-subject experi-

ments provide, treatment components not working as planned can be altered, abandoned, or supplemented.

The comprehensive data recorded over several single-subject designs can also be used to provide linkage between client characteristics and treatment success or failure. As more detailed information is gathered in time-series designs than in a typical group experiment, events in individual client lives and various client characteristics that coincide with declines in treatment efficacy can be identified and taken into consideration for subsequent clients. The advantage at this level is that variability due to sources other than treatment can be identified at the level of the individual. This means that when many cases are collected and analyzed, correlations between subject characteristics and treatment responsiveness can be more refined. For example, it may become apparent after conducting several single-subject designs mapping the effects of a given intervention that subjects with certain characteristics respond in characteristically similar ways. Such a hypothesis can be followed up using additional single subjects, or by using a group design. Subjects that fail to respond positively to a given treatment may do so because of a detectable reason, and this reason may point to an important aspect of a relevant theory. Outcomes like this critically depend on the foresight of the researcher. Potentially important background data, as indicated by theory and common sense, should be collected in every single-subject experiment.

The use of time-series designs also compels a clinician to focus on the careful description of patient problems and treatment characteristics, and how this data relates to treatment outcome. In such a manner, variables that are functionally important for treatment can become evident. Over a series of SCEDs, generalizations concerning the active and efficacious components of treatment can be made from such data.

Finally, analysis of SCEDs concentrates on the magnitude of treatment effects rather than their statistical significance. If the treatment analyzed in a properly conducted SCED is clinically significant, it will be clearly so.

3.02.2 ESSENTIAL COMPONENTS OF SINGLE CASE EXPERIMENTAL DESIGNS

Although various types of individual time-series designs exist, and are discussed in some detail later, several procedures common to all time-series designs are first described.

3.02.2.1 Repeated Measurement

The bedrock of single case experimental designs is repeated measurements of client functioning taken in relevant domains throughout the course of treatment (Barlow & Hersen (1984), Hayes, Barlow, and Nelson (1997), and Kazdin (1980) give information on specific measurement strategies). Repeated measurements enable the estimation of variability within a case over time to provide the sources of information about treatment, measurement error, and extraneous factors in a time-series approach.

In the real world of clinical evaluation, the goal is to use measures that are both high quality and highly practical. It is advisable that such measurements begin as soon as possible, ideally during the first session. It is also advisable, in choosing which instruments to administer to the client or research subject, that the researcher err on the side of caution and administer as many instruments as may be even partially relevant to the current experiment's concerns. Theory and even common sense should be used to guide the choice as to what instruments are relevant. Practical constraints also play an important part. If an adequate but imperfect instrument already exists and no time is currently available to create a new one, the adequate instrument may be used. Client self-monitoring and self-report is entirely acceptable. In fact, any method of collecting data is acceptable with single-subject designs, so long as the researcher deems it appropriate. Flexibility, again, is the by-word. But, as with any instrument, pay attention to its established reliability and validity before using or interpreting data. As treatment progresses, instruments useless or irrelevant to the current case can be discarded, but data not initially gathered can never be collected. It is worth spending a little extra time administering an instrument on a hunch on the chance that it will yield valuable information. Measurements are then ideally administered as frequently as is practical and meaningful.

3.02.2.2 Detailed Information

Specification of the particular intervention made with the client, including when each component is delivered and any possibly significant deviations from the standardized treatment, allows meaningful inferences to be made from collected data. To be meaningful indicators of the effects of a treatment and its components, the clinician must be able to temporally link specific phases of their intervention with the ongoing flow of outcome data

as described above. Details regarding the nature of the treatments, the environment that the therapy was delivered in, and characteristics of the therapist provide a level of detail conducive to proper replication, especially if the completed SCED is made available to others. Steps taken in group research to ensure treatment integrity can be taken here as well. For example, a colleague or student might be asked to assess a clinician's adherence to a designated treatment protocol, as well as the competence with which the treatment is delivered. Specification of the treatment requires that the researcher has a clear, theoretically-based idea of what they are attempting to accomplish and how to accomplish it. The type of treatment being used, its specific techniques, and the phases or subphases of each technique or strategy that are active should be noted. Enough detail should be added so that after the intervention is complete, an informed guess can be made as to what might have been responsible for observed effects.

Collection of detailed client information allows more meaningful inferences to be drawn from single-subject data. The recording of any information that might possibly affect the course and effectiveness of treatment may prove to be invaluable for data analysis. Seemingly relevant background information and significant events occurring in the client's life during the course of treatment qualify as important client information. If the client's spouse leaves her during the course of treatment, for example, notation of this event may serve as a possible explanation for a brief or sustained decline in the treatment's effectiveness. Of importance here is the chronicling of any information about the client or the client's life that might be expected to affect their response to treatment. Over a series of SCEDs, such information can be used to speculate as to why clients reacted differentially to treatment.

3.02.2.3 Graphing of Data

Analysis of an individual time-series design requires a visual representation of the data. A simple line graph, with time plotted on the x-axis and measurement score plotted on the y-axis, should be sufficient for most data because it presents an immediate picture of variability within a data series. Pragmatic considerations determine what unit of time to plot. Thus, if an instrument is measuring behaviors in frequent time intervals but the behavior itself is better thought of in temporally larger units, analysis may be facilitated if time intervals are collapsed (e.g., if daily measurements are summed and recorded as weekly measurements). Frequent and creative graphing of data, from various angles, using different units of time, composite scores from separate measures, etc., can allow insights into the effects of treatment.

3.02.2.4 Creative Use of Design Elements

Individual time-series design elements (discussed below) should be thought of as tools, not restrictive agents. If a complex phase change with an interaction element is initially planned, and the data indicates the client might benefit most from continuing with the current treatment, then continuation of treatment is clearly justified. Unexpected client or therapist vacations can be an opportunity for a return to baseline phase, allowing a chance to monitor the effectiveness, in contrast, of treatment. Clinical common sense and detailed understanding of the nature of the different design elements and when they are useful allows effective and serendipitous adaptation to events.

3.02.3 INTERPRETATION OF SINGLE-SUBJECT DATA

Time-series designs typically (though not always) consist of units of time called phases, each phase designating the continuous presence of a given condition (e.g., treatment, baseline, and so on). Data within each phase can be described as having various degrees of variability around a given level and trend. Use of statistical analyses is not necessary at the level of the individual, and indeed use of most inferential statistics with a single subject violates the assumptions of standard statistical tests. Clear graphing of data and a thorough understanding of interpreting such single-subject graphs are all that are needed to observe an effect. It is to the nature of variability, level, and trend, and to the opportunities they provide for the interpretation of the data, that we now turn.

3.02.3.1 Variability and Stability

Data within a phase is said to be stable to the extent that the effects of extraneous variables and measurement error, as reflected in variability within a subject across time, are sufficiently limited or identifiable that variability due to treatment can be ascertained. Determining stability requires that the clinician have some clarity about what treatment effects are large enough to be worth detection—the more variability due to extraneous factors or measurement error, the larger the treatment effect would have to be to be seen.

If the data are not stable (in the sense that important treatment effects might be obscured), the experimenter can (i) continue the phase until the data does become stable, (ii) examine the data using longer units of time if longer units are more sensible, or (iii) analyze the possible sources of variability. Each of these is defensible, but the last option is often the best because it can provide important information about the case.

3.02.3.2 Level

Level refers to the "height" on the *y*-axis at which the data tends to aggregate. For example, data taken during a treatment phase tending to stay at the upper points of the measurement scale would be notably distinguishable, in terms of level, from data congregating around the mid-point of a measurement scale.

3.02.3.3 Trend

Trend refers to the general linear direction in which data are moving across a given period of time. It takes a minimum of three data points to establish a trend and estimate variability around that trend.

Converging and diverging trends between phases can be analyzed to help differentiate variability due to treatment from variability due to extraneous sources. For example, if a client's data on a given measure shows a positive trend in baseline that continues when treatment is implemented and continues yet again when the baseline is reinstated, it is likely that something other than treatment is responsible for the improvement. Conversely, if a strong positive trend during a treatment phase levels out or especially reverses after a change to a baseline phase, the clinician can usually feel confident that treatment is responsible for the change (unless some potentially significant life change happened to co-occur with the phase change). Thus, trends are not only useful indicators as to the improvement or decline of clients on various measures, but are also useful indicators, coupled with phase changes, of the sources of those changes.

3.02.3.4 Use of Statistics with Single-subject Data

For the most part, inferential statistics were designed for use in between-group comparisons. The assumptions underlying the widely accepted classical model of statistics are usually violated when statistical tests based on the model are applied to single-subject data. To begin with, presentation of conditions is not generally random in single-subject designs, and randomization is a necessary prerequisite to statistical analysis. More importantly (and more constantly), the independence of data required in classical statistics is generally not achieved when statistical analyses are applied to time-series data from a single subject (Sharpley & Alavosius, 1988). Busk and Marascuilo (1988) found, in a review of 101 baselines and 125 intervention phases from various single-subject experiments, that autocorrelations between data, in most cases, were significantly greater than zero and detectable even in cases of low statistical power. Several researchers have suggested using analyses based on a randomization task to circumvent the autocorrelation problem (Edgington, 1980; Levin, Marascuilo, & Hubert, 1978; Wampold & Furlong, 1981). For example, data from an alternating treatment design or extended complex phase change design, where the presentation of each phase is randomly determined, could be statistically analyzed by a procedure based on a randomization task. Some controversy surrounds the issue (Huitema, 1988), but the consensus seems to be that classical statistical analyses are too risky to use in individual time-series data unless at least 35–40 data points per phase are gathered (Horne, Yang, & Ware, 1982). Very few researchers have the good fortune to collect so much data.

Time-series analyses where collected data is simply used to predict subsequent behavior (Gottman, 1981; Gottman & Glass, 1978) can also be used, and is useful when such predictions are desired. However, such an analysis is not suitable for series with less than 20 points, as serial dependence and other factors will contribute to an overinflated alpha in such cases (Greenwood & Matyas, 1990). In cases where statistical analysis indicates the data is not autocorrelated, basic inferential statistical procedures such as a *t*-test may be used. Finally, the Box–Jenkins procedure (Box & Jenkins, 1976) can technically be used to determine the presence of a main effect based on the departure of observed data from an established pattern. However, this procedure would require a minimum of about 50 data points per phase, and thus is impractical for all but a few single-subject analyses.

In addition, most statistical procedures are of unknown utility when used with single-subject data. As most statistical procedures and interpretations of respective statistical results were derived from between-group studies, use of these procedures in single-subject designs yields ambiguous results. The meaning of a statistically significant result with a lone subject does not mean the same thing as a statistically significant result with a group, and the assumptions and evidentiary base supporting classical statistics simply dose not tell us what a significant result with a single subject means. Beyond the technical incorrectness of using nomethetic statistical approaches to ideographic data, it is apparent that such use of these statistics is of extremely limited use in guiding further research and bolstering confidence about an intervention's efficacy with an individual subject. If, for example, a statistically significant result were to be obtained in the treatment of a given client, this would tell us nothing about that treatment's efficacy with other potential clients. Moreover, data indicating a clinically significant change in a single client would be readily observable in a well-conducted and properly graphed single-subject experiment. Statistics—so necessary in detecting an overall positive effect in a group of subjects where some improved, some worsened, and some remained unchanged—would not be necessary in the case of one subject exhibiting one trend at any given time.

3.02.4 VARIETIES OF SINGLE-SUBJECT DESIGNS

Time-series design elements can be classified either as within-series, between-series, or combined-series designs. Different types of time-series design elements within each group of designs are used for different purposes (Hayes et al., 1997). The nature of each type of element, as well as its purpose, will now be described.

3.02.4.1 Within-series Design Elements

A design element is classified as within-series if data points organized sequentially within a consistent condition are compared to other such sequential series that precede and follow. In such a design, the clinician is typically faced with a graphed data from a single measure or a homogenous group of measures, organized into a sequence of phases during which a consistent approach is applied. Phase changes occur, ideally, when data has stabilized. Otherwise, practical or ethical issues determine the time at which phases must change. For example, an extended baseline with a suicidal client would certainly not be possible, and time and financial constraints may determine phase changes in other cases. Aspects of specific design strategies that influence phase length are discussed at the appropriate points below.

Within-series design elements include the simple phase change, the complex phase change, the parametric design elements, and the changing criterion design. Each is described below. Note that specific phases are designated below by capital letters. Generally (but not always), the letter A refers to a baseline phase, and letters such as B and C refer to different interventions.

3.02.4.1.1 Simple phase change

If simply trying to determine a treatment's efficacy vs. no treatment at all for a given client, or comparing the relative efficacy of two validated treatments for a given client, then a simple phase change design is probably the right choice. Consider the case in which only a single treatment's efficacy is at issue. A similar approach can be taken to answer questions about the relative efficacy of two treatments.

In the standard simple phase change, baseline data on relevant client behaviors is typically taken for a period of time (enough time to estimate the level, trend, and variability around level and trend of the behavior of interest). This baseline phase can occur during initial sessions with the client while assessment (and no treatment *per se*) is taking place, while the client is on a waiting list, or through similar means. Treatment is then administered and while it is in place a second estimate is made of the level, trend, and variability around level and trend of the behavior of interest. If clear changes occur, treatment may have had an impact.

In order to control for extraneous events that might have co-occurred with the phase change from baseline to treatment, the phase change must be replicated. Usually this is done by changing from treatment back to baseline, but other options exist. Such a change, called a withdrawal, is useful in aiding the clinician in deciding whether it is indeed the treatment, and not some extraneous variable, that is responsible for any changes. However, certain ethical considerations must be made before a withdrawal is executed. If treatment definitely seems effective and is well-validated, it may not be necessary to withdraw the treatment to conclude that a treatment effect is likely. If the clinician is uncertain of the treatment's effectiveness, or if it is not well-validated, a withdrawal or some other means of replication is necessary in order to conclude that an effect has occurred. Even a short withdrawal can be sufficient if a clear trend is evident. Alternatively, a period of time where therapy is focused on a different, relatively unrelated problem can also be considered a withdrawal. Serendipitous opportunities for a return to a baseline phase can provide important information. Impromptu client or therapist vacations can be viewed as a chance to make more informed decisions regarding the treatment's efficacy.

More than one replication of the underlying phase change (such as an ABABAB design) may be necessary for the clinician to be confident of a treatment's effects for a particular client. Interpretation of the data is facilitated by referring to the specifics of stability, level and trends as discussed above.

Examples of well-conducted simple phase change designs include Gunter, Shores, Denny, and DePaepe (1994), who utilized the design to evaluate the effects of different instructional interactions on the disruptive behavior of a severely behaviorally disordered child. Gunter et al. (1994) used a simple phase change with reversal (in this case ABAB), with baseline or A phase consisting of a math assignment with between five and 15 difficult multiplication problems. The treatment or B phase consisted of equally difficult problems, but the experimenter would provide the correct answer and then present the same problem again whenever the subject incorrectly answered. Institution of the first treatment phase indicated a desirable effect, with the subject's rate of disruptive behavior falling from around 0.3 to around 0.1. Gunter et al. (1994) wisely decided to replicate the phase changes with the subject, allowing them to be more confident that extraneous variables such as time or (to some extent) order were not responsible for the changes.

Orsborn, Patrick, Dixon, and Moore (1995) provide another good, contemporary example of the simple phase change design (Figure 1). They used an ABAB design to evaluate the effect of reducing the frequency of teacher's questions and increasing the frequency of pauses on the frequency of student talk, using 21 first- and second-grade subjects. Both B phases showed a marked increase in student talk frequency relative to baseline phases. The strength of the design, however, could have been improved with the inclusion of more data points. Five data points were collected during baseline phases, and three in intervention phases. Three is an acceptable minimum, but more data points are advisable.

3.02.4.1.2 Complex phase change elements

A complex phase change combines a specific sequence of simple phase changes into a new logical whole.

(i) ABACA

When comparing the effectiveness of two (or more) treatments relative to each other and to

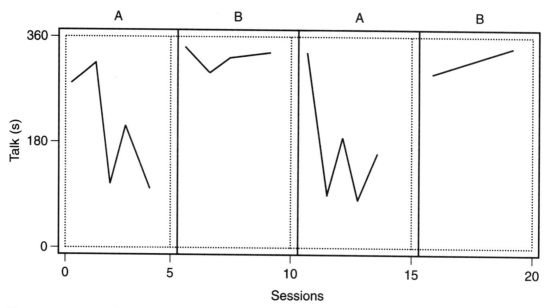

Figure 1   An adaptation of a simple phase change with reversal design. Data were relatively stable before phase changes (adapted from Orsborn et al., 1995).

no treatment, an ABACA complex phase change element might be used. Typically, the clinician would choose such a design when there is reason to believe that two treatments, neither yet well-validated, may be effective for a given client. When it is unclear whether either treatment will be effective, treatment phases can be interspersed with baseline phases. Phase changes conducted in such a manner will allow meaningful comparisons to be made between both treatments, as well as between each treatment and no treatment. After administering each treatment once, if one that results in clearly more desirable data level and trend, it may be reinstated. If each treatment's relative efficacy is still unclear, and the data gives no reason to believe that either may be iatrogenic, phase changes may be carried out as is practical. A sequence such as ABACACAB might not be unreasonable if the data and clinical situation warranted. Regardless of the sequence implemented, the clinician should remain aware that order effects in a complex phase change can be critical. The second treatment administered may be less effective simply because it is the second treatment. Counterbalancing of phase sequences in other cases can circumvent such ambiguity.

The clinician should stay alert to the possibility of introducing even a third treatment in such a design, if the original treatments do not appear to be having the desired effect. An example of such a situation is shown in a study by Cope, Moy, and Grossnickle (1988). In this study, McDonald's restaurants promoted the use of seat belts with an advertising campaign (phase B), and the distribution of instructive stickers for children asking them to "Make it Click" (phase C). These two interventions were tried repeatedly. Finally, an incentive program was implemented giving away soft drinks for drivers who arrived at McDonald's with their seat belt fastened. The design could be described as an ABCBCBDA. The spirit here, as always when using time-series approaches, should be one of flexible and data-driven decisions. With such a spirit, the clinician should be willing to abandon even an empirically validated treatment if it is clear, over a reasonable length of time, that there is no positive effect. No treatment is all things to all people.

Another well-conducted complex phase change design was reported by Peterson and Azrin (1992; Figure 2). Three treatments, including self-monitoring (phase B), relaxation training (phase C), and habit reversal (phase D), were compared with a baseline or no treatment (phase A). Six subjects were used, and the authors took advantage of the extra subjects by counterbalancing the presentation of phases. For example, while the first subject was presented with the phase sequence AAABCDCBDA, other subjects were presented with sequences such as AAADCBCD-BA, AAACDBDCBA, and AAACDBDCBA. A minimum of three data points were contained in each phase (generally four or more data points were used), and the authors more often than not waited until stability was achieved and clear trends were present before changing phases for subjects.

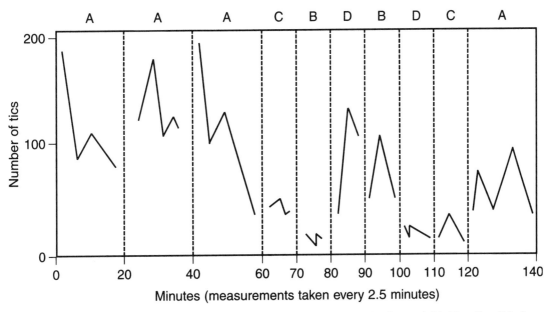

Figure 2 An example of a complex phase change. Waiting for the data in the first and third baseline (A) phase to stabilize (as well as the data in the first D phase) would have been preferable before initiating phase changes (adapted from Peterson and Azrin, 1992).

(ii) Interaction element

In an interaction element the separate and combined effects of intervention elements are examined. Use of this design element is appropriate both when a treatment is working and the clinician wishes to ascertain whether it will continue working without a particular (and costly in terms of time and/or money) component, or when a treatment is not maximally effective and the clinician believes adding or subtracting a specific component might enhance the treatment's efficacy.

White, Mathews, and Fawcett (1989) provide an example of the use of the interaction element. They examined the effect of contingencies for wheelchair push-ups designed to avoid the development of pressure sores in disabled children. Wheelchair push-ups were automatically recorded by a computer. After a baseline, two subjects were exposed to an alarm avoidance contingency (B), a beeper prompt (C), or a combination. An interaction design element was combined with a multiple baseline component. The design for one subject was an A/B + C/B/B + C/B/B + C/C/B + C, and for the other was A/B + C/C/B + C/C/B + C. Each component (B or C) was more effective than a baseline, but for both children the combined (B + C) condition was the most effective overall.

Shukla and Albin (1996) provided another good example when examining the effects of extinction vs. the effects of extinction plus functional communication training on problem behaviors of severely disabled subjects

(Figure 3). Extinction had previously been found to be effective in reducing the frequency of target behaviors, but it had the unfortunate effect of sometimes causing more problematic behaviors to emerge. By alternating phases consisting of extinction alone and extinction plus communication training, the authors were able to show that the second condition resulted in uniform decreases in problematic behavior.

(iii) Changing criterion

The changing criterion design element consists of a series of shifts in an expected benchmark for behavior, such that the correspondence between these shifts and changes in behavior can be assessed. It is particularly useful in the case of behaviors that tend to change gradually, provided that some benchmark, goal, criterion, or contingency is a key component of treatment.

The establishment of increasingly strict limits on the number of times a client smokes per day provides a simple example. A changing criterion design could be implemented when it is unclear as to whether the criteria themselves, and no other variable, were responsible for observed changes in smoking. As another example, a changing criterion design could be implemented to assess the degree to which changing minimum numbers of social contacts per day affects actual social contacts in a socially withdrawn client.

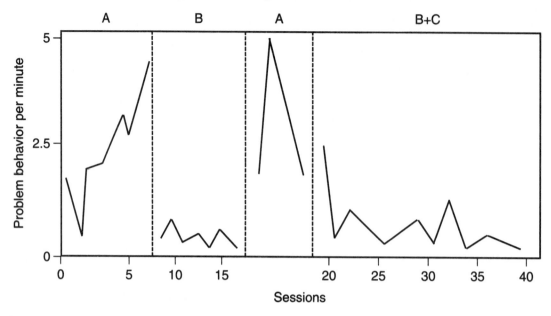

Figure 3   An interaction element design. The interaction (B + C) condition did not yield a better result than the B condition, but the demonstration of no further efficacy was still an important finding (adapted from Shukla & Albin, 1996).

In order to maximize the possibility that the data from a changing criterion design are correctly interpreted, five heuristics seem useful. First, the number of criterion shifts in the design should be relatively high. Each criterion shift is a replication of the effect of setting a criterion on subsequent client behavior. As with any type of experiment, the more frequently the results are replicated, the more confident the researcher can be of the effect and its causes. As a rule of thumb, four or more criterion shifts should occur when a changing criterion design is implemented.

Second, the length of the phase in which one level of the criterion is in effect should be long enough to allow the stability, level, and trend of the data to be interpreted relative to the criterion. Additionally, if a clear trend and level do not initially emerge, the criterion should remain in effect until a clear trend and level does emerge. Belles and Bradlyn (1987) provide a good example of properly timed criterion changes. The goal was to reduce the smoking rate of a long-time smoker who smoked several packs a day. The client recorded the number of cigarettes smoked each day (with reliability checks by the spouse). After a baseline period, goals were set by the therapist for the maximum number of cigarettes to be smoked. If the criterion was exceeded, the client sent a $25 check to a disliked charity. For each day the criterion was not exceeded, $3 went into a fund that could be used to purchase desirable items. Each criterion was left in place for at least three days, and the length of time, magnitude, and

direction of criterion shifts varied. It should also be noted that, as in the Belles and Bradlyn (1987) study, criterion changes should occur at irregular intervals. As certain behaviors may change in a cyclical or gradual manner naturally, criteria should be shifted after differing lengths of time. Thus, if the length of one criterion's phase happens to correspond to changes occurring naturally, the phase lengths of other levels of the criterion will be unlikely to continue this trend.

Third, criterion changes should occur at irregular intervals. As certain behaviors may change in a cyclical or gradual manner naturally, criteria should be shifted after differing lengths of time. Thus, if the length of one criterion's phase happens to correspond to changes occurring naturally, the phase lengths of other levels of the criterion will be unlikely to continue this trend.

Fourth, the magnitude of criterion shifts should be altered. If the data can be shown to track criterion changes of differing magnitudes, the statement that the criterion itself is responsible for observed changes can be made with a greater level of assurance.

Finally, a periodic changing of the direction of criterion shifts can be useful in assisting interpretations of effects. Such a strategy is similar to the reversal common in simple and complex phase changes. If client behavior can be shown to systematically track increasing and decreasing criteria, the data can be more confidently interpreted to indicate a clear effect of the changing criteria on those behavioral changes.

DeLuca and Holborn (1992) used the changing criterion design in analyzing the effects of a variable-ratio schedule on weight loss in obese and nonobese subjects (Figure 4). Phase sequences consisted of a baseline (no treatment) phase, three different criterion phases, an additional baseline phase, and finally a return to the third criterion phase. The criterion involved the number of revolutions completed on a stationary exercise bike during the allotted time in each phase. Criterion phases were determined by a calculation of 15% over the criterion in place for the previous phase; when the criterion was met, a subject would receive reinforcement in the form of tokens exchangeable for established reinforcers. Each phase (except for the five-session final phase) lasted for eight 30-minute sessions, resulting in eight data points per phase. The increasing variable ratio schedules were shown, through use of this design, to exert control over increased frequencies of revolution. Although the design did not exhibit some typical features of the changing criterion design, such as staggered phase length, criterion direction reversals, and varying phase change depths, the observation of clear effects were facilitated by the return to baseline phase and subsequent replication of the third criterion phase. In addition, the use of the design in an exercise program was prudent, as exercise involves gradual performance improvements of a type easily detected by the changing criterion design.

3.02.4.1.3 Parametric design

When it is suspected that different levels or frequencies of a component of an intervention might have a differential effect on client behavior, a parametric design can be implemented. Such designs are frequently used to assess the effects of different psychotropic drug dosages, but design is relevant for many other purposes. Kornet, Goosen, and Van Ree (1991) demonstrated the use of the parametric design in investigating the effects of Naltrexone on alcohol consumption.

Ideally, a kind of reversal can be incorporated into a parametric design, where levels of the independent variable in question were systematically increased and then decreased. As with the changing criterion element, showing that an effect tracks a raised and lowered standard bolsters the confidence with which an interpretation is made. Baseline data should usually be taken before and after changes in the parameter of interest. If certain levels of the parameter provide interesting or unclear data, alternations between those levels, even if not originally planned, can aid in clarification (e.g., if the sequence A/B/B′/B″/B‴/B″/B′/B/A was originally planned and the data spurs increased interest in the B and B′ levels, a sequence such as B/B′/B/B′ could be inserted or added).

An example of acceptable use of parametric design is provided by Stavinoah, Zlomke, Adams, and Lytton (1996). The experimenters

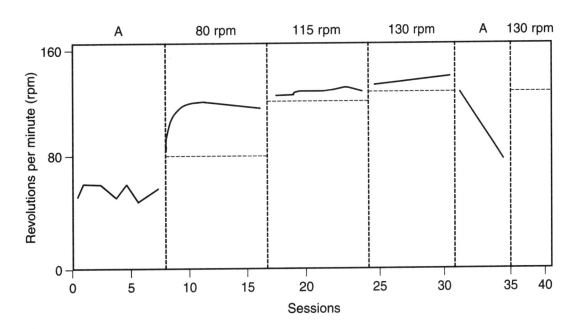

Figure 4 An example of a changing criterion design. Dotted horizontal lines indicate set criterion in each phase. The use of more than three criteria might have been preferable to further indicate experimental control over behavior, but the design seems adequate nonetheless (taken from DeLuca & Holborn, 1992).

systematically varied dosages of haloperidol and fluoxetine while measuring the frequency of the subject's impulsive aggressive behaviors (IABs). Dosages of haloperidol ranged from about 40 mg to 20 mg over the 40 weeks that it was administered. As a 40 mg dose initially resulted in an average of 10 IABs per week, dosage was reduced to 20 mg after 12 weeks. During the next 34 weeks, IABs increased to 13 per week, and the decision was made to increase the dosage back to 40 mg. This resulted in an average of 45 IABs per week for the four weeks this dosage was in place. The experimenters then administered a 20 mg dose of fluoxetine for the next 62 weeks, resulting in an average IAB frequency of near zero. A 40 mg dose of fluoxetine administered for 58 weeks yielded IAB frequencies of near zero. A subsequent reduction to 20 mg for five weeks resulted in an average IAB frequency of 12; the dosage was then returned to 40 mg, with a resulting IAB frequency of almost zero. Ideally, less time could have been spent at each dosage, and a greater variety of dosages could have been employed. But the experimenters did vary dosage and even drugs, and did so with a sufficient number of data points to determine the effect each drug and dosage had on behavior.

Lerman and Iwata (1996) provide a better example of use of the parametric design in treating the chronic hand mouthing of a profoundly retarded man (Figure 5). Sessions were conducted two or three times per day. Baseline frequencies (with no attempts to stop the hand mouthing behavior) were first calculated; baseline rates of three times per minute, on average, were recorded over several sessions. During the intervention phase, all subject attempts at hand mouthing were blocked by the experimenter putting his hand in front of the subject's mouth, resulting in less than one instance of hand mouthing per minute. Subsequently, attempts were blocked at a ratio of 1 block per 2 attempts, 1/4, 1/2, 2/3, and 3/4. The frequency of hand mouthing remained near zero over all levels. The experimenters properly used a descending/ascending order for levels, but also allowed subject behavior to determine what blocking schedule would be used. The experimenters thus remained responsive to the data, and their efforts yielded a less intensive intervention than one block per attempt.

3.02.4.1.4 Final suggestions for interpreting within-series data

Besides the suggestions listed above for interpreting various types of within-series data, additional general suggestions are offered here. First, as with any type of data-producing procedure, replicated effects are always more believable than nonreplicated effects. If an effect is consistently duplicated across several clients or across several different behaviors in the same client, the clinician can feel more confident in stating that the treatment in question is responsible for the effect. Each additional reinstatement of a treatment phase resulting in client improvement within a single series of data should also allow more confident statements about that treatment's efficacy with that client to be made. Second, effects are much more believable to the extent that they occur in a consistent manner. Third, changes of a greater magnitude (when parsing out changes apparently caused by extraneous variables) should generally be taken as more robust evidence of the treatment's effects. Fourth, effects occurring immediately after the onset of a treatment phase are logically stronger indicators that the treatment is responsible for the changes than are delayed effects, since fewer alternative explanations exist for the effects seen. Fifth, greater changes in the level and trend of the data are generally more indicative of a treatment's efficacy. Sixth, any effects not explainable by variables other than treatment should naturally be more convincing. Finally, all effects should be interpreted while considering the background variability of the data. The variability in the data around a given level and trends in a consistent condition provide an individual estimate of the impact of extraneous factors and measurement error against which any treatment effect is seen. If, for example, the level and/or trend of baseline data at times overlaps with the level and/or trend of treatment phase data, the clear possibility that factors other than treatment may be augmenting (or inhibiting) the treatment effect should be considered.

Brief mention of some commonly occurring conditions illustrate application of the guidelines discussed thus far. If a significant upward or downward data trend begins one to three data points before a phase change is planned, delay of the phase change until the data stabilizes is suggested. A trend is significant if it is of a greater degree than changes attributable to background variability, such as would be observed when a series of relatively stable data fluctuates around an average level. However, if an established and significant trend has emerged over a few (e.g., three or more) data points, a phase change might be acceptable if such results had been expected. Instability and unclear trends are obviously of less importance at the beginning of a phase than at the end; data at first uninterpretable often has a way of telling a clearer story after more data is collected. The

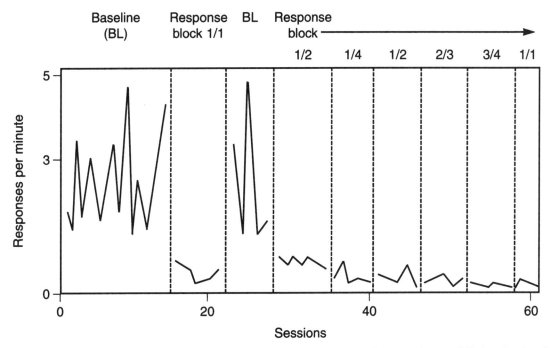

Figure 5 An example of a parametric design. Response block conditions refer to differing levels of intervention, that is, 14 translates to one response block per every four handmouthing attempts (adapted from Lerman & Iwata, 1996).

value of collecting as many data points as feasible (e.g., seven or more) becomes clear after only a few data points have been graphed.

3.02.4.2 Between-series Designs

Within-series designs involve comparisons of sequences of repeated measurements in a succession of consistent conditions. Between-series designs are based on a comparison of conditions that are concurrent or rapidly alternating, so that multiple data series are simultaneously created. Pure between-series designs consist of the alternating treatments design and the simultaneous treatment design.

3.02.4.2.1 *Alternating treatment design*

The alternating treatment design (ATD) consists of rapid and random or semirandom alteration of two or more conditions such that each has an approximately equal probability of being present during each measurement opportunity. As an example, it was observed during a clinical training case that a student therapist, during many sessions, would alternate between two conditions: leaning away from the client and becoming cold and predictable when he was uncomfortable, and leaning towards the client and becoming warm and open when feeling comfortable. The client would disclose less when the therapist leaned away, and more when

he leaned forward. If it were assumed that the therapist had preplanned the within-session alternations, an ATD as shown in Figure 6 would be obtained. The condition present in the example at any given time of measurement is rapidly alternating. No phase exists; however, if the data in each respective treatment condition are examined separately, the relative level and trend of each condition can be compared between the two data series (hence the name between-series designs).

An example of the ATD is provided by Jordan, Singh, and Repp (1989). In this study, two methods of reducing stereotypical behavior (e.g., rocking, hand-flapping) in retarded subjects were examined: gentle reaching (the use of social bonding and gentle persuasion with the developmentally disabled) and visual screening (covering the client's eyes for a few seconds following stereotypic behavior, thus reducing visual stimulation including that provided by these movements). Each of the two conditions were randomly alternated with a baseline condition. After a baseline period, visual screening produced a dramatic reduction in stereotypy, whereas gentle teaching had only a transient effect.

Another proper use of the alternating treatments design is provided by Van Houten (1993; Figure 7). Four children were taught subtraction using two different procedures (one procedure involved the use of a general rule,

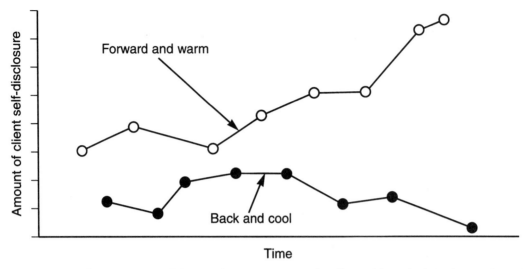

Figure 6   A hypothetical example of the use of an ATD to assess the effects of therapist behavior on client self-disclosure.

the other involved only rote learning). Use of the procedures was alternated randomly and every 15 minutes over the length of 15 or more sessions, and the subtraction problems used in each session were counterbalanced across the subjects so that effects could be attributed to the teaching methods and not the problem sets. The use of an ATD rather than a complex phase change was prudent, as the order the methods were presented in longer phases could probably have exerted a practice effect.

One of the benefits of the ATD is the simplicity with which it can be used to compare three or even more treatment conditions. Proper comparisons of three conditions in a within-series design can be difficult due to counter-balancing concerns, order effects, and the sheer number of phase changes that need to be executed over a relatively long period of time. With an ATD, three or even more conditions can be presented in a short time. The rapid and random alternations between conditions makes order effects less likely, but multiple treatment interference (the impact of one treatment is different due to the presence of another) is arguably likely. ATDs are ideally used with behaviors emitted at a relatively high frequency that correspondingly allows many instances of each alternate intervention to be applied. However, the design may be used with relatively infrequent behaviors if data is collected for a longer period of time. In addition, behaviors that tend not to have an impact for long after a discrete intervention is made and withdrawn make better targets for an ATD. If a change initiated by such a discrete intervention continues over a long period of time, effects of subsequent interventions are obscured and reliable data interpretation is often not possible.

ATDs hold several other advantages over standard within-series designs. First, treatment need not be withdrawn in an ATD—if treatment is periodically withdrawn, it can be for relatively short periods of time. Second, comparisons between components can be made more quickly. If a clear favorite emerges early in a well-conducted ATD, the clinician can be reasonably sure that its comparative efficacy will be maintained McCullough, Cornell, McDaniel, and Mueller (1974), for example, compared the relative efficacy of two treatments in four days using an ATD. ATDs can be used without collecting baseline data, or with baseline data through the creation of a concurrent baseline data series. Any background within-series trends (such as those due to maturation of the client or etiology of the disorder) are unlikely to obscure interpretation of the data because the source of data comparisons are purely between series, not within.

ATD requires a minimum of two alterations per data series. As both series can be combined to assist assessments of measurement error and extraneous factors, the number of data points required is less than with a within-series design. The collection of more than two data points per series is typical and highly useful, however. In a sense, each alternation is a replication and conclusions from all time-series designs can be stated with more confidence with each consistent replication.

When planning alternations, the clinician should be alert to the duration, after presentation, of a component's effect. An administered drug, for example, exerts an effect over a period of time, and presenting a new treatment component before that time has expired would confound interpretation.

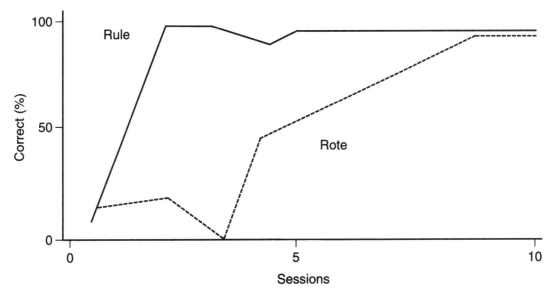

Figure 7 An ATD in which rule-learning trials are interspersed with rote-learning trials. A practice or generalization effect is apparent in the rote-learning condition beginning around session 8 (adapted from Van Houten, 1993).

One of the shortcomings of the ATD is that observed effects in the design can be due to the way in which conditions are presented and combined. Three areas of concern in this domain of multiple treatment interference are sequential confounding, carry-over effects, and alternation effects (Barlow & Hayes, 1979; Ullman & Sulzer-Aszaroff, 1975).

Sequential confounding occurs when there is a possibility that a treatment condition A yields different effects when presented before a treatment condition B than it does when presented after condition B. To control for sequential confounding, the clinician is encouraged to alternate treatment conditions randomly or at least semirandomly. With a randomly delivered sequence such as ABB-BAABABBBABBAAAABBAAABAA, if consistent differences between each condition's effects continue to show up throughout the sequence, despite the fact that the order and frequency of each conditions' presence differs through the sequence, the clinician can be relatively certain that observed effects are not an artifact of order of condition presentation.

A carry-over effect occurs when the presentation of one condition somehow affects the impact of the subsequent condition, regardless of the presentation order of the conditions. Potentially this can occur in two ways. The effects of two conditions can change in opposite directions, or in the same direction. For example, when a strong reinforcer is delivered after a weak reinforcer, the weak reinforcer can subsequently cease to reinforce the desired behavior at all while the other reinforcer has a strong effect. At times, exposure to one condition results in a similar response to a somewhat similar second condition. Implementing each condition for a relatively short period of time can help reduce these problems (O'Brien, 1968), as might clear separations between each treatment condition (such as introducing only one treatment condition per session).

Several procedures exist to help detect multiple treatment interference (Sidman, 1960). A simple phase change where one treatment condition is preceded by a baseline phase, when compared to another AB design containing the other treatment, and finally compared to an ATD combining both conditions, could be used to parse out the separate and interactive effects of the treatment conditions. Alternatively, the intensity of one treatment condition could be increased, with any subsequent changes in the following conditions (as compared to changes already witnessed in an ATD containing both conditions) attributable to carry-over effects.

Some additional caveats regarding proper use of the ATD are of note. First, although a baseline phase is not necessary in an ATD, inclusion of baseline data can be useful for both gathering further information on client functioning and interpreting the magnitude of treatment effects. If periodic baseline points can be included within the ATD itself, valuable information regarding background level, trend, and variability can also be gleaned, over and above what would be interpretable if treatment conditions alone were present.

Second, it is important to realize that although ATDs can effectively be used with four or even more treatment conditions and corresponding data series, an upper limit exists on the number of data series that can be meaningfully interpreted. One useful heuristic (Barlow, Hayes, & Nelson, 1984) is to count the number of data points that will likely be collected for the ATD's purpose and then divide this number by the desired number of data series. If several data points will be collected for each series, the clinician should be able to proceed as planned.

Third, the clinician must consider the amount of data overlap between data series when interpreting ATD results. Overlap refers to the duplication of level between series. Several issues must be considered if considerable overlap exists. First, the percentage of data points, relative to all data points in an involved series, that indeed overlap can be calculated. If this percentage is low, the likelihood of a differential effect is higher. Second, the stability of the measured behavior should be considered. If the frequency of a given behavior is known to vary widely over time, then some overlap on measures of that behavior between ATD conditions would be expected. Third, the clinician must note if any overlapping trends occur in the two conditions. If data in two series are similar not only in level but also in trend, then it seems plausible that a background variable, rather than the treatment conditions, might affect the data.

One final example is shown in Figure 8. These are the data from an airplane-phobic client in the study on the effect of cognitive coping on progress in desensitization (Hayes, Hussian, Turner, Anderson, & Grubb, 1983). Notice that there is a clear convergence as the two series progress. The orderliness of the data suggested that the results from cognitive coping were generalizing to the untreated scenes. Alternating a reminder not to use the coping statements with the usual statements then tested this possibility. The data once again diverged. When the original conditions were then reinstated, the data converged once more. This showed that the convergence was a form of systematic generalization, rather than a lack of difference between the two conditions. This is also a good example of the combination of design elements to answer specific questions. This particular design does not have a name, but it is a logical extension of design tools discussed above.

3.02.4.2.2 Simultaneous treatment design

Simultaneous treatment design (STD) is similar to ATD in which the two treatments are continuously present but are accessed by the choice of the subject. What is plotted is not the impact of the treatment but the degree to which it is accessed. In other words, an STD measures preference. As an example, suppose a clinician wished to assess the motivation of a disabled child for different kinds of sensory stimulation. Several kinds of toys that produced different sensory consequences could be placed in a room with the child and the percentage of time played with each kind of toy could be recorded and graphed. This would be an STD.

3.02.4.3 Combined-series Elements

Combined-series designs contain elements from both within- and between-series designs, and combine them into a new logical whole. Although many examples in the literature contain elements of both between- and within-series designs, true combined-series designs involve more than merely piecing components together. What distinguishes combined series elements from any combination of elements is that the combination yields analytical logic.

3.02.4.3.1 Multiple baseline

One of the more often encountered SCEDs is the multiple baseline. An adaptation of the simple phase change, the multiple baseline design allows control over some variables that often confound interpretation of within-series phase change data. Upon a phase change from baseline to treatment in a simple phase change, for example, the data would ideally indicate a sudden and very strong treatment effect. It would be arranged in such a way that background variability could be easily detected against the effects of the treatment. Even when this ideal outcome occurs, however, there is also the possibility that some extraneous variable having a strong effect on measured outcomes might co-occur with the onset of a treatment phase. Such an occurrence would have dire implications for interpretation of the simple phase change result. The multiple baseline design allows considerable control over such threats to validity.

Essentially, the multiple baseline typically involves a sort of simple phase change across at least three data series, such that the phase change between baseline and treatment occurs at different times in all three data series (Figure 9). The logic of the design is elegantly simple. Staggering the implementation of each respective phase change allows the effects of extraneous variables to be more readily observed. It is generally unlikely that any given extraneous occurrence will have an equal effect on phase changes occurring at three different points in time.

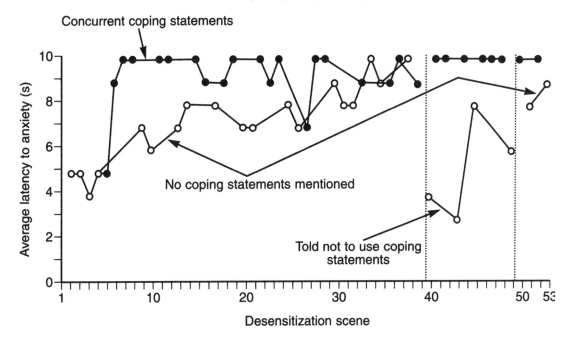

Figure 8 An example of series convergence in the ATD and its analysis by adding within-series components (redrawn from Hayes et al., 1983).

Implementation of a multiple baseline design greatly increases the potential number of comparisons that can be made between and within data series, ultimately strengthening the confidence with which conclusions are made from the data. Figure 3 details where such comparisons can be made. First, changes in level and trend within each data series (that is, between the baseline and treatment phase of each of the three data series) can be analyzed, just as with a simple AB design. Unlike a simple phase change, however, differences in level and trend between baseline and treatment can also be compared between three series of data. The design, in effect, contains replications of the phase change. If similar levels and trends are exhibited across all three series, the clinician can feel confident that the treatment is the most likely candidate for exerting the effect. Comparisons can also be made between the point of time at which the first phase change occurs, and the same points of time in the two remaining data series, where baseline data is still being collected. Such comparisons give the researcher information on whether some variable other than treatment might be responsible for observed changes. For example, a strong positive trend and marked change in level might be indicated by the data after the treatment phase is implemented. If similar changes occur in the other two data series at the same points in time, before treatment has even been implemented in those data series, it would seem clear that something besides treatment was exerting an

influence on the data. A similar comparison can be made between the point at which the second phase change is implemented and the corresponding data points on the third series of data.

The type of data recorded in each of the three series must be similar enough so that comparisons can be made between the series, yet different enough that effects in one series are not expected from a phase change in another series. The context in which the data in each of the three series is collected can be of three varieties. The multiple baseline across behaviors requires that three relatively discrete and problematic behaviors, each of which might be expected to respond to a given treatment, be chosen. The treatment is then implemented in staggered, multiple baseline fashion for each behavior. The clinician would probably wish to choose behaviors that are unlikely to be subject to some generalization effect, so that a treatment implemented with behavior 1 results in concomitant change in one or both of the other behaviors (because, for example, the client begins to apply the principles learned immediately to those other behaviors). Such an effect would be easily observed in between-series comparisons (i.e., when a data trend in a condition where the intervention has not yet been initiated resembles the trend exhibited in an intervention condition, a generalization effect may very likely be present). However, the clinician could not be absolutely certain in such a case that the changes across behaviors were due to some generalization effect and not an extraneous variable. In

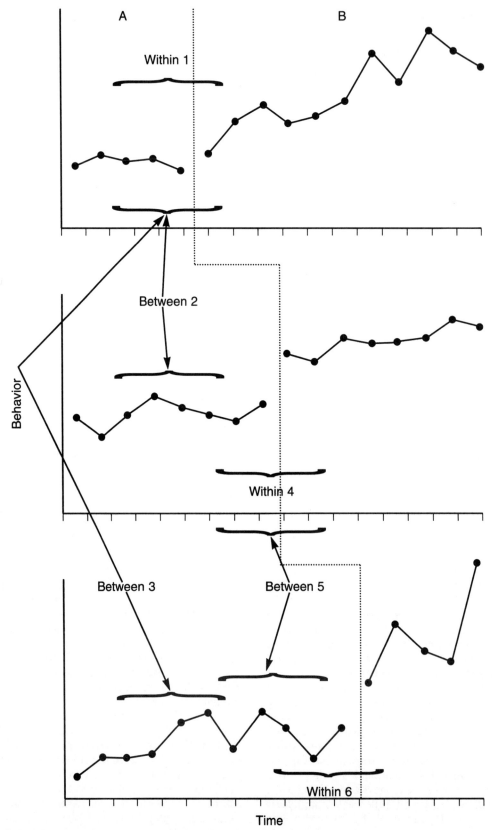

Figure 9 A hypothetical example of a multiple baseline, with between- and within-sources of data comparisons. Comparisons can be made between pre- and postphase change data within any of the three series, as well as between any two series at the points where an intervention is in place for one series and baseline conditions are still in effect for the second series.

general, if it seems theoretically likely that a generalization effect would occur under such circumstances, and no apparent confounding variable is present, then it is often safe to assume generalization occurred. Even if such an effect were observed, it might not be disastrous by any means. Implementing a treatment only to serendipitously find that it positively affects behaviors other than the targeted one could hardly be considered unfortunate.

An example of the multiple baseline across behaviors is provided by Trask-Tyler, Grossi, and Heward (1994). Developmentally disabled young adults were taught to use three cooking recipes of varying degrees of complexity (simple, trained, and complex), with the goal of the study being to determine whether or not specific skills would generalize across recipes. Simple tasks included preparing microwave popcorn while receiving specific instructions regarding its preparation. Trained tasks were analogs of previously taught simple tasks, where subjects used previously taught skills to prepare a different food (e.g., microwave french fries). Complex tasks consisted either of new tasks or novel combinations of previously trained tasks. Intervention phases were staggered across complexity levels, and occurred after a baseline phase where subjects completed recipes without instruction. Complexity level served as an appropriate analog for differing behaviors in this case, and the implementation of new phases were staggered with sufficient data points (i.e., three or over) occurring in each phase. The design use was also innovative in that it involved applied skills.

Alternately, the clinician may choose to implement a multiple baseline design across settings. If, for example, a client was socially withdrawn in a variety of circumstances (e.g., at work, at the gym, and on dates), social skills training might be implemented at different points in time across several of those circumstances. As another example, anger management training with an adolescent could be implemented in a staggered fashion at home, school, and at a part-time job site. As with the multiple baseline across behaviors, the clinician should be alert to the possibility of generalization effects.

An example of the multiple baseline across settings design is provided by Kennedy, Cushing, and Itkonen (1997; Figure 10). The study investigated the effects of an inclusion intervention on the frequency and quality of social contacts with nondisabled people, using two developmentally disabled children as subjects. The intervention included a number of components, such as placement in general school settings with nondisabled peers, and feedback. After a baseline where both subjects participated

in special education classes only, the design took the shape of a multiple baseline across classes. One subject eventually participated in four classes, the other in two. Phase lengths were more than adequate (minimum of five data points), and phase changes were appropriately staggered (levels and trends stabilized before onset of the intervention in a new setting). The intervention was effective in increasing the frequency and quality of peer interactions.

Finally, a multiple baseline design can be implemented across persons. Such a manifestation of the design would, of course, require access to three clients with fairly similar presenting concerns subjected to the same treatment. As it is probably unlikely that anyone but a therapist at a university or health center would have simultaneous access to three such clients, it is acceptable to collect data on new clients as they present for services (Hayes, 1985). Objections exist to this approach (Harris and Jenson, 1985), but we feel strongly that the practicality of the approach and the control against extraneous factors that the design possesses greatly outweigh the potential risks.

The multiple baseline across persons design is exemplified by Kamps et al. (1992). The effects of social skills groups on the frequency of social skills interactions of high functioning autistic subjects with normal peers were analyzed across three subjects. Baseline consisted of frequency counts of social interactions before social skills training. Phase changes within each series did not occur until data stabilized, and phase changes across subjects were staggered approximately 10 sessions apart. A minimum of seven data points (usually more) were present in each phase. Social skills training had a positive effect on social interactions.

Ideally, phase changes should wait until the data indicates a clear level and trend, and is stable, before the phase change is executed. This is advisable when changing from baseline to treatment within a given series, and especially when executing staggered phase changes in the second and third data series. If no clear effect is observable in a series, then co-occurring data points between a series cannot be meaningfully interpreted.

An example of the multiple baseline is provided by Croce (1990). A multiple baseline across persons was used to evaluate the effects of an aerobic fitness program on three obese adults, while weekly body fat and cardiovascular fitness measurements were taken. Over three weeks of baseline data was collected in all subjects before treatment was delivered to the first subject. Treatment for the second subject was implemented three weeks after the first, and treatment for the third subject was delayed an

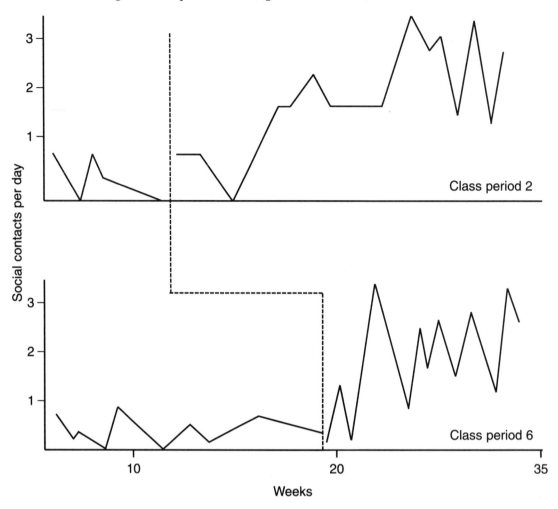

Figure 10 A multiple baseline across settings. Data was stable before phase changes in both settings, and comparisons between the settings indicate that the intervention was responsible for changes and that no generalization effect occurred (adapted from Kennedy et al., 1997).

additional three weeks. The data clearly indicated a desirable effect.

3.02.4.3.2 *Crossover design*

The crossover design essentially involves a modification of the multiple baseline allowing an additional degree of control over extraneous variables (Kazdin, 1980). It can be especially useful when only two (rather than three or even more) series of data can plausibly be gathered, as this added control tends to compensate for the control lost by the omission of a third series. This design has been widely used in pharmacological studies (Singh & Aman, 1981).

Execution of a crossover design simply involves simultaneous phase changes across two series of data such that, at any given point in time, opposite phases are in operation between each series. If series one's phase sequence was, for example, ABAB, a BABA sequence would be simultaneously delivered, with each phase

change occurring at the same time in both series, and after treatment phases of precisely equal lengths. Such an arrangement can make even a relatively weak effect evident, as each treatment (B phase) always has a corresponding baseline (A phase) in the other data series to allow finer interpretations of stability, level, and trend.

3.02.4.3.3 *Constant series control*

One final combined series design warrants brief mention. A constant series control can be added to a series of data when baseline data alone is collected concurrently on some other person, problem, or situation of interest. In adding a constant series control to an in-school anger management intervention with a child, for example, relevant behavioral data might be collected at the child's home (where the treatment is not considered active) throughout the period where an ABAB phase sequence is being implemented at school. Treatment B effects from the school setting can then be compared to concurrently gathered baseline data from the home setting to assist in interpretation of the treatment's effects. Such a control is extremely useful when used in conjunction with a simple or complex phase change design.

A study by O'Reilly, Green, and Braunling-McMorrow (1990) provides an example of a baseline-only constant series control. O'Reilly et al. were attempting to change the accident-prone actions of brain-injured individuals. A written safety checklist that listed, but did not specifically prompt hazard remediation, was prepared for each of several areas of the home. If improvement was not maximal in a given area, individualized task analyses were prepared that prompted change in areas that still required mediation. The design used was a multiple baseline across settings (living room, kitchen, bedroom, and bathroom). Although phase changes from baseline to checklist prompts to task analysis occurred in staggered multiple baseline across the first three settings, a baseline condition remained in effect for the entire 29 weeks of the study. Results indicated very little evidence of generalization across responses, and the baseline-only constant series control provided additional evidence that training was responsible for the improvements that were seen.

3.02.5 FUTURE DIRECTIONS

Widespread use of SCEDs by practicing clinicians could provide a partial remedy to two currently omnipresent concerns in the mental health care delivery field: a virtual lack of use and production of psychotherapy outcome literature by clinicians, and the demand for demonstrated treatment efficacy by the managed care industry.

3.02.5.1 Potential for Research Production and Consumption by Practicing Clinicians

Line clinicians currently produce very little research. This is unfortunate since it is widely recognized that assessment of the field effectiveness of treatment technology is a critical and largely absent phase in the research enterprise (Strosahl, Hayes, Bergan, & Romano, in press).

Single-subject designs are well suited to answer many of the questions most important to a clinician. They are useful tools in keeping the clinician in touch with client progress and informing treatment decisions. Most of the requirements of these designs fit with the requirements of good clinical decision making and with the realities of the practice environment.

This has been true for some time, and the research production using these designs in the on-line practice environment is still limited. That may be about to change, however, for the reason discussed next.

3.02.5.2 Managed Health Care, Single-subject Design, and the Demonstration of Efficacy

The managed health care revolution currently underway in the USA represents a force that, in all likelihood, will soon encompass nearly all US mental health services delivery systems (Strosahl, 1994; Hayes et al., in press). The hallmark of managed care organizations (MCOs) is the provision of behavioral health services in a way that is directed, monitored, not merely compensated.

In generation I of the managed care revolution, cost savings accrued mostly to cost reduction strategies. That phase seems nearly complete. In generation II, cost savings are accruing to quality improvement strategies. Uppermost in this approach is the development of effective and efficient treatment approaches, and encouragement of their use through clinical practice guidelines.

Time-series designs are relevant to MCOs in three ways. First, they can allow much greater accountability. Single-subject designs provide an excellent opportunity for the clinician to document client progress and provide sufficient justification to MCOs, HMOs, and PPOs for implementing treatments or treatment components. Even a simple AB is a big step forward in that area. Second, when cases are complex or treatment resistant, these designs provide a way of evaluating clinical innovation that might be useful for improving the quality of treatment for other cases not now covered by empirically supported treatments. Finally, these designs can be used to evaluate the impact of existing treatment programs developed by MCOs.

3.02.6 CONCLUSION

This chapter provides a brief overview of current single-subject design methodologies and their use in the applied environment. The design elements are a set of clinical tools that are effective both in maximally informing treatment decisions and generating and evaluating research hypotheses. Single-subject designs fill a vital role in linking clinical practice to clinical science. With the evolution of managed care, this link is now of significant economic importance to a major sector of our economy.

3.02.7 REFERENCES

Baer, D. M., Wolf, M. M., & Risley, T. R. (1968). Some current dimensions of applied behavior analysis. *Journal of Applied Behavior Analysis, 1,* 91–97.

Barlow, D. H., & Hayes, S. C. (1979). Alternating treatments design: One strategy for comparing the effects of two treatments in a single subject. *Journal of Applied Behavior Analysis, 12,* 199–210.

Barlow, D. H., Hayes, S. C., & Nelson, R. O. (1984). *The scientist practitioner: Research and accountability in clinical and educational setting.* New York: Pergamon.

Barlow, D. H., & Hersen, M. (1984). *Single case experimental designs: Strategies for studying behavior change* (2nd ed.). New York: Pergamon.

Belles, D., & Bradlyn, A. S. (1987). The use of the changing criterion design in achieving controlled smoking in a heavy smoker: A controlled case study. *Journal of Behavior Therapy and Experimental Psychiatry, 18,* 77–82.

Box, G. E. P., & Jenkins, G. M. (1976). *Time series analysis: Forecasting and control.* San Francisco: Holden-Day.

Busk, P. L., & Marascuilo, L. A. (1988). Autocorrelation in single-subject research: A counterargument to the myth of no autocorrelation: The autocorrelation debate. *Behavioral Assessment, 10*(3), 229–242.

Campbell, D. T. (1957). Factors relevant to the validity of experiments in social settings. *Psychological Bulletin, 54,* 297–312.

Cone, J. D. (1986). Idiographic, nomothetic, and related perspectives in behavioral assessment. In R. O. Nelson & S. C. Hayes (Eds.), *Conceptual foundations of behavioral assessment* (pp. 111–128). New York: Guilford Press.

Cope, J. G., Moy, S. S., & Grossnickle, W. F. (1988). The behavioral impact of an advertising campaign to promote safety belt use. *Journal of Applied Behavior Analysis, 21,* 277–280.

Croce, R. V. (1990). Effects of exercise and diet on body composition and cardiovascular fitness in adults with severe mental retardation. *Education and Training in Mental Retardation, 25*(2), 176–187.

Cronbach, L. J. (1975). Beyond the two disciplines of scientific psychology. *American Psychologist, 30,* 116–127.

Cummings, N. A., Cummings, J. L., & Johnson, J. N. (1997). *Behavioral health in primary care: A guide for clinical integration.* Madison, CT: Psychosocial Press.

Cummings, N. A., Pollack, M. S., & Cummings, J. L. (1996). *Surviving the demise of solo practice: Mental health practitioners prospering in the era of managed care.* Madison, CT: Psychosocial Press.

DeLuca, R. V., & Holborn, S. W. (1992). Effects of a variable ratio reinforcement schedule with changing criteria on exercise in obese and nonobese boys. *Journal of Applied Behavior Analysis, 25,* 671–679.

Edgington, E. S. (1980) Validity of randomization tests for one-subject experiments. *Journal of Educational Statistics, 5,* 235–251.

Ferster, C. B., & Skinner, B. F. (1957). *Schedules of reinforcement.* New York: Appleton-Century-Crofts.

Gottman, J. M. (1981). *Time-series analysis: A comprehensive introduction for social scientists.* Cambridge, UK: Cambridge University Press.

Gottman, J. M., & Glass, G. V. (1978). Analysis of interrupted time-series experiments. In T. R. Kratochwill (Ed.), *Single subject research: Strategies for evaluating change* (pp. 197–235). New York: Academic Press.

Greenwood, K. M., & Matyas, T. A. (1990). Problems with the application of interrupted time series analysis for brief single subject data. *Behavioral Assessment, 12,* 355–370.

Gunter, P. L., Shores, R. E., Jac, K. S. L., Denny, R. K., & DePaepe, P. A. (1994). A case study of the effects of altering instructional interactions on the disruptive behavior of a child identified with severe behavior disorders. *Education and Treatment of Children, 17*(3), 435–444.

Harris, F. N., & Jenson, W. R. (1985). Comparisons of multiple-baseline across persons designs and AB designs with replication: Issues and confusions. *Behavioral Assessment, 7*(2), 121–127.

Hayes, S. C. (1985). Natural multiple baselines across persons: A reply to Harris and Jenson. *Behavioral Assessment, 7*(2), 129–132.

Hayes, S. C., Barlow, D. H., & Nelson, R. O. (1997). *The scientist practitioner: Research and accountability in the age of managed care,* (2nd ed.). Boston: Allyn & Bacon.

Hayes, S. C., Hussian, R. A., Turner, A. E., Anderson, N. B., & Grubb, T. D. (1983). The effect of coping statements on progress through a desensitization hierarchy. *Journal of Behavior Therapy and Experimental Psychiatry, 14,* 117–129.

Hersen, M., & Barlow, D. H. (1976). *Single case experimental designs: Strategies for studying behavior change.* New York: Pergamon.

Horne, G. P., Yang, M. C. K., & Ware, W. B. (1982). Time series analysis for single subject designs. *Psychological Bulletin, 91,* 178–189.

Huitema, B. E. (1988). Autocorrelation: 10 years of confusion. *Behavioral Assessment, 10,* 253–294.

Jordan, J., Singh, N. N., & Repp, A. (1989). An evaluation of gentle teaching and visual screening in the reduction of stereotypy. *Journal of Applied Behavior Analysis, 22,* 9–22.

Kamps, D. M., Leonard, B. R., Vernon, S., Dugan, E. P., Delquadri, J. C., Gershon, B., Wade, L., & Folk, L. (1992). Teaching social skills to students with autism to increase peer interactions in an integrated first-grade classroom. *Journal of Applied Behavior Analysis, 25,* 281–288.

Kazdin, A. E. (1980). *Research design in clinical psychology.* New York: Harper & Row.

Kennedy, C. H., Cushing, L. S., & Itkonen, T. (1997). General education participation improves the social contacts and friendship networks of students with severe disabilities. *Journal of Behavioral Education, 7,* 167–189.

Koan, S., & McGuire, W. J. (1973). The Yin and Yang of progress in social psychology. *Journal of Personality and Social Psychology, 28,* 446–456.

Kornet, M., Goosen, C., & Van Ree, J. M. (1991). Effect of naltrexone on alcohol consumption during chronic alcohol drinking and after a period of imposed abstinence in free-choice drinking rhesus monkeys. *Psychopharmacology, 104*(3), 367–376.

Lerman, D. C., & Iwata, B. A. (1996). A methodology for distinguishing between extinction and punishment effects associated with response blocking. *Journal of Applied Behavior Analysis, 29,* 231–233.

Levin, J. R., Marascuilo, L. A., & Hubert, L. J. (1978). N = nonparametric randomization tests. In T. R. Kratochwill (Ed.), *Single subject research: Strategies for evaluating change* (pp. 167–196). New York: Academic Press.

McCullough, J. P., Cornell, J. E., McDaniel, M. H., & Mueller, R. K. (1974). Utilization of the simultaneous treatment design to improve student behavior in a first-grade classroom. *Journal of Consulting and Clinical Psychology, 42,* 288–292.

O'Brien, F. (1968). Sequential contrast effects with human subjects. *Journal of the Experimental Analysis of Behavior, 11,* 537–542.

O'Reilly, M. F., Green, G., & Braunling-McMorrow, D. (1990). Self-administered written prompts to teach home accident prevention skills to adults with brain injuries. *Journal of Applied Behavior Analysis, 23,* 431–446.

Orsborn, E., Patrick, H., Dixon, R. S., & Moore, D. W. (1995). The effects of reducing teacher questions and increasing pauses on child talk during morning news. *Journal of Behavioral Education, 5*(3), 347–357.

Paul, G. L. (1969). Behavior modification research: Design and tactics. In C. M. Franks (Ed.), *Behavior therapy: Appraisal and status* (pp. 29–62). New York: McGraw-Hill.

Peterson, A. L., & Azrin, N. H. (1992). An evaluation of behavioral treatments for Tourette Syndrome. *Behavior Research and Therapy, 30*(2), 167–174.

Shakow, D., Hilgard, E. R., Kelly, E. L., Luckey, B., Sanford, R. N., & Shaffer, L. F. (1947). Recommended graduate training program in clinical psychology. *American Psychologist, 2,* 539–558.

Sharpley, C. F., & Alavosius, M. P. (1988). Autocorrelation in behavioral data: An alternative perspective. *Behavioral Assessment, 10,* 243–251.

Shukla, S., & Albin, R. W. (1996). Effects of extinction alone and extinction plus functional communication training on covariation of problem behaviors. *Journal of Applied Behavior Analysis, 29*(4), 565–568.

Singh, N. N., & Aman, M. G. (1981). Effects of thioridazine dosage on the behavior of severely mentally retarded persons. *American Journal of Mental Deficiency, 85,* 580–587.

Snow, R. E. (1974). Representative and quasi-representative designs for research in teaching. *Review of Educational Research, 44,* 265–291.

Stavinoah, P. L., Zlomke, L. C., Adams, S. F., & Lytton, G. J. (1996). Treatment of impulsive self and other directed aggression with fluoxetine in a man with mild mental retardation. *Journal of Developmental and Physical Disabilities, 8*(4), 367–373.

Strosahl, K. (1994). Entering the new frontier of managed mental health care: Gold mines and land mines. *Cognitive and Behavioral Practice, 1,* 5–23.

Strosahl, K., Hayes, S. C., Bergan, J., & Romano, P. (in press). Evaluating the field effectiveness of Acceptance and Commitment Therapy: An example of the manipulated training research method. *Behavior Therapy.*

Thorne, F. C. (1947). The clinical method in science. *American Psychologist, 2,* 159–166.

Trask-Tyler, S. A., Grossi, T. A., & Heward, W. L. (1994). Teaching young adults with developmental disabilities and visual impairments to use tape-recorded recipes: Acquisition, generalization, and maintenance of cooking skills. *Journal of Behavioral Education, 4,* 283–311.

Ulman, J. D., & Sulzer-Azaroff, B. (1975). Multielement baseline design in educational research. In E. Ramp & G. Semb (Eds.), *Behavior analysis: Areas of research and application* (pp. 377–391). Englewood Cliffs, NJ: Prentice-Hall.

Van Houten, R. (1993). Rote vs. rules: A comparison of two teaching and correction strategies for teaching basic subtraction facts. *Education and Treatment of Children, 16,* 147–159.

Wampold, B. E., & Furlong, M. J. (1981). Randomization tests in single subject designs Illustrative examples. *Journal of Behavioral Assessment, 3,* 329–341.

White, G. W., Mathews, R. M., & Fawcett, S. B. (1989). Reducing risks of pressure sores: Effects of watch prompts and alarm avoidance on wheelchair pushups. *Journal of Applied Behavior Analysis, 22,* 287–295.

3.03
Group Comparisons: Randomized Designs

NINA R. SCHOOLER
Hillside Hospital, Glen Oaks, NY, USA

3.03.1 INTRODUCTION

A major function of clinical psychology is to provide treatment or other interventions for clients who suffer from mental illness or seek relief from problems. This chapter addresses the role of experimental evaluation of treatments as a source of data in deciding about the utility of a treatment. In the medical literature, such studies are referred to as randomized clinical trials (RCTs) (Pocock, 1983) and many recent studies of psychological treatments also use this terminology (e.g., Bickel, Amass, Higgins, Badger, & Esch, 1997). This chapter will consider the strengths and weaknesses of a number of strategies for judging treatment utility; review some historical background of the experimental study of treatment; examine the experimental designs that have been used to study psychological treatments and the circumstances under which such experiments are appropriate. In each of the sections regarding specific experimental designs, exemplar studies will be discussed in some detail in order to highlight relevant issues for evaluating the literature and for the design of future studies.

3.03.2 COMPARING STRATEGIES FOR TREATMENT EVALUATION

In order to set the experimental study of treatment into context, this section will review a variety of strategies for evaluation of treatment efficacy attending to their strengths and weaknesses.

3.03.2.1 Case Reports and Summaries of Case Series

This strategy represents perhaps the method with the longest history. For example, Brill (1938) cites a case treated in 1880 by Josef Breuer (cf p. 7) of a young girl with symptoms of "paralyses with contractures, inhibitions and states of psychic confusion." Under hypnosis she was able to describe the connections between her symptoms and past experiences and "... by this simple method he freed her of her symptoms." Another case described by Brill concerns a four-year-old child who became nervous, refused to eat, and had frequent crying spells and tantrums. The symptoms began shortly after the mother was separated from the child and she was "cured" soon after the mother returned. The mechanism that was posited to account for the effect was a disturbance in libido.

Much more recently, *Consumer Reports* (1994, 1995) report the results of a survey of 4000 subscribers who reported their experiences with psychotherapy broadly defined. Respondents to the survey reported in general that they had benefitted from their psychotherapy and, of particular interest, that more and longer psychotherapy was associated with greater benefit. This survey has been reviewed and received careful critique by psychologists (Brock, Green, Reich, & Evans, 1996; Hunt, 1996; Kotkin, Daviet, & Gurin, 1996; Kriegman, 1996; Mintz, Drake, & Crits-Christoph, 1996; Seligman, 1995, 1996).

These examples differ in a number of ways. The most obvious is that they span over a century. The more relevant one for the present purpose is that the *Consumer Reports* survey carries the weight of numbers and implied authority as a result. However, both single case reports and reports that summarize large numbers of cases share limitations. Neither can address the very compelling question regarding the reported outcomes—"compared to what?" In the *Consumer Reports* survey, there are a number of obvious hypotheses that can be entertained regarding the absent comparison groups that call into question the validity of the reported finding. The finding that psychotherapy was helpful could be because those who did not feel they had benefitted from their psychotherapy did not respond to the questionnaire. The finding that longer psychotherapy was more helpful could be because those who experienced benefit continued in treatment longer or because those who discontinued early needed to justify their discontinuation. Statistical modeling of alternative causal interpretations cannot fully exclude these interpretations. The common characteristic of both the attributed interpretations of findings from case reports or case series and the criticism of them is that there is no formal procedure for judging the accuracy of the interpretation.

Such reports serve the important function of generating hypotheses regarding treatments and interventions that can lead to well-designed studies. But they are not designed to test hypotheses and therefore cannot provide definitive evidence for treatment efficacy.

3.03.2.2 Single Case Experimental Designs

Chapter 2, this volume, on single case designs, discusses the methodologies for assessing causal relationships in individuals. A striking advantage of single case designs is that they can be used to evaluate treatments for individuals with very specifically defined characteristics. These characteristics do not need to be shared with large numbers of other patients or clients for the experiments to be valid. The applicability of the specific interventions studied to broader populations of clients will, of course, depend on the similarity of such clients to the subjects studied. An important disadvantage of single case designs is that they are only applicable in conditions in which return of the target complaints can be reliably demonstrated once the treatment has been removed. If a treatment results (or is hypothesized to result) in a change in personality or in the orientation of an individual to himself or others, then the repeated administration and withdrawal of treatment that is the hallmark of single case designs will not provide useful information. A further disadvantage is that the comparisons are all internally generated and generalization is accomplished only through assessment of multiple cases with similar individual characteristics and treatment.

3.03.2.3 Quasi-experimental Designs

These methods, described in detail in Chapter 4, this volume, take advantage of naturalistic treatment assignment or self-selection and use statistical methods to model outcome and to provide controls for the major limitation of these methods—namely that assignment to treatment is not random. A further advantage is that evaluation of treatment outcome can be independent of treatment delivery (and even blind to the knowledge of treatment) so that the effects of expectancy on outcome are controlled. The major weakness of such designs is that the biases of treatment selection are allowed full rein.

3.03.2.4 Randomized Experimental Designs

Randomization is the hallmark of these studies. Random assignment to intervention provides the potential to control for biases that treatment self-selection and choice introduce into the evaluation of treatment outcome. The disadvantages that randomized treatment studies have include the logistical difficulties in implementation and restrictions in generalizability. Generalizability is restricted to clients who are willing to consider randomization. Individuals who come to treatment facilities with a strong preference or expectation may well reject randomization to treatment as an option and insofar as matching to treatment influences outcome, the absence of such subjects reduces generalization. Subject refusal to participate, particularly if it occurs after treatment assignment is known, can further compromise the advantage that random assignment introduces. Refusal after treatment assignment is known implies that subjects whose expectations are met continue and that those who did not get the treatment they preferred have chosen not to participate. If such refusal is frequent, the principle of randomization has been compromised and interpretation of findings will encounter limitations similar to those described for quasi-experimental designs. Attrition from all causes may introduce bias (Flick, 1988). Despite these disadvantages, randomization offers insurance that, within the population studied, bias—particularly from unknown sources, has been contained. Randomized experimental studies share with quasi-experimental designs the potential advantages afforded by the separation of evaluation of outcome from provision of the intervention.

3.03.3 HISTORICAL BACKGROUND

Early research in psychotherapy ran on two relatively independent tracks: the first empha-sized the internal process of the psychotherapeutic encounter; the second was concerned with evaluating the effects of psychotherapy *per se*. In the latter studies the primary comparisons were between patients or clients who received psychotherapy and those who did not. Most controls centered around controls for treatment time such as deferred entry into treatment using waiting lists. In these experimental studies, attention to the content of the psychotherapy was descriptive. This position was strongly bolstered by the writings of theorists such as Frank (1971), who held that general constructs such as positive regard and the therapeutic alliance underlay the effects of psychotherapy.

Smith and Glass (1977) revolutionized the field with the publication of the first meta-analysis of the psychotherapy literature, demonstrating a moderate effect size for the comparison between psychotherapy and no treatment (see Chapter 15, this volume, for a discussion of current meta-analytic methods). At the same time, increased attention to measurement of change in psychotherapy (Waskow & Parloff, 1975) and the development of manualized treatments (see Chapter 9, this volume) signaled a change in the models that were available for the study of psychological treatments.

During the same period, attention to methodology in clinical psychology quickened (Campbell & Stanley, 1963, 1966; Cook & Campbell, 1979). The emergence of medications for the treatment of mental illness had inaugurated experimental studies of these treatments using rigorous designs drawn initially from clinical psychology that included randomization, double-blind administration of medication, placebo controls, diagnostic specificity, rating scales that paid attention to specific signs and symptoms of psychopathology (see Prien & Robinson, 1994, for a recent review of progress in methods for psychopharmacology). The demand for similar studies of psychological interventions became apparent. The modern era of experimental studies of psychotherapy and other psychological interventions was upon us.

3.03.4 APPROPRIATE CONDITIONS FOR RANDOMIZED GROUP DESIGNS

Experimentation is best suited to address comparative questions that would be biased if the groups being compared were self-selected. Random assignment of individuals to groups controls for biases introduced by self-selection. Some questions—for example, those regarding differences between young and old people or men and women—obviously will not be addressed experimentally, although later in the chapter the question of designs to study individual differences in relation to an experimental condition will be considered.

Some examples: does marital therapy prevent divorce?; is cognitive-behavior therapy helpful in depression?; does family psychoeducation potentiate the effects of medication in schizophrenia?; should children with attention deficit disorder receive medication or family support?; does respite care for Alzheimer's patients reduce physical illness in caregivers?; does medication reduce craving in alcohol dependent individuals? In all these examples, an intervention is either contrasted to others or in the cases where no comparison is stated, it is implied that the comparison is with a group that does not receive an alternate intervention.

The hallmark of all these questions is that they identify a group or condition and ask about an intervention. The implication is that the findings from the experiment will apply to members of the group who did not receive the intervention in the experimental study. This assumption represents a statistical assumption—it is required for the use of virtually all statistical tests applied in evaluating the questions under review. It also represents an important clinical concern. Experiments are not conducted solely for the benefit of the subjects who participate in the research. It is anticipated that the conclusions will be applicable to other individuals who share characteristics (ideally key characteristics) with those who were subjects in the research.

Perhaps the greatest threat to the validity of experimental studies is that there is something that distinguishes the members of the group (depressed patients, children with attention deficit disorder) who agree to randomization from those who will not participate in a study of randomized treatment. In the general medical clinical trials literature where the conditions to be treated are defined by readily measurable signs and symptoms or by physiological measurements (e.g., tumor size), that assumption is readily accepted and is therefore generally untested. In the psychological literature the question may be considered but there are very few studies that have actually drawn a sample of subjects from a population in order to know whether the subjects of a study are like the population from which they came. In other words, although we look to randomization as a control for bias in evaluating the effect of a treatment or intervention, there has been little attention paid to whether subjects who agree to randomization represent a bias that is negligible or substantial.

3.03.4.1 Ethical Requirements

Certain ethical conditions regarding the subjects and the treatments or interventions must be met (Department of Health and Human Services, 1994). Research participation requires informed consent from the participant or from an appropriately authorized surrogate, for example, a parent for a minor child. Even in cases where consent is obtained from a surrogate, the research participant (e.g., the child) must provide "assent." Assent is the term used for agreement to participate by individuals who are judged to lack the capacity to provide fully informed consent. Currently in the USA regulations are promulgated by the Department of Health and Human Services that define 12 elements of informed consent. They are:

(i) An explanation of the procedures to be followed, including specification of those that are experimental.

(ii) A description of the reasonably foreseeable attendant discomforts and risks and a statement of the uncertainty of the anticipated risks due to the inherent nature of the research process.

(iii) A description of the benefits that may be expected.

(iv) A disclosure of appropriate and available alternate procedures that might be advantageous for the subject.

(v) An offer to answer any inquiries concerning the procedures.

(vi) A statement that information may be withheld from the subject in certain cases when the investigator believes that full disclosure may be detrimental to the subject or fatal to the study design (provided, however, that the Institutional Review Board (IRB) has given proper approval to such withholding of information).

(vii) A disclosure of the probability that the subject may be given a placebo at some time during the course of the research study if placebo is to be utilized in the study.

(viii) An explanation in lay terms of the probability that the subject may be placed in one or another treatment group if randomization is a part of the study design.

(ix) An instruction that the subject may withdraw consent and may discontinue participation in the study at any time.

(x) An explanation that there is no penalty for not participating in or withdrawng from the study once the project has been initiated.

(xi) A statement that the investigator will inform the subject of any significant new information arising from the experiment or other ongoing experiments which may bear on the subject's choice to remain in the study.

(xii) A statement that the investigator will provide a review of the nature and results of the study to subjects who request such information.

All these essential elements must be included in an Informed Consent Form to insure adequate consent to participate in any research.

In studies that involve randomization to treatment, some elements are of particular importance because they represent concepts that are sometimes difficult for potential subjects to appreciate. The first, of course, is that of randomization itself—that treatment will be decided "as if tossing a coin." The second is that the clinician or treater will not choose "the best" treatment for the client. Other elements of informed consent that need to be emphasized for a truly informed process is that the subject is free to withdraw at any time and that those providing treatment may also discontinue the subject's participation if they believe it to be in the subject's best interest.

In most countries research involving human subjects must be reviewed by local Research Ethics Committees or IRBs that are mandated to insure that the research meets ethical standards, that all elements of informed consent are present, and that the interests of subjects are protected.

A number of issues regarding consent that go beyond the 12 critical items are currently a subject of debate. Participants in these deliberations include various regulatory bodies, independent commissions, and private individuals and groups that are self-declared protectors of those who may participate in experiments regarding treatments or interventions of interest to clinical psychology. Among these issues are the following: requiring that an independent person unaffiliated with a given research project oversee the consent process; expanding the definition of those who lack the capacity to provide informed consent to include populations such as all those diagnosed with schizophrenia and other illnesses; restricting the conduct of research that does not offer direct benefit to the participant subjects; elimination of the use of placebo treatment conditions in patient groups for whom there is any evidence of treatments that are effective. These potential changes may well alter the nature of experimental research regarding treatment and intervention.

In general, concerns about placebo treatment or no-treatment control conditions have been hotly debated in the arena of pharmacological treatment rather than psychological interventions. However, as evidence regarding the efficacy and effectiveness of psychological interventions becomes widely accepted, experimental strategies such as waiting list controls,

"usual care," and even nonspecified psychotherapies may require re-evaluation. One strategy that may receive increasing attention and popularity is that of treatment dosage. In other words, a comparison group may be defined as one that receives the intervention of interest but receives less of it.

Interventions and control conditions being compared should be potentially effective; there should be evidence regarding benefit. If this assertion is accepted, how can a "no-treatment" comparison group be included in an experiment? First, there should be provision for the subject to receive the potentially more effective intervention following study participation. In other words, the "no-treatment" group is really a delayed treatment or the time hallowed waiting list condition. This may be relatively easy to implement with short-term treatment interventions but more difficult for long-term interventions. Alternate solutions include the use of minimal treatment conditions. Later in the chapter, both of these conditions will be discussed in more detail from the substantive perspective. In the present context, both represent plausible solutions to the ethical dilemma of providing appropriate treatment for client populations for whom there exist a corpus of information regarding treatment effects. Obviously, these concerns are moot in specific patient or client populations where there are no data regarding treatment effects. The ethical dilemma is heightened when the intervention is long term or there may be substantial risk if treatment is deferred. For example, studies of treatment for depression generally exclude subjects who are suicidal.

3.03.4.2 Stage of Treatment Development

The ideal sequence of treatment development includes the following stages: innovation; preliminary description in practice, usually by the innovators or developers of the treatment; comparative experimental studies to determine treatment efficacy and investigate client characteristics that may be linked to treatment response; dissemination into clinical practice; and evaluation of outcome under conditions of usual clinical care. Experimental, randomized designs may take several forms during the sequence outlined. The first is often a study that compares the new treatment with no treatment. As indicated earlier, that condition is most likely to be defined by a waiting list condition or deferred treatment. Other studies that provide comparisons to other established treatments may follow. At the present time, studies that examine psychological interventions in relationship to medication are often carried out. These studies may address direct comparative questions regarding medication and a psychological intervention or they may address relatively complex questions regarding the additive or interactive effects of medication and a psychological intervention.

3.03.4.3 Treatment Specification: Definition of Independent Variables

As indicated above, randomized designs are most valuable when the interventions can be well-specified or defined. Since the goal of such research is generalization, the advantage of well-specified treatment interventions is that their reproduction by other clinicians is possible. Manuals such as those discussed in Chapter 9, this volume, represent the ideal model of treatment specification, but other methods can be considered. The training of the treatment provider can provide a plausible statement regarding specification. For example, clinical psychologists with a Ph.D. who are board certified and who have completed an established training course may represent an appropriate statement regarding a treatment specification.

Specification should also include such elements as treatment duration, frequency, and number of contacts. Duration and number may appear to be relatively simple constructs but in examining psychological interventions the duration of treatment may not be rigidly defined. In some cases, treatment adherence by clients will affect duration, frequency, and number. In other circumstances, treatment may be continued until a specified outcome is reached. Under these conditions, duration of treatment until a criterion of improvement is reached may represent an outcome itself.

Finally, the most careful specification needs to be matched by measurement of adherence to the specified treatment. Did therapists do what they were supposed to do? This represents an interesting shift in research on interventions. Earlier in the history of psychotherapy research, when the emphasis was on the process of psychotherapy, the evaluation of what happened during the psychotherapeutic encounter was of interest because it was assumed that psychotherapeutic interventions altered outcomes. One could draw an analogy to recording the practices of a gifted cook in order to ascertain the recipe. As the emphasis has shifted to the evaluation of outcomes, the interest in the nature of the interpersonal interactions that comprise the intervention has come to be seen as assurance of adherence or "fidelity" (Hollon, Waskow, Evans, & Lowery, 1984). The question now is to determine whether a given cook has followed the recipe.

3.03.4.4 Client/Subject Characteristics

Characterization of the clients in the randomized trial provides the means for communicating attributes of the population of clients who may be appropriate for the treatment in routine clinical practice. Currently, the most common strategy for characterizing clients is the use of diagnostic criteria that provide decision rules for determining whether clients fit categories. The most widely used are those of the World Health Organization's *International classification of diseases* (World Health Organization, 1992) and the American Psychiatric Association's *Diagnostic and statistical manual of mental disorders* (American Psychiatric Association, 1987, 1994). The use of specified diagnostic criteria (and even standardized instruments for ascertaining diagnosis) provides some insurance that clients participating in a given study share characteristics with those who have been participants in other studies and with potential clients who may receive the treatment at a later time. However, under some circumstances it may be preferable to specify client inclusion based on other methods—such as the reason for seeking clinical assistance rather than a formal clinical diagnosis. An advantage of using inclusion criteria other than diagnosis is that problem-focused inclusion criteria may make translation of findings from a randomized trial to clinical practice easier.

A second issue regarding client characteristics in randomized studies is insuring that important client characteristics which may influence outcome are balanced across treatment groups. One strategy is to conduct relatively large studies. Randomization is designed to minimize imbalance but, as anyone who has seen heads come up 10 times in a row knows, in the short term randomization may well result in imbalance. One of the most common ways to achieve balanced groups is to randomize to treatment or condition within a prespecified group; for example, gender or age to insure against the possibility that by chance disproportionate numbers of one group are randomized to one treatment condition. A second strategy is to use an adaptive randomization algorithm (Pocock & Simon, 1975; White & Freedman, 1978). In this method, several client characteristics that are known or hypothesized to affect the outcomes of interest in the study are identified. The goal of the randomization algorithm is to insure that the groups are relatively well balanced considering all of the characteristics simultaneously. A particular algorithm may specify a number of characteristics but when the number exceeds three or four, the overall balance is unlikely to be affected. The characteristics can also be weighted so that some are more likely to influence treatment assignment than others. Adaptive randomization is a dynamic process in which subject characteristics are fed into a program that generates a treatment assignment such that the identified characteristics will be well balanced across all groups.

What is central to randomization within groups or adaptive randomization is the premise that the chosen characteristics are known or hypothesized to affect the outcomes of interest in the study. Characteristics that are not expected to influence outcome do not need to be considered in this way. Section 3.03.6 discusses the use of individual differences among study participants in attempting to understand outcome differences among treatments or interventions.

3.03.4.5 Specification and Assessment of Outcome: Definition of Dependent Variables

To state the obvious, outcome criteria should reflect the intended effect of the interventions studied and the reliability and validity of the assessment instruments used should be established. In general, there are advantages to using some measures that are established in the field. This provides the opportunity to compare findings across studies and aids in the cumulative development of knowledge (Waskow & Parloff, 1975). In addition, it is valuable to include study-specific measures that focus on the particular intervention(s) under investigation and hypotheses being tested. In discussing examples of specific studies in later sections of this chapter, the issue of whether differences were found on standard measures or on measures that were idiosyncratic to the study in question will be considered.

Also of relevance is who assesses outcome. In pharmacologic clinical trials, double-blind procedures represent standard operating procedure. Concerns are often expressed that side effect patterns and other "clues" may serve to break the blind, but blinding preserves a measure of uncertainty regarding treatment assignment (Cole, 1968). In studies of psychological intervention, double-blind conditions are not possible. The subject and the treating clinician know what treatment the subject is receiving and commitment and enthusiasm for treatment are assumed to be present. For this reason, a common strategy is to include

independent assessors. It is not a perfect strategy. Such assessors have only limited opportunity to observe subjects and may not be sensitive to subtle but important cues because of their limited contact with the subjects. In this context, both initial training of assessors to insure reliability and ongoing monitoring of reliability are critical.

3.03.4.6 Study Duration

Study duration includes two components: duration of the intervention and duration of postintervention evaluation. Duration of the intervention should be theoretically driven, based on the nature of the clinical problem that is being addressed and the mechanism of action of the intervention. Short-term interventions are much easier to investigate, particularly short-term interventions for which manuals have been developed. It appears that manuals are easier to develop for short-term interventions. However, some questions will require longer-term intervention. Interventions whose duration are reckoned in months rather than weeks require additional care to avoid subject attrition and to insure that the treatment remains constant during the long period of time that it is being delivered.

Post-treatment evaluation or follow-up after treatment ends is common in studies of psychological interventions and addresses the important question of whether effects persist in the absence of continued treatment intervention. Such follow-up studies are subject to the criticism that uncontrolled interventions may have occurred during the post-treatment period and may bias the outcome. But, if an intervention is hypothesized to exert a long-lasting effect that may include change in personality or long-term functioning, such evaluation is required. Follow-up evaluations are also subject to increased problems of attrition and the risk that differential attrition may introduce bias. Comparisons of baseline and demographic characteristics are frequently made between those subjects who are ascertained at the end of follow-up and those who are lost. This provides some measure of comfort, but further important comparisons should include treatment group and measures of outcome at the completion of study treatment. An incorrect strategy that has fallen into disuse was to compare those not ascertained with the full cohort, including those lost to follow-up, so that those not ascertained were included in both groups.

In studies of pharmacologic treatment, reversal of effects on discontinuation of treatment has been taken as *prima facie* evidence of efficacy. In fact, a major research design strategy in psychopharmacology is to establish efficacy of treatment in a cohort and then to randomize subjects to continuation or disconti- nuation of medication. Differential levels of symptom severity after a fixed experimental period and time to symptom exacerbation are taken as evidence of treatment efficacy. In contrast, studies of psychological interventions have often considered persistence of effect following the end of treatment as evidence for the efficacy of the psychological intervention. The problem that these conflicting paradigms represent will be considered further in Section 3.03.5.3 which considers comparative effects of pharmacologic and psychological treatments.

3.03.5 STUDY DESIGNS

The choice of study design always involves compromise. The clever experimenter can al- ways think of additional controls and varia- tions. In the previous section some of the relevant issues have been highlighted. Ethical considerations may proscribe some scientifically appropriate conditions. For example, under some circumstances deferring treatment through the use of a "waiting list" control may be inappropriate. Financial resources may constrain designs. Aside from funding con- straints, availability of appropriate subjects may limit the number of conditions that can be studied. This may be stating the obvious, but the more conditions and the larger the number of subjects in a study, the longer it will take to complete the study and the longer an important clinical question will remain unanswered. Each additional group in a study increases both the cost and the duration of a study. Finally, there is no single, ideal design. Ultimately, the design of a clinical experiment represents a decision that is driven by the hypotheses that are under investigation. What is critical is the recognition by the investigator (and by the reader/critic of the research) of the hypotheses that can be tested, and conversely, the questions that are simply not addressed by a given study.

3.03.5.1 Simple Two-group Comparisons

Designs involving only two groups are often used in the early stages of research with a given form of psychotherapy. The comparison group may be a no-treatment waiting list for the duration of the treatment, treatment "as usual" in the treatment setting, or a nonspecific psychological intervention. Nonspecific psy- chological interventions are sometimes referred

to as "placebo" treatment in the literature. Comparisons of two specific psychological interventions also represent potential two- group comparisons. A final model may include a treatment and no-treatment comparison in the presence of a specified medication condition (see Section 3.03.5.3 for discussion of this design in the context of other designs that include medication conditions).

Such studies may evaluate the benefit of two specific psychological interventions, of a spe- cific intervention vs. a nonspecific control (usual care) or of intervention vs. none. The hypoth- eses and specific clinical questions that drive a given investigation should, in principle, drive the particular nature of the experimental and control groups. However, sometimes logistic considerations such as the nature of the treatment setting and the treatments that are routinely provided in the setting may influence the design of the experiment. A further, important factor may be the clinical needs of the clients and the urgency of providing some intervention.

There are limitations of two-group designs. Whatever the outcome, the design will not allow testing of a range of alternate hypotheses. If the study does not include a no-treatment control group, there is no control for time, spontaneous remission, or improvement. If the study does not include an alternate interven- tion group there is no control for nonspecific factors in treatment or for the specific characteristics of the designated experimental treatment. Further, if the study includes two specified interventions, there is no control for either receipt of any treatment or for non- specific factors in treatment.

Interpretation of the findings from two-group studies absent a no-treatment control is difficult if there are no differences in outcome between the groups. No difference can be interpreted as Lewis Carroll and the Red Queen would have us believe "that all have won and all shall have prizes" or that there is no effect of either. Interpretation of studies that do not include a no-treatment group may often depend on integrating findings from other prior studies that did include such controls—not necessarily a bad state of affairs. As the field of experimental studies of psychological interventions matures, it may become less appropriate to implement studies with no-treatment control groups.

In the following example of a two group design, Keane, Fairbank, Caddell, and Zimer- ing (1989) compared implosive (flooding) therapy to a waiting list control in 24 subjects with post-traumatic stress disorder (PTSD). Interestingly, the study design had originally included a stress management group, but for unspecified reasons, this condition was not successfully implemented, and those subjects are not included in the report. Thus, the two-group comparison is between a specified treatment and a no-treatment control. Implosive therapy was manual driven, following a manual (Lyons and Keane, as cited in Keane et al., 1989), and included between 14 and 16 sessions. The experimental group received baseline, post-treatment (elapsed time from baseline not reported), and a six-month follow-up assessment. The wait-list control group was assessed twice: at baseline prior to randomization and after, on average, four months. Half of the implosive therapy group and the majority of subjects in the wait-list group received anxiolytic medication because of, as the authors note, "... concerns about placebo groups and no treatment controls ... we didn't attempt to withdraw these patients from the medications which were prescribed to them" (Keane et al., 1989, p. 249). The authors maintain that the comparison of implosive therapy to subjects who were receiving pharmacotherapy (even if it was not systematically administered) represented a more stringent test of implosive therapy—although it was not a part of the original design. Subjects were assessed using well-known standardized assessments scales for depression, trait and state anxiety, and instruments specifically designed by the investigators for the assessment of PTSD. Post-test assessments were completed by the therapist who treated the subject in the implosive therapy group and by one of the same therapists for the wait-list group. In addition, the subjects rated themselves on depression, anxiety, and satisfaction with social adjustment in several life areas.

Implosive therapy appeared to improve depression and anxiety according to self-report and specific features of PTSD as rated by the therapists. No changes in social adjustment were seen.

Strengths of the study include randomization, specification of diagnosis, apparent absence of dropouts in both conditions, the existence of a manual for the experimental treatment, and the use of both standard outcome measures and measures tailored to the specific study hypotheses. Although subjects were randomly assigned to treatment, the randomization was compromised by the fact that treatment in one of three groups to which subjects were randomized was, for unspecified reasons, not fully implemented. In other words, this study was a two-group design in execution rather than intent. Another weakness is that assessments were completed by the therapists who treated the subjects and who therefore knew the treatment assignment. As discussed in Section 3.03.4.5, when treatment assignment is known, there is a potential bias.

3.03.5.2 Multiple-group Comparisons

Multiple-group comparisons offer the opportunity to test hypotheses simultaneously regarding comparisons of interventions (specificity of effects) and of intervention to a no-intervention control. If the interventions being studied derive from theoretical models, their comparison may test specific hypotheses regarding the psychological mechanisms that underlie the condition being treated. Other more pragmatic questions that can be addressed in multiple-group comparisons include group vs. individual contact and treatment intensity. However, it should be noted that when intensity or dosage of the intervention becomes a condition, control for amount of contact is lost. Again, there is no single "best" design. The appropriate design depends on the questions being asked and the appropriate questions depend on the stage of research. For example, questions of treatment duration or frequency are more likely to be asked after a particular treatment has been shown to have an effect.

Brown and Lewinsohn (1984) compared three psychoeducational approaches in treating depression that all used the same course materials: class, individual tutoring, brief telephone contact, and a delayed treatment control. Sixty-three individuals who met diagnostic criteria for unipolar depression and paid a course fee were randomly assigned to one of the four groups. Half the course fee was refunded if subjects completed all evaluations. Subjects in the three immediate treatment groups were assessed pre- and post-treatment and at two later follow-up points. The delayed treatment control group was assessed at baseline and at eight weeks, the time equivalent of post-treatment after which they received the class condition. All treatments focused on specific behaviors believed to be dysfunctional in depression (although not necessarily in the study subjects) and followed a syllabus that included a text (Lewinsohn, Munoz, Youngren, & Zeiss, 1978) and a workbook (Brown & Lewinsohn, 1984). An independent interviewer completed a standardized diagnostic assessment at baseline and of symptoms at later assessment points. Subjects completed three standardized self-report measures. The primary outcome measure was a factor-analytically derived score that included all three self-report measures.

Improvement was seen in all three immediate treatment groups on this single composite measure compared to the delayed treatment group. There were no differences among the active treatment groups either in self-report or in rate of diagnosed depression at follow-up. Comparison of high and low responders to treatment found few differences; none were a function of specific treatment. No detailed assessment of psychopathology or self-report measures was made.

The strengths of the study include randomization, a design that tested specific effects of a treatment modality and the method of delivery, the absence of drop-outs from treatment or assessment, specification of treatment conditions, the use of standardized measures of outcome assessment, and the use of independent assessors. The major weakness of the study is not in its design but the limited use made of the assessment battery. Ratings made by the independent assessors were only used to assess the presence or absence of diagnosable depression at the six-month follow-up and the use of a single summary score for all self-report measures may well conceal more than it reveals. A second weakness is the absence of assessments of implementation—how well the instructors used the course materials in the three conditions and whether all three conditions were implemented equally well.

It is difficult to decide whether charging subjects for treatment is a strength or a weakness. On the one hand, payment for treatment is characteristic of clinical treatment settings. All subjects completed the study and it could be argued that motivation to receive a 50% rebate on the course fee was a factor in enhancing study completion. On the other hand, the authors report that one of the major reasons that screened potential participants did not enter the study was inability to pay. Thus, the study population may have been biased by the exclusion of these subjects.

This study exemplifies a model that deconstructs a psychotherapeutic approach—in this case a psychoeducational approach to the treatment of depression—in order to identify which treatment delivery strategy offers advantages in outcome given that the strategies differ in the amount of clinical time and resources required to deliver the treatment. All subjects, including the delayed treatment group, reported significant improvement. The implication of these findings is that the least costly method of treatment delivery, brief telephone contact, should be implemented. However, there was no report regarding the acceptability of the method of treatment delivery and as noted earlier, there was no assessment of post-treatment symptoms. In the absence of these data, perhaps a firm clinical recommendation is premature.

3.03.5.3 Multiple-group Comparisons that Include Medication Conditions

Although in principle, designs that compare medication to psychological interventions can be classified in terms of whether they are simple comparisons (Section 3.03.5.1), multiple comparisons (Section 3.03.5.2) or represent factorial designs (Section 3.03.5.4), they entail unique research challenges and therefore merit separate consideration. The first design challenge was introduced earlier, namely the difference in the model of assessing effects. Follow-up assessments after treatment ends are seen as important sources of information in studies of psychological treatments. In contrast, such assessments are rare in studies of pharmacotherapy. Relapse or re-emergence of symptoms after treatment discontinuation is taken as evidence of efficacy. Therefore, discontinuation designs to study efficacy of treatment are common in psychopharmacology. A second design challenge is whether psychological and pharmacologic treatments should be introduced at the same time or are appropriate for different stages of an illness. Third, pharmacologic studies use double-blind methods as the preferred strategy to control assessor bias and therefore studies often rely on treating clinicians to assess outcome. Because it is not possible to blind treating clinicians to the psychological treatment they are providing, studies of psychological interventions rely on independent assessors who, although they will be blind to treatment assignment, have reduced opportunity to observe, and have minimal opportunity to develop rapport with the subjects they are assessing. For these reasons, evaluations by independent assessors may be less sensitive than those made by treating clinicans. Fourth, psychological interventions are often hypothesized to affect different aspects of outcome than pharmacologic interventions, so that direct comparisons of effects may be difficult.

Historically, pharmacologic clinical trials have relied more heavily on medical diagnoses of mental illness than studies of psychological interventions. But current research in both pharmacologic and psychological treatment is largely wedded to specific diagnoses derived from the *DSM* of the American Psychiatric Association (1987, 1994) or the *ICD* of the World Health Organization (1992). Parenthetically, one can question whether the increased reliance on medical diagnostic schemes such as *DSM* and *ICD* represents an advance in studies of psychological intervention. It has been argued that diagnostic specificity enhances reliability and therefore enhances replication and communication. On the other hand, clients who seek treatment do not necessarily seek help for a specific diagnostic label.

A wide range of designs have been used to examine the relationship of medications and psychological treatments. In the simplest, a medication or placebo is added to a uniform psychological intervention, or the converse, a psychological intervention or control condition is added to an established medication condition. These designs examine the additive effect of the modality that is superimposed. Questions like does naltrexone enhance abstinence in alcoholic subjects who are in a therapeutic milieu or does social skills training enhance social functioning in schizophrenic subjects who are maintained on antipsychotic medication can be addressed in this manner. The major design challenges faced by such studies are: the inclusion of appropriate outcome measures to evaluate change on psychological interventions; insuring that the treatment modality which represents the background condition remains relatively constant during the course of the study; and insuring an adequate timeframe in which to evaluate effects of psychological treatments (in the design where psychological intervention is manipulated).

The second class of studies adds a medication condition (or conditions) to a multiple-group design such as those discussed in the previous section. These studies examine the comparative effects of medication and psychological treatments and face greater challenges. They have been called "horse races" and may thereby contribute to guild conflicts between psychologists and psychiatrists (Kendall & Lipman, 1991).

Appropriate inclusion criteria for medication and psychological treatments may differ and compromises may be necessary. Such studies will generally include double-blind conditions for medication and also benefit from inclusion of independent assessors. The studies require expertise in both clinical psychopharmacology and the relevant psychological interventions. Insuring this expertise for a study usually requires close collaboration and mutual respect by investigators drawn from psychology and psychiatry. Outcome criteria need to include measures of dimensions that are hypothesized to be sensitive to change in both modalities being studied and the reasons for inclusion of specific outcome measures should be explicit. A detailed review of these and other methodological considerations can be found in an article by Kendall and Lipman (1991) and in the article detailing the research plan for the National Institute of Mental Health Treatment of Depression Collaborative Research Program (Elkin, Parloff, Hadley, & Autry, 1985).

Finally, factorial designs provide explicit tests of both additive and interactive effects of medication and psychological treatment. These designs will be considered in Section 3.03.5.4.

An example of a study that compared medication and a specific psychotherapy is the study of prevention of recurrence of depression by Frank et al. (1990). Patients characterized by recurrent depression (at least two prior episodes) were treated with medication and manual-based interpersonal psychotherapy (IPT) (Klerman, Weissman, Rounsaville, & Chevron, 1984) until symptom remission was documented and maintained for 20 weeks. One hundred and twenty-eight subjects were then randomized to one of five treatment conditions: a maintenance form of interpersonal psychotherapy (IPT-M) that was characterized by less frequent visits; IPT-M and an antidepressant (imipramine) at the acute treatment dose; IPT-M and medication placebo; medication clinic visits and imipramine; medication clinic visits; and medication placebo. Subjects were treated for three years. Therapists were trained and certified by the developers of IPT. The major difference from the published manual is described as visit frequency. The major outcome examined was recurrence of depressive episodes during the three-year period. The two treatment arms that included imipramine (IPT-M and imipramine; imipramine and clinic visits) had the lowest risk of recurrence. Mean survival time was more than 83 weeks. The two groups that received IPT-M without medication (IPT-M alone; IPT-M and placebo) had a higher risk of recurrence; mean survival time was more than 60 weeks. The lowest survival time was seen in the group that received placebo and medication clinic visits; survival time was 38 weeks on average. The authors conclude that medication, at a relatively high maintenance dose, affords the greatest protection from recurrence in individuals who have experienced recurrent depression. However, psychotherapy, absent medication, represents a distinct advantage over clinic attendance coupled with a placebo.

The study has a number of strengths. Patients were randomized to treatment condition. There was an extremely low dropout rate (17%) over the three-year study duration. The design included control conditions for medication (placebo) and psychotherapy was administered under three conditions: alone, in combination with imipramine, and in combination with imipramine placebo. The psychotherapy followed an established manual and therapists were trained by the originators of the therapy. Survival analysis represents the most powerful statistical method for evaluating risk of recurrence.

Weaknesses include the limited examination of clinical outcomes. Although the authors mention the importance of judging interepisode social functioning, the article only examined recurrence risk. Second, the study population was, by design, limited to those who both had recurrent episodes and recovered from them. Of the 230 patients who met the first criterion, fully 42% did not enter the randomized trial. This represents a substantial limitation to generalization of the findings to depression broadly defined.

3.03.5.4 Factorial Designs

Designs that include at least two factors allow for detection of main effects in each factor as well as interactive effects. In the simplest of these, 2×2 designs, there is a control condition or at least two defined levels of each factor, as shown in Figure 1. If the factors represent independently defined treatment modalities, then such designs can detect the ability of one treatment to potentiate the other or even to inhibit the effect of the other. For this reason, such designs are particularly suited to examining the relationship of medication and psychological interventions. Uhlenhuth, Lipman, and Covi (1969), Schooler (1978), and Hollon and DeRubeis (1981) have considered factorial models for the study of the interaction of medication and psychological treatments. According to Uhlenhuth et al. (1969), there are four possible forms that the interaction can take. These are shown in Figure 1. An additive effect is defined as the simple sum of the effects of the two treatment modalities. The effect in cell 1 is equal to the combined effects seen in cells 2 and 3. The treatments may potentiate each other. In that case, the combined effect (cell 1) is greater than the additive sum of the two treatment effects (cells 2 and 3). The treatment modalities may inhibit one another. In that case the combined effect (cell 1) is less than the effects of each treatment independently (cells 2 and 3). Finally, there may be an effect that they call reciprocal, in which the combined effect (cell 1) is equal to the main effect of the more effective treatment (the effect seen in either cell 2 or cell 3). Detection of all these effects depends on the factorial design and the presence of cell 4 which represents the combined control condition or as it has sometimes been dubbed, the double placebo.

Factorial designs are potentially a valuable model for examination of other important variables in understanding treatment, for example, to control for the effect of setting in studies that are conducted in more than one clinical setting. However, the most important use, from the perspective of this chapter, is to study the relationship of medication and psychological treatment.

Marks and his colleagues (1993) studied the effects of medication and a psychological treatment for panic disorder. There was prior evidence of efficacy for both the medication, alprazolam, an antianxiety drug, and the experimental psychological treatment, live exposure. One hundred and fifty-four subjects were randomly assigned to four treatment conditions: alprazolam and exposure (AE cell 1, Figure 1); alprazolam and relaxation, the control for the psychological treatment (AR cell 2, Figure 1); placebo and live exposure (PE cell 3, Figure 1); and placebo and relaxation, so-called double-placebo (PR cell 4, Figure 1). Pharmacologic and psychological treatment lasted for eight weeks, medication was tapered during the following eight weeks and subjects were followed for an additional six months to assess relapse or maintenance of gains following discontinuation of treatment. Both exposure and relaxation followed published guides, not treatment manuals (Marks, 1978; Wolpe & Lazarus, 1966). The study was conducted at two centers; one in London, UK, and the other in Toronto, Canada.

The primary outcome measures were: ratings of avoidance by an assessor and the subject; the number of major panics; work and social disability; and the clinician's rating of improvement. After eight weeks of treatment, there were significant main effects of both alprazolam and exposure. The effects of alprazolam, as would be expected for a pharmacologic treatment, did not persist during follow-up, whereas the effects of exposure persisted after treatment discontinuation. Interpretation of findings is complicated by the fact that there was substantial improvement in total major panic in the "double-placebo" group that received medication placebo and relaxation.

In addition to reporting statistical significance of outcome measures, the article also reports the effect size of various outcome measures (Cohen, 1988, 1992). With large samples, differences that are clinically uninteresting may be statistically significant, that is, they are unlikely to be due to chance. The effect size is less influenced by sample size and may therefore be considered a better indicator of clinical relevance. During the first eight weeks, when both treatments were being delivered and were significantly better than their controls, the effect size is larger for exposure than for alprazolam. According to the definitions of Uhlenhuth et al. (1969), this would be a

Psychological treatment

		Experimental	Control
Pharmacologic treatment	Experimental	**1** Alprazolam/exposure	**2** Alprazolam/relaxation
	Control	**3** Placebo/exposure	**4** Placebo/relaxation

reciprocal effect. Effect sizes are moderate to large for alprazolam and very large for exposure according to criteria defined by Cohen (1992). The effect sizes diminish over time for exposure but are still in the large to very large range after six months. Those for alprazolam are absent to small during the follow-up period. Effect size for total major panics are absent to small throughout the study because of the effect in the control group. In general, the findings show a greater effect for exposure and no consistent pattern of interaction between psychological treatment and medication.

The strengths of the study include an appropriate population for study. All subjects met stringent criteria for panic disorder and none had been nonresponders to either of the treatment modalities prior to study entry. Further, assignment to treatment was random, assessment was double-blind to medication and single-blind to psychological treatment, assessment included both self- and assessor-completed measures, and analyses addressed the range of assessments included.

The design reveals one of the problems inherent in studies designed to assess interactions of medication and psychological treatments. The discontinuation design, that was appropriate for the psychological treatment in the present study, is not optimal for assessment of pharmacologic treatments and the fact that pharmacologic effects were not maintained after discontinuation should come as no surprise. Analysis was restricted to 134 subjects who completed at least six weeks of treatment (a 16% dropout rate). Although the rate is relatively low compared to other studies of alprazolam, and there were no differences in baseline characteristics between the 20 subjects who withdrew from the study and the 134 who did not, it is unclear how their inclusion in analyses might have altered the results. The general wisdom regarding randomized clinical trials is unequivocal in stating that all subjects randomized must be included in analysis but a review of a standard journal in the field, *Controlled Clinical Trials*, during the past four years did not reveal a single specific citation.

3.03.6 INDIVIDUAL DIFFERENCES: WHAT TREATMENT WORKS FOR WHOM?

From a clinical perspective, perhaps the most important question regarding treatment is the appropriate matching of patient or client to treatment. The idea that a given treatment approach is appropriate for all (even all who share certain characteristics) runs counter to clinical and research experience. Although randomized experiments may not represent the optimal method for evaluating this question, they can provide useful information. Two rather different methods can be used in the context of randomized trials. The first is the use of factorial designs and the other is the *post hoc* examination of individual characteristics as predictors of treatment response. This section will consider these methods.

3.03.6.1 Individual Difference Variable

The use of an individual difference variable as a factor in a factorial design allows a direct experimental test of a hypothesis regarding differential effects of a patient or client characteristic in relation to a psychological treatment. This strategy is difficult to implement—each client characteristic included doubles the number of subjects needed in a study. Perhaps the most common example of a client characteristic studied in this way is the use of more than one center in a study so that the generalization across centers can be tested. Examples of this strategy are relatively common (e.g., Elkin et al., 1989; Marks et al., 1993), but it is unusual for hypothesized differential effects to be proposed. A second variable that is sometimes investigated in a factorial design is gender.

3.03.6.2 *Post hoc* Examination of Predictors of Treatment Response

In general, *post hoc* analyses of individual client characteristics as differential predictors of treatment response have been disappointing. For example, several of the studies that are reviewed in this chapter have attempted to identify characteristics of clients who fare particularly well in the treatments studied and as has been noted in the descriptions, reliable differences have not been found. Review of the psychopharmacology literature yields a similar conclusion.

Perhaps the most reliable finding regarding prediction of treatment outcome has been severity of symptoms. In a number of studies where symptom severity has been studied, the evidence suggests that it usefully discriminated response (e.g., Elkin et al., 1989). In that study, discrimination of differences between medications and psychotherapies was clearer among subjects with greater symptom severity.

Difficulty in reliable identification of individual characteristics that predict differential response may stem from a number of causes. The nihilistic view is that there simply are no reliable predictors. Two alternatives seem more reasonable. The first is that although studies may have adequate power to detect treatment differences, they do not have adequate power to examine individual characteristics. If this is the case, meta-analytic strategies could allow the examination of data regarding characteristics that are frequently considered such as gender, age, symptom severity, duration of symptoms, referral source, comorbid psychological problems, or diagnoses. See Chapter 15, this volume, for a discussion of this problem and methods to deal with it. The final alternative is that client characteristics which are predictive of treatment outcome are elusive and are not captured adequately in experimental studies. Characteristics such as motivation and client–therapist rapport come immediately to mind.

3.03.7 CONCLUSIONS

Randomized, experimental designs represent a useful method in the evaluation of psychological treatments. They allow unambiguous conclusions regarding the treatments that are studied in the subjects who receive them. This chapter has reviewed in some detail several generally excellent individual studies in order to identify their strengths and weaknesses. The astute reader will have noted that all the studies had both strengths and weaknesses. The goal of drawing attention to these is twofold. The first is to provide readers of the research literature with a framework within which to evaluate other studies. The second is to hope that the observations in this chapter may contribute to the ongoing process of improving the quality of experimental studies of psychological treatments. In this way we can maximize the value of the contributions made by subjects who agree to participate in experiments and improve the treatment and care of clients and patients.

3.03.8 REFERENCES

American Psychiatric Association (1987). *Diagnostic and statistical manual of mental disorders* (3rd ed. Rev.). Washington, DC: Author.

American Psychiatric Association (1994). *Diagnostic and statistical manual of mental disorders* (4th ed.). Washington, DC: Author.

Bickel, W. K., Amass, L., Higgins, S. T., Badger, G. J., & Esch, R. A. (1997). Effects of adding behavioral treatment to opioid detoxification with buprenorphine. *Journal of Consulting and Clinical Psychology, 65,* 803–810.

Brill, A. A. (1938). *The basic writings of Sigmund Freud.* New York: Modern Library.

Brock, T. C., Green, M. C., Reich, D. A., & Evans, L. M. (1996). The *Consumer Reports* Study of Psychotherapy: Invalid is Invalid. *American Psychologist, 51,* 1083.

Brown, R. A., & Lewinsohn, P. M. (1984). A psychoeducational approach to the treatment of depression: Comparison of group, individual, and minimal contact procedures. *Journal of Consulting and Clinical Psychology, 52,* 774–783.

Campbell, D. T., & Stanley, J. C. (1963). Experimental and quasi-experimental designs for research on teaching. In N. L. Gage (Ed.), *Handbook of research on teaching* (pp. 171–246). Chicago: Rand McNally.

Campbell, D. T., & Stanley, J. C. (1966). *Experimental and quasi-experimental designs for research.* Chicago: Rand McNally.

Cohen, J. (1992). A power primer. *Psychological Bulletin, 112,* 155–159.

Cohen, J. (1988). *Statistical power analysis for the behavioral sciences* (2nd ed.). Hillsdale, NJ: Erlbaum.

Cole, J. O. (1968). Peeking through the double blind. In D. H. Efron (Ed.), *Psychopharmacology. A review of progress 1957–1967* (pp. 979–984). Washington, DC: US Government Printing Office.

Consumer Reports (1994). Annual questionnaire.

Consumer Reports (1995, November). Mental health: Does therapy help? *Consumer Reports,* 734–739.

Cook, T. D., & Campbell, D. T. (Eds.) (1979). *Quasi-experimentation: design and analysis issues for field settings.* Boston, MA: Houghton Mifflin.

Department of Health and Human Services, Office of the Secretary (1994). Protection of Human Subjects. Title 45 of the Code of Federal Regulations, Sub-part 46. *OPRR Reports,* Revised June 18, 1991, Reprinted March 15, 1994.

Elkin, I., Parloff, M. B., Hadley, S. W., & Autry, J. H. (1985). NIMH Treatment of Depression Collaborative Research Program. Background and Research Plan. *Archives of General Psychiatry, 42,* 305–316.

Elkin, I., Shea, T., Watkins, J. T., Imber, S. O., Sotsky, S. M., Collins, J. F., Glass, D. R., Pilkonis, P. A., Leber, W. R., Docherty, J. P., Fiester, S. J., & Parloff, M. B. (1989). National Institute of Mental Health treatment of depression collaborative research program. General effectiveness of treatments. *Archives of General Psychiatry, 46,* 971–982.

Flick, S. N. (1988). Managing attrition in clinical research. *Clinical Psychology Review, 8,* 499–515.

Frank, E., Kupfer, D. J., Perel, J. M., Cornes, C., Jarrett, D. B., Mallinger, A. G., Thase, M. E., McEachran, A. B., & Grochocinski, V. J. (1990). Three-year outcomes for maintenance therapies in recurrent depression. *Archives of General Psychiatry, 47,* 1093–1099.

Frank, J. D. (1971). Therapeutic factors in psychotherapy. *American Journal of Psychotherapy, 25,* 350–361.

Hollon, S. D., & DeRubeis, R. J. (1981). Placebo–psychotherapy combinations: Inappropriate representations of psychotherapy in drug-psychotherapy comparative trials. *Psychological Bulletin, 90,* 467–477.

Hollon, S. D., Waskow, I. E., Evans, M, & Lowery, H. A. (1984). System for rating therapies for depression. Read before the annual meeting of the American Psychiatric Association, Los Angeles, May 9, 1984. For copies of the Collaborative Study Psychotherapy Rating Scale and related materials prepared under NIMH contract 278-81-003 (ER), order "System for Rating Psychotherapy Audiotapes" from US Dept of Commerce, National Technical Information Service, Springfield, VA 22161.

Hunt, E. (1996). Errors in Seligman's "The Effectiveness of Psychotherapy: The *Consumer Reports* Study." *American Psychologist, 51*(10), 1082.

Keane, T. M., Fairbank, J. A., Caddell, J. M., & Zimering, R. T. (1989). Implosive (flooding) therapy reduces symptoms of PTSD in Vietnam combat veterans. *Behavior Therapy, 20,* 245–260.

Kendall, P. C., & Lipman, A. J. (1991). Psychological and pharmacological therapy: Methods and modes for comparative outcome research. *Journal of Consulting and Clinical Psychology, 59,* 78–87.

Klerman, G. L., Weissman, M. D., Rounsaville, B. J., and Chevron, E. S. (1984). *Interpersonal psychotherapy of depression.* New York: Basic Books.

Kotkin, M., Daviet, C., & Gurin, J. (1996). The *Consumer Reports* Mental Health Survey. *American Psychologist, 51,* 1080–1082.

Kriegman, D. (1996). The effectiveness of medication: The *Consumer Reports* study. *American Psychologist, 51,* 1086–1088.

Lewinsohn, P. M., Munoz, R. F., Youngren, M. A., & Zeiss, A. M. (1978). *Control your depression.* Englewood Cliffs, NJ: Prentice-Hall.

Marks, I. M. (1978). *Living with fear.* New York: McGraw-Hill.

Marks, I. M., Swinson, R. P., Basoglu, M., Kuch, K., Noshirvani, H., O'Sullivan, G., Lelliott, P. T., Kirby, M., McNamee, G., Sengun, S., & Wickwire, K. (1993). Alprazolam and exposure alone and combined in panic disorder with agoraphobia. A controlled study in London and Toronto. *British Journal of Psychiatry, 162,* 776–787.

Mintz, J., Drake, R. E., & Crits-Christoph, P. (1996). Efficacy and Effectiveness of Psychotherapy: Two Paradigms, One Science. *American Psychologist, 51,* 1084–1085.

Pocock, S. J. (1983). *Clinical trials: a practical approach.* New York: Wiley.

Pocock, S. J., & Simon, R. (1975). Sequential treatment assignment with balancing for prognostic factors in the controlled clinical trial. *Biometrics, 31,* 103–115.

Prien, R. F., & Robinson, D. S. (Eds.) (1994). *Clinical evaluation of psychotropic drugs—principles and guidelines.* New York: Raven Press.

Schooler, N. R. (1978). Antipsychotic drugs and psychological treatment in schizophrenia. In M. A. Lipton, A. DiMascio, & K. F. Killam (Eds.), *Psychopharmacology—a generation of progress* (pp. 1155–1168). New York: Raven Press.

Seligman, M. E. P. (1995). The effectiveness of psychotherapy: The *Consumer Reports* study. *American Psychologist, 50,* 965–974.

Seligman, M. E. P. (1996). Science as an ally of practice. *American Psychologist, 51,* 1072–1079.

Smith, M. L., & Glass, G. V. (1977). Meta-analysis of psychotherapy outcome studies. *American Psychologist, 32,* 752–760.

Uhlenhuth, E. H., Lipman, R. S., & Covi, L. (1969). Combined pharmacotherapy and psychotherapy: Controlled studies. *Journal of Nervous and Mental Diseases, 148,* 52–64.

Waskow, I. E., & Parloff, M. B. (1975). *Psychotherapy change measures.* Washington, DC: National Institute of Mental Health, US Government Printing Office.

White, S. J., & Freedman, L. S. (1978). Allocation of patients to treatment groups in a controlled clinical study. *British Journal of Cancer, 37,* 849–857.

Wolpe, J., & Lazarus, A. (1966). *Behaviour therapy techniques.* Oxford, UK: Pergamon.

World Health Organization (1992). *International classification of diseases (ICD-10)* (10th ed.). Geneva, Switzerland: Author.

3.04
Multiple Group Comparisons: Quasi-experimental Designs

HANS-CHRISTIAN WALDMANN and FRANZ PETERMANN
Universität Bremen, Germany

3.04.1 INTRODUCTION

3.04.1.1 The Relevance of Experimentation in Clinical Psychology

Contributions of clinical psychology to health services have received widespread recognition and the benefits are undisputed. The parallel increase of costs in such services due to growing utilization of psychological aids, however, must be justified on grounds of the scientific method. There is a double need for valid and reliable demonstration of the value in technology derived from and offered by clinical psychology: efficacy in serving the customer and efficiency legitimizing it to the supplier must be shown. Quasi-experimental multiple group comparison designs are well-suited for this task: they account for the fact that randomization may often not be an adequate sampling strategy in real-life clinical research situations and still allow for assessment of absolute and relative efficacy of psychological interventions. They help evaluate the merits of different components in interventions and support decision making as regards implementation, monitoring, and optimization of respective programs. This practical, if not wholly pragmatic, research and reasoning contributes directly to either correction or refinement of the present state of scientific knowledge and development in the domain of clinical psychology. It is practice where results from clinical psychology are to be evaluated, and it will be seen that multiple group comparisons offer adequate tools to do so.

3.04.1.2 Terms: "True," "Quasi-," and "Non-" Experimental Studies

In this chapter, multiple group comparisons will be focused on by means of quasi-experimental designs. Delimiting characteristics to distinguish the three kinds of empirical research situations quoted above are subject assignment, modus of treatment, and control. It is agreed widely to speak of true experiments when both random subject assignment and creation of treatment or, in a broader sense, active manipulation of conditions occur. In a quasi-experimental setup the first condition is weakened, and in observational studies both conditions are completely released. Some authors refer to the term quasi-experimental as to the constraint that the researcher cannot deliberately assign subjects to conditions or that occurrence of a treatment is only a typical but not necessary feature (e.g., Spector, 1981). In this case, the differentiation to pure observational studies seems obsolete. It is argued that any experimental situation, be it "true" or "quasi," involves an arbitrary discernible kind of treatment, by creation or manipulation of conditions regardless of mode of subject assignment, and that quasi-experiments feature all elements of true experiments except randomization.

If there is no manipulation of subjects or conditions in order to evoke variation in dependent measures (and thus contrasts for testing), reference is made to "pure" observational studies (see Chapters 4 and 13, this volume). The main problem then lies with selecting a statistical model and further in devising an appropriate parametrization that reflects as closely as possible the structure of scientific hypotheses (in their original, verbal form). The objective of such inquiries may

comprehend the identification of latent traits and their structural composition (factor analysis), the identification of the dimensional metrics according to which subjects determine the relative value of different objects (multidimensional scaling/conjoint measurement), or in the identification of a time series regression model in order to predict value and stability of a criterion. In neither case is a treatment strictly required.

3.04.1.3 The Concept of an "Effect"

Multiple groups comparison experiments are conducted in order to demonstrate relative effects of treatment. Effect hypotheses refer to presence, size, and variability of effects with respect to certain criterion measurements. The major objective of multiple group comparison designs lies with the generation of data in order to test such hypotheses. Subjects or groups methods representing different levels of independent variables or being subjected to different kinds of treatment, eventually measured at different points of time, are compared on data obtained in the same way in each group and at each occurrence. Then a classical concept of an "effect" is identified with the interaction of the subject or group factor and time/treatment with respect to the outcome measure. For example, the idea of a case–control study to determine therapy effectiveness might be pointed out as "if you apply X (treatment, independent variable) in one group, while not in another, and you observe a significant difference in Y (some functional status, dependent varable) between both groups, then you have reason to believe that there is a relationship between X and Y, given all else being equal." It will be seen that it is the *ceteris paribus* condition in the given clause, and how it is tentatively realized, that makes (quasi-)experimentation a delicate challenge to researchers' creativity and expertise.

A worked example of a quasi-experiment is chosen to introduce into the present chapter an illustration of some of these challenges and ways to counter them.

Worked example: Outline

In a very well designed study, Yung and Kepner (1996) compared absolute and relative efficacy of both muscular and cognitive relaxation procedures on blood pressure in borderline hypertensives employing a multiple-treatment–multiple-control extension of design Number 6 in Figure 2. It is reported that most clinical applications make use of an amalgam of cognitive techniques like suggestion, sensational focusing, and strict behavioral training of muscle stretching relaxation. The authors aim at partialing out the effects of these various components by clearly separating instructions that target muscles directly and such instructions that try to mediate muscle tension by mental efforts. As a consequence, special attention is given to operational validity and treatment integrity. In order to counter confounding of subject characteristics and procedure variables the authors devise a rigorous subject selection and assignment policy which makes their work an excellent example for the case here.

Before engaging in describing various designs and methods of data analysis, and in evaluating this particular experiment, it seems instructive to outline a general process of experimental research.

Generally, it will not be possible to observe all possible instances of variable relations (which would innecessitate inference), but evidence for the hypotheses will be sought by investigating subsets of the population(s) in which these relations are considered to hold true. Sampling variability and measurement error lead to the use of statistical models in order to determine the genuity of an observed effect. Effect sizes (ES) serves to model the above "difference" in terms of statistical distributions (which, in turn, provide both the mathematical background and the factual means for testing effect size). The significance of statistical significance and the concept of reason based hereupon are evaluated in Chapter 14, this volume, and the issue of interpreting such a relationship as causal is briefly discussed in Section 3.04.3. But how does one arrive at effect hypotheses and corresponding statistical models in the first place?

3.04.2 THE LOGIC OF DESIGN IN THE COURSE OF EMPIRICAL RESEARCH

It is suggested that experimentation as a procedure is a special realization of a general process of empirical research, as depicted in Figure 1. Whether experimentation is seen as an appropriate access to address the problems in question depends on preceding decisions; if so, choice of design and sampling structure is conceived as an embedded level. Furthermore, it is proposed that this procedural outline is paralleled by a conceptual process of hypotheses derivation. Figure 1 illustrates this correspondence with hypotheses levels according to the deductive four-step model presented by Hager (1992):

(i) Generally agreeing with the hypothetico-deductive method, scientific hypotheses are derived from proposition structures in theory. Sometimes, mere need for evaluation or striking observations from practice must serve as a starting point for the research process.

(ii) Relative to marginal conditions (resources, time, etc.) and constraints in construct operationalization, a subject matter model is derived in terms of variables and their interrelation. Temporal ordering and other prerequisites of model theory guaranteed, predictions regarding empirical manifestations are derivable ("should then be higher than"). Devise a design now in order to translate a hypothesized structure of variables into a measurable one and a sampling strategy in order to actually perform the measurement. Hypotheses stating that certain strategies of verbal intervention in psychotherapy are of use for depressives might be translated into a "better-off" proposition as quoted in the text above. It is clear that, at this level, an experiment rationale is suggested: comparison of groups. Also, global aspects of testing are implied: assessment strategy (will psychometric tests be applied or will therapists rate patients' depressiveness by virtue of their expertise?), or inference conditions (will an effect be required to instantiate simultaneously on all criteria and to be stable for at least a year, thus calling for multiple post-tests, or will the whole study be replicated using different subjects and other therapists?). In transition to the next level, a set of decisions to be made is encountered that are known to statistical consultants as "how many" questions in project and design planning (how many subjects are enough per group in order to balance sensibly factors of sensitivity?, how many time intervals make up the optimal retest interval?, how many outliers can be tolerated in and across groups?, etc.).

(iii) Multiple group comparison as a conceptual strategy implies suppositions about structures in the data. Here, conceptually identified effect sizes receive an accurate, quantitative, and thereby testable formulation. A "pre–postdifference" between groups may now be specified in terms of an expectation of a difference in central tendency of an outcome variable, a kind of second-order comprehensive measure that can be tested easily for significance at the next level. More generally, statistical predictions formally denote compound suppositions about the "behavior" of data, and a "good" design generates data behavior that by maximum degree either confirms or contradicts behavior that would be expected by hypothesis.

(iv) Statistical hypotheses are statements about specific values, variability, and ordinal or metric relations of parameters of distributions which follow from statistical predictions. A common prototype for such a measure is

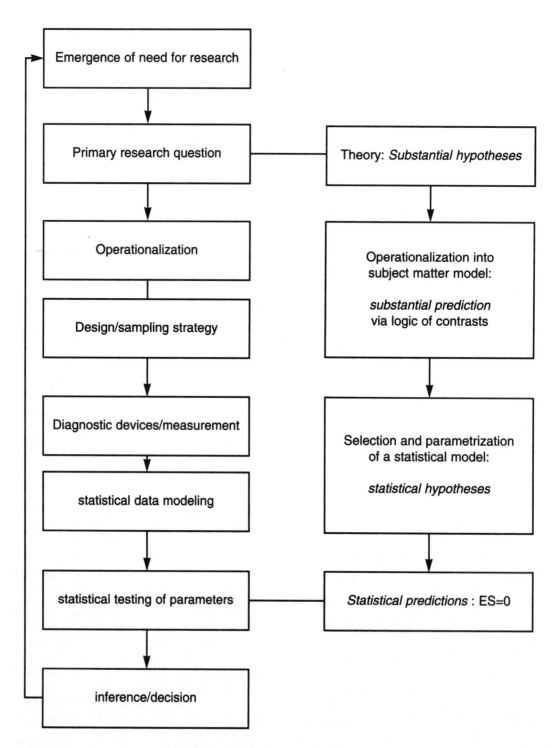

Figure 1 The process of empirical research.

given by $ES = (\mu_{treat} - \mu_{control})/\sigma_{control}$. Its problems not withstanding, this is considered a fairly reasonable and intuitive basic concept. Various other ES formulations can be translated to it (Cohen, 1988; Lipsey, 1990). For instance, in the example of therapy effectiveness, and effect is assumed to be present when statistical testing has determined that its ES differs from zero significantly, that is, beyond the expected limits of sampling error and with prespecified error probabilities of the α- and β- kind. In fact the probability is always estimated that there is no effect (therefore speaking of "null" hypotheses) or that, as it is frequently put in terms of sampling theory, comparison groups are samples that were drawn from the same population. In this case, observed differences merely reflect sampling error. Depending on the formulation of predictions, it is not always obvious at first sight whether these "null" probabilities are required to be high or low. Further complicating things, a statistical prediction must sometimes be further differentiated into a set of single-testable statistical hypotheses. It must then be decided whether an overall null (or alternative) hypothesis is conforming to the compound statistical prediction or what pattern of acceptance or rejection of individual hypotheses integrates to a favorable finding. Moreover, there is a need to decide whether integration of separate findings should follow a disjunctive (compensatory) or conjunctive rule (e.g., must depressives benefit on all scales applied in order to justifiably speak of an effect). As a consequence of this multiple testing, there is a need to control for accumulation of error probabilities. Note, however, that "difference" does not necessarily imply the comparison of means. It most cases, pretest-standardized differences in means are in fact used for this purpose because such measures have known statistical properties (e.g., distributions and standard errors) following normal theory and can thus be easily tested statistically. But a test might be made for a ratio to be greater than a prespecified number (as is done frequently when using differential model fit across groups as a criterion) or the inequality of regression intercept and slope parameters (as featured in regression continuity designs, see Section 3.04.5.7). The general rationale is to determine whether or not groups differ in any statistical parameter and to relate this difference to a reference sampling error estimate. (For details on procedures of significance testing see Cohen, 1988; Fisher, 1959; Giere, 1972; Mayo 1985.) Criteria like adequacy (on each level, hypotheses preserve to maximum degree classificatory, ordinal, or metric relations assumed on preceding level), sufficiency (a linearly predictable trend may not be tested for monotony only), decisiveness and unambiguous identification of theory-conforming empirical states (Hager, 1992) serve to estimate validity of hypothesis derivation. After statistical testing, however, there is a need to work backwards: what effect size is considered practically significant? Is there a failure in predicting things as they should occur in theory? Do the findings entitle inductive inferences to be drawn to higher levels in the hierarchy of hypotheses, leading to tentative confirmation of propositions in the theoretical frame of reference? Here have been introduced some of the most serious problems in philosophy of science, and there is a need to get still further into it before turning to techniques.

3.04.3 CRITERIA: SENSITIVITY, VALIDITY, AND CAUSALITY

Conventionally, the major objective of experimentation is seen in demonstrating a causal relationship between phenomena, or, as Cook and Campbell (1979) put it in more correct terms, in facilitating causal inference. The logic underlying experimental design is an implicit variation of the concepts of covariation, temporal precedence, and of ruling out alternatives. This means, in terms of experimentation, that the hypothesized "cause" should be capable of being omitted and control group esigns are preferable. One-shot case studies or pretest–post-test designs without at least one control or, in a broader sense, a comparison group, do by no degree allow for the kind of inference scientists are most interested in: causal ones. But, as was seen from Figure 1, experimentation ends up in statistics. The result of an experiment is that data are communicated in the form of statistical propositions. Whether statistical relationships should be taken as indicators only or be conceived as "causal," "functional," or "probabilistic" cannot be determined by simply rating how well the rules of experimentation were obeyed, but depends on affiliations in philosophy of science. Criteria for when to apply the predicate causal and be justified in doing so, are hardly available. But before drawing any such inferences it will be necessary to (i) ensure sensitivity in order to detect the effect and (ii) rely on it being a valid indicator for what is to be interpreted as causal. In the following section, a start is made on practice by introducing the key concepts whose consideration will hopefully establish a sensitive, valid, and meaningful design. It is clear, however, that an evaluation of meaning must rely on protoscientific argumentation.

3.04.3.1 Sensitivity

Sensitivity refers to the likelihood to detect an effect in sample-based investigations, given it is indeed present in the population from which samples were drawn. It is determined by sample size, total and direction of effect size, heterogenity of both subjects and treatment applications, and various undesired features of diagnostic devices (unreliability, etc.). While those factors affect experimental precision, others like prescribed error probabilities of both α and β type and the kind of statistical test used affect the associated concept on the level of statistical analysis: power. It must be borne in mind that sampling error stands for the variance of parameter estimates and is, thus, maximally dependent on sample size. As a consequence, an effect size however small will become significant in statistical terms with increasing sample size, while being wholly uninformative for practical considerations. For an ES of the kind presented above less than or equal to 0.3 to attain statistical significance at $\alpha = 0.05$, some $n = 300$ subjects would be in order; for an ES of 0.5 still a hundred or more. In a meta-analysis on psychotherapy efficacy Grawe (1992) found that 87% of 897 studies were using samples of $n = 30$ or less subjects in intervention groups. To attain statistical significance at the usual level an effect size of greater than 1.20 would then be required. This may be considered quite an unlikely prerequisite: in their meta-analysis on psychotherapy research Smith, Glass, and Miller (1980) reported an overall expectation of treatment effectiveness of no more than ES = 0.85. Tentative counterbalancing the determinants of effect sizes other than the "true" effect (population effect), namely sample size, error probability, and assumed ES, is best achieved using power tables as proposed in Cohen (1988). Since detecting an effect usually means observing an effect size that statistically differs from zero, the levels of design and data analysis in Figure 1 become mixed up when evaluating the whole procedure of quasi-experimental multiple group comparisons. It is the correspondence of design structure "giving" the data and statistical data model that establishes a "good" design. Sometimes data obtained from one design can be translated into different models (problem of parametrization) and effect sizes may be evaluated for their significance by various of statistical tests (problem of relative power).

3.04.3.2 Validity

Validity refers to the likelihood that the effect detected is in fact the effect of interest. Campbell and Stanley (1963), and Cook and Campbell (1979), originators of the concept, distinguish internal, external, and statistical validity as well as construct validity. The latter refers to operationalization problems (mono-operationalization bias, monomethod bias, evaluation apprehension, experimenter expectancies, etc.). Internal validity evaluates to which extent variation in measured dependent variables is attributable solely to variation of independent variables or treatment, respectively. Again, assuming an effect for a difference in the value of some statistical parameter calculated from data on dependent variables (e.g., the mean), internal validity assures that nothing but treatment "caused" this difference, and that, as Lipsey (1990) puts it, the observed difference parallels the fact that "the only difference between the treatment and the control conditions is the intervention of interest" (p. 11). This, of course, relies heavily on the experimenter's ability to control for other possible "sources of variation" or undesired confounding influences. External validity refers to the extent to which results obtained from a sample-based study may be generalized to a specified population from which samples were drawn in the first place and/ or across slightly different (sub)populations. Such extrapolation must be reasonably justified as regards target population (i.e., persons), settings, and future time. Note that representativeness is a prerequisite to external validity that not only holds for subject selection but also for situative conditions of experimentation itself: ecological validity must be given careful consideration especially in clinical fields.

Campbell and Stanley (1963) have raised the argument that internal validity can be thought of as a necessary while not sufficient condition for external validity. Note, however, that some methods of control depicted in the next section show conflicting effects on internal and external validity, and to compensate for these imbalances with a reasonable trade-off certainly is an art of its own. Most flaws in experimental and quasi-experimental design boil down to violations of factors of validity which is why a short outline is presented (see Table 1) of their respective factors as designated by Cook and Campbell (1979). A far more comprehensive listing of possible threats to validity and various other shortcomings in planning experimental research is presented in Hoole (1978). Special attention to external validity in evaluation contexts is given in Bernstein (1976).

Admittedly, full consideration of all these caveats, if not mere apprehension of this rather lengthy list, seems to discourage any use of (quasi-)experimental designs at all. The contrary is true, though. There will be a benefit from

Table 1 Factors of internal and external validity.

Internal validity	
History	In the time interval between pretest and post-test measure, various influences or sources of variation that are not of interest or that may even distort "true" findings may be in effect besides the applied treatment. This clearly leads to confounding. Also, these factors may be differently effective for different subjects, thereby introducing additional error variance. Controlling for such intrusion by elimination or by holding it constant to some degree is an appropriate method in laboratory settings but is almost impossible to achieve in real-world clinical (field) settings (apart from identifying such factors as relevant in the first place). Moreover, many disorders are known to be subject to seasonal variation or others periodicities.
Maturation	In longitudinal studies with fairly large restest intervals, effects may be confounded with or entirely due to "natural" change in subjects' characteristics that are correlated with the variables and treatments of interest. A prominent example in clinical research is spontaneous remission in psychotherapy studies. The hope is that such change takes effect equivalently in both groups of a case–control study (which again is rather a "large sample" argument but is usually held true for randomized samples).
Mortality	In repeated measures designs, attrition or loss of a certain proportion of subjects is to be expected on a regular basis. Differential loss, however, means that the observed drop-out pattern across groups seems not to be random but is dependent on variables that might correlate with treatment or outcome measure. This in turn introduces *post hoc* selection artifacts and is likely to erroneously contribute to effect size in that it may change value and variability of post-test statistics.
Statistical regression	A typical problem with measuring change lies with regression towards the mean. Subjects may shown gain or loss in scores from pretest to posttest solely due to the unreliability of the test. This may be compensated for to a certain degree by multivariate assessment of dependent variables. Moreover, differential effects are likely to fall into place depending on subjects" pretest or starting-off: "viewed more generally, statistical regression (a) operates to increase obtained pretest–post-test scores among low pretest scores, since this group's pretest scores are more likely to have been depressed by error, (b) operates to increase obtained change scores among persons with high pretest scores since their pretest scores are likely to have been inflated by error, and (c) does not affect change scores among scorers at the center of the pretest distribution since the group is likely to contain as many units whose pretest scores are inflated by error as units whose pretest scores are deflated by it."[a]
Testing, instrument reactivity, and sensitization	In repeated measures designs subjects are likely to become familiar with diagnostic devices or may carry over pretest scoring behavior. In addition, there are many ways that testing procedure itself may affect what is tested. Items that evoke strong emotional reactions may distort scoring in subsequent ability subtests by increasing subjects' unspecific arousal. Moreover, pretests may sensitize subjects for treatment reception by enhancing attention for certain attributes or by facilitating self-communication and introspection. Sometimes it is possible to control for this effect in quasi-experimental settings by applying strategies similar to the Solomon four-group design (see Chapter 3, this volume).
Selection/ interactions with selection	Selection is a threat to internal validity when an effect size—a difference in some parameter across groups—reflects pre-experimental differences between cases and controls rather than differential impact of treatment. Note that inference from such experimentation relies heavily on the *ceteris paribus* condition (denoted in the given clause in the outline in Section 3.04.1.3), and that systematic differences across groups due to selection bias are most pervasive in quasi-experimentation where we have to do without randomization. This is especially true in case of clinical treatment: one would not want to allot inhouse patients or program participants to different treatments (or exclude them to serve as controls) by random numbers but according to their individual needs and aptitude. Patients assigned for cases on behalf of equal (that is, equivocal) diagnoses may yet still differ from other patients in their group (error variance) as well as from controls in a whole pattern, of other variables that are likely to be related to both reception of treatment and outcome measures (e.g., hospitalization, socioeconomic status, verbal fluency, etc.). Note that most factors of internal validity listed so far may interact with subject selection, producing differential effects and thereby increasing experimental error.

Table 1   (continued)

Instrumentation	In the first place it must be ensured, of course, that diagnostic devices meet criteria of reliability, objectivity, and validity in terms of measurement and testing theory. In repeated measures designs, discrimination and differentiation capabilities of tests may change. Thus a gain in scores from one occasion to another may partly be due to enhanced performance of observers who improved skills with practice, and less due to differential effects of applied treatment at these occasions. A related problem lies with so-called floor or ceiling effects. Subjects scoring at the upper end of a scale on one occasion, say 6 on a 1–7 Likert scale, may easily report a decrease by half but will find it difficult to state a major increase of similar proportion. Note that clinical samples are often defined by a shift in mean in certain indicators with respect to a "normal" population.
Control group behavior	Besides the problem of recruiting and maintaining a control group, "compensatory rivalry" of respondents receiving less desirable treatment and "resentful demoralization" of such subjects are further threats to internal validity. In the first case, being assigned to the nonreceiving group may motivate subjects to behave competetively as to reduce the "true" effect (due to treatment) in counter-hypothesized direction. In the second case, the deprived get more deprived and less motivated: a patient that suffers from his disease is assigned for a control and thus kept from a therapy that is thought to be efficient by the experimenter. The "lose-heart" effect would then artificially enlarge effects. Both variants are of great practical importance in therapy effectiveness research.[a]
External validity	
Interaction of pretest and treatment, reactivity	It is well-known that mere knowledge to participate in a study or the awareness of being observed does affect behavior. Furthermore, due to sensitization effects or conditioning effects (see above), results obtained from samples that have completed a pretest cannot be fully generalized to populations that have not done so.
Interaction of selection and treatment	People that deliberately demand for psychological care or for access to health care programs are likely to be more susceptible to treatment or motivated than are accidental samples of convenience (collective of inpatients, rooms, etc.). Often, selection processes that have led to admission of subjects are unknown. It is clear, however, that results obtained from such samples cannot be generalized unreservedly.
Interfering treatments	Parallel, overlapping or interacting treatments lead to confounding and thus constitute a major threat to internal validity. But there are undesirable consequences for external validity as well. Suppose patients are receiving medical treatment in ascending dosage. Due to idiosyncratic effects of cumulation, conclusions drawn with respect to an intermediate level of dosage that generalize across people may be erroneous.
Nonrepresentative samples	Generally, target populations must be clearly specified in advance. In quasi-experimental design, representativeness cannot be ensured by random sampling on a large scale but instead take advantage of "natural" (nonmanipulative) sample formation. Often characteristics of research context naturally differentiate subjects into groups (rooming policies of hospital, record analysis, etc.). Strictly speaking, since there is no real sampling there is no point in making inferences. But this aside, sampling should not refer to subjects only: generalizing also includes care givers (therapists, etc.), hospitals, and regions. Therefore, another strategy lies with deliberate sampling for heterogeneity with respect for certain attributes relevant to the research question. Inference would then be across a wide range of units holding subsets of these attributes, but still limited to the respective superset. When dealing with clinical samples, this method seems fairly reasonable.

Source: Cook & Campbell (1979).[a]

it in that the degree to which attention is given to these issues prior to experimentation parallels the degree to which results can be interpreted and inferences drawn after experimentation. Factors of validity thus serve as criteria for comparative evaluation of quasi-experimental studies, they are not meant as a checklist for building the perfect one (remember that several factors exclude mutually). Another precaution must be added. While the bearings of internal validity on technical issues in research planning are widely agreed upon and factors listed above have nearly become codified into a guide on design construction, most important issues of construct validity often receive less recognition. But re-examining the procedural structure of empirical research, as sketched in Figure 1, the view that emerges is that everything begins and ends with valid operationalization of constructs into measurable variables, and of hypothesized relations into exercisable methods for "visualizing" them. Greater appreciation of construct and derivation validity is advocated before turning too readily to tactics and techniques of experimentation. For instance, one should examine treatment integrity well before constructing sophisticated application schedules in an interrupted time series design (see Section 3.04.5.3). Nonetheless, within the entire validity framework, causal inference is predicated on maximum appreciation mostly of internal validity. The question is what is meant by causal.

3.04.3.3 Causality, Practice, and Pragmatism

However sensitive and valid a design might be by these terms, an effect or statistical relationship cannot be interpreted as truly causal in an objectivist ontological sense or in the traditional Humean readings (for an introduction, see Cook & Campbell, 1979, and Salmon, 1966). Therefore, and for the following reasons, a wholly alternative view is pledged on these issues in the tradition of James and other pragmatist reviewers of methodology. Scientific inquiry and its results (e.g., explanations) should always bear technological relevance. As one consequence, the importance of manipulation, is re-emphasized as a feature of treatment in quasi-experimentation. Consider the following argument raised by Collingwood (1940):

> Suppose one claimed to have discovered cause of cancer, but added that his discovery would be of no practical use because the cause he had discovered was not a thing that could be produced or prevented at will. His dicovery would be denounced a shame. (p. 300)

Collingwood's point is that causal explanations are often valued for the leads they give about factors that can be manipulated. If the essential cause of some effect does not imply controlling the effect (e.g., cancer) through manipulating some factor, then knowledge of this cause is not considered useful by many persons (Cook & Campbell, 1979). Scientific inquiry and quasi-experimental research designs are conceived as concretization devices, as tools to obtain technological knowledge. Thus, research designs need to take into account the feasibility of manipulation of conditions that produce effects in order to at least allow for transfer into practice. It is practice where results from research in clinical psychology should be evaluated, which is why a concept of causality and explanation is needed that is of relevance.

Modern philosophers and methodologists have demonstrated successfully that pragmatist reasoning can be adapted successfully to methodology in social sciences, and have done so down to the level of hypotheses testing (Putnam, 1974). Of course there is no pragmatic explanation of its own right. But our attempts to explain phenomena on experimental or even statistical grounds can be justified pragmatically by introducing criteria beyond a "logic of discovery":

> The first and ineliminable criterion for the adequacy of an explanation must be based on what it does for a man who wants explanation. This depends on contextual factors that are not reflected in the forms of propositions or the structure of inferences. (Collins, 1966, p. 140)

> Knowledge of causal manipulanda, even the tentative, partial and probabilistic knowledge of which we are capable, can help improve social life. What policy makers and individual citizens seem to want from science are recipes that can be followed and that usually lead to the desired positive effects, even if understanding the micromediational is only partial and the positive effects are not *invariably* brought about. (Cook & Campbell, 1979, p. 28)

If efficacy of, say, a new drug has been demonstrated on a statistical basis by experimentation, it is not possible, strictly speaking, to conclude that deficiency in effective substance of the drug caused the disease or that the substance now reversed the pathogenetic process to regeneration. Having controlled for side effects, it is perfectly justifiable to maintain the drug as a successful therapy (and raise funds for further elaboration which might give new insights for science as well as for refinement of the drug). On a statistical level this "better-off" thinking in interpreting results from case–control studies translates into the concept of statistical relevance (Salmon, 1966) or into the notion of Granger causality. The latter derives from the theory of linear systems and defines causal relevance of independent variables ("causes") in terms of increased predictability of value and variability of dependent variables ("effects"). Prognosis should then be more precise with a relevant variable included in the model than with the variable removed, and good prognosis is definitely a very useful outcome of research (Granger, 1969). Good prognosis is, after all, a feature of operational models. This is what should be expected from experimentation in clinical psychology: identification of factors that influence etiology and the spread of disorders and derivation of operational models that in turn might aid to confront them.

3.04.4 CONTROL IN QUASI-EXPERIMENTAL DESIGN

Control aims at enhancing and balancing factors of internal and external validity following the max-con-min-rule formulated by Kerlinger (1973):

(i) *maxi*mize impact of independent variables on dependent ones,

(ii) while holding *con*stant factors of systematic intrusion, and

(iii) *mini*mizing the influence of unsystematic variables or error.

What is meant by factors, influences, and error? Control is always exerted over independent variables that contribute to effects. It is instructive to refine the term variable into four types relevant in experimentation. Systematic variance denotes differences between groups and, with reference to the definition of an effect size in Section 3.04.1.3, thus indicates the presence of "true" effects. In concept, it is solely attributed to explanatory variables, indicating treatment. Extraneous variables, however, are not a primary focus of a study but in cases of substantial correlation with dependent ones introduce error variance and do bias estimates of effects. Such variables may either be subjected to control or be left uncontrolled in one of two ways, depending on both sample size and subject assignment policy. In the latter case, randomized variables are let run freely in the hope that their effects will cancel out in the long run and thus equate groups in a probabilistic sense while confounded variables constitute a threat to validity that cannot be ruled out. It follows that controlled variables are extraneous but their impact on measures of effect is accounted for because error variance is reduced. If such erroneous influences are known to operate (by background knowledge introduced into the subject matter model, or simply by intuition), the techniques presented in Table 2 are used or at least an attempt is made to obtain accurate measures on them. Statistical techniques may, then, be used in order to separate *post hoc* the effect of treatment (in terms of ES) and selection differences.

In quasi-experimentation, control is exercised rather by means of subject selection or statistical analysis than by manipulating conditions. Because no randomization is used in quasi-experimental settings to wash out all initial differences in and across groups and because an effect has been defined in terms of post-test differences, credibility of findings will depend on the ability to demonstrate that groups have been alike as possible except for the difference in treatment they received. It will be noticed, however, that pretest equivalence does not lead, as might be implied by name, to equivalent groups. There may still be reliable and substantial differences on other factors relevant but left unconsidered (or even unmeasureable if known) that affect the phenomenon in question. The argument by Cook and Campbell (1979) is followed that only understanding the process of subject selection allows full understanding of subject differences that cannot be attributed to treatment, and that randomization must be considered the only model of such a process that can be completely understood.

The following is a worked example:—Control is by subject selection and assignment:

Of 307 recruited individuals, only 40 were eligible for participation. Persons showing habituation effects were excluded, because their high pressure in multiple baseline readings was assumed to be a reaction to the measurement situation itself (sensitization). To control for treatment interference persons currently engaged in other pressure control techniques were also excluded. Persons on medication were asked to present medical records to assure constant dosage for the time of their participation (history). The authors cite evidence for a linear relationship between blood pressure level prior to behavioral intervention and treatment change. They further attribute contradictory results in recent research on relaxation efficacy to the common practice of matching experimental groups with respect to the average on certain blood pressure parameters, which leaves differential treatment susceptibility in higher degrees of hypertension uncontrolled. Subjects were therefore orthogonally matched on systolic blood pressure, age, and sex to assure pretest equivalence.

Experimental error also leads to bias in effect size estimates. While disturbing marginal influences (disruptions due to periodicities in hospitals" daily routines, noise, etc.) may be held approximately constant or be eliminated thereby having their influence equated in and across groups, other undeliberate variations of experimental conditions (e.g., treatment inflation or interferences) and measurement effects are to a far lesser extent under the control of the experimenter. But in many field settings there may be no desire to exert artificial control over such (in theory) irregular components of overall effect. It may be preferrable to preserve or enhance external or ecological validity when finally turning to generalization. Since practice is defined as primary, however, bias due to naturally varying concomittants is something to be faced. There is no need to put research back into the laboratory by excellent control when findings need to be transferred into applications for a noncompliant world.

The worked example is continued to demonstrate trial structure and procedural control:

Table 2 Controlling subject-induced extraneous variables.

Matching	The rationale of matching is to fully equate groups with respect to pretest scores, so that differential post-test scoring could legitimately be interpreted as differential change. The more variables are called in for matching the greater a shrinkage in sample size must be expected, sometimes deflating degrees of freedom to an extent where statistical analysis is no longer possible. Moreover, such samples may no longer be representative for target populations to which one finally intends to generalize findings. By the way, there is great appeal in the idea to match subjects with themselves across treatment levels as is the case, for example, in crossover designs.
Parallel groups or aggregate matching	This means of control is, in a way, a weaker version of matching by taking resort to group statistics rather than to individual values. The influence of confounds or, more generally speaking, nuisance factors is considered not relevant if it is distributed evenly across groups. If such a variable has equal distribution in each group (with respect to first- and second-order moments, e.g., mean and variance), groups are said to be parallel on this variable. When dealing with intact groups or when assignment is guided by need or merit, this strategy would entail exclusion of subjects in one group in order to approximate the other or vice versa. Again, sample size would be reduced and groups may finally differ on other variables by selective exclusion. Control always seems to trade off with external validity, notably generalizability. Parallel groups, however, are much easier to obtain than samples matched by score.
Blocking	Blocking further draws variance out of the error term when nuisance factor(s) are known and measurable on a categorical level. The rationale is to match subjects with equal score on this measure into as many groups as there are levels of the nuisance factor. If, for example, $n_j = 10$ subjects are to be assigned to each of $J = 3$ treatment conditions (factor A), and another factor B is known to contribute to variance, one would obtain $K = 10$ levels of factor B with $n_k = 3$ subjects each and then randomly assign $n_{jk} = 1$ subjects per B-level to each of the J levels in A. An increase in numbers of blocks will further decrease error variance since scores within a block of subjects matched this way are less likely to vary due to selection differences to the same extent than would have to be expected in blocks comprising more or all (no blocking) subjects. Note that in this model blocks represent a randomly sampled factor in terms of mixed-model ANOVA[a] and thus can enter statistical analysis to have their effect as well as possible interactions with treatment tested for. As a result, blocking could be viewed as transition of matching (above) into factorization (below). On the other hand, matching is but an extreme case of blocking where any pair of matched subjects can be considered a separate block.
Factorization	Confounding can be completely removed from analysis when confounding variables are leveled (measured by assignment to categories or by recording their continuous scale into discrete divisions) and introduced into design as a systematic source of variation. This generally results in factorial designs where effects of factors can be quantified and tested (main effect and interaction in fully crossed designs, main effect only in hierarchical or incomplete structures).[a,b,c]
Analysis of covariance	While factorization is a pre-experimental device of control (it gives, after all, a sampling structure), analysis of covariance serves to *post hoc* correct results for concommittant variables or pretest differences.[d]
Holding constant elimination	If hospitalization must be expected to substantially mediate results, a most intuitive remedy lies with selecting subjects with the same inhouse time. Strictly speaking, there is no way of generalizing to other levels of the hospitalization variable.

Source: Hays (1990).[a] Pedhazur & Pedhazur (1991).[b] Spector (1981).[c] Cook & Campbell (1979).[d]

All subjects received treatment, placebo, or pure assessment in equal time spacing in eight experimental sessions. They were instructed to replicate these sessions for 30 days after the laboratory trial and to keep a record of their practice. After this follow-up period, all subjects were finally assessed on their blood pressure. Though this procedure implicated a loss in standardization, it certainly enhanced ecological validity and increased the clinical relevance of the study's findings. Light and temperature were held constant in all measurement situations, all equipment was visually shielded to prevent feedback effects. Measurement equipment was calibrated before each trial. All participants spent equal time in the measurement setting and were blinded with respect to assessment results until completion of the measurement occasion. To control for experimenter effects subjects received live relaxation instructions in three sessions followed by five sessions with taped instructions. This procedure further improved standardization of treatment situations. A training time of 18–20 minutes was justified as optimal by recurring to recent findings that shorter training lacks any effects and that longer training often results in loss of motivation to practice, increased dropout rates, and reduced stability of effects over time.

3.04.5 A PRIMER SYSTEM OF DESIGN

As will be obvious from Figure 2, basic forms of designs mostly differ in whether or not they use randomization to assure initial group equivalence and control groups to determine effects, and whether or not they dispose of pretest, multiple observations, multiple forms of treatment (applied, removed, reversed, faded, etc.) and different controls. Following on from this, the regression discontinuity approach is presented as leading to a class of designs in its own right. In the case of more than one explanatory independent variable, additional decisions must be made regarding logical and temporal order of treatment application (factorization into fully crossed and balanced plans, incomplete and hierachical plans, balancing sequence effects, etc.). These topics are more fully covered in Chapter 4, this volume. Note

that many important practical considerations and implications for choice of a statistical model for subsequent analysis are hidden completely in what is called the "data aquisition box" (or "O" in standard notation, see below). Here it must be decided on (i) number of dependent variables (uni- vs. multivariate analysis), (ii) various parameters of repeated measurement (number of occasions, lengths of retest intervals, etc.), (iii) order of dependent measures and error modeling (e.g., use of latent variable models), and (iv) scale characteristics of dependents (parametric vs. arbitrary distribution models).

Most authors, follow standard ROX terminology and notion introduced by Campbell and Stanley (1963): R stands for randomization, O stands for an observation or measurement occassion, X stands for treatment or intervention. Temporal sequence is expressed by left-to-right notation in a row, separate rows refer to different groups.

3.04.5.1 Selections from the General Scheme: Nonequivalent Group Designs

The designs shown in Figure 2, while not a focus of this chapter, will now be considered. Designs one and four are considered "pre-experimental" by Campbell and Stanley (1963):

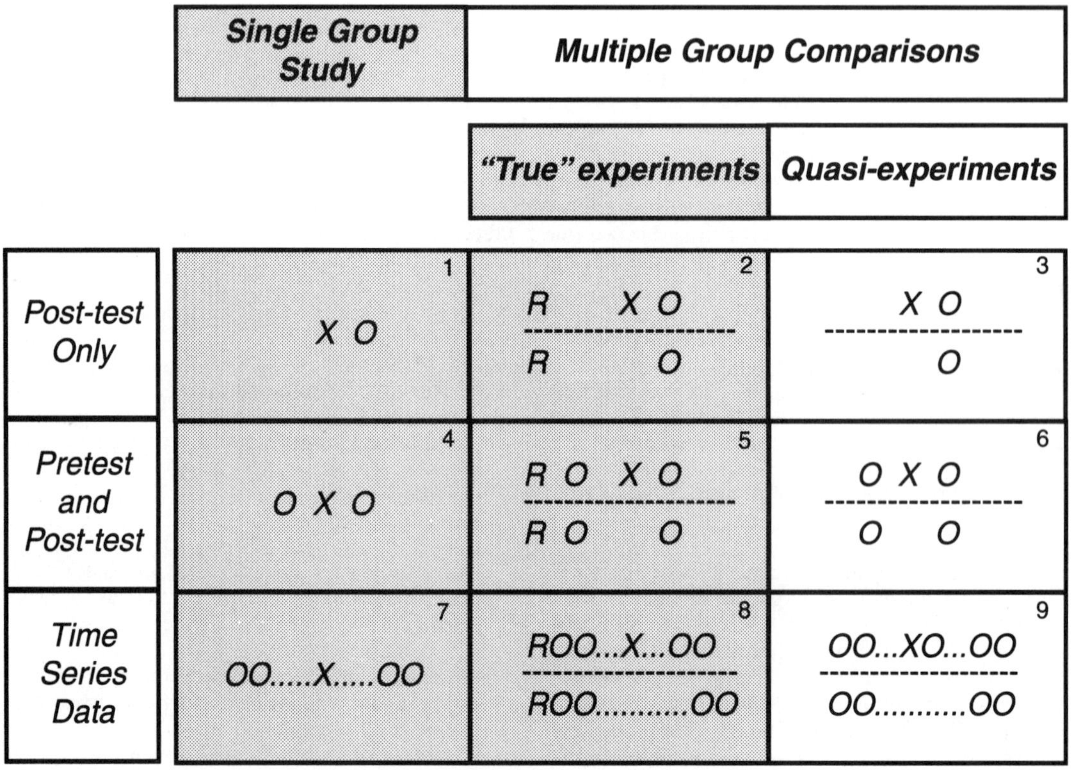

Figure 2　A basic system of designs.

findings from such studies are most ambiguous since almost any threat to internal validity listed above may be an effect and left uncontrolled. As a consequence, and because experimentation is meant to demonstrate effects by assessing comparative change due to treatment while ruling out alternative explanations, these designs are commonly held inconclusive of effects. They are not recommended for the purposes sketched in Sections 3.04.1 and 3.04.3. Design three does implement an independent control group, but still remains inconclusive as regards the genuity of effects due to selection differences. In design four, subjects serve as their own control. With two measures only, little can be inferred about true effects since maturation and other time-relevant threats to validity remain uncontrolled. Extending the principle to design seven, however, leads to a typical time series design for basic impact analysis that to some extent allows for more control. Suppose a trend line is fitted to both consecutive pretests and post-tests: a discernible shift in intercept and/or slope parallel to treatment application would indicate presence of an experimental effect (a conceptually different, but technically similar concept will be discussed with the regression discontinuity approach). Without determination of such a "natural" trend a higher post-test level might reflect what should be expected from extrapolation of regularities in pretest values only, disregarding treatment. In other words, dependent variables might show a change in value that is due to natural change over time (inflation, deflation, or periodicities of the phenomenon under study). Using multiple observations does not rule out this possibility as would using multiple observations and control groups, but still make it highly unlikely for such a trend to go undiscovered. Some authors argue that lack of a control group may be of less importance for this reason. Delay in effect instantiation or special forms of temporal calibration of effects can be modeled by univariate intervention (or interrupted time series) analyses (see McDowall, McCleary, Meidinger, & Hay, 1980). Note, however, that group designs are still being dealt with exclusively where $N > 1$. Single-subject designs, even when presented in the same notation, employ another rationale of contrasting and inference and are covered in Section 3.04.2. Multiple-group extensions to this design are covered in Section 3.04.5.3. Designs two, five, and eight have the most desirable properties: they implement randomization, repeated measurements, and control groups, with multiple observations additionally available in the last one. These designs are discussed in Chapter 4, this volume. From the preceding, it is clear that the rightmost column contains three nonequivalent group designs which do implement multiple group comparisons. Design three, however, is subject to the same reservations made for designs one and four. It lacks both randomization and pretesting as an approximation to the same end. Therefore designs six and nine, when used with appropriate care and caution, permit the testing of causal hypotheses, with causality being conceived as in Section 3.04.3.

The worked example is continued with aspects of design

In quasi-experimental design, the treatments to be compared serve as independent variables and experimental groups are built by assigning subjects to treatment conditions by nonrandom procedures. In the worked example study by Yung and Kepner (1996), the treatment factor comprised stretch release (SR), tense release (TR), and cognitive relaxation (COG) as well as a placebo attention group and a test-only control group (TOC) that remained wholly untreated. The placebo group was given a medicament by a physician with the ruse that it would reduce blood pressure in order to control for positive treatment expectancy effects. The control group were given pure assessments of their blood pressure to control for effects of the measurement process itself. Systolic and diastolic blood pressure as well as heart rate were chosen as dependent variables, entailing a multivariate setup for subsequent statistical analysis. All subjects were measured repeatedly several occasions (multiple baseline readings, with assessments before and after trial, follow-ups), which gives a multiple-treatment–multiple-control extension of design six in Figure 2.

Note that the study outlined above does in fact realize most of those items that make up the following sectional structure: conduct of pretests, multiple observations, different forms of treatment, different forms of control groups, and, introduced *post hoc* by means of statistical analysis, even combination of different designs.

3.04.5.2 Using a Pretest

3.04.5.2.1 Using pretest as a reference for gain scores

The major step from design three to design six clearly lies with the introduction of pretesting, seemingly indicating analysis of change. A natural concept of an ES would derive by subtracting pretest averages from post-test means and normalize the result with respect to a control group for a comparison. There has been extensive work on the question whether or not to use difference scores as an estimate of ES. Some main issues addressed in this context comprise the fact that difference scores (i) carry the unreliability of both their constituents, (ii) depend on correlation with initial (pretest) scores, (iii) depend on scale characteristics, and (iv) are subject to regression towards the mean. Various alternative techniques have been proposed among which are (i) standardizing prior to calculating differences, (ii) establishing "true" difference scores (Lord, 1963), (iii) using regression residuals (Cronbach & Furby, 1970) and, (iv) most commonly used, regression adjustment by means of analysis of covariance. Further, in terms of mathematical models, specification of correlation structure for error components of total scores, decomposition of error itself into various time-depending and static components, as well as the formulation of model-fit criteria and appropriate statistical testing, with serial dependence of data contradicting the "usual" (IIND) assumptions on error terms, are of major concern when analyzing change. These items denote not mere problems of statistical theory, but reflect substantial problems about a concept of empirical change. There is, however, no concern about all the complications that arise when trying to measure change but with the logic of design. For an introduction and further reading on the above issues, see Eye (1990), Diggle, Liang, and Zeger (1994) and for special topics as indicated Kepner and Robinson (1988) and Thompson (1991) (ordinal measures), Hagenaars (1990) and Lindsey (1993) (categorical data), Christensen (1991) and Toutenburg (1994) (generalized linear models), Vonesh (1992) (nonlinear models), Farnum and Stanton (1989) and Box, Jenkins, and Reinsel (1994) (forecasting), Petermann (1996) and Plewis (1985) (measurement).

3.04.5.2.2 *Using pretests as approximations to initial group equivalence*

In Section 3.04.2 the concept was introduced of an ES as the observable and testable formulation of what is sought in experimentation: effects. As can be seen from Figure 2, repeated measures are not strictly required to demonstrate effects. As is the case in design three differences may be observed in dependent measures across independent samples that underwent two different treatments (or none for a control) and state that one group scored higher on the average (this being favorable). Drawing any inferences or preferring this treatment over the other (or none) as a result of such a post-test-only design would rest entirely on the assumption that groups were equivalent with respect to dependent variables prior to treatment application. In "true" experiments, random subject assignment and/

or large samples may be relied upon to justify this assumption, but in quasi-experimental design performing a pretest is strictly required to obtain meaningful results. One still does not need to take gain scores or measures of different growing rates as a base for an effect size. In Section 3.04.2, they were not. But post-test differences can only be interpreted as monitoring effects when initial group equivalence is given as a common ground for comparison. As a consequence, subject assignment in quasi-experimental design is based upon techniques that require a pretest (see Table 2).

3.04.5.2.3 *When not to use a pretest*

Research situations can be imagined where conducting a pretest may not be recommended for even stronger reasons. Suppose that the phenomenon in question is likely to change qualitatively rather than quantitatively. A pretest would then presumably first measure something different than post-test. Second, a pretest may interact with treatment by differential sensitization (see factors of internal validity) or by producing such bias that results could not sensibly be attributed to treatment anymore (e.g., when using attitude tests). Third, retesting may be impossible because testing can only be set up once on the relevant variable because measurement must be assumed to distort or annul the phenomenon, or because no parallel form of a test is available. In such cases, the use of a proxy variable might be considered which, measuring something different but conceptually related to post-test criteria and, thus, (hopefully) being correlated to it in the statistical sense, serves as a substitute for evaluating initial group equivalence as a prerequisite for interpreting post-test differences (Rao & Miller, 1971). In extreme cases, when any kind of pretesting, be it on behalf of proxies or using the post-test instrument, seems impossible, using separate samples "from the same population" for pre- and post-test may be in order. From the preceding it is clear, however, that this variant of the basic design (six) provides a very weak basis for inference. Selection cohort designs as proposed in Cook and Campbell (1979) can be understood as a conceptually improved (while more demanding) extension of separate sample designs. When using self-selected samples it is obvious that subjects collected from cohorts that fall into place with regular periodicity because of characteristics of natural environment can be considered more alike than separate samples with obscure nonrandom selection processes. As this is most typically the case for institutions with cyclical (e.g., annual) turnover, like schools, such designs have been labeled "re-current institutional cycle designs" (Campbell & Stanley, 1963).

3.04.5.2.4 Outcome patterns

It is trivial to state that informational complexity of outcome pattern depends on the factorial complexity of design. It should be borne in mind, however, that sophisticated group and treatment structures do not necessarily entail higher levels of information or yield better causal models of a post-test. For example, the higher an order of interaction is allowed in fully crossed factorial designs, the less readable will be the results obtained and interpretation will be difficult. Pedhazur and Pedhazur (1991) give examples of how adding predictors to regression equations alters coefficients of former included predictors and changes overall results. Though the foregoing statements about validity and control may suggest a kind of "the more the better" strategy when designating independent and dependent variables for a design, the ultimate purpose of all modeling, simplification, should be recalled. The ultimate prerequisite in modeling, however, is of equal importance to the same end: unambiguous specification. Design six, for instance, when including two pretest occasions and being carried out on near-perfectly matched groups of sufficient size with near-constant treatment integrity, clearly outperforms a time series extension of the same design (see below) with uncontrolled subject attrition and carry-over effects.

A naturally expected, and in most cases desired, outcome of basic design six would obtain when the average post-test response of the treatment group is found to differ significantly in desired (hypothesized) direction from the control group post-test scoring, given pretest equivalence and given zero or nonsignificant trend in the control group pretest–post-test mean scores. But there are several variations of that scheme, largely due to selection–maturation interaction, regression artifacts, and scale characteristics (see Table 1). Cook and Campbell (1979) discuss at length such different outcomes of design six in its basic form (parallel trend lines, differential growing rates for groups, nonconstant controls, controls outperforming cases, treatment leading to post-test equivalence, trendline crossover ["switching means"]). Testers should not, however, as might be suggested by these authors and the foregoing presentation of all those threats to validity, too readily attribute findings not in line with expectations to design misspecification, artifact operation, and limitations of diagnostic

devices. It is true that there is always our obligation to evaluate and justify the whole procedure of research instead of its findings only. But having revised the process of hypotheses derivation that leads to design, and to data as a result, and having confirmed derivation validity to a maximum extent attainable within the limits offset by a concrete research context, there should be no complaints about reluctant and unruly reality.

3.04.5.3 Using Multiple Observations

It is obvious that design nine is but a generalization of standard design six, taking advantage of multiple observations pointed out above, and being subjected to the flaws of multiple repeated measurements. While the extension is straightforward as regards the logic of contrasts (the rationale for multiple group comparisons), the notion of an effect and according ES is more difficult to define. Time series analysis is usually carried out to detect and analyze patterns of change over time or to build models for forecasting. Multiple group comparisons enter when chosen to define an effect in terms of different time series evolution for cases and controls, conditional on a pre-intervention phase (baseline) and triggered by differential onset, intensity, and duration of treatment. Two major problems must be considered, then: first, how should treatment and observation phases be scheduled in the course of the whole study in order to set contrasts for obtaining effects while accounting for time-relevant threats to validity (see Section 3.04.5.4 using multiple forms of treatment); second, how to statistically analyze serially dependent data and interpret contrasts in the data in terms of within-subject (within-group) vs. between-subject (between groups) patterns (see Section 3.04.6).

The major benefit of using multiple observation has been presented in Section 3.04.5.1 (control for maturation and regression). Adding a control group further permits control of history and instrumentation for there is no *a priori* reason to suppose that untreated subjects experienced different environmental conditions during the study or that they should react differently to repeated measures. While non-spuriousness of treatment effects justifiably may be assumed by reference to significantly different pretreatment levels or increased/decreased slope of baseline, temporal persistence of effects can never be assured without comparison to an untreated control group.

As it is intended to dedicate the section on analysis mostly to handling design six and its nontime-series (i.e., simple pretest–post-test) extensions, a few words on statistical analysis of time series experiments are in order here. For more detail see Glass, Wilson, and Gottman (1975), Gottman (1981), and Lindsey (1993). Comparisons of intercepts (level), slopes (trend) and variance (stability, predictability) are mostly used for contrasting pre–post phases. Note that effects in time series designs need not instantiate immediately with treatment application and pertain. Impact of treatment may be delayed, with gradual or one-step onset, and various forms of nonconstancy show up over time (linear, nonlinear, or cyclic fading or gain, etc.). But such rather sophisticated parameters of time series data will only be used rarely for ES definition: statistical tests for directly comparing oscilation parameters or analytically derived characteristics like assymptotic behavior (e.g., speed of point convergence) are not readily available. While most one-sample time series parameters of interest to researchers concerned with intervention analyses can be identified, estimated, and tested for by transfer function models, between-sample comparisons often reduce to fitting an optimal model to one group and observing that fit indices decrease when obtained from application of the same model in another group. Cross-series statistics are, after all, hard to interpret in many cases (they require consideration of lead-lag relations, etc.). For an introduction to interrupted time series analysis for intervention designs see McDowall, et al., (1980) or Schmitz, (1989), and illustrated extensions to nonlinear and system models are presented in Gregson (1983).

3.04.5.4 Using Different Forms of Treatment

In this section concerns about implementing different forms of the same treatment instead of adding treatments like in a factorial design will be discussed. In basic pretest–post-test designs of type six, treatment is applied only once. Hence, variations concern application or removement only. Graduation in treatment application or withdrawal calls for multiple groups to undergo such graduation. This would be achieved, in concept, by stacking $k-1$ pretest–post-test designs without a control group over standard design six for k levels of treatment to be tested. The resulting model would conform to standard one-way analysis of variance for differences scores with a fixed or randomly sampled treatment factor (see Section 3.04 .6). In time series designs, however, some more challenging variations are at hand that further increase validity and clarity of inference, if properly implemented. Figure 3 gives an overview.

Design 10 replicates design four, with treatment removed in the second block in order for this block to serve as a "same-subjects" substitute for an otherwise nonavailable control group. Careful consideration must be given to the following questions:

(i) Are treatment effects of transient nature and be made to fade out (it is supposed, generally, that persistence of intervention effects is desired)? Ethical concerns, financial questions and potential attrition effects could be added to hesitations about mere feasibility of such designs.

(ii) Is it reasonable to expect that average scoring will return to a near-baseline level after removal of treatment?

(iii) Will it be expected that, after reintroduction of treatment as in design 12, effects will reinstall the same way (delay, size, stability, etc.) as in the first turn? (It is supposed that the reader is acquainted with general replication effects in experimenting like learning and resentment.) Then, and especially in case of high-amplitude treatment and obstrusive measurement, construct validity will be seriously affected.

If answers are favorable to these concerns then the designs that are particularly useful in evaluation of recurrent intervention components can be disposed of. Next should be considered the reversed treatment nonequivalent control design 11 with pretest and post-test. Cook and Campbell (1979) suggest that this design outperforms standard design six as regards construct validity since a treatment variable has to be specified rather rigorously in order to determine its logical reverse and an operational mode for it to be applied. Nevertheless the additional use of a wholly untreated control group is strongly advised in order to arrive at clear-cut results, in case trend lines do in fact depart from (assumed equivalent) pretest levels in opposite directions but in slopes that differ with respect to size and significance. Including a common reference for contradicting provides a very strong basis for inference. Finally design 13 (interrupted time series with switching replications) is considered. Due to delayed treatment application, one group can always serve as a control during treatment periods of the other ("reflexive controls," Rossi, Freeman, & Wright, 1979; "taking-turn controls," Fitz-Gibbon & Morris, 1987). The particular strength of this design lies with its capability to demonstrate simultaneously effects in two different settings and points of time with greatest parsimony. Still it is possible to overcome most threats to validity that are faced when using the above designs.

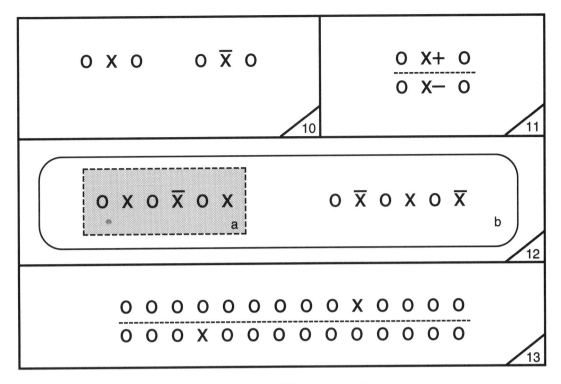

Figure 3 Designs using different forms of treatment.

3.04.5.5 Using Different Forms of Comparison Groups

It has been pointed out frequently that to use a control group is indispensible as a baseline for comparison in most cases of quasi-experimental research, and highly advocated in any other. Effects should be demonstrated by either relative change or post-test difference to rule out alternative explanations besides treatment impact. While this is widely agreed, there has been some controversy as regards various qualitative characteristics of controls. Are controls really untreated as assumed for inference? How can control groups be maintained (they do not receive, after all, any benefits of treatment)? Is there such a thing as placebo treatment? Do waiting groups (subjects scheduled for subsequent cycle of treatment, see design 13) differ in any substantial respect to wholly unaffiliated pools of control? In many cases the nature of a control group is determined simply by contextual factors like availability in terms of total number of subjects, financial resources, ethical considerations, or the time horizon of the study. While "real" control groups receive no treatment at all, placebo groups receive only irrelevant treatment. Conceptually, there are two forms of such irrelevance. In the first case, intervention neither in theory nor in statistical terms relates to the treatment variable of interest and is only meant to minimize motivation effects like resentful demoralization. A second version refers to treatments that in fact can be, or even are, expected to contribute to effects by operating through subjects' expectancies and external attributions that are hypothesized to go along with actual treatment. Perhaps the most prominent example is medication with a sugar pill. Note that such placebos work on psychological grounds and usually are implemented to separate such effects from "real," physical, or pharmacological treatment. As a consequence, it might be difficult to define a psychological placebo in psychotherapy research. For further detail on the issue of placebo groups, see a well-received article of Prioleau, Murdock, and Brody (1983), defending admission of such placebo treatment, and subsequent peer commentaries in *The Behavioral and Brain Sciences*. Waiting control groups differ from untreated groups in that they must be supposed to expect benefits from treatment to come. As a consequence, after assignment, such subjects may show more sensible behavior in any respects related to health and well-being or more medical compliance (thus "raising" baselines into trendlines). Waiting groups are, however, easiest to recruit and maintain, they naturally fall into place when treatment cannot be delivered unlimitedly, and there is no way of avoiding selection for admission. Still another concept of a control group emerges when using qualitatively different treatments in comparison groups, that is distributing treatment across groups. A way of treating a disease might, for instance, to compare against current or standard treatment, thus highlighting the relative merits of the new and saliently different features of the innovative treatment. Technically, within the ANOVA framework introduced below, treatment would represent a fixed factor with more than two levels (treat1, treat2, etc). It is clear that adding a further untreated control group is still preferable (see Section 3.04.5.6).

3.04.5.6 Using Combinations of Different Designs

There are three convincing arguments for combining designs. First, combining complete designs rather than extending one of their internal features (as discussed in above subsections) will generally enhance control. Second, broadly defining designs themselves as methods and using different methods and research plans in addressing the same question and phenomenon will always decrease monomethod bias and increase both construct validity and generalizability of results. Third, combining designs offers refined testing of hypotheses. For example, in Section 3.04.5.4 it was proposed, to multiply stack design four over design six. Consider now the application of different dosages of a drug as treatment variable. Given initially comparable groups (in the present, quasi-experimental sense), trend hypotheses about dosage could even be tested. Also, integral features of basic designs as depicted in Figure 2 may be tested for their mediating effects. For an example, if design six is stacked over design three a composite design is obtained that allows for separation of pretest and treatment effects and is named after its proposer Solomon (1949). Note that there are two fully crossed factors: whether treatment is applied or not (case–control factor), and whether pretesting is administered or not. This design may now be conceived as factorial (see Chapter 3, this volume) and an analysis of the main effect of treatment made (disregarding effects of pretest sensitization and the like), main effects of pretesting (effect obtained without regard to treatment), and interaction (treatment effects depend on pretest). If statistical testing has determined that such interaction is present, consideration of the main effects due to one sole factor (e.g., treatment) is sure to yield misleading results and inferences. But the latter is always true in cases where any design is used that both lacks randomization and pretest. As a

consequence, this rather sophisticated design is mostly applied in research situations that allow for randomization. Trivial as it may seem, another way of combining designs lies with replicating the whole basic design using the same samples and measurement occasions by simply obtaining multivariate measures of posttest indicators and, thus, testing multiple predictions concerning the same outcome criterion.

3.04.5.7 Regression Discontinuity

As if to provoke further discussion in order to put an end to presumed underutilization of regression discontinuity (RD) designs, Trochim (1984) stated that RD "is inherently counter-intuitive . . . not easy to implement . . . statistical analysis of the regression discontinuity design is not trivial . . . [there are] few good instance of the use" (pp. 46–47). So what is the point in these designs? In structure and objective, RD designs conform to the layout of design six. The major difference lies with assignment policy: while randomization is believed to guarantee fully equivalent groups (in the long run, that is) and pretest equivalence in nonequivalent group designs assures comparability with respect to the variables in questions only (leaving obscure presence and influence of other selection processes), it is maximum nonequivalence that serves as a rationale of regression discontinuity designs. This is achieved by ordering subjects according to their scores on the continuum of a pretest scale and subsequently defining a cut-off point for division into further subsets to be assigned to different conditions. Most commonly, subjects scoring below the cutting point would then be assigned to one group, subjects scoring below this point to another. If a "sharp" cut-off point is not desirable on theoretical grounds or because of known unreliability regions of scales, a midscale cut-off interval might be used instead, with interval width depending on estimates of measurement error similar standard deviation. Subjects within this range would then be assigned randomly to either treatment or control group condition. While it is true that the process of subject selection is still only imperfectly controlled because merely one factor (the dependent variable) is accounted for, it is perfectly known since being specified entirely by the researcher. It is clear that, in order to prevent cut-off point selection being rather arbitrary, strong theoretical grounds or consent on practical concerns (limited therapy resources, etc.) are called for.

Basically, analysis of RD designs means testing hypotheses of equality of regression equations across groups similar to analysis of covariance. The objective is to ask whether the trend or regression line obtained from analysis of the treatment group pretest and post-test scores is displaced significantly from the respective control group regression line. If displacement is due largely to greater (or lesser) intercept, while slopes are statistically equal (parallel line regression), a main efect has been successfully demonstrated. Stated differently, with no effect present, a single regression line would equally fit scores of both treatment and comparison group and, as a consequence, a trend in the treatment group could be predicted from the control group scores. Interaction effects are revealed by discontinuity in slope of regression lines at cut-off point. Note that, technically, regression need not necessarily be linear but can include parameters of any order, but that extrapolation of a trend line becomes extremely difficult then and often leads to false conclusions about effects (see Pedhazur & Pedhazur, 1991). These problems notwithstanding, more frequent use of these designs is recommended. In many intervention research contexts, subjects not only are in fact but also should be assigned to either treatment or control groups by need or similar, perhaps medical, criteria related to both treatment and outcome.

3.04.6 ANALYSIS

Having successfully derived and implemented a multiple group comparison design there is now a need to fit a statistical model to the data obtained in order to test the hypotheses on the "final" deductive level in the process model of empirical research (Figure 1). In particular, there is an interest in deriving ESs and whether they are different from zero. Note that from an epistemiological point of view, use of a different statistical model is made than observational methods (see Section 3.04.1.2). Here, models are considered as mere tools for hypotheses qualification and inference and are not of contentional value besides some implications of their structural assumptions (like additivity, linearity, etc.). Analysis of nonequivalent group designs is achieved in three major steps. First, the overall rationale of analysis is introduced by borrowing from the theory of generalized linear models. Second, its specification language is used to acquaint the reader with a system of models that indeed is a superset to nearly all models applicable in this context. Third, a closer look is taken at a subset of models that are most commonly employed in treating standard design six, namely analysis of variance with or without adjusting for a covariate and its

respective conceptual analogies when ordinal or categorical data have been obtained. Since there are many textbooks on statistical data analysis that cover technique in detail, attention is drawn merely to the principle and major formulae and dispensed with (references are given, however).

It is important to understand that until now discussion has been located entirely in the realm of logic. Nothing has been implied as regards scale and complexity of measurement and data. The point is that anything can be stored in O (Figures 2 and 3) and that structural complexity of whatever resides in this data aquisition box is logically independent of complexity in design structure. Enlarging designs by stacking sub-elements simply adds data boxes and obtains lots of data and can sometimes lead to technical difficulties in statistics, but both of these features should not complicate the idea or inference behind the material. In fact, there is only one condition: statistical parameters obtained from the data must be comparable on formal (i.e., mathematical) grounds (distributions, standard error of estimate, etc.). Now dominance of comparison-of-means-style models is readily explained: differences in means of normally distributed variables again follow normal distribution, and departure from zero is most easily tested using direct probabilities. In essence, value and standard error of any parameter's estimate should be determined and related to each other (e.g., in a ratio, giving standard t-test in case of metric dependents) or to another pair of parameters (e.g., in a double ratio, giving standard F-test, respectively). But there are many other ways besides of comparing distributions, some less strict but more straightforward or creative.

Why not obtain entire time series for one single data box in a multiply repeated measurements design? A time series model may be fitted to data at each occassion resulting in microstructural analysis. Stated differently: time series information has been condensed into some quantities that now enter macrostructural analysis reflecting design logic. Here, one might compare such aggregate measures in a pre–postfashion analysis like in standard design six, thus evaluating treatment impact by relative change in parameters of local change. Other studies involve entire structural equations systems in a single data box, constructed from covariance structure in multivariate data obtained at one occassion (Bentler, 1995; Duncan, 1975; Möbus & Bäumer, 1986; Jöreskog & Sörbom, 1993).

Most textbooks on the statistical analysis of experiments focus on analysis of variance and associates. While preference for models assuming variables on an interval or rational scale is perfectly understandable from the researchers point of view, it is felt that there is a rationale of testing that allows for far more variety. Appreciation of this variety is badly needed in order to be able to choose an analysis model for the design present, thus preserving the rather deductive idea of the process model in Figure 1, instead of being forced to the contrary: adapting design and idea to some analysis model readily at hand from common textbooks. Variety need not imply incomprehensible diversity if there is a model rationale. Here, the rationale states: all analysis, excepting some tests for ordinal data working on special ranking methods, boils down to regression. This holds true even in cases where it might not be expected that a regression structure presents at first glance (joint space analysis in multidimensional scaling, etc.). Most important, it is also true for analysis of variance and companions since these models can be written as regression equations of metric dependent variables on a set of coded vectors. These dummy variables, then, represent treatment in all its aspects (intensity, frequency, schedule of application, etc.). Encoding logic of designs into what is now called a design or hypotheses matrix for statistical analysis certainly is an art of its own (for an introduction, see Kerlinger (1973), or Pedhazur & Pedhazur (1991)). But here, regression stands for a whole family of models obeying a certain relational form. Thus, the rationale translates to concrete statistics by proposing that all variable relations (and contrasts are just a special relation) be specified in the form $y = f(x, \beta, e)$, where y denotes a possibly vector-valued set of responses (dependents) and x denotes a set of explanatory variables (independents, respectively) that are used to approximate the response with determinable residual or stochastic error e. A set of coefficients β quantify the intensity of an element of x (which can be interpreted as effect information), these parameters are estimated conditional to the data by minimizing a quality function ("least squares," "$(-2)*$maximum likelihood"). Finally, $f(.)$ denotes a characteristic link function that relates the explanatory or predictive determistic part of the model and error component to the response. Mostly used for this purpose are identity link (giving standard multiple regression), logit link (for binary response), and logarithmic links (leading to regression models involving polytoneous categorical data). In this way of thinking, the data are thought of as determined by the model but jammed by additional random error. Note that "error" does not denote anything false but is meant to incorporate, by definition, all factors in effect that remained unspecified or did not explicitly enter the model (i.e., remain uncontrolled).

To sum up, ingredients of a model are variables, parameters, a link function to algebraically interconnect all these, and an estimation strategy to optimally fit the resulting model to the data. The point in mapping most different ideas and objectives into a common-models structure is variable designation: using intensities can still mean single-attribute utilities, attitude strength, blood pressure. But $y = f(x, \beta, e)$ is too much in the abstract to be of use for this purpose, and even giving an outline on mathematical formulation and derivation of some less hard-to-handle submodels or estimation techniques would be beyond the limits of this chapter. For an advanced reading and a complete build-up of generalized linear model theory and practice see Arminger, Clogg, and Sobel (1995), Christensen (1991), and Diggle et al. (1994). But model specification terms summarized in Figure 4 can be used to figure out the greater proportions of the generalized linear model. Note that not everything goes along with anything else when crossing items on the utmost right side and that some models use parametrization strategies that do not satisfy the condition of formal comparability of parameters across groups. What is required now is careful examination of the nature of the variables and the justifiability of assumed form of relations among them. Never follow the impression possibly implied that all it takes is simply picking up a model from the scheme and applying it to the data if the marginal parameters are met. While it is true that with the exceptions mentioned above almost any statistical model of interest for analysis of designs can be integrated in or extrapolated from the generalized linear models scheme, the fit of design and analysis model is never guaranteed from this alone.

Several submodels can be located from that scheme that are most commonly used in analyzing experiments of type three and six (in Figure 2) and that may now be arranged in a more readable tabular system. If groups or discrete time are assumed for a single independent variable of categorical nature, and an arbitrary scale for a single dependent manifests, variables measured in discrete time and everything else in Figure 4 is dispensed with, the following table results (Table 3). In view of practice, that is, software, some submodels present not as rigorously special cases of the Generalized Linear Model (though they all can be specified accordingly), but rather as "stand-alone" implementations of tests. They serve the same purpose and are integrated in all major statistical software packages.

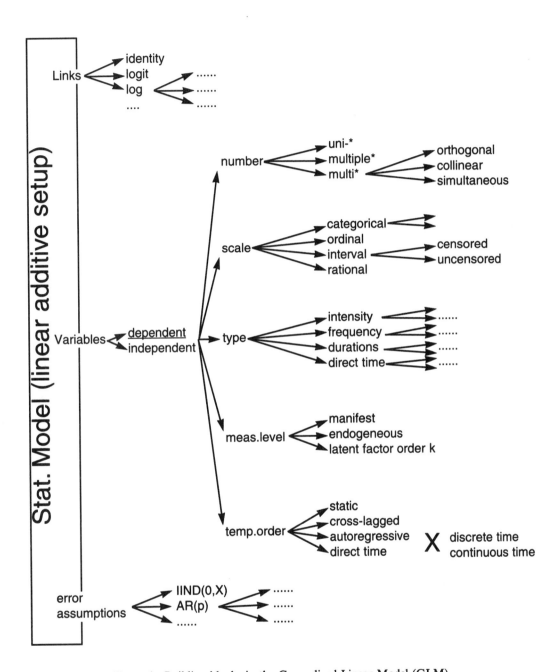

Figure 4 Building blocks in the Generalized Linear Model (GLM).

Table 3 Common models for analysis of designs three/six.

Idea of effect	Independent (group-time)	Scale of single dependent	Analysis/test
Simple change	One sample pre–post	categorical ordinal metric	McNemar test Wilcoxon test dep. *t*-test
	One sample *k* times	categorical ordinal metric	Cochran Q-test Friedman test One-way ANOVA rep. meas.
Post-test differences	Two samples	categorical ordinal metric	Simple χ^2 Mann–Whitney test indep. *t*-test
m samples		categorical ordinal metric	Logit/Loglinear models Kruskal–Wallis test One-way ANOVA
Relative change (interaction)	*m* samples *k* times each	categorical ordinal metric	Logit/Loglinear models Loglinear models *m*-way ANOVA rep. meas.

Further insight can he gained by the introduction of the analyses of variance. These models are considered the standard for analyses of multiple group comparison designs, but there is no hope of covering its various features and the richness of its submodels in detail. For the time being, do not bother with the distinction of fixed-effect, random-effect, and mixed models but with the rationale of analysis (for details, see Hays, (1980). Especially in the case of repeated measurement models, there are, however, some ideas and assumptions that must be understood before actually using these techniques, most prominent and important among these are: heteroscedasticity, additivity, orthogonality, balance, degrees of freedom, compound symmetry sphericity. In addition, further precautions as regards covariance structure are in order when extending the model to multivariate analysis of several dependent variables. For advanced reading on these topics whose consideration is indispensible for enhanced statistical conclusion validity, see Toutenburg (1994) or Christensen (1991).

Consider that response data $\vec{y} = [y_1 y_2 \ldots y_m \ldots y_M]$ on M dependent variables are obtained on interval-scale level for $k = 2 \ldots k \ldots K$ samples of equal size; for convenience, $n = 1 \ldots i \ldots N$ at $t = 1, 2 \ldots t \ldots T$ occasions. A categorical independent variable (or factor $f1$ denoting treatment(s) $f1 = (f1_1, \ldots, f1_{\bar{k}}, \ldots, f1^K)$ has been realized at least twice in one sample or independently across different samples at any occasion $1 < t < T$. Treatment $f1_{\bar{t}}$ denotes "no treatment" for implementing nonequivalent control group(s). If $\hat{y}$ offers data on more than

one dimension ($M > 1$), multivariate analysis (MANOVA) is called for, if it reduces to a scalar ($M = 1$) but extends in time ($T > 1$), univariate repeated measures ANOVA is applicable. For $M = 1$ and $T = 1$, effects are evaluated using a post-test-differences-only-given-pretest-equivalence rationale as presented in the first row in Table 3 (performed with a *t*-test for $k = 2$ both uni- and multivariate and any (M)ANOVA for $k > 2$). With repeated measures carrying effect information ($T > 1$) as it holds for both other rationales, data setup is a bit more sophisticated. Common software packages usually take repeated measures of one variable for separate variables (maybe with the same root name: p.ex. *out*1 *out*2 *out*3 ... for criterion variable *out* at three occasions). It follows that a multivariate data setup of the input data matrix is required. Note that when more than one genuine variable besides *out* enters analysis, a doubly multivariate procedure is called for. Stated differently, M variables are to be analyzed whose respective T time-dependent realizations are coded as T different variables, giving $M \times T$ data columns in a typical data entry spreadsheet of minimal logical dimension $(N * K) \times (M * T)$ since data are obtained for K groups of N subjects each. This holds true, so far, for any one-way (M)ANOVA with a *k*-level treatment-factor, affecting one or more metric dependent variables. In most instances, however, it is likely that this root design will be extended by introducing:

(i) further experimental factors subject to manipulation (e.g., single vs. group therapy),

(ii) further cross-classifying factors that fall

into place from basic sample analyses (e.g., age, sex, hospitality, etc.),

(iii) further metric time-invariant covariates (e.g., onset of disease, initial dosage of medication), and

(iv) further metric time-varying covariates (e.g., ongoing medication).

The general idea of analysis of variance is rather simple: if means between k groups and/or t occasions differ, and this is what is called an effect, roughly, then they are supposed to vary from the grand mean μ obtained from collapsing over all $M \times K$ data points disregarding groups and treatments or collapsing over occasions giving the grand mean as a "no-change" profile of t equal means. If they do vary significantly then this variation should be to a certain proportion greater than variation present within groups (i.e., with respect to the mean in a group). More specifically, a partitioning of total variance found in the data matrix into (at least) two components is attempted: variance of *groups'* means reflects the systematic ("causal model") part that is solely attributable to variation of treatment (be it in time or across groups), whereas variance of subjects' measurements within a group is generated by interindividual differences (i.e., violation pretest-equivalence or lack-in-treatment integrity) and is therefore taken as an "error term" against which the other part must be evaluated. Remember that the ratio of two variances or two sums of squares divided according to degrees of freedom constitutes on F-value when certain assumptions on data (Hays, 1980) are met: statistical significance is readily tested for. In this way, model variance due to effects, possibly containing interactions when more independent variables are present and error variance due to anything else, add up to give the total variance (assuming a fixed effect model). In the case of repeated measures analysis, there is also variance among t different measures of a single variable within one subject. To sum up: three main effect sources of variation are accounted for by standard ANOVA models:

(i) differences between individuals, to be further decomposed into differences between k groups (disregarding the individual by taking means and thereby constituting a "true value" outcome measure for this treatment) and differences between subjects within a group, obtained from subtracting the individual's measure from the group mean. In analyses with no repeated measures factor present, these differences contribute to error variance against which the first kind of variation is evaluated. In the case of f-way ANOVAs, interactions of independent variables (factors) must be taken into account as well.

(ii) Differences within repeated measures of a subject and according interactions with factors varied between groups in f-way analyses. This variation may be further decomposed into three sources: a main effect of retesting (supposed to be present in each subject's profile over time), an interaction of treatment and retesting, and differential reactions to retesting (specific to each of the subjects). In case of analyses with no between-factors present, the latter source of variation is taken to contribute to residual variance. In multiway repeated measures analyses of variance, determination of appropriate components for a F-ratio in order to test for statistical significance of a factor or an interaction of some factors, can be very complicated; excellent advice is given in Bortz (1993).

For design six, a differential change would be required for an effect by testing the interaction term of a repeated measures "within" factor and the case–control "between" factor for significance using the appropriate F ratio. Change takes place but in different directions (or none) depending on whether receiving treatment or not. Suppose one group of aggressive children received behavior modification training while another group of equal size is still waiting for admission and thus serves as a control group. Both groups are considered equivalent on the dependent variable of interest beforehand. Take it that $t = 3$ measures on each of $N_1 + N_2$ individuals in $k = 2$ groups: pretest, post-test after training, and a follow-up retest six months after intervention to estimate the stability of possible effects. Formally expressing the above sources of variation in a structural model for the individual measure, as is common for GLM submodels, and dispensing with explicit notation of associated dummies for discrete independent variables leads to:

$$y_{ikt} = \mu + a_k + \beta_t + (\alpha\beta)_{kt} + \gamma_{ik} + \epsilon_{ikt}$$

where α_k refers to effect of being in either treatment or control group, β_t refers to differences solely attributable to time or change, $(\alpha\beta)_{kt}$ stands for the interaction of both main effects and thus denotes differential change as sketched above and in greater detail in Section 3.04.1.3, γ_{ikt} refers to a random (= erroneous) effect of a single subject i in the kth kind of treatment (training vs. control, in the case present), maybe for individual specific reaction types to either form of treatment at any occassion, and ϵ_{ikt} accounts for anything not covered by the model (error term).

For full coverage of mathematical assumptions underlying this model, see Toutenburg (1994). As mentioned before, statistical hypotheses are formulated as null hypotheses conjecturing "no effect" of the according term in the model. In addition, for the present example, effects of several levels of an independent variable are required, coded by an according contrast in the hypothesis matrix (see above), which add up to zero. Hypotheses testable in this model include:

$H_0: \alpha_1 = \alpha_2$

There is no difference between treatment and control group with respect to the outcome variable (dependent), disregarding point of time of measurement. More generally speaking, such between hypotheses state homogeneity of measurement levels in groups. Note that no differences at pretest time are expected. Moreover, differences possibly present at post-test time (near termination of intervention) tend to attenuate up until the follow-up testing. It is not known whether group differences were at maximum by consideration of this main effect of group membership alone.

$H_0: \beta_{c1(t)} = \beta_{c2(t)}$

specific formulation depending on contrasts $c(t)$ for time effects. There is no overall change between occasions disregarding group membership. Again more generally speaking, the hypothesis states homogeneous influence of time effects in the course of experimentation. Considering this time main effect alone, it is known that whatever change occurred applied unspecifically to both groups and can therefore not be attributed to treatment. Obviously, this effect does not carry the information sought. When certain assumptions on covariance structure in time are met (sphericity condition, see above), a $t - 1$ to orthonormal linear contrasts may be used to evaluate change at certain periods using univariate and averaged tests. These assumptions assure, roughly speaking, that present differences are due to inhomogeneity of means rather than of variances (for details, see Toutenberg, 1994). Major software packages offer correction methods to compensate for violations of these assumptions (e.g., by correcting components of the F-test) or have alternatives available.

$H_0: (\alpha\beta)_{ij} = 0$

This hypothesis states parallelism of progressive forms in groups or, equivalently, the absence of differential change. If this hypothesis can be rejected, there is an interaction of treatment and the repeated measurement factor in the sense that (at least) one group apparently took a different course from pretest to post-test and follow-up as regards the outcome criteria. This is precisely what was presented as the standard notion of an effect in Section 3.04.3. Such a change can be attributed to treatment because the overall effects like common linear trends and so on, have been accounted for by the time of main effect. In more complex cases, there may also be interest in differential growth rates or whether one group arrived sooner at a saturation level (suggesting earlier termination of treatment).

Actual testing of these hypotheses might be performed using "means models" available with the (M)ANOVA procedures or by parameterizing the above equation to fit the general linear model regression equation with identity link. In essence, this is done by building a parameter vector β of semipartial regression coefficients from all effects noted ($\mu, \alpha_1, \ldots \alpha_{k-1}, \beta_{c_1(t)} \cdots \beta_{ct-1}$), associated by the corresponding hypotheses matrix X (made up from coded vectors of contrasted independent variables) and an additive error term. This right-hand part of the equation is regressed on to the vector $\vec{y}$ giving a standard Gauss–Markov–Aitken estimate of $\beta = (X'\Sigma^{-1}X)^{-1}X'\Sigma^{-1}y$ from least squares normal equations. A typical printout from respective software procedures includes parameter value, associated standard error, and t value, confidence limits for parameter estimate, η^2 effect size, F-noncentrality parameter, and power estimate. When interpreting results, remember that an effect is conceptualized as a difference of respective group (= treatment) mean from the grand mean, and that effects are usually normalized to add up to zero over all treatments (for details and exceptions, see Hays, 1980).

Analysis of the worked example study was carried out as follows:

A one-way ANOVA with repeated measurements was used to test statistical significance of recorded difference in three dependent variables for five experimental conditions at pre, post, and follow-up occasions. There was no significant overall main group effect. Only systolic blood pressure was found to differ across groups at follow-up time with greatest reduction present in a comparison of TR to TOC. Group-time-interactions for testing differential change were carried out by an ANOVA using repeated contrasts (pre vs. post; post vs. follow-up). Systolic blood pressure decreased significantly over time in all relaxation groups and the placebo group, but not in the control group. TR muscle relaxation showed greatest reduction of diastolic pressure, whereas SR and COG significantly lowered heart rate. Pooled treatment effects were evaluated against nontreatment groups by special ANOVA contrasts, showing significant reduction in systolic pressure when compared to control group and significant reduction in diastolic pressure when compared to the placebo group. There were no effects on heart rate in comparison to either one of the nontreatment groups. The results indicate a strong placebo attention effect. It is suggested that independence of heart rate and significant blood pressure reduction is in line with the findings in the field.

With additional restrictions put on Σ, this rationale of testing easily extends to multivariate and doubly multivariate cases (Toutenburg, 1994). Also, there is much appeal in the idea of comparing groups on entire linear systems obtained from all measured variables by structural equations modeling (SEM; see Duncan, 1975). Here, measurement error in both independent and dependent variables is accounted for explicitly. For an introduction to multiple-group covariance structure analyses and to models additionally including structured means see Bentler (1995), Möbus and Bäumer (1986), and Sörbom (1979). MANOVA and SEM are compared on theoretical and practical grounds in Cole, Maxwell, Arvey, and Salas (1993). Note that the latest formulations of these models and associated software packages can now deal with nonnormal and categorical data.

When ordinal measures have been obtained, ANOVA on ranks of subjects" measures (with respect to the order in their respective group) rather than on absolute values may be applied instead of "genuine" ordinal methods as listed in Table 3. In the case of categorical measures, frequencies mostly have been obtained denoting the number of subjects with the characteristic feature of the category level in question present relative to the total number of subjects over the range of all possible levels of that categorical variable. Basically, analysis is carried out on an aggregate level (groups or subpopulations) rather than on the individual level, and link functions other than identity link are employed to regress independent variables (which have been of a categorical nature all the time: group membership, etc.) on to categorical outcome measures (now dependent variables have also become categorical). Regression coefficients must be interpreted differently, though, when dependent variables have been reconceptualized in this way. A positive β indicates that the probability of a specific category of a dependent variable is positively affected (risen) relative to another category, including the case of simply not being in that very category, when the characteristic feature of the category for an independent variable is present in a subject. In the case of a dichotomous dependent variable (logit models) interpretation is facilitated: β quantifies the effect of the independent variable on the odds, that is, the ratio of favorable to unfavorable responses (e.g., whether or not cancer is or will be present given the information available from independent variables). On a more formal level a nonzero regression coefficient in log-linear models indicates that the expected cell frequency in the category r of R categories or "levels" of the dependent variable departs from what would be expected in the "null" case of no effects, that is $n_r = n. = N/R$.

As with the metric case, regression coefficients are considered effect parameters and tested for statistical significance by evaluating their standard error. Multiple group comparisons can be obtained in one of two ways: by introducing an independent variable denoting group membership, or by testing whether there is a significant change in the associated overall model fit indices from the more saturated model incorporating the effect in question (H_1) to the more restricted model dispensing with it (H_0).

3.04.7 CONCLUSION

In the last section are described the statistical models for multiple group comparisons. In most cases, however, analysis will be carried out using techniques presented in Table 3. It is re-emphasized that it is not the complexity or elegance of the final data model that puts a good end to the process of quasi-experimental research: it is the fit of research questions or hypotheses and according methodological tools to tackle them. This is why a major part in this chapter is devoted to a presentation of an idealized procedural outline of this research process as sketched in Figure 1, and on discussing validity affairs. Generally speaking, the last step in this process lies with reversing it inductively and with introducing evaluative elements. It must be decided by which degree present patterns of statistical significance justify the induction that predictions derived from substantial hypotheses have instantiated as they should and whether validity issues have been attended to a degree that inference to the level of theory is admissible. Limitations in generalizability should be examined and problems encountered in the course of the study must be evaluated in order to point to future directions of research. With reference to Section 3.04.3.3, implications to clinical practice should be derived and be evaluated. In publications, these issues are usually covered in the "Results" and "Discussion" sections.

In the worked example study, the following discussion is offered:

A result most relevant to clinical practice lies with the fact that cognitive and muscular relaxation both significantly reduce blood pressure and therapists may therefore choose from both methods with respect to their individual clients" special needs and aptitudes (differential indication). The critical prerequisite for this conclusion in terms of validity lies with clear separation of experimental instructions concerning either musculary or cognitively induced relaxation. It might be argued that any instruction relevant to improving irritating bodily sensations does feature cognitive elements, like expectancy, that contribute to intervention

88 *Multiple Group Comparisons: Quasi-experimental Designs*

effects. It might be better to differentiate between techniques involving direct muscular practice and a pool of techniques that dispense with the behavioral element. In the end, all relaxation techniques affect muscle tension. But persons might well vary on the degree to which they can benefit from direct or indirect techniques. It is known that more susceptible persons, or persons with greater ability to engage in and maintain vivid imagination and concentration, will benefit more from cognitive techniques, and that physical disabilities often rule out application of muscularly directed interventions. On the other hand, muscle relaxation instructions are considered easier to follow, and, after all, straight muscle relaxation techniques showed the greatest overall effect in the present study, thus pointing to a "safe-side" decision. These arguments refer to client selection in clinical practice as a parallel to the referred effects of subject selections in experimentation.

Accounting for the demand for both methodologically valid and practically relevant methods, the following guidelines for quasi-experimental research may be offered:
(i) preference for case–control designs,
(ii) preference for repeated measures designs, thus preference for diagnostic devices and statistical methods sensitive to (relative) change,
(iii) specification of hypotheses in terms of effect sizes,
(iv) consideration of multiple indicators per criterion, entailing a multivariate data setup, and
(v) special attention to balancing N (sample size), T (rep. measures level), ES (effect size), and other factors determining both statistical and practical significance of results presented in Section 3.04.3.1.

3.04.8 REFERENCES

Arminger, G., Clogg, C. C., & Sobel, M. E. (Eds.) (1995). *Handbook of statistical modeling for the social and behavioral sciences.* New York: Plenum.
Bentler, P. M. (1995). *EQS structural equations program manual.* Encino, CA: Multivariate Software.
Bernstein, I. N. (Ed.) (1976). *Validity issues in evaluative research.* Beverly Hills, CA: Sage.
Bortz, J. (1993). *Statistik.* Berlin: Springer.
Box, G. E., Jenkins, G. M., & Reinsel, G. C. (1994). *Time series analysis: forecasting and control.* Englewood Cliffs, NJ: Prentice-Hall.
Campbell, D. T., & Stanley, J. C. (1963). *Experimental and quasi-experimental design for research on teaching.* In N. L. Gage (Ed.), *Handbook for research on teaching,* (pp. 171–246). Chicago: Rand McNally.
Christensen, R. (1991). *Linear models for multivariate, time series, and spatial data.* New York: Springer.
Cohen, J. (1988). *Statistical power analysis for the behavioral sciences.* Hillsdale, NJ: Erlbaum.
Cole, D. A., Maxwell, S. E., Arvey, R., & Salas, E. (1993). Multivariate group comparison of variable systems: MANOVA and structural equation modeling. *Psychological Bulletin, 114,* 174–184.
Collingwood, R. G. (1940). *An essay on metaphysics.* Oxford, UK: Oxford University Press.
Collins, A. W. (1966). The use of statistics in explanation. *British Journal for the Philosophy of Science, 17,* 127–140.
Cook, T. D., & Campbell, D. T. (1979). *Quasi-experimentation: Design and analysis issues for field settings.* Chicago: Rand McNally.
Cronbach, L. J., & Furby, L. (1970). How should we measure "change"—or should we? *Psychological Bulletin, 74,* 68–80.
Diggle, P. J., Liang, K. Y., & Zeger, S. L. (1994). *Analysis of longitudinal data.* Oxford, UK: Oxford University Press.
Duncan, O. D. (1975). *Introduction to structural equations models.* New York: Academic Press.
Eye, A. V. (Ed.) (1990). *Statistical methods for longitudinal research.* Boston: Academic Press.
Farnum, N. R., & Stanton, L. W. (1989). *Quantitative forecasting methods.* Boston: Kent Publishing.
Fisher, R. A. (1959). *Statistical method and statistical inference.* Edinburgh, UK: Oliver & Boyd.
Fitz-Gibbon, C. T., & Morris, L. L. (1991). *How to design a program evaluation. Program evaluation kit, 3.* Newbury Park, CA: Sage.
Giere, R. N. (1972). The significance test controversy. *British Journal for the Philosophy of Science, 23,* 170–181.
Glass, G. V., Willson, V. L., & Gottman, J. M. (1975). *Design and analysis of time series experiments.* Boulder, CO: Associated University Press.
Gottman, J. M. (1981). *Time series analysis.* Cambridge, UK: Cambridge University Press.
Granger, C. W. (1969). Investigating causal relations by econometric models and cross-spectral methods. *Econometrica, 37,* 424–438.
Grawe, K. (1992). Psychotherapieforschung zu Beginn der neunziger Jahre. *Psychologische Rundschau, 43,* 132–168.
Gregson, R. (1983). *Times series in Psychology.* Hillsdale, NJ: Erlbaum.
Hager, W. (1992). *Jenseits von Experiment und Quasiexperiment: Zur Struktur psychologischer Versuche und zur Ableitung von Vorhersagen.* Göttingen, Germany: Hogrefe.
Hagenaars, J. A. (1990). *Categorical longitudinal data: log-linear panel, trend and cohort analysis.* Newbury Park, CA: Sage.
Hays, W. (1980). *Statistics for the social sciences.* New York: Holt, Rinehart, & Winston.
Hoole, F. W. (1978). *Evaluation research and development activities.* Beverly Hills, CA: Sage.
Jöreskog, K., & Sörbom, D. (1993). *LISREL 8 user's reference guide.* Chicago: Scientific Software International.
Kepner, J. L., & Robinson, D. H. (1988). Nonparametric methods for detecting treatment effects in repeated measures designs. *Journal of the American Statistical Association, 83,* 456–461.
Kerlinger, F. (1973). *Foundations of behavioral research* (2nd ed.). New York: Holt, Rinehart, & Winston.
Lindsey, J. K. (1993). *Models for repeated measurements. Oxford statistical science series, 10.* Oxford, UK: Claredon Press.
Lipsey, M. W. (1990). *Design sensitivity: statistical power for experimental research.* Newbury Park, CA: Sage.
Lord, F. M. (1963). Elementary models for measuring change. In C. W. Harris (Ed.), *Problems in measuring change.* Madison, WI: University of Wisconsin Press.
Mayo, D. (1985). Behavioristic, evidentialist and learning models of statistical testing. *Philosophy of Science, 52,* 493–516.
McDowall, D., & McCleary, R., Meidinger, E. E., & Hay, R. A. (1980). *Interrupted time series analysis.* Newbury Park, CA: Sage
Möbus, C., & Bäumer, H. P. (1986). *Strukturmodelle für*

Längsschnittdaten und Zeitreihen. Bern, Switzerland: Huber.

Pedhazur, E. J., & Pedhazur, L. (1991). *Measurement, design and analysis: an integrated approach.* Hillsdale, NJ: Erlbaum.

Petermann, F. (Ed.) (1996). *Einzelfallanalyse* (3rd ed.). München, Germany: Oldenbourg.

Prioleau, L., Murdock, M., & Brody, N. (1983). An analyis of psychotherapy versus placebo studies. *The Behavioural and Brain Sciences, 6,* 275–285.

Plewis, I. (1985). *Analysing change: measurement and explanation using longitudinal data.* New York: Wiley.

Putnam, H. (1991). The "Corroboration" of theories. In R. Boyd, P. Gasper, & J. D. Trout (Eds.), *The philosophy of science* (pp. 121–137). Cambridge, MA: MIT Press.

Rao, P., & Miller, R. L. (1971). *Applied econometrics.* Belmont, CA: Wadsworth.

Rossi, P. H., Freeman, H. E., & Wright, S. R. (1979). *Evaluation: a systematic approach.* Beverly Hills, CA: Sage.

Salmon, W. C. (1966). *The foundations of scientific inference.* Pittsburg, OH: University of Pittsburgh Press.

Schmitz, B. (1989). *Einführung in die Zeitreihenanalyse.* Bern, Switzerland: Huber.

Smith, M. L, Glass, V. G., & Miller, T. I. (1980). *The benefits of psychotherapy.* Baltimore: Johns Hopkins University Press.

Solomon, R. L. (1949). An extension of control group design. *Psychological Bulletin, 46,* 137–150.

Sörbom, D. (1979). A general model for studying differences in factor means and factor structure between groups. In K. G. Jöreskog & D. Sörbom (Eds.), *Advances in factor analysis and structural equation models* (pp. 207–217). Cambridge, MA: Abt Books.

Spector, P. E. (1981). *Research designs.* Beverly Hills, CA: Sage.

Thompson, G. L. (1991). A unified approach to rank tests for multivariate and repeated measures designs. *Journal of the American Statistical Association, 86,* 410–419.

Toutenburg, H. (1994). *Versuchsplanung und Modellwahl: statistische Planung und Auswertung von Experimenten mit stetigem oder kategorialem Response.* Heidelberg, Germany: Physica.

Trochim, W. M. (1984). *Research design for program evaluation: the regression-discontinuity approach. Contemporary evaluation research, 6.* Beverly Hills, CA: Sage.

Vonesh, E. F. (1992). Non-linear models for the analysis of longitudinal data. *Statistics in Medicine, 11,* 1929–1954.

Yung, P. M. B., & Kepner, A. A. (1996). A controlled comparison on the effect of muscle and cognitive relaxation procedures on blood pressure: implications for the behavioral treatment of borderline hypertensives. *Behavioral Research and Therapy, 34,* 821–826.

3.05
Epidemiologic Methods

WILLIAM W. EATON
Johns Hopkins University, Baltimore, MD, USA

3.05.1 INTRODUCTION

3.05.1.1 Epidemiology and Clinical Psychology

Is psychological epidemiology an oxymoron? The primary goals of psychology differ from the primary goals of epidemiology. Psychology seeks to understand the general principles of psychological functioning of individual human beings. Epidemiology seeks to understand pathology in populations. These two differences—general principles vs. pathology, and individuals vs. populations—form the foundations for ideologic differences which have led to failures of linkage between the two disciplines, and many missed opportunities for scientific advances and human betterment. The gap between the two is widened by their location in different types of institutions: liberal arts universities vs. medical schools.

Various definitions of epidemiology reflect the notion of pathology in populations. Mausner and Kramer define epidemiology as "the study of the distribution and determinants of diseases and injuries in human populations" (1985, p. 1). Lilienfeld and Stolley use a very similar definition but include the notion that "epidemiologists are primarily interested in the occurrence of disease as categorized by time, place, and persons" (1994, p. 1). A less succinct, but nevertheless classic, statement is by Morris (1975), who listed seven "uses" of epidemiology:

(i) To study the hertory of health of populations, thus facilitating projections into the future.

(ii) To diagnose the health of the community, which facilitates prioritizing various health problems and identifying groups in special need.

(iii) To study the working of health services, with a view to their improvement.

(iv) To estimate individual risks, and chances of avoiding them, which can be communicated to individual patients.

(v) To identify syndromes, by describing the association of clinical phenomena in the population.

(vi) To complete the clinical picture of chronic diseases, especially in terms of natural hertory.

(vii) To search for causes of health and disease.

The seventh use is regarded by Morris as the most important, but, in reviewing the literature on psychiatric disorders for the third (1975) edition of his text, he was surprised at

The sad dearth of hard fact on the causes of major as well as minor mental disorders, and so on how to prevent them ... [and] the dearth of epidemiological work in search of causes ... Lack of ideas? Methods? Money? It wants airing. Of course, the popular trend open-endedly to hand over to psychiatry (and to social work), in hope or resignation, the whole of the human condition is no help. (p. 220)

3.05.1.2 Dichotomy and Dimension

Pathology is a process, but diseases are regarded as present or absent. Psychologists have been interested historically in promoting health and in understanding the nature of each individual's phenomenology, leading to emphasis on dimensions of behavior; but epidemiologists have focused on disorders without much regard to individual differences within a given diagnostic category, leading to focus on dichotomies. For clinical psychologists adopting the epidemiologic perspective, the phrase "psychiatric epidemiology" could describe their work accurately (Tsuang, Tohen, & Zahner, (1995). Another area of work for psychologists in epidemiology focuses on psychological contributors to diseases in general, which can include psychiatric disorders but not be limited to them. This type of epidemiology might be termed "psychosocial epidemiology" (Anthony, Eaton, & Henderson, (1995), and receives less attention in this chapter.

Interest in normal functioning, or in deviations from it, has led psychologists to focus on statistical measures related to central tendency, such as the mean, and the statistical methods oriented toward that parameter, such as the comparison of means and analysis of variance. Epidemiology's base in medicine has led it to focus on the dichotomy of the presence or absence of disease. There is the old adage in epidemiology: "The world is divided into two types of persons: those who think in terms of dichotomies, and those who do not." The result for statistical analysis is recurring focus on forms involving dichotomies: rates and proportions (Fleiss, 1981), the two-by-two table (Bishop, Fienberg, & Holland, 1975), the life table (Lawless, 1982), and logistic regression (Kleinbaum, Kupper, & Morgenstern, 1982).

The epidemiologic approach is focused on populations. A population is a number of individuals having some characteristic in common, such as age, gender, occupation, nationality, and so forth. Population is a broader term than group, which has awareness of itself, or structured interactions: populations typically are studied by demographers, whereas groups typically are studied by sociologists. The general population is not limited to any particular class or characteristic, but includes all persons without regard to special features. In the context of epidemiologic research studies, the general population usually refers to the individuals who normally reside in the locality of the study. Many epidemiologic studies involve large populations, such as a nation, state, or a county of several hundred thousand inhabitants. In such large studies, the general population includes individuals with a wide range of social and biological characteristics, and this variation is helpful in generalizing the results. In the broadest sense, the general population refers to the human species. The fundamental parameters used in epidemiology often are conceptualized in terms of the population: for example, prevalence sometimes is used to estimate the population's need for health care; incidence estimates the force of morbidity in the population. Generally diseases have the characteristic of rarity in the population. As discussed below, rates of disease often are reported per 1000, 10 000, or 100 000 population.

Much of the logic that distinguishes the methods of epidemiology from those of psychology involves the epidemiologic focus on rare dichotomies. The case–control method maximizes efficiency in the face of this rarity by searching for and selecting cases of disease very intensively, for example, as in a hospital or a catchment area record system, and selecting controls at a fraction of their representation in the general population. Exposures can also be rare, and this possibility is involved in the logic of many cohort studies which search for and select exposed individuals very intensively, for example, as in an occupational setting with toxins present, and selecting nonexposed controls at a fraction of their representation in the general population. In both strategies the cases, exposed groups, and controls are selected with equal care, and in both strategies they are drawn, if possible, to represent the population at risk of disease onset: the efficiency comes in the comparison to a relatively manageable sample of controls.

3.05.1.3 Exemplar Study: Ecological Approach to Pellagra

The ecologic approach compares populations in geographic areas as to their rates of disease, and has been a part of epidemiology since its beginnings. A classic ecologic study in epidemiology is Goldberger's work on pellagra psychosis (Cooper & Morgan, 1973). The pellagra research also illustrates the concept of the causal chain and its implications for prevention. In the early part of the twentieth century, pellagra was most prevalent in the lower classes in rural villages in the southeastern US. As the situation may be in the 1990s for many mental disorders (Eaton & Muntaner, 1996), the relationship of pellagra prevalence to low social class was a consistent finding: a leading etiologic clue among many others with less consistent evidence. Many scientists felt that pellagra psychosis was infectious, and that lower class living situations promoted breeding of the infectious agent. But Goldberger noticed that there were striking failures of infection, for example, aides in large mental hospitals, where pellagra psychosis was prevalent, seemed immune. He also observed certain exceptions to the tendency of pellagra to congregate in the lower class, among upper-class individuals with unusual eating habits. Goldberger became convinced that the cause was a nutritional deficiency which was connected to low social class. His most powerful evidence was an ecologic comparison of high and low rate areas: two villages which differed as to the availability of agricultural produce. The comparison made a strong case for the nutritional theory using the ecological approach, even though he could not identify the nutrient. He went so far as to ingest bodily fluids of persons with pellagra to demonstrate that it was not infectious. Eventually a deficiency in vitamin B was identified as a necessary causal agent. Pellagra psychosis is now extremely rare in the US, in part because of standard supplementation of bread products with vitamin B.

Goldberger understood that low social class position increased risk of pellagra, and he also believed that nutritional deficiencies which resulted from lower class position were a necessary component in pellagra. With the advantage of hindsight, nutritional deficiency appears to have a stronger causal status, because there were many lower class persons who did not have pellagra, but few persons with pellagra who were not nutritionally deprived: vitamin B deprivation is a necessary cause, but lower social class position is a contributing cause. The concept of the causal chain points to both causes, and facilitates other judgements about the importance of the cause. For example, which cause produces the most cases of pellagra? (Since they operate in a single causal chain, the nutritional deficiency is more important from this point of view.) Which cause is antecedent in time? (Here the answer is lower social class position.) Which cause is easiest to change in order to prevent pellagra? The answer to this question is not so obvious, but, from the public health viewpoint, it is the strongest argument about which cause deserves attention. Which cause is consistent with an accepted framework of disease causation supportive of the ideology of a social group with power in society? Here the two causes diverge: funneling resources to the medical profession to cure pellagra is one approach to the problem consistent with the power arrangement in the social structure; another approach is redistributing income so that nutritional deficiency is less common. As it happens, neither approach would have been effective. The consensus to redistribute income, in effect, to diminish social class differences, is not easy to achieve in a democracy, since the majority are not affected by the disease. Bread supplementation for the entire population was a relatively cost-effective public health solution. The more general point is that Goldberger's work encompassed the complexity of the causal process.

Epidemiology accepts the medical framework as defining its dependent variable, but it is neutral as to discipline of etiology. Goldberger did not eliminate one or the other potential cause due to an orientation toward social vs. biological disciplines of study. He did not favor one or the other potential cause because it focused on the individual vs. the collective level of analysis. This eclecticism is an important strength in epidemiology because causes in different disciplines can interact, as they did in the case of pellagra, and epidemiology still provides a framework for study. The public health approach is to search for the most important causes, and to concentrate on those that are malleable, since they offer possibilities for prevention.

3.05.2 RATES

An early and well-known epidemiologist, Alexander Langmuir, used to say that "stripped to its basics, epidemiology is simply a process of obtaining the appropriate numerator and denominator, determining the rate, and interpreting that rate" (cited in Foege, 1996, p. S11). In the sense in which Langmuir was speaking, the term rates includes proportions such as the prevalence "rate" as well as the incidence rate, as explained below. Table 1 shows the minimum design requirements, and the definitions of numerators and denominators, for various types of the rates and proportions. The table is ordered from top to bottom by increasing difficulty of longitudinal follow-up.

3.05.2.1 Prevalence

Prevalence is the proportion of individuals ill in a population. Temporal criteria allow for several types of prevalence: point, lifetime, and period. Point prevalence is the proportion of individuals in a population at a given point in time. The most direct use of point prevalence is as an estimate of need for care or potential treatment load, and it is favored by health

services researchers. It is also useful because it identifies groups at high risk of having a disorder, or greater chronicity of the disorder, or both. Finally, the point prevalence can be used to measure the impact of prevention programs in reducing the burden of disease on the community.

Lifetime prevalence is the proportion of individuals, who have ever been ill, alive on a given day in the population. As those who die are not included in the numerator or denominator of the proportion, the lifetime prevalence is sometimes called the proportion of survivors affected (PSA). It differs from the lifetime risk because the latter attempts to include the entire lifetime of a birth cohort, both past and future, and includes those deceased at the time of the survey. Lifetime risk is the quantity of most interest to geneticists. Lifetime prevalence also differs from the proportion of cohort affected (PCA), which includes members of a given cohort who have ever been ill by the study date, regardless of whether they are still alive at that time.

Lifetime prevalence has the advantage over lifetime risk and PCA in that it does not require ascertaining who is deceased, whether those deceased had the disorder of interest, or how likely those now alive without the disorder are to develop it before some given age. Thus, lifetime prevalence can be estimated from a cross-sectional survey. The other measures require either following a cohort over time or asking relatives to identify deceased family members and report symptoms suffered by them. Often these reports must be supplemented with medical records. The need for these other sources adds possible errors: relatives may forget to report persons who died many years before or may be uninformed about their psychiatric status; medical records may be impossible to locate or inaccurate; and the prediction of onset in young persons not yet affected requires the assumption that they will fall ill at the same rate as the older members of the sample and will die at the same ages if they do not fall ill. If risks of disorder or age-specific death rates change, these predictions will fail.

Lifetime prevalence requires that the diagnostic status of each respondent be assessed over his or her lifetime. Thus, accuracy of recall of symptoms after a possible long symptom-free period is a serious issue, since symptoms and disorders that are long past, mild, short-lived, and less stigmatizing are particularly likely to be forgotten. For example, data from several cross-sectional studies of depression seem to indicate a rise in the rate of depression in persons born after World War II (Cross-National Collaborative Group, 1992; Klerman & Weissman, 1989).

Table 1 Rates and proportions in epidemiology.

Rate	Minimum design	Numerator	Denominator
Lifetime prevalence	Cross-section	Ever ill	Alive
Point prevalence	Cross-section	Currently ill	Alive
Period prevalence (1)	Cross-section	Ill during period	Alive at survey
Period prevalence (2)	Two waves	Ill during period	Alive during period
First incidence	Two waves	Newly ill	Never been ill
Attack rate	Two waves	Newly ill	Not ill at baseline
Proportion of cohort affected	Birth to present	Ever ill	Born and still alive
Lifetime risk	Birth to death	Ever ill	Born

These persons are older, however, and it may be that they have forgotten episodes of depression which occurred many years prior to the interview (Simon & Von Korff, 1995). Data showing that lifetime prevalence of depressive disorder actually declines with age (Robins et al., 1984) is consistent with the recall explanation.

Period prevalence is the proportion of the population ill during a specified period of time. Customarily the numerator is estimated by adding the prevalent cases at the beginning of the defined period to the incident (first and recurrent) cases that develop between the beginning and the end of the period. This form is shown as period prevalence (2) in Table 1. In research based on records, all cases of a disorder found over a one-year period are counted. The denominator is the average population size during the interval. Thus, the customary definition of period prevalence requires at least two waves of data collection. Both Mausner and Kramer (1985) and Kleinbaum et al. (1982) have noted the advantages of period prevalence for the study of psychiatric disorders, where onset and termination of episodes is difficult to ascertain exactly (e.g., the failure to distinguish new from recurrent episodes is unimportant in the estimation of period prevalence). Furthermore, the number of episodes occurring during the follow-up is unimportant; it is important only to record whether there was one or more vs. none. The disadvantage of period prevalence is that it is not as useful in estimating need as point prevalence, nor as advantageous in studying etiology as incidence.

Another type of period prevalence, sometimes labeled by a prefix denoting the period, such as one-year prevalence, is a hybrid type of rate, conceptually mixing aspects of point and period prevalence, which has been found useful in the ECA Program (Eaton et al., 1985). This type of period prevalence is labeled period prevalence (1) in Table 1. It includes in the numerator all those surveyed individuals who have met the criteria for disorder in the past year, and as denominator all those interviewed.

It is not a point prevalence rate because it covers a longer period of time, which can be defined as six months, two years, and so forth, as well as one year. But one-year prevalence is not a period prevalence rate because some individuals in the population who are ill at the beginning of the period are not successfully interviewed, because they either die or emigrate. As the time period covered in this rate becomes shorter, it approximates the point prevalence; as the time period becomes longer, the rate approaches the period prevalence. If there is large mortality, the one-year prevalence rate will diverge markedly from period prevalence.

3.05.2.2 Incidence

Incidence is the rate at which new cases develop in a population. It is a dynamic or time-dependent quantity and can be expressed as an instantaneous rate, although, usually, it is expressed with a unit of time attached, in the manner of an annual incidence rate. In order to avoid confusion, it is essential to distinguish first incidence from total incidence. The distinction itself commonly is assumed by epidemiologists but there does not appear to be consensus on the terminology. Most definitions of the incidence numerator include a concept such as "new cases" (Lilienfeld & Stolley, 1994, p. 109), or persons who "develop a disease" (Mausner & Kramer, 1985, p. 44). Morris (1975) defines incidence as equivalent to our "first incidence," and "attack rate" as equivalent to our "total incidence." First incidence corresponds to the most common use of the term "incidence," but since the usage is by no means universal, keeping the prefix is preferred.

The numerator of first incidence for a specified time period is composed of those individuals who have had an occurrence of the disorder for the first time in their lives and the denominator includes only persons who start the period with no prior history of the disorder. The numerator for attack rate (or total incidence) includes all individuals who have had an occurrence of the disorder during the time period under investigation, whether or not it is the initial episode of their lives or a recurrent episode. The denominator for total incidence includes all population members except those cases of the disorder which are active at the beginning of the follow-up period.

A baseline and follow-up generally are needed to estimate incidence. Cumulative incidence (not shown in Table 1) is the proportion of the sample or population who become a case for the first time between initial and followup interviews (Kleinbaum et al., 1982). But incidence generally is measured per unit of time, as a rate. When the follow-up period extends over many years, the exposure period of the entire population at risk is estimated by including all years prior to onset for a given individual in the denominator, and removing years from the denominator when an individual has onset or dies. In this manner, the incidence is expressed per unit time per population: for example, "three new cases per 1000 person years of exposure." This method of calculating facilitates comparison between studies with different lengths of follow-up and different mortality. When the mean interval between initial and follow-up interview is approximately 365 days, then the ratio of new cases to the number of followed up respondents, who were ascertained as being with a current or past history of the disorder at the time of the initial interview, can serve as a useful approximation of the disorder's annual first incidence.

First incidence also can be estimated by retrospection if the date of onset is obtained for each symptom or episode, so that the proportion or persons who first qualified in the year prior to the interview can be estimated. For this type of estimate (not shown in Table 1), only one wave of data collection is needed. This estimate of first incidence is subject to the effects of mortality, however, because those who have died will not be available for the interview.

The preference for first or total incidence in etiologic studies depends on hypotheses and assumptions about the way causes and outcomes important to the disease ebb and flow. If the disease is recurrent and the causal factors vary in strength over time, then it might be important to study risk factors not only for first but for subsequent episodes (total incidence): for example, the effects of changing levels of stress on the occurrence of episodes of neurosis (Tyrer, 1985) or schizophrenia (Brown, Birley, & Wing, 1972). For a disease with a presumed fixed progression from some starting point, such as dementia, the first occurrence might be the most important episode to focus on, and first incidence is the appropriate rate. In the field of

psychiatric epidemiology, there are a range of disorders with both types of causal structures operating, which has led us to focus on this distinction in types of incidence.

The two types of incidence are related functionally to different measures of prevalence. Kramer et al. (1980) have shown that lifetime prevalence (i.e., the proportion of persons in a defined population who have ever had an attack of a disorder) is a function of first incidence and mortality in affected and unaffected populations. Point prevalence (i.e., the proportion of persons in a defined population on a given day who manifest the disorder) is linked to total incidence by the queuing formula $P = f(I \times D)$ (Kleinbaum et al., 1982; Kramer, 1957), that is, point prevalence is a function of the total number of cases occurring and their duration. In the search for risk factors that have etiologic significance for the disorder, comparisons based on point prevalence rates suffer the disadvantage that differences between groups as to the chronicity of the disorder: that is, the duration of episodes; the probability that episodes will recur; or the mortality associated with episodes; affect the comparisons (Kramer, (1957). For example, it appears that Blacks may have episodes of depression of longer duration than Whites (Eaton & Kessler, 1981). If so, the point prevalence of depression would be biased toward a higher rate for Blacks, based solely on their greater chronicity.

3.05.2.3 Incidence and Onset

Dating the onset of episodes is problematic for most mental disorders for many reasons. One is that the diagnostic criteria for the disorders themselves are not well agreed upon, and continual changes are being made in the definition of a case of disorder, such as the recent fourth revision of the *Diagnostic and statistical manual of mental disorders* (*DSM-III*; American Psychiatric Association, 1994). The *DSM-IV* has the advantage that criteria for mental disorders are more or less explicitly defined, but it is nevertheless true that specific mental disorders are often very difficult to distinguish from nonmorbid psychological states. Most disorders include symptoms that, taken by themselves, are part of everyone's normal experience: for example, feeling fearful, being short of breath or dizzy, and having sweaty palms are not uncommon experiences, but they are also symptoms of panic disorder. It is the clustering of symptoms, often with the requirement that they be brought together in one period of time or "spell," that generally forms the requirement for diagnosis. Although the clustering criteria are fairly explicit in the

DSM, it is not well established that they correspond to the characteristics generally associated with a disease, such as a predictable course, a response to treatment, an association with a biological aberration in the individual, or an associated disability. Thus, the lack of established validity of the criteria-based classification system exacerbates problems of dating the onset of disorder.

The absence of firm data on the validity of the classification system requires care about conceptualizing the process of disease onset. One criterion of onset used in the epidemiology of some diseases is entry into treatment, but this is unacceptable in psychiatry since people with mental disorders so often do not seek treatment for them. Another criterion of onset sometimes used is detectability, that is, when the symptoms first appear, but this is also unacceptable because experiences analogous to the symptoms of most psychiatric disorders are so widespread. It is preferable to conceptualize onset as a continuous line of development towards manifestation of a disease. There is a threshold at which the development becomes irreversible, so that at some minimal level of symptomatology it is certain that the full characteristics of the disease, however defined, will become apparent. This use of irreversibility is consistent with some epidemiological uses (Kleinbaum et al., 1982). Prior to this point, the symptoms are thought of as "subcriterial." At the state of knowledge in psychiatry in the 1990s, longitudinal studies in the general population, such as the ECA program and others mentioned above, are needed to determine those levels of symptomatology at which irreversibility is achieved.

There are at least two ways of thinking about development towards disease. The first way is the increase in severity or intensity of symptoms. An individual could have all the symptoms required for diagnosis but none of them be sufficiently intense or impairing. The underlying logic of such an assumption may well be the relatively high frequency of occurrence of the symptoms in milder form, making it difficult to distinguish normal and subcriterial complaints from manifestations of disease. For many chronic diseases, it may be inappropriate to regard the symptom as ever having been "absent," for example, personality traits giving rise to deviant behavior, categorized as personality disorders on Axis II of the *DSM* (APA, 1994). This type of development can be referred to as "symptom intensification," indicating that the symptoms are already present and have become more intense during a period of observation. This concept leads the researcher to consider whether there is a crucial level of severity of a given symptom or symptoms in which the rate of development towards a full-blown disease state is accelerated, or becomes irreversible.

A second way of thinking about progress towards disease is the occurrence of new symptoms which did not exist before. This involves the gradual acquisition of symptoms so that clusters are formed which increasingly approach the constellation required to meet specified definitions for diagnosis. A cluster of symptoms which occur more often together than would be expected by their individual prevalence in the population, that is, more often than expected by chance, is a syndrome. "Present" can be defined as occurrence either at a nonsevere or at a severe level, thus, decisions made about the symptom intensification process complicate the idea of acquisition. This idea leads the researcher to consider the order in which symptoms occur over the natural history of disease, and in particular, whether one symptom is more important than others in accelerating the process.

Figure 1 is an adaptation of a diagram used by Lilienfeld and Lilienfeld (1980, Figure 6.3) to visualize the concept of incidence as a time-oriented rate which expresses the force of morbidity in the population. In their original figure, (1(a)), the horizontal axis represents time and the presence of a line indicates disease. The adaptations (1(b) and 1(c)) give examples of the several distinct forms that onset can take when the disorder is defined by constellations of symptoms varying in intensity and co-occurrence, as is the case with mental disorders. In Figure 1(b), the topmost subject (1) is what might be considered the null hypothesis, and it corresponds to simple onset as portrayed in the original. Figure 1(b) shows how intensity, represented by the vertical width of the bars, might vary. The threshold of disease is set at four units of width, and in the null hypothesis subject 1 progresses from zero intensity to four units, becoming a case during the observation period. Subject 2 changes from nearly meeting the criteria (width of three units) to meeting it (four units) during the year. Both subjects 1 and 2 are new cases, even though the onset was more sudden in subject 1 than in subject 2, that is, the force of morbidity is stronger in subject 1 than subject 2. Subjects 3 and 4 are not new cases, even though their symptoms intensify during the year as much or more than those of subject 2.

Figure 1(c) adapts the same original diagram to conceptualize acquisition of symptoms and the development of syndromes. At one point in time there is no correlation between symptoms, but the correlation gradually develops, until there is a clear separation of the population into one group, with no association of symptoms,

Incidence and Intensification

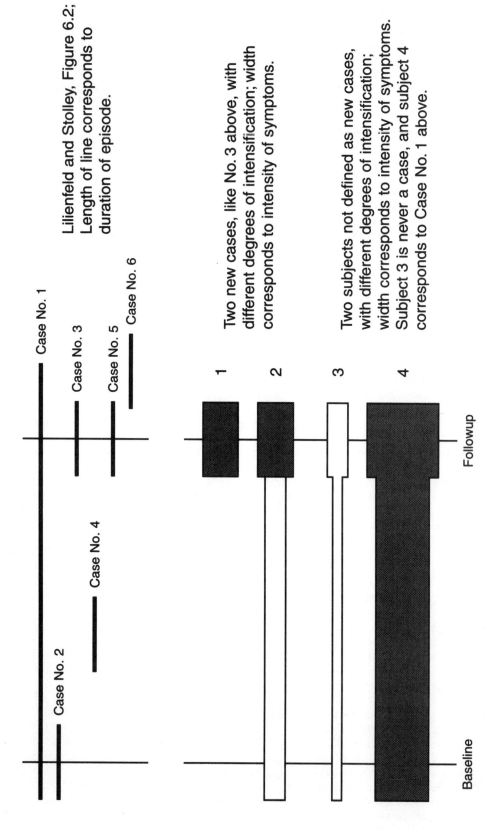

Case No. 1

Case No. 3

Case No. 5

Case No. 6

Case No. 2

Case No. 4

Lilienfeld and Stolley, Figure 6.2; Length of line corresponds to duration of episode.

Two new cases, like No. 3 above, with different degrees of intensification; width corresponds to intensity of symptoms.

Two subjects not defined as new cases, with different degrees of intensification; width corresponds to intensity of symptoms. Subject 3 is never a case, and subject 4 corresponds to Case No. 1 above.

1

2

3

4

Baseline

Followup

Figure 1(a) and (b) Incidence and intensification.

Incidence and Development of Syndromes

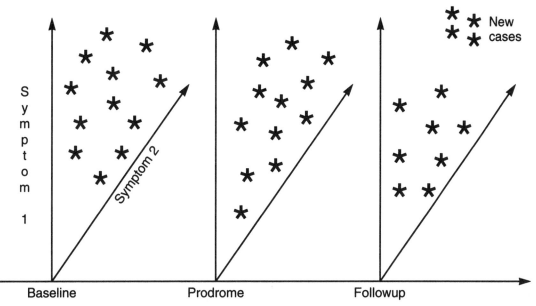

Figure 1(c)   Incidence and the development of syndromes.

and another group where the two symptoms co-occur. This example could be expanded to syndromes involving more than two symptoms.

Acquisition and intensification are indicators of the force of morbidity in the population, as are more traditional forms of incidence rate. But they are not tied to any one definition of caseness. Rather, these concepts allow study of disease progression independently of case definition. Risk factors at different stages of the disease may be differentially related to disease progression only above or below the threshold set by the diagnosis. In this situation, we might reconsider the diagnostic threshold.

3.05.3 MORBIDITY SURVEYS

Morbidity surveys are cross-sectional surveys of the general population. They are used to estimate prevalence of disease in the population as well as to estimate need for care. Morbidity surveys address Morris's (1975, discussed above) second "use" of epidemiology, "diagnosing the health of the community, prioritizing health problems and identifying groups in need;" as well as the third use "studying the working of health services;" and the fifth use, "identifying syndromes." Morbidity surveys are sometimes called the descriptive aspect of epidemiology, but they can also be used to generate hypotheses about associations in the population, and to generate control samples for cohort and case–control studies.

3.05.3.1 Exemplar Study: The Epidemiologic Catchment Area (ECA) Program

An example of a morbidity survey is the Epidemiologic Catchment Area (ECA) Program, sponsored by the United States National Institute of Mental Health from 1978 through 1985. The broad aims of the ECA Program were "to estimate the incidence and prevalence of mental disorders, to search for etiological clues, and to aid in the planning of health care facilities" (Eaton, Rogier, Locke, & Taube, 1981). The Program involved sample surveys of populations living in the catchment areas of already designated Community Mental Health Centers. The broad goals of the ECA Program are described in Eaton et al. (1981), the methods are described in Eaton and Kessler (1985), and Eaton et al. (1984), the cross-sectional results are described in Robins and Regier (1991), and the incidence estimates are described in Eaton, Kramer, Anthony, Chee, and Shapiro (1989).

A principal advantage of the morbidity survey is that it includes several or many disorders, which helps in assessing their relative importance from the public health point of view. Another advantage is that estimates of prevalence and association are measured without regard to the treatment status of the sample (Shapiro et al., 1984). Figure 2 displays results from the ECA study, showing the relatively high prevalence of phobia and relatively low prevalence of schizophrenia. The figure also shows the proportion meeting criteria for a given

100

Epidemiologic Methods

disorder within the last six months, who had seen either a physician or mental health specialist during that period. These proportions are well under 50%, with the exception of schizophrenia and panic disorder. For depression, which is disabling and highly treatable, less than a third of those with the disorder have received treatment.

3.05.3.2 Defining and Sampling the Population

Defining the target population for the morbidity survey is the first step. The best way to define the target population is not always clear, and different definitions have implications for the ultimate value of the results, as well as the feasibility of the study. A good definition of a target population is an entire nation, such as in the National Comorbidity Survey, or, better yet, a birth cohort of an entire nation, such as the British Perinatal Study, which included all births in Britain during a single week in March of 1958 (Butler & Alberman, 1969). Other studies usually involve compromises of one form or another. The goal of the sampling procedure is that each respondent is selected into the sample with a known, and nonzero,

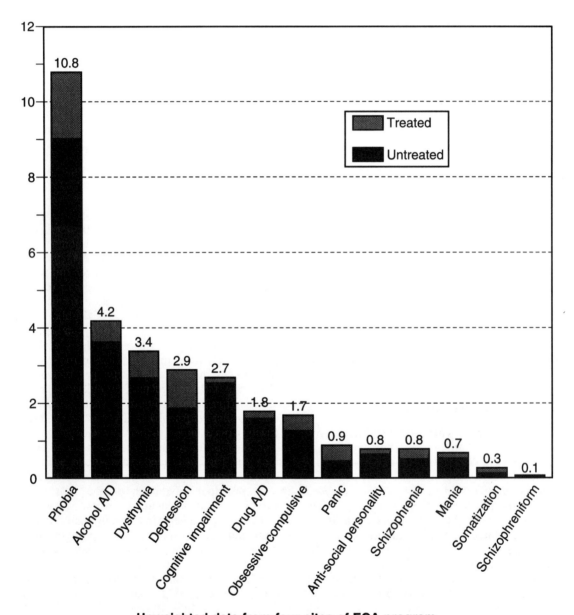

Unweighted data from four sites of ECA program

Figure 2   Prevalence of disorder in percent in six months prior to interview.

probability. Strict probabilistic sampling characterizes high-quality epidemiologic surveys, and is a requirement for generalization to the target population.

Most surveys are of the household residing, noninstitutionalized population, where the survey technology for sampling and interviewing individuals is strongest (e.g., Sudman, 1976). The ECA design defined the target population as "normal" residents of previously established catchment areas. Sampling was conducted in two strata, as shown in Figure 3. The household residing population was sampled via area probability methods or household listings provided by utility companies (e.g., as in Sudman, 1976). This stratum included short-stay group quarters such as jails, hospitals, and dormitories. After making a list of the residents in each household, the interviewer asked the person answering the door as to whether there were any other individuals who "normally" resided there but were temporarily absent. "Normally" was defined as the presence of a bed reserved for the individual at the time of the interview. Temporarily absent residents were added to the household roster before the single respondent was chosen randomly. If an individual was selected who was temporarily absent, the interviewer made an appointment for a time after their return, or conducted the interview at their temporary group quarters residence (i.e., in hospital, jail, dormitory, or other place). The ECA sampled the institutional populations separately, by listing all the institutions in the catchment area, as well as all those nearby institutions who admitted residents of the catchment area. Then the inhabitants of each institution were rostered and selected probabilistically. Sampling the institutional population required many more resources, per sampled individual, than the household sample, because each institution had to be approached individually. Inclusion of temporary and long-stay group quarters is important for health services research because many of the group quarters are involved in provision of health services, and because residents of group quarters may be high utilizers. The ultimate result of these procedures in the ECA was that each normal resident of the catchment area was sampled with a known probability.

It is not enough to crisply define a geographic area, because different areas involve different limitations on the generalizability of results. A nationally representative sample, such as the National Comorbidity Survey (NCS; Kessler et al., 1994), may seem to be the best. But how are the results of the national sample to be applied to a given local area, where decisions about services are made? In the ECA the decision was made to select five separate sites of research in order to provide the possibility of replication of results across sites, and to better understand the effects of local variation (Eaton et al., 1981). The ECA target population thus consisted, not of the nation, but rather of an awkward aggregation of catchment areas. Nevertheless, the ECA data were considered as benchmarks for a generation of research (Eaton, 1994) because there was sufficient variation in important sociodemographic variables to allow generalization to other large populations, that is, sufficiently large subgroups of young and old, men and women, married and unmarried, rich and poor, and so forth. Generalization to other target populations, such as Asian-Americans or Native Americans, or to rural areas, was not logical from the ECA. But note that generalization from a national random sample to all rural areas, or to small ethnic groups, would likewise not always be possible. The point is that the target population should be chosen with a view toward later generalization.

3.05.3.3 Sample Size

General population surveys are not efficient designs for rare disorders or unusual patterns of service use. Even for research on outcomes that are not rare, sample sizes are often? larger than one thousand. A common statistic to be estimated is the prevalence, which is a proportion. For a proportion, the precision is affected by the square root of the sample size (Blalock, 1979). If the distribution of the proportion is favorable, say, 30–70%, then a sample size of 1000 produces precision which may be good enough for common sample surveys such as for voter preference. For example, a proportion of 0.50 has a 95% confidence interval from 0.47 to 0.53 with a sample of 1000. For rarer disorders, the confidence interval grows relative to the size of the proportion (i.e., 0.82–0.118 for a proportion of 0.10; 0.004–0.160 for a proportion of 0.01). Often, there is interest in patterns broken down by subpopulations, thus challenging the utility of samples with as few as 1000 individuals. Many community surveys, such as the ECA, have baseline samples in excess of 3000. It is important to estimate the precision of the sample for parameters of interest, and the power of the sample to test hypotheses of interest, before beginning the data collection.

3.05.3.4 Standardization of Data Collection

Assessment in epidemiology should ideally be undertaken with standardized measurement instruments which have known and acceptable

Sampling Strata for Residents
ECA Study Design

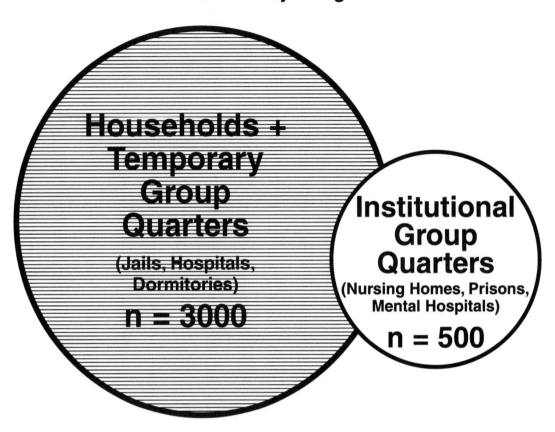

Figure 3 Sampling strata for residents: ECA study design.

reliability and validity. In community surveys, and automated record systems, reliable and valid measurement must take place efficiently and in "field conditions." The amount of training for interviewers in household studies depends on the nature of the study. Interviewers in the Longitudinal Study on Aging (LSOA; Kovar, 1992), a well-known cohort study in the United States, received about 1.5 days of training (Fitti & Kovar, 1987), while ECA interviewers received slightly more than a week (Munson et al., 1985). Telephone interviews, such as in the LSOA, can be monitored systematically by recording or listening in on a random basis (as long as the subject is made aware of this possibility), but it is difficult to monitor household interviews, since it cannot be predicted exactly when and where the interview will take place.

The ECA Program involved a somewhat innovative interview called the Diagnostic Interview Schedule, or DIS (Robins, Helzer, Croughan, & Ratcliff, 1981). The DIS was designed to resemble a typical psychiatric interview, in which questions asked are highly dependent on answers already given. For example, if an individual responds positively to a question about the occurrence of panic attacks, a series of questions about that particular response are asked, but if the response to the question on panic is negative, the interviewer skips to the next section. In effect, the interview adapts to the responses of the subject, so that more questions are asked where more information is needed. The high degree of structure in the DIS required more than one week of training, as well as attention to the visual properties of the interview booklet itself. The result was that the interviewer could follow instructions regarding the flow of the interview, and the recording of data, smoothly, so as not to offend or alienate the respondent. Household survey questionnaires are becoming increasingly adaptive and response dependent, because more information can be provided in a shorter amount of time with adaptive interviews. Inexpensive laptop computers will facilitate such adaptive interviewing. Self-administered, computerized admission procedures are becoming more widely disseminated in the health care system, expanding the database, and facilitating the retrieval and linkage of records.

The reliability and validity of measurement are usually assessed prior to beginning a field study. Usually, the assessment involves pilot tests on samples of convenience to determine the optimal order of the questions, the time required for each section, and whether any questions are unclear or offensive. Debriefing subjects in these pilot tests is often helpful. The next step is a test of reliability and validity. Many pretests select samples from populations according to their health or services use characteristics in order to generate enough variation on responses to adequately estimate reliability and validity. In order to economize, such pretests are often conducted in clinical settings. But such pretests do not predict reliability and validity under the "field" conditions of household interviews. The ECA Program design involved reliability and validity assessment in a hospital setting (Robins et al., 1981), and later under field conditions (Anthony et al., 1985). The reliability and validity of the DIS were lower in the household setting.

3.05.4 EXPOSURE AND DISEASE

Two basic research designs in epidemiology are the cohort and the case–control design. These designs are used mostly in addressing Morris' seventh "use" of epidemiology, the search for causes. This is sometimes called the analytic aspect of epidemiology. These designs differ in their temporal orientation to collection of data (prospective vs. retrospective), and in the criteria by which they sample (by exposure or by caseness), as shown in Table 2.

3.05.4.1 Cohort Design

In a cohort design, incidence of disorder is compared in two or more groups which differ in some exposure thought to be related to the disorder (Table 2). The cohort design differs from the morbidity survey in that it is prospective, involving longitudinal follow-up of an identified cohort of individuals. As well as the search for causes, the cohort design addresses Morris' fourth "use" of epidemiology, "estimating individual risks;" and the sixth "use," that is, "completing the clinical picture, especially the natural history." The entire cohort can be sampled, but when a specific exposure is hypothesized, the design can be made more efficient by sampling for intensive measurement on the basis of the putative exposure, for example, children living in an area of toxic exposures, or with parents who have been convicted of abuse, or who have had problems during delivery, and a control group from the general population. Follow-up allows comparison of incidence rates in both groups.

3.05.4.2 Exemplar Study: the British Perinatal Study

An example is the British Perinatal Study, a cohort study of 98% of all births in Great Britain during a single week in March, 1958 (Butler & Alberman, 1969; Done, Johnstone, & Frith, 1991; Sacker, Done, Crow, & Golding, 1995). The cohort had assessments at the ages of 7 and 11 years, and, later, mental hospital records were linked for those entering psychiatric hospitals between 1974 and 1986, by which time the cohort was 30 years old. Diagnoses were made from hospital case notes using a standard system. There was some incompleteness in the data, but not too large, for example, 12 of the 49 individuals diagnosed as "narrow" schizophrenia were excluded because they were immigrants, multiple births, or because they lacked data. It is difficult to say how many individuals in the cohort had episodes of disorder that did not result in hospitalization, but that does not necessarily threaten the results, if the attrition occurred equally for

Table 2 Case–control and cohort studies.

		Case–control study		
		Cases	Controls	
Cohort	Exposed	a	b	$a + b$
Study	Not exposed	c	d	$c + d$

$$\text{Relative risk} = \frac{a / (a + b)}{c / (c + d)}$$

$$\text{Relative odds} = \frac{a / b}{c / d} = \frac{ad}{bc}$$

different categories of exposure. Table 3 shows results for one of 37 different variables related to birth, that is, "exposures," that were available in the midwives' report: birth weight under 2500 g. With *n* given at the head of the columns in Table 3, the reader can fill in the four cells of a two-by-two table, as in Table 2, for each of the four disorders. For example, the cells, labeled as in Table 2, for narrow schizophrenia, are: a–5; b–706; c–30; d–16 106. The number with the disorder is divided by the number of births to generate the risk of developing the disorder by the time of follow-up: the cumulative incidence. The risks can be compared across those with and without the exposure. In Table 2, the incidence of those with exposure is $a/(a+b)$, and the incidence of those without exposure is $c/(c+d)$. The relative risk is a comparison of the two risks: $[a/(a+b)]/[c/(c+d)]$. For narrow schizophrenia the relative risk is (RR $= [5/711]/[30/16 136]$), or 3.78.

The relative risk is closely related to causality since it quantifies the association in the context of a prospective study, so the temporal ordering is clear. The relative risk is approximated closely by the relative odds or odds ratio, which does not include the cases in the denominator (i.e., OR $= [5/706]/[30/16 106] = 3.80$, not 3.78). The odds ratio has many statistical advantages for epidemiology. It is easy to calculate in the two-by-two table by the cross-products ratio (i.e., ad/bc). The odds ratio quantifies the association without being affected by the prevalence of the disorder or the exposure, which is important for the logic of cohort and case–control studies, where these prevalences may change from study to study, depending on the research design. This lack of dependence on the marginal distribution is not characteristic of many measures of association typically used in psychology, such as the correlation coefficient, the difference in proportions, or the kappa coefficient (Bishop et al., 1975). The odds ratio is a standard result of logistic regression, and can be adjusted by

other factors such as gender, age, and so forth. The odds ratio for low birth weight and narrow schizophrenia in the British Perinatal Study, as it happens, was 3.9, after adjustment for social class and other demographic variables.

The logic of the cohort study includes assessing the natural history of the disorder, that is, the study of onset and chronicity, in a population context without specific intervention by the researcher. Study of natural history requires repeated follow-up observations. In the British Perinatal Study, there were assessments of the cohort at the ages of 7 and 11. Once the case groups had been defined, it was possible to study their reading and mathematics performance well before hospitalization. Those destined to become schizophrenic had lower reading and mathematics scores at both 7 and 11 years of age (Crow, Done, & Sacker, 1996). Males who would eventually be diagnosed schizophrenic had problems relating to conduct during childhood, while females were anxious, as compared to children who did not end up being hospitalized with a diagnosis of schizophrenia later. Later follow-ups in this study may economize by studying only those who have had onset, and a small random subsample of others, to estimate such factors as the length of episodes, the probability of recurrences, prognostic predictors, and long-term functioning.

3.05.4.3 Case–Control Design

In the case–control study, it is the disease or disorder which drives the logic of the design, and many factors can be studied efficiently as possible causes of the single disorder (Schlesselman, 1982). The case–control study may be the most important contribution of epidemiology to the advancement of public health, because it is so efficient in searching for causes when there is little knowledge. For example, adenocarcinoma of the vagina occurs so rarely, that, prior to 1966, not a single case under the age of 50 years

Table 3 Mental disorder and low birth weight: British Perinatal study.

| | Cumulative incidence per 1000 | | |
Disorder	Low birth weight (n = 727)	Normal birth weight (n = 16 812)	Odds ratio
Narrow schizophrenia (n = 35)	7.03	1.86	3.8
Broad schizophrenia (n = 57)	9.82	3.09	3.2
Affective psychosis (n = 32)	8.43	1.61	5.3
Neurosis (n = 76)	4.23	4.51	0.9

Source: Adapted from Sacker et al. (1995).

had been recorded at the Vincent Memorial Hospital in Boston. A time-space clustering of eight cases, all among young women born within the period 1946–1951, was studied (Herbst, Utfeder, & Poskanzer, 1971). There was almost no knowledge of etiology. A case–control study was conducted, matching four controls to each case. The study reported a highly significant ($p < 0.00001$) association between treatment of the mothers with estrogen diethylstilbestrol during pregnancy and the subsequent development of adenocarcinoma of the vagina in the daughters. The results led to recommendations to avoid administering stilbestrol during pregnancy. Logistic regression, developed by epidemiologists and used in case–control studies, has distinct advantages over analysis of variance, ordinary least-squares regression, discriminant function analysis, and probit regression, developed by agronomists, psychologists, economists, and educational psychologists, especially when the dichotomous dependent variable has a very skew distribution, that is, is very rare.

3.05.4.4 Exemplar Study: Depression in Women in London

The most convincing demonstration of social factors in the etiology of any mental disorder is *The social origins of depression*, by Brown and Harris (1978). That study used the case–control method to demonstrate the importance of life-event stresses and chronic difficulties as causal agents provoking the onset of depression. The method involved indepth diagnostic and etiologic interviews with a sample of 114 patients and a sample of 458 household residents. The target population is that residing in the Camberwell area in south London.

The analysis presented by Brown and Harris is logical but does not always follow the standard epidemiologic style. Table 4 presents the crucial findings in the typical epidemiologic manner (following Table 2). Two case groups are defined: the 114 women presenting at clinics and hospitals serving the Camberwell area, diagnosed by psychiatrists using a standardized clinical assessment tool called the Present

Examination, and 76 women in the community survey (17%) who were depressed at the time of the survey, as judged by a highly trained, nonmedical interviewer using a shortened version of the same instrument. Sixty-one percent of the patient cases (70/114) and 68% of the survey cases (52/76) experienced the "provoking agent" of a severe life event during the year prior to the onset of depression. Twenty percent (76/382) of the healthy controls experienced such an event in the year prior to the interview. Patient cases had 6.4 times the odds of having experienced a life event than the controls (i.e., [70/44]/[76/306]).

The case–control study is very efficient, especially when the disease is rare, because it approximates the statistical power of a huge cohort study with a relatively limited number of controls. For a disease like schizophrenia, which occurs in less than 1% of the population, 100 cases from hospitals or a psychiatric case register can be matched to 300 controls from the catchment area of the hospital. A cohort study of this number would involve measurements on 10 000 persons instead of 400! Since the disease is rare, it may be unnecessary to conduct diagnostic examinations on the group of controls, which would have only a small number of cases. Furthermore, a few cases distributed among the controls would weaken the comparison of cases to controls, generating a conservative bias. The statistical power of the case–control study is very close to that of the analogous cohort study, and, as shown above, the odds ratio is a close estimate of the relative risk. The case–control study can be used to test hypotheses about exposures, but it has the very great ability to make comparisons across a wide range of possible risk factors, and can be useful even when there are very few hypotheses available.

3.05.5 USING AVAILABLE RECORDS

3.05.5.1 Government Surveys

There are many sources of data for psychiatric epidemiologic research which are available to the public. These include statistics from

Table 4 Depression and life events and difficulties in London.

	Cases (patients)		Cases (survey)		Controls (survey)	
One or more severe event	70	61%	52	68%	76	20%
No severe events	44	39%	24	32%	306	80%
	114	100%	76	100%	382	100%

Source: Brown & Harris (1978).

treatment facilities and from large sample surveys of the populations conducted by a large organization such as national governments. Often the measures of interest to psychologists are only a small part of the survey, but the availability of a range of measures, drawn from other disciplines, can be a strong advantage. In the United States an important source of data is the National Center for Health Statistics (NCHS). For example, the Health and Nutrition Examination Survey (HANES) is a national sample survey conducted by the NCHS involving physical examinations of a sample of the United States population. Its first phase included the Center for Epidemiologic Studies Depression Scale as part of its battery of measures, which included anthropometric measures, nutritional assessments, blood chemistry, medical history, and medical examinations (Eaton & Kessler, 1981; Eaton & McLeod, (1984).

Later phases of the HANES included portions of the DIS. The Health Interview Survey conducts health interviews of the general population of the United States, and includes reports by the respondent of named psychiatric disorders such as schizophrenia, depressive disorder, and so forth. The National Medical Care Utilization and Expenditure Survey (MCUES) is conducted by the NCHS to help understand the health service system and its financing. The MCUES samples records of practitioners from across the nation, and there are several questions on treatment for psychological problems.

Some governments also sponsor national surveys which focus on psychological disorders. The ECA is one such example, although it was not, strictly speaking, a sample of the nation. The later National Comorbidity Survey includes 8058 respondents from a probability sample of the US, with its major measurement instrument being a version of the Composite International Diagnostic Interview (CIDI), a descendant of the DIS used in the ECA surveys (Kessler et al., 1994). The British government conducted a large survey of psychological disorders in a national sample, using a similar instrument to the DIS and CIDI (Meltzer, Gill, Pettirew, & Hindi, 1995a, 1995b). Anonymous, individual level data from the ECA, the British survey, and the NCS are available at nominal cost.

3.05.5.2 Vital Statistics

Governments generally assimilate data on births, deaths, and marriages from states, provinces, or localities, ensuring some minimal degree of uniformity of reporting and creating data files for public use. The mortality files usually list the cause of death, including suicide. These data files are often available from the government at nominal cost.

3.05.5.3 Record-based Statistics and Record Linkage

Statistics originating from treatment facilities can also be put to good use in psychiatric epidemiology. Many early epidemiologic studies used hospital statistics as the numerators in estimating rates, and census statistics in the denominators (Kramer, 1969). The utility of rates estimated in this manner is dependent on the degree to which the clinical disorder is associated with treatment, a stronger association for severe schizophrenia than for mild phobia, presumably. The value of these rates also depends on the relative scarcity or abundance of treatment facilities. In the United States, Medicaid and Medicare files, which include such data as diagnosis and treatment, are available for research use. Many Health Maintenance Organizations maintain data files which could be used in psychological epidemiological research.

Statistics from treatment facilities are enhanced considerably by linkage with other facilities in the same geographic area, serving the same population (Mortensen, 1995). Although the number has declined, there still exist several registers which attempt to record and link together all psychiatric treatment episodes for a given population (ten Horn, Giel, Gulbinar, & Henderson, 1986). Linkage across facilities allows multiple treatment episodes for the same individual (even the same episode of illness) to be combined into one record (so-called "unduplicating"). Linkage across time allows longitudinal study of the course of treatment. Linkage with general health facilities, and with birth and mortality records, provides special opportunities. The best known example of a comprehensive health registry is the Oxford Record Linkage Study (ORLS; Acheson, Baldwin, & Graham, 1987), which links together all hospital treatment episodes in its catchment area. The database of the ORLS consists of births, deaths, and hospital admissions, which is a strong limitation. However, due to the catchmenting aspect of the British National Health Service, the data are not limited to the household-residing population, as is the National Comorbidity Survey, for example, or the LSOA. In automated data collection systems such as the ORLS, the recordation is often done under the auspices of the medical record systems, with data recorded by the physician, such as the diagnosis. It cannot be presumed that physician's diagnosis is "standardized" and therefore more reliable than other interview or record data. In fact, there is significant variation in diagnosis among physicians. Research using measurements and diagnoses recorded by the physician, as in record linkage systems such as the ORLS, should ideally include studies of reliability and validity (e.g., Loffler et al., 1994).

3.05.5.4 Exemplar Study: the Danish Adoption Study

An example of the benefits of record linkage in psychological research is the adoption study of schizophrenia in Denmark (Kety, Rosenthal, Wender, Schulsinger, & Jacobsen, 1975). Familial and twin studies of schizophrenia suggested strongly that schizophrenia was inherited, but these studies were open to the interpretation that the inheritance was cultural, not genetic, because family members are raised together, and identical twins may be raised in social environments which are more similar than the environments of fraternal twins. The Danish Adoption Study ingeniously combined the strategy of file linkage with interviews of cases, controls, and their relatives. In Denmark, each individual receives a number at birth which is included in most registration systems. The registration systems are potentially linkable, after appropriate safeguards and clearances. In the adoption study, three registers were used. First, all 5483 individuals in the county and city of Copenhagen who had been adopted by persons or families other than their biological relatives, from 1924 through 1947, were identified from a register of adoptions (Figure 4). These were linked to the psychiatric case register, wherein it was determined that 507 adoptees had ever been admitted to a psychiatric hospital. From case notes in the hospitals, 34 adoptees who met criteria for schizophrenia (about 0.5% of of the total number of adoptees) were selected, and matched on the basis of age, sex, socioeconomic status of the adopting family, and time with biologic family, or in institution, prior to adoption. The relatives of these 68 cases and controls were identified by linkage with yet another register in Denmark which permits locating families, parents, and children. After allowing for mortality, refusal, and a total of three who were impossible to trace, a psychiatric interview was conducted on 341 individuals (including 12 on whom the interview was not conducted but sufficient information for diagnosis was obtained). Eleven of the 118 biologic relatives of the index adoptees were schizophrenic (9%), vs. one in the 35 relatives of adoptive families of the index adoptees (3%), and three of the 140 biologic

relatives of the control adoptees (2%). The findings for schizophrenia spectrum disorders (including uncertain schizophrenia and schizoid personality) also show a pattern consistent only with genetic inheritance (26/118 in the biologic relatives of index cases, or 22%, vs. 16/140 biologic relatives of control adoptees, or 14%).

3.05.6 PREVENTIVE TRIALS

3.05.6.1 The Logic of Prevention

Some of the earliest epidemiologists used interventions in the community to stop an epidemic or to gather information about the causes of diseases in the population. This is sometimes called the experimental aspect of epidemiology. The best known experiment is that conducted by Snow in the cholera epidemic in London. Snow's work exemplifies epidemiologic principles in several ways (Cooper & Morgan, 1973). It was widely believed that cholera was spread through the air, in a miasma, leading many to seek safety by retreating to rural areas. Snow showed with ecologic data in London that areas serviced by a water company taking water from upstream in the Thames had lower rates of cholera than areas serviced by a company taking water from downstream. This ecologic comparison suggested that cholera was borne by water. In the context of a single cholera epidemic, Snow identified individual cases of cholera, showing that they tended to cluster around a single water pump at Broad Street. He further showed that many exceptional cases, that is, cases of cholera residing distant from the pump, had actually drawn or drank water from that pump (e.g., on their way home from work). His action to remove the handle of the pump, which roughly coincided with the termination of the epidemic, is regarded as an early instance of experimental epidemiology.

In epidemiology, as with medicine generally, intervention is valued if it is effective, regardless of whether the causation of the disease is understood or not. Table 5 shows examples of preventive measures which were implemented well prior to knowledge of the cause, discovered much later in many cases. This logic leads to experimentation even in the absence of causal information.

Various conceptual frameworks have been used to organize the area of prevention research. The Commission on Chronic Illness (1957) divided prevention into three types, dependent on the stage of the disease the intervention was designed to prevent or treat. Prior to onset of the disease, the prevention was primary, and its goal was to reduce incidence; after disease onset, the intervention was directed at promoting

Epidemiologic Methods

Danish Adoption Study

Research Design

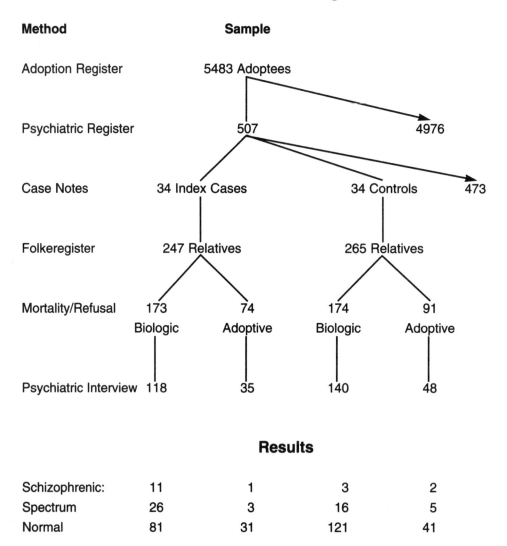

Figure 4 Danish adoption study: research design and results.
Source: Kety, Rosenthal, Wender, Schulsinger, and Jacobsen (1975).

recovery, and its goal was to reduce prevalence, so-called secondary prevention. Tertiary prevention was designed to prevent impairment and handicap which might result from the disease. The Institute of Medicine (Mrazek & Haggerty, 1994) integrated this framework into that of Gordon (1983), who directed attention at the population to which the preventive intervention was directed: universal preventions at the entire general population; targeted interventions at subgroups at high risk of development of disorder; and indicated interventions, directed at individuals who have already manifest signs and symptoms of the disease.

The results of integrating the two frameworks are shown in Figure 5. Curative medicine generally operates in the area of secondary prevention, with indicated interventions. Rehabilitative medicine is in the area of tertiary prevention. Primary, universal, and targeted interventions are the province of experimental epidemiology. Prominent examples of universal interventions in the area of epidemiology are various smoking cessation campaigns, and such studies as the Stanford Five-City Project, which was designed to reduce risk of heart disease by lowering levels of several associated risk factors (Farquhar et al., 1990).

Table 5 Knowledge of prevention and etiology.

	Prevention			Etiology		
Disease	Discoverer	Year	Agent	Discoverer	Year
Scurvy	Lind	1753	Ascorbic acid	Szent-Gyorgi	1928
Pellagra	Casal	1755	Niacin	Goldberger	1924
Scrotal cancer	Pott	1775	Benzopyrene	Cook	1933
Smallpox	Jenner	1798	Orthopoxvirus	Fenner	1958
Puerperal fever	Semmelwies	1847	Streptococcus	Pasteur	1879
Cholera	Snow	1849	Vibrio cholerae	Koch	1893
Bladder cancer	Rehn	1895	2-Napththylamine	Hueper	1938
Yellow fever	Reed	1901	Flavirus	Stokes	1928
Oral cancer	Abbe	1915	N-Nitrosonornicotine	Hoffman	1974

Source: Wynder (1994).

3.05.6.2 Attributable Risk

From among many possibilities, how should interventions be selected? Epidemiology provides a helpful tool in the form of the Population Attributable Risk, sometimes called the Attributable Fraction or the Etiologic Fraction (Lilienfeld & Stolley, 1994, p. 202). The attributable risk is the maximum estimate of the proportion of the incidence of disease that would be prevented if a given risk factor were eliminated. For a given disease, the attributable risk combines information from the relative risk for a given exposure with the prevalence of the exposure in the population. The formula for attributable risk is:

$$\text{Attributable Risk} = \frac{P(RR - 1)}{P(RR - 1) + 1}$$

where:
P = Prevalence of Exposure, and
RR = Relative Risk of Exposure to Disease

The relative risk can be estimated from a cohort study, as described above, and the prevalence of the exposure can be estimated from a separate survey. A simple case–control study also provides the information for attributable risk, under certain conditions. The relative risk is approximated by the relative odds, as discussed above. If the controls are selected from the general population, the level of exposure can be estimated from them. For example, case–control studies of smoking and lung cancer in the early 1950s showed that the odds of dying from lung cancer were about 15 times higher for smokers as for nonsmokers. About half the population smoked, leading to the attributable risk estimate of about 80%. In the United States, this meant that about 350 000 of the 400 000 annual deaths due to lung cancer would

not occur if smoking were eliminated totally. In the situation of many possible risk factors, the attributable risk is a tool which helps prioritize them.

Epidemiologic cohort studies can provide information which may help to stage the intervention at the most appropriate time. The intervention should occur before most onsets in the population have taken place, but not so far before onset that the effects of the intervention wash out before the process of disease development has begun. The appropriate stage for prevention in many situations would appear to be that of precursors, in which there are subgroups which can be identified at high risk, but before the disease prodrome has started (Eaton et al., 1995).

3.05.6.3 Developmental Epidemiology

Epidemiologists are gradually becoming aware of the need for life course perspective (Kellam & Werthamer-Larson, 1986). In social and psychological research on human beings, cohort studies may suggest regularities in human development which can be considered etiologic clues. The clues consist of temporal sequences of various behaviors over several years, with only a probabilistic connection between each behavior. The behaviors may have a common antecedent, such as a genetic background, or they may depend on the sequence of environments that the individual experiences, and the interaction between environments, genetic traits, and habits formed by the history of prior behaviors. The epidemiologic notion of exposures, developed in the context of infectious agents and toxins, is too simple to be useful in these multicausal, developmental sequences. For example, aggressive behavior by boys in early elementary school years is followed by conduct problems in middle

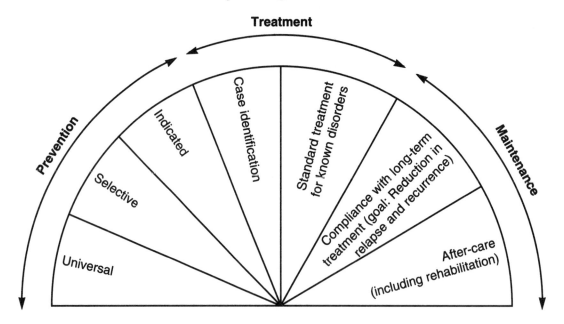

Figure 5 The mental health intervention spectrum for mental disorders.

school; later behaviors such as smoking cigarettes, having sexual relations at an early age, and drinking alcohol, in high school, and, eventually, the diagnosis of antisocial personality disorder as an adult. Which of these are essential causes, and which simply are associated behaviors which have no influence on the causal chain to the outcome (in this example, the diagnosis of antisocial personality disorder)? Since the chain of causes is probabilistic and multicausal, the notion of attributable risk (discussed above) is too simplistic, and it is unlikely that any estimate of attributable risk would be even moderate in size. A preventive intervention trial with random or near-random assignment to conditions which manipulate a putative cause may be the only way to generate an understanding of the causal chain. The preventive trial serves the traditional purpose in epidemiology of testing the efficacy of the intervention, but it also serves as an examination of the developmental pathway leading to disorder, for building and testing theories.

3.05.6.4 Exemplar Study: the Johns Hopkins Prevention Trial

An example of a preventive intervention trial is the Johns Hopkins Prevention Trial (Kellam, Rebek, Ialongo, & Mayer, 1994). The trial was designed to examine developmental pathways generally occurring after two important characteristics which could be identified in first graders: success at learning (especially, learning to read) and aggressive behavior. Table 6 shows the design of the trials, using the notation of

experimental and quasi-experimental design in psychology (Campbell & Stanley, 1971). The population for the trial was carefully defined in epidemiologic terms to include all first graders in public schools in an area of Baltimore. The Baltimore City Public School system was an active participant in the research. The 19 schools were divided into five levels, with three or four schools per level, based on the socioeconomic characteristics of the areas they served. At each of the five levels there was a control school and two experimental schools. For the study of aggressive behavior, 153 children were assigned at random to eight separate classrooms in which the teacher used a special classroom procedure called the "Good Behavior Game," which had been shown to reduce the level of aggressive behavior in classrooms. Nine classrooms with 163 children received an intervention to improve reading mastery, and there were 377 children who were in control classrooms. The control classrooms consisted of classrooms in the same school as the experimental, but who did not receive the intervention; and classrooms in schools in the same area of Baltimore, where there were no interventions at all. One outcome of the Good Behavior Game Trial was that the median level of aggressive behavior went down during the period of the trial for those in the experimental group. For controls, the level of aggressive behavior was relatively stable. The most impressive result was that aggressive behavior continued to decline in the experimental group, even after discontinuation of the intervention in third grade, at least through the spring of sixth grade.

Table 6 Intervention and assessment for Johns Hopkins Preventive Trials in 19 public elementary schools.

	Number of classrooms	Number of students	Grade 1 1985–1986 F|S	Grade 2 1986–1987 F|S	Grade 3 1987–1988 F|S	Grade 4 1988–1989 F|S	Grade 5 1989–1990 F|S	Grade 6 1990–1991 F|S
Good behavior game	8	153	RO/XO	XO/O	/O	/O	/O	/O
Mastery learning	9	163	RO/XO	XO/O	/O	/O	/O	/O
Controls	24	377	RO/O	O/O	/O	/O	/O	/O

Source: Kellam et al. (1994).   F = fall; S = spring; O = observation; X = intervention; R = random assignment.

3.05.7 BIAS

Epidemiologic research entails bias, and it is beneficial to anticipate bias in designing research studies. Common biases in epidemiology take a slightly different form than in typical psychological research (e.g., as enumerated in Campbell & Stanley, 1971), but the principle of developing a language to conceptualize bias, and to attempts to anticipate, eliminate, or measure bias is common to both disciplines. In this section five basic types of bias are considered: sampling bias, divided into three subtypes of treatment bias, prevalence bias, and response bias; and measurement bias, divided into subtypes of diagnostic bias and exposure bias.

3.05.7.1 Sampling Bias

Sampling bias arises when the sample studied does not represent the population to which generalization is to be made. An important type of sampling bias is treatment bias. The case–control design often takes advantage of treatment facilities for finding cases of disorder to compare with controls. With severe diseases which invariably lead to treatment, there is less bias than for disorders which are less noticeable, distressing, or impairing to the individual. As shown in Figure 2, data from the ECA Program indicate that among the mental disorders, only for schizophrenia and panic disorder are as many as half the current cases under treatment. In 1946, Berkson showed that, where the probability of treatment for a given disorder is less than 1.0, cases in treatment over-represented individuals with more than one disorder, that in, comorbid cases. In studying risk factors for disorder with the case–control design, where cases are found through clinics, the association revealed in the data may be an artifact of the comorbidity, that is, exposure x may appear to be associated with disease y, the focus disorder of the study, but actually related to disease z (perhaps not measured in the study). This type of bias is so important in epidemiologic research, especially case–control studies, it is termed "Berkson's bias," or sometimes "treatment bias." The existence of this bias is possibly one factor connected to little use of the case–control design in studies of psychiatric disorders.

Another type of sampling bias very common in case–control studies arises from another type of efficiency in finding cases of disorder, that in, the use of prevalent cases. This is sometimes termed prevalence bias, or the clinician's illusion (Cohen & Cohen, 1984). The ideal is to compare relative risks among exposed and nonexposed populations, which entails comparison of incidence rates, as discussed above. But the rate of incidence is often too low to generate sufficient cases for analysis, and necessitates extending the data collection over a period of months or years during which new cases are collected. Prevalent cases are easier to locate, either through a cross-sectional survey, or, easier yet, through records of individuals currently under treatment. The problem with study of current cases is that the prevalence is a function of the incidence and chronicity of the disorder, as discussed above. Association of an exposure with the presence or absence of disease mixes up influences on incidence with influences on chronicity. Influences on chronicity can include treatment. For example, comparing the brain structure of prevalent cases of schizophrenia to controls showed differences in the size of the ventricles, possibly an exciting clue to the etiology of schizophrenia. But a possible bias is that phenothiazine or other medication, used to treat schizophrenia, produced the changes in brain structure. Later studies of brain structure had to focus on schizophrenics who had not been treated in order to eliminate this possibility. The study of depression among women in London is possibly subject to prevalence bias since cases were selected on the basis of presentation to treatment, and controls via a cross-sectional (prevalence) survey. Thus, it may be that provoking agents such as life events contribute only to the recurrence of episodes of depression, not necessarily to their initial onset.

Response bias is a third general threat to the validity of findings from epidemiologic research. The epidemiologic design includes explicit statements of the population to which generalization is sought, as discussed above. The sampling procedure includes ways to designate individuals thought to be representative of that population. After designation as respondents, before measurements can be taken, some respondents become unavailable to the research, usually through one of three mechanisms: death, refusal, or change of residence. If these designated-but-not-included respondents are not a random sample, there will be bias in the results. The bias can result from differences in the distribution of cases vs. noncases as to response rate, or to differences in distribution of exposures, or both. In cross-sectional field surveys (Von Korff et al., 1985) and in follow-up surveys (Eaton, Anthony, Tepper, & Dryman, 1992), the response bias connected to psychopathology has not been extremely strong. Persons with psychiatric diagnoses are not more likely to refuse to participate, for example. Persons with cognitive impairment are more likely to die during a follow-up interval, and persons with antisocial personality disorder, or abuse of illegal drugs, are more likely to change address and be difficult to locate. Differential response bias is particularly threatening to studies with long follow-up periods, such as the British Perinatal Study and the Danish Adoption Study, since there was sizable attrition in both studies.

3.05.7.2 Measurement Bias

Bias in measurement is called invalidity in psychology, and this term is also used in epidemiology. But the study of validity in epidemiology has been more narrowly focused than in psychology. The concentration in epidemiology has been on dichotomous measures, as noted above. The medical ideology has ignored the notion that concepts for disease and pathology might actually be conventions of thought. Where the psychometrician takes as a basic assumption that the true state of nature is not observable, the epidemiologist tends to think of disease as a state whose presence is essentially knowable. As a result, discussion of face validity, content validity, or construct validity are rare in epidemiologic research. Instead the focus has been on sensitivity and specificity, which are two aspects of criterion validity (also a term not used much in epidemiologic research).

Sensitivity is the proportion of true cases that are identified as cases by the measure (Table 7). Specificity is the proportion of true noncases that are identified as noncases by the measure. In psychological research, validity is often estimated with a correlation coefficient, but this statistic is inappropriate because the construct of disease is dichotomous and differences in rarity of the disorder will constrain the value of the correlation coefficient. Furthermore, use of sensitivity and specificity has the advantage over correlation that it forces quantification of both types of error, that is, false-positive and false-negative error. These errors, and the calibration of the measurement to adapt to them, depend heavily on the prevalence of the disorder, on the importance of locating cases, and on the expense of dealing with those cases that are located. Choice of a threshold to define disorder as present or absent has important consequences, and is aided by detailed study of the effects of different thresholds (sometimes termed response operating characteristic (ROC) analysis, as in Murphy, 1987). There are simple procedures for correcting prevalence estimates according to the sensitivity and specificity of the

measurement (Rogan & Gladen, 1978). Procedures for correcting measures of association, such as the odds ratio, are more complicated since they depend on the precise study design.

Bias also exists in the measurement of exposure. The epidemiologist's tendency to categorical measurement leads to the term "misclassification" for this type of bias. A well-known example is the study of Lilienfeld and Graham (1958: cited in Schlesselman, 1982, pp. 137–138), which compared male patients' declarations as to whether they were circumcised to the results of a doctor's examination. Of the 84 men judged to be circumcised by the doctor (the "gold standard" in this situation), only 37 reported being circumcised (44% sensitivity). Eighty-nine of the 108 men who were not circumcised in the view of the doctor reported not being circumcised (82% specificity). In psychological research, the exposures are often subjective psychological happenings, such as emotions, or objective events recalled by the subject, such as life events, instead of, for example, residence near a toxic waste dump, as might be the putative exposure in a study of cancer. The importance of psychological exposures, or subjective reporting of exposures, threatens the validity of the case–control design in psychiatric epidemiology, and may be one reason it has been used so little. The cases in a case–control study by definition have a disease or problem which the controls do not. In any kind of case–control study where the measure of exposure is based on recall by the subjects, the cases may be more likely than controls to recall exposures, because they wish to explain the occurrence of the disease. In the study of depression in London, depressed women may be more likely to recall a difficult life event that happened earlier in their lives, because of their current mood, than women who are not depressed; or depressed women may magnify the importance of a given event which actually did occur. These problems of recall raise the importance of strictly prospective designs in psychological epidemiological research.

3.05.8 CONCLUSION: THE FUTURE OF PSYCHOLOGY IN EPIDEMIOLOGY

Epidemiology is developing rapidly in ways that will promote effective collaboration with psychology. The traditional interest of psychologists in health as well as illness links up to epidemiologists' growing interest in the development of host resistance. The traditional interest of psychologists in phenomenology is beginning to link up with epidemiologists'

Table 7   Sensitivity and specificity.

		True disease status		
		Present	Absent	
Test results	Present	a (True-positives)	b (False-positives)	$a + b$
	Absent	c (False-negatives)	d (True-negatives)	$c + d$
		$a + c$	$b + d$	

Sensitivity = $a / (a + c)$
Specificity = $d / (b + d)$

growing interest in measurement and complex nosology. In statistics, techniques of multivariate analysis are being adapted increasingly well to the developmental perspective. Developments in the field of physiological and biological measurement, including nearly noninvasive assessments of DNA, hormones, and brain structure and functioning, have led to concepts like "molecular epidemiology," which will lead to vast increases in knowledge about how psychological functioning affects diseases across the spectrum of mental and physical illness. Many of these measures are efficient enough to be applied in the context of a large field survey. In a few decades, the concept of the "mind–body split" may be an anachronism. Finally, the increasing use of laptop computers for assistance in assessment of complex human behaviors and traits will increase the utility of questionnaires and interview data. For all these reasons psychologists should look forward to increasingly productive collaborations in the field of epidemiology.

ACKNOWLEDGMENTS

Production of this paper was supported by NIMH grants 47447, and by the Oregon Social Learning Center. The author is grateful to Nina Schooler and Ray Lorion for comments on early drafts.

3.05.9 REFERENCES

Acheson, E. D., Baldwin, J. A., & Graham, W. J. (1987). *Textbook of medical record linkage*. New York: Oxford University Press.

American Psychiatric Association (1994). *Diagnostic and statistical manual of mental disorders* (4th ed.). Washington, DC: Author.

Anthony, J. C., Eaton, W. W., & Henderson, A. S. (1995). Introduction: Psychiatric epidemiology (Special Issue of Epidemiologic Reviews). *Epidemiologic Reviews, 17*(1), 1–8.

Anthony, J. C., Folstein, M. F., Romanoski, A., Von Korff, M., Nestadt, G., Chahal, R., Merchant, A., Brown, C. H., Shapiro, S., Kramer, M., & Gruenberg, E.

M. (1985). Comparison of the lay Diagnostic Interview Schedule and a standardized psychiatric diagnosis: Experience in Eastern Baltimore. *Archives of General Psychiatry, 42*, 667–675.

Berkson, J. (1946). Limitations of the application of fourfold table analysis to hospital data. *Biometrics, 2*, 47–53.

Bishop, Y. M. M., Fienberg, S. E., & Holland, P. W. (1975). *Discrete multivariate analysis: Theory and practice*. Cambridge, MA: MIT Press.

Blalock, H. M. (1979). *Social statistics* (2nd ed.). New York: McGraw-Hill.

Brown, G. W., Birley, J. L. T., & Wing, J. K. (1972). Influence of family life on the course of schizophrenic disorders: a replication. *British Journal of Psychiatry, 121*, 241–258.

Brown, G. W., & Harris, T. (1978). *The social origins of depression: A study of psychiatric disorder in women*. London: Tavistock.

Butler, N. R., & Alberman, E. D. (1969). *Perinatal Problems: The Second Report of the 1958 British Perinatal Survey*. Edinburgh, Scotland: Livingstone.

Campbell, D. T., & Stanley, J. C. (1971). *Experimental and Quasi-Experimental Designs for Research*. Chicago: Rand McNally.

Cohen, P., & Cohen, J. (1984). The Clinician's Illusion. *Archives of General Psychiatry, 41*, 1178–1182.

Commission on Chronic Illness (1957). *Chronic illness in the United States*. Cambridge, MA: Harvard University Press.

Cooper, B., & Morgan, H. G. (1973). *Epidemiological psychiatry*. Springfield, IL: Charles C. Thomas.

Cross-National Collaborative Group (1992). The changing rate of major depression: cross-national comparisons. *Journal of the American Medical Association, 268*, 3098–3105.

Crow, T. J., Done, D. J., & Sacker, A. (1996). Birth cohort study of the antecedents of psychosis: Ontogeny as witness to phylogenetic origins. In H. Hafner & W. F. Gattaz (Eds.), *Search for the causes of schizophrenia* (Vol. 3, pp. 3–20). Heidelberg, Germany: Springer.

Done, D. J., Johnstone E. C., Frith, C. D., et al. (1991). Complications of pregnancy and delivery in relation to psychosis in adult life: data from the British perinatal mortality survey sample. *British Medical Journal, 302*, 1576–1580.

Eaton, W. W. (1994). The NIMH epidemiologic catchment area program: Implementation and major findings. *International Journal of Methods in Psychiatric Research, 4*, 103–112.

Eaton, W. W. (1995). Studying the natural history of psychopathology. In M. Tsuang, M. Tohen, & G. Zahner (Eds.), *Textbook in psychiatric epidemiology* (pp. 157–177). New York: Wiley Lisa, Inc.

Eaton, W. W., Anthony, J. C., Tepper, S., & Dryman, A. (1992). Psychopathology and Attrition in the Epidemiologic Catchment Area Surveys. *American Journal of Epidemiology, 135,* 1051–1059.

Eaton, W. W., Badawi, M., & Melton, B. (1995). Prodromes and precursors: Epidemiologic data for primary prevention of disorders with slow onset. *American Journal of Psychiatry, 152*(7), 967–972.

Eaton, W. W., Holzer, C. E., Von Korff, M., Anthony, J. C., Helzer, J. E., George, L., Burnam, A., Boyd, J. H., Kessler, L. G., & Locke, B. Z. (1984). The design of the Epidemiologic Catchment Area surveys: the control and measurement of error. *Archives of General Psychiatry, 41,* 942–948.

Eaton, W. W., & Kessler, L. G. (1981). Rates of symptoms of depression in a national sample. *American Journal of Epidemiology, 114,* 528–538.

Eaton, W. W., Kramer, M., Anthony, J. C., Chee, E. M. L., & Shapiro, S. (1989). Conceptual and methodological problems in estimation of the incidence of mental disorders from field survey data. In B. Cooper & T. Helgason (Eds.), *Epidemiology and the prevention of mental disorders* (pp. 108–127). London: Routledge.

Eaton, W. W., & McLeod, J. (1984). Consumption of coffee or tea and symptoms of anxiety. *American Journal of Public Health, 74,* 66–68.

Eaton, W. W., & Muntaner, C. (1996). Socioeconomic stratification and mental disorder. In A. V. Horwitz & T. L. Scheid (Eds.), *Sociology of mental health and illness.* New York: Cambridge University Press.

Eaton, W. W., Regier, D. A., Locke, B. Z., & Taube, C. A. (1981). The Epidemiologic Catchment Area Program of the National Institute of Mental Health. *Public Health Report 96,* 319–325.

Eaton, W. W., Weissman, M. M., Anthony, J. C., Robins, L. N., Blazer, D. G., & Karno, M. (1985). Problems in the definition and measurement of prevalence and incidence of psychiatric disorders. In W. W. Eaton & L. G. Kessler (Eds.), *Epidemiologic Field Methods in Psychiatry: The NIMH Epidemiologic Catchment Area Program* (pp. 311–326). Orlando, FL: Academic Press.

Farquhar, J. W., Fortmann, S. P., Flora, J. A., Taylor, C. B., Haskell, W. L., Williams, P. T., Maccoby, N., & Wood, P. D. (1990). Effects of communitywide education on cardiovascular disease risk factors: The Stanford Five-City Project. *Journal of the American Medical Association, 264*(3), 359–365.

Fitti, J. E., & Kovar, M. G. (1987). *The Supplement on Aging to the 1984 National Health Interview Survey. Vital and Health Statistics.* Washington, DC: Government Printing Office.

Fleiss, J. L. (1981). *Statistical methods for rates and proportions* (2nd ed.). New York: Wiley.

Foege, W. H. (1996). Alexander D. Langmuir: His impact on public health. *American Journal of Epidemiology, 144*(8) (Suppl.), S11–S15.

Gordon, R. (1983). An operational classification of disease prevention. *Public Health Reports, 98,* 107–109.

Herbst, A. L., Ulfelder, H., & Poskanzer, D. C. (1971). Adenocarcinoma of the vagina. Association of maternal stilbestrol therapy with tumor appearance in young women. *The New England Journal of Medicine, 284*(16), 878–881.

Kellam, S. G., & Werthamer-Larsson, L. (1986). Developmental epidemiology: a basis for prevention. In M. Kessler & S. E. Goldston (Eds.), *A Decade of Progress in Primary Prevention* (pp. 154–180). Hanover, NH: University Press of New England.

Kellam, S. G., Rebok, G. W., Ialongo, N., & Mayer L.S. (1994). The course and malleability of aggressive behavior from early first grade into middle school: Results of a developmental epidemiologically-based preventive trail. *Journal of Child Psychology and Psychiatry, 35*(2), 259–281.

Kessler, R. C., McGonagle, K. A., Zhao, S., Nelson, C. B., Hughes, M., Eshelman, S., Wittchen, H., & Kendler, K. S. (1994). Lifetime and 12-month prevalence of *DSM-III-R* psychiatric disorders in the United States. *Archives of General Psychiatry, 51,* 8–19.

Kety, S. S., Rosenthal, D., Wender, P. H., Schulsinger, F., & Jacobsen, B. (1975). Mental illness in the biological and adoptive families of adopted individuals who have become schizophrenic: a preliminary report based on psychiatric interviews. In R. R. Fieve, D. Rosenthal, & H. Brill (Eds.), *Genetic Research in Psychiatry* (pp. 147–165). Baltimore, MD: Johns Hopkins University Press.

Kleinbaum, D. G., Kupper, L. L., & Morgenstern, H. (1982). *Epidemiologic Research. Principles and Quantitative Methods.* Belmont, CA: Lifetime Learning.

Klerman, G. L., & Weissman, M. M. (1989). Increasing rates of depression. *JAMA, 261,* 2229–2235.

Kovar, M. (1992). *The Longitudinal Study of Aging: 1984–90.* Hyattsville, MD: US Department of Health and Human Services.

Kramer, M. (1957). A discussion of the concepts of incidence and prevalence as related to epidemiologic studies of mental disorders. *American Journal of Public Health & Nation's Health, 47*(7), 826–840.

Kramer, M. (1969). *Applications of Mental Health Statistics: Uses in mental health programmes of statistics derived from psychiatric services and selected vital and morbidity records.* Geneva: World Health Organization.

Kramer, M., Von Korff, M., & Kessler, L. (1980). The lifetime prevalence of mental disorders: estimation, uses and limitations. *Psychological Medicine, 10,* 429–435.

Lawless, J. F. (1982). *Statistical models and methods for lifetime data* (Wiley Series in Probability and Mathematical Statistics). New York: Wiley.

Lilienfeld, A., & Lilienfeld, D. (1980). *Foundations of epidemiology.* New York: Oxford University Press.

Lilienfeld, D. E., & Stolley, P. D. (1994). *Foundations of epidemiology.* New York: Oxford University Press.

Loffler, W., Hafner, H., Fatkenheuer, B., Maurer, K., Riecher-Rossler, A., Lutzhoft, J., Skadhede, S., Munk-Jorgensen, P., & Stromgren, E. (1994). Validation of Danish case register diagnosis for schizophrenia. *Acta Psychiatrica Scandinavica, 90,* 196–203.

Mausner, J. S., & Kramer, S. (1985). *Mausner & Bahn epidemiology: An introductory text* (2nd ed.). Philadelphia: Saunders.

Meltzer, H., Gill, B., Petticrew, M., & Hinds, K. (1995a). *Physical complaints, service use and treatment of adults with psychiatric disorders.* London: Her Majesty's Stationery Office.

Meltzer, H., Gill, B., Petticrew, M., & Hinds, K. (1995b). *Prevalence of psychiatric morbidity among adults living in private households.* London: Her Majesty's Stationery Office.

Morris, J. N. (1975). *Use of epidemiology* (3rd ed.). Edinburgh: Churchill Livingstone.

Mortensen, P. B. (1995). The untapped potential of case registers and record-linkage studies in psychiatric epidemiology. *Epidemiologic Reviews, 17*(1), 205–209.

Mrazek, P. J., & Haggerty, R. J. (1994). *Reducing risks for mental disorders.* Washington, DC: National Academy Press.

Munson, M. L., Orvaschel, H., Skinner, E. A., Goldring, E., Pennybacker, M., & Timbers, D. M. (1985). Interviewers: Characteristics, training and field work. In W. W. Eaton & L. G. Kessler (Eds.), *Epidemiologic Field Methods in Psychiatry: The NIMH Epidemiologic Catchment Area Program* (pp. 69–83). Orlando, FL: Academic Press.

Murphy, J. M., Berwick, D. M., Weinstein, M. C., Borus, J. F., Budman, S. H., & Klerman, G. L. (1987). Performance of Screening and Diagnostic Tests: Application of receiver operating characteristic analysis. *Archives of General Psychiatry, 44,* 550–555.

Robins, L. N., Helzer, J. E., Croughan, J., & Ratcliff, K. S. (1981). National Institute of Mental Health Diagnostic Interview Schedule: Its history, characteristics, and validity. *Archives of General Psychiatry, 38,* 381–389.

Robins, L. N., Helzer, J. E., Weissman, M. M., Orvaschel, H., Gruenberg, E. M., Burke, J. D., & Regier, D. A. (1984). Lifetime prevalence of specific psychiatric disorders in three sites. *Archives of General Psychiatry, 41,* 949–958.

Robins, L. N., & Regier, D. A. (Eds.) (1991). *Psychiatric disorders in America: The epidemiologic catchment area study.* New York: Free Press.

Rogan, W. J., & Gladen, B. (1978). Estimating Prevalence from the Results of a Screening Test. *American Journal of Epidemiology, 107,* 71–76.

Sacker, A., Done, J., Crow, T. J., & Golding, J. (1995). Antecedents of schizophrenia and affective illness obstetric complications. *British Journal of Psychiatry, 166,* 734–741.

Schlesselman, J. J. (1982). *Case–control studies: Design, conduct, analysis.* New York: Oxford University Press.

Shapiro, S., Skinner, E. A., Kessler, L. G., Von Korff, M., German, P. S., Tischler, G. L., Leaf, P. J., Benham, L., Cottler, L., & Regier, D. A. (1984). Utilization of health and mental health services, three epidemiologic catchment area sites. *Archives of General Psychiatry, 41,* 971–978.

Simon, G. E., & Vor Korff, M. (1995). Recall of Psychiatric History in Cross-sectional Surveys: Implications for Epidemiologic Research. *Epidemiologic Reviews, 17*(1), 221–227.

Sudman, S. (1976). *Applied sampling.* New York: Academic Press.

ten Horn, G. H., Giel, R., Gulbinat, W. H., & Henderson, J. H. (Eds.) (1986). *Psychiatric case registers in public health—A worldwide inventory 1960–1985.* Amsterdam: Elsevier Science.

Tsuang, M., Tohen, M., & Zahner, G. (1995). *Textbook in psychiatric epidemiology.* New York: Wiley-Liss.

Tyrer, P. (1985). Neurosis divisible? *Lancet, 1,* 685–688.

Von Korff, M., Cottler, L., George, L. K., Eaton, W. W., Leaf, P. J., & Burnam, A. (1985). Nonresponse and nonresponse bias in the ECA surveys. In W. W. Eaton & L. G. Kessler (Eds.), *Epidemiologic field methods in psychiatry: The NIMH Epidemiologic Catchment Area Program* (pp. 85–98). Orlando, FL: Academic Press.

Wynder, E. L. (1994). Studies in mechanism and prevention: Striking a proper balance. *American Journal of Epidemiology, 139*(6), 547–549.

3.06
Qualitative and Discourse Analysis

JONATHAN A. POTTER
Loughborough University, UK

3.06.1 INTRODUCTION: QUALITATIVE RESEARCH IN CONTEXT

For many researchers the words "qualitative method" spell out psychology's most notorious oxymoron. If there is one thing that qualitative methods are commonly thought to lack it is precisely an adequate methodic way of arriving at findings. Indeed, for much of the twentieth century quantification has been taken as the principle marker of the boundary between a mature scientific psychology and common-sense, intuitive approaches. Since the late 1980s, however, there has been a remarkable increase in interest in qualitative research in psychology. This partly reflects a broader turn to qualitative research across the social sciences, although qualitative research of one kind or another has long been an established feature of disciplines such as education, sociology, and, most prominently, anthropology.

In psychology there is a handbook of qualitative research (Richardson, 1996) as well as a range of volumes and special journal issues whose major focus is on developing qualitative approaches to psychological problems (Antaki, 1988; Bannister, Burman, Parker, Taylor, & Tyndall, 1994; Henwood & Parker, 1995; Henwood & Nicolson, 1995; Smith, Harré, & van Langenhove, 1995). Psychology methods books and collections are increasingly serving up qualitative methods to accompany the more usual diet of experiments, questionnaires, and surveys. At the same time, an increasing permeability of boundaries between the social sciences has provided the environment for a range of trans-disciplinary qualitative methods books including a useful doorstop-sized handbook (Denzin & Lincoln, 1994) and varied edited and authored works (Bogdan & Taylor, 1975; Bryman & Burgess, 1994; Coffey & Atkinson, 1996; Gilbert, 1993; Lofland & Lofland, 1984; Miles & Huberman, 1994; Miller & Dingwall, 1997; Silverman, 1993, 1997a). These general qualitative works are complemented by a mushrooming range of books and articles devoted to specific methods and approaches.

Why has there been this increase in interest in qualitative research? Three speculations are proferred. First, there is a widespread sense that traditional psychological methods have not proved successful in providing major advances in the understanding of human life. Despite regular promissory notes, psychology seems to offer no earth-moving equivalent of the transistor, of general relativity, or of molecular genetics. Second, as is discussed below, views of science have changed radically since the 1950s, making it much harder to paint qualitative researchers, as either antiscientific extremists or merely sloppy humanists. Third, psychology is no longer as insulated from other social sciences as it has been in the past. Of course, for much of its twentieth century existence psychology has been invigorated by infusions from other sciences such as physiology and linguistics. However, in recent years there has been increasing exchange with disciplines where qualitative methods have been more established such as sociology and anthropology. This is reflected in contemporary theoretical developments such as constructionism (Gergen, 1994) and poststructuralism (Henriques, Hollway, Irwin, Venn, & Walkerdine, 1984) that have swept right across the human sciences.

This is, then, an exciting time for qualitative researchers, with new work and new opportunities of all kinds. Yet it should also be emphasised that qualitative research in psychology is in a chaotic state, with a muddle of inconsistent questions and approaches being blended together. Much poor work has involved taking questions formulated in the metaphysics of experimental psychology and attempting to plug them into one or more qualitative methods. At its worst such research peddles unsystematic and untheorized speculations about the influences on some piece of behavior which are backed up with two or three quotes from an interview transcript. This expanding literature and variable quality creates some problems for the production of a useful overview. This chapter selects what are seen as the most coherent and successful qualitative approaches from a range of possibilities, as well as focusing on those approaches which are being used, and have prospects for success, in clinical settings. A range of references is provided for those who wish to follow up alternative methods.

3.06.1.1 Historical Moments in Qualitative Research in Clinical Settings

In one sense a large proportion of twentieth century clinical therapeutic practice was based on qualitative methods. The process of conducting some kind of therapy or counseling with clients and then writing them up as case histories, or using them as the basis for inferences about aspects of the psyche, behavior, or cognitive processes, has been a commonplace of clinical work. Freud's use of case histories in the development of psychoanalytic thinking is probably the most influential. Although it is an approach to clinical knowledge that overwhelmingly eschews quantification, it is hard to say much about its methodic basis. For good or bad, it is dependent on the unformulated skills and intuitions of the therapist/researcher. In the hands of someone as brilliant as Freud the result can be extraordinary; elsewhere the product has often been merely ordinary. The problem for the readers of such research is that they can do little except either take it on trust or disagree. The process through which certain claims are established is not open to scrutiny. However, Freud's study of the case of Little Hans is exceptional in this regard, and so it is briefly worth considering (see Billig, 1998).

Although Freud initially based his arguments for the existence of the Oedipus complex on the interpretation of what patients told him in the course of therapy sessions, he attempted, unusually, to support this part of psychoanalytic theory with more direct evidence. He asked some of his followers to collect observations from their own children. The music critic Max Graf was most helpful in this regard and presented Freud with copious notes on conversations between his son, Hans, and other family members, as well as descriptions of dreams he had recounted. The published case history (Freud, 1977 [1909]) contains more than 70 pages of reports about Hans which Freud describes as reproduced "just as I received them" without "conventional emendations" (1977, pp. 170). Here is an example:

Another time he [Hans] was looking on intently while his mother undressed before going to bed. "What are you staring like that for?" she asked. *Hans*: "I was only looking to see if you'd got a widdler too." *Mother*: "Of course. Didn't you know that?" *Hans*: "No. I thought you were so big you'd have a widdler like a horse." (1977, p. 173)

Freud's fascinating materials and striking interpretations beg many of the questions that have been central to qualitative research ever since. For example, what is the role of Max Graf's expectations (he was already an advocate of Freud's theories) in his selection and rendering of conversations with Hans? How closely do the extracts capture the actual interactions (including the emphasis, nonvocal elements, and so on)? What procedure did Freud use to select the examples that were reproduced from the full corpus? And, most importantly, what is the basis of Freud's interpretations? His inter-

pretations are strongly derived from his theory, as is shown by his willingness to straightforwardly rework the overt sense of the records. Take this example:

Hans (aged four and a half) was again watching his little sister being given her bath, when he began laughing. On being asked why he was laughing, he replied. "I'm laughing at Hanna's widdler." "Why?" "Because her widdler's so lovely."
Of course his answer was a disingenuous one. In reality her widdler had seemed to him funny. Moreover, this is the first time he has recognized in this way the distinction between male and female genitals instead of denying it. (1977, p. 184)

Note the way Graf here, and implicitly Freud in his text, treat the laughter as the real indicator of Hans understanding of events, and his overt claim to find his sister's "widdler" lovely as a form of dissembling. Hans is not delighted by the appearance of his sister's genitals but is amused, in line with psychoanalytic theory, by their difference from his own. Again, the issue of how to treat the sense of records of interaction, and what interpretations should be made from them to things going on elsewhere such as actions or cognitions, is a fundamental one in qualitative research (Silverman, 1993).

Some 40 years later another of clinical psychology's great figures, Carl Rogers, advocated the use of newly developed recording technology to study the use of language in psychotherapy itself, with the aim of understanding and improving therapeutic skills. For him such recordings offered "the first opportunity for an adequate study of counseling and therapeutic procedures, based on thoroughly objective data" (Rogers, 1942, p. 433). Rogers envisaged using such recordings in the development of a scale to differentiate the styles of different counselors and studies of the patterns of interaction; for example, "what type of counselor statement is most likely to be followed by statements of the client's feeling about himself?" (1942, p. 434).

Rogers' emphasis on the virtue of recordings was followed up in two major "microscopic" studies of psychotherapeutic discourse. The first by Pettinger, Hockett, and Danehy (1960) focused on the initial portion of an initial interview. A typical page of their study has just a few words of transcript coupled with an extended discussion of their sense. Much of the focus was on the prosodic cues—the intonation and stress—provided in the interview and their contextual significance. Prosody is, of course, a feature of interaction which is almost impossible to reliably capture in *post hoc* notes made by key informants and so highlights the virtue of the new technology. A second study by Labov and Fanshell (1977) also focused on the opening stages of a therapy session, in this case five episodes of interaction from the first 15 minutes of a psychoanalytic therapy session with Rhoda, a 19-year-old girl with a history of anorexia nervosa.

The classic example of ethnographic work in the history of clinical psychology is Goffman's study of the everyday life of a mental hospital published under the title *Asylums* (1961). It is worth noting that although Goffman was a sociologist, the various essays that make up *Asylums* were initially published in psychiatry journals. Rather than utilize tape recording technology to capture the minutiae of some social setting, Goffman used an ethnographic approach. He spent a year working ostensibly as an assistant to the athletic director of a large mental hospital, interacting with patients and attempting to build up an account of the institution as viewed by the patients. His justification for working in this way is instructive for how the strengths and weaknesses of qualitative work have been conceptualized:

> Desiring to obtain ethnographic detail regarding selected aspects of patient social life, I did not employ usual kinds of measurements and controls. I assumed that the role and time required to gather statistical evidence for a few statements would preclude my gathering data on the tissue and fabric of patient life. (1961, p. 8)

As an ethnographic observer, he developed an understanding of the local culture and customs of the hospital by taking part himself. He used the competence generated in this way as the basis for his writing about the life and social organization in a large mental hospital.

3.06.1.2 Background Issues

Before embarking on a detailed overview of some contemporary qualitative approaches to clinical topics there are some background issues that are worth commenting on, as they will help make sense of the aims and development of qualitative approaches. In some cases it is necessary to address issues that have been a long-standing source of confusion where psychologists have discussed the use of qualitative methods.

3.06.1.2.1 *Philosophy, sociology, and changing conceptions of science*

As noted above, the development of qualitative work in psychology has been facilitated by the more sophisticated understanding of the

nature of science provided by philosophers and sociologists since the 1970s. The image of the lone scientist harvesting facts, whose truth is warranted through the cast-iron criterion of replication, has intermittently been wheeled on to defend supposedly scientific psychology against a range of apparently sloppier alternatives. However, this image now looks less than substantial (see Chalmers, 1992; Potter, 1996a; Woolgar, 1988).

The bottom-line status of scientific observation has been undermined by a combination of philosophical analyses and sociological case studies. Philosophers have highlighted the logical relationships between observation statements and theoretical notions (Hesse, 1974; Kuhn, 1962; Popper, 1959). Their argument is that even the simplest of scientific descriptions is dependent on a whole variety of theoretical assumptions. Sociologists have supplemented these insights with studies of the way notions of observations are used in different scientific fields. For example, Lynch (1994) notes the way the term observation is used in astronomy as a loose device for collecting together a range of actions such as setting up the telescope, attaching sensors to it, building up traces on an oscilloscope, converting these into a chart and canvassing the support of colleagues. Knorr Cetina (1997) documents the different notions of observation that appear in different scientific specialities, suggesting that high energy physicists and molecular biologists, for example, work with such strikingly different notions of what is empirical that they are best conceived of as members of entirely different epistemic cultures.

The idea that experimental replication can work as a hard criterion for the adequacy of any particular set of research findings has been shown to be too simple by a range of sociological studies of replication in different fields (Collins, 1981). For example, Collins (1985) has shown that the achievement of a successful replication is closely tied to the conception of what counts as a competent experiment in the first place—and this itself was often as much a focus of controversy as the phenomenon itself. In a study of gravity wave researchers, Collins found that those scientists who believed in gravity waves tended to treat replications that claimed to find them as competent and replications that failed to find them as incompetent. The reverse pattern was true of nonbelievers. What this meant was that replication did not stand outside the controversy as a neutral arbiter of the outcome, but was as much part of the controversy as everything else.

Philosophical and sociological analysis has also shown that the idea that a crucial experiment can be performed which will force the abandonment of one theory and demonstrate the correctness of another is largely mythical (Lakatos, 1970; Collins & Pinch, 1993). Indeed, historical studies suggest that so-called crucial experiments are not merely insufficient to effect the shift from one theory to another, they are often performed, or at least constructed as crucial, after the shift to provide illustration and legitimation (Kuhn, 1977).

Let us be clear at this point. This research does not show that careful observation, skilful replication, and theoretically sophisticated experiments are not important in science. Rather, the point is that none of these things are bottom-line guarantees of scientific progress. Moreover, these sociological studies have suggested that all these features of science are embedded in, and inextricable from, its communal practices. Their sense is developed and negotiated in particular contexts in accordance with *ad hoc* criteria and a wide range of craft skills which are extremely hard to formulate in an explicit manner (Knorr Cetina, 1995; Latour & Woolgar, 1986). The message taken from this now very large body of work (see Jasanoff, Markle, Pinch, & Petersen, 1995) is not that psychologists must adopt qualitative methods, or that qualitative methods will necessarily be any better than the quantitative methods that they may replace or supplement; it is that those psychologists who have argued against the adoption of such methods on the principle that they are unscientific are uninformed about the nature of science.

3.06.1.2.2 *Investigatory procedures vs. justificatory rhetoric*

There are a number of basic linguistic and metatheoretical difficulties in writing about qualitative methods for psychologists. Our terminology for methodological discussion—reliability, validity, sampling, factors, variance, hypothesis testing, and so on—has grown up with the development of quantitative research using experiments and surveys. The language has become so taken-for-granted that it is difficult to avoid treating it as obvious and natural. However, it is a language that is hard to disentangle from a range of metatheoretical assumptions about the nature of behavior and processes of interaction. Traditional psychology has become closely wedded to a picture of factors and outcomes which, in turn, cohabits with the multivariate statistics which are omnipresent where data is analyzed. For some forms of qualitative research, particularly most discourse and ethnographic work, such a picture is inappropriate. This does not mean

that such research is incoherent or unscientific, merely that it should not be construed and evaluated using the family of concepts whose home is experimental journal articles. Likewise the psychological model of hypothesis testing is just one available across the natural and human sciences. Qualitative research that utilizes theoretically guided induction, or tries to give a systematic description of some social realm, should not be criticized on the grounds that it is unscientific, let alone illegitimate. Ultimately, the only consistent bottom line for the production of excellent qualitative work is excellent scholarship (Billig, 1988).

Another difference between traditional quantitative and qualitative work is that in the traditional work the justification of research findings is often taken to be equivalent to the complete and correct carrying out of a set of codified procedures. Indeed, methods books are often written as if they were compendia of recipes for achieving adequate knowledge. Sampling, operationalization of variables, statistical tests, and interpretation of significance levels are discussed with the aid of tree diagrams and flow charts intended to lead the apprentice researcher to the correct conclusion. In one sense, much qualitative work is very different to this, with the procedures for justifying the research claims being very different to the procedures for producing the work. Thus, the manner in which a researcher arrives at some claims about the various functions of "mm hm's" in psychiatric intake interviews, say, may be rather different from the manner in which they justify the adequacy of the analysis. Yet, in another sense the difference between qualitative and quantitative research is more apparent than real, for studies of the actual conduct of scientists following procedural rules of method show that such rules require a large amount of tacit knowledge to make them understandable and workable, and that they are often more of a rhetorical device used to persuade other scientists than an actual constraint on practice (Gilbert & Mulkay, 1984; Polyani, 1958). As Collins (1974) showed in an innovative ethnographic study, when a group of scientists wrote a paper offering the precise technical specification of how to make a new laser, the only people who were able to build a working laser of their own had actually seen one built; just reading the paper was not enough.

This presents something of a dilemma for anyone writing about qualitative methods. Should they write to help people conduct their research so as better to understand the world, or should they work to provide the sorts of formalized procedural rules that can be drawn on in the methods sections of articles to help persuade the psychologist reader? In practice, most writing does some of each. However, the difficulty that psychologists often report when attempting qualitative work is probably symptomatic of the failure to fully explicate the craft skills that underpin qualitative work.

3.06.1.2.3 Quality and quantity

There are different views on how absolute the quantity/quality divide is. Arguments at different levels of sophistication have been made for future integration of qualitative and quantitative research (Bryman, 1988; Silverman, 1993). It is undoubtedly the case that at times proponents of both quantitative and qualitative research have constructed black and white stereotypes with little attempt at dialog (although a rare debate about the relative virtues of quantitative and qualitative research on the specific topic of attitudes towards mental hospitalisation is revealing—Weinstein, 1979, 1980; Essex et al., 1980). It is suggested that quantification is perfectly appropriate in a range of situations, dependent on appropriate analytic and theoretical judgements.

In many other research situations the goal is not something that can be achieved through counting. For example, if the researcher is explicating the nature of "circular questioning" in Milan School Family Therapy, that goal is a prerequisite for a study which considers the statistical prevalence of such questioning. Moreover, there are arguments for being cautious about quantification when studying the sorts of discursive and interactional materials which have often been central to qualitative research because of distortions and information loss that can result (see Schegloff, 1993, and papers in Wieder, 1993). Some of the grounds for caution come from a range of qualitative studies of quantification in various clinical settings (Ashmore, Mulkay, & Pinch, 1989; Atkinson, 1978; Garfinkel, 1967a; Potter, Wetherell, & Chitty, 1991).

3.06.1.3 Qualitative Research and Theory

It is hard to overestimate how close the relationship is between the theories, methods, and questions used by psychologists. Theories specify different positions on cognition and behavior, different notions of science, different views of the role of action and discourse, different understandings of the role of social settings, and, most fundamentally, different objects for observation.

For both psychoanalytic theory and most of the mass of theories and perspectives that make up modern cognitivism the objects of observation are hypothetical mental entities (the Oedipus complex, attributional heuristics). Psychoanalytic researchers have generally preferred to engage in an interpretative exercise of reconstructing those entities from the talk of patients undergoing therapy. Cognitive psychologists have typically used some hypothetico-deductive procedure where predictions are checked in experiments which investigate, say, the attributional style of people classified as depressed. Note that in both of these cases they are using people's discourse—talk in the therapy session, written responses to a questionnaire—yet in neither case is the discourse as such of interest. In contrast, for researchers working with different perspectives such as social constructionism or discursive psychology, the talk or writing itself, and the practices of which it is part, is the central topic. For these researchers there is a need to use procedures which can make those practices available for study and allow their organization to be inspected and compared.

To take another example, behaviorist psychologists have done countless studies on the effects of particular regimes of reward and punishment on target behaviors such as compulsive hand washing. However, such studies are typically focused on outcomes and statistical associations, whereas a theoretical perspective such as symbolic interactionism or, to give a more psychological example, Vygotskyan activity theory, encourage a more ethnographic examination of the settings in which rewards are administered and of the sense that those behaviors have in their local context

Without trying to flesh out these examples in any detail, the important practical point they make is that it is a mistake to attempt simply to import a question which has been formulated in the problematics of one theoretical system, and attempt to answer it using a method developed for the problematics of another. The failure to properly conceptualize a research question that fits with the research method is a major source of confusion when psychologists start to use qualitative methods.

3.06.1.4 Boundaries of Qualitative Research and Coverage of the Current Chapter

What distinguishes qualitative research from quantitative? And what qualitative approaches are there? These questions are not as straightforward as they seem. In the past the qualitative/quantitative distinction has sometimes been treated as the equivalent of the distinction between research that produces objective and subjective knowledge—a distinction which makes little sense in the light of recent sociology and philosophy of science. Sometimes certain approaches using numbers have been treated as qualitative. For example, content analysis has occasionally been treated as a qualitative method because it is used to deal with "naturally occurring" objects such as diaries, novels, transcripts of meetings, and so on. Content analysis was meant to eliminate many of the potential "reactive" effects that bedevil social research and thereby avoid the problem in experimental and survey research, of how findings relate to what goes on in the real world; for these are records of (indeed, examples of) what is actually going on. However, in this chapter content analysis is treated as quantitative, and therefore outside the scope of this survey, on the grounds that it (i) transforms phenomena into numerical counts of one kind or another and (ii) typically attempts to statistically relate these counts to some broader factors or variables. For useful introductions to content analysis related to psychological topics see Holsti (1969) and Krippendorf (1980).

For similar reasons repertory grid analysis associated with personal construct theory, and the "Q" methodology developed by William Stephenson, have sometimes been treated as qualitative. The rationale for this was probably that they were often focused on understanding the reasoning or cognitive organization of single individuals rather than working exclusively from population statistics. However, as they involve quantitative manipulation of elicited responses from participants they will not be dealt with here. The ideographic/nomathetic distinction will be treated as orthogonal to the qualitative/quantitative one! For accessible introductions to these approaches, see Smith (1995) on repertory grid methods and Stainton Rogers (1995) on Q methodology.

In addition to these methods which are excluded as not properly qualitative, a wide range of methods have not been discussed which nevertheless satisfy the criterion of being at least minimally methodic and generally eschewing quantification. For simplicity, Table 1 lists nine methods or approaches which have been excluded, along with one or two references that would provide a good start point for any researcher who was interested in learning more about them. It would take some time to make explicit the reasons for excluding all of them. Generally, the problem is that they have not been, and are unlikely to be in the future, particularly useful for studying problems in the area of clinical psychology (e.g., focus groups—although, see Piercy & Nickerson, 1996). In some cases, the approaches are not coherent

enough to warrant discussion. In others, their central problematics are better addressed by the approaches that are discussed.

The most controversial exclusion is probably humanistic methods given that humanistic psychology developed in settings which had a broad emphasis on therapy and psychological well-being. It is suggested that the romanticism of much humanistic psychology is attractive, but ultimately unconvincing. However, it is often, quite legitimately, more concerned with developing participants' skills and sensitivity than developing propositional claims and arguments; as such it is often offering a set of techniques for expanding human potential rather than developing methods for research. Feminist methods are excluded, despite an appreciation of the importance of feminist issues in clinical settings, because the arguments for the existence of specifically feminist methods (as opposed to theories or arguments) are not convincing. This is particularly true where such claims give a major epistemological role for experience or intuition (Ellis, Kiesinger, & Tillmann-Healy, 1997). These are topics for decomposition and analysis rather than bottom-lines for knowledge. For some arguments in both directions on this topic see Gelsthorpe (1992), Hammersley (1992), Ramazanoglu (1992), and Wilkinson (1986).

Finally, it should be stressed that qualitative work is not seen as having some overall coherence. Quite the contrary, it is fragmented and of highly variable quality. Nor is some overall coherence seen as a desirable goal. Those workers who talk of a qualitative paradigm (Guba & Lincoln, 1994, Reason & Rowan, 1981) unhelpfully blur over a range of theoretical and metatheoretical differences (see Henwood & Pidgeon, 1994).

3.06.2 GROUNDED THEORY

Grounded theory has the most clear-cut origin of any of the approaches discussed here. The term was coined by two sociologists in an influential book: *The discovery of grounded theory* (Glaser & Strauss, 1967). Some of its key features and concerns were a product of its birthplace within sociology, where it was developed to counter what the authors saw as a preoccupation, on the one hand, with abstract grand theories and, on the other, with testing those theories through large scale quantitative studies. Grounded theory was intended to link theoretical developments (conceived as plausible relations among concepts and sets of concepts—Strauss & Corbin, 1994) more closely to the particulars of settings, to ground

Table 1   Varieties of qualitative research not covered.

Qualitative research method	Source
Action research	Argyris, Putnam, & Smith, 1985, Whyte, 1991
Documentary studies	Hodder, 1994, Scott, 1990
Ethogenics	Harré, 1992
Feminist approaches	Olesen, 1994, Reinharz, 1992
Focus groups	Krueger, 1988, Morgan, 1997
Humanistic, participative research	Reason & Rowan, 1981, Reason & Heron, 1995
Life histories	Plummer, 1995, Smith, 1994
Role play	Yardley, 1995
Semiotics	Manning & Cullum-Swan, 1994

middle range theories in actual qualitative data rather than to start from preconceived hypotheses. It is important to stress that grounded theory is not a theory as such, rather it is an approach to theorising about data in any domain. Moreover, since its inception in the 1960s, work on the theory ladenness of data has made the idea of "grounding" theory increasingly problematic.

Much grounded theory research has been done outside of psychology; however, psychologists have become increasingly interested in the approach in general (Charmaz, 1995; Henwood and Pidgeon, 1995; Pidgeon, 1996; Pidgeon and Henwood, 1996; Rennie, Phillips & Quartaro, 1988), and have carried out specific studies in health (Charmaz, 1991, 1994) and clinical (Clegg, Standen, & Jones, 1996) settings.

3.06.2.1 Questions

Grounded theory is designed to be usable with a very wide range of research questions and in the context of a variety of metatheoretical approaches. Rather like the statistical analyses that psychologists are more familiar with, it deals with patterns and relationships. However, these are not relationships between numbers but between ideas or categories of things, and the relationships can take a range of different forms. In some respects the procedures in grounded theory are like the operation of a sophisticated filing system where entries are cross-referenced and categorized in a range of different ways. Indeed, this is one qualitative approach that can be effectively helped by the use of computer packages such as NUDIST, which was itself developed to address grounded theory notions.

Grounded theory has proved particularly appropriate for studying people's understandings of the world and how these are related to their social context. For example, Turner (1994; Turner & Pidgeon, 1997) has used grounded theory to attempt to explain the origins of

manmade disasters like fires and industrial accidents; Charmaz (1991) has studied the various facets that make up people's experience of chronic illness; Clegg, Standen, and Jones (1996) focused on the staff members' understanding of their relationship with adults with profound learning disabilities. In each case, a major concern was to incorporate the perspectives of the actors as they construct their particular social worlds. Grounded theory methods can help explicate the relation of actions to settings (how does the behavior of key personnel in the evolution of a major fire follow from their individual understanding of events and physical positioning?); it can be used for developing typologies of relevant phenomena (in what different ways do sufferers of chronic illness conceptualize their problem?); and it can help identify patterns in complex systems (how does the information flowing between social actors help explain the development of a laboratory smallpox outbreak?).

Like most of the qualitative approaches discussed here, grounded theory is not well suited to the kinds of hypothesis testing and outcome evaluation that have traditionally been grist to the mill of clinical psychology, because of its open-ended and inductive nature. Although the researcher is likely to come to a topic with a range of more or less explicit ideas, questions, and theories, it is not necessary for any or all of these to be formally stated before research gets under way. The approach can start with a specific problem or it may be more directed at making sense of an experience or setting.

Grounded theory can be applied to a range of different textual materials such as documents, interview transcripts and records of interaction, and this makes it particularly suitable for certain kinds of questions. It can deal with records which exist prior to the research and it can deal with materials specifically collected. The processes of coding allow quite large amounts of material to be dealt with. For example, while Turner studied a single (lengthy) official report of a major fire in a holiday complex, Charmaz studied 180 interviews with 90 different people with chronic illnesses. The requirement is only that the material can be coded.

3.06.2.2 Procedures

The procedures for conducting grounded theory work are straightforward to describe, if less so to follow in practice. Pidgeon and Henwood (1996, p. 88) provide a useful diagram to explicate the process (Figure 1).

3.06.2.2.1 Materials

In line with the general emphasis on participants' perspectives and on understanding patterns of relationships, researchers often attempt to obtain rich materials such as documents and conversational, semistructured interviews. These may be supplemented by participant observation in the research domain, generating fieldnotes which can be added to other data sets or simply used to improve the researcher's understanding so they can better deal with the other materials.

After data is collected and stored the intensive process that is most characteristic of grounded theory is performed. This involves coding the data, refining the coding and identifying links between categories, and writing "memos" which start to capture theoretical concepts and relationships.

3.06.2.2.2 Coding

Different grounded theory researchers approach coding in different ways. For example, it can involve generating index cards or making annotations next to the relevant text. The researcher works through the text line by line, or paragraph by paragraph, labeling the key concepts that appear. Charmaz (1995, p. 38)

suggests a series of specific questions that are useful for picking out the key concepts:
(i) What is going on?
(ii) What are the people doing?
(iii) What is the person saying?
(iv) What do these actions and statements take for granted?
(v) How do structure and context serve to support, maintain, impede, or change these actions and statements?
More broadly, Pidgeon and Henwood suggest that this phase of coding is answering the question: "what categories or labels do I need in order to account for what is of importance to me in this paragraph?" (1996, p. 92).

Such coding is intensive and time consuming. For example, Table 2 shows an example by Charmaz of line-by-line coding of just a brief fragment of one of her 180 interviews. Note the way that the interview fragment is coded under a number of different topics. There is no requirement in grounded theory that categories apply exclusively.

3.06.2.2.3 Method of constant comparison

Coding is not merely a matter of carefully reading and labeling the materials. As the coding continues the researcher will be starting to identify categories that are interesting or relevant to the research questions. They will refine their indexing system by focused coding which will pick out all the instances from the data coded as, for example "avoiding disclosure." When such a collection has been produced the researcher can focus on the differences in the use of this category according to the setting or the actors involved. This is what grounded theorists refer to as the "method of constant comparison." In the course of such comparisons the category system may be reworked; some categories will be merged together and others will be broken up, as the close reading of the data allows an increasingly refined understanding.

Table 2 Line-by-line coding.

Coding	Interview
Shifting symptoms, having inconsistent days	If you have lupus, I mean one day it's my liver; one day it's my joints; one day it's my head, and
Interpreting images of self given by others	it's like people really think you're a hypochondriac if you keep complaining about
Avoiding disclosure	different ailments. . . . It's like you don't want to say anything because people are going to start
Predicting rejection	thinking, you know, "God, don't go near her,
Keeping others unaware	all she is—is complaining about this."

Source: Charmaz (1995, p. 39)

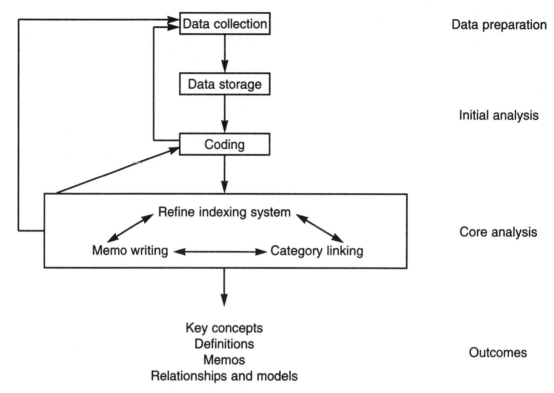

Figure 1   Procedures for conducting grounded theory research.

3.06.2.2.4 Memo writing

Throughout this stage of coding and comparison grounded theorists recommend what they call memo writing. That is, writing explicit notes on the assumptions that underly any particular coding. Memo writing is central to the process of building theoretical understandings from the categories, as it provides a bridge between the categorization of data and the writing up of the research. In addition to the process of refining categories, a further analytic task involves linking categories together. The goal here is to start to model relationships between categories. Indeed, one possibility may be the production of a diagram or flow chart which explicitly maps relationships.

As Figure 1 makes clear, these various elements in grounded theory analysis are not discrete stages. In the main phase of the analysis, refining the indexing system is intimately bound up with the linking of categories, and memo writing is likely to be an adjunct to both. Moreover, this analysis may lead the researcher back to the basic line-by-line coding, or even suggest the need to collect further material for analysis.

3.06.2.2.5 Validity

There is a sense in which the general methodological procedures of grounded theory are together designed to provide a level of validation as they force a thoroughgoing engagement with the research materials. Line-by-line coding, constant comparison, and memo writing are all intended to ensure that the theoretical claims made by the analyst are fully grounded in the data. That, after all, was the original key idea of grounded theory. However, some specific procedures of validation have been proposed.

Some grounded theorists have suggested that respondent validation could be used as a criterion. This involves the researcher taking back interpretations to the participants to see if they are accepted. The problem with such an approach is that participants may agree or disagree for a range of social reasons or they may not understand what is being asked of them. Other approaches to validation suggest that research should be generative, that is, facilitate further issues and questions; have rhetorical power, that is, prove effective in persuading others of its effectiveness; or that there could be an audit trail which would allow another researcher to check how the conclusions were reached (Henwood & Pidgeon, 1995; Lincoln & Guba, 1985).

3.06.2.3 Example: Clegg, Standen, and Jones (1996)

There is no example in clinical psychology of the sorts of full-scale grounded theory study that Charmaz (1991) conducted on the experience of illness or Glaser and Strauss (1968) carried out on hospital death. Nevertheless, a modest study by Clegg et al. (1996) of the relationships between staff members and adults with profound learning disabilities illustrates some of the potential of grounded theory for clinical work.

In line with the grounded theory emphasis on the value of comparison, 20 staff members from four different residential settings were recruited. Each member of staff was videotaped during eight sessions of interaction with a single client that they had known for over three months. Each staff member was subsequently interviewed about their work, their relationship with the client, a specific experience with the client, and their understanding of the client's view of the world. These conversational interviews were tape recorded and transcribed, and form the data for the major part of the study.

The study followed standard grounded theory procedures in performing a range of codings developing links between categories and building up theoretical notions from those codings. The range of different outcomes of the study is typical of grounded theory. In the first place, they identify four kinds of relationships that staff may have with clients: provider (where meeting of the client's needs is primary); meaning-maker (where making sense of the client's moods or gestures is primary); mutual (where shared experience and joy at the client's development is primary); companion (where merely being together is treated as satisfying). The authors go on to explore the way different settings and different client groups were characterized by different relationships. Finally, they propose that the analysis supports four propositions about staff–client relationships: some types of relationship are better than others (although this will vary with setting and client); staff see the balance of control in the relationship as central; families can facilitate relationships; professional networks create dilemmas.

3.06.2.4 Virtues and Limitations

Grounded theory has a range of virtues. It is flexible with respect to forms of data and can be applied to a wide range of questions in varied domains. Its procedures, when followed fully, force the researcher into a thorough engagement with the materials; it encourages a slow-motion reading of texts and transcripts that should avoid the common qualitative research trap of trawling a set of transcripts for quotes to illustrate preconceived ideas. It makes explicit some of the data management procedures that

are commonly left inexplicit in other qualitative approaches. The method is at its best where there is an issue that is tractable from a relatively common sense actor's perspective. Whether studying disasters, illness, or staff relationships, the theoretical notions developed are close to the everyday notions of the participants. This makes the work particularly suitable for policy implementation, for the categories and understandings of the theory are easily accessible to practitioners and policy makers.

Some problems and questions remain, however. First, although there is a repeated emphasis on theory—after all, it is in the very name of the method—the notion of theory is a rather limited one strongly influenced by the empiricist philosophy of science of the 1950s. The approach works well if theory is conceived in a limited manner as a pattern of relationships between categories, but less well if theories are conceived of as, say, models of underlying generative mechanisms (Harré, 1986).

Second, one of the claimed benefits of grounded theory work is that it works with the perspective of participants through its emphasis on accounts and reports. However, one of the risks of processes such as line-by-line coding is that it leads to a continual pressure to assign pieces of talk or elements of texts to discrete categories rather than seeing them as inextricably bound up with broader sequences of talk or broader textual narratives. Ironically this can mean that instead of staying with the understandings of the participants their words are assigned to categories provided by the analyst.

Third, grounded theorists have paid little attention to the sorts of problems in using textual data that ethnomethodologists and discourse analysts have emphasised (Atkinson, 1978; Gilbert & Mulkay, 1984; Silverman, 1993; Widdicombe & Wooffitt, 1995). For example, how far is the grounding derived not from theorizing but from reproducing common sense theories as if they were analytic conclusions? How far are Clegg's et al. (1996) staff participants, say, giving an accurate picture of their relationships with clients, and how far are they drawing on a range of ideas and notions to deal with problems and work up identities in the interview itself?

Some practitioners are grappling with these problems in a sophisticated manner (Pidgeon & Henwood, 1996). As yet there is not a large enough body of work with clinical materials to allow a full evaluation of the potential of this method. For more detailed coverage of grounded theory the reader should start with the excellent introductions by Pidgeon (1996) and Pidgeon and Henwood (1996); Charmaz (1991) provides a full scale research illustration of the potential of grounded theory; Rafuls and Moon (1996) discuss grounded theory in the context of family therapy; and, despite its age, Glaser and Strauss (1967) is still an informative basis for understanding the approach.

3.06.3 ETHNOGRAPHY AND PARTICIPANT OBSERVATION

Ethnography is not a specific method so much as a general approach which can involve a number of specific research techniques such as interviewing and participant observation. Indeed, this has been a source of some confusion as rather different work is described as ethnography in anthropology, sociology, and other disciplines such as education or management science. The central thrust of ethnographic research is to study people's activities in their natural settings. The concern is to get inside the understanding and culture, to develop a subtle grasp of how members view the world, and why they act as they do. Typically, there is an emphasis on the researcher being involved in the everyday world of those who are being studied. Along with this goes a commitment to working with unstructured data (i.e., data which has not been coded at the point of data collection) and a tendency to perform intensive studies of small numbers of cases. Ethnography is not suited to the sorts of hypothetico-deductive procedures that are common in psychology.

Two important tendencies in current ethnographic work can be seen in their historical antecedents in anthropology and sociology. In the nineteenth century, anthropology often involved information collected by colonial administrators about members of indigenous peoples. Its use of key informants and its focus on revealing the details of exotic or hidden cultures continue in much work. Sociologists of the "Chicago School" saw ethnography as a way of revealing the lives and conditions of the US underclass. This social reformism was married to an emphasis on understanding their participants' lives from their own perspective.

3.06.3.1 Questions

Ethnography comes into its own where the researcher is trying to understand some particular sub-cultural group in a specific setting. It tends to be holistic, focusing on the entire experience participants have of a setting, or their entire cosmology, rather than focusing on discrete variables or phenomena. This means that ethnographic questions tend to be general: What happens in this setting? How do this group understand their world? In Goffman's

(1961) *Asylums* he tried to reveal the different worlds lived by the staff and inmates, and to describe and explicate some of the ceremonies that were used to reinforce boundaries between the two groups. A large part of his work tracked what he called the "moral careers" of inmates from prepatient, through admission, and then as inpatients. Much of the force and influence of Goffman's work derived from its revelations about the grim "unofficial" life lived by patients in large state mental hospitals in the 1950s. In this respect it followed in the Chicago school tradition of exposé and critique. Rosenhan's (1973) classic study of hospital admission and the life of the patient also followed in this tradition. Famously it posed the question of what was required to be diagnosed as mentally ill and then incarcerated, and discovered that it was sufficient to report hearing voices saying "empty," "hollow," and "thud." This "pseudo-patient" study was designed with a very specific question about diagnostic criteria in mind; however, after the pseudopatients were admitted they addressed themselves to more typically ethnographic concerns, such as writing detailed descriptions of their settings, monitoring patient contact with different kinds of staff, and documenting the experience of powerlessness and depersonalization.

Goffman's and Rosenhan's work picks up the ethnographic traditions of revealing hidden worlds and providing a basis for social reform. Jodelet (1991) illustrates another analytic possibility by performing an intensive study of one of the longest running community care schemes in the world, the French colony of Ainay-le-Château where mental patients live with ordinary families. Again, in line with the possibilities of ethnography, she attempted to explore the whole setting, including the lives of the patients and their hosts and their understandings of the world. Her work, however, is notable for showing how ethnography can explore the representational systems of participants and relate that system to the lives of the participants. To give just one small example, she shows the way the families' representation of a close link between madness and uncleanliness relates to practices such as taking meals separately from the lodgers.

Another topic for ethnographic work has been the practice of psychotherapy itself (Gubrium, 1992; Newfield, Kuehl, Joanning, & Quinn, 1990, 1991). These studies are interested in the experience of patients in therapy and their conceptions of what therapy is, as well as the practices and conceptions of the therapists. Such studies do not focus exclusively on the interaction in the therapy session itself, but on the whole setting.

Although ethnography is dependent on close and systematic description of practices it is not necessarily atheoretical. Ethnographic studies are often guided by one of a range of theoretical conceptions. For example, Jodelet's (1991) study was informed by Moscovici's (1984) theory of social representations and Gubrium's (1992) study of family therapy was guided by broader questions about the way the notion of family and family disorder are constructed in Western society. Ethnography has sometimes been treated as particularly appropriate for feminist work because of the possibility of combining concerns with experience and social context (e.g., Ronai, 1996).

3.06.3.2 Procedures

Ethnography typically involves a mix of different methods with interviews and participant observation being primary, but often combined with nonparticipant observation and the analysis of documents of one kind or another. Such a mixture raises a large number of separate issues which will only be touched on here. There are whole books on some elements of ethnographic work such as selecting informants (Johnson, 1990), living with informants (Rose, 1990), and interpreting ethnographic writings (Atkinson, 1990). The focus here is on research access, field relations, interviewing, observing, fieldnotes, and analysis (see Ellen, 1984; Fetterman, 1989; Fielding, 1993; Hammersley & Atkinson, 1995; Rachel, 1996; Toren, 1996; Werner & Schoepfle, 1987).

3.06.3.2.1 Access

Research access is often a crucial issue in ethnography, as a typical ethnographic study will require not only access to some potentially sensitive group or setting but may involve the researcher's bodily presence in delicate contexts. Sitting in on a family therapy session, for example, may involve obtaining consent from a range of people who have different concerns and has the potential for disrupting, or at least subtly changing, the interaction that would have taken place. There are only restricted possibilities for the ethnographer to enter settings with concealed identities, as Goffman did with his mental hospital study, and Rosenhan's pseudopatients did. Moreover, such practices raise a host of ethical and practical problems which increasingly lead ethnographers to avoid deception. Access can present another problem in sensitive settings if it turns out that it is precisely unusual examples where access is granted, perhaps because the participants view them as models of good practice.

3.06.3.2.2 Field relations

Field relations can pose a range of challenges. Many of these follow from the nature of the participation of the researcher in the setting. How far should researchers become full participants and how far should they stay uninvolved observers? The dilemma here is that much of the power of ethnography comes from the experience and knowledge provided by full participation, and yet such participation may make it harder to sustain a critical distance from the practices under study. The ethnographer should not be converted to the participants' cultural values; but neither should they stay entirely in the Martian role that will make it harder to understand the subtle senses through which the participants understand their own practices. Field relations also generate many of practical, prosaic, but nevertheless important problems which stem from the sheer difficulty of maintaining participant status in an unfamiliar and possibly difficult setting for a long period of time. At the same time there are a whole set of skills required to do with building productive and harmonious relationships with participants.

3.06.3.2.3 Fieldnotes

One of the central features of participant observation is the production of fieldnotes. Without notes to take away there is little point in conducting observation. In some settings it may be possible to take notes concurrently with the action but often the researcher will need to rely on their memory, writing up notes on events as soon as possible after they happened. A rule of thumb is that writing up fieldnotes will take just as much time as the original period of observation (Fielding, 1993). In some cases it may be possible to tape record interaction as it happens. However, ethnographers have traditionally placed less value on recording as they see the actual process of note taking as itself part of the process through which the researcher comes to understand connections between processes and underlying elements of interaction.

Ethnographers stress that fieldnotes should be based around concrete descriptions rather than consisting of abstract higher-order interpretations. The reason for this is that when observation is being done it may not yet be clear what questions are to be addressed. Notes that stay at low levels of inference are a resource that can be used to address a range of different questions. Fielding argues that fieldnotes are expected:

> to provide a running description of events, people and conversation. Consequently each new setting observed and each new member of the setting

merits description. Similarly, changes in the human or other constituents of the setting should be recorded. (1993, p. 162)

It is also important to distinguish in notes between direct quotation and broad précis of what participants are saying. A final point emphasised by ethnographers is the value of keeping a record of personal impressions and feelings.

3.06.3.2.4 Interviews

Ethnographers make much use of interviews. However, in this tradition interviews are understood in a much looser manner than in much of psychology. Indeed, the term interview may be something of a misnomer with its image of the researcher running through a relatively planned set of questions with a single passive informant in a relatively formal setting. In ethnography what is involved is often a mix of casual conversations with a range of different participants. Some of these may be very brief, some extended, some allowing relatively formal questioning, others allowing no overt questioning. In the more formal cases the interview may be conducted with a planned schedule of questions and the interaction is recorded and transcribed.

3.06.3.2.5 Analysis

There is not a neat separation of the data collection and analytic phases of ethnographic research. The judgements about what to study, what to focus on, which elements of the local culture require detailed description, and which can be taken for granted, are already part of analysis. Moreover, it is likely that in the course of a long period of participant observation, or a series of interviews, the researcher will start to develop accounts for particular features of the setting, or begin to identify the set of representations shared by the participants. Such interpretations are refined, transformed, and sometimes abandoned when the fieldwork is completed and the focus moves on to notes and transcripts.

Fielding (1993, p. 192) suggests that the standard pattern of work with ethnographic data is straightforward. The researcher starts with the fieldnotes and transcripts and searches them for categories and patterns. These themes form a basis for the ethnographic account of the setting, and they also structure the more intensive analysis and probably the write-up of the research. The data will be marked or cut up (often on computer text files) to collect these themes together. In practice, the ethnographer is unlikely to attempt a complete account of a setting, but will concentrate on a small subset of themes which are most important or which relate to prior questions and concerns.

The analytic phase of ethnography is often described in only the sketchiest terms in ethnography guidebooks. It is clear that ethnographers often make up their own ways of managing the large amount of materials that they collect, and for using that material in convincing research accounts. At one extreme, ethnography can be considered an approach to develop the researcher's competence in the community being studied—they learn to be a member, to take part actually and symbolically, and they can use this competence to write authoritatively about the community (Collins, 1983). Here extracts from notes and interview transcripts become merely exemplars of the knowledge that the researcher has gained through participation. At the other extreme, ethnography blurs into grounded theorizing, with the notes and transcripts being dealt with through line-by-line coding, comparison of categories, and memo writing. Here the researcher's cultural competence will be important for interpreting the material, but the conclusions will ultimately be dependent on the quality of the fieldnotes and transcripts and what they can support.

3.06.3.2.6 Validity

One of the virtues of ethnography is its rich ecological validity. The researcher is learning directly about what goes on in a setting by observing it, by taking part, and/or by interviewing the members. This circumvents many of the inferences that are needed in extrapolating from more traditional psychological research tools—questionnaires, experimental simulations—to actual settings. However, the closeness of the researcher to the setting does not in itself ensure that the research that is produced will be of high quality.

The approach to validity most often stressed by ethnographers is triangulation. At the level of data this involves checking to see that different informants make the same sorts of claims about actions or events. At the level of method, it involves checking that conclusions are supported by different methods, for example, by both interviews and observation. However, triangulation is not without its problems. Discourse researchers have noted that in practice the sheer variability in and between accounts makes triangulation of only limited use (Potter & Wetherell, 1987) and others have identified conceptual problems in judging what a successful triangulation between methods would be (Silverman, 1993).

3.06.3.3 Example: Gubrium (1992)

There are only a small number of ethnographies done in clinical settings or on clinical topics. For instance, many of the clinical examples in Newfield, Sells, Smith, Newfield, & Newfield's (1996) chapter on ethnography in family therapy are unpublished dissertations. The body of ethnographic work is small but increasing rapidly. I have chosen Gubrium's (1992) study of family therapy in two institutions as an example because it is a book-length study, and it addresses the therapeutic process itself rather than concentrating solely on the patients' lives in hospital or community care schemes. However, it is important to stress that Gubrium's focus was as much on what the therapy revealed about the way notions of family and order are understood in American culture as in therapeutic techniques and effectiveness. He was concerned with the way behaviours such as truancy take their sense as part of a troubled family and the way service professionals redefine family order as they instigate programmes of rehabilitation.

Gubrium's choice of two contrasting institutions is a commonplace one in ethnography. The small number enables an intensive approach; having more than one setting allows an illuminating range of comparisons and contrasts. In this case one was inpatient, one outpatient; one more middle class than the other; they also varied in their standard approaches to treatment. The virtues of having two field sites shine through in the course of the write-up, although it is interesting to note that the selection was almost accidental as the researcher originally expected to be successful in gaining access to only one of the institutions.

The fieldwork followed a typical ethnographic style of spending a considerable amount of times at the two facilities, talking to counselors, watching them at work in therapy sessions, reviewing videos of counseling, and making fieldnotes. The study also drew on a range of documents including patients' case notes and educational materials. In some ways this was a technically straightforward setting for ethnographic observation as many of the participants were themselves university trained practitioners who made notes and videos as part of the general workings of the facilities.

One of the striking differences between this ethnographic study of therapy and a typical process or outcome study is that the therapy is treated as a part of its physical, institutional, and cultural contexts. For instance, time is spent documenting the organization of the reception areas of the two facilities and the way the counselors use the manner in which the families seat themselves in that area as evidence of family dynamics. Gubrium writes about the important role of tissue boxes in both signaling the potential for emotional display and providing practical support when such display occurs:

> I soon realized that tissues were about more than weeping and overall emotional composure during therapy. Tissues mundanely signaled the fundamental reality of the home as locally understood: a configuration of emotional bonds. For Benson [a counselor] their usage virtually put the domestic disorder of the home on display, locating the home's special order in the minutiae of emotional expression. (Gubrium, 1992, p. 26)

The ethnographic focus on events in context means that therapy is treated as a product of actual interactions full of contingency and locally managed understandings. It shows the way abstract notions such as family systems or tough love are managed in practice, and the way the various workers relate to each other as well as to the clients. It provides an insight into the world of family therapy quite different from most other styles of research.

3.06.3.4 Virtues and Limitations

Much of the power of ethnographic research comes from its emphasis on understanding people's actions and representations both in context and as part of the everyday practices that make up their lives, whether they are Yanomami Indians or family therapists. It can provide descriptions which pick out abstract organizations of life in a setting as well as allowing the reader rich access. Ethnography can be used in theory development and even theory testing (Hammersley & Atkinson, 1995). It is flexible; research can follow up themes and questions as they arise rather than necessarily keeping to preset goals.

Ethnographic research can be very time consuming and labor intensive. It can also be very intrusive. Although Gubrium was able to participate in some aspects of family therapy, this was helped by the sheer number of both staff and family members who were involved. It is less easy to imagine participant observation on individual therapy.

One of the most important difficulties with ethnographic work is that the reader often has to take on trust the conclusions because the evidence on which they are based is not available for assessment (Silverman, 1993). Where field notes of observations are reproduced in ethnographies—and this is relatively rare—such notes are nevertheless a ready-theorized version of events. Descriptions of actions and events are always bound up with a range of judgments (Potter, 1996a). Where analysis depends on the claims of key informants the problem is assessing how these claims relate to any putative activities that are described. Ethnographers deal with these problems with varying degrees of sophistication (for discussion see Nelson, 1994). However, some researchers treat them as inescapable and have turned to some form of discourse analysis instead.

For more detailed discussions of ethnography readers should start with Fielding's (1993) excellent brief introduction and then use Hammersley and Atkinson (1995) as an authoritative and up to date overview. Two of the most comprehensive, although not always most sophisticated, works are Werner and Schoepfle (1987) and Ellen (1984). Both were written by anthropologists, and this shows in their understanding of what is important. Newfield, Sells, Smith, Newfield, and Newfield (1996) provide a useful discussion of ethnography in family therapy research.

3.06.4 DISCOURSE ANALYSIS

Although both grounded theorizing and ethnographic work in clinical areas has increased, the most striking expansion has been in research in discourse analysis (Soyland, 1995). This work is of variable quality and often done by researchers isolated in different subdisciplines; moreover, it displays considerable terminological confusion. For simplicity, discourse analysis is taken as covering a range of work which includes conversation analysis and ethnomethodology (Heritage, 1984; Nofsinger, 1991), some specific traditions of discourse analysis and discursive psychology (Edwards & Potter, 1992a; Potter & Wetherell, 1987), some of the more analytically focused social constructionist work (McNamee & Gergen, 1992), and a range of work influenced by post-structuralism, Continental discourse analysis, and particularly the work of Foucault (Burman, 1995; Madigan, 1992; Miller & Silverman, 1995). In some research these different themes are woven together; elsewhere strong oppositions are marked out.

The impetus for discourse analysis in clinical settings comes from two directions. On the one hand, there are practitioner/researchers who have found ideas from social constructionism, literary theory, and narrative useful (e.g., Anderson & Goolishian, 1988; White & Epston, 1990). On the other, there are academic researchers who have extended analytic and theoretical developments in discourse studies to clinical settings (e.g., Aronsson & Cederborg, 1996; Bergmann, 1992; Buttny, 1996; Edwards, 1995; Lee, 1995). Collections such as Siegfried (1995), Burman, Mitchel, and Salmon (1996), and Morris and Chenail (1995) reflect both types of work, sometimes in rather uneasy combination (see Antaki, 1996).

This tension between an applied and academic focus is closely related to the stance taken on therapy. In much discourse analysis, therapy is the start point for research and the issue is how therapy gets done. For example, Gale's (1991; Gale & Newfield, 1992) intensive study of one of O'Hanlon's therapy sessions considered the various ways in which the goals of solution focused family therapy were realized in the talk between therapist and client. However, some conversation analysts and ethnomethodologists resist assuming that conversational interaction glossed by some parties as therapy (solution focused, Milan School, or whatever) must have special ingredient X—therapy—that is absent in, say, the everyday "troubles talk" done with a friend over the telephone (Jefferson, 1988; Jefferson & Lee, 1992; Schegloff, 1991; Watson, 1995).

This is a significant point for all researchers into therapy and counseling, so it is worth illustrating with an example. In Labov and Fanshel's classic study, the therapy session starts in the following manner:

Rhoda:	I don't (1.0) know, whether (1.5) I-I think I did- the right thing, jistalittle situation came up (4.5) an' I tried to uhm (3.0) well, try to (4.0) use what I- what I've learned here, see if it worked (0.3)
Therapist:	Mhm
Rhoda:	Now, I don't know if I did the right thing. Sunday (1.0) um- my mother went to my sister's again.
Therapist:	Mm-hm
Rhoda:	And she usu'lly goes for about a day or so, like if she leaves on Sunday, she'll come back Tuesday morning. So- it's nothing. But- she lef' Sunday, and she's still not home.
Therapist:	O- oh.

(1977, p. 263)

Labov and Fanshel provide many pages of analysis of this sequence. They identify various direct and indirect speech acts and make much of what they call its therapeutic interview style, particularly the vague reference terms at the start: "right thing" and "jistalittle situation." This vagueness can easily be heard as the 19-year-old anorexia sufferer struggling to face up to her relationship with her difficult mother. However, in a reanalysis from a conversation analytic perspective, Levinson (1983) suggests that this sequence is characteristic of mundane news telling sequences in everyday conversation. These typically have four parts: the pre-announcement, the go ahead, the news telling, and the news receipt. For example:

D:	I forgot to to tell you the two best things that happen' to me today.	preannouncement
R:	Oh super = what were they.	go ahead turn
D:	I got a B+ on my math test ... and I got an athletic award	news telling
R:	Oh excellent. (Levinson, 1983, p. 349—slightly modified)	news receipt

A particular feature of preannouncements is their vagueness, for their job is to prefigure the story (and thereby check its newsworthiness), not to actually tell it. So, rather than following Labov and Fanshel (1977) in treating this vagueness as specific to a troubled soul dealing with a difficult topic in therapy, Levinson (1983) proposes that it should be understood as a commonplace characteristic of mundane interaction.

This example illustrates a number of features typical of a range of discursive approaches to therapy talk. First, the talk is understood as performing actions; it is not being used as a pathway to cognitive processes (repression, say) or as evidence of what Rhoda's life is like (her difficult mother). Second, the interaction is understood as sequentially organized so any part of the talk relates to what came immediately before and provides an environment for what will immediately follow. The realization of how far interaction gets its sense from its sequential context has critical implications for approaches such as content analysis and grounded theory which involve making categorizations and considering relations between them; for such categorizations tend to cut across precisely the sequential relations that are important for the sense of the turn of talk.

The third feature is that the talk is treated as ordered in its detail not merely in its broad particulars. For example, Levinson (1983) highlights a number of orderly elements in what we might easily mistake for clumsiness in Rhoda's first turn:

R's first turn is ... formulated to prefigure (i) the telling of something she did (*I think I did the right thing*), and (ii) the describing of the situation that led to the action (*jistalittle situation came up*). We are therefore warned to expect a story with two components; moreover the point of the story and its relevance to the here and now is also prefigured (*use what I've learned here, see if it worked*). (1983, p. 353)

Even the hesitations and glottal stops in Rhoda's first turn, which seem so redolent of a troubled young person are "typical markings of self-initiated self-repair, which is characteristic of the production of first topics" (Levinson, 1983, p. 353). This emphasis on the significance of detail has an important methodological consequence—if interaction is to be understood properly it must be represented in a way that captures this detail. Hence the use of a transcription scheme that attempts to represent a range of paralinguistic features of talk (stress, intonation) on the page as well as elements of the style of its delivery (pauses, cut-offs).

A fourth feature to note here is the comparative approach that has been taken. Rather than focus on therapy talk alone Levinson is able to support an alternative account of the interaction by drawing on materials, and analysis, taken from mundane conversations. Since the mid 1980s there has been a large amount of work in different institutional settings as well as everyday conversation, and it is now possible to start to show how a news interview, say, differs from the health visitor's talk with an expectant mother, and how that differs in turn from conversation between two friends over the telephone (Drew & Heritage, 1992a).

A fifth and final feature of this example is that it is an analysis of interaction. It is neither an attempt to reduce what is going on to cognitions of the various parties—Rhoda's denial, say, or the therapist's eliciting strategies—nor to transform it into countable behaviors such as verbal reinforcers. This style of discourse work develops a Wittgensteinian notion of cognitive words and phrases as elements in a set of language games for managing issues of blame, accountability, description, and so on (Coulter, 1990; Edwards, 1997; Harré & Gillett, 1994). Such a "discursive psychology" analyzes notions such as attribution and memory in terms of the situated practices through which responsibility is assigned and the business done by constructing particular versions of past events (Edwards & Potter, 1992b, 1993).

3.06.4.1 Questions

Discourse analysis is more directly associated with particular theoretical perspectives—

ethnomethodology, post-structuralism, discursive psychology—than either grounded theory or ethnography. The questions it addresses focus on the practices of interaction in their natural contexts and the sorts of discursive resources that are drawn on those contexts.

Some of the most basic questions concern the standardized sequences of interaction that take place in therapy and counseling (Buttny & Jensen, 1995; Lee, 1995; Peräkylä, 1995; Silverman, 1997b). This is closely related to a concern with the activities that take place. What is the role of the therapist's tokens such as "okay" or "mm hm" (Beach, 1995; Czyzewski, 1995)? How do different styles of questioning perform different tasks (Bergmann, 1992; Peräkylä, 1995; Silverman, 1997b)? What is the role of problem formulations by both therapists and clients, and how are they transformed and negotiated (Buttny, 1996; Buttny & Jensen, 1995; Madill & Barkham, 1997)? For example, in a classic feminist paper Davis (1986) charts the way a woman's struggles with her oppressive social circumstances are transformed into individual psychological problems suitable for individual therapy. While much discourse research is focused on the talk of therapy and counseling itself, studies in other areas show the value of standing back and considering clinical psychology as a set of work practices in themselves, including management of clients in person and as records, conducting assessments, delivering diagnoses, intake and release, stimulating people with profound learning difficulties, case conferences and supervisions, offering advice, and managing resistance (see Drew & Heritage, 1992a). Discourse researchers have also been moving beyond clinical settings to study how people with clinical problems or learning difficulties manage in everyday settings (Brewer & Yearley, 1989; Pollner & Wikler, 1985; Wootton, 1989).

Another set of questions are suggested by the perspective of discursive psychology. For example, Edwards (1997) has studied the rhetorical relationship between problem formulations, descriptions of activities, and issues of blame in counseling. Cheston (1996) has studied the way descriptions of the past in a therapy group of older adults can create a set of social identities for the members. Discursive psychology can provide a new take on emotions, examining how they are constructed and their role in specific practices (Edwards, 1997).

From a more Foucaultian inspired direction, studies may consider the role of particular discourses, or interpretative repertoires in constructing the sense of actions and experiences (Potter & Wetherell, 1987). For example, what are the discursive resources that young women draw on to construct notions of femininity, agency, and body image in the context of eating disorders (Malson & Ussher, 1996; Wetherell, 1996)? What discourses are used to construct different notions of the person, of the family, and of breakdown in therapy (Burman, 1995; Frosh, Burck, Strickland-Clark, & Morgan, 1996; Soal & Kotter, 1996)? This work is often critical of individualistic conceptions of therapy.

Finally, discourse researchers have stood back and taken the administration of psychological research instruments as their topic. The intensive focus of such work can show the way that the sort in idiosyncratic interaction that takes place when filling in questionnaires or producing records can lead to particular outcomes (Antaki & Rapley, 1996; Garfinkel, 1967b; Rapley & Antaki, 1996; Soyland, 1994).

Different styles of discourse work address rather different kinds of questions. However, the conversation analytic work is notable in commonly starting from a set of transcribed materials rather than preformulated research questions, on the grounds that such questions often embody expectations and assumptions which prevent the analyst seeing a range of intricacies in the interaction. Conversation analysis reveals an order to interaction that participants are often unable to formulate in abstract terms.

3.06.4.2 Procedures

The majority of discourse research in the clinical area has worked with records of natural interaction, although a small amount has used open-ended interviews. There is not space here to discuss the role of interviews in discourse analysis or qualitative research generally (see Kvale, 1996; Mischler, 1986; Potter & Mulkay, 1985; Widdicombe & Wooffitt, 1995). For simplicity discourse work will be discussed in terms of seven elements.

3.06.4.2.1 Research materials

Traditionally psychologists have been reluctant to deal with actual interaction, preferring to model it experimentally, or reconstruct it via scales and questionnaires. Part of the reason for this is the prevalent cognitivist assumptions which have directed attention away from interaction itself to focus on generative mechanisms within the person. In contrast, discourse researchers have emphasised the primacy of practices of interaction themselves. The most obvious practice setting for clinical work is the therapy session itself, and this has certainly received the most attention. After all, there is an elegance in studying the "talking cure" using methods designed to acquire an understanding of the nature of talk. However, there is a danger that such an exclusive emphasis underplays mundane aspects of clinical practices: giving advice, offering a diagnosis, the reception of new clients, casual talk to clients' relatives, writing up clinical records, case conferences, clinical training, and assessment.

Notions of sample size do not translate easily from traditional research as the discourse research focus is not so much on individuals as on interactional phenomena of various kinds. Various considerations can come to the fore here, including the type of generalizations that are to be made from the research, the time and resources available, and the nature of the topic being studied. For example, if the topic is the role of "mm hms" in therapy a small number of sessions may generate a large corpus; other phenomena may be much rarer and require large quantities of interaction to develop a useful corpus. For some questions, single cases may be sufficient to underpin a theoretical point or reveal a theoretically significant phenomena.

3.06.4.2.2 *Access and ethics*

One of the most difficult practical problems in conducting discourse research involves getting access to sometimes sensitive settings in ways which allow for informed consent from all the parties involved. Experience suggests that more often than not it is the health professionals rather than the clients who are resistant to their practices being studied, perhaps because they are sensitive to the difference between the idealized version of practices that was used in training and the apparently more messy procedures in which they actually engage. Sometimes reassurances about these differences can be productive.

Using records of interaction such as these raise particular issues for ensuring anonymity. This is relatively manageable with transcripts where names and places can be changed. It is harder for audio tape and harder still with video. However, technical advances in the use of digitized video allow for disguising of identity with relatively little loss of vocal information.

3.06.4.2.3 *Audio and video recording*

There is a range of practical concerns in recording natural interaction, some of them pulling in different directions. An immediate issue is whether to use audio or video recording. On the one hand, video provides helpful information about nonverbal activities that may be missed from the tape, and good quality equipment is now compact and cheap. On the other hand, video can be more intrusive, particularly where the recording is being done by one of the participants (a counselor, say), and may be hard to position so it captures gestures and expressions from all parties to an interaction. Video poses a range of practical and theoretical problems with respect to the transcription of nonvocal activity which can be both time consuming and create transcript that is difficult to understand. Moreover, there is now a large body of studies that shows high quality analysis can, in many cases, be performed with an audio tape alone. One manageable solution is to use video if doing so does not disrupt the interaction, and then to transcribe the audio and work with a combination of video tape and audio transcript. Whether audio or video is chosen, the quality (clear audibility and visibility) is probably the single most consequential feature of the recording for the later research.

Another difficulty is how far the recording of interaction affects its nature. This is a subtle issue. On the one hand, there are a range of ways of minimizing such influences including acclimatizing participants and giving clear descriptions of the role of the research. On the other, experience has shown that recording has little influence on many, perhaps most, of the activities in which the discourse researcher is interested. Indeed, in some clinical settings recordings may be made as a matter of course for purposes of therapy and training, and so no new disruption is involved.

3.06.4.2.4 *Transcription*

Producing a high-quality transcript is a crucial prerequisite for discourse research. A transcript is not a neutral, simple rendition of the words on a tape (Ochs, 1979). Different transcription systems emphasize different features of interaction. The best system for most work of this kind was developed by the conversation analyst Gail Jefferson using symbols that convey features of vocal delivery that have been shown to be interactionally important to participants (Jefferson, 1985). At the same time the system is designed to use characters and symbols easily available on wordprocessors making it reasonably easy to learn and interpret. The basic system is summarized in Table 3. For fuller descriptions of using the system see Button and Lee, (1987), Ochs, Schegloff, and Thompson (1996), and Psathas and Anderson (1990).

Producing high quality transcript is very demanding and time consuming. It is hard to give a standard figure for how long it takes

Table 3   Brief transcription notation.

Um::	colons represent lengthening of the preceding sound; the more colons, the greater the lengthening.
I've-	a hyphen represents the cut-off of the preceding sound, often by a stop.
↑Already	up and down arrows represent sharp upward and downward pitch shifts in the following sounds. Underlining represents stress, usually by volume; the more underlining the greater the stress.
settled in his = Mm = own mind.	the equals signs join talk that is continuous although separated across different lines of transcript.
hhh hh .hh P(h)ut	'h' represents aspiration, sometimes simply hearable breathing, sometimes laughter, etc.; when preceded by a superimposed dot, it marks in-breath; in parenthesis inside a word it represents laugh infiltration.
hhh[hh .hh] [I just]	left brackets represent point of overlap onset; right brackets represent point of overlap resolution.
.,?	punctuation marks intonation, not grammar; period, comma and 'question mark' indicate downward, 'continuative', and upward contours respectively.
( )	single parentheses mark problematic or uncertain hearings; two parentheses separated by an oblique represent alternative hearings.
(0.2)(.)	numbers in parentheses represent silence in tenths of a second; a dot in parentheses represents a micro-pause, less than two tenths of a second.
°mm hmm°	the degree signs enclose significantly lowered volume.

Source: Modified from Schegloff (1997, pp. 184–185).

because much depends on the quality of the recording (fuzzy, quiet tapes can quadruple the time needed) and the type of interaction (an individual therapy session presents much less of a challenge than a lively case conference with a lot of overlapping talk and extraneous noise); nevertheless, a ratio of one hour of tape to twenty hours of transcription time is not unreasonable. However, this time should not be thought of as dead time before the analysis proper. Often some of the most revealing analytic insights come during transcription because a profound engagement with the material is needed to produce good transcript— it is generally useful to make analytic notes in parallel to the actual transcription.

3.06.4.2.5 Coding

In discourse research the principle task of coding is to make the task of analysis more straightforward by sifting relevant materials from a large body of transcript. In this it differs from both grounded theory and traditional content analysis where coding is a more intrinsic

part of the analysis. Typically coding will involve sifting through materials for instances of a phenomenon of interest and copying them into an archive. This coding will often be accompanied by preliminary notes as to their nature and interest. At this stage selection is inclusive—it is better to include material that can turn out to be irrelevant at a later stage than exclude it for ill-formulated reasons early on. Coding is a cyclical process. Full analysis of a corpus of materials can often take the researcher back to the originals as a better understanding of the phenomenon reveals new examples. Often initially disparate topics merge together in the course of analysis while topics which seemed unitary can be separated.

3.06.4.2.6 Analysis

There is no single recipe for analyzing discourse. Nevertheless, there are five considerations which are commonly important in analysis. First, the researcher can use variation in and between participants' discourse as an analytic lever. The significance of variation is that it can be used for identifying and explicating the activities that are being performed by talk and texts. This is because the discourse is constructed in the specific ways that it is precisely to perform these actions; a description of jealousy in couple counseling can be assembled very differently when excusing or criticizing certain actions (Edwards, 1995). The researcher will benefit from attending to variations in the discourse of single individuals, between different individuals, and between what is said and what might have been said.

Second, discourse researchers have found it highly productive to attend to the detail of discourse. Conversation analysts such as Sacks (1992) have shown that the details in discourse—the hesitations, lexical choice, repair, and so on—are commonly part of the performance of some act or are consequential in some way for the outcome of the interaction. Attending to the detail of interaction, particularly in transcript, is one of the most difficult things for psychologists who are used to reading through the apparently messy detail for the gist of what is going on. Developing analytic skills involves a discipline of close reading.

Third, analysis often benefits from attending to the rhetorical organization of discourse. This involves inspecting discourse both for the way it is organized to make argumentative cases and for the way it is designed to undermine alternative cases (Billig, 1996). A rhetorical orientation refocuses the analyst's attention away from questions about how a version—description of a psychological disorder, say—relates to some putative reality and focuses it on how it relates to competing alternatives.

Concern with rhetoric is closely linked to a fourth analytic concern with accountability. That is, displaying one's activities as rational, sensible, and justifiable. Ethnomethodologists have argued that accountability is an essential and pervasive character of the design and understanding of human conduct generally (Garfinkel, 1967c; Heritage, 1984). Again an attention to the way actions are made accountable is an aid for understanding precisely what those actions are.

A fifth and final analytic consideration is of a slightly different order. It is an emphasis on the virtue of building on prior analytic studies. In particular, researchers into interaction in an institutional setting such as a family therapy setting will almost certainly benefit from a familiarity with research on mundane talk as well as an understanding of how the patterning of turn taking and activities change in different institutional settings.

The best way to think of these five considerations is not as specific rules for research but as elements in an analytic mentality that the researcher will develop as they become more and more skilled. It does not matter that they are not spelled out in studies because they are separate from the procedures for validating discourse analytic claims.

3.06.4.2.7 Validity

Discourse researchers typically draw on some combination of four considerations to justify the validity of analytic claims. First, they make use of participants' own understandings as they are displayed in interaction. One of the features of a conversation is that any turn of talk is oriented to what came before and what comes next, and that orientation typically displays the sense that the participant makes of the prior turn. Thus, at its simplest, when someone provides an answer they thereby display the prior turn as a question and so on. Close attention to this turn-by-turn display of understanding provides one important check on analytic interpretations (see Heritage, 1988).

Second, researchers may find (seemingly) deviant cases most useful in assessing the adequacy of a claim. Deviant cases may generate problems for a claimed generalization, and lead the researcher to abandon it; but they may also display in their detailed organization precisely the reason why a standard pattern should take the form that it does.

Third, a study may be assessed in part by how far it is coherent with previous discourse studies. A study that builds coherently on past research is more plausible than one that is more anomalous.

Fourth, and most important, are readers' evaluations. One of the distinctive features of discourse research is its presentation of rich and extended materials in a way that allows the reader to make their own judgements about interpretations that are placed along side of them. This form of validation contrasts with much grounded theory and ethnography where interpretations often have to be taken on trust; it also contrasts with much traditional experimental and content analytic work where it is rare for "raw" data to be included or more than one or two illustrative codings to be reproduced.

Whether they appear singly or together in a discourse study none of these procedures guarantee the validity of an analysis. However, as the sociology of science work reviewed earlier shows, there are no such guarantees in science.

3.06.4.3 Example: Peräkylä (1995)

Given the wide variety of discourse studies with different questions and styles of analysis it is not easy to chose a single representative study. The one selected is Peräkylä's (1995) investigation of AIDS counseling because it is a major integrative study that addresses a related set of questions about interaction, counseling, and family therapy from a rigorous conversation analytic perspective and illustrates the potential of discourse work on clinical topics. It draws heavily on the perspective on institutional talk surveyed by Drew and Heritage (1992b) and is worth reading in conjunction with Silverman's (1997b) related study of HIV + counseling which focuses more on advice giving.

Peräkylä focused on 32 counseling sessions conducted with HIV + hemophilic mainly gay identified men and their partners at a major London hospital. The sessions were videotaped and transcribed using the Jeffersonian system. A wider archive of recordings (450 hours) was drawn on to provide further examples of phenomena of interest but not otherwise transcribed. The counselors characterized their practices in terms of Milan School Family Systems Theory and, although this is not the startpoint of Peräkylä's study, he was able to explicate some of the characteristics of such counseling.

Part of the study is concerned with identifying the standard turn-taking organization of the counseling. Stated baldly it is that (i) counselors ask questions; (ii) clients answer; (iii) counselors comment, advise, or ask further questions. When laid out in this manner the organization may not seem much of a discovery. However, the power of the study is showing how this organization is achieved in the interaction and how it can be used to address painful and delicate topics such as sexual behavior, illness, and death.

Peräkylä goes on to examine various practices that are characteristic of family systems theory such as "circular questioning," where the counselor initially questions the client's partner or a family member about the client's feelings, and "live open supervision," where a supervisor may offer questions to the counselor that are, in turn, addressed to the client. The study also identifies some of the strategies by which counselors can address "dreaded issues" in a manageable way. Take "circular questioning," for example. In mundane interaction providing your partial experience of some event or experience is a commonplace way of "fishing" for a more authoritative version (Pomerantz, 1980). For example:

A: Yer line's been busy.
B: Yeuh my fu (hh)- .hh my father's
        wife called me

In a similar way, the use of questioning where a client's partner, say, offers their understanding of an experience "can create a situation where the clients, in an unacknowledged but most powerful way, elicit one another's descriptions of their inner experiences" (Peräkylä, 1995, p. 110). In the following extract the client is called Edward; his partner and the counselor are also present.

Counselor: What are some of things that you think E:dward might have to do. = He says he doesn't know where to go from here maybe: and awaiting results and things. (0.6)
Counselor: What d'you think's worrying him. (0.4)
Partner: Uh::m hhhhhh I think it's just fear of the unknow:n.
Client: Mm[:
Counselor: [Oka:y.
Partner: [At- at the present ti:me. (0.2) Uh:m (.) once: he's (0.5) got a better understanding of (0.2) what could happen
Counselor: Mm:
Partner: uh:m how .hh this will progre:ss then: I think (.) things will be a little more [settled in his =
Counselor: [Mm
Partner: = own mi:nd.
Counselor: Mm:
          (.)
Client: Mm[:
Counselor: [Edward (.) from what you know::
          ((sequence continues with Edward responding to a direct question with a long and detailed narrative about his fears))
          (Peräkylä, 1995, p. 110)

Peräkylä emphasizes the way that the client's talk about his fears is elicited, in part, through the counsellor asking the partner for his own view of those fears. The point is not that the client is forced to reveal his experiences, rather it is that the prior revelation of his partner's partial view produces an environment where such a revelation is expected and nonrevelation will itself be a delicate and accountable matter. In effect, what Peräkylä is documenting here are the conversational mechanisms which family therapists characterize as using circular questioning to overcome clients' resistance.

3.06.4.4 Virtues and Limitations

Given the variety of styles of work done under the rubric of discourse analysis it is difficult to give an overall summary of virtues and limitations. However, the virtue of a range of studies in the conversation and discourse analytic tradition is that they offer, arguably for the first time in psychology, a rigorous way of directly studying human social practices. For example, the Peräkylä study discussed above is notable in studying actual HIV+ counseling in all its detail. It is not counseling as recollected by participants while filling in rating scales or questionnaires; it is not an experimental simulation of counseling; it does not depend on *post hoc* ethnographic reconstructions of events; nor are the activities immediately transformed into broad coding categories or used as a mere shortcut to underlying cognitions.

A corollary of this emphasis on working with tapes and transcripts of interaction is that these are used in research papers to allow readers to evaluate the adequacy of interpretations in a way that is rare in other styles of research.

Studies in this tradition have started to reveal an organization of interaction and its local management that has been largely missed from traditional psychological work from a range of perspectives. Such studies offer new conceptions of what is important in clinical practice and may be particularly valuable in clinical training which has often been conducted with idealized or at least cleaned up examples of practice.

Discourse research is demanding and requires a considerable investment of the researcher's time to produce satisfactory results. It does not fit neatly into routines that can be done by research assistants. Indeed, even transcription, which may seem to be the most mechanical element in the research, requires considerable skill and benefits from the involvement of the primary researchers. Analysis also requires considerable craft skills which can take time to learn.

With its focus on interaction, this would not necessarily be the perspective of choice for researchers with a more traditional cognitive or behavioral focus, although it has important implications for both of these. Some have claimed that it places too much emphasis on verbal interaction at the expense of nonverbal elements, and broader issues of embodiment. Others have claimed that it places too much emphasis on the importance of local contexts of interaction rather than on broader issues such as gender or social class. For some contrasting and strongly expressed claims about the role of discourse analysis in the cognitive psychology of memory, see papers in Conway (1992).

An accessible general introduction to various practical aspects of doing discourse analysis is provided in Potter and Wetherell (1987; see also Potter, 1996b, 1997). Potter and Wetherell (1995) discuss the analysis of broader content units such as interpretative repertoires, while Potter and Wetherell (1994) and Wooffitt (1993) discuss the analysis of how accounts are constructed. For work in the distinctive conversation analytic tradition Drew (1995) and Heritage (1995) provide clear overviews and Heath and Luff (1993) discuss analysis which incorporates video material; Gale (1996) explores the use of conversation analysis in family therapy research.

3.06.5 FUTURE DIRECTIONS

The pace of change in qualitative research in clinical settings is currently breathtaking, and it is not easy to make confident predictions. However, it is perhaps useful to speculate on how things might develop over the next few years. The first prediction is that the growth in the sheer quantity of qualitative research will continue for some time. There is so much new territory, and so many possibilities have been opened up by new theoretical and analytic developments, that they are bound to be explored.

The second prediction is that research on therapy and counseling talk will provide a particular initial focus because it is here that discourse analytic approaches can clearly provide new insights and possibly start to provide technical analytically grounded specifications of the interactional nature of different therapies in practice, as well as differences in interactional style between therapists. There may well be conflicts here between the ideological goals of constructionist therapists and the research goals of discourse analysts.

The third prediction is that the growth of qualitative work will encourage more researchers to attempt integrations of qualitative and quantitative research strategies. There will be attempts to supplement traditional outcomes research with studies of elements of treatment which are not easily amenable to quantification. Here the theoretical neutrality of grounded theory (ironically) is likely to make for easier integration than the more theoretically developed discourse perspectives. The sheer difficulty of blending qualitative and quantitative work should not be underestimated—research that has attempted this has often found severe problems (see Mason, 1994, for a discussion).

The final prediction is that there will be an increased focus on clinical work practices embodied within settings such as clinics and networks of professional and lay relationships. Here the richness of ethnographic work will be drawn on, but increasingly the conversation analytic discipline of working with video and transcript will replace field notes and recollections. Such work will have the effect of respecifying some of the basic problems of clinical research. Its broader significance, however, may depend on the course of wider debates in Psychology over the development and success of the cognitive paradigm and whether it will have a discursive and interaction based successor.

ACKNOWLEDGMENTS

I would like to thank Alan Bryman, Karen Henwood, Alexa Hepburn, Celia Kitzinger, and Denis Salter for making helpful comments on an earlier draft of this chapter.

3.06.6 REFERENCES

Anderson, H., & Goolishian, H. A. (1988). Human systems as linguistic systems: Preliminary and evolving ideas about the implications for clinical theory. *Family Process, 27,* 371–393.
Antaki, C. (Ed.) (1988). *Analysing everyday explanation.* London: Sage.
Antaki, C. (1996). Review of *The talk of the clinic. Journal of Language and Social Psychology, 15,* 176–81.
Antaki, C., & Rapley, M. (1996). "Quality of life" talk: The liberal paradox of psychological testing. *Discourse and Society, 7,* 293–316.
Argyris, C., Putnam, R., & Smith, D. M. (1985). *Action Science: Concepts, methods, and skills for research and intervention.* San Francisco: Jossey-Bass.
Aronsson, K., & Cederborg, A.-C. (1996). Coming of age in family therapy talk: Perspective setting in multiparty problem formulations. *Discourse Processes, 21,* 191–212.
Ashmore, M., Mulkay, M., & Pinch, T. (1989). *Health and efficiency: A sociological study of health economics.* Milton Keynes, UK. Open University Press.
Atkinson, J. M. (1978). *Discovering suicide: Studies in the social organization of sudden death.* London: Macmillan.
Atkinson, P. (1990). *The ethnographic imagination: The textual construction of reality.* London: Routledge.
Bannister, P., Burman, E., Parker, I., Taylor, M., & Tindall, C. (1994). *Qualitative methods in psychology: A research guide.* Buckingham, UK: Open University Press.
Beach, W. A. (1995). Preserving and constraining options: "Okays" and "official" priorities in medical interviews. In G. H. Morris & R. J. Chenail (Eds.), *The talk of the clinic: Explorations in the analysis of medical and therapeutic discourse* (pp. 259–289). Hillsdale, NJ: Erlbaum.
Bergmann, J. R. (1992). Veiled morality: Notes on discretion in psychiatry. In P. Drew & J. Heritage (Eds.), *Talk at work: Interaction in institutional settings* (pp. 137–162). Cambridge, UK: Cambridge University Press.
Billig, M. (1988). Methodology and scholarship in understanding ideological explanation. In C. Antaki (Ed.), *Analysing everyday explanation: A casebook of methods* (pp. 199–215). London: Sage.
Billig, M. (1996). *Arguing and thinking: A rhetorical approach to social psychology* (2nd ed.). Cambridge, UK: Cambridge University Press.
Billig, M. (1998). Dialogic repression and the Oedipus Complex: Reinterpreting the Little Hans case. *Culture and Psychology, 4,* 11–47.
Bogdan, R., & Taylor, S. J. (1975). *Introduction to*

qualitative research methods: A phenomenological approach to social sciences. New York: Wiley.
Brewer, J. D., & Yearley, S. (1989). Stigma and conversational competence: A conversation-analytic study of the mentally handicapped. *Human Studies, 12,* 97–115
Bryman, A. (1988). *Quantity and quality in social research.* London: Unwin Hyman.
Bryman, A., & Burgess, R. G. (Eds.) (1994). *Analyzing qualitative data.* London: Routledge.
Burman, E. (1995). Identification, subjectivity, and power in feminist psychotherapy. In J. Siegfried (Ed.), *Therapeutic and everyday discourse as behaviour change: Towards a micro-analysis in psychotherapy process research* (pp. 469 490). Norwood, NJ: Ablex.
Burman, E., Mitchell, S., & Salmon, P. (Eds.) (1996). *Changes: An International Journal of Psychology and Psychotherapy (special issue on qualitative methods), 14,* 175–243.
Buttny, R. (1996). Clients' and therapists' joint construction of the clients' problems. *Research on Language and Social Interaction, 29,* 125–153.
Buttny, R., & Jensen, A. D. (1995) Telling problems in an initial family therapy session: The hierarchical organization of problem-talk. In G. H. Morris & R. J. Chenail (Eds.), *The talk of the clinic: Explorations in the analysis of medical and therapeutic discourse* (pp. 19–48). Hillsdale, NJ: Erlbaum.
Button, G., & Lee, J. R. E. (Eds.) (1987). *Talk and social organization.* Clevedon, UK: Multilingual Matters.
Chalmers, A. (1992). *What is this thing called science?: An assessment of the nature and status of science and its methods* (2nd ed.), Milton Keynes, UK: Open University Press.
Charmaz, K. (1991). *Good days, bad days: The self in chronic illness and time.* New Brunswick, NJ: Rutgers University Press.
Charmaz, K. (1994). Identity dilemmas of chronically ill men. *The Sociological Quarterly, 35,* 269–288.
Charmaz, K. (1995). Grounded theory. In J. A. Smith, R. Harré, & L. van Langenhove (Eds.), *Rethinking methods in pychology* (pp. 27–49). London: Sage.
Cheston, R. (1996). Stories and metaphors: Talking about the past in a psychotherapy group for people with dementia. *Ageing and Society, 16,* 579–602.
Clegg, J. A., Standen, P. J., & Jones, G. (1996). Striking the balance: A grounded theory analysis of staff perspectives. *British Journal of Clinical Psychology, 35,* 249–264.
Coffey, A., & Atkinson, P. (1996). *Making sense of qualitative data: Complementary research strategies.* London: Sage.
Collins, H. M. (1974). The TEA Set: Tacit knowledge and scientific networks. *Science Studies, 4,* 165–186.
Collins, H. M. (Ed.) (1981). Knowledge and controversy: Studies of modern natural science. *Social Studies of Science (special issue),* 11.
Collins, H. M. (1983). The meaning of lies: Accounts of action and participatory research. In G. N. Gilbert & P. Abell (Eds.), *Accounts and action* (pp. 69–76). Aldershot, UK: Gower.
Collins, H. M. (1985). *Changing order: Replication and induction in scientific practice.* London: Sage.
Collins, H. M., & Pinch, T. (1993) *The Golem: What everyone should know about science.* Cambridge, UK: Cambridge University Press.
Conway, M. (Ed.) (1992). Developments and debates in the study of human memory (special issue). *The Psychologist, 5,* 439–461.
Coulter, J. (1990). *Mind in action.* Cambridge, UK: Polity.
Czyzewski, M. (1995). "Mm hm" tokens as interactional devices in the psychotherapeutic intake interview. In P. ten Have & G. Psathas (Eds.), *Situated order: Studies in the social organization of talk and embodied activities* (pp. 73–89). Washington, DC: International Institute for

Ethnomethodology and Conversation Analysis & University Press of America.

Davis, K. (1986). The process of problem (re)formulation in psychotherapy. *Sociology of Health and Illness, 8,* 44–74.

Denzin, N. K., & Lincoln, Y. S. (Eds.) (1994) *Handbook of qualitative research.* London: Sage.

Drew, P. (1995). Conversation analysis. In J. Smith, R. Harré, & L. van Langenhove (Eds.), *Rethinking methods in psychology* (pp. 64–79). London: Sage.

Drew, P., & Heritage, J. (Eds.) (1992a). *Talk at work: Interaction in institutional settings.* Cambridge, UK: Cambridge University Press.

Drew, P., & Heritage, J. (1992b). Analyzing talk at work: An introduction. In P. Drew & J. Heritage (Eds.), *Talk at work: Interaction in institutional settings* (pp. 3–65). Cambridge, UK: Cambridge University Press.

Edwards, D. (1995). Two to tango: Script formulations, dispositions, and rhetorical symmetry in relationship troubles talk. *Research on Language and Social Interaction, 28,* 319–350.

Edwards, D. (1997). *Discourse and cognition.* London: Sage.

Edwards, D., & Potter, J. (1992a). *Discursive psychology.* London: Sage.

Edwards, D., & Potter, J. (1992b). The chancellor's memory: Rhetoric and truth in discursive remembering. *Applied Cognitive Psychology, 6,* 187–215.

Edwards, D., & Potter, J. (1993). Language and causation: A discursive action model of description and attribution. *Psychological Review, 100,* 23–41.

Ellen, R. F. (1984). *Ethnographic research: A guide to general conduct.* London: Academic Press.

Ellis, C., Kiesinger, C., & Tillmann-Healy, L. M. (1997) Interactive interviewing: Talking about emotional experience. In R. Hertz (Ed.), *Reflexivity and Voice.* Thousand Oaks, CA: Sage.

Essex, M., Estroff, S., Kane, S., McLanahan, J., Robbins, J., Dresser, R., & Diamond, R. (1980). On Weinstein's "Patient attitudes toward mental hospitalization: A review of quantitative research." *Journal of Health and Social Behaviour, 21,* 393–396.

Fetterman, D. M. (1989). *Ethnography: Step by step.* London: Sage.

Fielding, N. (1993). Ethnography. In N. Gilbert (Ed.), *Researching social life* (pp. 154–171). London: Sage.

Freud, S. (1977). *Case histories. I: "Dora" and "Little Hans."* London: Penguin.

Frosh, S., Burck, C., Strickland-Clark, L., & Morgan, K. (1996). Engaging with change: A process study of family therapy. *Journal of Family Therapy, 18,* 141–161.

Gale, J. E. (1991). *Conversation analysis of therapeutic discourse: The pursuit of a therapeutic agenda.* Norwood, NJ: Ablex.

Gale, J. E. (1996). Conversation analysis: Studying the construction of therapeutic realities. In D. H. Sprenkle & S. M. Moon (Eds.), *Research methods in family therapy* (pp. 107–124). New York: Guilford.

Gale, J. E., & Newfield, N. (1992). A conversation analysis of a solution-focused marital therapy session. *Journal of Marital and Family Therapy, 18,* 153–165.

Garfinkel, H. (1967a). "Good" organizational reasons for "bad" clinical records. In H. Garfinkel (Ed.), *Studies in ethnomethodology* (pp. 186–207). Englewood Cliffs, NJ: Prentice-Hall.

Garfinkel, H. (1967b). Methodological adequacy in the quantitative study of selection criteria and selection practices in psychiatric outpatient clinics. In H. Garfinkel (Ed.), *Studies in ethnomethodology* (pp. 208–261). Englewood Cliffs, NJ: Prentice-Hall.

Garfinkel, H. (1967c). *Studies in ethnomethodology.* Englewood Cliffs, NJ: Prentice-Hall.

Gelsthorpe, L. (1992). Response to Martyn Hammersley's paper "On feminist methodology." *Sociology, 26,* 213–218.

Gergen, K. J. (1994). *Realities and relationships: Soundings in social construction.* Cambridge, MA: Harvard University Press.

Gilbert, G. N. (Ed.) (1993). *Researching social life.* London: Sage.

Gilbert, G. N., & Mulkay, M. (1984). *Opening Pandora's box: A sociological analysis of scientists' discourse.* Cambridge, UK: Cambridge University Press.

Glaser, B., & Strauss, A. L. (1967). *The discovery of grounded theory: Strategies for qualitative research.* Chicago: Aldine.

Glaser, B., & Strauss, A. L. (1968). *Time for dying.* Chicago: Aldine.

Goffman, E. (1961). *Asylums: Essays on the social situation of mental patients and other inmates.* London: Penguin.

Guba, E. G., & Lincoln, Y. S. (1994). Competing paradigms in qualitative research. In N. K. Denzin & Y. S. Lincoln (Eds.), *Handbook of qualitative research* (pp. 105–117). London: Sage.

Gubrium, J. F. (1992). *Out of control: Family therapy and domestic disorder.* London: Sage.

Hammersley, M. (1992). On feminist methodology. *Sociology, 26,* 187–206.

Hammersley, M., & Atkinson, P. (1995). *Ethnography: Principles in practice* (2nd ed.). London: Routledge.

Harré, R. (1986). *Varieties of realism.* Oxford, UK: Blackwell.

Harré, R. (1992). *Social being: A theory for social psychology* (2nd ed.). Oxford, UK: Blackwell.

Harré, R., & Gillett, G. (1994). *The discursive mind.* London: Sage.

Heath, C., & Luff, P. (1993) Explicating face-to-face interaction. In N. Gilbert (Ed.), *Researching social life* (pp. 306–326) London: Sage.

Henriques, J., Hollway, W., Irwin, C., Venn, C., & Walkerdine, V. (1984). *Changing the subject: Psychology, social regulation and subjectivity.* London: Methuen.

Henwood, K., & Nicolson, P. (Eds.) (1995). Qualitative research methods (special issue). *The Psychologist, 8,* 109–129.

Henwood, K., & Parker, I. (1994). Qualitative social psychology (special issue). *Journal of Community and Applied Social Psychology, 4,* 219–223.

Henwood, K., & Pidgeon, N. (1994). Beyond the qualitative paradigm: A framework for introducing diversity within qualitative psychology. *Journal of Community and Applied Social Psychology, 4,* 225–238.

Henwood, K., & Pidgeon, N. (1995). Grounded theory and psychological research. *The Psychologist, 8,* 115–118.

Heritage, J. C. (1984). *Garfinkel and ethnomethodology.* Cambridge, UK: Polity.

Heritage, J. C. (1988). Explanations as accounts: A conversation analytic perspective. In C. Antaki (Ed.), *Analysing everyday explanation: A casebook of methods* (pp. 127–144). London: Sage.

Heritage, J. C. (1995). Conversation analysis: Methodological aspects. In U. Quasthoff (Ed.), *Aspects of oral communication.* (pp. 391–418). Berlin, Germany: De Gruyter.

Hesse, M. B. (1974). *The structure of scientific inference.* London: Macmillan.

Hodder, I. (1994). The interpretation of documents and material culture. In N. K. Denzin & Y. S. Lincoln (Eds.), *Handbook of qualitative research* (pp. 395–402). London: Sage.

Holsti, O. R. (1969). *Content analysis for the social sciences and humanities.* Reading, MA: Addison-Wesley.

Jasanoff, S., Markle, G., Pinch T., & Petersen, J. (Eds.) (1995). *Handbook of science and technology studies.* London: Sage.

Jefferson, G. (1985). An exercise in the transcription and

analysis of laughter. In T. van Dijk (Ed.), *Handbook of discourse analysis* (Vol. 3, pp. 25–34). London: Academic Press.

Jefferson, G. (1988). On the sequential organization of troubles-talk in ordinary conversation. *Social Problems, 35,* 418–441.

Jefferson, G., & Lee, J. R. E. (1992). The rejection of advice: Managing the problematic convergence of a "troubles-telling" and a "service encounter." In P. Drew & J. Heritage (Eds.), *Talk at work: Interaction in institutional settings* (pp. 521–548). Cambridge, UK: Cambridge University Press.

Jodelet, D. (1991). *Madness and social representations.* London: Harvester/Wheatsheaf.

Johnson, J. C. (1990). *Selecting ethnographic informants.* London: Sage.

Knorr Cetina, K. (1995). Laboratory studies: The cultural approach to the study of science. In S. Jasanoff, G. Markle, T. Pinch, & J. Petersen (Eds.), *Handbook of science and technology studies.* London: Sage.

Knorr Cetina, K. (1997). *Epistemic cultures: How scientists make sense.* Chicago: Indiana University Press.

Krippendorff, K. (1980). *Content analysis: An introduction to its methodology.* London: Sage.

Krueger, R. A. (1988). *Focus groups: A practical guide for applied research.* London: Sage.

Kuhn, T. S. (1977). *The essential tension: Selected studies in scientific tradition and change.* Chicago: University of Chicago Press.

Kvale, S. (1996). *InterViews: An introduction to qualitative research interviewing.* London: Sage.

Labov, W., & Fanshel, D. (1977). *Therapeutic discourse: Psychotherapy as conversation.* London: Academic Press.

Lakatos, I. (1970). Falsification and the methodology of scientific research programmes. In I. Lakatos & A. Musgrave (Eds.), *Criticism and the growth of knowledge* (pp. 91–195). Cambridge, UK: Cambridge University Press.

Latour, B., & Woolgar, S. (1986). *Laboratory life: The construction of scientific facts* (2nd ed.). Princeton, NJ: Princeton University Press.

Lee, J. R. E. (1995). The trouble is nobody listens. In J. Siegfried (Ed.), *Therapeutic and everyday discourse as behaviour change: Towards a micro-analysis in psychotherapy process research* (pp. 365–390). Norwood, NJ: Ablex.

Levinson, S. (1983). *Pragmatics.* Cambridge, UK: Cambridge University Press.

Lincoln, Y. S., & Guba, E. G. (1985). *Naturalistic inquiry.* London: Sage.

Lofland, J., & Lofland, L. H. (1984). *Analyzing social settings: A guide to qualitative observation and analysis.* Belmont, CA: Wadsworth.

Lynch, M. (1994). Representation is overrated: Some critical remarks about the use of the concept of representation in science studies. *Configurations: A Journal of Literature, Science and Technology, 2,* 137–149.

Madigan, S. P. (1992). The application of Michel Foucault's philosophy in the problem externalizing discourse of Michael White. *Journal of Family Therapy, 14,* 265–279.

Madill, A., & Barkham, M. (1997). Discourse analysis of a theme in one successful case of brief psychodynamic-interpersonal psychotherapy. *Journal of Counselling Psychology, 44,* 232–244.

Malson, H., & Ussher, J. M. (1996). Bloody women: A discourse analysis of amenorrhea as a symptom of anorexia nervosa. *Feminism and Psychology, 6,* 505–521.

Manning, P. K., & Cullum-Swan, B. (1994) Narrative, content and semiotic analysis. In N. K. Denzin & Y. S. Lincoln (Eds.), *Handbook of qualitative research* (pp. 463–477). London: Sage.

Mason, J. (1994). Linking qualitative and quantitative data analysis. In A. Bryman & R. G. Burgess (Eds.), *Analyzing qualitative data.* London: Routledge.

McNamee, S., & Gergen, K. (Eds) (1992). *Therapy as social construction.* London: Sage

Miles, M. B., & Huberman, A. M. (1994). *Qualitative data analysis: An expanded sourcebook* (2nd Ed.). London: Sage.

Miller, G., & Dingwall, R. (Ed.) (1997). *Context and method in qualitative research.* London: Sage

Miller, G., & Silverman, D. (1995). Troubles talk and counseling discourse: A comparative study. *The Sociological Quarterly, 36,* 725–747.

Mischler, E. G. (1986). *Research interviewing: Context and narrative.* Cambridge, MA: Harvard University Press.

Morgan, D. L. (1997). *Focus groups as qualitative research* (2nd ed.). London: Sage.

Morris, G. H., & Chenail, R. J. (Eds.) (1995). *The talk of the clinic: Explorations in the analysis of medical and therapeutic discourse.* Hillsdale, NJ: Erlbaum.

Moscovici, S. (1984). The phenomenon of social representations. In R. M. Farr & S. Moscovici (Eds.), *Social representations* (pp. 3–69). Cambridge, UK: Cambridge University Press.

Nelson, C. K. (1994). Ethnomethodological positions on the use of ethnographic data in conversation analytic research. *Journal of Contemporary Ethnography, 23,* 307–329.

Newfield, N. A., Kuehl, B. P., Joanning, H. P., & Quinn, W. H. (1990). A mini ethnography of the family therapy of adolescent drug abuse: The ambiguous experience. *Alcoholism Treatment Quarterly, 7,* 57–80.

Newfield, N., Sells, S. P., Smith, T. E., Newfield, S., & Newfield, F. (1996). Ethnographic research methods: Creating a clinical science of the humanities. In D. H. Sprenkle & S. M. Moon (Eds.), *Research Methods in Family Therapy.* New York: Guilford.

Newfield, N. A., Kuehl, B. P., Joanning, H. P., & Quinn, W. H. (1991). We can tell you about "Psychos" and "Shrinks": An ethnography of the family therapy of adolescent drug abuse. In T. C. Todd & M. D. Slekman (Eds.), *Family therapy approaches with adolescent substance Abusers* (pp. 277–310). London: Allyn & Bacon.

Nofsinger, R. (1991). *Everyday conversation.* London: Sage.

Ochs, E. (1979). Transcription as theory. In E. Ochs & B. Schieffelin (Eds.), *Developmental pragmatics* (pp. 43–47). New York: Academic Press.

Ochs, E., Schegloff, E., & Thompson, S. A. (Eds.) (1996). *Interaction and grammar.* Cambridge, UK: Cambridge University Press.

Olesen, V. (1994), Feminisms and models of qualitative research. In N. K. Denzin & Y. S. Lincoln (Eds.), *Handbook of qualitative research* (pp. 158–174). London: Sage.

Peräkylä, A. (1995). *AIDS counseling: Institutional interaction and clinical practice.* Cambridge, UK: Cambridge University Press.

Pettinger, R. E., Hockett, C. F., & Danehy, J. J. (1960). *The first five minutes: A sample of microscopic interview analysis.* Ithica, NY: Paul Martineau.

Pidgeon, N. (1996). Grounded theory: Theoretical background. In J. T. E. Richardson (Ed.), *Handbook of qualitative research methods for psychology and the social sciences* (pp. 75–85). Leicester, UK: British Psychological Society.

Pidgeon, N., & Henwood, K. (1996). Grounded theory: Practical implementation. In J. T. E. Richardson (Ed.), *Handbook of qualitative research methods for psychology and the social sciences* (pp. 86–101). Leicester, UK: British Psychological Society.

Piercy F. P., & Nickerson, V. (1996). Focus groups in family therapy research. In D. H. Sprenkle & S. M.

Moon (Eds.), *Research methods in family therapy* (pp. 173–185). New York: Guilford.

Plummer, K. (1995). Life story research. In J. A. Smith, R. Harré, & L. van Langenhove (Eds.), *Rethinking methods in psychology* (pp. 50–63). London: Sage.

Polanyi, M. (1958). *Personal knowledge*. London: Routledge and Kegan Paul.

Pollner, M., & Wikler, L. M. (1985). The social construction of unreality: A case study of a family's attribution of competence to a severely retarded child. *Family Process, 24*, 241–254.

Pomerantz, A. M. (1980). Telling my side: "limited access" as a fishing device. *Sociological Inquiry, 50*, 186–198.

Popper, K. (1959). *The logic of scientific discovery*. London: Hutchinson.

Potter, J. (1996a). *Representing reality: Discourse, rhetoric and social construction*. London: Sage.

Potter, J. (1996b). Discourse analysis and constructionist approaches: Theoretical background. In J. T. E. Richardson (Ed.), *Handbook of qualitative research methods for psychology and the social sciences*. Leicester, UK: British Psychological Society.

Potter, J. (1997). Discourse analysis as a way of analysing naturally occurring talk. In D. Silverman (Ed.), *Qualitative research: Theory, method and practice* (pp. 144–160). London: Sage.

Potter, J., & Mulkay, M. (1985). Scientists' interview talk: Interviews as a technique for revealing participants' interpretative practices. In M. Brenner, J. Brown, & D. Canter (Eds.), *The research interview: Uses and approaches* (pp. 247–271). London: Academic Press.

Potter, J., & Wetherell, M. (1987). *Discourse and social psychology: Beyond attitudes and behaviour*. London: Sage.

Potter, J., & Wetherell, M. (1994) Analyzing discourse. In A. Bryman & B. Burgess (Eds.), *Analyzing qualitative data*. London: Routledge.

Potter, J., & Wetherell, M. (1995). Discourse analysis. In J. Smith, R. Harré, & L. van Langenhove (Eds.), *Rethinking methods in psychology* (pp. 80–92). London: Sage.

Potter, J., Wetherell, M., & Chitty, A. (1991). Quantification rhetoric—cancer on television. *Discourse and Society, 2*, 333–365.

Psathas, G., & Anderson, T. (1990). The "practices" of transcription in conversation analysis. *Semiotica, 78*, 75–99.

Rachel, J. (1996). Ethnography: Practical implementation. In J. T. E. Richardson (Ed.), *Handbook of qualitative research methods for psychology and the social sciences* (pp. 113–124). Leicester, UK: British Psychological Society.

Rafuls, S. E., & Moon, S. M. (1996). Grounded theory methodology in family therapy research. In D. H. Sprenkle & S. M. Moon (Eds.), *Research methods in family therapy* (pp. 64–80). New York: Guilford.

Ramazanoglu, C. (1992). On feminist methodology: Male reason versus female empowerment. *Sociology, 26*, 207–212.

Rapley, M., & Antaki, C. (1996). A conversation analysis of the "acquiescence" of people with learning disabilities. *Journal of Community and Applied Social Psychology, 6*, 207–227.

Reason, P., & Heron, J. (1995). Co-operative inquiry. In J. A. Smith, R. Harré, & L. van Langenhove (Eds.), *Rethinking methods in psychology* (pp. 122–142). London: Sage.

Reason, P., & Rowan, J. (Eds.) (1981). *Human inquiry: A sourcebook of new paradigm research*. Chichester, UK: Wiley.

Reinharz, S. (1992). *Feminist methods in social research*. New York: Oxford University Press.

Rennie, D., Phillips, J., & Quartaro, G. (1988). Grounded theory: A promising approach to conceptualisation in psychology? *Canadian Psychology, 29*, 139–150.

Richardson, J. E. (Ed.) (1996). *Handbook of qualitative research methods for psychology and the social sciences*. Leicester, UK: British Psychological Society.

Rogers, C. R. (1942). The use of electrically recorded interviews in improving psychotherapeutic techniques. *American Journal of Orthopsychiatry, 12*, 429–434.

Ronai, C. R. (1996). My mother is mentally retarded. In C. Ellis & A. P. Bochner (Eds.), *Composing ethnography: Alternative forms of qualitative writing*. Walnut Creek, CA: AltaMira Press.

Rose, D. (1990). *Living the ethnographic life*. London: Sage.

Rosenhan, D. L. (1973). On being sane in insane places. *Science, 179*, 250–258.

Sacks, H. (1992). *Lectures on conversation*. (Vols. I & II). Oxford, UK: Blackwell.

Schegloff, E. A. (1991). Reflections on talk and social structure. In D. Boden & D. H. Zimmerman (Eds.), *Talk and social structure* (pp. 44–70). Berkeley, CA: University of California Press.

Schegloff, E. A. (1993). Reflections on quantification in the study of conversation. *Research on Language and Social Interaction, 26*, 99–128.

Schegloff, E. A. (1997) Whose text? Whose Context? *Discourse and Society, 8*, 165–187.

Scott, J. (1990). *A matter of record: Documentary sources in social research*. Cambridge, UK: Polity.

Siegfried, J. (Ed.) (1995). *Therapeutic and everyday discourse as behaviour change: Towards a micro-analysis in psychotherapy process research*. Norwood, NJ: Ablex.

Silverman, D. (1993). *Interpreting qualitative data: Methods for analysing talk, text and interaction*. London: Sage.

Silverman, D. (Ed.) (1997a). *Qualitative research: Theory, method and practice*. London: Sage.

Silverman, D. (1997b). *Discourses of counselling: HIV counselling as social interaction*. London: Sage.

Smith, L. M. (1994). Biographical method. In N. K. Denzin & Y. S. Lincoln (Eds.), *Handbook of qualitative research* (pp. 286–305) London: Sage.

Smith, J. A. (1995). Repertory grids: An interactive, case-study perspective. In J. A. Smith, R. Harré, & L. van Langehove (Eds.), *Rethinking methods in psychology* (pp. 162–177). London: Sage.

Smith, J. A., Harré, R., & van Langenhove, L. (Eds.) (1995). *Rethinking methods in psychology*. London: Sage.

Soal, J., & Kottler, A. (1996). Damaged, deficient or determined? Deconstructing narratives in family therapy. *South African Journal of Psychology, 26*, 123–134.

Soyland, A. J. (1994). Functions of a psychiatric case-summary. *Text, 14*, 113–140.

Soyland, A. J. (1995). Analyzing therapeutic and professional discourse. In J. Siegfried (Ed.), *Therapeutic and everyday discourse as behaviour change: Towards a micro-analysis in psychotherapy process research* (pp. 277–300). Norwood, NJ: Ablex.

Stainton Rogers, R. (1995). Q methodology. In J. A. Smith, R. Harré, & L. van Langenhove (Eds.), *Rethinking methods in psychology* (p. 178–192). London: Sage.

Strauss, A. L., & Corbin, J. (1994). Grounded theory methodology: An overview. In N. K. Denzin, & Y. S. Lincoln (Eds.), *Handbook of qualitative research* (pp. 273–285). London: Sage.

Toren, C. (1996). Ethnography: Theoretical background. In J. T. E. Richardson (Ed.), *Handbook of qualitative research methods for psychology and the social sciences* (pp. 102–112). Leicester, UK: British Psychological Society.

Turner, B. A. (1994). Patterns of crisis behaviour: A qualitative inquiry. In A. Bryman & R. G. Burgess (Eds.), *Analyzing qualitative data* (pp. 195–215). London: Routledge.

Turner, B. A., & Pidgeon, N. (1997). *Manmade disasters* (2nd ed.). Oxford, UK: Butterworth-Heinemann.

Watson, R. (1995). Some potentialities and pitfalls in the

144 *Qualitative and Discourse Analysis*

analysis of process and personal change in counseling and therapeutic interaction. In J. Siegfried (Ed.), *Therapeutic and everyday discourse as behaviour change: Towards a micro-analysis in psychotherapy process research* (pp. 301–339). Norwood, NJ: Ablex.

Weinstein, R. M. (1979). Patient attitudes toward mental hospitalization: A review of quantitative research. *Journal of Health and Social Behavior, 20,* 237–258.

Weinstein, R. M. (1980). The favourableness of patients' attitudes toward mental hospitalization. *Journal of Health and Social Behavior, 21,* 397–401.

Werner, O., & Schoepfle, G. M. (1987). *Systematic fieldwork: Foundations of ethnography and interviewing* (Vol. 1). London: Sage.

Wetherell, M. (1996). Fear of fat: Interpretative repertoires and ideological dilemmas. In J. Maybin & N. Mercer (Eds.), *Using English: From conversation to canon* (pp. 36–41). London: Routledge.

White, M., & Epston, D. (1990). *Narrative means to therapeutic ends.* New York: Norton.

Whyte, W. F. (1991). *Participatory action research.* London: Sage.

Widdicombe, S., & Wooffitt, R. (1995). *The language of youth subcultures: Social identity in action.* Hemel Hempstead, UK: Harvester/Wheatsheaf.

Wieder, D. L. (Ed.) (1993). Colloquy: On issues of quantification in conversation analysis. *Research on Language and Social Interaction, 26,* 151–226.

Wilkinson, S. (1986). Introduction. In S. Wilkinson (Ed.), *Feminist social psychology* (pp. 1–6). Milton Keynes, UK: Open University Press.

Wooffitt, R. (1993). Analysing accounts. In N. Gilbert (Ed.), *Researching social life* (pp. 287–305). London: Sage.

Woolgar, S. (1988). *Science: The very idea.* London: Tavistock.

Wootton, A. (1989). Speech to and from a severely retarded young Down's syndrome child. In M. Beveridge, G. Conti-Ramsden, & I. Leudar (Eds.), *The language and communication of mentally handicapped people* (pp. 157–184). London: Chapman-Hall.

Yardley, K. (1995). Role play. In J. A. Smith, R. Harré & L. van Langenhove (Eds.), *Rethinking methods in psychology* (pp. 106–121). London: Sage.

3.07
Personality Assessment

THOMAS A. WIDIGER and KIMBERLY I. SAYLOR
University of Kentucky, Lexington, KY, USA

3.07.1 INTRODUCTION

Most domains of psychology have documented the importance of personality traits to adaptive and maladaptive functioning, including the fields of behavioral medicine (Adler & Matthews, 1994), psychopathology (Watson, Clark, & Harkness, 1994; Widiger & Costa, 1994), and industrial-organizational psychology (Hogan, Curphy, & Hogan, 1994). The assessment of personality is perhaps fundamental to virtually all fields of applied psychology. However, there are as many as 4500 different personality traits, or at least 4500 different trait terms within the English language (Goldberg, 1990) and there might be almost as many personality assessment instruments. There are instruments for the assessment of individual traits (e.g., tender-mindedness), for collections of traits (e.g., the domain of agreeableness, which includes tender-mindedness, trust, straightforwardness, altruism, compliance, and modesty), for constellations of traits (e.g., the personality syndrome of psychopathy, which includes such traits as arrogance, superficial charm, impulsivity, callousness, arrogance, deception, irresponsibility, and low empathy), and for traits identified by theorists for which there might not yet be a specific term within the language (e.g., extratensive experience balance; Exner, 1993).

There are also different methods for the assessment of personality traits. The primary methods used in personality research are self-report inventories, semistructured interviews, and projective techniques. Self-report inventories consist of written statements or questions, to which a person responds in terms of a specified set of options (e.g., true vs. false or agree vs. disagree along a five-point scale). Semistructured interviews consist of a specified set of verbally administered questions, accompanied by instructions (or at least guidelines) for follow-up questions and for the interpretation and scoring of responses. Projective techniques consist of relatively ambiguous stimuli or prompts, the possible responses to which are largely open-ended, accompanied by instructions (or at least guidelines) for their scoring or interpretation. The distinctions among these three methods, however, is somewhat fluid. A self-report inventory is equivalent to a fully structured, self-administered interview; semistructured interviews are essentially verbally administered self-report inventories that include at least some open-ended questions; and fully structured interviews are essentially verbally administered self-report inventories.

Each of the methods will be considered below, including a discussion of issues relevant to or problematic for that respective method. However, the issues discussed for one method of assessment will apply to another. Illustrative instruments for each method are also presented.

3.07.2 SELF-REPORT INVENTORIES

The single most popular method for the assessment of personality by researchers of normal personality functioning is a self-report inventory (SRI). The advantages of SRIs, relative to semistructured interviews and projective techniques, are perhaps self-evident. They are substantially less expensive and time-consuming to administer. Data on hundreds of persons can be obtained, scored, and analyzed at relatively little cost to the researcher. Their inexpensive nature allows collection of vast amounts of normative data that are unavailable for most semistructured interviews and projective techniques. These normative data in turn facilitate substantially their validation, as well as their interpretation by and utility to researchers and clinicians.

The high degree of structure of SRIs has also contributed to much better intersite reliability than is typically obtained by semistructured interviews or projective techniques. The findings of SRIs are very sensitive to the anxious, depressed, or angry mood states of respondents, contributing at times to poor test–retest reliability (discussed further below). However, the correlation between two SRIs is much more likely to be consistent across time and across research sites than the correlation between two semistructured interviews or two projective techniques. SRIs might be more susceptible to mood state distortions than semistructured interviews, but this susceptibility may itself be observed more reliably across different studies than the lack of susceptibility of semistructured interviews.

The specific and explicit nature of SRIs has also been very useful in researching and understanding the source and nature of subjects' responses. Much more is known about the effects of different item formats, length of scales, demographic variables, base rates, response sets, and other moderating variables from the results of SRIs than from semistructured interviews or projective techniques. Five issues to be discussed below are (i) item analyses; (ii) gender, ethnic, and cultural differences; (iii) individual differences; (iv) response distortion; and (v) automated assessments.

3.07.2.1 Item Analyses

There are a variety of methods for constructing, selecting, and evaluating the items to be included within an SRI (Clark & Watson, 1995). However, it is useful to highlight a few points within this chapter as such analyses are of direct importance to personality assessment research.

An obvious method for item construction, often termed the rational approach, is to construct items that describe explicitly the trait being assessed. For example, the most frequently used SRI in clinical research for the assessment of personality disorders is the Personality Diagnostic Questionnaire-4 (PDQ-4; Hyler, 1994). Its items were written to inquire explicitly with respect to each of the features of the 10 personality disorders included in the American Psychiatric Association's (APA) *Diagnostic and statistical manual of mental disorders* (*DSM-IV*; APA, 1994). For example, the dependent personality criterion, "has difficulty expressing disagreement with others because of fear of loss of support or approval" (APA, 1994, p. 668) is assessed by the PDQ-4 item, "I fear losing the support of others if I disagree with them" (Hyler, 1994, p. 4).

The content validity of an SRI is problematic to the extent that any facets of the trait being assessed are not included or are inadequately represented, items representing other traits are included, or the set provides a disproportionately greater representation of one facet of the trait relative to another (Haynes, Richard, & Kubany, 1995). "The exact phrasing of items can exert a profound influence on the construct that is actually measured" (Clark & Watson, 1995, p. 7) yet the content of items often receives little consideration in personality assessment research. Widiger, Williams, Spitzer, and Frances (1985) concluded from a systematic content analysis of the Millon Clinical Multiaxial Inventory (MCMI; Millon, 1983) that the MCMI failed to represent adequately many significant features of the antisocial personality disorder.

> Many of the [personality] traits are not sampled at all (e.g., inability to sustain consistent work behavior, lack of ability to function as a responsible parent, inability to maintain an enduring attachment to a sexual partner, failure to plan ahead or impulsivity, and disregard for the truth), including an essential requirement of the *DSM-III* antisocial criteria to exhibit significant delinquent behavior prior to the age of 15. (Widiger et al., 1985, p. 375)

Many MCMI-III items are written in part to represent an alternative theoretical formulation for the *DSM-IV* personality syndromes (Millon et al., 1996).

High content validity, however, will not ensure a valid assessment of a respective personality trait. Although many of the PDQ-4 dependency items do appear to represent adequately their respective diagnostic criteria, it is difficult to anticipate how an item will actually perform when administered to persons with varying degrees of dependency and to persons with varying degrees of other personality traits, syndromes, or demographic characteristics. Most authors of SRIs also consider the findings of internal consistency analyses (Smith & McCarthy, 1995). "Currently, the single most widely used method for item selection in scale development is some form of internal consistency analysis" (Clark & Watson, 1995, p. 313).

Presumably, an item should correlate more highly with other items from the same scale (e.g., dependent personality traits) than items from another scale (e.g., borderline personality traits), consistent with the basic principles of convergent and discriminant validity. However, these assumptions hold only for personality syndromes that are homogeneous in content and that are distinct from other syndromes, neither of which may be true for syndromes that involve overlapping constellations of personality traits (Pilkonis, 1997; Shea, 1995). Confining a scale to items that correlate highly with one another can result in an overly narrow assessment of a construct, and deleting items that correlate highly with other scales can result in false distinctions and a distorted representation of the trait being assessed (Clark & Watson, 1995; Smith & McCarthy, 1995). For example, the APA (1994) criteria set for the assessment of antisocial personality disorder does not include such items as lacks empathy and arrogant self-appraisal that are included in alternative criteria sets for this personality syndrome (Hare, 1991) in part because these items are already contained within the *DSM-IV* criteria set for the narcissistic personality disorder. Their inclusion within the criteria set for antisocial personality disorder would complicate the differentiation of the antisocial and narcissistic personality syndromes (Gunderson, 1992), but the failure to include these items may also provide an inadequate description and assessment of antisocial (psychopathic) personality traits (Hare, Hart, & Harpur, 1991).

Overlapping scales, on the other hand, have their own problems, particularly if they are to be used to test hypotheses regarding the relationships among or differences between the traits and syndromes being assessed (Helmes & Reddon, 1993). For example, the MCMI-III personality scales overlap substantially (Millon, Millon, & Davis, 1994). Scale overlap was in part a pragmatic necessity of assessing 14 personality disorders and 10 clinical syndromes with no more than 175 items. However, this overlap was also intentional to ensure that the scales be consistent with the overlap of the personality constructs being assessed. "Multiple keying or item overlapping for the MCMI inventories was designed to fit its theory's polythetic structure, and the scales constructed to represent it" (Millon, 1987, p. 130). However, the MCMI-III cannot then be used to assess the validity of this polythetic structure, or to test hypotheses concerning the covariation, differentiation, or relationship among the personality constructs, as the findings will be compelled by the scale overlap (Helmes & Reddon, 1993). For example, the MCMI-III provides little possibility for researchers to fail to confirm a close relationship between, or comparable findings for, sadistic and antisocial personality traits, given that eight of the 17 antisocial items (47%) are shared with the sadistic scale. The same point can be made for studies using the Minnesota Multiphasic Personality Inventory (MMPI-2) antisociality and cynicism scales, as they share approximately a third of their items (Helmes & Reddon, 1993). It was for this reason that Morey, Waugh, and Blashfield (1985) developed both overlapping and nonoverlapping MMPI personality disorder scales.

Scale homogeneity and interscale distinctiveness are usually emphasized in SRIs constructed through factor analyses (Clark & Watson, 1995). For example, in the construction of the NEO Personality Inventory-Revised (NEO-PI-R), Costa and McCrae (1992)

> adopted factor analysis as the basis for item selection because it identifies clusters of items that covary with each other but which are relatively independent of other item clusters—in other words, items that show convergent validity with respect to other items in the cluster and divergent validity with respect to other items [outside the cluster]. (p. 40)

Reliance upon factor analysis for scale construction has received some criticism (Block, 1995; Millon et al., 1996) and there are, indeed, instances in which factor analyses have been conducted with little appreciation of the limitations of the approach (Floyd & Widaman, 1995), but this is perhaps no different than for any other statistical technique. Factor analysis remains a powerful tool for identifying underlying, latent constructs, for data reduction, and for the validation of an hypothesized dimensional structure (Smith & McCarthy, 1995; Watson et al., 1994). In any case, the construction of the NEO-PI-R through factor analysis was consistent with the theoretical model for the personality traits being assessed (Clark & Watson, 1995; Costa & McCrae, 1992; Goldberg, 1990). Additional illustrations of theoretically driven factor analytic scale constructions are provided by the Dimensional Assessment of Personality Pathology—Basic Questionnaire (DAPP-BQ; Livesley & Jackson, in press), the Schedule for Nonadaptive and Adaptive Personality (SNAP; Clark, 1993), the Interpersonal Adjective Scales (IAS; Wiggins & Trobst, 1997), the Multidimensional Personality Questionnaire (MPQ; Tellegen & Waller, in press), and the Temperament and Character Inventory (TCI; Cloninger & Svrakic, 1994).

The most informative item analyses will be correlations with external validators of the personality traits, including the ability of items to identify persons with the trait in question, correlations with hypothesized indicators of the trait, and an absence of correlations with variables that are theoretically unrelated to the trait (Smith & McCarthy, 1995). These data typically are discussed under a general heading of construct validity, including data concerning items' concurrent, postdictive, predictive, convergent, and discriminant validity (Ozer & Reise, 1994). Illustrative studies with SRIs include Ben-Porath, McCully, and Almagor (1993), Clark, Livesley, Schroeder, and Irish (1996), Lilienfeld and Andrews (1996), Robins and John (1997), and Trull, Useda, Coasta, and McCrae (1995).

The MMPI-2 clinical scales exemplify the purely empirical approach to scale construction. "The original MMPI (Hathaway & McKinley, 1940) was launched with the view that the content of the items was relatively unimportant and what actually mattered was whether the item was endorsed by a particular clinical group" (Butcher, 1995, p. 302). This allowed the test to be "free from the restriction that the subject must be able to describe his own behavior accurately" (Meehl, 1945, p. 297). For example, one of the items on the MMPI hysteria scale was "I enjoy detective or mystery stories" (keyed false; Hathaway & McKinley, 1982).

Indicating that one does not enjoy detective or mystery stories does not appear to have any obvious (or perhaps even meaningful) relationship to the presence of the mental disorder of hysteria, but answering false did correlate significantly with the occurrence of this disorder. "The literal content of the stimulus (the item) is entirely unimportant, and even irrelevant and potentially misleading. Sophisticated psychometric use of test items dictates that the test interpreter ignore item content altogether lest he or she be misled" (Ben-Porath, 1994, p. 364). Limitations to this approach, however, are suggested below.

A sophisticated approach to item analysis is item response theory (IRT; Hambleton, Swaminathan, & Rogers, 1991). Its most unique datum is the probability of a response to a particular item given a particular level of the personality trait being assessed. IRT analyses demonstrate graphically how items can vary in their discriminative ability at different levels of the trait being assessed (assuming that the anchoring items are not themselves systematically biased). It is not the case that all items perform equally well, nor does any particular item perform equally well at all levels of the trait. It may be the case that none of the items on a scale provide any discrimination at particular levels of a trait, or that the scale is predominated by items that discriminate at high rather than moderate or low levels of the trait. For example, it is possible that the MMPI-2 items to assess the personality domain of neuroticism are weighted toward a discrimination of high levels of neuroticism, providing very little discrimination at low levels. IRT analyses might allow researchers to maximize the sensitivity of a test to a particular population (e.g., inpatient hospital vs. prison setting) by deleting items that work poorly within certain settings (Embretson, 1996). IRT analyses have been used widely with tests of abilities and skills, and are now being applied to measures of personality (Ozer & Reise, 1994). Illustrative applications include analyses of items from the MPQ (Tellegen & Waller, in press) by Reise and Waller (1993), items from a measure of alexithymia by Hendryx, Haviland, Gibbons, and Clark (1992) and items from a psychopathy semistructured interview by Cooke and Michie (1997).

3.07.2.2 Gender, Ethnic, and Cultural Differences

Differences among gender, ethnic, cultural, and other demographic populations with respect to personality traits are often socially sensitive, politically controversial, and difficult to explain (Eagly, 1995). There is substantial SRI research to indicate differences, on average, between males and females for a wide variety of personality traits, as assessed by research with SRIs (Sackett & Wilk, 1994). For example, males obtain higher scores on measures of assertiveness and self-esteem; whereas females obtain higher scores on measures of anxiousness, trust, gregariousness, and tender-mindedness (Feingold, 1994).

Separate norms therefore have been developed for the interpretation of most SRI personality scales (e.g., Costa & McCrae, 1992; Graham, 1993; Millon et al., 1994). However, the rationale for providing different norms for each sex (gender) is unclear. Sackett and Wilk (1994) "searched test manuals, handbooks, and the like for a discussion of the rationale for the practice. We typically found none" (p. 944). They indicated, with some surprise, that the provision of separate norms for males and females "does not seem to have been viewed as at all controversial" (Sackett & Wilk, 1994, p. 944). If the SRI is indicating an actual difference between males and females (Feingold, 1994) it is unclear why this difference showed then be eliminated or diminished in SRI assessments of males and females (Kehoe & Tenopyr, 1994; Sackett & Wilk, 1994).

For example, males and females with the same raw score on the psychopathic deviate scale of the MMPI-2 will be given different final scores due to the use of different norms. Different raw scores for males and females can then result in the same final score (Graham, 1993). The extent of psychopathy in females is then relative to other females; it is not a measure of the actual (absolute) extent to which they are psychopathic. A male who has more traits (or symptoms) of psychopathy could be described by the MMPI-2 as being less psychopathic than a female with the same number of traits. The separate norms provided for males and females on SRIs are never so substantial as to eliminate entirely the differences between the sexes, but the rationale for reducing or minimizing any differences is unclear.

The provision of separate norms for males and females by SRIs is inconsistent with other domains of assessment, including most semistructured interview and projective assessments of personality variables. For example, the same threshold is used for males and females by the most commonly used semistructured interview for the assessment of psychopathy, the (revised) Psychopathy Checklist (Hare, 1991). Separate norms are not provided for females and males in the assessment of intelligence, nor are they provided for different cultural and ethnic groups in the assessment of personality. Although statistically significant differences have also been obtained across ethnic and cultural groups for SRI personality measures, "none of the major personality measures ... offered norm scoring based on race or ethnicity either as a routine aspect of the scoring system or as a scoring option" (Sackett & Wilk, 1994, p. 947). It is unclear whether separate norms should be provided for ethnic groups, but it does appear to be inconsistent to provide separate norms for gender and not for ethnicity.

Separate norms would be appropriate if there is reason to believe that the SRI items are biased against a particular gender, ethnic, or cultural group. "Bias is the extent to which measured group differences are invalid ... Group differences are invalid to the extent that the constructs that distinguish between groups are different from the constructs the measures were intended to represent" (Kehoe & Tenopyr, 1994, p. 294). Consider, for example, the MMPI item cited earlier, "I enjoy detective or mystery stories" (Hathway & McKinley, 1982, p. 3). The MMPI reliance upon a blind empiricism for item selection can be problematic if the basis for the item endorsement is for reasons other than, or in addition to, the presence of the construct being assessed. Lindsay and Widiger (1995) suggested that this item might have been correlated with hysteria because hysteria was itself correlated with female gender. Significantly more females than males are diagnosed with hysteria and significantly more females than males respond negatively to an interest in detective or mystery stories; therefore, the item may have correlated with hysteria because it was identifying the presence of females rather than the presence of hysteria. In addition, because such an item concerns normal behavior that occurs more often in one sex than in the other, we would consider it to be sex biased because its errors in prediction (false positives) will occur more often in one sex than in the other. (Lindsay & Widiger, 1995, p. 2)

One would never consider including as one of the *DSM-IV* diagnostic criteria for histrionic personality disorder, "I have often enjoyed reading Cosmopolitan and Ms. Magazine" but many such items are included in SRIs to diagnose the presence of a personality disorder. For example, responding false to the item "in the past, I've gotten involved sexually with many people who didn't matter much to me," is used for the assessment of a dependent personality disorder on the MCMI-II (Millon, 1987, p. 190). Not getting involved sexually with many people who do not matter much is hardly an indication of a dependent personality disorder (or of any dysfunction), yet it is used to diagnose the presence of this personality disorder.

There are also data to suggest that the same items on an SRI may have a different meaning to persons of different ethnic, cultural, or gender groups (Okazaki & Sue, 1995), although the magnitude, consistency, and significance of these differences has been questioned (Ozer & Reise, 1994; Timbrook & Graham, 1994). Applications of IRT analyses to the assessment of bias would be useful (Kehoe & Tenopyr, 1994). For example, Santor, Ramsay, and Zuroff (1994) examined whether men and women at equal levels of depression respond differentially to individual items. They reported no significant differences for most items, but bias was suggested for a few, including a body-image dissatisfaction item. Females were more likely to endorse body-image dissatisfaction than males even when they were at the same level of depression as males, suggesting that the endorsement of the item by women (relative to men) reflected their gender independently of their level of depression.

3.07.2.3 Individual Differences

The provision of any set of norms may itself be questioned. Personality description with SRIs traditionally has been provided in reference to individual differences. "Raw scores on personality inventories are usually meaningless—responses take on meaning only when they are compared to the responses of others" (Costa & McCrae, 1992, p. 13). However, this individual differences approach can itself be problematic. "The individual differences research paradigm, which has thoroughly dominated empirical personality research throughout the present century, is fundamentally inadequate for the purposes of a science of personality" (Lamiell, 1981, p. 36). Lamiell's scathing critique of individual differences research raised many important and compelling concerns. For example, he noted how the test–retest reliability of a personality scale typically is interpreted as indicating the extent to which the expression of a trait is stable in persons across time, but most analyses in fact indicate the extent to which persons maintain their relative position on a scale over time. The test–retest reliability of relative position may itself correlate highly with the test–retest reliability of the magnitude within each person, but it need not. For example, the reliability of a measure of height, assessed across 100 persons using a product-moment correlation, would suggest substantial stability between the ages of eight and 15, despite the fact that each person's actual height would have changed substantially during this time. Height is not at all consistent or stable across childhood, yet a measure of stability in height would be very high if the relative height among the persons changed very little. This confusion, however, would be addressed by alternative reliability statistics (e.g., an intra-class correlation coefficient).

Interpreting personality test scores relative to a particular population is not necessarily problematic as long as the existence of these norms and their implications for test interpretation are understood adequately. For example, a score on an MMPI-2 social introversion scale does not indicate how introverted a person is, but how much more (or less) introverted the person is relative to a particular normative group. The MMPI-2 social introversion scale does not indicate the extent to which an Asian-American male is socially introverted, it indicates how more (or less) introverted he is relative to a sample of 1138 American males who provided the normative data, only 1% of whom were Asian-American (Graham, 1993).

Nevertheless, researchers and clinicians will at times refer to SRI results as if they are providing an absolute measure of a personality trait. For example, researchers and clinicians will describe a person as having high self-esteem, low self-monitoring, or high dependency, when in fact the person is simply higher or lower than a particular comparison group. It is common in personality research to construct groups of subjects on the basis of median splits on SRI scores for such traits as self-esteem, self-monitoring, dependency, autonomy, or some other personality construct. Baumeister, Tice, and Hutton (1989) searched the literature for all studies concerning self-esteem. "Most often . . .

high and low self-esteem groups are created by performing a median split on the self-esteem scores across the sample" (p. 556). Persons above the median are identified as having "high self-esteem" whereas persons below the median are identified as having "low self-esteem." However, interpreting SRI data in this manner is inaccurate and potentially misleading. Persons below a median would indeed have less self-esteem than the persons above a median, but it is unknown whether they are in fact either high or low in self-esteem. All of the subjects might be rather high (or low). This method of assessing subjects is comparable to providing a measure of psychopathy to a sample of nuns to identify a group of psychopaths and nonpsychopaths, or a measure of altruism to convicts within a prison to identify a group of saints and sinners. Yet, many researchers will provide measures of self-esteem (self-monitoring, dependency, narcissism, or some other SRI measure) to a group of well-functioning college students to identify persons high and low in self-esteem. Baumeister et al. (1989) indeed found that "in all cases that we could determine, the sample midpoint was higher (in self-esteem) than the conceptual midpoint, and generally the discrepancy was substantial and significant" (p. 559).

3.07.2.4 Response Distortion

SRIs rely substantially on the ability of the respondent to provide a valid self-description. To the extent that a person does not understand the item, or is unwilling or impaired in his or her ability to provide an accurate response, the results will be inaccurate. "Detection of an attempt to provide misleading information is a vital and necessary component of the clinical interpretation of test results" (Ben-Porath & Waller, 1992, p. 24).

The presence of sufficiently accurate self-description is probably a reasonable assumption in most instances (Costa & McCrae, 1997). However, it may also be the case that no person will be entirely accurate in the description of this or her personality. Each person probably evidences some degree of distortion, either minimizing or exaggerating flaws or desirabilities. Such response distortion will be particularly evident in persons characterized by personality disorders (Westen, 1991). Antisocial persons will tend to be characteristically dishonest or deceptive in their self-descriptions, dependent persons may self-denigrate, paranoid persons will often be wary and suspicious, borderline persons will tend to idealize and devalue, narcissistic persons will often be

arrogant or self-promotional, and histrionic persons will often be overemotional, exaggerated, or melodramatic in their self-descriptions (APA, 1994). Response distortion may also be common within some populations, such as forensic, disability, or psychiatric settings, due in part to the higher prevalence of personality disorder symptomatology within these populations but due as well to the pressures, rewards, and inducements within these settings to provide inaccurate self-descriptions (Berry, 1995).

A substantial amount of research has been conducted on the detection of response distortion (otherwise known as response sets or biases), particularly with the MMPI-2 (Butcher & Rouse, 1996). There are self-report scales to detect nonresponsiveness (e.g., random responding, yea-saying or nay-saying), overreporting of symptoms (e.g., malingering, faking bad, exaggeration, or self-denigration), and underreporting (e.g., faking good, denial, defensiveness, minimization, or self-aggrandizement). These scales often are referred to as validity scales, as their primary function has been to indicate the extent to which the scores on the personality (or clinical) scales are providing an accurate or valid self-description, and they do appear to be generally successful in identifying the respective response distortions (Berry, Wetter, & Baer, 1995).

However, it is not always clear whether the prevalence of a respective form of response distortion is frequent enough to warrant its detection within all settings (Costa & McCrae, 1997). Acquiescence, random responding, and nay-saying might be so infrequent within most settings that the costs of false positive identifications (i.e., identifying a personality description as invalid when it is in fact valid) will outweigh the costs of false negatives (identifying a description as valid when it was in fact invalid). In addition, much of the research on validity scales has been confined to analogue studies in which various response distortions are simulated by college students, psychiatric patients, or other persons. There is much less data to indicate that the inclusion of a validity scale as a moderator or suppressor variable actually improves the validity of the personality assessment. For example, it is unclear whether the correlation of a measure of the personality trait of neuroticism with another variable (e.g., drug usage) would increase when variance due to a response distortion (e.g., malingering or exaggeration) is partialled from the measure of neuroticism (Costa & McCrae, 1997).

In some contexts, such as a disability evaluation, response distortions are to be avoided, whereas in other contexts, such as the assessment of maladaptive personality traits, they may be what the clinician is seeking to identify (Ozer & Reise, 1994). Validity scales typically are interpreted as indicators of the presence of misleading or inaccurate information, but the response tendencies assessed by validity scales are central to some personality disorders. For example, an elevation on a malingering scale would indicate the presence of deception or dishonesty, suggesting perhaps that the information provided by the subject in response to the other SRI items was inaccurate or misleading. However, one might not want to partial the variance due to malingering from an SRI measure of antisocial or psychopathic personality. The validity of a measure of psychopathy would be reduced if variance due to deception or dishonesty was extracted, as dishonesty or deception is itself a facet of this personality syndrome (APA, 1994; Hare, 1991; Lilienfeld, 1994). It might be comparably misleading to extract variance due to symptom exaggeration from a measure of borderline personality traits, self-aggrandizement from a measure of narcissism, or self-denigration from a measure of dependency. Validity scales are not just providing a measure of response distortion that undermines the validity of personality description; they are also providing valid descriptions of highly relevant and fundamental personality traits.

For example, a response distortion that has been of considerable interest and concern is social desirability. Persons who are instructed to attribute falsely to themselves good, desirable qualities provide elevations on measures of social desirability, and many researchers have therefore extracted from a measure of personality the variance that is due to this apparent response bias. However, extracting this variance typically will reduce rather than increase the validity of personality measures because much of the socially desirable self-description does in fact constitute valid self-description (Borkenau & Ostendorf, 1992; McCrae & Costa, 1983). Persons who characteristically describe themselves in a socially desirable manner are not simply providing false and misleading information. Much of the variance within a measure of social desirability is due to persons either describing themselves accurately as having many desirable personality traits or, equally accurately, as having a personality disposition of self-aggrandizement, arrogance, or denial. This problem could be addressed by first extracting the variance due to valid individual differences from a measure of social desirability before it is used as a moderater variable, but then it might obviously fail to be useful as a moderater variable to the personality scales.

3.07.2.5 Automated Assessment and Base Rates

The structured nature of the responses to SRIs has also facilitated the development of automated (computerized) systems for scoring and interpretation. The researcher or clinician simply uses score sheets that can be submitted for computerized scanning, receiving in return a complete scoring and, in most cases, a narrative description of the subject's personality derived from the theoretical model of, and the data considered by, the author(s) of the computer system. Automated systems are available for most of the major personality SRIs, and their advantages are self-evident. "The computer can store and access a much larger fund of interpretive literature and base-rate data than any individual clinician can master, contributing to the accuracy, objectivity, reliability, and validity of computerized reports" (Keller, Butcher, & Slutske, 1990, p. 360).

Automated interpretive systems can also be seductive. They might provide the appearance of more objectivity and validity than is in fact the case (Butcher, 1995). Clinicians and researchers should always become closely familiar with the actual data and procedures used to develop an automated system, and the subsequent research assessing its validity, in order to evaluate objectively for themselves the nature and extent of the empirical support. For example,

> while any single clinician may do well to learn the norms and base rates of the client population he or she sees most often, a computer program can refer to a variety of population norms and, if programmed to do so, will always "remember" to tailor interpretive statements according to modifying demographic data such as education, marital status, and ethnicity. (Keller et al., 1990, p. 360)

This is an excellent sentiment, describing well the potential benefits of an automated report. However, simply providing a subject's education, marital status, and ethnicity to the automated computer system does not necessarily mean that this information will in fact be used. As noted above, very few of the SRIs consider ethnicity.

A purported advantage of the MCMI-III automated scoring system is that "actuarial base rate data, rather than normalized standard score transformations, were employed in calculating scale measures" (Millon et al., 1994, p. 4). The cutoff points used for the interpretation of the MCMI-III personality scales are based on the base rates of the personality syndromes within the population. "The BR [base rate] score was designed to anchor cut-off points to the prevalence of a particular attribute in the psychiatric population" (Millon et al., 1994, p. 26). This approach appears to be quite sophisticated, as it is seemingly responsive to the failure of clinicians and researchers to consider the effect of base rates on the validity of an SRI cutoff point (Finn & Kamphuis, 1995). "These data not only provide a basis for selecting optimal differential diagnostic cut-off scores but also ensure that the frequencies of MCMI-III diagnoses and profile patterns are comparable to representative clinical prevalence rates" (Millon et al., 1994 p. 4).

However, the MCMI-III automated scoring system does not in fact make adjustments to cutoff points depending upon the base rate of the syndrome within a local clinical setting. The MCMI-III uses the same cutoff point for all settings and, therefore, for all possible base rates. The advantage of setting a cutoff point according to the base rate of a syndrome is lost if the cutoff point remains fixed across different base rates (Finn & Kamphuis, 1995). "The use of the MCMI-III should be limited to populations that are not notably different in background from the sample employed to develop the instrument's base rate norms" (Millon et al., 1994, p. 35). It is for this reason that Millon et al. discourage the use of the MCMI-III within normal (community or college) populations (a limitation not shared by most other SRIs). In fact, the population sampled for the MCMI-III revision might have itself been notably different in background from the original sample used to develop the base rate scores. Retzlaff (1996) calculated the probability of having a personality disorder given the obtainment of a MCMI-III respective cutoff point, using the data provided in the MCMI-III test manual. Retzlaff concluded that "as determined by currently available research, the operating characteristics of the MCMI-III scales are poor" (p. 437). The probabilities varied from 0.08 to a high of only 0.32. For example, the probability of having an avoidant personality disorder if one surpassed the respective cutoff point was only 0.17, for the borderline scale it was only 0.18, and for the antisocial scale it was only 0.07. As Retzlaff indicated, "these hit rate statistics are well under one-half of the MCMI-II validities" (Retzlaff, 1996, p. 435).

Retzlaff (1996) suggested that there were two possible explanations for these results, either "the test is bad or that the validity study was bad" (p. 435) and he concluded that the fault lay with the MCMI-III cross-validation data. "At best, the test is probably valid, but there is no evidence and, as such, it cannot be trusted until better validity data are available" (Retzlaff, 1996, p. 435). However, it is unlikely that any new data will improve these statistics, unless the

new study replicates more closely the population characteristics of the original derivation study. A third alternative is to have the cutoff points for the scales be adjusted for different base rates within local settings, but no automated scoring system currently provides this option.

3.07.2.6 Illustrative Instruments

There are many SRIs for the assessment of normal and maladaptive personality traits, including the SNAP (Clark, 1993), the DAPP-BQ (Livesley & Jackson, in press), the Personality Assessment Inventory (Morey, 1996), the MPQ (Tellegen & Waller, in press), the MCMI-III (Millon et al., 1994), the PDQ-4 (Hyler, 1994), the IAS (Wiggins & Trobst, 1997), the Wisconsin Personality Inventory (Klein et al., 1993), and the TCI (Cloninger & Svrakic, 1994). Space limitations prohibit a consideration of each of them. A brief discussion, however, will be provided for the two dominant SRIs within the field of clinical personality assessment, the MMPI-2 (Graham, 1993; Hathaway et al., 1989) and the NEO-PI-R (Costa & McCrae, 1992).

3.07.2.6.1 Minnesota Multiphasic Personality Inventory-2

The MMPI-2 is an SRI that consists of 566 true/false items (Graham, 1993; Hathaway et al., 1989). It is the most heavily researched and validated SRI, and the most commonly used in clinical practice (Butcher & Rouse, 1996). Its continued usage is due in part to familiarity and tradition, but its popularity also reflects the obtainment of a substantial amount of empirical support and normative data over the many years of its existence (Graham, 1993).

The MMPI-2 is described as "the primary self-report measure of abnormal personality" (Ben-Porath, 1994, p. 363) but its most common usage is for the assessment of anxiety, depressive, substance, psychotic, and other such (Axis I) mental disorders rather than for the assessment of personality traits (Ozer & Reise, 1994). "The MMPI-2 clinical scales are ... measures of various forms of psychopathology ... and not measures of general personality" (Greene, Gwin, & Staal, 1997, p. 21). This is somewhat ironic, given that it is titled as a personality inventory (Helmes & Reddon, 1993).

However, the MMPI-2 item pool is extensive and many additional scales have been developed beyond the basic 10 clinical and three validity scales (Graham, 1993). For example, some of the new MMPI-2 content scales (Ben-Porath, 1994; Butcher, 1995), modeled after the seminal research of Wiggins (1966), do assess personality traits (e.g., cynicism, social discomfort, Type A behavior, and low self-esteem). The Morey et al. (1985) personality disorder scales have also been updated and normed for the MMPI-2 (Colligan, Morey, & Offord, 1994) and an alternative set of MMPI-2, *DSM-IV* personality disorder scales are being developed by Somwaru and Ben-Porath (1995). Harkness and McNulty (1994) have developed scales (i.e., the PSY-5) to assess five broad domains of personality (i.e., neuroticism, extraversion, psychoticism, aggressiveness, and constraint) that are said to provide the MMPI-2 assessment of, or an alternative to, the five-factor model of personality (Ben-Porath, 1994; Butcher & Rouse, 1996). "Other measures of five-factor models of normal personality will need to demonstrate incremental validity in comparison to the full set of MMPI-2 scales (including the PSY-5) to justify their use in clinical practice" (Ben-Porath, 1994, p. 393). However, there are important distinctions between the PSY-5 and the five-factor model constructs, particularly for psychoticism and aggressiveness (Harkness & McNulty, 1994; Harkness, McNulty, & Ben-Porath, 1995; Widiger & Trull, 1997). In addition, the utility of the MMPI-2 for personality trait description and research may be limited by the predominance of items concerning clinical symptomatology and the inadequate representation of important domains of personality, such as conscientiousness (Costa, Zonderman, McCrae, & Williams, 1985) and constraint (DiLalla, Gottesman, Carey, & Vogler, 1993)

3.07.2.6.2 *Neo Personality Inventory-Revised*

The most comprehensive model of personality trait description is provided by the five-factor model (Saucier & Goldberg, 1996; Wiggins & Pincus, 1992). Even the most ardent critics of the five-factor model acknowledge its importance and impact (e.g., Block, 1995; Butcher & Rouse, 1996; Millon et al., 1996). And, the predominant measure of the five-factor model is the NEO-PI-R (Costa & McCrae, 1992, 1997; Ozer & Reise, 1994; Widiger & Trull, 1997).

The 240 item NEO-PI-R (Costa & McCrae, 1992) assesses five broad domains of personality: neuroticism, extraversion (vs. introversion), openness (vs. closedness), agreeableness (vs. antagonism), and conscientiousness. Each item is rated on a five-point scale, from strongly disagree to strongly agree. Each domain is differentiated into six underlying facets. For example, the six facets of agreeableness vs. antagonism are trust vs. mistrust, altruism vs. exploitiveness, compliance vs. oppositionalism

or aggression, tender-mindedness vs. tough-mindedness (lack of empathy), modesty vs. arrogance, and straightforwardness vs. deception or manipulation. The domains and facets of the NEO-PI-R relate closely to other models of personality, such as the constructs of affiliation and power within the interpersonal circumplex model of personality (McCrae & Costa, 1989; Wiggins & Pincus, 1992). The NEO-PI-R assessment of the five-factor model also relates closely to the *DSM-IV* personality disorder nomenclature, despite its original development as a measure of normal personality functioning (Widiger & Costa, 1994).

The application of the NEO-PI-R within clinical settings, however, may be problematic, due to the absence of extensive validity scales to detect mood state and response-set distortion (Ben-Porath & Waller, 1992). A valid application of the NEO-PI-R requires that the respondent be capable of and motivated to provide a reasonably accurate self-description. This is perhaps a safe assumption for most cases (Costa & McCrae, 1997), but the NEO-PI-R might not be successful in identifying when this assumption is inappropriate. Potential validity scales for the NEO-PI-R, however, are being researched (Schinka, Kinder, & Kremer, 1997).

3.07.3 SEMISTRUCTURED INTERVIEWS

The single most popular method for clinical assessments of personality by psychologists working in either private practice, inpatient hospitals, or university psychology departments, is an unstructured interview (Watkins, Campbell, Nieberding, & Hallmark, 1995). Whereas most researchers of personality disorder rely upon semistructured interviews (SSI) (Rogers, 1995; Zimmerman, 1994), there are but a few SSIs for the assessment of normal personality functioning (e.g., Trull & Widiger, 1997) and none of the psychologists in a survey of practicing clinicians cited the use of a semistructured interview (Watkins et al., 1995).

Unstructured clinical interviews rely entirely upon the training, expertise, and conscientiousness of the interviewer to provide an accurate assessment of a person's personality. They are problematic for research as they are notoriously unreliable, idiosyncratic, and prone to false assumptions, attributional errors, and misleading expectations (Garb, 1997). For example, many clinical interviewers fail to provide a comprehensive assessment of a patient's maladaptive personality traits. Only one personality disorder diagnosis typically is provided to a patient, despite the fact that most patients will meet criteria for multiple diagnoses (Gunderson, 1992). Clinicians tend to diagnose personality traits and disorders hierarchically. Once a patient is identified as having a particular personality disorder (e.g., borderline), clinicians will fail to assess whether additional personality traits are present (Herkov & Blashfield, 1995). Alder, Drake, and Teague (1990) provided 46 clinicians with case histories of a patient that met the *DSM-III* criteria for four personality disorders (i.e., histrionic, narcissistic, borderline, and dependent). "Despite the directive to consider each category separately ... most clinicians assigned just one [personality disorder] diagnosis" (Adler et al., 1990, p. 127). Sixty-five percent of the clinicians provided only one diagnosis, 28% provided two, and none provided all four.

Unstructured clinical assessments of personality also fail to be systematic. Morey and Ochua (1989) provided 291 clinicians with the 166 *DSM-III* personality disorder diagnostic criteria (presented in a randomized order) and asked them to indicate which personality disorder(s) were present in one of their patients and to indicate which of the 166 diagnostic criteria were present. Kappa for the agreement between their diagnoses and the diagnoses that would be given based upon the diagnostic criteria they indicated to be present, ranged from 0.11 (schizoid) to only 0.58 (borderline). In other words, their clinical diagnoses agreed poorly with their own assessments of the diagnostic criteria for each disorder. The results of this study were replicated by Blashfield and Herkov (1996). Agreement in this instance ranged from 0.28 (schizoid) to 0.63 (borderline). "It appears that the actual diagnoses of clinicians do not adhere closely to the diagnoses suggested by the [diagnostic] criteria" (Blashfield & Herkov, 1996, p. 226).

Clinicians often base their personality disorder assessments on the presence of just one or two features, failing to consider whether a sufficient number of the necessary features are present (Blashfield & Herkov, 1996). In addition, the one or two features that one clinician considers to be sufficient may not be consistent with the feature(s) emphasized by another clinician, contributing to poor interrater reliability (Widiger & Sanderson, 1995; Zimmerman, 1994) and to misleading expectations and false assumptions. For example, a number of studies have indicated that many clinicians tend to overdiagnose the histrionic personality disorder in females (Garb, 1997). Clinicians tend to perceive a female patient who has just one or two histrionic features as having a histrionic personality disorder, even when she may instead meet the diagnostic criteria for an alternative personality disorder (Blashfield & Herkov, 1996; Ford & Widiger, 1989; Morey &

Ochoa, 1989). This overdiagnosis of histrionic personality disorder in females is diminished substantially when the clinician is compelled to assess systematically each one of the features. "Sex biases may best be diminished by an increased emphasis in training programs and clinical settings on the systematic use and adherence to the [diagnostic] criteria" (Ford & Widiger, 1989, p. 304).

The reluctance to use semistructured interviews within clinical practice, however, is understandable. Semistructured interviews that assess all of the *DSM-IV* personality disorder diagnostic criteria can require more than two hours for their complete administration (Widiger & Sanderson, 1995). This is unrealistic and impractical in routine clinical practice, particularly if the bulk of the time is spent in determining the absence of traits. However, the time can be diminished substantially by first administering an SRI to identify which domains of personality functioning should be emphasized and which could be safely ignored (Widiger & Sanderson, 1995).

Unstructured interviews are also preferred by clinicians because they find SSIs to be too constraining and superficial. Most clinicians prefer to follow leads that arise during an interview, adjusting the content and style to facilitate rapport and to respond to the particular needs of an individual patient. The questions provided by an SSI can appear, in comparison, to be inadequate and simplistic. However, SSIs are considered to be semistructured because they require (or allow) professional judgment and discretion in their administration and scoring. They are not simply mindless administrations of an SRI. The responsibility of an SSI interviewer is to assess for the presence of a respective trait, not to just record a subject's responses to a series of structured questions. Follow-up questions that must be sensitive and responsive to the mood state, defensiveness, and self-awareness of the person being interviewed are always required and are left to the expertise and discretion of the interviewer (Widiger, Frances, & Trull, 1989). There are only a few fully structured interviews for the assessment of personality traits and they may be inadequate precisely because of their excessive constraint and superficiality (Perry, 1992).

The questions provided by an SSI are useful in ensuring that each trait is assessed, and that a set of questions found to be useful in prior studies is being used in a consistent fashion. Systematic biases in clinical assessments are more easily identified, researched, and ultimately corrected with the explicit nature of SSIs and their replicated use across studies and research sites. A highly talented and skilled clinician can outperform an SSI, but it is risky to presume that one is indeed that talented clinician or that one is consistently skilled and insightful with every patient (Dawes, 1994). It would at least seem desirable for talented clinicians to be informed by a systematic and comprehensive assessment of a patient's personality traits.

3.07.3.1 Personality, Mood States, and Mental Disorders

Personality traits typically are understood to be stable behavior patterns present since young adulthood (Wiggins & Pincus, 1992). However, few SRIs emphasize this fundamental feature. For example, the instructions for the MMPI-2 make no reference to age of onset or duration (Hathaway et al., 1989). Responding true to the MMPI-2 borderline item, "I cry easily" (Hathaway et al., p. 6) could be for the purpose of describing the recent development of a depressive mood disorder rather than a characteristic manner of functioning. Most MMPI-2 items are in fact used to assess both recently developed mental disorders as well as long-term personality traits (Graham, 1993).

SRIs that required a duration since young adulthood for the item to be endorsed would be relatively insensitive to changes in personality during adulthood (Costa & McCrae, 1994), but SSIs are generally preferred over SRIs within clinical settings for the assessment of personality traits due to the susceptibility of SRIs to mood-state confusion and distortion (Widiger & Sanderson, 1995; Zimmerman, 1994). Persons who are depressed, anxious, angry, manic, hypomanic, or even just agitated are unlikely to provide accurate self-descriptions. Low self-esteem, hopelessness, and negativism are central features of depression and will naturally affect self-description. Persons who are depressed will describe themselves as being dependent, introverted self-conscious, vulnerable, and pessimistic (Widiger, 1993). Distortions will even continue after the remission of the more obvious, florid symptoms of depression (Hirschfeld et al., 1989).

Piersma (1989) reported significant decreases on the MCMI-II schizoid, avoidant, dependent, passive–aggressive, self-defeating, schizotypal, borderline, and paranoid personality scales across a brief inpatient treatment, even with the MCMI-II mood state correction scales. Significant increases were also obtained for the histrionic and narcissistic scales, which at first appeared nonsensical (suggesting that treatment had increased the presence of histrionic and narcissistic personality traits), until it was recognized that these scales include many items that involve self-confidence, assertion, and gregariousness. Piersma concluded that "the MCMI-II is not able to measure long-term personality characteristics ('trait' characteristics) independent of symptomatology ('state' characteristics)" (p. 91). Mood state distortion, however, might not be problematic within outpatient and normal community samples (Trull & Goodwin, 1993).

SSIs appear to be more successful than SRIs in distinguishing recently developed mental disorders from personality traits, particularly if the interviewers are instructed explicitly to make this distinction when they assess each item. Loranger et al. (1991) compared the assessments provided by the Personality Disorder Examination (PDE; Loranger, in press) at admission and one week to six months later. Reduction in scores on the PDE were not associated with depression or anxiety. Loranger et al. concluded that the "study provides generally encouraging results regarding the apparent ability of a particular semistructured interview, the PDE, to circumvent trait-state artifacts in diagnosing personality disorders in symptomatic patients" (p. 727).

However, it should not be presumed that SSIs are resilient to mood state distortions. O'Boyle and Self (1990) reported that "PDE dimensional scores were consistently higher (more symptomatic) when subjects were depressed" (p. 90) and Loranger et al. (1991) acknowledged as well that all but two of the PDE scales decreased significantly across the hospitalization. These changes are unlikely to reflect actual, fundamental changes in personality secondary to the brief psychiatric hospitalization.

The methods by which SRIs and SSIs address mood state and mental disorder confusion should be considered in future research (Zimmerman, 1994). For example, the *DSM-IV* requires that the personality disorder criteria be evident since late adolescence or young adulthood (APA, 1994). However, the PDE (Loranger, in press) requires only that one item be present since the age of 25, with the others present for only five years. A 45-year old adult with a mood disorder might then receive a dependent, borderline, or comparable personality disorder diagnosis by the PDE, if just one of the diagnostic criteria was evident since the age of 25.

3.07.3.2 Dissimulation and Distortion

Unstructured and semistructured interviewers base much of their assessments on the self-descriptions of the respondent. However, a substantial proportion of the assessment is also based on observations of a person's behavior and mannerisms (e.g., the schizotypal trait of odd or eccentric behavior; APA, 1994) the manner in which a person responds to questions (e.g., excessive suspiciousness in response to an innocuous question), and the consistency of the responses to questions across the interview. SSIs will also require that respondents provide examples of affirmative responses to ensure that the person understood the meaning or intention of a question. The provision of follow-up queries provides a significant advantage of SSIs relative to SRIs. For example, schizoid persons may respond affirmatively to an SRI question, "do you have any close friends," but further inquiry might indicate that they never invite these friends to their apartment, they rarely do anything with them socially, they are unaware of their friends' personal concerns, and they never confide in them. Widiger, Mangine, Corbitt, Ellis, and Thomas (1995) described a person who was very isolated and alone, yet indicated that she had seven very close friends with whom she confided all of her personal feelings and insecurities. When asked to describe one of these friends, it was revealed that she was referring to her seven cats.

In sum, none of the SSIs should or do accept a respondent's answers and self-descriptions simply at face value. Nevertheless, none of the personality disorder SSIs includes a formal method by which to assess defensiveness, dissimulation, exaggeration, or malingering. An assessment of exaggeration and defensiveness can be very difficult and complicated (Berry et al., 1995) yet it is left to the discretion and expertise of the interviewer in the assessment of each individual personality trait. Some interviewers may be very skilled at this assessment, whereas others may be inadequate in the effort or indifferent to its importance.

SSIs should perhaps include validity scales, comparable to those within self-report inventories. Alterman et al. (1996) demonstrated empirically that subjects exhibiting response sets of positive or negative impression management as assessed by the PAI (Morey, 1996) showed similar patterns of response distortion on two semistructured interviews, yet the interviewers appeared to be "essentially unaware of such behavior" (Alterman et al., 1996, p. 408). "The findings suggest that some individuals do exhibit response sets in the context of a structured interview and that this is not typically detected by the interviewer" (Alterman et al., 1996, p. 408). Much of the assessment of psychopathic personality traits by the revised Psychopathy Checklist (PCL-R; Hare, 1991) is based on a review of institutional file data rather than answers to interview questions, given the expectation that psychopathic persons will be characteristically deceptive and dishonest during an interview. It is unclear whether the PCL-R could provide a valid assessment of psychopathy in the absence of this additional, corroboratory information (Lilienfeld, 1994; Salekin, Rogers, & Sewell, 1996).

A notable exception to the absence of SSI validity scales is the Structured Interview of Reported Symptoms (SIRS; Rogers, Bagby, & Dickens, 1992) developed precisely for the assessment of subject distortion and dissimulation. The SIRS includes 172 items (sets of questions) organized into eight primary and five supplementary scales. Three of the primary scales assess for rare, improbable, or absurd symptoms, four assess for an unusual range and severity of symptoms, and the eighth assesses for inconsistencies in self-reported and observed symptoms. A substantial amount of supportive data has been obtained with the SIRS, particularly within forensic and neuropsychological settings (Rogers, 1995).

3.07.3.3 Intersite Reliability

The allowance for professional judgment in the selection of follow-up queries and in the interpretation of responses increases significantly the potential for inadequate interrater reliability. Good to excellent interrater reliability has been consistently obtained in the assessment of maladaptive personality traits with SSIs (Widiger & Sanderson, 1995; Zimmerman, 1994), but an SSI does not ensure the obtainment of adequate interrater reliability. An SSI only provides the means by which this reliability can be obtained. Most SSI studies report inadequate to poor interrater reliability for at least one of the domains of personality being assessed (see Widiger & Sanderson, 1995; Zimmerman, 1994). The obtainment of adequate interrater reliability should be assessed and documented in every study in which an SSI is being used, as it is quite possible that the personality disorder of particular interest is the one for which weak interrater reliability has been obtained.

The method by which interrater reliability has been assessed in SSI research is also potentially misleading. Interrater reliability has traditionally been assessed in SSI research with respect to the agreement between ratings provided by an interviewer and ratings provided by a person listening to an audiotaped (or videotaped) recording of this interview (Zimmerman, 1994). However, this methodology assesses only the agreement regarding the ratings of the respondents' statements. It is comparable to confining the assessment of the interrater reliability of practicing clinicians' personality assessments to the agreement in their ratings of a recording of an unstructured clinical interview. The poor interrater reliability that has been reported for practicing clinicians has perhaps been due largely to inconsistent, incomplete, and idiosyncratic interviewing (Widiger & Sanderson, 1995). It is unclear whether personality disorder SSIs have actually resolved this problem as few studies have in fact assessed interrater reliability using independent administrations of the same interview.

The misleading nature of currently reported SSI interrater reliability is most evident in studies that have used telephone interviews. Zimmerman and Coryell (1990) reported kappa agreement rates of 1.0 for the assessment of the schizotypal, histrionic, and dependent personality disorders using the Structured Interview for *DSM-III* Personality (SIDP; Pfohl, Blum, & Zimmerman, in press). However, 86% of the SIDP administrations were by telephone. Telephone administrations of an SSI will tend to be more structured than face-to-face interviews, and perhaps prone to brief and simplistic administrations. They may degenerate into a verbal administration of an SRI. Interrater agreement with respect to the ratings of subjects' affirmative or negative responses to MMPI-2 items (i.e., highly structured questions) is not particularly informative.

There is reason to believe that there might be poor agreement across research sites using the same SSI. For example, the prevalence rate of borderline personality disorder within psychiatric settings has been estimated at 15% (Pilkonis et al., 1995), 23% (Riso, Klein, Anderson, Ouimette, & Lizardi, 1994), 42% (Loranger et al., 1991), and 71% (Skodol, Oldham, Rosnick, Kellman, & Hyler, 1991), all using the same PDE (Loranger, in press). This substantial disagreement is due to many different variables (Gunderson, 1992; Pilkonis, 1997; Shea, 1995), but one distinct possibility is that there is an inconsistent administration and scoring of the PDE by Loranger et al. (1991), Pilkonis et al. (1995), Riso et al. (1994), and Skodol et al. (1991). Excellent interrater reliability of a generally unreliably administered SSI can be obtained within one particular research site through the development of local (idiosyncratic) rules and policies for the administration of follow-up questions and the scoring of respondents' answers that are inconsistent with the rules and policies developed for this same SSI at another research site.

3.07.3.4 Self and Informant Ratings

Most studies administer the SSI to the person being assessed. However, a method by which to address dissimulation and distortion is to administer the SSI to a spouse, relative, or friend who knows the person well. Many personality traits involve a person's manner of relating to others (McCrae & Costa, 1989; Wiggins & Trobst, 1997) and some theorists suggest that personality is essentially this manner of relating to others (Kiesler, 1996; Westen, 1991; Wiggins & Pincus, 1992).

A useful source for the description of these traits would then be persons with whom the subject has been interacting. These "informants" (as they are often identified) can be intimately familiar with the subject's characteristic manner of relating to them, and they would not (necessarily) share the subject's distortions in self-description. The use of peer, spousal, and other observer ratings of personality has a rich tradition in SRI research (Ozer & Reise, 1994).

An interview with a close friend, spouse, employer, or relative is rarely uninformative and typically results in the identification of additional maladaptive personality traits. However, it is unclear which source will provide the most valid information. Zimmerman, Pfohl, Coryell, Stangl, and Corenthal (1988) administered an SSI to both a patient and an informant, and obtained rather poor agreement, with correlations ranging from 0.17 (compulsive) to only 0.66 (antisocial). The informants identified significantly more dependent, avoidant, narcissistic, paranoid, and schizotypal traits, but Zimmerman et al. (1988) concluded that "patients were better able to distinguish between their normal personality and their illness" (p. 737). Zimmerman et al. felt that the informants were more likely to confuse patients' current depression with their longstanding and premorbid personality traits than the patients' themselves. Similar findings have been reported by Riso et al. (1994). Informants, like the patients themselves, are providing subjective opinions and impressions rather than objective descriptions of behavior patterns, and they may have their own axes to grind in their emotionally invested relationship with the identified patient. The fundamental attribution error is to overexplain behavior in terms of personality traits, and peers might be more susceptible to this error than the subjects themselves.

3.07.3.5 Convergent Validity Across Different Interviews

One of the most informative studies on the validity of personality disorder SSIs was provided by Skodol et al. (1991). They administered to 100 psychiatric inpatients two different SSIs on the same day (alternating in morning and afternoon administrations). Agreement was surprisingly poor, with kappa ranging from a low of 0.14 (schizoid) to a high of only 0.66 (dependent). Similar findings have since been reported by Pilkonis et al. (1995). If this is the best agreement one can obtain with the administration of different SSIs to the same persons by the same research team on the same day, imagine the disagreement that must be obtained by different research teams with different SSIs at different sites (however, both studies did note that significantly better agreement was obtained when they considered the dimensional rating of the extent to which each personality syndrome was present).

Skodol et al. (1991) concluded that the source of the disagreement they obtained between the Structured Clinical Interview for *DSM-III-R* Personality Disorders (SCID-II; First, Gibbon, Spitzer Williams, & Benjamin, in press) and the PDE (Loranger, in press) was the different questions (or items) used by each interview. "It is fair to say that, for a number of disorders (i.e., paranoid, schizoid, schizotypal, narcissistic, and passive–aggressive) the two [interviews] studied do not operationalize the diagnoses similarly and thus yield disparate results" (Skodol et al., p. 22).

There appear to be important differences among the SSIs available for the assessment of personality disorders (Clark,1992; Widiger & Sanderson, 1995; Zimmerman, 1994). Table 1 presents the number of structured questions (i.e., answerable by one word, such as "yes" or "frequently"), open-ended questions, and observational ratings provided in each of the five major personality disorder SSIs. It is evident from Table 1 that there is substantial variation across SSIs simply with respect to the number of questions provided, ranging from 193 to 373 with respect to structured questions and from 20 to 69 for open-ended questions. There is also variability in the reliance upon direct observations of the respondent. The PDE, Diagnostic Interview for *DSM-IV* Personality Disorders (DIPD-IV), and SIDP-IV might be more difficult to administer via telephone, given the number of observational ratings of behavior, appearance, and mannerisms that are required (particularly to assess the schizotypal and histrionic personality disorders).

There is also significant variability in the content of the questions used to assess the same personality trait (Clark, 1992; Widiger & Sanderson, 1995; Zimmerman, 1994). Table 2 presents the questions used by each of the five major SSIs to assess the borderline trait of identity disturbance, defined in *DSM-IV* as a markedly and persistently unstable sense of self-image or sense of self (APA, 1994). All five SSIs do ask about significant or dramatic changes in self-image across time. However, there are also notable differences. For example, the DIPD-IV and SIDP-IV refer specifically to feeling evil; the SIDP-IV highlights in particular a confusion regarding sexual orientation; the SCID-II appears to emphasize changes or fluctuations in self-image, whereas the DIPD-IV appears to emphasize an uncertainty or absence of self-image; and the Personality Disorder Interview-4 (PDI-IV) includes more open-ended self-descriptions.

It is possible that the variability in content of questions across different SSIs may not be as important as a comparable variability in questions across different SRIs, as the interviews may converge in their assessment through the unstructured follow-up questions, queries and clarifications. However, the findings of Pilkonis et al. (1995) and Skodol et al. (1991) suggest otherwise. In addition, as indicated in Table 1, most of the questions within the five SSIs are relatively structured, resulting perhaps in very little follow-up query.

3.07.3.6 Illustrative Instruments

The three most commonly used SSIs within clinical research for the assessment of the *DSM* personality disorders are the SIDP-IV (Pfohl et al., in press), the SCID-II (First et al., in press), and the PDE (Loranger, in press). The SIDP-IV has been used in the most number of studies. A distinctive feature of the PDE is the inclusion of the diagnostic criteria for the personality disorders of the World Health Organization's (WHO) *International Classification of Diseases* (*ICD-10*; 1992). However, using this international version of the PDE to compare the *DSM-IV* with the *ICD-10* is problematic, as the PDE does not in fact provide distinct questions for the *ICD-10* criteria. It simply indicates which of the existing PDE questions, developed for the assessment of the *DSM-IV* personality disorders, could be used to assess the *ICD-10* criteria. The *DSM-IV* and *ICD-10* assessments are not then independent. The DIPD (Zanarini, Frankenburg, Sickel, & Yong, 1996) is the youngest SSI, but it is currently being used in an extensive multi-site, longitudinal study of personality disorders.

3.07.3.6.1 SIDP-IV

The SIDP-IV (Pfohl et al., in press) is the oldest and most widely used SSI for the

Table 1 Amount of structure in personality disorder semistructured interviews.

	Number of questions				
Interview	Structured	Open-ended	Examples	Total	Observations
DIPD-IV	373	20	5	398	19
PDE	272	69	196	537	32
PDI-IV	290	35		325	3
SCID-II	193	35	75	303	7
SIDP-IV	244	58	35	337	16

Note. Examples = specified request for examples (PDI-IV instructs interviewers to always consider asking for examples, and therefore does not include a specified request for individual items); DIPD-IV = Diagnostic Interview for *DSM-IV* Personality Disorders (Zanarini et al., 1996); PDE = Personality Disorder Examination (Loranger, in press); PDI-IV = Personality Disorder Interview-4 (Widiger et al., 1995); SCID-II = Structured Clinical Interview for *DSM-IV* Axis II Personality Disorders (First, et al., in press); SIDP-IV = Structured Interview for *DSM-IV* Personality (Pfohl et al., in press).

assessment of the *DSM* personality disorders (Rogers, 1995; Widiger & Sanderson, 1995; Zimmerman, 1994). It includes 353 items (337 questions and 16 observational ratings) to assess the 94 diagnostic criteria for the 10 *DSM-IV* personality disorders. Additional items are provided to assess the proposed but not officially recognized negativistic (passive–aggressive), depressive, self-defeating, and sadistic personality disorders. It is available in two versions, one in which the items are organized with respect to the diagnostic criteria sets (thereby allowing the researcher to assess only a subset of the disorders) and the other in which the items are organized with respect to similar content (e.g., perceptions of others and social conformity) to reduce repetition and redundancy. Each diagnostic criterion is assessed on a four-point scale (0 = not present, 1 = subthreshold, 2 = present, 3 = strongly present). Administration time is about 90 minutes, depending in part on the experience of the interviewer and the verbosity of the subject. A computerized administration and scoring system is available. The accompanying instructions and manual are limited, but training videotapes and courses are available.

3.07.3.6.2 PDI-IV

The PDI-IV (Widiger et al., 1995) is the second oldest SSI for the assessment of the *DSM* personality disorders. It is comparable in content and style to the SIDP-IV, although it has fewer observational ratings and more open-ended inquiries. The PDI-IV has been used in substantially fewer studies than the SIDP-IV, PDE, or SCID-II, it lacks supportive training material, and only one of the published studies using the PDI-IV was conducted by independent investigators (Rogers, 1995). However, its accompanying man-

ual is the most systematic and comprehensive, providing extensive information regarding the history, rationale, and common assessment issues for each of the *DSM-IV* personality disorder diagnostic criteria.

3.07.4 PROJECTIVE TECHNIQUES

Projective techniques are not used as often as SRIs in personality research, "and many academic psychologists have expressed the belief that knowledge of projective testing is not as important as it used to be and that use of projective tests will likely decline in the future" (Butcher & Rouse, 1996, p. 91). However, "of the top 10 assessment procedures [used by clinicians] ... 4 are projectives, and another (Bender-Gestalt) is sometimes used for projective purposes" (Watkins et al., 1995, p. 59). Butcher and Rouse (1996) document as well that the second most frequently researched clinical instrument continues to be the Rorschach. "Predictions about the technique's demise appear both unwarranted and unrealistic" (Butcher & Rouse, 1996, p. 91). "Whatever negative opinions some academics may hold about projectives, they clearly are here to stay, wishing will not make them go away ... and their place in clinical assessment practice now seems as strong as, if not stronger than, ever" (Watkins et al., 1995, p. 59).

The term "projective," however, may be somewhat misleading, as it suggests that these tests share an emphasis upon the interpretation of a projection of unconscious conflicts, impulses, needs, or wishes onto ambiguous stimuli. This is true for most projective tests but it is not in fact the case for the most commonly used scoring system (i.e., Exner, 1993) for the most commonly used projective test (i.e., the Rorschach). The Exner (1993) Comprehensive

Table 2 Semistructured interview questions for the assessment of identity disturbance.

DIPD-IV

1. During the past two years, have you often been unsure of who you are or what you're really like?
2. Have you frequently gone from feeling sort of OK about yourself to feeling that you're bad or even evil?
3. Have you often felt that you had no identity?
4. How about that you had no idea of who you are or what you believe in?
5. That you don't even exist?

PDE

1. Do you think one of your problems is that you're not sure what kind of person you are?
2. Do you behave as though you don't know what to expect of yourself?
3. Are you so different with different people or in different situations that you don't behave like the same person?
4. Have others told you that you're like that? Why do you think they've said that?
5. What would you like to accomplish during your life? Do your ideas about this change often?
6. Do you often wonder whether you've made the right choice of job or career? (If housewife, ask:) Do you often wonder whether you've made the right choice in becoming a housewife? (If student, ask:) Have you made up your mind about what kind of job or career you would like to have?
7. Do you have trouble deciding what's important in life?
8. Do you have trouble deciding what's morally right and wrong?
9. Do you have a lot of trouble deciding what type of friends you should have?
10. Does the kind of people you have as friends keep changing?
11. Have you ever been uncertain whether you prefer a sexual relationship with a man or a woman?

PDI-IV

1. How would you describe your personality?
2. What is distinct or unique about you?
3. Do you ever feel that you don't know who you are or what you believe in?
4. Has your sense of who you are, what you value, what you want from life, or what you want to be, been fairly consistent, or has this often changed significantly?

SCID-II

1. Have you all of a sudden changed your sense of who you are and where you are headed?
2. Does your sense of who you are often change dramatically?
3. Are you different with different people or in different situations so that you sometimes don't know who you really are?
4. Have there been lots of sudden changes in your goals, career plans, religious beliefs, and so on?

SIDP-IV

1. Does the way you think about yourself change so often that you don't know who you are anymore?
2. Do you ever feel like you're someone else, or that you're evil, or maybe that you don't even exist?
3. Some people think a lot about their sexual orientation, for instance, trying to decide whether or not they might be gay (or lesbian). Do you often worry about this?

Note. *DIPD-IV* = Diagnostic Interview for *DSM-IV* Personality Disorders (Zanarini et al., 1996, pp. 25–26); PDE = Personality Disorder Examination (Loranger, in press, pp. 58–60, 83, & 117); PDI-IV = Personality Disorder Interview-4 (Widiger et al., 1995, p. 92); SCID-II = Structured Clinical Interview for *DSM-IV* Axis II Personality Disorders (First et al., in press, p. 37); SIDP-IV = Structured Interview for *DSM-IV* Personality (Pfohl et al., in press, p. 19).

System does include a few scores that appear to concern a projection of personal needs, wishes, or preoccupations (e.g., morbid content) but much of the scoring concerns individual differences in the perceptual and cognitive processing of the form or structure of the shapes, textures, details, and colors of the ambiguous inkblots. Exner (1989) has himself stated that "unfortunately, the Rorschach has been erroneously mislabeled as a projective test for far too long" (p. 527).

The label "projective test" is also contrasted traditionally with the label "objective test" (e.g., Keller et al., 1990) but this is again misleading. The Exner (1993) Comprehensive System scoring for the Rorschach is as objective as the scoring of an MMPI-2 (although not as reliable). In addition, clinicians often can interpret MMPI-2 profiles in an equally subjective manner.

A more appropriate distinction might be a continuum of structure vs. ambiguity with respect to the stimuli provided to the subject and the range of responses that are allowed. Most of the techniques traditionally labeled as projective do provide relatively more ambiguous stimuli than either SRIs or SSIs (e.g., inkblots or drawings). However, many SRI items can be as ambiguous as an item from a projective test. Consider, for example, the MMPI-2 items "I like mechanics magazines," "I used to keep a diary," and "I would like to be a journalist" (Hathaway et al., 1989, pp. 5, 8, 9). These items are unambiguous in their content, but the trait or characteristic they assess is very ambiguous (Butcher, 1995). There is, perhaps, less ambiguity in the meaning of the stems provided in a sentence completion test, such as "My conscience bothered me most when," "I used to dream about" and "I felt inferior when" (Lah, 1989, p. 144) than in many of the MMPI-2 items.

SRIs, on the other hand, are much more structured (or constraining) in the responses that are allowed to these stimuli. The only responses can be "true" or "false" to an ambiguous MMPI-2 item, whereas anything can be said in response to a more obvious sentence completion stem. Projective tests are uniformly more open-ended than SRIs in the responses that are allowed, increasing substantially the potential for unreliability in scoring.

However, SSIs can be as open-ended as many projective tests in the responses that are allowed. For example, the PDI-IV SSI begins with the request of "having you tell me the major events, issues, or incidents that you have experienced since late childhood or adolescence" (Widiger et al., 1995, p. 245). This initial question is intentionally open-ended to ensure that the

most important events or incidents are not neglected during the interview (Perry, 1992). However, such open-ended inquiries will contribute to problematic intersite reliability.

3.07.4.1 Rorschach

The Rorschach consists of 10 ambiguously shaped inkblots, some of which include various degrees of color and shading. The typical procedure is to ask a person what each inkblot might be, and to then follow at some point with inquiries that clarify the bases for the response (Aronow, Reznikoff, & Moreland, 1994; Exner, 1993). The Rorschach has been the most popular projective test in clinical practice since the Second World War, although the Thematic Apperception Test (TAT) and sentence completion tests are gaining in frequency of usage (Watkins et al., 1995).

There is empirical support for many Rorschach variables (Bornstein, 1996; Exner, 1993; Weiner, 1996), although the quality of some of this research has been questioned, including the support for a number of the fundamental Exner variables, such as the experience ratio (Kleiger, 1992; Wood, Nezworski, & Stejskal, 1996). The Rorschach can be administered and scored in a reliable manner, but the training that is necessary to learn how to score reliably the 168 variables of the Exner Comprehensive System is daunting, at best. SRIs and SSIs might provide a more cost-efficient method to obtain the same results (although profile interpretation of the MMPI-2 clinical scales can at times be equally complex; Helmes & Reddon, 1993). Exner (1996) has acknowledged, at least with respect to a depression index, that "there are other measures, such as the [MMPI-2], that might identify the presence of reported depression much more accurately than the Rorschach" (p. 12). The same point can perhaps be made for the assessment of personality traits, such as narcissism and dependency. Bornstein (1995), however, has argued that the Rorschach provides a less biased measure of sex differences in personality (dependency, in particular) because its scoring is less obvious to the subject. He suggested that the findings from SRIs and SSIs have provided inaccurate estimates of dependency in males because males are prone to deny the extent of their dependent personality traits in response to SRIs and SSIs.

An additional issue for the Rorschach is that its relevance to personality research and assessment is at times unclear. For example, the cognitive-perceptual mechanisms assessed by the Exner Comprehensive system do not appear to be of central importance to many theories of personality and personality disorder (Kleiger, 1992). "It is true that the Rorschach does not offer a precise measure for any single personality trait" (Exner, 1997, p. 41). How a person perceptually organizes an ambiguous inkblot may indeed relate to extratensive ideational activity, but constructs such as introversion, conscientiousness, need for affection, and empathy have a more direct, explicit relevance to current personality theory and research. More theoretically meaningful constructs are perhaps assessed by content (e.g., Aronow et al., 1994; Bornstein, 1996) or object-relational (e.g., Lerner, 1995) scoring systems. Content interpretations of the Rorschach are more consistent with the traditional understanding of the instrument as a projective stimulus, but this approach also lacks the empirical support of the cognitive-perceptual scoring systems and may only encourage a return to less reliable and subjective interpretations (Acklin, 1995).

3.07.4.2 Thematic Apperception Test

The TAT (Cramer, 1996) consists of 31 cards: one is blank, seven are for males, seven for females, one for boys or girls, one for men or women and one each for a boy, girl, man, and woman (the remaining 10 are for anyone). Thus, a complete set for any particular individual could consist of 20 stimulus drawings, although only 10 typically are used per person. Most of the drawings include person(s) in an ambiguous but emotionally provocative context. The instruction to the subject is to make up a dramatic story for each card, describing what is happening, what led up to it, what is the outcome, and what the persons are thinking and feeling. It is common to describe the task as a test of imaginative intelligence to encourage vivid, involved, and nondefensive stories.

The TAT is being used increasingly in personality research with an interpersonal or object-relational perspective (e.g., Westen, 1991). The TAT's provision of cues for a variety of interpersonal issues and relationships make it particularly well suited for such research, and the variables assessed are theoretically and clinically meaningful (e.g., malevolent vs. benevolent affect and the capacity for an emotional investment in relationships). The necessary training for reliable scoring is also less demanding than for the Rorschach, although a TAT administration remains time-consuming. There are many SRI measures of closely related interpersonal constructs that are less expensive and complex to administer and score (e.g., Kiesler, 1996; Wiggins & Trobst, 1997).

3.07.5 CONCLUSIONS

The assessment of personality is a vital component of clinical research and practice, particularly with the increasing recognition of the importance of personality traits to the development and treatment of psychopathology (Watson et al., 1994). The assessment of adaptive and maladaptive personality functioning is fundamental to virtually all fields of applied psychology.

It is then surprising and regrettable that clinical psychology training programs provide so little attention to the importance of and methods for obtaining comprehensive and systematic interviewing. The primary method for the assessment of personality in clinical practice is an unstructured interview that has been shown to be quite vulnerable to misleading expectations, inadequate coverage, and gender and ethnic biases. Training programs will devote a whole course, perhaps a whole year, to learning different projective techniques, but may never even inform students of the existence of any particular semistructured interview.

The preferred method of assessment in personality disorder research appears to be SSIs (Zimmerman, 1994), whereas the preferred method in normal personality research are SRIs (Butcher & Rouse, 1996). However, the optimal approach for both research and clinical practice would be a multimethod assessment, using methods whose errors of measurement are uncorrelated. No single approach will be without significant limitations. The convergence of findings across SRI, SSI, and projective methodologies would provide the most compelling results.

3.07.6 REFERENCES

Acklin, M. W. (1995). Integrative Rorschach interpretation. *Journal of Personality Assessment, 64,* 235–238.
Adler, D. A., Drake, R. E., & Teague, G. B. (1990). Clinicians' practices in personality assessment: Does gender influence the use of DSM-III Axis II? *Comprehensive Psychiatry, 31,* 125–133.
Adler, N., & Matthews, K. (1994) Health psychology: Why do some people get sick and some stay well? *Annual Review of Psychology, 45,* 229–259.
Alterman, A. I., Snider, E. C., Cacciola, J. S., Brown, L. S., Zaballero, A., & Siddiqui, N. (1996). Evidence for response set effects in structured research interviews. *Journal of Nervous and Mental Disease, 184,* 403–410.
American Psychiatric Association (1994). *Diagnostic and statistical manual of mental disorders.* (4th ed.). Washington, DC: Author.
Aronow, E., Reznikoff, M., & Moreland, K. (1994). *The Rorschach technique: Perceptual basics, content, interpretation and applications.* Boston: Allyn and Bacon.
Baumeister, R. F., Tice, D. M., & Hutton, D. G. (1989). Self-presentational motivations and personality differences in self-esteem. *Journal of Personality, 57,* 547–579.
Ben-Porath, Y. S. (1994). The MMPI and MMPI-2: Fifty

years of differentiating normal and abnormal personality. In S. Strack & M. Lorr (Eds.), *Differentiating normal and abnormal personality* (pp. 361–401). New York: Springer.

Ben-Porath, Y. S., McCully, E., & Almagor, M. (1993). Incremental validity of the MMPI-2 content scales in the assessment of personality and psychopathology by self-report. *Journal of Personality Assessment, 61,* 557–575.

Ben-Porath, Y. S., & Waller, N. G. (1992). "Normal" personality inventories in clinical assessment: General requirements and the potential for using the NEO Personality Inventory. *Psychological Assessment, 4,* 14–19.

Berry, D. T. R. (1995). Detecting distortion in forensic evaluations with the MMPI-2. In Y. S. Ben-Porath, J. R. Graham, G. C. N. Hall, R. D. Hirschman, & M. S. Zaragoza (Eds.), *Forensic applications of the MMPI-2* (pp. 82–102). Thousands Oaks, CA: Sage.

Berry, D. T. R., Wetter, M. W., & Baer, R. A. (1995). Assessment of malingering. In J. N. Butcher (Ed.), *Clinical personality assessment. Practical approaches* (pp. 236–248). New York: Oxford University Press.

Blashfield, R. K., & Herkov, M. J. (1996). Investigating clinician adherence to diagnosis by criteria: A replication of Morey and Ochoa (1989). *Journal of Personality Disorders, 10,* 219–228.

Block, J. (1995). A contrarian view of the five-factor approach to personality description. *Psychological Bulletin, 117,* 187–215.

Bornstein, R. F. (1995). Sex differences in objective and projective dependency tests: A meta-analytic review. *Assessment, 2,* 319–331.

Bornstein, R. F. (1996). Construct validity of the Rorschach oral dependency scale: 1967–1995. *Psychological Assessment, 8,* 200–205.

Borkenau, P., & Ostendorf, F. (1992). Social desirability scales as moderator and suppressor variables. *European Journal of Personality, 6,* 199–214.

Butcher, J. N. (1995). Item content in the interpretation of the MMPI-2. In J. N. Butcher (Ed.), *Clinical personality assessment. Practical approaches* (pp. 302–316). New York: Oxford University Press.

Butcher, J. N. (1995). How to use computer-based reports. In J. N. Butcher (Ed.), *Clinical personality assessment. Practical approaches* (pp. 78–94). New York: Oxford University Press.

Butcher, J. N., & Rouse, S. V. (1996). personality: Individual differences and clinical assessment. *Annual Review of Psychology, 47,* 87–111.

Clark, L. A. (1992). Resolving taxonomic issues in personality disorders. The value of large-scale analysis of symptom data. *Journal of Personality Disorders, 6,* 360–376.

Clark, L. A. (1993). *Manual for the schedule for nonadaptive and adaptive personality.* Minneapolis, MN: University of Minnesota Press.

Clark, L. A., Livesley, W. J., Schroeder, M. L., & Irish, S. L. (1996). Convergence of two systems for assessing specific traits of personality disorder. *Psychological Assessment, 8,* 294–303.

Clark, L. A., & Watson, D. (1995). Constructing validity: Basic issues in objective scale development. *Psychological Assessment, 7,* 309–319.

Cloninger, C. R., & Svrakic, D. M. (1994). Differentiating normal and deviant personality by the seven factor personality model. In S. Strack & M. Lorr (Eds.), *Differentiating normal and abnormal personality* (pp. 40–64). New York: Springer.

Colligan, R. C., Morey, L. C., & Offord, K. P. (1994). The MMPI/MMPI-2 personality disorder scales. Contemporary norms for adults and adolescents. *Journal of Clinical Psychology, 50,* 168–200.

Cooke, D. J., & Michie, C. (1997). An item response theory analysis of the Hare Psychopathy Checklist-Revised. *Psychological Assessment, 9,* 3–14.

Costa, P. T., & McCrae, R. R. (1992). *Revised NEO Personality Inventory (NEO PI-R) and NEO Five-Factor Inventory (NEO-FFI) professional manual.* Odessa, FL: Psychological Assessment Resources.

Costa, P. T., & McCrae, R. R. (1994). Set like plaster? Evidence for the stability of adult personality. In T. F. Heatherton & J. L. Weinberger (Eds.), *Can personality change?* (pp. 21–40). Washington, DC: American Psychological Association.

Costa, P. T., & McCrae, R. R. (1997). Stability and change in personality assessment: The Revised NEO Personality Inventory in the year 2000. *Journal of Personality Assessment, 68,* 86–94.

Costa, P. T., Zonderman, A. B., McCrae, R. R., & Williams, R. B. (1985). Content and comprehensiveness in the MMPI: An item factor analysis in a normal adult sample. *Journal of Personality and Social Psychology, 48,* 925–933.

Cramer, P. (1996). *Storytelling, narrative, and the Thematic Apperception Test.* New York: Guilford.

Dawes, R. M. (1994). *House of cards. Psychology and psychotherapy built on myth.* New York: Free Press.

DiLalla, D. L., Gottesman, I. I., Carey, G., & Vogler, G. P. (1993). Joint factor structure of the Multidimensional Personality Questionnaire and the MMPI in a psychiatric and high-risk sample. *Psychological Assessment, 5,* 207–215.

Eagly, A. H. (1995). The science and politics of comparing women and men. *American Psychologist, 50,* 145–158.

Embretson, S. E. (1996). The new rules of measurement. *Psychological Assessment, 8,* 341–349.

Exner, J. E. (1989). Searching for projection in the Rorschach. *Journal of Personality Assessment, 53,* 520–536.

Exner, J. E. (1993). *The Rorschach: A comprehensive system* (Vol. 1). New York: Wiley.

Exner, J. E. (1996). A comment on "The Comprehensive System for the Rorschach: A critical examination." *Psychological Science, 7,* 11–13.

Exner, J. E. (1997). The future of Rorschach in personality assessment. *Journal of Personality Assessment, 68,* 37–46.

Feingold, A. (1994). Gender differences in personality: A meta-analysis. *Psychological Bulletin, 116,* 429–456.

Finn, S. E., & Kamphuis, J. H. (1995). What a clinician needs to know about base rates. In J. N. Butcher (Ed.), *Clinical personality assessment. Practical approaches* (pp. 224–235). New York: Oxford University Press.

First, M. B., Gibbon, M., Spitzer, R. L., Williams, J. B. W., & Benjamin, L. S. (in press). *User's guide for the Structured Clinical Interview for DSM-IV Axis II Personality Disorders.* Washington, DC: American Psychiatric Press.

Floyd, F. J., & Widaman, K. F. (1995). Factor analysis in the development and refinement of clinical assessment instruments. *Psychological Assessment, 7,* 286–299.

Ford, M. R., & Widiger, T. A. (1989). Sex bias in the diagnosis of histrionic and antisocial personality disorders. *Journal of Consulting and Clinical Psychology, 57,* 301–305.

Garb, H. N. (1997). Race bias, social class bias, and gender bias in clinical judgment. *Clinical Psychology: Science and Practice.*

Goldberg, L. R. (1990). An alternative "Description of personality": The Big Five factor structure. *Journal of Personality and Social Psychology, 59,* 1216–1229.

Graham, J. R. (1993). *MMPI-2. Assessing personality and psychopathology* (2nd ed.). New York: Oxford University Press.

Greene, R. L., Gwin, R., & Staal, M. (1997). Current status of MMPI-2 research: A methodologic overview. *Journal of Personality Assessment, 68,* 20–36.

Gunderson, J. G. (1992). Diagnostic controversies. In A. Tasman & M. B. Riba (Eds.), *Review of psychiatry* (Vol. 11, pp. 9–24). Washington, DC: American Psychiatric Press.

Hambleton, R. K., Swaminathan, H., & Rogers, H. J. (1991). *Fundamentals of item response theory.* Newbury Park, CA: Sage.

Hare, R. D. (1991). *Manual for the Revised Psychopathy Checklist* Toronto, Canada: Multi-Health Systems.

Hare, R. D., Hart, S. D., & Harpur, T. J. (1991). Psychopathy and the DSM-IV criteria for antisocial personality disorder. *Journal of Abnormal Psychology, 100,* 391–398.

Harkness, A. R., & McNulty, J. L. (1994). The Personality Psychopathology Five (PSY-5): Issue from the pages of a diagnostic manual instead of a dictionary. In S. Strack & M. Lorr (Eds.), *Differentiating normal and abnormal personality* (pp. 291–315). New York. Springer.

Harkness, A. R., McNulty, J. L., & Ben-Porath, Y. S. (1995). The Personality Psychopathology Five (PSY-5): Constructs and MMPI-2 scales. *Psychological Assessment, 7,* 104–114.

Hathaway, S. R., & McKinley, J. C. (1940). A multiphasic personality schedule (Minnesota): I. Construction of the schedule. *Journal of Psychology, 10,* 249–254.

Hathaway, S. R., & McKinley, J. C. (1982). *Minnesota Multiphasic Personality Inventory test booklet.* Minneapolis, MN: University of Minnesota.

Hathaway, S. R., McKinley, J. C., Butcher, J. N., Dahlstrom, W. G., Graham, J. R., & Tellegen, A. (1989). *Minnesota Multiphasic Personality Inventory test booklet.* Minneapolis, MN: Regents of the University of Minnesota.

Haynes, S. N., Richard, D. C. S., & Kubany, E. S. (1995). Content validity in psychological assessment: A functional approach to concepts and methods. *Psychological Assessment, 7,* 238–247.

Helmes, E., & Reddon, J. R. (1993). A perspective on developments in assessing psychopathology: A critical review of the MMPI and MMPI-2. *Psychological Bulletin, 113,* 453–471.

Hendryx, M. S., Haviland, M. G., Gibbons, R. D., & Clark, D. C. (1992). An application of item response theory to alexithymia assessment among abstinent alcoholics. *Journal of Personality Assessment, 58,* 506–515.

Herkov, M. J., & Blashfield, R. K. (1995). Clinician diagnoses of personality disorders: Evidence of a hierarchical structure. *Journal of Personality Assessment, 65,* 313–321.

Hirschfeld, R. M., Klerman, G. L., Lavori, P., Keller, M., Griffith, P., & Coryell, W. (1989). Premorbid personality assessments of first onset of major depression. *Archives of General Psychiatry, 46,* 345–350.

Hogan, R., Curphy, G. J., & Hogan, J. (1994). What we know about leadership. Effectiveness and personality. *American Psychologist, 49,* 493–504.

Hyler, S. E. (1994). *Personality Diagnostic Questionnaire-4 (PDQ-4).* Unpublished test. New York: New York State Psychiatric Institute.

Kehoe, J. F., & Tenopyr, M. L. (1994). Adjustment in assessment scores and their usage: A taxonomy and evaluation of methods. *Psychological Assessment, 6,* 291–303.

Keller, L. S., Butcher, J. N., & Slutske, W. S. (1990). Objective personality assessment. In G. Goldstein & M. Hersen (Eds.), *Handbook of psychological assessment* (2nd ed., pp. 345–386). New York: Pergamon.

Kiesler, D. J. (1996). *Contemporary interpersonal theory & research, personality, psychopathology, and psychotherapy.* New York: Wiley.

Kleiger, J. H. (1992). A conceptual critique of the EA;es comparison in the Comprehensive Rorschach System. *Psychological Assessment, 4,* 288–296.

Klein, M. H., Benjamin, L. S., Rosenfeld, R., Treece, C., Husted, J., & Greist, J. H. (1993). The Wisconsin Personality Disorders Inventory: development, reliability, and validity. *Journal of Personality Disorders, 7,* 285–303.

Lah, M. I. (1989). Sentence completion tests. In C. S. Newmark (Ed.), *Major psychological assessment instruments* (Vol. II, pp. 133–163). Boston: Allyn & Bacon.

Lamiell, J. T. (1981). Toward an idiothetic psychology of personality. *American Psychologist, 36,* 276–289.

Lerner, P. M. (1995). Assessing adaptive capacities by means of the Rorschach. In J. N. Butcher (Ed.), *Clinical personality assessment. Practical approaches* (pp. 317–325). New York: Oxford University Press.

Lilienfeld, S. O. (1994). Conceptual problems in the assessment of psychopathy. *Clinical Psychology Review, 14,* 17–38.

Lilienfeld, S. O., & Andrews, B. P. (1996). Development and preliminary validation of a self-report measure of psychopathic personality traits in noncriminal populations. *Journal of Personality Assessment, 66,* 488–524.

Lindsay, K. A., & Widiger, T. A. (1995). Sex and gender bias in self-report personality disorder inventories: Item analyses of the MCMI-II, MMPI, and PDQ-R. *Journal of Personality Assessment, 65,* 1–20.

Livesley, W. J., & Jackson, D. (in press). *Manual for the Dimensional Assessment of Personality Pathology-Basic Questionnaire.* Port Huron, MI: Sigma.

Loranger, A. W. (in press). *Personality disorder examination.* Washington, DC: American Psychiatric Press.

Loranger, A. W., Lenzenweger, M. F., Gartner, A. F., Susman, V. L., Herzig, J., Zammit, G. K., Gartner, J. D., Abrams, R. C., & Young, R. C. (1991). Trait-state artifacts and the diagnosis of personality disorders. *Archives of General Psychiatry, 48,* 720–728.

McCrae, R. R., & Costa, P. T. (1983). Social desirability scales: More substance than style. *Journal of Consulting and Clinical Psychology, 51,* 882–888.

McCrae, R. R., & Costa, P. T. (1989). The structure of interpersonal traits: Wiggins' circumplex and the Five-Factor Model. *Journal of Personality and Social Psychology, 56,* 586–595.

Meehl, P. E. (1945). The dynamics of "structured" personality tests. *Journal of Clinical Psychology, 1,* 296–303.

Millon, T. (1983). *Millon Clinical Multiaxial Inventory manual* (3rd ed.). Minneapolis, MN: National Computer Systems.

Millon, T. (1987). *Manual for the MCMI-II* (2nd ed.). Minneapolis, MN: National Computer Systems.

Millon, T., Davis, R. D., Millon, C. M., Wenger, A. W., Van Zuilen, M. H., Fuchs, M., & Millon, R. B. (1996). *Disorders of personality. DSM-IV and beyond.* New York: Wiley.

Millon, T., Millon, C., & Davis, R. (1994). *MCMI-III manual.* Minneapolis, MN: National Computer Systems.

Morey, L. C. (1996). *An interpretive guide to the Personality Assessment Inventory (PAI).* Odessa, FL: Psychological Assessment Resources.

Morey, L. C., & Ochoa, E. S. (1989). An investigation of adherence to diagnostic criteria: Clinical diagnosis of the DSM-III personality disorders. *Journal of Personality Disorders, 3,* 180–192.

Morey, L. C., Waugh, M. H., & Blashfield, R. K. (1985). MMPI scales for DSM-III personality disorders: Their derivation and correlates. *Journal of Personality Assessment, 49,* 245–251.

O'Boyle, M., & Self, D. (1990). A comparison of two interviews for DSM-III-R personality disorders. *Psychiatry Research, 32,* 85–92.

Okazaki, S., & Sue, S. (1995). Methodological issues in assessment research with ethnic minorities. *Psychological Assessment, 7,* 367–375.

Ozer, D. J., & Reise, S. P. (1994). Personality assessment. *Annual Review of Psychology, 45,* 357–388.

Perry, J. C. (1992). Problems and considerations in the valid assessment of personality disorders. *American Journal of Psychiatry, 149,* 1645–1653.

Pfohl B., Blum, N., & Zimmerman, M. (in press). *Structured Interview for DSM-IV Personality.* Washington, DC: American Psychiatric Press.

Piersma, H. L. (1989). The MCMI-II as a treatment outcome measure for psychiatric inpatients. *Journal of Clinical Psychology, 45,* 87–93

Pilkonis, P. A. (1997). Measurement issues relevant to personality disorders. In H. H. Strupp, M. J. Lambert, & L. M. Horowitz (Eds.), *Measuring patient change in mood, anxiety, and personality disorders: Toward a core battery* (pp. 371–388). Washington, DC: American Psychological Association.

Pilkonis, P. A., Heape, C. L., Proietti, J. M., Clark, S. W., McDavid, J. D., & Pitts, T. E. (1995). The reliability and validity of two structured diagnostic interviews for personality disorders. *Archives of General Psychiatry, 52,* 1025–1033.

Reise, S. P., & Waller, N. G. (1993). Traitedness and the assessment of response pattern scalability. *Journal of Personality and Social Psychology, 65,* 143–151.

Retzlaff, P. (1996). MCMI-III diagnostic validity: Bad test or bad validity study. *Journal of Personality Assessment, 66,* 431–437.

Riso, L. P., Klein, D. N., Anderson, R. L., Ouimette, P. C., & Lizardi, H. (1994). Concordance between patients and informants on the Personality Disorder Examination. *American Journal of Psychiatry, 151,* 568–573.

Robins, R. W., & John, O. P. (1997). Effects of visual perspective and narcissism on self-perception. Is seeing believing? *Psychological Science, 8,* 37–42.

Rogers, R. (1995). *Diagnostic and structured interviewing. A handbook for psychologists.* Odessa, FL: Psychological Assessment Resources.

Rogers, R., Bagby, R. M., & Dickens, S. E. (1992). *Structured Interview of Reported Symptoms (SIRS) professional manual.* Odessa, FL: Psychological Assessment Resources.

Sackett, P. R., & Wilk, S. L. (1994). Within-group norming and other forms of score adjustment in preemployment testing. *American Psychologist, 49,* 929–954.

Santor, D. A., Ramsay, J. O., & Zuroff, D. C. (1994). Nonparametric item analyses of the Beck Depression Inventory: Evaluating gender item bias and response option weights. *Psychological Assessment, 6,* 255–270.

Salekin, R. T., Rogers, R., & Sewell, K. W. (1996). A review and meta-analysis of the Psychopathy Checklist and Psychopathy Checklist-Revised: Predictive validity of dangerousness. *Clinical Psychology: Science and Practice, 3,* 203–215.

Saucier, G., & Goldberg, L. R. (1996). The language of personality: Lexical perspectives on the five-factor model. In J. S. Wiggins (Ed.), *The five-factor model of personality. Theoretical perspectives* (pp. 21–50). New York: Guilford.

Schinka, J. A., Kinder, B. N., & Kremer, T. (1997). Research validity scales for the NEO-PI-R: Development and initial validation. *Journal of Personality Assessment, 68,* 127–138.

Shea M. T. (1995). Interrelationships among categories of personality disorders. In W. J. Livesley (Ed.), *The DSM-IV personality disorders* (pp. 397–406). New York: Guilford.

Skodol, A. E., Oldham, J. M., Rosnick, L., Kellman, H. D., & Hyler, S. E. (1991). Diagnosis of DSM-III-R personality disorders: A comparison of two structured interviews. *International Journal of Methods in Psychiatric Research, 1,* 13–26.

Smith, G. T., & McCarthy, D. M. (1995). Methodological considerations in the refinement of clinical assessment instruments. *Psychological Assessment, 7,* 300–308.

Somwaru, D. P., & Ben-Porath, Y. S. (1995). *Development and reliability of MMPI-2 based personality disorder scales.* Paper presented at the 30th Annual Workshop and Symposium on Recent Developments in Use of the MMPI-2 & MMPI-A. St. Petersburg Beach, FL.

Tellegen, A., & Waller, N. G. (in press). Exploring personality through test construction: Development of the Multidimensional Personality Questionnaire. In S. R. Briggs & J. M. Cheek (Eds.), *Personality measures: Development and evaluation* (Vol. 1). Greenwich, CT: JAI Press.

Timbrook, R. E., & Graham, J. R. (1994). Ethnic differences on the MMPI-2? *Psychological Assessment, 6,* 212–217.

Trull, T. J., & Goodwin, A. H. (1993). Relationship between mood changes and the report of personality disorder symptoms. *Journal of Personality Assessment, 61,* 99–111.

Trull, T. J., Useda, J. D., Costa, P. T., & McCrae, R. R. (1995). Comparison of the MMPI-2 Personality Psychopathology Five (PSY-5), the NEO-PI, and the NEO-PI-R. *Psychological Assessment, 7,* 508–516.

Trull, T. J., & Widiger, T. A. (1997). *Structured Interview for the Five-Factor Model of Personality professional manual.* Odessa, FL: Psychological Assessment Resources.

Watkins, C. E., Campbell, V. L., Nieberding, R., & Hallmark, R. (1995). Contemporary practice of psychological assessment by clinical psychologists. *Professional Psychology: Research and Practice, 26,* 54–60.

Watson, D., Clark, L. A., & Harkness, A. R. (1994). Structure of personality and their relevance to psychopathology. *Journal of Abnormal Psychology, 103,* 18–31.

Weiner, I. B. (1996). Some observations on the validity of the Rorschach inkblot method. *Psychological Assessment, 8,* 206–213.

Westen, D. (1991). Social cognition and object relations. *Psychological Bulletin, 109,* 429–455.

Widiger, T. A. (1993). Personality and depression: Assessment issues. In M. H. Klein, D. J. Kupfer, & M. T. Shea (Eds.), *Personality and depression. A current view* (pp. 77–118). New York: Guilford.

Widiger, T. A., & Costa, P. T. (1994). Personality and personality disorders. *Journal of Abnormal Psychology, 103,* 78–91.

Widiger, T. A., Frances, A. J., & Trull, T. J. (1989). Personality disorders. In R. Craig (Ed.), *Clinical and diagnostic interviewing* (pp. 221–236). Northvale, NJ: Aronson.

Widiger, T. A., Mangine, S., Corbitt, E. M., Ellis, C. G., & Thomas, G. V. (1995). *Personality Disorder Interview-IV. A semistructured interview for the assessment of personality disorders.* Odessa, FL: Psychological Assessment Resources.

Widiger, T. A., & Sanderson, C. J. (1995). Assessing personality disorders. In J. N. Butcher (Ed.), *Clinical personality assessment. Practical approaches* (pp. 380–394). New York: Oxford University Press.

Widiger, T. A., & Trull, T. J. (1997). Assessment of the five factor model of personality. *Journal of Personality Assessment, 68,* 228–250.

Widiger, T. A., Williams, J. B. W., Spitzer, R. L., & Frances, A. J. (1985). The MCMI as a measure of DSM-III. *Journal of Personality Assessment, 49,* 366–378.

Wiggins, J. S. (1966). Substantive dimensions of self-report in the MMPI item pool. *Psychological Monographs, 80,* (22, Whole No. 630).

Wiggins, J. S., & Pincus, A. L. (1992). Personality: Structure and assessment. *Annual Review of Psychology, 43*, 473–504.

Wiggins, J. S., & Trobst, K. K. (1997). Prospects for the assessment of normal and abnormal interpersonal behavior. *Journal of Personality Assessment, 68*, 110–126.

Wood, J. M., Nezworski, M. T., & Stejskal, W. J. (1996). The Comprehensive System for the Rorschach: A critical examination. *Psychological Science, 7*, 3–10.

World Health Organization. (1992). *The ICD-10 classification of mental and behavioural disorders. Clinical descriptions and diagnostic guidelines*. Geneva, Switzerland: Author.

Zanarini, M. C., Frankenburg, F. R., Sickel, A. E., &

Yong, L. (1996). *Diagnostic Interview for DSM-IV Personality Disorders (DIPD-IV)*. Boston: McLean Hospital.

Zimmerman, M. (1994). Diagnosing personality disorders. A review of issues and research methods. *Archives of General Psychiatry, 51*, 225–245.

Zimmerman, M., & Coryell, W. H. (1990). Diagnosing personality disorders in the community. A comparison of self-report and interview measures. *Archives of General Psychiatry, 47*, 527–531.

Zimmerman, M., Pfohl, B., Coryell, W., Stangl, D., & Corenthal, C. (1988). Diagnosing personality disorders in depressed patients. A comparison of patient and informant interviews. *Archives of General Psychiatry, 45*, 733–737.

3.08
Assessment of Psychopathology: Nosology and Etiology

NADER AMIR
University of Georgia, Athens, GA, USA

and

CATHERINE A. FEUER
University of Missouri at St. Louis, MO, USA

3.08.1 INTRODUCTION

The history of clinical psychology, similar to the history of medicine, has been characterized by the quest for knowledge of pathological processes. This knowledge enables practitioners in both fields to treat and prevent disorders that threaten the quality of life. Health practitioners must be able to identify and conceptualize the problem, communicate research and clinical findings to other members of their field, and ideally, to reach a scientific understanding of the disorder. Diagnostic taxonomies have evolved in part to achieve these goals (Millon, 1991). Classification systems have a long history, first in the basic sciences and medicine, and later in psychopathology. Modern psychopathology taxonomies owe much to the work of earlier medical diagnosticians, and their development has often paralleled that of medical systems (Clementz & Iacono, 1990). Both medical and psychopathological classification systems have served the purposes of improving diagnostic reliability, guiding clinical conceptualization and treatment, and facilitating research and scientific advancement (Blashfield, 1991; Clark, Watson, & Reynolds, 1995). Despite the usefulness of classification systems in psychopathology, no system is accepted universally. Furthermore, some have questioned the utility of classification systems as a whole, favoring behavioral descriptions of individual presentations instead (Kanfer & Saslow, 1965; Ullman & Krasner, 1975). The purpose of this chapter is to review the issues related to the assessment, diagnosis, and classification of psychopathology. The chapter will begin with a brief outline of the history of medical and psychopathological classification. Next, it will review the systems in use in the late 1990s, and evaluate these systems from the standpoint of clinical utility, research facilitation, and scientific understanding. It will then discuss the alternative approaches and future directions in the classification of psychopathology. Finally, the role of assessment strategies in informing this debate will be examined.

3.08.2 HISTORY OF CLASSIFICATION

3.08.2.1 Medical Classification

As Clementz and Iacono (1990) point out, medical classification systems have relied historically on careful observation of patients and their symptoms. The importance of observation as an adjunct to theorizing was recognized as long ago as the seventeenth century by thinkers such as Thomas Sydenham (1624–1689). Observations were used to make inferences about the causes of disease. The practice of medical observation and classification gained momentum with the advent of medical instruments. The most notable of these was the stethoscope, developed in 1819 by Rene Theophile Hyacinthe-Laennec (1787–1826). This advance in instrumentation led to the use of objective signifiers of pathology in diagnosing disease and a diminished interest in less technologically sophisticated observations or subjective reports of symptoms. The continuous development of new technologies increased the ability of physicians to determine the function of organs and their modes of operation when healthy. This novel conceptualization of dysfunction as related to the functioning of organs led the French physician Broussais (1772–1838) to propose the radical idea that specific symptom clusters could not define a disease adequately because of the high overlap between different disorders. He suggested that in order to identify a disease one needs to study the patient's physiological processes and constitution. Mid-nineteenth century advances in the various basic sciences (such as anatomy, histology, and biology) led to the further decline of the practice of observation in favor of the experimental study of physiological disease processes. Although this emphasis on understanding function was a great benefit to the various basic sciences, it culminated in the near abandonment of the practice of clinical observation (Clementz & Iacono, 1990). The increasing popularity of laboratory research also resulted in an emphasis on specific symptoms, rather than on the phenomenology of disease. This topographic or symptom-based approach to the study of pathology lent itself to a descriptive system of classification. However, this approach had its critics, as far back as the 1800s. Some investigators (e.g., Trousseau, 1801–1867) believed that a more comprehensive approach to diagnosis, incorporating both clinical observation and laboratory findings, would better allow the recognition of disorders and their treatment.

The field of genetics provided another major development in the science of classification. Mendel, working in an isolated monastery, pioneered the science of genetics. His efforts were continued by others (e.g., Garrod, 1902) who applied his work to humans. Watson and Crick's (1953a, 1953b) detailed description of the structure of human genetic material supplied yet another powerful tool for identifying the presence and etiology of certain disorders. A classification system based on genetic and biological etiology may seem promising. However, researchers soon realized that the specificity of genetics is less than perfect. This lack of specificity seemed particularly evident in the psychiatric disorders. We now know several psychiatric disorders are at least partly genetic. This is revealed by the finding that individuals with identical genetic make-up have higher concordance rates for developing the same disease than those who do not. However, because the concordance rate between identical twins is less than 100% (e.g., schizophrenia; Dworkin; Lenzenwenger, Moldin & Cornblatt, 1987), not all the variance in psychiatric disorders can be explained by genetic inheritance. These findings have led to the view that genetic make-up provides a diathesis for a particular disorder, which, when interacting with the environmental factors, may produce a disease.

3.08.2.2 Early Nosology of Psychopathology

Emil Kraepelin (1856–1926) was the first to adapt a medical classification framework for psychiatric illnesses (Blashfield, 1991; Kraepelin, 1971). He considered psychopathology to be the result of underlying disease states and advocated the scientific investigation of illnesses. He coined the term "dementia praecox" (later known as schizophrenia) to describe what had previously been considered distinct pathologies. Kraepelin's thinking regarding psychopathology and classification was shaped by the rapid advances in German medical science in the nineteenth century and by his training in behaviorism from Wilhelm Wundt (Berrios & Hauser, 1988). German medicine during Kraepelin's lifetime emphasized the interpretation of mental disorders as diseases of the brain (Menninger, 1963).

Kraepelin's training with Wundt contributed to his use of behavioral descriptions for clusters of symptoms he believed were linked by a common etiology. Kraepelin's psychopathology classification became influential through the publication of his textbooks on psychiatry. His categories later became the basis for the first official classification adopted by the American Psychiatric Association (APA) in 1917 (Menninger, 1963), and revised in 1932 (APA, 1933).

A contemporary of Kraepelin's, Sigmund Freud (1856–1939), was also influential in forming our understanding of psychopathology. In contrast to Kraepelin, Freud placed little emphasis on the phenomenology of disorders, stressing the importance of diagnoses based on the underlying cause of patients' manifest symptoms. Kraepelin, however, opposed Freudian theory and psychoanalytic practice because of its nonempirical orientation (Kahn, 1959). Freud's theories were well articulated, however, and by the 1950s had come to dominate American psychiatry (Blashfield, 1991). Psychoanalytic thought did not lose its foothold until the community-based mental health movement of the 1960s, which pointed out that psychoanalysis was only accessible to the wealthy. Other factors that contributed to the decline of psychoanalytic thought include the development of alternative interventions such as psychotropic medications and behavioral intervention, as well as a general shift toward empiricism. Around this time, there was a resurgence of Kraepelinian thought, mainly by a group of psychiatrists at Washington University in St. Louis (Robins & Guze, 1970). They believed that psychiatry had drifted too far from its roots in medicine, and that it was necessary to identify the biological bases of psychopathology. They advocated an emphasis on classification as a tool for helping psychopathology to evolve as a field (Blashfield, 1991; Klerman, 1978).

3.08.3 CLASSIFICATION OF MENTAL ILLNESS

3.08.3.1 History of Classification of Mental Illness

After World War II, the armed forces developed a more comprehensive nomenclature to facilitate the treatment of World War II servicemen. During this same period, the World Health Organization (WHO) published the first version of the *International classification of diseases* (*ICD-6*; WHO, 1992) that included psychiatric disorders. The authors of the *ICD-6* relied heavily on the work of various branches of the armed forces in the development of their taxonomy of psychopathology. The first version of the *Diagnostic and statistical manual of mental disorders* (*DSM*), a variant on the *ICD-6*, was published in 1952 by the APA's Committee on Nomenclature and Statistics. This nomenclature was designed for use in the civilian population, and focused on clinical utility (APA, 1994). The *DSM* (APA, 1994) was originally created as a means of standardizing the collection of statistics in psychiatric hospitals in the early 1900s. By the release of the second edition of the *DSM* (*DSM-II*) (1975), the authors had moved toward the elimination of exclusion rules and provision of more explicit and descriptive diagnostic criteria. The inclusion of explicit diagnostic criteria in the *DSM-II* was inspired by the 1972 work of a group of Neo-Kraeplinian theorists, Feighner, Baran, Furman, and Shipman at the Washington University School of Medicine in St. Louis (Feighner et al., 1972). This group had originally created a six-category system as a guideline for researchers in need of homogenous subject groups.

In 1978 and 1985, Spitzer and his colleagues modified and expanded the Washington University system and labeled it the Research Diagnostic Criteria (RDC). The RDC established criteria for 25 major categories, with an emphasis on the differential diagnosis between schizophrenia and the affective disorders. The authors of the *DSM-III* (1980) followed the example of the Washington University and RDC groups, including diagnostic criteria for each disorder and exclusion criteria for 60% of all *DSM-III* disorders. Most of these exclusion rules described hierarchical relationships between disorders, in which a diagnosis is not given if its symptoms are part of a more pervasive disorder.

As a result of these changes, the *DSM-III* and *DSM-III-R* are based almost exclusively on descriptive criteria. These criteria are grouped into distinct categories representing different disorders. The *DSM-IV* continues this tradition, using a categorical model in which patients are assigned to classes that denote the existence of a set of related signs and symptoms. The constituent signs and symptoms are thought to reflect an underlying disease construct. Researchers who advocate a categorical model of disease (e.g., Kraepelin) propose that disorders differ qualitatively from each other and from the nondisordered state. Although later editions of the *DSM* have relied progressively more on research findings in their formulation, the stated goal of *DSM-IV* remains the facilitation of clinical practice and communication (Frances et al., 1991). The *DSM* system has evolved as a widely used manual in both clinical and research settings. However, the structure and the stated goals of the *DSM* have been at the core of many controversies regarding the assessment, diagnosis, and classification of psychopathology.

3.08.3.2 Current Classification Systems

Two systems of classification are currently in common use: the *DSM-IV* (APA, 1994) and the ICD-10 (WHO, 1992). A detailed description of these systems is beyond the scope of this chapter and the interested reader should consult recent reviews of these systems (Frances, 1998; Regier, et al., 1998; Spitzer, 1998). A brief overview of each system is provided below.

The *DSM-IV* is a multiaxial classification system. The individual is rated on five separate axes. Axis I includes all diagnoses except personality disorders and mental retardation, the later being rated on Axis II. The rationale for the separation of these axes is to ensure that

the presence of long-term disturbances is not overlooked in favor of current pathology. Together, these axes constitute the classification of abnormal behavior. The remaining three axes are not needed to make a diagnosis but contribute to the recognition of factors, other than the individuals' symptoms, that should be considered in determining the person's diagnosis. General medical conditions are rated on Axis III, psychosocial and environmental problems are coded on axis IV, and the individual's current level of functioning is rated on axis V.

The 10th Revision of the *ICD* (*ICD-10*) is a multiaxial system. Axis I includes clinical diagnoses for both mental and physical disorders, Axis II outlines disabilities due to impairments produced by the disorder, and Axis III lists the environmental, circumstantial, and personal lifestyle factors that influence the presentation, course, or outcome disorders. *ICD-10* differs from other multiaxial classifications in that it: (i) records all medical conditions on the same axis (Axis I), (ii) assesses comorbid disorders (Axis II) in specific areas of functioning without ascribing a specific portion to each disorder, and (iii) allows expression of environmental (Axis III) factors determined by clinical practice and epidemiological evidence (Janca, Kastrup, Katschnig, Lopez-Ibor, 1996).

One purpose for the collaboration between *DSM-IV* and *ICD-10* authors was to foster the goal of the transcultural applicability of *ICD-10* (Uestuen, Bertelsen, Dilling, & van Drimmelen, 1996). A multiaxial coding format in both *DSM-IV* and *ICD-10* was adopted in order to provide unambiguous information with maximum clinical usefulness in the greatest number of cases (WHO, 1996). Although not explicitly stated by the authors of either manual, both the *DSM-IV* and *ICD-10* are examples of the "neo-Kraepelinian revolution" in psychiatric diagnostic classification (Compton & Guze, 1995).

The progress toward the shared goals of the two systems include two areas: general clinical use of the systems; and fostering international communication and cultural sensitivity. Regarding general clinical use, a multicenter field trial evaluating aspects of the *ICD-10* and *DSM-IV* involving 45 psychiatrists and psychologists in seven centers was conducted in Germany (Michels et al., 1996). Results revealed moderate inter-rater reliability for the *ICD-10* Axis I and Axis II. However, the number of relevant psychosocial circumstances coded on Axis III by the different raters varied greatly. The authors concluded that the multiaxial system was generally well accepted by participating clinicians, and that it is worth studying empirically and revising accordingly.

Clinicians specializing in several specific areas have not been as positive in their comments about the *ICD-10*. For instance, Jacoby (1996) has argued that neither the *DSM-IV* nor the *ICD-10* is adequate in its categorization of certain disorders associated with the elderly, such as certain dementias and psychotic disorders. Others have argued that specific *ICD-10* diagnoses show poor levels of stability of diagnosis across time. Specifically, a 1997 study found that neurotic, stress-related, adjustment, generalized anxiety, and panic disorders as well as some psychoses and personality disorders showed low rates of reliability across interviews at different time points (Daradkeh, El-Rufaie, Younis, & Ghubash, 1997).

Issues regarding the fostering of international communication and cultural sensitivity were addressed by a Swiss study published in 1995 that assessed the inter-rater reliability and confidence with which diagnoses could be made using the *ICD Diagnostic Criteria for Research* (*ICD-10 DCR*), as well as examining the concordance between *ICD-10 DCR*, *ICD-10 Clinical Descriptions and Diagnostic Guidelines*, and other classification systems including the *DSM-IV*. Field trials were carried out at 151 clinical centers in 32 countries by 942 clinician/ researchers who conducted 11 491 individual patient assessments. The authors report that most of the clinician/researchers found the criteria to be explicit and easy to apply and the inter-rater agreement was high for the majority of diagnostic categories. In addition, their results suggested that the use of operational criteria across different systems increases levels of inter-rater agreement.

Regier, Kaelber, Roper, Rae, and Sartorius (1994) cited findings suggesting that while overall inter-rater reliability across 472 clinicians in the US and Canada was good, the clinician tended to make more use of multiple coding for certain disorders than clinicians from other countries. This suggests that certain aspects of the *DSM* system (e.g., its encouragement of multiple diagnoses) may make the transition and agreement between the two systems somewhat more difficult.

The *ICD's* efforts to place psychiatric disorders in the context of the world community's different religions, nationalities, and cultures has received praise in the literature (Haghighat, 1994), while the *DSM-IV* may be seen as somewhat less successful in achieving this goal. The *ICD's* increased cultural sensitivity was at the expense of increased length, but efforts to omit cultural-biased criteria were largely successful. However, other authors have argued that the attempts to improve cultural sensitivity to the degree of a "universal" understanding of mental illness may be misguided (Patel & Winston, 1994). Specifically, while mental illness as a phenomenon may be universal, specific categories of mental illness as outlined by the *DSM* and *ICD* may require identification and validation of particular diagnoses within specific cultures (Patel & Winston, 1994).

3.08.3.3 Tools for Clinical Assessment

A comprehensive review of assessment measures for psychopathology is beyond the scope of this chapter. The interested reader should consult comprehensive reviews of this topic (e.g., Baumann, 1995; Bellack & Hersen, 1998; Sartorius & Janca, 1996). One useful method of classifying assessment techniques is to consider two classes of measures: those that aim to aid in diagnosis and those that aim to assess the severity of symptoms relatively independent of diagnosis. Examples of the first category include The Structured Clinical Interview for *DSM-IV* Diagnoses (SCID; First, Spitzer, Gibbon, & Williams, 1995) and the Composite International Diagnostic Interview (CIDI; Robins et al., 1988). These measures are mapped closely on the diagnostic systems on which they are based (*DSM-IV* and *ICD-10*, respectively). The second class of assessment instruments use a dimensional approach and aim to assess severity of symptoms relatively independently of diagnosis. Examples of such instruments include the Hamilton Depression Inventory (HAM-D; Riskind, Beck, Brown, & Steer, 1987) and the Yale-Brown Obsessive-Compulsive Scale (Y-BOCS; Goodman, Price, Rasmussen, & Mazure, 1989a). The advantages and disadvantages of these assessment techniques are tied closely to advantages and disadvantages of the categorical and dimensional approaches to classification and will be discussed in Section 3.08.5.2.3.

An important aspect of developing new knowledge in psychopathology is the improvement and standardized use of assessment tools across studies of psychopathology. The vast majority of studies of *DSM* disorders have used self-report or interview-based measures of symptoms. In some cases, behavioral checklists (either self- or other-reports) or psychological tests have been employed. In this section, issues such as the accuracy, reliability, and discriminate validity of such assessment tools and how they may influence findings in psychopathology studies will be examined.

Self-report measures may be the most time- and labor-efficient means of gathering data about psychological symptoms and behaviors. However, individuals often are inconsistent in their observations of their own behaviors, and the usefulness of these reports depends heavily on often limited powers of self-observation. Psychometric methods for enhancing the usefulness of self-report data generally focus on increasing the consistency (i.e., reliability and accuracy or validity) of the measures. A number of psychometrically sophisticated scales are available for several different types of disorders (e.g., anxiety; BAI; Beck, Epstein, Brown, & Steer, 1988; PSS; Foa, Riggs, Dancu, & Rothbaum, 1993; Y-BOCS; Goodman et al., 1989a, 1989b). Many of the traditional psychometric approaches classify disorders into state (transitory feelings) and trait (stable personality) attributes (e.g., state anxiety vs. trait anxiety, STAI; Spielberger, Gorsuch, & Lushene, 1970). The accuracy of these scales is most often evaluated by comparing results on the measure to results on other measures of the same emotion or disorder (e.g., interviews, physiological assessments, observations of behavior). By assessing various aspects of an emotion or disorder, the investigator tries to create a composite gauge of an emotion for which no single indicator offers a perfect yardstick.

One impediment to discovering which symptoms may be shared across disorders has been the structure of many clinical measures. Examples of widely-used measures of psychological states are the Beck Depression Inventory (BDI; Beck & Steer, 1987), the Beck Anxiety Inventory (BAI; Beck et al., 1988), the Minnesota Multiphasic Personality Inventory (MMPI-2; Butcher, Dahlstrom, Graham, Tellegen, & Kaemmer, 1989), and structured interview scales such as the Diagnostic Inventory Scale (DIS; Helzer & Robins, 1988) and the Structured Clinical Interview for *DSM-IV* Diagnoses (SCID; First et al., 1995).

These self-report and clinician-rated scales usually assess "modal" symptoms, as they focus on core aspects of each syndrome rather than on all possible variants. Structured interviews, such as the SCID-IV or the DIS, often allow "skip outs" in which the interviewer need not necessarily assess all of the symptoms of all disorders. Many studies have examined the convergent and divergent validity patterns of self-report (e.g., modal) measures of various disorders (e.g., Foa et al., 1993). These measures tend to yield strongly convergent assessments of their respective syndromes, but there is little specificity in their measurement, especially in nonpatient samples. The data often suggest the presence of a large nonspecific component shared between syndromes such as anxiety and depression (Clark & Watson, 1991). Some scales appear to be more highly loaded with the nonspecific distress factor than others. There-

fore, in order to efficiently discriminate between disorders, future research should emphasize identification of symptoms which optimally discriminate between diagnoses. Watson and Clark (1992) found that even when factor analytically derived mood measures such as the Profile of Moods (POMS; McNair, Lorr, & Droppleman, 1981) and the Positive and Negative Affectivity Scale (PANAS; Watson, Clark, & Tellegen, 1988) are used, certain basic affects (i.e., anxiety and depression) are only partially differentiable. Their data suggest that the overlap between basic affects represents a shared component inherent in each mood state, which must be measured in order to understand the overlap between different mood states and disorders.

3.08.4 CURRENT ISSUES IN THE CLASSIFICATION OF PSYCHOPATHOLOGY

As noted earlier, the classification of psychopathology has been a controversial topic since inception. Currently, the discussions revolve primarily around the *DSM* system, although many of the debates predate the *DSM*. The most common topics of controversy in the classification of psychopathology are: (i) the definition of psychopathology; (ii) the artificially high rates of comorbidity found between disorders when using the *DSM* system (Frances, Widiger, & Fyer, 1990; Robins, 1994; (iii) the balance between a focus on clinical utility and the facilitation of research and scientific progress (Follette, 1996); and (iv) organizational problems, both within and across disorders in the *DSM* (Brown & Barlow, 1992; Quay, Routh, & Shapiro, 1987).

3.08.4.1 Definition of Psychopathology

There is a lack of agreement about the definition of psychopathology. Early versions of both the *ICD* and the *DSM* attempted to guide the categorization of mental disorders without addressing the definition of psychopathology (Spitzer, Endicott, & Robins, 1978). Some contend that this lack of agreement about the definition of psychopathology remains the current state of affairs (e.g., Bergner, 1997). Others (e.g., Kendell, 1975, 1982) have noted that physicians frequently diagnose and treat disorders for which there is no specific definition, and which, in many cases, are not technically considered disorders (e.g., pregnancy). The controversy over the definition of mental disorder may be fueled by the fact that such illnesses are signified commonly by behaviors, and distinguishing between "normal" and "deviant" or "disordered" behaviors is viewed by some as having serious cultural and sociological implications (Mowrer, 1960; Szasz, 1960). According to Gorenstein (1992), attempts at defining mental illness have fallen historically into several categories. Some have relied on statistical definitions based on the relative frequency of certain characteristics in the general population. Others have employed a social definition in which behaviors which conflict with the current values of society are considered deviant. Still other approaches have focused on the subjective discomfort caused by the problem, as reported by the individual. Finally, some definitions of psychopathology have been based on psychological theories regarding states or behaviors thought to signify problems within the individual. The *DSM-IV* (APA, 1994) defines a mental disorder as a "clinically significant behavioral or psychological syndrome or pattern that occurs in an individual and ... is associated with present distress ... or disability ... or with a significant increased risk of suffering death, pain, disability or an important loss of freedom." The disorder should not be an "expectable and culturally sanctioned response to an event," and must be considered a manifestation of dysfunction in the individual. Wakefield has expanded and refined this idea in his concept of "harmful dysfunction" (Wakefield, 1992, 1997c). This concept is a carefully elaborated idea considered by some to be a workable solution to the problem of defining abnormality (e.g., Spitzer, 1997). In essence, the harmful dysfunction concept means that behaviors are abnormal to the extent that they imply something is not working properly as would be expected based on its evolutionary function. Specifically, Wakefield (1992) states that a mental disorder is present

> if and only if, a) the condition causes some harm or deprivation of benefit to the person as judged by the standards of the person's culture (the value criteria), and b) the condition results from the inability of some mental mechanism to perform its natural function, wherein a natural function is an effect that is part of the evolutionary explanation of the existence and structure of the mental mechanism (the explanatory criterion). (p. 385)

Critics of Wakefield's concept argue that it represents a misapplication of evolutionary theory (Follette & Houts, 1996). They contend that evolutionary selection was not meant to apply on the level of behavioral processes, that is, it is not possible to know the function of a part or process of the individual by examining evolutionary history because random variation precludes a straightforward interpretation of the "design" of various parts of organisms (Mayr, 1981; Tattersall, 1995). Proponents of the "harmful dysfunction" definition suggest that it may provide a useful starting point for research in psychopathology, although further research needs to identify the specific mechanisms that are not functioning properly (Bergner, 1997).

3.08.4.2 Comorbidity

The term comorbidity was first used in the medical epidemiology literature and has been defined as "the co-occurrence of different diseases in the same individual" (Blashfield, 1990; Lilienfeld, Waldman, & Israel, 1994). Many factors potentially may contribute to the comorbidity rates of psychiatric disorders. Reported comorbidity rates are influenced by the actual co-occurrence of disorders, the populations considered, the range, severity, and base rates of the disorders considered, the method of assessment, and the structure of the classification system used.

3.08.4.2.1 *Actual co-occurrence of disorders*

In the medical literature, comorbidity often refers to diagnoses which occur together in an individual, either over one's lifetime or simultaneously. This concept emphasizes the recognition that different diagnoses potentially are related in several ways. One disease can signal the presence of another, predispose the patient to the development of another, or be etiologically related to another disorder (Lilienfeld et al., 1994). Lilienfeld et al. suggest that the increased attention to comorbidity in psychopathology is due to acknowledgment of the extensive co-occurrence and covariation that exists between diagnostic categories (Lilienfeld et al. ; Widiger & Frances, 1985). For example, Kessler et al. (1994) reported the results of a study on the lifetime and 12-month prevalence of *DSM-III-R* disorders in the US, in a random sample of 8098 adults. Forty-eight percent of the subjects reported at least one lifetime disorder, with the vast majority of these individuals, 79%, reporting comorbid disorders. Other studies using large community samples report that more than 50% of the participants diagnosed with one *DSM* disorder also meet criteria for a second disorder (Brown & Barlow, 1992). It has been argued that the common etiological factors across different diagnoses are of greater importance than the etiological factors specific to one disorder (Andrews, 1991; Andrews, Stewart, Morris-Yates, Holt, & Henderson, 1990).

3.08.4.2.2 Populations considered

One factor that affects comorbidity rates is the population under study. Kessler et al. (1994) found that people with comorbid disorders were likely to report higher utilization of services than those without a comorbid disorder. Similarly, higher rates of comorbidity were found among urban populations than rural populations, despite the higher rates of single psychiatric disorders and financial problems among rural participants. The race of the population studied also seems to influence comorbidity rates. African-American participants in the Kessler et al. study reported lower comorbidity rates than Caucasian participants, after controlling for the effects of income and education. However, Caucasian participants reported lower rates of current comorbid disorders than Hispanics. Disparities in prevalence of reported comorbidity were also found between respondents of different age groups, with people aged between 25 and 34 years reporting the highest rates. The income and education of the participants were also associated with reported comorbidity in the Kessler et al. study.

3.08.4.2.3 Range, severity, and base rates of disorders considered

The rates of comorbidity are also influenced by the disorders studied. Specifically, the range, severity, and base rates of certain disorders increase the likelihood that these disorders will be comorbid with another disorder. Certain diagnostic categories, including childhood disorders (Abikoff & Klein, 1992; Biederman, Newcorn, & Sprich, 1991), anxiety disorders (Brown & Barlow, 1992; Goldenberg et al., 1996), and personality disorders (Oldham et al., 1992; Widiger & Rogers, 1989), appear to be comorbid with other disorders. For example, 50% of patients with a principal anxiety disorder reported at least one additional clinically significant anxiety or depressive disorder in a large-scale study by Moras, DiNardo, Brown, and Barlow (1991). Similarly, anxiety disorders are not only highly likely to be comorbid with each other but also with mood, substance use, and personality disorders (Brown & Barlow, 1992). These high rates of comorbidity may in part be due to the degree to which the different anxiety disorders include overlapping features (Brown & Barlow, 1992). Finally the degree of comorbidity is influenced directly by thresholds set to determine the presence or absence of various disorders. The choice of threshold appears to affect comorbidity rates differentially, depending on the disorder. For instance, certain disorders (e.g., social phobia) appear to be more likely to accompany other anxiety disorders when considered at subclinical levels (Rapee, Sanderson, & Barlow, 1988). Conversely, Frances et al. (1990) have suggested that the severity of mental health problems in a sample will influence comorbidity rates, in that a patient with a severe presentation of one disorder is more likely to report other comorbid disorders.

In addition to the range and severity thresholds of disorders, the base rates of a particular disorder have a strong influence on the apparent comorbidity rates. Conditions that are frequently present in a given sample will tend to be diagnosed together more often than those that are infrequent. This may help explain the comorbidity rates of certain highly prevalent disorders such as anxiety, depression, and substance abuse.

3.08.4.2.4 Assessment methods

The choice of assessment methods may influence comorbidity rates in much the same way as aspects of the disorders. Disagreement regarding comorbidity rates may be partly due to differences in the definition of comorbidity. For example, comorbidity has been defined as within-episode co-occurrence (or dual diagnosis) among disorders by some (August & Garfinkel, 1990; Fulop, Strain, Vita, Lyons, & Hammer, 1987), lifetime co-occurrence by others (Feinstein, 1970; Shea, Widiger, & Klein, 1992, p. 859), and covariation among diagnoses (i.e., across individuals) by still other researchers (Cole & Carpentieri, 1990; Lewinsohn, Rohde, Seeley, & Hops, 1991). Even when researchers agree on a definition, their estimates of comorbidity may differ based on the type of assessment tool they use. As Lilienfeld et al. (1994) point out, assessment techniques have error variance that by definition is not related to the construct(s) of interest or may artificially inflate the actual comorbidity rate.

Furthermore, individual raters may hold biases or differing endorsement thresholds for behaviors which are common to a variety of disorders. Likewise, raters may have specific beliefs about which disorders tend to covary. These types of biases may affect both self-report and interviewer-based data. Similarly, studies utilizing structured interviews may differ from studies in which severity thresholds are not described as concretely. Therefore, differing rates of comorbidity across studies may be an artifact of the types of measurement used, or the biases of raters involved (Zimmerman, Pfohl, Coryell, Corenthal, & Stangl, 1991).

3.08.4.2.5 Structure of the classification system

Frances et al. (1990) argue that the classification system used in the various versions of the *DSM* increases the chance of comorbidity in comparison to other, equally plausible systems. The early systems (e.g., *DSM-III*) attempted to address the comorbidity issue by proposing elaborate hierarchical exclusionary rules specifying that if a disorder was present in the course of another disorder that took precedence, the second disorder was not diagnosed (Boyd et al., 1984). Thus, disorders which may have been truly comorbid were overlooked. Examination of these issues resulted in the elimination of this exclusionary criterion in *DSM-III-R*. This new method of diagnosis, however, has been criticized for artificially inflating comorbidity between various disorders.

Frances et al. (1990) point out that new editions of the *DSM* expanded coverage by adding new diagnoses. This was done by "splitting" similar disorders into subtypes. They argue that the tendency to split diagnoses creates much more comorbidity than would "lumping" systems of classification. This is because disorders that share basic underlying features are viewed as separate.

Much of the "splitting" in the *DSM* has resulted from the increasing reliance on prototypical models of disorders (Blashfield, 1991). The creators of the *DSM* increasingly have relied on prototypes, defining a diagnostic category by its most essential features, regardless of whether these features are also present in other diagnoses. McReynolds (1989) argued that categories with a representative prototype and indistinct or "fuzzy" boundaries are the basis of the most utilitarian classification systems because they are representative of categories in nature. The use of this type of prototype-based classification has improved the sensitivity and clinical utility of the *DSM* system. However, these gains are achieved at the expense of increased comorbidity and decreased specificity of differential diagnosis due to definitional overlap. Thus, this system of diagnostic classification makes it unclear whether there is any true underlying affinity between disorders currently considered to have high rates of comorbidity.

The stated approach of the *DSM-IV* is a descriptive method relying on observable signs and symptoms rather than underlying mechanisms. The sets of signs and symptoms that constitute the different diagnoses are, by definition, categorical, that is, the presence of the required number and combination of symptoms indicates a diagnosis and the absence of the required number of symptoms precludes a diagnosis. The symptoms are not weighted, implying that they are of equal importance in defining the disorder. For many diagnoses, the structure of this system makes it possible for two individuals to meet the same diagnostic criteria without sharing many symptoms. Conversely, it is possible for one person to meet the criteria while another person who shares all but one feature does not meet the criteria. As a result, patients who actually form a fairly heterogeneous group may be "lumped" into one homogeneous diagnostic category.

Combined with unweighted symptoms and a lack of attention to severity of symptoms, this "lumping" can lead to what Wakefield (1997a) refers to as "overinclusiveness" of diagnostic criteria. Specifically, people who do not truly suffer from a mental disorder may nonetheless receive the diagnosis, thus lowering the conceptual validity of *DSM* diagnostic categories. Conversely, minute differences in reported symptoms may result in dichotomizing between disordered and nondisordered individuals, or between individuals with one disorder as opposed to another (e.g., avoidant personality disorder vs. generalized social phobia), creating heterogeneity where there may actually be none.

This point is further elaborated by Clark et al. (1995), who point out that within-category heterogeneity constitutes a serious challenge to the validity of the *DSM*. These authors view comorbidity and heterogeneity as related problems, that is, within-group heterogeneity of symptoms found across diagnostic categories leads to increased rates of comorbidity among the disorders. Homogenous categories, on the other hand, lead to patient groups that share defining symptoms and produce lower rates of both comorbidity and heterogeneity. This is in part because of polythetic systems that require some features of a disorder for diagnosis. In contrast, a monothetical system would require all features of a disorder for diagnosis. Because the monothetic approach to diagnosis produces very low base rates for any diagnosis (Morey, 1988), researchers generally have used the polythetic approach. However, this approach promotes within-category heterogeneity because individuals who do not share the same symptom profiles can receive the same diagnosis. This poses a problem for any categorical system, including the *DSM*. Because of the inherent heterogeneity in patient profiles, a categorical system must address this issue by either proposing artificial methods of limiting heterogeneity (e.g., *DSM-III*), using unrealistic homogeneous categories, or acknowledging the heterogeneity (e.g., *DSM-IV*; Clark et al., 1995). Schizophrenia is an example of a diagnosis that has proved to have within-group heterogeneity. For example, current nosology (e.g., *DSM-IV*) assumes that schizophrenia and affective illness are distinct disorders. However, shared genetic vulnerability has been proposed for schizophrenia and some affective disorders (Crow, 1994). Taylor (1992) reviewed the evidence for this continuum and suggested that the discrimination of these disorders by their signs and symptoms is inadequate (Taylor & Amir, 1994). The need to know whether psychoses vary along a continuum is obviously critical to our understanding of their pathogenesis and etiology.

To address within-group heterogeneity of disorders, researchers have attempted to create subtypes (e.g., positive vs. negative symptoms of schizophrenia; Andreasen, Flaum, Swayze, Tyrell, & Arndt, 1990). Consistent with this conceptualization, researchers have correlated negative symptoms of schizophrenia with cognitive deficits (Johnstone et al., 1978), poor premorbid adjustment (Pogue-Geile & Harrow, 1984), neuropathologic and neurologic abnormalities (Stevens, 1982), poor response to neuroleptics (Angrist, Rotrosen, & Gershon, 1980), and genetic factors (Dworkin & Lenzenweger, 1984). On the other hand, positive symptoms have been correlated with attention (Cornblatt, Lenzenweger, Dworkin, Erlenmeyer-Kimling, 1992) and a positive response to neuroleptics (Angrist et al., 1980). Despite these differences, some investigators have questioned the reliability of these findings (Carpenter, Heinrichs, & Alphs, 1985; Kay, 1990) and the clinical clarity of the subtypes (Andreasen et al., 1990). The majority of these studies included patients with schizophrenia but not affective disorders, and some assessed only limited symptoms (e.g., only negative symptoms; Buchanan & Carpenter, 1994; Kay, 1990). These approaches are potentially problematic because they assume implicitly that the psychoses are distinct, and that the specific types of psychopathology are easily discriminated.

In summary, the issue of comorbidity poses what is potentially the greatest challenge to diagnosis. Factors including the populations considered, the range, severity, and base rates of the disorders considered, the method of assessment, and the structure of the classification system contribute to reported comorbidity rates. These factors are often extremely difficult to distinguish from the true comorbidity of disorders. A full understanding of the common factors and shared etiologies of psychiatric disorders will most likely require an understanding of their true comorbidity. It is likely, then, that this will remain a highly controversial topic in psychopathology assessment.

3.08.4.3 Clinical and Research Applications of Classification Systems

Classification serves various purposes, depending on the setting in which it is used. In clinical settings, classification is used for treatment formulation, whereas in research settings it allows researchers to formulate and communicate ideas. The *DSM-IV* taskforce has stated that the various uses of classification are usually compatible (APA, 1994, p. xv). It is not clear whether this assertion has been tested empirically, or whether steps have been taken to resolve any divergence between the various uses of classification. The goals of clinical utility and outcome of research are not inherently inconsistent, but situations may arise in which the two diverge in their application. The majority of the modifications made to recent versions of the *DSM* were designed to improve clinical utility by simplifying or improving everyday diagnostic procedures. While not necessarily empirically driven, these changes do not appear to have adversely impacted the validity of the diagnoses they affect. Assigning diagnoses facilitates information storage and retrieval for both researchers and clinicians (Blashfield & Draguns; 1976; Mayr, 1981). However, problematic issues have been raised about the use and structure of diagnostic systems in both clinical and research settings.

The use of classification and the reliance on the *DSM* appears to be increasing (Follette, 1996). This is partly because of the trend toward the development and empirical examination of treatments geared toward specific diagnoses (Wilson, 1996). Although the use of diagnostic classification is beneficial in conceptualizing cases, formulating treatment plans, and communicating with other providers, some have argued that assigning a diagnosis may have a negative impact on patients (Szasz, 1960), that is, decisions about what constitutes pathology as opposed to normal reactions to stressors may be arbitrary (Frances, First, & Pincus, 1995), gender-based, and culturally or socioeconomically based. Furthermore, the choice of which behaviors are considered pathological (de Fundia, Draguns, & Phillips, 1971) may be influenced by the characteristics of the client (Broverman, Broverman, Clarkson, Rusenkrantz, & Vogel, 1970; Gove, 1980; Hamilton, Rothbart, & Dawes, 1986).

Diagnostic categories may also have adverse consequences on research. For example, although the diagnostic categories defined by the classifications systems are well studied and easily compared across investigations, patients who do not clearly fit a diagnosis are ignored. Furthermore, frequent and generally clinically-driven changes in the diagnostic criteria for a particular disorder make sustained investigation of the disorder difficult (Davidson & Foa, 1991). This situation is further exacerbated by the frequent addition of new diagnostic categories to the *DSM* (Blashfield, 1991). The *DSM-IV* taskforce addressed this issue by explicitly recommending that the diagnostic classifications be used as a "guideline informed by clinical judgment," as they "are not meant to be used in a cookbook fashion" (APA, 1994, p. xxiii). This suggestion, while useful in a clinical setting, may not be as applicable in research settings.

The proliferation of diagnostic criteria in recent versions of the *DSM* have successfully improved diagnostic reliability, but have done so at the expense of external validity (Clementz & Iacono, 1990). That may adversely affect research findings (Carey & Gottesman, 1978; Meehl, 1986). According to Clementz and Iacono (1990), the achievement of high reliability in a diagnostic classification is often taken to signify either validity or a necessary first step toward demonstrating validity. However, this is not the case in situations in which disorder criteria are designed significantly to increase reliability (i.e., by using a very restrictive definition). In such situations, validity may actually suffer greatly due to the increase in false categorizations of truly disordered people as unaffected. Conversely, the generation of specific behavioral criteria (e.g., Antisocial Personality Disorder in *DSM-III-R*) may increase reliability but lead to overinclusion (e.g., criminals in the antisocial category) while entirely missing other groups (e.g., "successful" psychopaths who have avoided legal repercussions of the behavior) (Lykken, 1984).

Clearly there are possible negative impacts of our current diagnostic system for research. More broadly, some have argued that nosological questions involve "value judgments" (Kendler, 1990, p. 971) and as such are nonempirical. But, as Follette and Houts (1996) point out, the classification of pathology, even in physical medicine, requires the identification of desirable endstates which are culturally rather than biologically defined. Furthermore, value judgments lie in the choices made between competing theories (Widiger & Trull, 1993) and the attempt by the authors of the *DSM* to remain theoretically "neutral" is inherently problematic. In its attempt to remain "neutral," the DSM actually adopts a model of shared phenomenology, which implicitly accepts a theory of the underlying structure of psychopathology (Follette & Houts, 1996). This implicit theory is problematic on several related fronts. First, the *DSM* professes to be theory-

neutral while it may arguably be considered theory-bound. Second, because the authors of the *DSM* do not explicitly recognize any theory, specific theories cannot be empirically tested against competing theories of psychopathology.

3.08.4.4 Organizational Problems in the *DSM*

Several of the issues regarding assessment and classification revolve around the organization of the *DSM*. These problems can be classified into two broad categories: problems with the multiaxial system and problems concerning the placement and utilization of specific categories of disorders (Clark et al., 1995).

The multiaxial system of the *DSM* has no doubt accomplished its goal of increasing the attention given to various (e.g., personality) aspects of functioning. However, the distinction between certain personality (Axis II) disorders and some Axis I disorders are problematic. For example, there is now ample data suggesting that there is a high degree of overlap between avoidant personality disorder and generalized social phobia (Herbert, Hope, & Bellack, 1992; Widiger, 1992). Similarly, it is difficult to distinguish schizotypal personality disorder and schizophrenia on empirical grounds (Grove et al., 1991).

The second type of organizational issue relates to the placement and utilization of individual disorders. For example, because post-traumatic stress disorder (PTSD) shares many features (e.g., depersonalization, detachment) with the dissociative disorders, some (e.g., Davidson & Foa, 1991) have argued for its placement with the dissociative disorders instead of the anxiety disorders. Likewise, the overly exclusive diagnostic categories of the *DSM* have led to situations in which clearly disordered patients exhibiting symptoms of several disorders do not fit into any specific category. The authors of the *DSM* have attempted to remedy this by creating "not otherwise specified" (NOS) categories for several classes of disorders. While at times it is difficult to distinguish the meaning of NOS categories, they are often utilized in clinical practice. Clark et al (1995) view the high prevalence of subthreshold and atypical forms of the disorders commonly classified as NOS as contributing to the problem of heterogeneity. For example, various diagnoses including mood disorders (Mezzich, Fabrega, Coffman, & Haley, 1989), dissociative disorders (Spiegel & Cardena, 1991), and personality disorders (Morey, 1992) are characterized by high rates of NOS. One method of combating the high NOS rates would be to create separate categories to accommodate these individuals. For example, the rate of bipolar disorder NOS was reduced by the inclusion of the subcategories I and II in *DSM-IV*. Another method addressing the NOS problems is to include clear examples of individuals who would meet the NOS criteria. This second approach has been tested for some potential diagnostic groups, such as the mixed anxiety-depression category (Clark & Watson, 1991; Zinbarg & Barlow, 1991; Zinbarg et al., 1994).

3.08.5 ALTERNATIVE APPROACHES TO CLASSIFICATION

While many well-articulated criticisms of the classification system have been presented, the literature contains far fewer suggested alternatives (Follette, 1996). There is great disagreement among authors who have suggested other taxonomic models about not only the type of model, but also its content, structure, and methodology. The study of psychopathology has been pursued by researchers from different theoretical schools, including behaviorists, neurochemists, phenomenologists, and psychodynamicists (Millon, 1991). These approaches rely on unique methodologies and produce data regarding different aspects of psychopathology. No one conceptualization encompasses the complexity of any given disorder. These differing views are not reducible to a hierarchy, and cannot be compared in terms of their objective value (Millon, 1991). Biophysical, phenomenological, ecological, developmental, genetic, and behavioral observations have all been suggested as important contents to include in the categorization of psychopathology. How to structure or organize content has also been a topic of much debate. In this section the structural and methodological approaches to creating classification systems will be reviewed. Models of psychopathology will be discussed, including the Neo-Kraepelinian model, prototype models, and dimensional and categorical models. Finally, the use of etiological factors in the categorization of psychopathology (J. F. Kihlstrom, personal communication, September 2, 1997, SSCPnet) will be examined and other research and statistical methodologies will be outlined that may potentially lead to better systems of classification (J. F. Kihlstrom, personal communication, September 11, 1997, SSCPnet; D. Klein, personal communication, September 2, 1997, SSCPnet).

3.08.5.1 Types of Taxonomies

As knowledge about features best signifying various disorders increases, determinations must be made about the structure that best suits their classification. Before undertaking an investigation of the specific psychopathology classifications which have been proposed, the structural design of diagnostic taxonomies in general will be outlined briefly. The frameworks suggested fall into three categories: hierarchical, multiaxial, and circular. The hierarchical model organizes disorders into sets with higher-order diagnoses subsuming lower-order classifications. The multiaxial model assigns parallel roles for the different aspects of a disorder. Finally, the circular model assigns similar disorders to adjoining segments of a circle and dissimilar disorders to opposite sides of the circle (Millon, 1991). These three conceptualizations are not mutually exclusive, and many taxonomies share aspects of more than one structure. Within each of these three general frameworks, taxa may be considered categorical or dimensional. The current *DSM* combines both hierarchical and multiaxial approaches. Circular frameworks, which generally employ the dimensional approach, have been used in theories of personality. The model that is the basis for the *DSM* system, the Neo-Kraepelian model will be examined first, and then prototype and dimensional models will be considered Finally, suggested methodological and statistical approaches to improving the classification of psychopathology will be covered.

3.08.5.2 Taxonomic Models

3.08.5.2.1 *Neo-Kraepelinian* (DSM) *model*

The Neo-Kraepelinian model, inspired by the 1972 work of the Washington University group and embodied in the recent versions of the *DSM*, is the current standard of psychopathology classification. According to the Neo-Kraepelinian view, diagnostic categories represent medical diseases, and each diagnosis is considered to be a discrete entity. Each of the discrete diagnostic categories is viewed as having a describable etiology, course, and pattern of occurrence. Clearly specified operational criteria are used to define each category and foster objectivity. This type of classification is aided by the use of structured interviews in gathering relevant symptom information to assign diagnoses. Diagnostic algorithms specify the objective rules for combining symptoms and reaching a diagnosis (Blashfield, 1991). In this view, the establishment of the reliability of diagnostic categories is considered necessary before any type of validity can be established. Categories that refer to clearly described patterns of symptoms are considered to have good internal validity, while the utility of a diagnosis in predicting the course and treatment response of the disorder are seen as markers of good external validity. Despite its many shortcomings, the widespread adoption of the *DSM* system in both clinical work and research is a testament to the utility of the Neo-Kraepelinian model.

3.08.5.2.2 Prototype model

The prototype model has been suggested as a viable alternative to the current Neo-Kraepelinian approach (Cantor, Smith, French, & Mezzich, 1980; Clarkin, Widiger, Frances, Hurt, & Gilmore, 1983; Horowitz, Post, French, Wallis, & Siegelman, 1981; Livesley, 1985a, 1985b). In this system, patients' symptoms are evaluated in terms of their correlation with a standard or prototypical representation of specific disorders. A prototype consists of the most common features of members of a category, and is the standard against which patients are evaluated (Horowitz et al., 1981).

The prototype model differs from the Neo-Kraepelinian model in several ways. First, the prototype model is based on a philosophy of nominalism, in which diagnostic categories represent concepts used by mental health professionals (Blashfield, 1991). Diagnostic groups are not viewed as discrete, but individuals may warrant membership in a category to a greater or lesser degree. The categories are defined by exemplars, or prototypes, and the presentation of features or symptoms in an individual is neither necessary nor sufficient to determine membership in a category. Rather, the prototype model holds that membership in a category is correlated with the number of representative symptoms the patient has. The prototype model suggests that the degree of membership to a category is correlated with the number of features that a member has, so defining features are neither necessary nor sufficient.

Some authors have described the *DSM* system as a prototype model, primarily because it uses polythetic, as opposed to monothetic, definitions (Clarkin et al., 1983; Widiger & Frances, 1985). Although the *DSM* does use polythetic definitions, it does not constitute a prototypical model because specific subsets of symptoms are sufficient for making a diagnosis. Prototype and polythetic models allow variability among features within a category, however, they view category definition differently. Prototype models focus on definition by example, polythetic models focus on category membership as achieved by the presence of certain features that are sufficient. In a prototype model the level of membership is correlated with number of features present, and features are neither necessary nor sufficient since membership is not an absolute. Furthermore, categories in the prototype model have indistinct boundaries, and the membership decision relies largely on clinician judgment. It is likely that the adoption of this model would result in a decrease in reliability compared to the *DSM*. However, proponents argue that this model is more reflective of real-world categories in psychopathology (Chapman & Chapman, 1969).

3.08.5.2.3 Dimensional and categorical models

An alternative to the categorical classification system is the dimensional approach. In dimensional models of psychopathology, symptoms are assessed along several continua, according to their severity. Several dimensional models have been suggested (Eysenck, 1970; Russell, 1980; Tellegen, 1985). Dimensional models are proposed as a means of increasing the empirical parsimony of the diagnostic system. The personality disorders may be most readily adapted to this approach (McReynolds, 1989; Widiger, Trull, Hurt, Clarkin, & Frances, 1987; Wiggins, 1982) but this approach is by no means limited to personality disorders and has been suggested for use in disorders including schizophrenia (Andreasen and Carpenter, 1993), somatoform disorder (Katon et al., 1991), bipolar disorder (Blacker & Tsuang, 1992), childhood disorders (Quay et al., 1987), and obsessive-compulsive disorder (Hollander, 1993). Dimensional models are more agnostic (i.e., making fewer assumptions), more parsimonious (i.e., possibly reducing the approximately 300 diagnosis classifications in the *DSM* to a smaller subset of dimensions), more sensitive to differences in the severity of disorders across individuals, and less restrictive.

While a dimensional approach might simplify some aspects of the diagnostic process, it would undoubtedly create new problems. First, categorical models are resilient because of the psychological tendency to change dimensional concepts into categorical ones (Cantor & Genero, 1986; Rosch, 1978). Second, implementation of dimensional systems would require a major overhaul of current practice in the mental health field. Third, replacing the *DSM* categorical model with a dimensional model will undoubtedly meet with much resistance from proponents of clinical descriptiveness, who believe that each separate category provides a more richly textured picture of the disorder. Finally, there are currently no agreed upon dimensions to be included in such a classification model (Millon, 1991).

Thus, the task of advocates of the dimensional approach is twofold. First, they must determine the type and number of dimensions that are necessary to describe psychopathology. Second, they will need to demonstrate that it is possible to describe the entire range of psychopathology using a single set of dimensions. At this stage, the most useful starting point may be examination of the role of various dimensions in the description of psychopathology, as opposed to arguing the virtues and limitations of categorical and dimensional approaches to psychopathology.

3.08.5.3 The Use of Etiological Factors for Diagnosis

Another proposed remedy to the problems facing current classification systems is to examine the role of etiology. Andreasen and Carpenter (1993) point out the need to identify etiologic mechanisms in order to understand a disorder. In addition, understanding etiologic factors may help explain the heterogeneity and comorbidity of the disorders currently listed in the *DSM*. The authors of the *DSM* have generally avoided making statements regarding the etiology of disorders in keeping with the "theoretically neutral" stance. However, some authors have argued that this caveat is only loosely enforced in *DSM* as it is, as exemplified by life-stress based disorders such as PTSD and adjustment disorder (Brett, 1993).

Traditional models of etiology have focused on either the biological or environmental causes of psychopathology. Wakefield (1997b) has warned against the assumption that the etiology of psychopathological disorders will necessarily be found to be a physiological malfunction. He argued that the mind can begin to function abnormally without a corresponding brain disorder. More recent conceptualizations of the etiology of psychopathology acknowledge the role of both biological and environmental factors, and debate the ratio of the contribution from each. As would be expected, etiological studies of psychopathology tend to reflect the underlying theories of mental disorders accepted by the researchers who conduct them. For example, biological theorists attempt to identify biological markers of certain disorders (e.g., Clementz & Iacono, 1990; Klein, 1989). Environmental theories attempt to identify specific events that are necessary or sufficient to produce a disorder. These approaches have achieved varying degrees of success depending on which diagnostic groups were considered. One explanation for the limited success of attempts to identify etiological factors in psychopathology is

the limited number of techniques available for the examination of potential factors. For example, the history of psychiatry and medicine is replete with examples of major findings due in part to advances in technology (e.g., computerized axial tomography [CAT] scans as a method of examining the function of internal organs). An alternative explanation for the limited success of etiological studies is that most researchers have relied on theoretical perspectives that assume distinct categories of illness. Specifically, the assumption of distinct diagnostic entities masks the possibility that multiple etiological factors may lead to the development of the same disorder, and that biological and environmental factors may ameliorate the effect of strong etiological factors. Even when a diagnosis may seem to have a clear etiology (e.g., PTSD), the picture is not clear. For example, although the diagnosis of PTSD requires a clear stressor it is known that not all individuals who experience that stressor develop PTSD and not all stressors are likely to create PTSD (Foa & Rothbaum, 1998). Furthermore, the presence of a stressor alone is not sufficient to warrant the diagnosis. In fact, research suggests that etiologic factors entirely outside the diagnostic criteria (e.g., IQ; Macklin et al., 1998; McNally & Shin, 1995) may ameliorate the effects of the identified etiologic factors on the development of the disorder.

Much of the controversy about assessment and classification in psychopathology stems from the conflict about the use of value judgments as opposed to data-driven theory testing in creating diagnostic categories. Some have suggested that a combination of the two perspectives, including the use of both theory and data, may be the most workable approach (Blashfield & Livesley, 1991; Morey, 1991). This approach would amount to a process of construct validation depending on both theory and evaluation of the theory by data analysis. As in other areas of theory development, testability and parsimony would play a crucial role in choosing between competing theories. In the following section, the need for the adoption of new research methodologies in the field of assessment and classification of psychopathology will be considered. Next some of the areas of research which illustrate promising methods, most of which focus on identifying etiologic factors in psychopathology, will be discussed.

As mentioned earlier, researchers have called for a move away from a system of diagnosis based on superficial features (symptoms) toward diagnosis based on scientifically-based theories of underlying etiology and disease processes. This focus parallels that of medical diagnosis of physical illness. Physicians do not diagnose based on symptoms. Instead, patient reports of symptoms are seen as indicators of potential illnesses. Diagnoses are not made until specific indicators of pathology (e.g., biopsies, masses, blood draws, etc.) have been examined. The interpretation of such laboratory results requires an understanding of the differences between normal and abnormal functioning of the cell or organ in question. In order for assessment of psychopathology to follow this route, researchers must continue to amass information on normal mental and behavioral functioning (J. F. Kihlstrom, personal communication, September 11, 1997, SSCPnet). This endeavor can be facilitated by technological advances in experimental paradigms and measurement techniques and devices. The issue of what constitutes a great enough deviation from "normal" functioning to warrant treatment has been and most likely will continue to be controversial. However, such decisions are a necessary hurdle if psychopathology is to evolve as a science.

It is likely that the identification of etiological factors in psychopathology will not rely entirely on biological factors. The validation of etiological constructs in psychopathology will undoubtedly include studies designed to identify potential contributing causes including environmental, personality, and physiological factors. Examples of research methods and paradigms which may prove useful in determining the etiology of psychiatric disorders are becoming increasingly evident in the literature. Possible methodologies include: psychopharmacological efficacy studies (Harrison et al., 1984; Hudson & Pope, 1990; Papp et al., 1993; Quitkin et al., 1993; Stein, Hollander, & Klein, 1994); family and DNA studies (Fyer et al., 1996); treatment response studies (Clark et al., 1995, Millon, 1991); *in vivo* monitoring of physiological processes (Martinez et al., 1996); and identification of abnormal physiological processes (Klein, 1993, 1994; Pine et al., 1994). These approaches may prove informative in designing future versions of psychopathology classification systems. Other researchers have chosen a more direct approach, as is evidenced in a series of articles in a special section of the *Journal of Consulting and Clinical Psychology* (*JCCP*) entitled "Development of theoretically coherent alternatives to the *DSM-IV*" (Follette, 1996). The authors of this special issue of *JCCP* pose radical alternatives to the *DSM*. The alternative classification systems are proposed from a clearly stated behavioral theoretical viewpoint, which differs considerably from many of the more biologically-based approaches described above.

A number of the alternatives and improvements suggested in the 1996 *JCCP* are based on

functional analysis, the identification of the antecedents, and consequences of each behaviors (Hayes, Wilson, Gifford, Follette, & Strosahl, 1996; Scotti, Morris, McNeil, & Hawkins, 1996; Wulfert, Greenway, & Dougher, 1996). Wulfert et al. (1996) use the example of depression as a disorder which may be caused by a host of different factors (biological, cognitive, social skills deficits, or a lack of reinforcement). They argue that the fact that functionally similar behavior patterns may have very different structures may contribute to the heterogeneity found in the presumably homogenous *DSM* categories. These authors contend that functional analysis may constitute one means of identifying homogenous subgroups whose behavior share similar antecedents and consequences. This approach could be used to refine the existing *DSM* categories, and to inform treatment strategies. Hayes et al. (1996) describe a classification system based on functional analysis as a fundamentally different alternative to the current syndromal classification system. They proposed that a classification system could be based on dimensions derived from the combined results of multiple functional analyses tied to the same dimension. Each dimension would then be associated with specific assessment methods and therapy recommendations. The authors describe one such functional dimension, "experiential avoidance," and illustrate its utility across disorders such as substance abuse, obsessive-compulsive disorder, panic disorder, and borderline personality disorder (Hayes et al.). This model provides an alternative to the current *DSM* syndromal model, using the methodological approach of functional analysis. Scotti et al. (1996) proposed a similar system of categorization of childhood and adolescent disorders utilizing functional analysis. Hayes et al. (1996), Scotti et al. (1996), and Wulfert et al. (1996) have all successfully illustrated that alternatives or improvements to the current *DSM* system are possible.

However, functional analysis is a distinctly behavioral approach which assumes that a learned stimulus–response connection is an important element in the development or maintenance of psychopathology. Other authors, for example, proponents of genetic or biological explanations of psychopathology described above, might strongly oppose a classification system based purely on the methodology and tenets of a behavioral approach. Others disagree with the notion of any unified system of classification of psychopathology, arguing that no one diagnostic system will be equally useful for all of the classes of disorders now included in the *DSM* (e.g., what works for Axis I may not apply to the personality or childhood disorders). Several of these authors have taken a more radical stance, asserting the need for separate diagnostic systems for different classes of disorder (Kazdin & Kagan, 1994; Koerner, Kohlenberg, & Parker, 1996).

3.08.6 CONCLUSIONS

The assessment and classification of psychopathology is relatively new and controversies abound. However, the heated debates regarding issues such as comorbidity, types of taxonomies, and alternative approaches are indicators of the strong interest in this area. Comparisons between the classification of psychopathology and taxonomies in the basic sciences and medicine can be informative. However, the classification of psychopathology is a difficult task, and the methods used in other fields are not always applicable. It is likely that the systems of classification, informed by the continuing debates and research on the topic, will continue to evolve at a rapid pace. As Clark et al. (1995) remarked, the science of classification has inspired research in new directions and helped to guide future developments of psychopathology.

ACKNOWLEDGMENTS

We would like to thank Amy Przeworski and Melinda Freshman for their help in editing this chapter.

3.08.7 REFERENCES

Abikoff, H., & Klein, R. G. (1992). Attention-deficit hyperactivity and conduct disorder: Comorbidity and implications for treatment. *Journal of Consulting and Clinical Psychology, 60*(6), 881–892.

American Psychiatric Association (1933). Notes and comment: Revised classification of mental disorders. *American Journal of Psychiatry, 90*, 1369–1376.

American Psychiatric Association (1994). *Diagnostic and statistical manual of mental disorders* (4th ed.). Washington, DC: Author.

Andreasen, N. C., & Carpenter, W. T. (1993). Diagnosis and classification of schizophrenia. *Schizophrenia Bulletin, 19*(2), 199–214.

Andreasen, N. C., Flaum, M., Swayze, V. W., Tyrrell, G., & Arndt, S. (1990). Positive and negative symptoms in schizophrenia: A critical reappraisal. *Archives of General Psychiatry, 47*, 615–621.

Angrist, B., Rotrosen, J., & Gershon, S. (1980). Differential effects of amphetamine and neuroleptics on negative vs. positive symptoms in schizophrenia. *Psychopharmacology, 72*, 17–19.

August, G. J., & Garfinkel, B. D. (1990). Comorbidity of ADHD and reading disability among clinic-referred children. *Journal of Abnormal Child Psychology, 18*, 29–45.

Baumann, U. (1995) Assessment and documentation of psychopathology, *Psychopathology, 28* (Suppl.1), 13–20.

Beck, A. T., Epstein, N., Brown, G., & Steer, R. A. (1988). An inventory for measuring anxiety: Psychometric properties. *Journal of Consulting and Clinical Psychology, 56*(6), 893–897.

Beck, A. T., & Steer, R. A. (1987). *Beck depression inventory manual*. San Antonio, TX: The Psychological Corporation.

Bellack, A. S., & Hersen, M. (Eds.) (1998). *Behavioral assessment: A practical handbook*. Needham Heights, MA: Allyn & Bacon.

Bergner, R. M. (1997). What is psychopathology? And so what? *Clinical Psychology: Science and Practice, 4*, 235–248.

Berrios, G. E., & Hauser, R. (1988). The early development of Kraepelin's ideas on classification: A conceptual history. *Psychological Medicine, 18*, 813–821.

Biederman, J., Newcorn, J., & Sprich, S. (1991). Comorbidity of attention deficit hyperactivity disorder with conduct, depressive, anxiety, and other disorders. *American Journal of Psychiatry, 148*(5), 564–577.

Blacker, D., & Tsuang, M. T. (1992). Contested boundaries of bipolar disorder and the limits of categorical diagnosis in psychiatry. *American Journal of Psychiatry, 149*(11), 1473–1483.

Blashfield, R. K. (1990). Comorbidity and classification. In J. D. Maser & C. R. Cloninger (Eds.), *Comorbidity of mood and anxiety disorders* (pp. 61–82). Washington, DC: American Psychiatric Press.

Blashfield, R. K. (1991). Models of psychiatric classification. In M Hersen & S. M. Turner (Eds.), *Adult psychopathology and diagnosis* (pp. 3–22). New York: Wiley.

Blashfield, R. K., & Draguns, J. G. (1976). Toward a taxonomy of psychopathology: The purpose of psychiatric classification. *British Journal of Psychiatry, 129*, 574–583.

Blashfield, R. K., & Livesley, W. J. (1991). Metaphorical analysis of psychiatric classification as a psychological test. *Journal of Abnormal Psychology, 100*, 262–270.

Boyd, J. H., Burke, J. D., Gruenberg, E., Holzer, C. E., Rae, D. S., George, L. K., Karno, M., Stoltzman, R., McEvoy, L., & Nestadt, G. (1984). Exclusion criteria of *DSM-III*. *Archives of General Psychiatry, 41*, 983–989.

Brett, E. A. (1993). Classifications of posttraumatic stress disorder in *DSM-IV*: Anxiety disorder, dissociative disorder, or stress disorder? In J. R. T. Davidson & E. B. Foa (Eds.), *Posttraumatic stress disorder: DSM-IV and beyond* (pp. 191–204). Washington, DC: American Psychiatric Press.

Broverman, I. K., Broverman, D. M., Clarkson, F. E., Rosenkrantz, P. S., & Vogel, S. R. (1970). Sex-role stereotypes and clinical judgments of mental health. *Journal of Consulting and Clinical Psychology, 34*(1), 1–7.

Brown, T. A., & Barlow, D. H. (1992). Comorbidity among anxiety disorders: Implications for treatment and *DSM-IV*. *Journal of Consulting and Clinical Psychology, 60*(6), 835–844.

Buchanan, R. W., & Carpenter, W. T. (1994). Domains of psychopathology: an approach to the reduction of heterogeneity in schizophrenia. *The Journal of Nervous and Mental Disease, 182*(4), 193–204.

Butcher, J. N., Dahlstrom, W. G., Graham, J. R., Tellegen, A., & Kaemmer, B. (1989). *Minnesota multiphasic personality inventory (MMPI-2). Administration and scoring*. Minneapolis, MN: University of Minnesota Press.

Cantor, N., & Genero, N. (1986). Psychiatric diagnosis and natural categorization: A close analogy. In T. Millon & G. L. Klerman (Eds.) *Contemporary directions in psychopathology—toward the DSM-IV* (pp. 233–256). New York: Guildford Press.

Carey, G., & Gottesman, I. I. (1978). Reliability and validity in binary ratings: Areas of common misunderstanding in diagnosis and symptom ratings. *Archives of General Psychiatry, 35,* 1454–1459.

Clark, L. A., & Watson, D. (1991). Tripartite model of anxiety and depression: Psychometric evidence and taxonomic implications. *Journal of Abnormal Psychology, 100*(3), 316–336.

Clark, L. A., Watson, D., & Reynolds, S. (1995). Diagnosis and classification of psychopathology: Challenges to the current system and future directions. *Annual Review of Psychology, 46,* 121–153.

Clarkin, J. F., Widiger, T. A., Frances, A. J., Hurt, S. W., & Gilmore, M. (1983). Prototypic typology and the borderline personality disorder. *Journal of Abnormal Psychology, 92*(3), 263–275.

Clementz, B. A., & Iacono, W. G. (1990). Nosology and diagnosis. In L. Willerman & D. B. Cohen (Eds.), *Psychopathology,* New York: McGraw-Hill.

Cole, D. A., & Carpentieri, S. (1990). Social status and the comorbidity of child depression and conduct disorder. *Journal of Consulting and Clinical Psychology, 58,* 748–757.

Compton, W. M., & Guze, S. B., (1995). The neo-Kraepelinian revolution in psychiatric diagnosis. *European Archives of Psychiatry & Clinical Neuroscience, 245,* 196–201.

Cornblatt, B. A., Lenzenweger, M. F., Dworkin, R. H., & Erlenmeyer-Kimling, L. (1992). Childhood attentional dysfunctions predict social deficits in unaffected adults at risk for schizophrenia. *British Journal of Psychiatry, 161,* 59–64.

Crow, T. J. (1994). The demise of the Kraepelinian binary system as a prelude to genetic advance. In E. S. Gershon, & C. R. Cloninger (Eds.), *Genetic approaches to mental disorders* (pp. 163–192). Washington, DC: American Psychiatric Press.

Daradkeh, T. K., El-Rufaie, O. E. F., Younis, Y. O., & Ghubash, R. (1997). The diagnostic stability of ICD-10 psychiatric diagnoses in clinical practice. *European Psychiatry, 12,* 136–139.

Davidson, J. R. T., & Foa, E. B. (1991). Diagnostic issues in posttraumatic stress disorder: Considerations for the *DSM-IV. Journal of Abnormal Psychology, 100*(3), 346–355.

de Fundia, T. A., Draguns, J. G., & Phillips, L. (1971). Culture and psychiatric symptomatology: A comparison of Argentine and United States patients. *Social Psychiatry, 6*(1), 11–20.

Dworkin, R. H., & Lenzenweger, M. F. (1984). Symptoms and the genetics of schizophrenia: Implications for diagnosis. *American Journal of Psychiatry, 141*(12), 1541–1546.

Dworkin, R. H., Lenzenwenger, M. F., Moldin, S. O., & Cornblatt, B. A. (1987). Genetics and the phenomenology of schizophrenia. In P. D. Harvey & E. F. Walker (Eds.), *Positive and negative symptoms of psychosis: Description, research and future directives* (pp. 258–288). Hillsdale, NJ: Erlbaum.

Eysenck, H. J. (1970). A dimensional system of psycho-diagnostics. In A. R. Mahrer (Ed.), *New approaches to personality classification* (pp. 169–207). New York: Columbia University Press.

Feighner, A. C., Baran, I. D., Furman, S., & Shipman, W. M. (1972). Private psychiatry in community mental health. *Hospital and Community Psychiatry, 23*(7), 212–214.

Feinstein, A. R. (1970). The pre-therapeutic classification of co-morbidity in chronic disease. *Journal of Chronic Diseases, 23,* 455–468.

First, M. B., Spitzer, R. L., Gibbon, M., & Williams, K. B. W. (1995). *Structured clinical interview for DSM-IV Axis I Disorders.* Washington, DC: American Psychiatric Press.

Foa, E. B., Riggs, D. S., Dancu, C. V., & Rothbaum, B. O.

(1993). Reliability and validity of a brief instrument for assessing post-traumatic stress disorder. *Journal of Traumatic Stress, 6,* 459–473.

Foa, E. B., & Rothbaum, B. (1998). *Treating the trauma of rape.* New York: Guilford Press.

Follette, W. C. (1996). Introduction to the special section on the development theoretically coherent alternatives to the *DSM* system. *Journal of Consulting and Clinical Psychology, 64,* 1117–1119.

Follette, W. C., & Houts, A. C. (1996) Models of scientific progress and the role of theory in taxonomy development: A case study of the *DSM. Journal of Consulting and Clinical Psychology, 64,* 1120–1132.

Frances, A. J. (1998). Problems in defining clinical significance in epidemiological studies. *Archives of General Psychiatry, 55,* 119.

Frances, A. J., First, M. B., & Pincus, H. A. (1995). *DSM-IV guidebook.* Washington, DC: American Psychiatric Press.

Frances, A. J., First, M. B., Widiger, T. A., Miele, G. I., M., Tilly, S. M., Davis, W. W., & Pincus, H. A. (1991). An A to Z guide to *DSM-IV* conundrums. *Journal of Abnormal Psychology, 100*(3), 407–412.

Frances, A. J., Widiger, T. A., & Fyer, M. R. (1990). The influence of classification methods on comorbidity. In J. D. Maser & C. R. Cloninger (Eds.), *Comorbidity of mood and anxiety disorders* (pp. 41–59). Washington, DC: American Psychiatric Press.

Fulop, G., Strain, J., Vita, J., Lyons, J. S. & Hammer, J. S. (1987). Impact of psychiatric comorbidity on length of hospital stay for medical/surgical patients: A preliminary report *American Journal of Psychiatry, 144,* 878–882.

Fyer, A.J., Mannuzza, S., Chapman, T. F., Lipsitz, J., Martin, L. Y. & Klein, D. F. (1996). Panic disorder and social phobia: Effects of comorbidity on familial transmission. *Anxiety 2,* 173–178.

Goldenberg, I. M., White, K., Yonkers, K., Reich, J., Warshaw, M. G., Goisman, R. M., & Keller, M. B. (1996). The infrequency of "Pure Culture" diagnoses among the anxiety disorders. *Journal of Clinical Psychiatry, 57*(11), 528–533.

Goodman, W. K., Price, L. H., Rasmussen, S. A., & Mazure, C. (1989a). The Yale-Brown obsessive compulsive scale: I. Development, use and reliability. *Archives of General Psychiatry, 46,* 1006–1011.

Goodman, W. K., Price, L. H., Rasmussen, S. A., & Mazure, C. (1989b). The Yale-Brown obsessive compulsive scale: II. Validity. *Archives of General Psychiatry, 46,* 1012–1016.

Gorenstein, E. E. (1992). *The science of mental illness.* New York: Academic Press.

Gove, W. R. (1980). Mental illness and psychiatric treatment among women. *Psychology of Women Quarterly, 4,* 345–362.

Grove, W. M., Lebow, B. S., Clementz, B. A., Cerri, A., Medus, C., & Iacono, W. G. (1991). Familial prevalence and coaggregation of schizotypy indicators: A multitrait family study. *Journal of Abnormal Psychology, 100,* 115–121.

Haghighat, R. (1994). Cultural sensitivity: *ICD-10* versus *DSM-III-R. International Journal of Social Psychiatry, 40,* 189–193.

Hamilton, S., Rothbart, M., & Dawes, R. (1986). Sex bias, diagnosis and *DSM-III. Sex Roles, 15,* 269–274.

Harrison, W. M., Cooper, T. B., Stewart, J. W., Quitkin, F. M., McGrath, P. J., Liebowitz, M. R., Rabkin, J. R., Markowitz, J. S., & Klein, D. F. (1984). The tyramine challenge test as a marker for melancholia. *Archives of General Psychiatry, 41*(7), 681–685.

Hayes, S. C., Wilson, K. G., Gifford, E. V., Follette, V. M., & Strosahl, K. D. (1996). Experiential avoidance and behavioral disorders: A functional dimensional approach to diagnosis and treatment. *Journal of Consulting*

& *Clinical Psychology, 64*(6), 1152–1168.

Helzer, J. E., & Robins, L. N. (1988). The Diagnostic interview schedule: Its development, evolution, and use. *Social Psychology and Psychiatric Epidemiology, 23*(1), 6–16.

Herbert, J. D., Hope, D. A., & Bellack, A. S. (1992). Validity of the distinction between generalized social phobia and avoidant personality disorder. *Journal of Abnormal psychology, 101*(2), 332–339.

Hollander, E. (1993). Obsessive-compulsive spectrum disorders: An overview. *Psychiatric Annals, 23*(7), 355–358.

Horowitz, L. M., Post, D. L, French, R. S., Wallis, K. D., & Siegelman, E. Y. (1981). The prototype as a construct in abnormal psychology: II. Clarifying disagreement in psychiatric judgments, *Journal of Abnormal Psychology, 90*(6), 575–585.

Hudson, J. I., & Pope, H. G. (1990). Affective spectrum disorder: Does antidepressant response identify a family of disorders with a common pathophysiology? *American Journal of Psychiatry, 147* (5), 552–564.

Jacoby, R. (1996). Problems in the use of ICD-10 and DSM-IV in the psychiatry of old age. In N. S. Costas & H. Hanns (Eds.), *Neuropsychiatry in old age: An update. Psychiatry in progress series* (pp. 87–88). Gottingen, Germany: Hogrefe & Huber.

Janca, A., Kastrup, M. C., Katschnig, H., & Lopez-Ibor, J. J., Jr. (1996). The ICD-10 multiaxial system for use in adult psychiatry: Structure and applications. *Journal of Nervous and Mental Disease, 184*, 191–192.

Johnstone, E. C., Crow, T. J., Frith, C. D., Stevens, M., Kreel, L., & Husband, J. (1978). The dementia of dementia praecox. *Acta Psychiatrica Scandanavia, 57*, 305–324.

Kanfer, F. H., & Saslow, G. (1965). Behavioral analysis. *Archives of General Psychiatry, 12*, 529–538.

Kahn, E. (1959). The Emil Kraepelin memorial lecture. In D. Pasamanick (Ed.), *Epidemiology of mental disorders.* Washington, DC: American Association for the Advancement of Science. (As cited in M. Hersen & S. M. Turner (Eds.), *Adult psychopathology and diagnosis* (p. 20). New York: Wiley).

Katon, W., Lin, E., Von Korff, M., Russo, J., Lipscomb, P., & Bush, T. (1991). Somatization: A spectrum of severity. *American Journal of Psychiatry, 148*(1), 34–40.

Kay, S. R. (1990). Significance of the positive-negative distinction in schizophrenia. *Schizophrenia Bulletin, 16* (4), 635–652.

Kazdin, A. E., & Kagan, J. (1994). Models of dysfunction in developmental psychopathology. *Clinical Psychology-Science & Practice, 1*(1), 35–52.

Kendell, R. E. (1975). The concept of disease and its implications for psychiatry. *British Journal of Psychiatry, 127*, 305–315.

Kendell, R. E. (1982). The choice of diagnostic criteria for biological research. *Archives of General Psychiatry, 39*, 1334–1339.

Kendler, K. S. (1990). Toward a scientific psychiatric nosology. *Archives of General Psychiatry, 47*, 969–973.

Kessler, R. C., McGonagle, K. A., Zhao, S., Nelson, C. B., Hughes, M., Eshelman, S., Wittchen, H. U., & Kendler, K. S. (1994). Lifetime and 12-month prevalence of DSM-III-R psychiatric disorders in the United States. *Archives of General Psychiatry, 51*, 8–19.

Klein, D. F. (1989). The Pharmacological validation of psychiatric diagnosis. In L. N. Robins & J. E. Barrett (Eds.), *The validity of psychiatric diagnosis* (pp. 203–214). New York: Raven Press.

Klein, D. F. (1993). False suffocation alarms, spontaneous panics, and related conditions: An integrative hypothesis. *Archives of General Psychiatry, 50*, 306–317.

Klein, D. F. (1994). Testing the suffocation false alarm theory of panic disorder. *Anxiety, 1*, 1–7.

Klerman, G. L. (1978). The evolution of a scientific nosology. In J. C. Shershow (Ed.), *Schizophrenia: Science and practice* (pp. 99–121). Cambridge, MA: Harvard University Press.

Koerner, K., Kohlenberg, R. J., & Parker, C. R. (1996). Diagnosis of personality disorder: A radical behavioral alternative. *Journal of Consulting & Clinical Psychology, 64*(6), 1169–1176.

Kraeplin, E. (1971). *Dementia praecox and paraphrenia* (R. M. Barklay, Trans.). Huntington, NY: Krieger. (Original work published in 1919).

Lewinsohn, P. M., Rohde, P., Seeley, J. R., & Hops, H. (1991). Comorbidity of unipolar depression: I. Major depression with dysthymia. *Journal of Abnormal Psychology, 100*(2), 205–213.

Lilienfeld, S. O., Waldman, I. D., & Israel, A. C. (1994). A critical examination of the use of the term and concept of comorbidity in psychopathology research. *Clinical Psychology-Science & Practice, 1*(1), 71–83.

Livesley, W. J. (1985a). The classification of personality disorder: I. The choice of category concept. *Canadian Journal of Psychiatry, 30*(5), 353–358.

Livesley, W. J. (1985b). The classification of personality disorder: II. The problem of diagnostic criteria. *Canadian Journal of Psychiatry, 30*(5), 359–362.

Lykken, D. T. (1984). Psychopathic personality. In R. I. Corsini (Ed.), *Encyclopedia of psychology* (pp. 165–167). New York, Wiley. (As cited in B. A. Clementz & W. E. Iacono (1990). In L. Willerman & D. B. Cohen (Eds.), *Psychopathology*, New York: McGraw-Hill.)

Macklin, M. L., Metzger, L. J., Litz, B. T., McNally, R. J., Lasko, N. B., Orr, S. P., & Pitman, R. K. (1998). Lower precombat intelligence is a risk factor for posttraumatic stress disorder. *Journal of Consulting and Clinical Psychology, 66*, 323–326

Martinez, J. M., Papp, L. A., Coplan, J. D., Anderson, D. E., Mueller, C. M., Klein, D. F., & Gorman, J. M. (1996). Ambulatory monitoring of respiration in anxiety. *Anxiety, 2*, 296–302.

Mayr, E. (1981). Biological classification: Toward a synthesis of opposing methodologies. *Science, 214*(30), 510–516.

McNair, D. M., Lorr, M., & Droppleman, L. F. (1981). *POMS manual* (2nd ed.). San Diego: Educational and Industrial Testing Service.

McNally, R., & Shin, L. M. (1995). Association of intelligence with severity of posttraumatic stress disorder symptoms in Vietnam combat veterans. *American Journal of Psychiatry, 152*(6), 936–938.

McReynolds, P. (1989). Diagnosis and clinical assessment: Current status and major issues. *Annual Review of Psychology, 40*, 83–108.

Meehl, P. E. (1986). Diagnostic taxa as open concepts: Metatheoretical and statistical questions about reliability and construct validity in the grand strategy of nosological revision. In T. Millon & G. L. Klerman (Eds.), *Contemporary directions in psychopathology: Toward the DSM-IV* (pp. 215–231). New York: Guilford Press.

Menninger, K. (1963). *The vital balance: The life process in mental health and illness.* New York: Viking Press.

Mezzich, J. E., Fabrega, H., Coffman, G. A., & Haley, R. (1989). DSM-III disorders in a large sample of psychiatric patients: Frequency and Specificity of diagnoses. *American Journal of Psychiatry, 146*(2), 212–219.

Michels, R., Siebel, U., Freyberger, H. J., Stieglitz, R. D., Schaub, R. T., & Dilling, H. (1996). The multiaxial system of ICD-10: Evaluation of a preliminary draft in a multicentric field trial. *Psychopathology, 29*, 347–356.

Millon, T. (1991). Classification in psychopathology: Rationale, alternatives and standards. *Journal of Abnormal Psychology, 100*, 245–261.

Moras, K., DiNardo, P. A., Brown, T. A., & Barlow, D. H. (1991). Comorbidity and depression among the DSM-III-R anxiety disorders. Manuscript as cited in Brown, T.

A. & Barlow, D. H. (1992). Comorbidity among anxiety disorders: Implications for treatment and DSM-IV. *Journal of Consulting and Clinical Psychology, 60*(6), 835–844.

Morey, L. C. (1988). Personality disorders in DSM-III and DSM-III-R: Convergence, coverage, and internal consistency. *American Journal of Psychiatry, 145*(5), 573–577.

Morey, L. C. (1991). Classification of mental disorder As a collection of hypothetical constructs. *Journal of Abnormal Psychology, 100*(3), 289–293.

Morey, L. C. (1992). *Personality disorder NOS: Specifying patterns of the otherwise unspecified.* Paper presented at the 100th Annual Convention of the American Psychological Association. Washington, DC: USA.

Mowrer, O. H. (1960). "Sin," the lesser of two evils. *American Psychologist, 15,* 301–304.

Oldham, J. M., Skodal, A. E., Kellman, H. D., Hyler, S. E., Rosnick, L., & Davies, M. (1992). Diagnosis of DSM-II-R personality disorders by two structured interviews: Patterns of comorbidity. *American Journal of Psychiatry, 149,* 213–220.

Papp, L. A., Klein, D. F., Martinez, J., Schneier, F., Cole, R., Liebowitz, M. R., Hollander, E., Fyer, A. J., Jordan, F., & Gorman, J. M. (1993). Diagnostic and substance specificity of carbon dioxide-induced panic. *American Journal of Psychiatry, 150,* 250–257.

Patel, V., & Winston, M. (1994). "Universality of mental illness" revisited: Assumptions, artefacts and new directions. *British Journal of Psychiatry, 165,* 437–440.

Pine, D. S., Weese-Mayer, D. E., Silvestri, J. M., Davies, M., Whitaker, A., & Klein, D. F. (1994). Anxiety and congenital central hypoventilation syndrome. *American Journal of Psychiatry, 151,* 864–870.

Pogue-Geile, M. F., & Harrow, M. (1984). Negative and positive symptoms in schizophrenia and depression: A follow-up. *Schizophrenia Bulletin, 10*(3), 371–387.

Quay, H. C., Routh, D. K., & Shapiro, S. K. (1987). Psychopathology of childhood: From description to validation. *Annual Review of Psychology, 38,* 491–532.

Quitkin, F. M., Stewart, J. W., McGrath, P. J., Tricamo, E., Rabkin, J. G., Ocepek-Welikson, K., Nunes, E., Harrison, W., & Klein, D. F. (1993). Columbia atypical depression: A sub-group of depressives with better response to MAOI than to tricyclic antidepressants or placebo. *British Journal of Psychiatry, 163,* 30–34.

Rapee, R. M., Sanderson, W. C., & Barlow, D. H. (1988). Social phobia features across the DSM-III-R anxiety disorders. *Journal of Psychopathology and Behavioral Assessment, 10*(3), 287–299.

Regier, D. A., Kaelber, C. T., Rae, D. S., Farmer, M. E., Knauper, B., Kessler, R. C., & Norquist, G. S. (1998) Limitations of diagnostic criteria and assessment instruments for mental disorders. Implications for research and policy. *Archives of General Psychiatry, 55,* 109–115.

Regier, D. A., Kaelber, C. T., Roper, M. T., Rae, D. S. & Sartorius, N. (1994). The ICD-10 clinical field trial for mental and behavioral disorders: Results in Canada and the United States. *American Journal of Psychiatry, 151,* 1340–1350.

Riskind, J. H., Beck, A. T., Brown, G., & Steer, R. A. (1987). Taking the measure of anxiety and depression. Validity of the reconstructed Hamilton scale. *Journal of Nervous and Mental Disease, 175*(8), 474–479.

Robins, E., & Guze, S. B. (1970). Establishment of diagnostic validity in psychiatric illness: Its application to schizophrenia. *American Journal of Psychiatry, 126,* 983–987.

Robins, L. N. (1994). How recognizing "comorbidities" in psychopathology may lead to an improved research nosology. *Clinical Psychology: Science and Practice, 1,* 93–95.

Robins, L. N., Wing, J., Wittchen, H. J., Helzer, J. E.,

Barbor, T. F., Burke, J. D., Farmer, A., Jablenski, A., Pickens, R., Reiger, D. A., Sartorius, N., & Towle, L. H. (1988). The composite international Diagnostic Interview: An epidemiological instrument suitable for use in conjunction with different diagnostic systems and different cultures. *Archives of General Psychiary, 45,* 1069–1077.

Rosch, E. H. (1978). Principles of categorization. In E. H. Rosch & B. B. Lloyd (Eds.), *Cognition and categorization* (pp. 27–48). Hillsdale, NJ: Erlbaum.

Russell, J. A. (1980). A circumplex model of affect. *Journal of Personality and Social Psychology, 39*(6), 1161–1178.

Sartorius, N., & Janca, A. (1996). Psychiatric assessment instruments developed by the World Health Organization. *Social Psychiatry and Psychiatric Epidemiological, 32,* 55–69.

Scotti, J. R., Morris, T. L., McNeil, C. B., & Hawkins, R. P. (1996). DSM-IV and disorders of childhood and adolescence: Can structural criteria be functional? *Journal of Consulting & Clinical Psychology, 64*(6), 1177–1191.

Shea, M. T., Widiger, T. A., & Klein, M. H. (1992). Comorbidity of personality disorders and depression: Implications for treatment. *Journal of Consulting and Clinical Psychology, 60,* 857–868.

Spiegel, D., & Cardena, E. (1991). Disintegrated experience: The dissociative disorders revisited. *Journal of Abnormal Psychology, 100*(3), 366–378.

Spielberger, C. D., Gorsuch, R. R., & Lushene, R. E. (1970). *State-trait anxiety Inventory: Test manual for form X.* Palo Alto, CA: Consulting Psychologists Press.

Spitzer, R. B. (1997). Brief comments for a psychiatric nosologist weary from his own attempts to define mental disorder: Why Ossorio's definition muddles and Wakefield's "Harmful Dysfunction" illuminates the issues. *Clinical Psychology: Science and Practice, 4,* 259–261.

Spitzer, R. B. (1998). Diagnosis and need for treatment are not the same. *Archieves of General Psychiatry, 55,* 120.

Spitzer, R. B., Endicott, J., & Robins, E. (1978). Research diagnostic criteria: Rationale and reliability. *Archives of General Psychiatry, 35*(6), 773–782.

Stein, D. J., Hollander, E., & Klein, D. F. (1994). Biological markers of depression and anxiety. *Medicographia, 16*(1), 18–21.

Stevens, J. R. (1982). Neuropathology of schizophrenia. *Archives of General Psychiatry, 39,* 1131–1139.

Szasz, T. (1960). The myth of mental illness. *American Psychologist, 15,* 113–118.

Tattersall, I. (1995). The fossil trail: How we know what we think we know about human evolution. New York: Oxford University Press. (As cited in Follette, W. C., & Houts, A. C. (1996). Models of scientific progress and the role of theory in taxonomy development: A case study of the DSM. *Journal of Consulting and Clinical Psychology, 64,* 1120–1132.)

Taylor, M. A. (1992). Are schizophrenia and affective disorder related? A selective literature review. *American Journal of Psychiatry, 149,* 22–32.

Taylor, M. A., & Amir, N. (1994). Are schizophrenia and affective disorder related?: The problem of schizoaffective disorder and the discrimination of the psychoses by signs and symptoms. *Comprehensive Psychiatry, 35*(6), 420–429.

Tellegen, A. (1985). Structures of mood and personality and their relevance to assessing anxiety, with an emphasis on self-report. In A. H. Tuma & J. D. Maser (Eds.), *Anxiety and the anxiety disorders* (pp. 681–706). Hillsdale, NJ: Erlbaum.

Uestuen, T. B., Bertelsen, A., Dilling, H., & van Drimmelen, J. (1996). *ICD-10 casebook: The many faces of mental disorders—Adult case histories according to ICD-10.* Washington, DC: American Psychiatric Press.

Ullman, L. P., & Krasner, L. (1975). *A psychological*

approach to abnormal behavior. Englewood Cliffs, NJ: Prentice-Hall.

Wakefield, J. C. (1992). Disorder as harmful dysfunction: A conceptual critique of DSM-III-R's definition of mental disorder. *Psychological Review, 99,* 232–247.

Wakefield, J. C. (1997a). Diagnosing DSM-IV, Part I: DSM-IV and the concept of disorder. *Behavioral Research Therapy, 35*(7), 633–649.

Wakefield, J. C. (1997b). Diagnosing DSM-IV, Part II: Eysenck (1986) and the essential fallacy. *Behavioral Research Therapy, 35*(7), 651–665.

Wakefied, J. C. (1997c). Normal inability versus pathological disability: Why Ossorio's definition of mental disorder is not sufficient. *Clinical Psychology: Science and Practice, 4,* 249–258.

Watson, D., & Clark, L. A. (1992). Affects separable and inseparable: On the hierarchical arrangement of the negative affects. *Journal of Personality and Social Psychology, 62*(3), 489–505.

Watson, D., Clark, L. A., & Tellegen, A. (1988). Development and validation of brief measures of positive and negative affect: The PANAS scales. *Journal of Personality and Social Psychology, 54*(6), 1063–1070.

Watson, J. D., & Crick, F. H. C. (1953a). General implications of the structure of deoxyribose nucleic acid. *Nature, 171,* 964–967. (As cited in Clementz B. A., & Iacono, W. G. (1990). In L. Willerman & D. B. Cohen (Eds.), *Psychopathology.* New York: McGraw-Hill.)

Watson, J. D., & Crick, F. H. C. (1953b). A structure for deoxyribose nucleic acid. *Nature, 171,* 737–738. (As cited in Clementz, B. A., & Iacono, W. G. (1990). In L. Willerman & D. B. Cohen (Eds.), *Psychopathology.* New York: McGraw-Hill.

Widiger, T. A. (1992). Categorical versus dimensional classification: Implications from and for research. *Journal of Personality Disorders, 6*(4), 287–300.

Widiger, T. A., & Frances, A. (1985). The DSM-III personality disorders: Perspectives form psychology. *Archives of General Psychiatry, 42,* 615–623.

Widiger, T. A., & Rogers, J. H. (1989). Prevalence and comorbidity of personality disorders. *Psychiatric Annals, 19*(3), 132–136.

Widiger, T. A., & Trull, T. J. (1993). The Scholarly development of DSM-IV. In J. A. Costa, E. Silva, & C. C. Nadelson (Eds.), *International Review of Psychiatry* (pp. 59–78). Washington DC, American Psychiatric Press.

Widiger, T. A., Trull, T. J., Hurt, S. W., Clarkin, J., & Frances, A. (1987). A multidimensional scaling of the DSM-III personality disorders. *Archives of General Psychiatry, 44,* 557–563.

Wiggins, J. S. (1982). Circumplex models of interpersonal behavior in clinical psychology. In P. C. Kendall & J. N. Butcher (Eds.), *Handbook of research methods in clinical psychology* (pp. 183–221). New York: Wiley.

Wilson, G. T. (1996). Empirically validated treatments: Realities and resistance. *Clinical Psychology-Science & Practice, 3*(3), 241–244.

World Health Organization (1992). *International statistical classification disease, 10th revision (ICD-10).* Geneva, Switzerland: Author.

World Health Organization (1996). *Multiaxial classification of child and adolescent psychiatric disorders: The ICD-10 classification of mental and behavioral disorders in children and adolescents.* Cambridge, UK: Cambridge University Press.

Wulfert, E., Greenway, D. E., & Dougher, M. J. (1996). A logical functional analysis of reinforcement-based disorders: Alcoholism and pedophilia. *Journal of Consulting and Clinical Psychology, 64*(6), 1140–1151.

Zimmerman, M., Pfohl, B., Coryell, W. H., Corenthal, C., & Stangl, D. (1991). Major depression and personality disorder. *Journal of Affective Disorders, 22,* 199–210.

Zinbarg, R. E., & Barlow, D. D. (1991). Mixed anxiety-depression: A new diagnostic category? In R. M. Rapee & D. H. Barlow (Eds.), *Chronic anxiety: Generalized anxiety disorder and mixed anxiety-depression* (pp. 136–152). New York: Guilford Press.

Zinbarg, R. E., Barlow, D. H., Liebowitz, M., Street, L., Broadhead, E., Katon, W., Roy-Byrne, P., Lepine, J. P., Teherani, M., Richards, J., Brantley, P., & Kraemer, H. (1994). The DSM-IV field trial for mixed anxiety-depression. *American Journal of Psychiatry, 151*(8), 1153–1162.

3.09
Intervention Research: Development and Manualization

JOHN F. CLARKIN
Cornell University Medical College, New York, NY, USA

3.09.1 INTRODUCTION

Psychotherapy research can progress only if the treatments that are investigated can be replicated by each of the therapists within the study, and the therapy can be described to the consumers of the research results. Standards of psychotherapy research have reached a point that one cannot communicate about results without a written manual describing the treatment and methods for demonstrating thera-

pists' adherence and competence in the delivery of the treatment. In the recent history of psychotherapy research, the manual has played a vital role in the specification of clinical trials. In addition, if a science and not just an art of psychotherapy is to flourish, there must be methods to teach clinicians how to perform the various therapies with adherence to the specific treatment strategies and techniques, and with competence in this complex interpersonal process. It is in this context that the written description of psychotherapies for specific patient populations in the form of manuals has become an essential fixture in the psychotherapy world.

There has been much lament that clinical research has little if any impact on clinical practice (Talley, Strupp, & Butler, 1994). Researchers complain that their findings are ignored. Clinicians argue that the research on rarified samples yield findings that are detailed, tedious, and irrelevant to their heterogeneous patients. It may be that the psychotherapy treatment manuals will provide a bridge between clinical research and clinical practice. The treatment manual is an accessible yield of clinical research that the clinician may find helpful, if not necessary as health delivery systems change.

This chapter draws upon various sources to describe the contents of the psychotherapy manual, provides some examples of the therapy manual movement, and discusses the advantages and disadvantages of this technology both for research and the instruction of therapists. It is interesting that, although medication management is a social process between patient and physician, with many similarities to psychotherapy, there has been little development of manuals for medication management. The informative exception is the medication management manual used in the multisite treatment study of depression (Elkin et al., 1989). Despite the fact that medication adherence is often variable and generally poor, and that there is great variation in physician behavior in dispensing medications, this area has attracted little attention, apparently because researchers and clinicians assume that providing medication is a simple and standardized behavior. We suspect this assumption is false, and that more sophisticated medication and medication–psychotherapy studies in the future will have manuals with validity checks on both psychotherapy and medication management.

3.09.2 AIMS AND INGREDIENTS OF A TREATMENT MANUAL

The concept of a treatment manual has quickly evolved in the research and clinical communities. The treatment manual was acclaimed (Luborsky & DeRubeis, 1984) as a quantum leap forward which introduced a new era in clinical research. Since that time there has been the development of numerous treatment manuals. There are even special series geared around treatment manuals, and at times accompanying materials for patients as well. In addition, the intellectual community is moving forward in defining what should be included in a treatment manual to meet standards for treatment development.

An example of the development of standards for treatment manuals is the National Institute on Drug Abuse (NIDA, Moras, 1995). The experts on this panel suggested that the aims of a treatment manual are to:

(i) make the therapy reproducible by therapists other than the immediate research group;

(ii) include information on those issues the investigator thinks are important determinants of therapy response;

(iii) delineate the knowledge base and skills needed by a therapist to learn from the manual.

Given these aims, the group suggested the following content for the manual:

(i) theory and principles of the treatment (theory underpinning the therapy, decision rules and principles to guide the therapists, information on the therapy that therapists should have to help them adopt the requisite attitude about it, i.e., belief in the treatment);

(ii) elements of the treatment (therapists, primary interpersonal stance in relation to the patient, common and unique elements of therapy);

(iii) intervention strategies for handling problems commonly encountered in delivering the therapy (miscellaneous interventions, specification of interventions not to be used in the therapy);

(iv) companion videotapes for teaching the treatment; and

(v) criteria and method of assessing therapist competence in the treatment.

In essence, these are the criteria by which one can judge the adequacy of any treatment manual.

These criteria are used to assess existing treatment manuals, some of which are used as illustrations in this chapter. As noted previously (Kazdin, 1991), it seems clear that the manuals are often incomplete, as they do not reflect the complexity of treatment and the full scope of the exchanges between therapist and patient. However, the development of treatment manuals has and continues to help the field move forward.

It should be noted that there is a difference between a treatment manual and a book published and marketed that has many but not all of the attributes of a practical, ever-changing treatment manual. In an attempt to make a book of publishable size, things that might be included in the working manual, such as clinician work sheets or rating scales might be eliminated from the book. A notable exception is the work by Linehan which includes both a book (Linehan, 1993a) and an accompanying workbook (Linehan, 1993b) with therapist work sheets and other material most useful in practical delivery of the treatment. The treatment manual of the near future will probably be both a written description of the treatment in book form, and an accompanying CD-ROM that provides video demonstration of the treatment (using therapists and actor/patients).

3.09.3 DIMENSIONS ALONG WHICH THE MANUALS VARY

The existing treatment manuals can be compared not only to the content as specified by the NIDA experts, but also by differences in aspects of the treatment, including: the process by which the authors generated and elucidated their treatment; the patient population for which the treatment is intended; the knowledge base of the disorder being treated; treatment strategies and techniques, duration, and format; and level of abstraction in which the manual is written.

3.09.3.1 Process of Manual Generation and Elucidation

What was the process of manual generation by the authors? Was the manual generated from extensive experience with a patient population, followed by a codification of the techniques that seem to work on a clinical basis? Conversely, was the manual generated from a theoretical understanding of the patient population followed by treatment contact? Was it generated from a specific treatment orientation, for example, cognitive-behavioral, that is then applied to a specific patient population? Is the manual generated by clinical researchers or by clinicians? Was the manual generated during extensive clinical research, profiting from that research, or without research experience? Does the manual have accompanying aids, such as audiotapes and work sheets?

3.09.3.2 Patient Population

Therapy manuals differ in the extent to which they specify for which patients the manual is intended and for which patients the manual has not been attempted, or, indeed, for whom the treatment does not work. Since psychotherapy research funding is focused on *DSM*-diagnosed patient groups, many of the manuals describe treatments for patient groups defined by diagnosis. This fact has both positive and negative aspects. Some diagnoses are close to phenomenological descriptions of behavioral problems, so the diagnoses are immediate descriptions of problems to be solved. An example is the treatment of phobic anxiety,

agoraphobia, and panic attacks. In contrast, the diagnosis of depression is more distant from specific behaviors, so the manuals describing treatments for depression have implicit theories about the nature of depression, such as the interpersonal treatment or the cognitive treatment. Linehan's manual for the treatment of parasuicidal individuals is an interesting transitional one, from a behavior (repetitive suicidal behavior) to a diagnosis that sometimes includes the behavior (borderline personality disorder). In contrast, there are manuals written not for patients with specific diagnoses but for those with certain problems such as experiencing emotions (Greenberg, Rice, & Elliott, 1993).

An additional way the manual being considered is specific to a population is the attention given to the details of patient assessment. Ideally, the assessment section would inform the reader of the patients included and excluded, and the subgroups of patients within the diagnosis/category treated by this manual, but treated with the differences in mind depending on such factors as comorbid conditions.

One difficulty that is becoming more clear is that, for those manuals that have been written for a specific disorder, how do they apply to patients with the disorder but with a common comorbid disorder? For example, the interpersonal psychotherapy manual was constructed with ambulatory, nonpsychotic patients with depression in mind, but gives little indication of its application when there are prominent Axis II disorders. Of course, this point also relates to the accumulation of knowledge that occurs all the time, so that a manual published a few years ago may need modification and updating as more data becomes available.

3.09.3.3 Knowledge Base of the Disorder

One could make a cogent argument that a treatment for a particular disorder cannot (should not) be developed until there is sufficient information on the natural course of the disorder at issue. Only with the background of the natural development of the disorder can one examine the impact of intervention. Furthermore, the age of the patients to whom the treatment is applied is most relevant in the context of the longitudinal pattern of the disorder in question. However, in light of the clinical reality of patients in pain needing intervention, the development of intervention strategies cannot wait for longitudinal investigations of the disorder. Both arguments are sound, but we can describe intervention manuals based on the natural history of the disorder versus those that do not have such a database upon which to build.

3.09.3.4 Treatment Strategies and Techniques

Obviously, treatment manuals differ in the strategies and techniques that are described. This would include manualization of treatments that use behavioral, cognitive, cognitive-behavioral, systems, supportive, and psychodynamic techniques. Less obvious is the fact that it may be easier to manualize some strategies/techniques more than others. In fact, some therapies may be more technique oriented and others relatively more interpersonally oriented, and this may have implications for the method of manualization and the results.

An issue related to strategies and techniques is the degree to which the treatment manual describes the stance of the therapist with respect to the patient, the induction of the patient into the treatment roles and responsibilities, and the development of the therapeutic relationship or alliance. Often, it is the ambivalent patient who questions the value of the treatment, is prone to drop out, or to attend therapy with little investment and involvement (e.g., does not carry out therapy homework) that provides a serious challenge to the therapist. The more complete manuals note the typical difficulties and challenges to full participation in the treatment that have been observed in experience with the patient population, and offer guidelines for the therapist in overcoming these challenges.

3.09.3.5 Treatment Duration

Most manuals describe a brief treatment of some 12–20 sessions. The methods for manualizing longer treatments may present a challenge to the field. A brief treatment can be described in a manual session by session. Each session can be anticipated in a sequence and described. This is especially true if the treatment is cognitive-behavioral in strategies and techniques, and can be anticipated as applied to the particular condition/disorder. In contrast, as the treatment becomes longer, and as the treatment deviates from a cognitive-behavioral orientation to one that depends more on the productivity and nature of the individual patient (e.g., interpersonal and psychodynamic treatment), the manual will of necessity become more principle based and reliant on what the patient brings to the situation.

3.09.3.6 Treatment Format

Psychotherapy is delivered in individual, group, marital, and family treatment formats. It would seem to be simpler, if not easier, to articulate a treatment manual for two participants (i.e., therapist and one patient), rather than a manual for therapist and many patients (i.e., family and group treatment). As the number of patients in the treatment room increases, the number of patient-supplied interactions increases, as does the potential for treatment difficulties and road blocks.

3.09.3.7 Level of Abstraction

The very term "manual" conjures up an image of the book that comes in the pocket of a new car. It tells how to operate all the gadgets in the car, and provides a guide as to when to get the car serviced. Diagrams and pictures are provided. It is a "how to" book on repair and maintenance of your new car. Thus, the term "treatment manual" promises to describe how to do the treatment in step-by-step detail.

More relevant to psychotherapy manuals are the manuals that inform the reader—often with graphs and pictures—how to sail a boat or play tennis. This is a more apt analogy because the manual attempts in written (and graphic) form to communicate how to achieve complex cognitive and motor skills. Opponents of treatment manuals will point to golfers who have read all the manuals, and hack their way around the course with less than sterling skill. (To us, this does not argue against the manual, but speaks of its limitations and how it should be used in the context of other teaching devises.)

Ignoring the critics for the moment, this discussion raises the issue of what level of concreteness or abstraction is the manual best formulated. Some manuals describe the treatment session by session, and within the individual session the flow of the session and details about its construction are indicated. Obviously, this is easier to do the shorter the treatment, and the more the treatment can be predicted from the beginning (i.e., the more the treatment is driven by the therapist and little influenced by patient response or spontaneous contribution). Probably the best manuals are those that constantly weave abstract principles and strategies of the treatment with specific examples in the form of clinical vignettes that provide illustrations of the application of the principles to the individual situation.

3.09.4 RANGE OF TREATMENT MANUALS

An exhaustive list of existing treatment manuals cannot be provided for many reasons, not the least of which is that the list would be out of date before this chapter goes to print. The American Psychological Association (APA), Division 12, Task Force on Psychological

Interventions lists the so-called efficacious treatments (Chambless et al., 1998) and has also listed treatment manuals that are relevant to the efficacious treatments (Woody & Sanderson, 1998). Some 33 treatment manuals are listed for 13 disorders and/or problem areas including bulimia, chronic headache, pain associated with rheumatic disease, stress, depression, discordant couples, enuresis, generalized anxiety disorder, obsessive-compulsive disorder, panic disorder, social phobia, specific phobia, and children with oppositional behavior. Not all of the manuals listed here have been published, and must be sent for to the originator. Further, this list is limited to only those treatments that have been judged by the Task Force of Division 12 to meet their criteria for efficaciousness.

3.09.5 REPRESENTATIVE TREATMENT MANUALS

In contrast, a listing of representative treatment manuals is provided here, using as the structure for such sampling the diagnoses in the *Diagnostic and statistical manual of mental disorders* (4th ed., *DSM-IV*).

This chapter uses three treatment manuals to illustrate the present state of the art in manualization of psychotherapy: *Interpersonal psychotherapy of depression* (IPT; Klerman, Weissman, Roundsaville, & Chevron, 1984), the dialectical behavioral treatment (DBT) for borderline personality disorder (BPD) and related self-destructive behaviors (Linehan, 1993a), and the family treatment of bipolar disorder (Miklowitz & Goldstein, 1997). One of these treatments and related treatment manuals (IPT) has achieved recognition in the APA Division 12 listing of efficacious treatments. One (DBT for BPD) is listed as a "probably efficacious treatment." The third (family treatment for bipolar disorder) is not listed at this time. These manuals are also selected because they relate to existing *DSM* diagnostic categories which are central to research data and to insurance company procedures for reimbursement of treatment. These manuals for the specified disorders are also chosen because they represent three levels of severity of disorder that face the clinician. Ambulatory patients with depression of a nonpsychotic variety are treated with IPT. BPD is a serious disorder, often involving self-destructive and suicidal behavior. Finally, bipolar disorder is a psychiatric condition with biological and genetic causes that can be addressed by both the empirically efficacious medications and psychotherapy. In addition, these three treatment manuals provide some

heterogeneity in terms of treatment format, strategies and level of treatment development. IPT is delivered in an individual treatment format (patient and individual therapist), the treatment format that is the simplest to manualize. DBT involves both an individual and a group treatment format. The family treatment of bipolar disorder involves the treatment of the individual with bipolar disorder and family or marital partner. There is less diversity among these three treatments in terms of treatment strategies and techniques. Two (DPT and family treatment of bipolar) are informed by cognitive-behavioral strategies and techniques, but the latter introduces the intriguing concepts of family dynamics and systems issues. The remaining (IPT) is interpersonal in focus and orientation. The three manuals vary in terms of treatment duration. IPT is brief, the family treatment of bipolar is intermediate, and DBT is the longest, presenting the most challenge to issues of manualization and therapist adherence across a longer period of time. A comparison of these three manuals gives a sense of development in this area, as the IPT manual was one of the first, and the latter two provide a view of recent manuals and their contents.

3.09.5.1 IPT: An Early Manual

One of the earliest and most influential manuals is *Interpersonal psychotherapy of depression* by Klerman et al. (1984). This manual was written as a time-limited, outpatient treatment for depressed individuals. The treatment focuses on the current rather than on past interpersonal situations and difficulties. While making no assumption about the origin of the symptoms, the authors connect the onset of depression with current grief, role disputes and/or transitions, and interpersonal deficits.

This brief intervention has three treatment phases which are described clearly in the manual. The first is an evaluation phase during which the patient and therapist review depressive symptoms, give the syndrome of depression a name, and induce the patient into a sick role. (Interestingly, the role of the therapist is not described explicitly.) The patient and therapist discuss and, hopefully, agree upon a treatment focus limited to four possibilities: grief, role disputes, role transitions, or interpersonal deficits. The middle phase of treatment involves work between therapist and patient on the defined area of focus. For example, with current role disputes the therapist explores with the patient the nature of the disputes and options for resolution. The final phase of treatment involves reviewing and consolidating therapeutic gains. A recent addition is the publication of a client workbook (Weissman, 1995) and client assessment forms.

IPT has been used in many clinical trials, the first of which was in 1974 (Klerman, DiMascio, Weissman, Prusoff, & Paykel, 1974). In addition to the IPT manual, a training videotape has been produced and an IPT training program is being developed (Weissman & Markowitz, 1994).

IPT provides a generic framework guiding patient and therapist to discuss current difficulties and this framework has been applied to symptom conditions other than depression. For example, the format has been applied to patients with bipolar disorder (Ehlers, Frank, & Kupfer, 1988), drug abuse (Carroll, Rounsaville, & Gawin, 1991; Rounsaville, Glazer, Wilber, Weissman, & Kleber, 1983), and bulimia (Fairburn et al., 1991). In addition to its initial use of treating depression in ambulatory adult patients, it has now been utilized as an acute treatment, as a continuation and maintenance treatment (Frank et al., 1990), and has been used for geriatric (Reynolds et al., 1992) and adolescent patients (Mufson, Moreau, Weissman, & Klerman, 1993) and in various settings such as primary care and hospitalized elderly. The success of IPT seems to be the articulation of a rather straightforward approach to discussion between patient and therapist, of current situations without the use of more complicated procedures such as transference interpretation.

The IPT manual was one of the first in the field, and its straightforward description of a common-sense approach to patients with depression is readily adopted by many clinicians. However, the process of treatment development and amplification is also relevant to this, one of the earliest and best treatment manuals. It is now clear that depression is often only partially responsive to brief treatments, such as IPT, and that many patients relapse. It would appear that maintenance treatment with IPT may be useful (Frank et al., 1991), and the IPT manual must therefore be amplified for this purpose. Furthermore, it has become clear that depressed individuals with personality disorders respond to treatment less thoroughly and more slowly than depressed individuals without personality disorders (Clarkin & Abrams, 1998). This would suggest that IPT may need modification for those with personality disorders, either in terms of how to manage the personality disorder during treatment, or to include treatment of relevant parts of the personality disorder to the depression.

In order to place IPT in perspective, one could compare it to the cognitive therapy of depression in its earliest articulation (Beck, Rush, Shaw, & Emery, 1979) and with more recent additions (Beck, 1995).

3.09.5.2 Cognitive-behavioral Treatment of BPD

Linehan's (1993a, 1993b) cognitive-behavioral treatment of the parasuicidal individual is an example of the application of a specific school of psychotherapy adapted to a specific patient population defined both by a personality disorder diagnosis (BPD) and repetitive self-destructive behavior.

The rationale and data upon which the patient pathology is understood as related to the treatment is well described and thorough. Linehan points out that theories of personality functioning/dysfunctioning are based upon world views and assumptions. The assumption behind DBT is that of dialectics. The world view of dialectics involves notions of inter-relatedness and wholeness, compatible with feminist views of psychopathology, rather than an emphasis on separation, individuation, and independence. A related principle is that of polarity, that is, all propositions contain within them their own oppositions. As related to the borderline pathology, it is assumed that within the borderline dysfunction there is also function and accuracy. Thus, in DBT, it is assumed that each individual, including the borderline clients, are capable of wisdom as related to their own life and capable of change. At the level of the relationship between borderline client and DBT therapist, dialectics refers to change by persuasion, a process involving truth not as an absolute but as an evolving, developing phenomenon.

Borderline pathology is conceptualized as a dialectical failure on the part of the client. The thinking of the BPD patient has a tendency to become paralyzed in either the thesis or antithesis, without movement toward a synthesis. There is a related dialectical theory of the development of borderline pathology. BPD is seen primarily as a dysfunction of the emotion regulation system, with contributions to this state of malfunction from both biological irregularities and interaction over time with a dysfunctional environment. In this point of view, the BPD client is prey to emotional vulnerability, that is, high sensitivity to emotional stimuli, emotional intensity, and a slow return to emotional baseline functioning. The invalidating environment, seen as crucial to the BPD development, is one in which interpersonal communication of personal and private experiences is met by others in the environment with trivialization and/or punishment. In such an environment, the developing individual does not learn to label private experiences, nor does the individual learn emotion regulation.

These assumptions and related data on the developmental histories and cross-sectional behaviors of those with BPD provide the rationale and shape of the treatment. The major tasks of the treatment are, therefore, to teach the client skills so that they can modulate emotional experiences and related mood-dependent behaviors, and to learn to trust and validate their own emotions, thoughts and activities. The relevant skills are described as four in type: skills that increase interpersonal effectiveness in conflict situations, strategies to increase self-regulation of unwanted affects, skills for tolerating emotional distress, and skills adapted from Zen meditation to enhance the ability to experience emotions and avoid emotional inhibition.

The manual provides extensive material on basic treatment strategies (e.g., dialectical strategies), core strategies of emotional validation (e.g., teaching emotion observation and labeling skills), behavioral validation (e.g., identifying, countering and accepting "shoulds"), and cognitive validation (e.g., discriminating facts from interpretations), and problem-solving strategies. Problem solving consists of analysis of behavior problems, generating alternate behavioral solutions, orientation to a solution behavior, and trial of the solution behavior. The core of the treatment is described as balancing problem-solving strategies with validation strategies.

This manual is exceptional, and provides a new and very high standard in the field for treatment manuals. There are a number of exemplary features. First, the patient population is defined by *DSM* criteria in addition to specific problematic behaviors, that is, parasuicidal behaviors. Second, the treatment manual was generated in the context of clinical research. The treatment was developed in the context of operationalization and discovery, that is, how to operationalize a treatment for research that fits the pathology of the patients who are selected and described by specific criteria. The skills training manual (Linehan, 1993b) notes that it has evolved over a 20 year period, and has been tested on over 100 clients. The treatment generated in this context has been used in diverse treatment settings to teach therapists of various levels of expertise and training to address BPD patients. This process of teaching the treatment to therapists of multiple levels of competence and training can foster the articulation of the treatment and enrich its adaptability to community settings. This treatment has a duration of one year or more because it is addressed to a very difficult and seriously

disturbed group of individuals, and provides the challenge of extending treatment manuals beyond brief treatments. A most important and practical addition to the book is an accompanying workbook with work sheets for therapist and patients.

To put DBT in context one could compare it to other cognitive approaches to the personality disorders (Beck & Freeman, 1990), to an interpersonal treatment delivered in a group format (Marziali & Munroe-Blum, 1994), to a modified psychodynamic treatment (Clarkin, Yeomans, & Kernberg, in press), and to a supportive treatment (Rockland, 1992) for these patients.

3.09.5.3 Psychosocial Treatment For Bipolar Disorder

Capitalizing on their years of clinical research with patients with schizophrenia and bipolar disorder and their families, Miklowitz and Goldstein (1997) have articulated a treatment manual for patients with bipolar disorder and their spouses or family members.

The rationale for the treatment is threefold. An episode of bipolar disorder in a family member affects not only the patient but the entire family. Thus, with each episode of the disorder (and this is a recurring disorder) there is a crisis and disorganization of the entire family. Thus, the family treatment is an attempt to assist the patient and family to cooperatively deal with this chronic illness. Finally, both in the rationale for the treatment and in the psychoeducational component of the treatment, the authors espouse a vulnerability–stress model of the disorder, which would argue for a treatment that reduces patient and family stress.

The therapeutic stance of the clinician conducting this treatment is explicated well. The clinician is encouraged to be approachable, open and emotionally accessible. It is recommended that the clinician develop a "Socratic dialogue" with the family in providing information, and develop a give and take between all parties. Although the treatment has a major psychoeducational component, the clinician is encouraged to be ready to explore the emotional impact of the information, and not to be simply a classroom teacher. In dealing with both difficult news (e.g., you have a life-long illness) and tasks (e.g., problem solving helps reduce stress), the clinician is encouraged to be reasonably optimistic about what the patient and family can accomplish if they give the treatment and its methods a chance to succeed.

The treatment is described in the manual in terms of three major phases or modules that have a clear sequence to them. The first phase of psychoeducation is intended to provide the patient and family with information that gives them an understanding of bipolar disorder and its treatment. It is hoped that this information may have practical value in informing the patient and family as to things they should do (e.g., medication compliance) that assists in managing the illness. The second phase or module of treatment is a communication enhancement training phase. The aim of this phase is to improve and/or enhance the patient and family's ability to communicate with one another clearly and effectively, especially in the face of the stress-producing disorder. The third or problem-solving phase provides the patient and family with training in effective conflict resolution. Prior to extensive explanation of the three phases of the treatment is information on connecting and engaging with patient and family, and conducting initial assessment. The authors also examine carefully patient and family criteria for admission to this family intervention. Interestingly, they do not rule out patients who are not medication compliant at present, nor those who are currently abusing substances, both common situations in the history of many bipolar patients. This is an articulated treatment broad enough to encourage those patients who are on the cusp of what is actually treatable.

This manual raises directly the issue of patient medication compliance and the combination of psychosocial treatment with medication treatment. Bipolar patients are responsive to certain medications, and medication treatment is considered a necessity. Thus, this treatment manual provides psychoeducation around the need for medication, and encourages patient and family agreement about continuous medication compliance.

This treatment manual can be placed in context by comparing it to a treatment for bipolar disorder in the individual treatment format (Basco & Rush, 1996). This manual should also be seen in the context of quite similar treatments for patients with schizophrenia and their families (such as those articulated by Anderson, Reiss, & Hogarty, 1986; Bellack, Mueser, Gingerich, & Agresta, 1997; Falloon, Boyd, & McGill, 1984).

3.09.5.4 Other Treatment Manuals

Beyond the three manuals chosen for illustration, it is interesting to note the patient diagnoses and problem areas that are currently addressed by a manual describing a psychotherapy. As noted in Table 1, there are treatments described in manuals for major Axis I disorders such as schizophrenia, bipolar disorder, major depression, anxiety disorders, substance abuse and eating disorders. Treatments for Axis II disorders are less well developed and manualized, except for BPD. Problem areas such as marital discord, sexual dysfunction and problematic emotion expression are also addressed. Further development will probably come in addressing common comorbid conditions. In addition, there has been more funding and research for brief treatments with a cognitive-behavioral orientation. Longer treatments, maintenance treatment for chronic conditions, and the development of manuals for strategies and techniques other than cognitive-behavioral ones can be expected in the future. With the heavy incursion of managed care with its emphasis on cost-cutting, more development of treatments delivered in a group format may also be seen.

3.09.6 ADVANTAGES OF TREATMENT MANUALS

It is clear that the introduction of the treatment manual has had tremendous impact. The very process of writing a treatment manual forces the author to think through and articulate the details of the treatment that may not have been specified before. In this way, the era of the written treatment manual has fostered fuller articulation of treatment by the treatment originators, and furthered the ability of teachers of the treatment to explicate the treatment to trainees.

Manuals provide an operationalized statement of the treatment being delivered or researched so that all can examine it for its foci and procedures. It cannot be assumed that the treatment described in the written manual was delivered as described by the therapists in the study or in a treatment delivery system. This gap between the manual and the treatment as delivered highlights the need for rating scales to assess the faithful (i.e., adherent and competent) delivery of the treatment as described in the manual.

Manuals provide a training tool for clinical research and for clinical practice. It has been noted (Chambless, 1996; Moras, 1993) that students learn treatment approaches much more quickly from their systematic depiction in manuals than through supervision alone.

3.09.7 POTENTIAL DISADVANTAGES AND LIMITATIONS OF TREATMENT MANUALS

Dobson and Shaw (1988) have noted six disadvantages of treatment manuals: (i) the

Table 1 Representative treatment manuals.

Disorder/problem area	Reference
Panic	Barlow and Cerny (1988)
Obsessive-compulsive disorder	Steketee (1993)
	Turner and Beidel (1988)
PTSD	Foy (1992)
Depression	Beck, Rush, Shaw, and Emery (1979)
	Klerman, Weissman, Rounsaville, and Chevron (1984)
Bipolar	Miklowitz and Goldstein (1997)
	Basco and Rush (1996)
Schizophrenia	Bellack (1997)
	Anderson, Reiss, and Hogarty (1986)
	Falloon, Boyd, and McGill (1984)
Borderline	Linehan (1993a, 1993b)
	Clarkin, Yeomans, and Kernberg (in press)
	Marzialli and Munroe-Blum (1994)
	Rockland (1992)
Marital discord	Baucom and Epstein (1990)
Sexual dysfunction	Wincze and Carey (1991)
Alcohol abuse	Sobell and Sobell (1993)
Binge eating	Fairburn, Marcus, and Wilson (1993)
Problematic emotion schemas	Greenberg, Rice, and Elliott (1993)

inability to assess the effects of therapists' variables, (ii) the diminished ability to study the therapy process, (iii) a focus on treatment fidelity rather than on competence, (iv) the increased expense for research, (v) the over-researching of older and more codified therapy procedures; and (vi) the promotion of schools of psychotherapy. It is important to distinguish the limitations of the manuals as they have been developed up to now, from the limitations of manuals as they can be if the field continues to improve them. There is no reason why many of the concerns listed above cannot be incorporated into future manuals. Some are already being included, such as therapist variables, process, and competence.

Probably the most extensively debated issue around manuals is the issue of therapist flexibility in the execution of the treatment. Some would argue that a manual seriously curtails the flexibility and creativity of the therapist, thus potentially eliminating the therapeutic effectiveness of talented therapists. This is the type of issue that, unless infused with data, could be debated intensely for a very long time. Jacobson et al. (1989) compared two versions of behavioral marital therapy, one inflexible and the other in which therapists had flexibility. The outcome of the flexibility condition was no better than that of the inflexible condition. There was a trend for less relapse at follow-up in the flexibly treated couples.

Wilson (1996) notes that allowing therapists to pursue their own somewhat ideographic case formulations rather than following validated treatment in manuals on average might reduce effectiveness rather than enhance it (Schulte, Kuenzel, Pepping, & Schulte-Bahrenberg, 1992). When research therapy programs are transferred to a clinic setting, there tends to be an increase in effectiveness (Weisz, Donenberg, Han, & Weiss, 1995). A number of studies show that greater adherence to the psychotherapy protocol predicts better outcome (Frank et al., 1991; Luborsky, McLellan, Woody, O'Brien, & Auerbach, 1985).

However, it has been pointed out that adherence to manualized treatments may lead to certain disruptive therapists' behaviors (Henry, Schacht, Strupp, Butler, & Binder, 1993). There is the possibility that therapists delivering a manualized treatment, especially those that are just learning the treatment and adhering with concentration, will deliver it with strict adherence but without competence. At its extreme, it might be argued that the use of the treatment manual may de-skill the therapist and interfere with therapist competence. In fact, rigid adherence could lead to poor therapy, and a mockery of what the treatment is intended to be.

In a study reported by Castonguay, Goldfried, Wiser, Raue, and Hayes (1996), when therapists were engaged in an abstract cognitive intervention the outcome appeared worse. However, those interventions were related to a bad outcome only when practiced to the detriment of the therapeutic alliance.

Jacobson and Hollon (1996) point out that the measurement of therapist adherence to treatments as manualized has received much attention, but the measurement of competence is at a rudimentary stage. The manual should provide instruments that have been shown to reliably assess therapist adherence to the treatment as described in the manual, and competence in the delivery of that treatment. Many books that proport to be treatment manuals do not include such instrumentation. The instruments are helpful in further specifying necessary therapist behaviors, and may be useful to the clinical supervisor.

A major limitation of manual development is the number of patients who appear for treatment who are not addressed in the existing treatment manuals. Some of this is due to the research focus of manuals, that is, the need for clinical research to have a narrowly and carefully defined patient population for whom the treatment is intended. Unfortunately, many if not most patients who appear in clinical settings would not fit into a research protocol because of comorbidity, not quite meeting criteria for a specific diagnosis (e.g., personality disorder NOS, not otherwise specified). Some of this is simply due to the newness of manuals and the little time there has been in their development.

3.09.8 USE AND ROLE OF TREATMENT MANUALS

Treatment manuals have had a brief but exciting and productive history. There is an extreme position that something as complex, unique and creative as a psychotherapy between two individuals cannot be manualized. It is thought that experience indicates that this is an extreme view, and that manualization has been useful to the field. The issues are how best to utilize a manual and what is the role of the manual in clinical research and training?

Whether in the early stages of clinical research or in a clinical training program, the treatment manual can serve as a tool to be used by the expert therapist who is teaching the treatment. It has been noted that the manual enables the student to learn the treatment more quickly than with supervision alone (Chambless, 1996; Moras, 1993). It is our experience, however, that the manual has a place in the teaching toolbox, but is less important than supervision and watching experts doing the treatment on videotape. The manual provides a conceptual overview of the treatment. Videotapes provide a visual demonstration of the manual being applied to a particular patient, in the style of a particular therapist model. Supervision allows the expert to help the trainee apply the manual to a specific patient in a specific treatment, which will always produce some situations that are not exactly covered in the written manual.

It is a naive and false assumption that a clinician can simply read a treatment manual, and thereby be enabled to deliver the treatment with skill. It is interesting that the authors of a treatment manual (Turner & Beidel, 1988) felt the need to argue that just reading a manual is not enough to train an individual in the competent delivery of the treatment in question to the individual patient.

3.09.8.1 Efficacy to Effectiveness

There is currently much discussion about the need to extend clinical trials of empirically validated treatments, that is treatments that have been shown to be efficacious, to larger, community samples with average therapists (effectiveness research). It may be that treatment manuals can play an important role in this work. Indeed, the ultimate value of a treatment manual and the training system within which it operates will be the result that clinicians can perform the treatment with adherence and competence. Manuals that are most useful will contain scales developed to measure therapist adherence and competence, and most current manuals are lacking this feature.

3.09.9 SUMMARY

Although treatment manuals have been effective in specifying psychotherapy for clinical research, the step from clinical efficacy studies to demonstration of clinical effectiveness of the treatments that have been manualized is still lacking. This is an issue of knowledge transfer. That is, given the demonstration that a specific therapy (that has been manualized) has shown clinical efficacy in randomized clinical trials with a homogeneous patient population and with carefully selected therapists, can this treatment also show clinical benefits when transferred to a setting in which the patients are less homogeneous and the therapists are those who are working at the local level? The written treatment manual may play a role in this transfer of expertise from a small, clinical research group to a larger group of therapists. However, this step has yet to be demonstrated. Thus, the test of a manual, and the entire teaching package within which it resides, is to demonstrate that a wider group of therapists can do the treatment with adherence and competence.

It is interesting to speculate about the future of training in psychotherapy given the advances in the field, including the generation of treatment manuals. For sake of argument, we indicated that there are some 33 manuals for 13 disorders for which there are efficacious treatments in the field of clinical psychology. Should these manuals form the basis of the training in psychotherapy of future psychologists? Or can one generate principles of treatment out of these disparate treatments for various disorders and conditions, and teach these principles? There are obvious redundancies across the manuals, and one could imagine a supermanual with branching points for various disorders. For example, most manuals have an assessment phase, followed by the phase of making an alliance with the patient and describing the characteristics of the treatment to follow, with some indication of the roles of patient and therapist. These are obvious skills that a therapist must learn, with nuances depending upon the patient and the disorder in question. For those manuals that are cognitive behavioral in strategies and techniques, there seems to be great redundancy in terms of the selected finite number of techniques that are used.

What is missing is the assessment of the patient in which there is no indication of what the problem is, the diagnosis, or which manual or manuals to use for treatment. Each manual seems to presume that clinicians can properly identify patients for that manual. Unfortunately, one cannot train a psychologist to treat only the 13 disorders/problem areas in the list, as many patients suffer from other conditions not covered. To compound things even further, many patients (if not most, depending on the clinical setting) do not suffer from just one condition, but from several.

Our own approach to training is the one implied by Roth, Fonagy, Parry, Target, and Woods (1996), with emphasis on the initial assessment of the patient with specific clinical hypotheses about the situation, proceeding to the most relevant treatment that has been validated to various degrees. This is a less black-and-white world of the empirically supported treatment approach and more related to the complex condition we call clinical work. Treatment manuals will play some role in this process, but it might be less than the quantum leap suggested by Luborsky and DeRubeis (1984). In our experience, trainees read the treatment manual if they must, but they look forward to seeing experts do the treatment on videotape, and they see supervision from an expert in the treatment as a matter of course.

3.09.10 REFERENCES

Anderson, C. M., Reiss, D. J., & Hogarty, G. E. (1986). *Schizophrenia and the family.* New York: Guilford Press.

Barlow, D. H., & Cerny, J. A. (1988). *Psychological treatment of panic.* New York: Guilford Press.

Basco, M. R., & Rush, A. J. (1996). *Cognitive-behavioral therapy for bipolar disorder.* New York: Guilford Press.

Baucom, D. H., & Epstein, N. (1990). *Cognitive-behavioral marital therapy.* New York: Brunner/Mazel.

Beck, A. T., & Freeman, A. M. (1990). *Cognitive therapy of personality disorders.* New York: Guilford Press.

Beck, A. T., Rush, A. J., Shaw, B. F., & Emery, G. (1979). *Cognitive therapy of depression.* New York: Guilford Press.

Beck, J. S. (1995). *Cognitive therapy: Basics and beyond.* New York: Guilford Press.

Bellack, A. S., Mueser, K. T., Gingerich, S., & Agresta, J. (1997). *Social skills training for schizophrenia: A step-by-step guide.* New York: Guilford Press.

Carroll, K. M., Rounsaville, B. J., & Gawin, F. H. (1991). A comparative trial of psychotherapies for ambulatory cocaine abusers: Relapse prevention and interpersonal psychotherapy. *American Journal of Drug and Alcohol Abuse, 17,* 229–247.

Castonguay, L. G., Goldfried, M. R., Wiser, S., Raue, P. J., & Hayes, A. M. (1996). Predicting the effect of cognitive therapy for depression: A study of unique and common factors. *Journal of Consulting and Clinical Psychology, 64,* 497–504.

Chambless, D. L. (1996). In defense of dissemination of empirically supported psychological interventions. *Clinical Psychology: Science and Practice, 3*(3), 230–235.

Chambless, D. L., Baker, M. J., Baucom, D. H., Beutler, L. E., Calhoun, K. S., Crits-Christoph, P., Daiuto, A., DeRubeis, R., Detweiler, J., Haaga, D. A. F., Johnson, S. B., McCurry, S., Mueser, K. T., Pope, K. S., Sanderson, W. C., Shoham, V., Stickle, T., Williams, D. A., & Woody, S. R. (1998). Update on empirically validate therapies. II. (1998). *Clinical Psychologist, 51,* 3–13.

Clarkin, J. F., & Abrams, R. (1998). Management of personality disorders in the context of mood and anxiety disorders. In A. J. Rush (Ed.), *Mood and anxiety disorders* (pp. 224–235). Philadelphia: Current Science.

Clarkin, J. F., Yeomans, F., & Kernberg, O. F. (in press). *Psychodynamic psychotherapy of borderline personality organization: A treatment manual.* New York: Wiley.

Dobson, K. S., & Shaw, B. F. (1988). The use of treatment manuals in cognitive therapy: Experience and issues. *Journal of Consulting and Clinical Psychology, 56,* 673–680.

Ehlers, C. L., Frank E., & Kupfer, D. J. (1988). Social zeitgebers and biological rhythms: A unified approach to understanding the etiology of depression. *Archives of General Psychiatry, 45,* 948–952.

Elkin, I., Shea, M. T., Watkins, J. T., Imber, S. D., Sotsky, S. M., Collins, J. F., Glass, D. R., Pilkonis, P. A., Leber, W. R., Docherty, J. P., Fiester, S. J., & Parloff, M. B. (1989). National Institute of Mental Health Treatment of Depression Collaborative Research Program: General effectiveness of treatments. *Archives of General Psychiatry, 46,* 971–982.

Fairburn, C. G., Jones, R., Peveler, R. C., Carr, S. J., Solomon, R. A., O'Connor, M. E., Burton, J., & Hope, R. A. (1991). Three psychological treatments for bulimia nervosa: A comparative trial. *Archives of General Psychiatry, 48,* 463–469.

Fairburn, C. G., Marcus, M. D. & Wilson, G. T. (1993). Cognitive-behavioral therapy for binge eating and bulimia nervosa: A comprehensive treatment manual. In C. G. Fairburn & G. T. Wilson (Eds.), *Binge eating: Nature, assessment and treatment* (pp. 361–404). New York: Guilford Press.

Falloon, I. R. H., Boyd, J. L., & McGill, C. W. (1984). *Family care of schizophrenia*. New York: Guilford Press.

Foy, D. W. (Ed.) (1992). *Treating PTSD: Cognitive-behavioral strategies. Treatment manuals for practitioners.* New York: Guilford Press.

Frank, E., Kupfer, D. J., Perel, J. M., Cornes, C., Jarrett, D. B., Mallinger, A. G., Thase, M. E., McEachran, A. B., & Grochociniski, V. J. (1990). Three-year outcomes for maintenance therapies in recurrent depression. *Archives of General Psychiatry, 47,* 1093–1099.

Frank, E., Kupfer, D. J., Wagner, E. F., McEachran, A. B., & Cornes, C. (1991). Efficacy of interpersonal psychotherapy as a maintenance treatment of recurrent depression. *Archives of General Psychiatry, 48,* 1053–1059.

Greenberg, L. S., Rice, L. N., & Elliott, R. K. (1993). *Facilitating emotional change: The moment-by-moment process.* New York: Guilford Press.

Henry, W. P., Schacht, T. E., Strupp, H. H., Butler, S. F., & Binder, J. L. (1993). Effects of training in time-limited dynamic psychotherapy: Mediators of therapists responses to training. *Journal of Consulting and Clinical Psychology, 61,* 441–447.

Jacobson, N. S., & Hollon, S. D. (1996). Prospects for future comparisons between drugs and psychotherapy: Lessons from the CBT-versus-pharmacotherapy exchange. *Journal of Consulting and Clinical Psychology, 64,* 104–108.

Jacobson, N. S., Schmaling, K. B., Holtzworth-Munroe, A., Katt, J. L., Wood, L. F., & Follette, V. M. (1989). Research-structured vs. clinically flexible versions of social learning-based marital therapy. *Behaviour Research and Therapy, 27,* 173–180.

Kazdin, A. E. (1991). Treatment research: The investigation and evaluation of psychotherapy. In M. Hersen, A. E. Kazdin, & A. S. Bellack (Eds.), *The clinical psychology handbook* (2nd ed., pp. 293–312). New York: Pergamon.

Klerman, G. L., DiMascio, A., Weissman, M., Prusoff, B., Paykel, E. S. (1974). Treatment of depression by drugs and psychotherapy. *American Journal of Psychiatry, 131,* 186–191.

Klerman, G. L., Weissman, M. M., Rounsaville, B. J., & Chevron, E. S. (1984). *Interpersonal psychotherapy of depression.* New York: Basic Books.

Linehan, M. M. (1993a). *Cognitive-behavioral treatment of borderline personality disorder.* New York: Guilford Press.

Linehan, M. M. (1993b). *Skills training manual for treating borderline personality disorder.* New York: Guilford Press.

Luborsky, L., & DeRubeis, R. J. (1984). The use of psychotherapy treatment manuals: A small revolution in psychotherapy research style. *Clinical Psychology Review, 4,* 5–14.

Luborsky, L., McLellan, A. T., Woody, G. E., O'Brien, C. P., & Auerbach, A. (1985). Therapists success and its determinants. *Archives of General Psychiatry, 42,* 602–611.

Marziali, E., & Munroe-Blum, H. (1994). *Interpersonal group psychotherapy for borderline personality disorder.* New York: Basic Books.

Miklowitz, D. J., & Goldstein, M. J. (1997). *Bipolar disorders: A family-focused treatment approach.* New York: Guilford Press.

Moras, K. (1993). The use of treatment manuals to train psychotherapists: Observations and recommendations. *Psychotherapy, 30,* 581–586.

Moras, K. (1995, January). Behavioral therapy development program workshop (Draft 2, 3/24/95). National Institute on Drug Abuse, Washington, DC.

Mufson, L., Moreau, D., Weissman, M. M., & Klerman, G. L. (Eds.) (1993). *Interpersonal psychotherapy for depressed adolescents.* New York: Guilford Press.

Reynolds, C. F., Frank, E., Perel, J. M., Imber, S. D., Cornes, C., Morycz. R. K., Mazumdar, S., Miller, M., Pollock, B. G., Rifai, A. H., Stack, J. A., George, C. J., Houck, P. R., & Kupfer, D. J. (1992). Combined pharmacotherapy and psychotherapy in the acute and continuation treatment of elderly patients with recurrent major depression: A preliminary report. *American Journal of Psychiatry, 149,* 1687–1692.

Rockland, L. H. (1992). *Supportive therapy for borderline patients: A psychodynamic approach.* New York: Guilford Press.

Roth, A., Fonagy, P., Parry, G., Target, M., & Woods, R. (1996). *What works for whom? A critical review of psychotherapy research.* New York: Guilford Press.

Rounsaville, B. J., Glazer, W., Wilber, C. H., Weissman, M. M., & Kleber, H. D. (1983). Short-term interpersonal psychotherapy in methadone-maintained opiate addicts. *Archives of General Psychiatry, 40,* 629–636.

Schulte, D., Kuenzel, R., Pepping, G., & Schulte-Bahrenberg, T. (1992). Tailor-made versus standardized therapy of phobic patients. *Advances in Behaviour Research and Therapy, 14,* 67–92.

Sobell, M. B., & Sobell, L. C. (1993). *Problem drinkers: Guided self-change treatment.* New York: Guilford Press.

Steketee, G. (1993). *Treatment of obsessive compulsive disorder.* New York: Guilford Press.

Talley, P. F., Strupp, H. H., & Butler, S. F. (Eds.) (1994). *Psychotherapy research and practice: Bridging the gap.* New York: Basic Books.

Turner, S. M., & Beidel, D. C. (1988). *Treating obsessive-compulsive disorder.* Oxford, UK: Pergamon.

Weissman, M. M. (1995). *Mastering Depression: A patient's guide to interpersonal psychotherapy.* San Antonio, TX: Psychological Corporation.

Weissman, M. M., & Markowitz, J. C. (1994). Interpersonal psychotherapy: Current status. *Archives of General Psychiatry, 51,* 599–606.

Weisz, J. R., Donenberg, G. R., Han, S. S., & Weiss, B. (1995). Bridging the gap between laboratory and clinic in child and adolescent psychotherapy. *Journal of Consulting and Clinical Psychology, 63,* 688–701.

Wilson, G. T. (1996). Empirically validated treatments: Realities and resistance. *Clinical Psychology, 3,* 241–244.

Wincz. J. P., & Carey, M. P. (1991). *Sexual dysfunction: A guide for assessment and treatment.* New York: Guilford Press.

Woody, S. R., & Sanderson, W. C. (1998). Manuals for empirically supported treatments: 1998 update. *Clinical Psychologist, 51,* 17–21.

3.10
Internal and External Validity of Intervention Studies

KARLA MORAS
University of Pennsylvania, Philadelphia, PA, USA

3.10.1 INTRODUCTION

The concepts of internal and external validity (IV and EV) were introduced by Campbell and Stanley in 1963. IV and EV concern the validity of inferences that can be drawn from an intervention study, given its design and methods. The concepts are used to assess the extent to which a study's outcome findings can be confidently: (i) interpreted as evidence for hypothesized causal relationships between interventions and outcomes (IV), and (ii) assumed to generalize beyond the study situation (EV). IV and EV are conceptual tools that guide deductive (IV) and inductive (EV) thinking about the impact of a study's design and methods on the validity of the conclusions that can be drawn from it. The concepts are not only of academic interest. Evaluation of a study's IV and EV is a logical, systematic way to judge if its outcome findings provide compelling evidence that an intervention merits implementation in public sector settings.

This chapter is written at a unique time in the history of IV and EV. The concepts have been at the forefront of a contemporary, often contentious debate in the USA about the public health value of alternative methods and designs for intervention research (e.g., Goldfried Wolfe, 1998; Hoagwood, Hibbs, Bren, & Jensen, 1995; Jacobson & Christensen, 1996; Lebowitz & Rudorfer, 1998; Mintz, Drake, & Crits-Christoph, 1996; Newman & Tejeda, 1996; Seligman, 1996; Wells & Sturm, 1996). The alternatives are referred to as "efficacy" vs. "effectiveness" studies. In current parlance, efficacy studies have high IV due to designs and methods that reflect a priority on drawing causal conclusions about the relationship between interventions and outcomes (e.g., Elkin et al., 1989). Effectiveness studies have high EV due to designs and methods that reflect the priority of obtaining findings that can be assumed to generalize to nonresearch intervention settings and clinic populations (e.g., Speer, 1994). Typically, effectiveness studies are done to examine the effects of interventions with demonstrated efficacy in high IV studies, when the interventions are used in standard community treatment settings. A related term, "clinical utility research," has started to appear (Beutler & Howard, 1998). The types of research questions connoted by clinical utility are broader than those connoted by effectiveness research (Howard, Moras, Brill, Martinovich, & Lutz, 1996; Kopta, Howard, Lowry, & Beutler, 1994; Lueger, 1998).

The efficacy vs. effectiveness debate is prominent in mental health intervention research. IV and EV often are viewed as competing rather than complimentary research aims (Kazdin,

1994; Roth & Fonagy, 1996). An alternative view is that EV questions only can be asked about a study's findings after the study's IV has been established (Flick, 1988; Hoagwood et al., 1995). A recent trend is to encourage investigators to design studies that can optimize both IV and EV (Clarke, 1995; Hoagwood et al., 1995). The topic is pursued later in the chapter.

This chapter is intended to provide a relatively concise, simplified explication of IV and EV that will be useful to neophyte intervention researchers and to consumers of intervention research. The main aims are to enhance the reader's sophistication as consumer of intervention research, and ability to use the concepts of IV and EV to design intervention studies. IV and EV are discussed and illustrated mainly from the perspective of research on interventions of a certain type: psychological therapies for mental health problems (Bergin & Garfield, 1971, 1994; Garfield & Bergin, 1978, 1986).The topics covered are: (i) definitions of IV and EV and of two newer, closely related concepts, construct validity (CV) and statistical conclusion validity (SCV); (ii) threats to IV, EV, CV, and SCV; (iii) designs and methods that are commonly used in mental health intervention research to enhance IV, EV, CV, and SCV; and (iv) suggested strategies from the efficacy vs. effectiveness debate to optimize the scientific validity, generalizability, and public health value of intervention studies. Finally, two intervention studies that were designed to meet both IV and EV aims are used to illustrate application of the concepts.

3.10.2 DEFINITIONS

3.10.2.1 Overview of IV, EV, CV, and SCV

Kazdin (1994) provided a concise overview of IV, EV, CV, and SCV, and of common threats to each type of validity (Table 1). The discussion of the four concepts in this chapter is based on Cook and Campbell's (1979) conceptualizations, as is Kazdin's table. Campbell and Stanley's (1963, 1966) original conceptualizations of IV and EV were extended and slightly revised by Cook and Campbell in 1979. The arguments and philosophy of science assumptions that underpin Cook and Campbell's (1979) perspective have been challenged (Cronbach, 1982). A key criticism is that they overemphasized the value of high IV studies in a way that was inconsistent with EV (generalizability) trade-offs often associated with such studies (Shadish, 1995). Cook and Campbell's views were adopted in this chapter because, challenges notwithstanding, they have had a major influence on mental health intervention research since the late 1960s.

Table 1 Types of experimental validity, questions they address, and their threats to drawing valid inferences.

Type of validity	Questions addressed	Threats to validity
Internal validity	To what extent can the intervention, rather than extraneous influences, be considered to account for the results, changes, or group differences?	Changes due to influences other than the experimental conditions, such as events (history) or processes (maturation) within the individual, repeated testing, statistical regression, and differential loss of subjects
External validity	To what extent can the results be generalized or extended to persons, settings, times, measures, and characteristics other than those in this particular experimental arrangement?	Possible limitations on the generality of the findings because of characteristics of the sample; therapists; or conditions, context, or setting of the study
Construct validity	Given that the intervention was responsible for change, what specific aspects of the intervention or arrangement were the causal agents; that is, what is the conceptual basis (construct) underlying the effect?	Alternative interpretations that could explain the effects of the intervention, that is, the conceptual basis of the findings, such as attention and contact with the subject, expectancies of subjects or experimenters, cues of the experiment
Statistical conclusion validity	To what extent is a relation shown, demonstrated, or evident, and how well can the investigation detect effects if they exist?	Any factor related to the quantitative evaluation that could affect interpretation of the findings, such as low statistical power, variability in the procedures, unreliability of the measurement, inappropriate statistical tests

Source: Kazdin (1994).

A basic premise of Cook and Campbell's definitions of IV and EV is that the term "validity" can only be used in an approximate sense. They would say, for example, that judgments of the validity of the conclusions that can be drawn from a study must always be understood as approximate because, from an epistemological perspective, we can never definitively know what is true, only that which has not been shown to be false.

3.10.2.2 Internal Validity

Simply stated, IV refers to the extent to which causal conclusions can be correctly drawn from a study about the relationship between an independent variable (e.g., a type of therapy) and a dependent variable (e.g., symptom change). The full definition reads: "Internal validity refers to the approximate validity with which we infer that a relationship between two variables is causal or that the absence of a relationship implies the absence of cause" (Cook & Campbell, 1979, p. 37).

3.10.2.3 External Validity

EV refers to the extent to which causal conclusions from a study about a relationship between interventions and outcomes can be assumed to generalize beyond the study's specific features (e.g., the patient sample, the therapists, the measures of outcome, the study setting). The full definition of EV is: " ... the approximate validity with which we can infer that the presumed causal relationship can be generalized to and across alternative measures of the cause and effect and across different types of persons, settings, and times" (Cook & Campbell, 1979, p. 37).

3.10.2.4 Construct Validity

In their 1979 update of Campbell and Stanley (1963, 1966), Cook and Campbell highlighted two new concepts that are closely linked to IV and EV: CV and SCV. Both have been incorporated into contemporary thinking about experimental design and threats to IV and EV (e.g., Kazdin, 1994).

Cook and Campbell (1979) focused their discussion of CV on the "putative causes and effects" (i.e., interventions and outcomes) of intervention studies. CV reflects the addition of a concept developed earlier by Cronbach and Meehl (1955) to Cook and Campbell's (1979) model of experimental validity. Simply stated, CV is the goodness of fit between the methods used to operationalize constructs (interventions and outcome variables) and the referent constructs. In other words, CV is the extent to which the methods used to measure and operationalize interventions and outcomes are likely to reflect the constructs that the investigators say they studied (e.g., cognitive therapy and depression). A more precise definition of CV is: " ... the possibility that the operations which are meant to represent a particular cause or effect construct can be construed in terms of more than one construct, each of which is stated at the same level of reduction" (p. 59). For example, the more possible it is to construe measures in terms of constructs other than those named by the investigators, the lower the CV.

CV also can be described as "what experimental psychologists are concerned with when they worry about 'confounding'" (Cook & Campbell, 1979, p. 59). An example of a threat to CV is the possibility that the effects of a medication for depression are due largely to the treating psychiatrist's concern for a patient and nonjudgmental reactions to his or her symptoms, rather than to neurochemical effects of the drug. Such alternative interpretations of the therapeutic cause of outcomes in medication intervention studies lead to: (i) the inclusion of pill placebo control conditions, (ii) randomized assignment to either active drug or pill placebo, and (iii) the use of double-blind procedures, that is, neither treater nor patient knows if the patient is receiving active drug or placebo.

Cook and Campbell (1979) link CV to EV. They say that generalizability is the essence of both. However, an integral aspect of CV is the adequacy with which the central variables of an intervention study (the interventions and outcomes) are operationalized. Thus, CV is also necessarily linked to IV: the CV of the methods used to measure and operationalize interventions and outcomes affects the validity of any causal conclusions drawn about a relationship between the designated interventions and outcomes.

3.10.2.5 Statistical Conclusion Validity

SCV is described by Cook and Campbell (1979) as a component of IV. SCV refers to the effects of the statistical methods used to analyze study data on the validity of the conclusions about a relationship (i.e., covariation) between interventions and outcomes. SCV concerns "particular reasons why we can draw false conclusions about covariates" (Cook & Campbell, 1979, p. 37). It "is concerned ... with sources of random error and with the appropriate use of statistics and statistical tests" (p. 80). For example, a determinant of SCV is whether the assumptions of the statistical test used to analyze a set of outcome data were met by the data.

3.10.3 COMMON THREATS TO IV, EV, CV, AND SCV

A study's IV, EV, CV, and SCV are determined by its design and methods, by the psychometric adequacy of its measures and operationalizations of central constructs, and by the appropriateness of the statistical tests used to analyze the data. All must be assessed to evaluate a study's IV, EV, CV, and SCV. "Design" refers to elements of a study's construction (the situation into which subjects are placed) that determine the probability that causal hypotheses about a relationship between the independent and dependent variables can validly be tested. For example, a design feature is the inclusion of a no-treatment control group of some type (e.g., pill placebo) in addition to the treatment group. A no-therapy group provides outcome data to compare with the outcomes of the treated group. The comparison allows examination of the possibility that changes associated with the treatment also occur without it and, thus, cannot be causally attributed to it.

"Methods" refers to a wide variety of procedures that are used to implement study designs, such as random assignment of subjects to each intervention group included in a study. A study's methods and design together determine the degree to which any relationship found between interventions and outcomes can validly be attributed to the interventions rather than to something else. In other words, study methods and design determine whether alternative or rival interpretations of findings can be dismissed as improbable. Designs and methods that affect a study's IV, EV, CV, and SCV are discussed in Section 3.10.4.

The use of IV, EV, CV, and SCV to guide study design and critical appraisal of study findings is assisted by knowledge of common threats to each type of validity. Cook and Campbell (1979) discussed several threats to each type. They cautioned, however, that no list is perfect and that theirs was derived from their own research experience and from reading about potential sources of fallacious inferences.

The threats to each type of validity identified by Cook and Campbell are listed in Tables 2–5. The tables also present examples of designs and methods that can offset the various threats ("antidotes"). The interested reader is encouraged to review Cook and Campbell's discussion of threats to IV, EV, CV, and SCV; design and methodological antidotes to the threats; and limitations of common antidotes.

In the following sections, the four types of threats to validity are discussed in turn. In each section, examples of designs and methods are described that are used in contemporary psychological and pharmacological mental health treatment research to enhance that type of validity. Only a sampling of designs and methods relevant to each type of validity is described due to space limitations.

3.10.4 EXPERIMENTAL DESIGNS AND METHODS THAT ENHANCE IV, EV, CV, AND SCV

Each design and method discussed in the sections that follow is limited in the extent to which it can ensure that a particular type of experimental validity is achieved. Some limitations result mainly from the fact that patient-subjects are always free to deviate from research treatment protocols they enter, by dropping out of treatment, for example. Other limitations arise because research methods that can enhance IV can simultaneously reduce EV. For example, using psychotherapists who are experts in conducting a form of therapy can both increase IV and reduce EV.

One point merits emphasis. The experimental validity potential of alternative designs and methods is always contingent on the match between study hypotheses and a study's design and methods. For example, the IV potential of a particular design differs if the main aim of a study is to obtain data that can be interpreted as evidence for a therapy's hypothesized effects vs. to obtain data that can be interpreted as evidence for the comparative efficacy of alternative therapies for the same problem.

3.10.4.1 IV Methods and Designs

Table 2 lists and defines common IV threats. The text that follows elaborates on some of the information in Table 2.

3.10.4.1.1 *Random assignment*

Random assignment of subjects to all intervention groups in a study design is a *sine qua non* of IV. Broadly defined, random assignment means that a procedure is used to ensure that each new subject has an equal chance to be assigned to every intervention condition in a study. A simple random assignment procedure is the coin flip: heads the subject is assigned to one intervention in a two-intervention study; tails he or she receives the other one. Various procedures are used for random assignment including sophisticated techniques like urn randomization (Wei, 1978). Urn randomization simultaneously helps ensure that subjects are randomly assigned to interventions, and that the subjects in each one are matched on preidentified characteristics (e.g., co-present problems) that might moderate the effects of an intervention (Baron & Kenny, 1986).

Random assignment contributes to IV by helping to ensure that any differences found between interventions can be attributed to the interventions rather than to the subjects who received them. The rationale for randomization is that known and unknown characteristics of subjects that can affect outcomes will be equally distributed across all intervention conditions. Hence, subject features will not systematically affect (bias) the outcomes of any intervention.

Random assignment has limitations as a way to enhance IV. For example, it is not a completely reliable method to ensure that all outcome-relevant, preintervention features of subjects are equally distributed across intervention conditions. Even when randomization is used, by chance some potentially outcome-relevant subject characteristics can be more prevalent in one intervention than another (Collins & Elkin, 1985). This fact can be discovered *post hoc* when subjects in each intervention are found to differ on a characteristic (e.g., marital status) that is also found to relate to outcome. This happened, for example, in the US National Institute of Mental Health's Treatment of Depression Collaborative Research Program study (Elkin et al., 1989).

Attrition (e.g., of subjects, of subjects' outcome data) also limits the IV protection provided by random assignment (Flick, 1988; Howard, Cox, & Saunders, 1990; Howard, Krause, & Orlinsky, 1986). For example, subjects can always drop out of treatment or fail to provide data at all required assessment points. Both are examples of postinclusion attrition in Howard, Krause et al. (1986) terminology. The problems associated with, and types of, attrition have been carefully explicated (Flick, 1988; Howard, Krause et al. 1986). For example, the core IV threat associated with dropout is that the subjects who drop out of each study intervention might differ somehow (e.g., severity of symptoms). This would create differences in the subjects who complete each intervention and simultaneously

Table 2 Internal validity.

Threat	Description	Example antidote
Historical factors	Events that occur between pre- and postintervention measurement could be responsible for the intervention effects found (e.g., a public information campaign to reduce drug use in teenagers coincides with an adolescent drug treatment intervention study)	If historical the event does not overlap completely with the study period, the outcome data can be analyzed separately for subject cohorts that received the intervention before the event vs. during it, and results compared to estimate the intervention's effects independent of the event
Maturation	Changes in subjects that naturally occur with the passage of time could be responsible for pre- to postintervention changes in outcomes	Include a no or minimal treatment control condition in the study, and randomize subjects to treatment conditions
Testing	Pre- to postintervention changes on outcome measures could be due to repeated administration of the measures, rather than to change in the outcome variables assessed	Evaluate the impact of repeated testing by administering the outcome measures to a randomly selected subset of subjects only at postintervention. Compare the final scores with those of subjects to whom the measures were repeatedly administered. Use the Solomon Four-Group design (Campbell & Stanley, 1963; Rosenthal & Rosnow, 1991) to examine both the effects of repeated testing and any interaction of testing and interventions
Instrumentation	Pre- to postintervention differences in the way an outcome measure is administered could be responsible for intervention effects (e.g., different diagnosticians administer a structured diagnostic interview at pre- and at post-test to the same subject)	Keep instruments and administration procedures constant throughout a study (e.g., recalibrate laboratory instruments and human assessors during study)
Statistical regression	Change in pre- to postintervention scores include "normal" drift toward more moderate scores whenever an initial score is either higher or lower than the average (mean) tendency of the group	Use the statistical technique of covarying preintervention scores from termination scores in outcome analyses (e.g., analysis of covariance, multiple regression)
Selection	Differences between subjects assigned to a study's intervention conditions could account for outcome differences in the interventions	Randomly assign subjects to intervention conditions
Attrition or mortality	Differences between subjects who complete each study intervention (e.g., due to dropout from the interventions) could be responsible for differences in intervention outcomes	Collect outcome data at every planned assessment point from *all* subjects (including dropouts and those withdrawn due to deterioration) and conduct outcome analyses on the 'intention-to-treat' sample (see text)
Ambiguity about the direction of causal influence	The study design does not make it possible to determine if A causes B or B causes A, although the hypotheses assume undirectional causality (e.g., in a correlational study it cannot be determined whether improvement in the therapeutic alliance enhanced outcome or if a subject's improvement enhanced the therapeutic alliance)	Do not use cross-sectional designs and standard correlational statistics if causal conclusions are desired. When theory and empirical findings exist to support causal hypotheses, one alternative is to develop and test causal models on data that lack experimental controls needed to infer causality (e.g., Kenny, 1979)

Table 2 (continued)

Threat	Description	Example antidote
Diffusion or imitation of treatments	The putative active elements of a study intervention are somehow disseminated to subjects in other intervention and/or control conditions (e.g., subjects who receive a treatment for drug addiction give copies of their treatment workbooks to subjects in the control condition)	When informed consent is administered, emphasize the requirement to refrain from discussing one's treatment with other subjects. Guarantee all subjects the opportunity to receive a study treatment (e.g., at the end of the study)
Compensatory equalization of treatments	Personnel who have control over desirable interventions compromise the study design by somehow making them available to all subjects. For example, in a study in which therapists serve as their own controls (the same therapists administer the interventions and control treatment conditions), therapists have difficulty refraining from using elements of the study's "active" interventions in the therapy sessions of subjects who are in the control condition	Ensure that subjects who do not get the desirable intervention during the study will have access to them after the study. Let subjects know at the beginning of the study that this will happen. Antidotes for the therapist example are to audiotape all therapy sessions and monitor the tapes for therapists' adherence to the intervention conditions. Immediately give therapists feedback when they deviate from adherence requirements. Also, offer all subjects who are randomized to control conditions the opportunity to receive the (putative) active treatments at the end of the study; inform therapists at the study outset that control subjects will have the opportunity to receive an active treatment
Compensatory rivalry by respondents receiving less desirable treatments	Subjects are aware of all intervention conditions in the study, and those in a "standard" condition are motivated to outperform those in "special" intervention conditions. Thus, any differences or lack of differences found between intervention and/or control conditions cannot be attributed to the interventions	This threat applies only to some types of intervention studies. For example, it can occur when a study setting is an intact unit (such as a department) and subjects in the standard condition expect some negative personal effect (e.g., lose their jobs) of study findings. Investigators need to be aware of the potential relevance of this threat to a study and either redesign the project or take actions to reduce its potential influence (e.g., see above antidote for compensatory equalization)
Resentful demoralization of respondents receiving less desirable treatments	This threat is the opposite of the threat of compensatory rivalry. Subjects in a control or other intervention condition underperform relative to their capacity and thereby contribute to artificial differences between the intervention outcomes	Investigators need to be aware of the relevance of this threat to a particular study and either redesign the project or take actions to reduce its potential influence (promise subjects in the less desirable intervention condition the opportunity to receive it at the end of the study)

Statements in the first two columns and some in the third are abstracted from Cook and Campbell (1979).

in those who provide outcome data. This type of threat of attrition to IV has been called the "differential sieve" (Hollon, Shelton, & Loosen, 1991), an apt metaphor. If differential attrition by intervention occurs, any outcome differences could be due to the subjects from whom assessments were obtained rather than to the interventions examined.

One methodological antidote to the IV problems posed by attrition due to dropout is to conduct outcome analyses on the "intention-to-treat" sample (Gillings & Koch, 1991). The intention-to-treat sample can be defined in different ways. For example, one definition is all subjects who were randomized to study interventions. Another definition is all subjects who attended at least one intervention session. The latter type of definition is often used when investigators want to generalize outcome findings only to patients who at least are willing to try an intervention.

Intention-to-treat analyses ideally require outcome assessments of all dropouts (and of all others who discontinued treatment prematurely, such as by being withdrawn by the investigators due to treatment noncompliance or deterioration) at the time(s) when they would have been assessed if they had remained in treatment. The intent-to-treat analytic strategy also contributes to a study's EV by maximizing the probability that the findings can be assumed to generalize to all individuals who would meet the study entry criteria.

Unfortunately, intention-to-treat analyses have limitations with respect to protecting a study's IV. The reader is referred to Flick (1988) and to Howard, Krause et al. (1986) for comprehensive discussions of other methods to evaluate and reduce the effects of attrition on a study's IV and EV.

3.10.4.2 Untreated or Placebo-treated Control Group

The inclusion of a no-treatment group (e.g., wait list) or putative sham treatment (e.g., pill placebo) in a study design is required to validly answer causal questions like "Does an intervention have certain effects?" A no-treatment or placebo condition to which subjects are randomly assigned and which continues for the same duration as a putative active treatment allows several rival explanations for a relationship between a treatment and outcomes to be dismissed. For example, if the outcomes associated with an active treatment are statistically better than the outcomes associated with a control treatment, then the active treatment outcomes cannot be attributed solely to changes that occur naturally with the passage of time, maturation, or "spontaneous remission."

The inclusion of control treatment conditions of some type is logically very compelling as a way to increase an intervention study's IV. Unfortunately, the compelling logic is not mirrored in practice. Reams have been written on problems associated with designing placebo therapies that meet IV goals (e.g., O'Leary & Borkovec, 1978). For example, credibility is one issue (Parloff, 1986). How can a placebo psychotherapy be developed that has no theoretically active therapeutic ingredients but that seems equally credible to subjects as a putative active treatment?

Pill placebo conditions used in psychopharmacology research are often thought to be free of the IV limitations associated with psychotherapy placebos. However, pill placebo conditions are also limited in terms of IV. For example, active medications almost always have side effects. Thus, the placebo pill used should mimic the side effects of the active drug. It also is important that both the subject and the prescribing therapist be blind (uninformed) about who is getting placebo and who is getting active medication. Experienced psychopharmacologists often, probably typically, can tell which subjects are receiving active medication (Greenberg, Bornstein, Greenberg, & Fisher, 1992; Margraf et al., 1991; Ney, Collins, & Spensor, 1986; Rabkin et al., 1986). The failure of the blinding procedure is problematic because therapists' impressions could be associated with different behavior toward placebo and active medication subjects. For example, a therapist might be less encouraging about the possibility of improvement if he or she suspects that a subject is getting placebo rather than medication. Differential therapist behavior toward placebo and active medication subjects could affect outcomes and thereby reduce the IV of the study design.

Another common threat to the IV value of no-treatment and placebo treatment conditions is contamination or diffusion. Putative therapeutic elements of an intervention can somehow infiltrate the control condition. A well-known example of this is the "MRFIT" study conducted in the USA. It was designed to evaluate an educational intervention to reduce the incidence of heart disease in men. The intervention provided information about diet, smoking, and exercise as a way to lower cholesterol and other risks of heart disease (Gotto, 1997; Multiple Risk Factor Trial Interventions Group, 1977). The study design was a randomized, controlled comparison of men who received the intervention with men who received "usual care." During the years that the study was done, information used in the intervention was widely disseminated in the US media, thus threatening the IV value of the usual care control sample.

Another way contamination of a control treatment can occur is via contact between the control subjects and those receiving the active treatments. For example, subjects in active treatments might give control subjects intervention materials (e.g., copies of intervention self-help workbooks). To help prevent this threat to IV, subjects can be required, as part of the study informed consent, to refrain from sharing information about their respective treatments while a study is in progress.

3.10.4.3 Specification of Interventions

A relatively new set of IV methods focuses on detailed specification of the interventions examined in a study. These methods have been adopted widely in psychotherapy research since the 1980s. Their primary aims are to facilitate replication of studies and to ensure that interventions are properly implemented. The methods include the preparation of treatment manuals (e.g., Beck, 1995; Klerman, Weissman, Rounsaville, & Chevron, 1984), for example. Such manuals describe the treatment rationale, the therapeutic techniques to be used, and the circumstances that should prompt therapists to choose between alternative techniques (Lambert & Ogles, 1988). The methods also include the development of therapist adherence measures to be used by observer-judges of therapy session material (e.g., audiotapes) to assess the extent to which treatments were delivered by study therapists as specified in the manual (Waltz, Addis, Koerner, & Jacobson, 1993).

Treatment specification methods are described more fully in Section 3.10.4.7 on CV. They are cross-referenced here to emphasize the fundamental dependence of a study's IV on the CV of its intervention variables. The dependence is essentially the same as that between the psychometric adequacy of the measures and methods used to operationalize independent and dependent variables, and the possibility of conducting a valid test of hypotheses about the relationship between independent and dependent variables (Kraemer & Telch, 1992). The validity of conclusions about hypotheses is necessarily contingent on the adequacy of the operationalization of central study variables or constructs. The preceding point, albeit basic, merits emphasis because it is often ignored or not understood well in mental health intervention research (Kraemer & Telch, 1992).

3.10.4.4 Process Research Methods

"Process" research refers to a highly developed methodology that has been used in adult psychotherapy research since at the 1950s (Greenberg & Pinsof, 1986; Kiesler, 1973; Rice & Greenberg, 1984; Russell, 1987). Described generally, process research is the application of measurement methods to therapy session material, such as videotaped recordings or transcripts of therapy sessions. A typical strategy for process research consists of four basic steps. First, a measure is developed of a theoretically important therapy construct (e.g., therapeutic alliance). The measure is designed to be rated by trained judges, based on observation of some type of therapy session material (e.g., video-

tapes of sessions). Judges are selected and trained to apply the measure. Psychometric studies are done to evaluate and ensure that judges' ratings on the measure meet standards for inter-rater reliability. A plan for sampling material from therapy sessions for judges to rate is developed. The sampling plan is designed to provide a valid idea of the construct. Judges then rate the selected material. In addition to the foregoing basic steps, it is also important to conduct psychometric evaluations of measure (e.g., the internal consistency reliability of ratings).

Process methods are used to examine a host of research questions (for comprehensive reviews see Orlinsky & Howard, 1986; Orlinsky, Grawe, & Parks, 1994). One of the most valuable uses of process research methods is to test the theories of therapeutic change that are associated with different types of psychotherapy. A standard treatment outcome study is designed to ask questions like "Does a treatment work?" and "Does a therapy work better than an alternative one for the same problem?" Process methods allow the next logical questions to be asked, for example, "Does a therapy work for the reasons it is theoretically posited to?" and "What are the therapeutically active elements of a therapy?" Viewed in terms of Cook and Campbell's (1979) types of experimental validity, process research methods contribute mainly to IV and CV.

Process methods can contribute to a study's IV when they are used to test hypothesized relationships about theoretically causal elements of a therapy (such as specific therapeutic techniques) and targeted outcomes. The precision of the causal conclusions that can be drawn from intervention studies is limited when patients are randomly assigned to treatments, receive treatment, and then outcomes are measured. Even when intervention outcome studies yield positive findings, many fundamental and important questions remain unanswered. Are a therapy's effects mediated by the theoretically hypothesized activities of therapists? Alternatively, are the effects primarily due to nonspecific features of the therapy (e.g., the therapist's empathy and understanding) rather than to its specific techniques (e.g., cognitive restructuring)? (Ilardi & Craighead, 1994; Kazdin, 1979; Strupp & Hadley, 1979). Are all of the recommended therapeutic techniques necessary; are any necessary and sufficient?

Process methods can be used to examine questions of the foregoing type. When used in such ways, they contribute to a study's IV because they help elucidate causality, that is, the extent to which specific elements of a therapeutic intervention can validly be assumed to play a causal role in the outcomes obtained

(Gomes-Schwartz, 1978). Furthermore, when process research methods yield answers to mechanisms of action questions like those stated above, the findings can be used to refine and improve existing treatments, for example, to increase their efficiency and efficacy, and to modify the theories of therapeutic change on which treatments are founded.

Process methods can also contribute to CV. For example, process methods are used both to develop instruments to assess therapists' adherence to manualized treatments (e.g., Evans, Piasecki, Kriss, & Hollon, 1984), and to develop a rating strategy (e.g., plan for sampling from the therapy session material to be rated by judges) to assess therapist adherence for intervention studies (e.g., Hill, O'Grady, & Elkin, 1992). More detail is provided on process research methods that contribute to CV in Section 3.10.4.3.

3.10.4.5 EV Methods

Table 3 presents three types of threats to EV that were highlighted by Cook and Campbell (1979). Each threat is described as an interaction between a study feature and the study treatment(s). This is because Cook and Campell emphasized the difference between generalizing *across* subject populations, settings, etc., vs. generalizing *to* target subject populations, settings. Cook and Campbell chose to focus on the former because the latter requires sophisticated random sampling methods which are rarely used in intervention research.

As stated earlier, EV concerns the extent to which outcome findings validly can be assumed to generalize beyond a study's specific therapists, subjects, setting(s), measures, and point in time when a study was conducted. For about the past eight years in the USA, criticisms have been raised increasingly often about intervention studies with apparent low EV (e.g., Lebowitz & Rudorfer, 1998). The criticisms are part of the efficacy vs. effectiveness debate. For example, it is said that the outcomes of therapies done by study therapists who are trained in a therapy and then receive ongoing supervision during a study (to ensure that they continue to adhere to the therapy manual) cannot be assumed to generalize to community therapists who might provide the treatment. The generalizability point is a valid one. At minimum, it underscores the need for therapist training methods and materials to be made widely available for interventions found to be efficacious in high IV studies.

Contemporary controversies aside, methods that can contribute to EV are described next. Some of their limitations are also noted.

3.10.4.5.1 *Naturalistic treatment settings*

The ultimate aim of psychotherapy intervention studies is to identify therapies that can be provided effectively in settings where individuals who have the problems that are targeted by the therapy are treated. However, studies with the highest IV, for example, those that include random assignment and a placebo treatment, are often done in university-affiliated clinic settings. Such settings are where researchers tend to be located. The settings also tend to be most amenable to the implementation of research methods that are needed for high IV studies.

University-affiliated clinical settings differ in many ways from other settings in which mental health interventions are provided, such as urban and rural community mental health clinics and private practice offices. The differences between a study's setting(s) and the settings to which it is important to generalize its findings reduce EV only if the differences affect the outcomes of the interventions being tested. Thus, to accurately evaluate a study's EV with respect to nonstudy settings, one must know which setting features affect the outcomes of the interventions. Unfortunately, research generally is not done on the foregoing topic. In the absence of knowledge, the prevailing convention seems to be to adopt a conservative position: namely, the more similar to "typical" mental health treatment settings that an intervention study setting is, the greater the study's probable EV.

The foregoing convention results in recommendations like: a study protocol that has high IV should be implemented in a variety of public and private mental health treatment settings, both urban and rural, and in different sections of a country (i.e., in large countries where areas exist that have different subcultures). Unfortunately, the preceding strategy to enhance the EV of settings is rife with limitations (cf. Clarke, 1995). Cook and Campbell (1979) extensively discussed the problems, which they referred to as "major obstacles to conducting randomized experiments in field settings." They also discussed social forces and field settings that are conducive to randomized intervention studies.

A common obstacle is that all community clinics have standard operating procedures. The need to introduce the key IV-enhancing experimental method, random assignment, typically is an enormous challenge in such settings. At minimum, it requires that all regular clinic staff, or at least a representative sample of them, be willing to learn and to correctly implement a new intervention. Assuming that the staff are interested in being trained in a new intervention,

Table 3 External validity (generalizability).

Threat	Description	Example antidote
Interaction of selection and treatment	The study's subject inclusion and exclusion criteria and/or other requirements of study participation could result in a sample that responds differently to the intervention(s) than would other individuals of the type for whom the intervention(s) was designed.	Make entry into the study as convenient as possible to maximize the representativeness of the sample of the desired population. Attempt to replicate the study using modified inclusion criteria (e.g., drop the prerandomization study induction procedure that was used in the original study)
Interaction of setting and treatment	Features unique to the study setting(s) could contribute to the intervention effects (e.g., the setting was a well-known treatment and research clinic, famous for one of the interventions)	Attempt to replicate the study by simultaneously or consecutively carrying out the same design and procedure in two or more settings
Interaction of history and treatment	Features unique to the time when the study was done could contribute to the intervention effects (e.g., a study of therapies for depression was conducted during the same year that the US National Institute of Mental Health ran a major public information campaign on the efficacy of psychological therapies for depression)	Attempt to replicate the study

Statements in the first two columns and some in the third are abstracted from Cook and Campbell (1979). The threats are listed as interactions between variables and study treatments because the threats apply when the intention is to generalize *across* populations, settings, etc., rather than *to* target populations, settings, etc. Cook and Campbell provide an extended discussion of the difference.

training time must be made available to them. The need for training can pose a major hurdle because staff work days typically are fully booked with existing job responsibilities.

An alternative is to hire new clinic staff specifically to conduct treatments for a study. This strategy typically is associated with pragmatic limitations such as office space. Also, hiring new staff can compromise the setting EV goal, the main reason for wanting to conduct an intervention study in a field setting.

3.10.4.6 Inclusive Subject Selection

Mental health interventions are developed to be helpful to individuals who have particular types of problems. Hence, subject EV is a critical type of EV for an intervention study. Several threats to subject EV that are associated with procedures which enhance IV have been described (e.g., Howard, Cox, & Saunders, 1990; Howard, Krause et al., 1986). For example, IV requires that subjects accept random assignment to any intervention condition in a study. Some study applicants will refuse to participate due to this requirement. Such refusal is a threat to EV

because the study sample will not be representative of all individuals for whom the study intervention is believed to be appropriate. Also, studies with high IV typically require subjects to participate in research assessments, often extensive ones. Some require subjects to agree to audio- or videorecording of therapy sessions. A portion of potential subjects are likely to refuse participation due to assessment requirements, thereby reducing the subject EV of study findings. All of the preceding examples are types of preinclusion attrition.

The fundamental threat to IV posed by subject dropout from treatment studies (post-inclusion attrition) was described previously. Dropout is also a serious, predictable, and often intractable EV threat. Researchers' careful selection, implementation, and description of subject inclusion and exclusion criteria all potentially enhance a study's EV by providing specific information on the types of individuals to whom the findings are most likely to generalize. The loss of outcome data that typically is associated with subject dropout compromises the confidence with which it can be concluded that a study's findings generalize to individuals like those selected for the study. The threat to EV of subject dropout is another reason why it is critically important to try to obtain data at all required assessment points from all subjects who enter a study, dropouts and remainers alike.

One of the most frequent subject EV criticisms of contemporary US studies with high IV is their psychodiagnostic inclusion and exclusion criteria (e.g., American Psychiatric Association, 1994). The criticism is that the use of specific diagnostic critieria for sample selection yields subjects who are unrepresentative of individuals who would receive the interventions in community settings. Study samples are said to be highly selected, consisting of "pure" types that are unrepresentatively homogeneous compared to treatment-seeking individuals who contact field clinical settings (e.g., Lebowitz & Rudorfer, 1998; Seligman, 1995).

The preceding subject of EV concern is a relatively new one. It relates directly to a mental health intervention research strategy that developed in the USA after 1980, when the third edition of the *Diagnostic and statistical manual of mental disorders* (*DSM*; American Psychiatric Association, 1980) was published. Shortly thereafter, sociopolitical forces converged to contribute to the requirement that applications for federal grant funding for mental health intervention efficacy studies be focused on specific diagnoses (e.g., major depressive disorder; social phobia) as defined in the *DSM*. Previously, the sample selection criteria for such studies were very broad, for example, treatment-seeking adults who complained of a variety of "problems in living" but who had no history of a psychotic disorder or current drug addictions.

The validity of the foregoing subject of EV criticism merits examination. It is true that the trend in intervention research in the USA since 1980 has been to develop and test interventions for relatively specific symptoms and syndromes (e.g., depression). However, study reports generally do not include comprehensive descriptions of co-present diagnoses (i.e., comorbidity patterns) of subjects. Thus, the extent to which most study samples are indeed more homogeneous than community setting patients for whom an intervention would be recommended typically cannot be determined. Also, some evidence from research clinics is beginning to appear that does not support the homogeneity criticism (e.g., Kendall & Brady, 1995).

3.10.4.6.1 Staff therapists

Another commonly mentioned threat to EV is the use of specially selected therapists. For example, sometimes investigators limit study therapists to a subset who meet a criterion of skillfulness. The rationale is that delivery of study interventions by therapists who are optimally skilled will provide the most accurate test of an intervention's efficacy. However, the strategy also poses a threat to EV. Can the outcomes of a study in which expert therapists delivered the interventions be assumed to generalize to less skilled therapists? The most conservative answer to this EV question is probably not. However, many contemporary intervention studies with high IV also specify (i) methods to identify therapists like those selected for a study, and (ii) therapist training programs that include ways to measure skill attained before therapists start to treat study patients. Thus, high IV studies that meet current methodological standards describe ways to identify and train nonstudy therapists who are like study therapists and, thus, who are likely to provide treatments that have outcomes similar to those obtained (cf. Kazdin, Kratochwill, & VandenBos, 1986).

3.10.4.6.2 CV Methods

Table 4 summarizes threats to CV and lists some antidotes. The text that follows elaborates on some of the information in Table 4.

In Cook and Campbell's 1979 discussion of CV, they opined that "most applied experimental research is much more oriented toward high construct validity of effects than of causes" (p. 63). Their observation was accurate for psychotherapy intervention research at the time but, notably, does not hold for therapy research published since about 1990 (e.g., Elkin et al., 1989). A methodological revolution in psychotherapy research enabled the CV of putative causes, that is, therapeutic interventions, to be enhanced. The relevant new methods are described in Sections 3.10.4.7.1–3.10.4.7.3.

3.10.4.6.3 Specification of interventions: treatment manuals

Cook and Campbell (1979) highlighted the dependence of CV on careful pre-operationalization explication of the essential features of study constructs. Prestudy preparation of treatment manuals, discussed in Section 3.10.4.1.3, is a research method that achieves pre-operationalization explication of the intervention construct, if done well. Criticisms of the treatment manual revolution in therapy research have been frequent and heated, despite the critical contribution of manuals to both the IV and potential EV of psychotherapy intervention studies

Table 4 Construct validity of putative causes and effects.

Threat	Description	Example antidote
Inadequate preoperational explication of construct	The researchers' elucidation of one or more of the main study constructs (i.e., the interventions and outcome) was not adequate to guide valid operationalization (measurement) of them	Devote necessary resources to identifying or developing valid operationalizations of interventions and outcomes because high construct validity of intervention and outcome variables is essential to conducting interpretable intervention research
Mono-operation bias	Reasonable variation in the implementation of an intervention does not occur (e.g., only male therapists are used) which reduces the validity of the operationalization of the intervention	Vary putatively irrelevant features of study interventions (e.g., use male and female therapists who represent a wide age range to deliver interventions)
Monomethod bias	Only one measurement method is used to assess central variables (e.g., all outcome measures use the paper and pencil self-report method) which confounds variance in scores due to method with variance that reflects the variable of interest	Include measures of central variables that are based on more than one assessment method (e.g., self-report and behavioral observation of symptoms)
Hypothesis-guessing within experimental conditions	Subjects try to intuit the study hypotheses and skew their responses based on what they think the hypotheses are	Try to make hypotheses hard to guess or intentionally tell subjects false hypotheses (and debrief them after the study is over). Tell subjects who are in a treatment outcome study that honest, candid responses are more useful to the research than trying to "help" the researcher by showing improvement on measures.
Evaluation apprehension	Subjects might present themselves more positively (or more negatively) than their honest self-evaluation when they are being assessed by experts in personality, psychopathology, or basic human skills	Use paper and pencil self-report measures of the same constructs that "expert" interviewers assess; include measures of social desirability response style, and use them as covariates if they are correlated with scores on outcome measures. Administer measures of socially undesirable variables at a prestudy baseline point and again immediately before study begins. Assume that the second administration is likely to be the more valid (candid) index
Experimenter expectancies	Investigators' biases influence the study findings	Investigators should not administer study interventions. Conduct the same study protocol in two or more settings, each of which is overseen by an investigator with a different preference (bias) for the interventions examined
Confounding constructs and levels of constructs	Some interventions might be differentially efficacious when provided at different levels or strengths (e.g., doses of psychotropic medications; a psychotherapy conducted with two sessions per week for the first 12 weeks vs. once weekly for the first 12 weeks)	Conduct a study to examine whether an intervention's effects differ by the strength of the "dose" administered

Table 4 (continued)

Threat	Description	Example antidote
Interaction of different treatments	Subjects concurrently receive nonstudy interventions and the study intervention (e.g., some subjects in a psychotherapy study start taking psychotropic medications; in a study of medication treatment for drug addiction, some subjects also receive medical and housing help at the study clinic)	Use procedures to reduce the probability that subjects will receive treatments other than the study treatments. For example, as a criterion for study participation, require subjects to refrain from taking psychotropic medications or having any other psychotherapeutic treatment while in the study. Check throughout a study for use of proscribed treatments and either withdraw subjects from study or exclude the data of subjects who use proscribed treatments from outcome analyses
Interaction of testing and treatment	The study assessment procedures affected the response of subjects to study interventions (e.g., a preintervention measure sensitized subjects in a way that enhanced their response to the study intervention)	Examine the presence of this threat experimentally by administering the measures to two subject samples. Administer tests to one sample at pre- and postintervention; administer to other only at postintervention. A complete Solomon four-group design (Campbell & Stanley, 1963) can also be used
Restricted generalizability across constructs	Interventions can affect many important outcome variables. However, effects on outcomes (constructs) of interest often are not highly correlated (generalizable)	Include measures that are closely related to the main outcomes sought with an intervention, in addition to the key outcomes (e.g., in a study of treatments for depression, include measures of severity of depression symptoms, work functioning [number of sick days], and marital conflict

Statements in the first two columns and some in the third are abstracted from Cook and Campbell (1979).

(Wilson, 1996). However, the CV of intervention constructs requires more than manuals. It also requires prestudy therapist training procedures to teach therapists how to conduct the interventions as specified in the manual. A final step is to evaluate and ensure the effectiveness of the training "manipulation" before therapists are permitted to conduct therapies with study subjects. Methods for this are discussed next.

3.10.4.6.4 Specification of interventions: therapist adherence measures

The previously mentioned process research methodology, observer-judge ratings of therapy session material, provides the most valid index available to date of the extent to which a therapist has acquired a requisite skill level with a study intervention. Some research findings support the preceding conclusion. For example, trainee therapists' scores on written tests about a therapy were not highly correlated with

supervisors' judgments of trainees' skill in conducting a therapy. Likewise, supervisors' impressions of trainees' competence with a therapy, based on trainees' descriptions of therapy sessions, were not highly correlated with supervisors' ratings of trainees' competence based on videotapes of therapy sessions (Chevron & Rounsaville, 1983).

The use of process methods to assess the extent to which therapists conduct treatments as specified requires the development of adherence measures (e.g., Evans et al., 1984). Adherence measures typically consist of items that operationally define what the developers of an intervention believe to be its essential therapeutic elements. Judges review therapy session material and rate the extent to which a therapist enacts (verbally and/or behaviorally) each item as specified by the adherence measure. The development of a psychometrically sound therapist adherence measure for an intervention, including a system for sampling the therapy session material to which the measure should be applied, is a time-consuming and sophisticated research methodology.

The use of self-report therapist adherence measures recently has been proposed as a substitute for judge-rated measures (Carroll, Nich, & Rounsaville, in press). Self-report adherence measures have interesting uses in therapy research, perhaps particularly in therapy development research. However, the only psychometric examination to date of the validity of such methods as indices of therapists' adherence to a treatment as specified in a manual yielded negative results (Carroll et al., in press).

Therapist adherence measures are a way to assess the CV of study interventions. Adherence measures can be applied to systematically sampled therapy session material to yield an index of the extent to which study therapies were conducted as specified. The contribution of psychometrically sound therapist adherence measures to both CV and IV cannot be overemphasized: they allow us to evaluate whether or not the designated interventions (the independent variables) were delivered as intended in intervention studies.

The preceding discussion is a simplified explication of the issues involved. The advent of therapist adherence methodology was associated with recognition of the difference between two constructs, adherence and competence (e.g., Waltz et al., 1993). Basically, adherence denotes a therapist's *fidelity* to the therapeutic techniques that are described in a treatment manual; competence denotes *skill* in implementing the techniques (e.g., tailoring a technique to increase its acceptability to a particular client). Reseach to date is consistent with the conclusion that inter-rater reliability is more achievable with adherence measures than with competence measures. Recruiting experts in a particular form of therapy to judge competence does not solve the reliability problem (a "problem" which signals needed directions for psychotherapy outcome research at this time).

3.10.4.6.5 Distinctiveness of interventions

The main aim of some intervention studies is to compare the outcomes of alternate treatments for the same problem. A fundamental assumption of comparative treatment studies, albeit sometimes implicit, is that the interventions being compared are distinctive in terms of their putative therapeutically active elements. For example, a study that is designed to compare the outcomes of a form of cognitive therapy for depression with another type of

psychotherapy for depression is based on the assumption that the therapies are substantively different somehow. The assumed distinction is what makes it worthwhile to compare therapies in a single study. In CV terms, a comparative intervention study design reflects the assumption that the intervention constructs are distinguishable. While the issue might seem moot, it is not. Therapies that sound distinct based on their theories of therapeutic change and prescribed techniques might not be distinguishable in practice, that is, when they are implemented (operationalized) in words and behaviors by therapists.

Therapist adherence measures for different interventions provide a systematic way to evaluate the distinctiveness of putatively different forms of psychotherapy and, hence, a way to evaluate the CV of comparative intervention studies. The general methodology is to apply the therapist adherence measure for each intervention to the intervention for which it was developed and to the other interventions in a study (e.g., cognitive therapy, psychodynamic therapy, and placebo therapy sessions each are rated on a cognitive therapy adherence scale and a psychodynamic therapy adherence scale). The scores obtained on the adherence measures for each intervention can then be compared to *a priori* criterion scores that are established to indicate the distinctiveness of the interventions. Hill et al. (1992) exemplifies the methodology.

3.10.4.6.6 Adjunctive therapies

When an intervention study is described as a test of a specific intervention, it is assumed that the intervention is the only one that the subjects received. However, sometimes study subjects are allowed to participate in adjunctive interventions (e.g., Alcoholics Anonymous) or are provided with additional interventions on an as-needed basis (e.g., aid from a case worker for housing and other needs; psychotropic medications). Participation in adjunctive interventions constitutes a threat to the CV of the study intervention, as well as to the study's IV. Outcome findings cannot be validly interpreted as due to the designated intervention(s) when adjunctive interventions are allowed but not controlled in some way.

3.10.4.6.7 Assessment procedures

Repeated testing on the same outcome measures is a CV threat that often is ignored. Cook and Campbell (1979) frame the issue as follows: can an intervention–outcome relationship be generalized to testing conditions other than those used in the study to assess outcomes?

For example, if an outcome measure was administered both pre- and postintervention, would the same outcomes have been obtained if the measure was administered only at post-intervention? One way to examine the threat of repeated testing to the CV of outcome scores is to compare findings of two randomly assigned intervention groups: one that was both pre- and post-tested, and another that only was post-tested.

A related CV threat is the possibility that study outcome measures interact with interventions. For example, studies of cognitive-behavioral (CB) therapy for panic disorder have been criticized for the possibility that CB affects a primary outcome measure used in such studies, self-reported frequency of panic attacks, mainly by teaching subjects to redefine panic attack rather than by reducing the actual frequency of attacks. To the extent that the criticism is valid, differences in panic attack frequency found between a control intervention and CB have low IV because the outcome measure in the CB condition has low CV. The measure does not reflect change in frequency of panic attacks, it reflects change in subjects' definitions of panic attack. The Solomon Four-Group Design (Campbell & Stanley, 1963; Rosenthal & Rosnow, 1991) can be used to simultaneously evaluate main effects of repeated testing on outcome measures and interactions of interventions and measures.

A common way to reduce CV threats to an outcome measure like the one just described for panic is to include other measures of closely related constructs in a study. The other measures should not be vulnerable to the same CV threat. For example, a spouse could be asked to provide ratings of the frequency and intensity of a subject's panic attacks. (This solution is, of course, associated with other types of CV concerns.)

3.10.4.7 SCV Methods

Only a few SCV-relevant methods are discussed here due to space limitations and to the technical detail associated with many SCV issues. The reader is referred to Cook and Campbell (1979) for a more complete review and to Table 5 for a synopsis of their discussion of SCV.

3.10.4.7.1 Statistical power analysis

Conducting a statistical power analysis at the planning phase of an intervention study is critical to its SCV (Cohen, 1977, 1992; Kraemer & Thiemann, 1987; Rosenthal & Rosnow,

1991). A power analysis helps an investigator determine the minimum sample size needed to detect a statistically significant outcome difference of a magnitude that he or she regards as clinically meaningful (e.g., Jacobson & Truax, 1991), given his or her willingness to risk making a type II error (i.e., accept the null hypothesis of no difference when it should be rejected). The smaller the sample size, the greater the risk of type II error when standard statistical procedures like analysis of variance are used in intervention research. However, the larger the sample size, the more expensive, time-consuming, and less feasible a study typically becomes.

A prestudy power analysis is a computation that allows investigators to enhance a study's SCV by determining the minimum sample size needed to statistically detect an outcome difference of a specified magnitude, given expected variances in the outcome measures. Ideally, an investigator can draw on criteria of some type to determine the size of a difference (effect size) that will have applied significance, that is, be clinically meaningful (Jacobson & Truax, 1991). For example, a clinically meaningful difference is one that experienced therapists would regard as a compelling reason to recommend one treatment over another for a particular problem.

The rationale for a power analysis is as follows. The magnitude of the variances of outcome measures and the study sample size are major determinants of whether or not an outcome difference of a certain magnitude between interventions will be statistically significant (i.e., unlikely to be due to chance). The same absolute difference between mean outcome scores of two interventions could be statistically significant if the sample size in each group was 30, but not if it was 15. Another perspective on the situation is that the smaller a study's sample size, the higher the probability of a type II error if the conventional $p \leqslant 0.05$ is used to indicate statistical significance. Rosnow and Rosenthal (1989) present a compelling perspective on the fundamental importance of the foregoing issues.

3.10.4.7.2 Controlling for the type I error rate

Statistical tests commonly used in intervention research (e.g., the F-test in analysis of variance) are associated with probability values, for example, $p < 0.05$. A p value indicates the probability that a difference found between interventions is due to chance rather than a true difference. Thus, for example, a statistical test that meets the $p \leqslant 0.05$ significance level means that a difference of the same magnitude would

Table 5 Statistical conclusion validity.

Threat	Description	Example antidote
Low statistical power	Limited potential of a study to yield statistically significant intervention effects (i.e., low potential to reject the null hypothesis) due to sample size and to the probable variances of outcome measures	Conduct a power analysis (e.g., Cohen, 1977, 1992; Rosenthal & Rosnow, 1991) during the design phase of a study to determine the sample size needed to detect an intervention effect of a predetermined size
Violated assumptions of statistical tests	Failure to ensure that a study's outcome data meet the assumptions of the statistical tests used to analyze it	Know the crucial assumptions of all statistical tests used and conduct analyses needed to evaluate whether the study data meet the assumptions. Seek expert statistical consultation if needed.
Fishing and the error rate problem	Several unplanned (i.e., *a posteriori* rather than *a priori*) statistical tests of effects (fishing) are conducted but no adjustments are made to reduce the likelihood that statistically significant findings are due to chance. In other words, the probability of type II error is larger than indicated by the reported *p* values	Consult statistics textbooks for methods to handle the error rate problem (e.g., Bonferroni correction; Tukey or Scheffé multiple comparison tests)
Reliability of measures	Low test–retest reliability (stability) and/or low internal consistency reliability of outcome measures inflates the error variance in scores and thus reduces the probability of finding intervention effects	Rely on psychometric properties of measures to guide selection of study measures. Choose measures with strong psychometric properties over measures with poor or unknown psychometric properties that might have better "face validity" as measures of the construct of interest (Kraemer & Telch, 1992)
Reliability of treatment implementation	Variability in the implementation of an intervention with different subjects (lack of standardization across subjects) inflates error and, thus, reduces the probability of finding intervention effects	Train study therapists to a criterion level of adherence to interventions before they treat any study patients; monitor their adherence to the treatment manual throughout the study and intervene if drift occurs (e.g., Shaw, 1984)
Random irrelevancies in the experimental setting	Features of a study setting other than the interventions could affect outcome scores (e.g., two research assistants administer the outcome measures to subjects: one is warm and friendly and the other is abrupt and distant)	Code features of the study setting that are likely to affect outcome measures as variables and include them in the data analyses to reduce error (e.g., research assistant who administered outcome measures is coded as a variable and included as a factor in an analysis of variance that is used to test for treatment effects)
Random heterogeneity of subjects	Differences in subjects could affect scores on the outcome measures independent of any intervention effects	Measure subject characteristics that are likely to be correlated with scores on outcome measures; use the characteristics as covariates or as blocking variables

Statements in the first two columns and some in the third are abstracted from Cook and Campbell (1979).

be expected to be obtained on average five times or fewer if 100 of the statistical tests were done, if the null hypothesis of no difference between interventions were true. The use of *p* values in conjunction with statistical tests is the principal way investigators guard against type I error (rejecting the null hypothesis of no difference when it should be accepted) when interpreting study findings. Thus, conducting statistical tests in ways that maintain the interpretability of *p* values is crucial to a study's SCV.

The interpretation of a *p* value is compromised when multiple statistical tests are done but no precautions are taken to ensure that the degree of protection against a type I error remains constant. A variety of procedures exist to maintain a specified level of protection against type I error when several statistical tests are performed. Statistics textbooks describe proce-dures such as the Bonferroni correction (e.g., Rosenthal & Rosnow, 1991). The main point for present purposes is that conducting multiple statistical tests without adjusting the probability level of the tests compromises a study's SCV. Unfortunately, this is a common type of threat to SCV in intervention research (Dar, Serlin, & Omer, 1994).

3.10.4.7.3 *Testing assumptions of statistical tests*

One fundamental assumption of the statis-tical tests that are commonly used for outcome analyses is that the dependent (outcome) variable is normally distributed. If the data do not meet the normality assumption, then the validity of the statistical test is compromised, that is, the study SCV is threatened. A special class of statistical procedures, nonparametric statistics (Leach, 1979), exist for analyzing data that are not normally distributed. Alterna-tively, procedures exist to transform data (e.g., square root transformation) to make their distribution more symmetrical before applying statistical tests (Atkinson, 1985; Carroll & Rupert, 1988).

3.10.5 FROM IV VS. EV TO IV + EV IN MENTAL HEALTH INTERVENTION RESEARCH

One illustration of the centrality of IV and EV to intervention research is the aforementioned controversy on efficacy vs. effectiveness studies (e.g., Goldfried & Wolfe, 1998; Jacobson & Christensen, 1996; Lebowitz & Rudorfer, 1998; Mintz et al., 1996; Seligman, 1995, 1996). The controversy took center stage largely as a side effect of dramatic shifts in health care delivery in the USA since the mid-1980s. Two forces were particularly valent in drawing the attention of intervention researchers and consumers of their research to efficacy (IV) and effectiveness (EV) methods. The forces were (i) a move from indemnity insurance coverage for health care to managed care coverage to control costs, and (ii) the US Congress's attempt in 1993 to reform national health care. Both forces highlighted the need for valid information about interventions to guide decisions of government policymakers and managed care entrepreneurs. Both groups were motivated to make decisions rapidly that would impact the interventions that millions of Americans could receive in insured programs. The need for valid findings to inform the decisions was keenly felt by all interested parties, including researchers. Limitations of

information from existing studies became widely and painfully evident. Lively debates later appeared about how intervention research in the USA, particularly federally funded research, should be designed (e.g., Clarke, 1995; Jacobson & Christensen, 1996; Lebowitz & Rudorfer, 1998; Newman & Tejeda, 1996; Seligman, 1995, 1996; Speer, 1994; Wells & Sturm, 1996).

A question at the core of the debate is how to design intervention studies to maximize three aims: (i) the value of findings in terms of definitive public health implications and en-hancement, (ii) the speed with which valid and useful findings can be obtained, and (iii) the public health policy yield from relatively scarce federal funding for mental health intervention studies. Personal biases are evident in positions taken by many who have spoken on the issues (e.g., pragmatism vs. concern that policy decisions that affect large numbers of people will be made based on scientifically weak findings). However, a valuable product of the debate has been creative thinking about how IV and EV goals might be maximized, for example, via new study questions and methods, and the use of statistical techniques such as causal modeling (Kenny, 1979). Interestingly, Cook and Campbell (1979) were keenly aware of all three of the aforementioned aims in the late 1970s. The ideas developed in all editions of their book, particularly in the sections on quasiexperimental designs, were largely in-tended to address them.

The current debate illustrates the importance of being fully fluent with the concepts of IV and EV for both creators and consumers of intervention research. A few suggestions from the debate for mounting studies that have both high IV and EV are described next. Then, two illustrative IV + EV studies are reviewed in terms of IV and EV.

3.10.5.1 Strategies for Efficacy + Effectiveness (IV + EV) Intervention Studies

Most strategies for designing intervention studies that optimize both IV and EV that have emerged so far from the efficacy vs. effectiveness debate are intended to maximize the applied public health (utilitarian) information that is obtained from studies. However, to test treat-ments that hold promise as marked advances over currently available interventions, high IV designs and methods are likely to be the most informative research strategies, due to their suitability for theory-testing and for testing causal hypotheses (Jacobson & Christensen, 1996; Mintz et al., 1996). The IV + EV strategies described here were selected to illustrate the diversity of approaches that have been proposed. Each strategy is described briefly, in a way intended to highlight its essence.

3.10.5.1.1 The conventional "phase" strategy

Before the recent efficacy vs. effectiveness debate, federal agencies that funded mental health research in the USA endorsed a phase model to meet the goals of IV and EV inference. According to Hoagwood et al. (1995), the phase model was adapted from one used by the US National Cancer Institute. Described in a simplified way, the model is to conduct efficacy studies of interventions for which promising outcome data were obtained in prior, preliminary research; the next phase is to conduct effectiveness studies of interventions for which compelling efficacy data are obtained.

3.10.5.1.2 A dimensional adaptation of the phase model

Hoagwood et al. (1995) identified several reasons why the phase model, although elegant, is rarely fully realized. A major hurdle has been moving interventions with demonstrated efficacy to effectiveness studies. A typical stumbling block to the transfer is introducing research methods into community settings to conduct effectiveness studies. Hoagwood et al. presented an alternative strategy, the essence of which is to conceptualize efficacy and effectiveness goals "in terms of continuous dimensions, rather than discrete phases" (p. 685). The authors describe a conceptual framework, not a model *per se*. It is linked specifically to mental health interventions for children, adolescents, and families.

The framework emphasizes three bipolar dimensions of intervention research, each of which can be described as having an IV and an EV pole. The dimensions are types of validity, types of intervention modalities and parameters, and types of outcomes. For example, at the IV pole of the intervention dimension are short-term (e.g., three months), highly structured, single modality therapies that are operationalized in detailed manuals; at its EV pole are longer-term, less well-specified treatments that allow for the integration of more than one therapy modality.

3.10.5.1.3 Stakeholder's model to guide data selection

Newman and Tejada (1996) highlighted the need to collect data that are sought by all parties who have a vested interest in mental health interventions (the stakeholders). The authors endorsed the view that high IV studies have an essential role in intervention research because they provide scientifically well-founded, important information about interventions, for example, their potential effects and their safety. EV goals are accomplished in the stakeholders model mainly by *collecting certain kinds of outcome and other data* about interventions that can help inform the decisions of all stakeholders in mental health treatment (e.g., government policymakers and corporate officials of managed care companies; potential recipients of interventions; family members and others who are directly affected by those who receive mental health interventions).

Types of data emphasized by Newman and Tejada (1996) include costs of interventions and estimates of the amount of therapeutic effort required to obtain specified behavioral outcomes. Hoagwood et al. (1995) also included cost data in their framework. The need for cost data (e.g., cost-effectiveness, cost-offset, comparative cost) is a dominant theme in research strategies that have been proposed for efficacy + effectiveness studies. This emphasis is largely a response to increasing concerns about, and concomitant restrictions on, health care costs in the USA. Cost data have not been standard products of federally funded efficacy studies in the USA for the past 30 years. Yates (1997) has presented guidelines for psychotherapy researchers on how to collect cost data. Wolff, Helminiak, and Tebes (1997) illustrate the impact of different assumptions on cost estimates in mental health treatment research. Other relevant references are Knapp (1995) and Yates (1996). Research strategies to examine the amount of therapeutic effort required to obtain specific outcomes have been available for some time in the psychotherapy research literature (e.g., Howard, Koptka, Krause, & Orlinsky, 1986; Kopta et al., 1994).

3.10.5.1.4 Mediator's model

The crux of a model proposed by Clarke (1995) is to use IV experimental methods to examine crucial generalizability (EV) questions about an interventions' outcomes. For example, a study design could include two or more intervention conditions distinguished mainly by the degree to which an intervention is implemented as specified in its manual. The essence of Clarke's (1995) model is to use IV methods to evaluate the effects of several potential mediator variables on the outcomes that can be achieved with an intervention. Examples of relevant mediators are the degree to which therapists adhere to the structure of a therapy as specified in its manual, heterogeneity of the patients treated, and the adjunctive therapeutic context in which an intervention is provided (e.g., used as a stand-alone intervention vs. included in an intervention package).

3.10.5.2 Examples of Efficacy + Effectiveness Intervention Studies

This section illustrates the use of the concepts of IV and EV to evaluate intervention studies. Two highly regarded US studies that were designed to meet both IV and EV aims are reviewed: Drake, McHugo, Becker, Anthony, and Clark (1996) and Schulberg et al. (1995). The main intent of each review is to illustrate how the concepts that are the focus of this chapter can be applied to help determine the conclusions that can validly be drawn from an intervention study. The reviews obviously are not complete or definitive evaluations of either study.

3.10.5.2.1 *Schulberg et al. (1995)*

The investigators' interest in integrating IV and EV considerations in a single study is evident in the study's two main aims. One aim was to compare the outcomes of a type of psychotherapy and a medication when used to treat depression in patients who were being seen in general medical clinics, not psychiatric settings. Both of the interventions were tested previously in randomized controlled studies and found to be efficacious for depression in psychiatric outpatients. A second aim was to compare the effects on depression of each of the two tested interventions with the effects of a third intervention of "usual care," that is, treatments of the type typically provided to depressed patients by doctors in primary care settings.

Central IV features of the study were: random assignment of patients to all three treatment conditions, use of sample selection procedures to identify patients who met standard psychiatric diagnostic criteria for depression, and outcome analyses on an intention-to-treat sample. IV and EV were simultaneously enhanced by other methods. The same study protocol was implemented concurrently at four primary care clinic settings. Procedures were used to help ensure that the psychotherapy was conducted in ways consistent with its manual but that also were minimally intrusive into the conduct of the therapies. Central EV features of the study were: it was conducted in primary care settings (although all four settings had academic affiliations), outcome data were obtained from patients who were randomly assigned to usual care, and the natural course of the usual care condition was preserved as much as possible.

A noteworthy EV threat was substantial preinclusion attrition of eligible subjects due to refusal to participate and other reasons. An IV threat was that therapists were "nested" in a treatment condition. That is, the medical professionals who provided usual care were not the same professionals who provided the psychotherapy intervention or the pharmacological intervention. Thus, better outcomes of the previously tested (efficacious) interventions compared to usual care could not be attributed validly to the therapies *per se*. Findings of this type were, in fact, obtained. However, it can be argued that the confounding of therapists and treatments does not pose an important IV limitation to this particular study. Rather, the confound enhances the generalizability of findings to standard practice (EV) because in the public sector, primary medical care providers are not the same as those who provide specific forms of psychotherapy for depression or those who specialize in psychopharmacological treatments for depression.

3.10.5.2.2 *Drake et al. (1996)*

Drake et al. (1996) integrated IV and EV methods in a study designed to examine interventions of a very different type from those examined by Schulberg et al. (1995). Their main aim was to compare two vocational programs for individuals with severe mental disorders (SMD) such as schizophrenia. Drake et al. described the interventions as differing in two primary ways. One intervention was provided by a professional rehabilitation agency external to the mental health clinics where individuals with SMD were treated; the other was integrated with mental health services and provided at the clinics. A second difference was in the structure of the interventions. The external intervention ("group skills training," GST) started with three months of pre-employment skills training; the mental health clinic intervention ("individual placement and support," IPS) started immediately with job placement activities.

The central IV feature of the study was random assignment to each of the intervention conditions. A key EV enhancement design feature was that each intervention was concurrently tested at two sites. However, the full EV value of the multisite design was compromised because GST staff who had central training roles overlapped at the two GST sites. Also, the GST and IPS interventions each were conducted at different sites. Thus, as the authors point out, interventions and sites were confounded. This type of confound notably compromises IV, that is, the confidence with which outcome findings can be attributed primarily to interventions.

The study illustrates that sample selection criteria can simultaneously increase the homogeneity of a study sample and enhance EV. The inclusion and exclusion criteria constitute minimal, yet realistic, qualifications for SMD clients to receive vocational interventions (e.g., lack of noteworthy memory impairment; clinical stability as indicated by not being hospitalized for at least one month; unemployment for at least one month but interest in employment). The potential subject EV enhancement associated with the sample selection criteria was reduced by another procedure, a "prerandomization group experience." SMD clients who were interested in participating in the study were required to attend a minimum of four weekly research induction group sessions. One purpose of the prerandomization group attendance requirement was to ensure that potential participants were "motivated" for the project interventions.

Prerandomization and pretreatment "orientation" or "stabilization" phases are sometimes used in mental health intervention research, particularly with populations in which high treatment failure and/or dropout rates are expected, such as drug abusers. EV is one trade-off for the use of such procedures. On the other hand, the procedures can have an IV advantage. They can create samples of individuals who are most likely to respond to an intervention, thereby yielding findings on its efficacy with individuals hypothesized to be most responsive to it. One potential risk is that the sample will consist of individuals who are likely to benefit from many incidental life/ environmental experiences and who, therefore, might not need the study interventions to achieve its targeted outcomes. The foregoing IV threat can be offset by the inclusion of a placebo control intervention of some type in the design.

Drake et al. (1996) also illustrates the critical impact on a study's CV, IV, and EV of the methods used to operationalize the interventions. The study report does not indicate if the interventions were specified in manuals or the type of training that counselors received before implementing them for the study. A related threat to the CV of the interventions and, thus, to the IV of study findings, is that the methods used to evaluate the success of the operationalization of the interventions (i.e., counselor adherence to GST and to IPS) are described too vaguely to evaluate. An additional IV threat is that it is not clear from the report if the IPS intervention was always provided by a counselor other than a client's SMD therapist. This is an IV consideration because the GST interventions were always provided by someone other than the client's SMD therapist.

One point illustrated by the preceding intervention-related aspects of the study is that the less clear and complete the description of methods used to implement interventions is, the less possible it is to evaluate their CV and, consequently, the IV of outcome findings. Thus, the public health significance of findings cannot be evaluated confidently. In turn, study findings can have less impact than they otherwise might.

An additional IV threat due to intervention procedures was site differences in the implementation of both interventions. The investigators intervened at one of the sites to correct deviations from the IPS model. However, the corrective attempts were not notably effective. The implementation of IPS is described as "weaker" at one site. Also, the GST counselors "concentrated their efforts" in one of their sites.

The study findings highlight the crucial importance to IV of intervention implementation procedures (intervention CV). In some analyses, the interventions differed on the major outcome variable (employment), favoring IPS; in others, the interventions did not differ. Interpretation of mixed findings about interventions' comparative effects is seriously compromised when the intervention CV is either poor or difficult to evaluate from information provided in a study report.

The foregoing review of Drake et al. (1996) from the perspective of IV and EV threats might seem inconsistent with the fact that it is widely regarded as one of the best IV + EV mental health intervention studies available. If it is assumed that the preceding IV and EV analysis itself is valid, what might be concluded? One conclusion is that difficulties maintaining the CV of interventions in studies that are done in natural settings to enhance EV can be costly in terms of IV. In turn, this analysis suggests that a cost-effective use of resources in high EV studies is to invest in methods that achieve and maintain the CV of interventions.

3.10.6 A CONCLUDING OBSERVATION

IV and EV considerations, and the related efficacy vs. effectiveness debate, highlight two vital applied aims of intervention research. The aims are: (i) to obtain findings that can be used directly and quickly in public mental health delivery systems, and (ii) to obtain findings that can markedly improve, ideally revolutionize, the effectiveness of treatments available in the public health sector. Both aims have clear public health significance. Aim (i) is most consistent with using designs and methods that are firmly tied to contemporary constraints on clinical practice in "real world" settings and obtaining findings that can affect practice in the short run. Aim (ii) is consistent with using scientific methods that are most likely to foster discovery and methods that can rule out rival interpretations of obtained covariation between interventions and outcomes. Immediate generalizability to current practice of findings from aim (ii) studies cannot be a central criterion of their public health significance.

The efficacy vs. effectiveness debate no doubt was partially fueled by efficacy researchers' frustration. Many of them observed that years of findings from high IV studies that support the value of certain types of psychotherapy (Task Force on the Promotion and Dissemination of Psychological Procedures, 1995) were eschewed by many who focused on the EV of those studies. Also, emphasizing EV limitations of well-done, high IV studies can impede implementation of tested therapies in public sector settings. By default, then, the use of untested, "treatment as usual" interventions is supported and maintained. This is the current situation in the USA.

A partial antidote to the preceding problem, a serious problem from the public health standpoint, was suggested by Kazdin et al. in 1986. Their suggestion is consistent with a point made earlier in this chapter. Mental health intervention research advances since the late 1980s include methods to systematically train therapists in therapies with demonstrated efficacy, and to evaluate the skillfulness that therapists attain from the training. Many therapist training and adherence assessment research methods generalize directly to public sector therapists. Thus, rather than look at findings from high IV studies and ask the therapist EV question: "Does the study provide evidence that therapists in the public health sector will be able to get the same results?," the question could be refocused: "Does the study provide methods that enable therapists to be identified and trained to get the same outcomes in public treatment settings?"

ACKNOWLEDGMENTS

Preparation of this chapter was supported by National Institute of Mental Health Grant K02 MH01443 to Karla Moras. Sincere thanks are extended to those who provided consultations, comments, or other contributions to the preparation of the manuscript: Phyllis Solomon, Elizabeth McCalmont, Christine Ratto, Heidi Grenke, J. R. Landis, and Jesse Chittams.

3.10.7 REFERENCES

American Psychiatric Association (1980). *Diagnostic and statistical manual of mental disorders* (3rd ed.). Washington, DC: Author.
American Psychiatric Association (1994). *Diagnostic and statistical manual of mental disorders* (4th ed.). Washington, DC: Author.
Atkinson, A. C. (1985). *Plots, transgressions and regression: An introduction to graphical methods of diagnostic regression analysis.* New York: Oxford University Press.
Baron, R. M., & Kenny, D. A. (1986). The moderator-mediator variable distinction in social psychological research: conceptual, strategic, and statistical considerations. *Journal of Personality and Social Psychology, 51,* 1173–1182.
Beck, J. S. (1995). *Cognitive therapy: Basics and beyond.* New York: Guilford Press.
Bergin, A. E., & Garfield, S. L. (Eds.) (1971). *Handbook of psychotherapy and behavior change* (1st ed.). New York: Wiley.
Bergin, A. E., & Garfield, S. L. (Eds.) (1994). *Handbook of psychotherapy and behavior change* (4th ed.). New York: Wiley.
Beutler, L. E., & Howard, K. I. (1998). Clinical utility research: An introduction. *Journal of Clinical Psychology, 54,* 297–301.
Campbell, D. T., & Stanley, J. C. (1963). Experimental and quasi-experimental designs for research on teaching. In N. L. Gage (Ed.), *Handbook of research on teaching* (pp. 171–246). Chicago: Rand McNally.
Campbell, D. T., & Stanley, J. C. (1996). *Experimental and quasi-experimental designs for research.* Chicago: Rand McNally.
Carroll, K. M., Nich, C., & Rounsaville, B. J. (in press). Use of observer and therapist ratings to monitor delivery of coping skills treatment for cocaine abusers: Utility of therapist session checklists. *Psychotherapy Research.*
Carroll, R. J., & Ruppert, D. (1988). *Transformation and weighting in regression.* New York: Chapman and Hall.
Chevron, E. S., & Rounsaville, B. J. (1983). Evaluating the clinical skills of psychotherapists: A comparison of techniques. *Archives of General Psychiatry, 40,* 1129–1132.
Clarke, G. N. (1995). Improving the transition from basic efficacy research to effectiveness studies: Methodological issues and procedures. *Journal of Consulting and Clinical Psychology, 63,* 718–725.
Cohen, J. (1977). *Statistical power analysis for the behavioral sciences* (Rev. ed.) New York: Academic Press.
Cohen, J. (1992). Quantitative methods in psychology: A power primer. *Psychological Bulletin, 112,* 155–159.
Collins, J. F., & Elkin, I. (1985). Randomization in the NIMH treatment of depression collaborative research program. In R. F. Boruch & W. Wothke (Eds.), *Randomization and field experimentations: New directions for program evaluation.* San Francisco: Jossey-Bass.
Consumer Reports (1995, November). Mental health: Does therapy help? (pp. 734–739).
Cook, T. D., & Campbell, D. T. (Eds.) (1979). *Quasi-experimentation: design and analysis issues for field settings.* Boston: Houghton Mifflin.
Cronbach, L. J. (1982). *Designing evaluations of educational and social programs.* San Francisco: Jossey-Bass.
Cronbach, L. J., & Meehl, P. E. (1955). Construct validity in psychological tests. *Psychological Bulletin, 52,* 281–302.
Dar, R., Serlin, R. C., & Omer, H. (1994). Misuse of statistical tests in three decades of psychotherapy research. *Journal of Consulting and Clinical Psychology, 62,* 75–82.
Drake, R. E., McHugo, G. J., Becker, D. R., Anthony, W.

A., & Clark, R. E. (1996). The New Hampshire study of supported employment for people with severe mental illness. *Journal of Consulting and Clinical Psychology, 64,* 391–399.

Elkin, I., Shea, M. T., Watkins, J. T., Imber, S. D., Sotsky, S. M., Collins, J. F., Glass, D. R., Pilkonis, P. A., Leber, W. R., Docherty, J. P., Fiester, S. J., & Parloff, M. B. (1989). NIMH Treatment of Depression Collaborative Research Program: I. General effectiveness of treatments. *Archives of General Psychiatry, 46,* 971–982.

Evans, M. E., Piasecki, J. M., Kriss, M. R., & Hollon, S. D. (1984). *Raters' manual for the Collaborative Study Psychotherapy Rating Scale—form 6.* Minneapolis. University of Minnesota and the St. Paul-Ramsey medical Center. (Available from the US Department of Commerce, National Technical Information Service, Springfield, VA 22161.)

Flick, S. N. (1988). Managing attrition in clinical research. *Clinical Psychology Review, 8,* 499–515.

Garfield, S. L., & Bergin, A. E. (Eds.) (1978). *Handbook of psychotherapy and behavior change* (2nd ed.). New York: Wiley.

Garfield, S. L., & Bergin, A. E. (Eds.) (1986). *Handbook of psychotherapy and behavior change* (3rd ed.). New York: Wiley.

Gibbons, R. D., Hedeker, D., Elkin, I., et al. (1993). Some conceptual and statistical issues in analysis of longitudinal psychiatric data. *Archives of General Psychiatry, 50,* 739–750.

Gillings, D., & Koch, G. (1991). The application of the principle of intention-to-treat to the analysis of clinical trials. *Drug Information Journal, 25,* 411–424.

Goldfried, M. R., & Wolfe, B. E. (1998). Toward a more clinically valid approach to therapy research. *Journal of Consulting and Clinical Psychology, 66,* 143–150.

Gomes-Schwartz, B. (1978). Effective ingredients in psychotherapy: Prediction of outcome from process variables. *Journal of Consulting & Clinical Psychology, 46,* 1023–1035.

Gotto, A. M. (1997). The multiple risk factor intervention trial (MRFIT): A return to a landmark trial. *Journal of the American Medical Association, 277,* 595–597.

Greenberg, L., & Pinsof, W. M. (Eds.) (1986). *The psychotherapeutic process: A research handbook.* New York: Guilford Press.

Greenberg, R. P., Bornstein, R. F., Greenberg, M. D., & Fisher, S. (1992). A meta-analysis of anti-depressant outcome under "blinder" conditions. *Journal of Consulting and Clinical Psychology, 60,* 664–669.

Hill, C. E., O'Grady, K. E., & Elkin, I. (1992). Applying the Collaborative Study Psychotherapy Rating Scale to rate therapist adherence in cognitive-behavior therapy, interpersonal therapy, and clinical management. *Journal of Consulting and Clinical Psychology, 60,* 73–79.

Hoagwood, K., Hibbs, E., Bren, T. D., & Jensen, P. (1995). Introduction to the special section: Efficacy and effectiveness in studies of child and adolescent psychotherapy. *Journal of Consulting and Clinical Psychology, 63,* 683–687.

Hollon, S. D., Shelton, R. C., & Loosen, P. T. (1991). Cognitive therapy and pharmacotherapy for depression. *Journal of Consulting and Clinical Psychology, 59,* 88–99.

Howard, K. I., Cox, W. M., & Saunders, S. M. (1990). Attrition in substance abuse comparative treatment research: the illusion of randomization. In L. S. Onken & J. D. Blaine (Eds.), *Psychotherapy and counseling in the treatment of drug abuse* (DHHS Publication No. (ADM)90–1722, pp. 66–79). Washington, DC: NIDA Research Monograph 104.

Howard, K. I., Kopta, S. M., Krause, M. S., & Orlinsky, D. E. (1986). The dose–effect relationship in psychotherapy. *American Psychologist, 41,* 159–164.

Howard, K. I., Krause, M. S., & Orlinsky, D. E. (1986).

The attrition dilemma: Toward a new strategy for psychotherapy research. *Journal of Consulting and Clinical Psychology, 54,* 106–107.

Howard, K. I., Moras, K., Brill, P. L., Martinovich, Z., & Lutz, W. (1996). Evaluation of psychotherapy: Efficacy, effectiveness, and patient progress. *American Psychologist, 51,* 1059–1064.

Ilardi, S. S., & Craighead, W. E. (1994). The role of nonspecific factors in cognitive-behavior therapy for depression. *Clinical Psychology: Science & Practice, 1,* 138–156.

Jacobson, N. S., & Christensen, A. (1996). Studying the effectiveness of psychotherapy: How well can clinical trials do the job? *American Psychologist, 51,* 1031–1039.

Jacobson, N. S., & Truax, P. (1991). Clinical significance: A statistical approach to defining meaningful change in psychotherapy research. *Journal of Consulting and Clinical Psychology, 59,* 12–19.

Kazdin, A. E. (1979). Nonspecific treatment factors in psychotherapy outcome research. *Journal of Consulting & Clinical Psychology, 47,* 846–851.

Kazdin, A. E. (1994). Methodology, design, and evaluation in psychotherapy research. In A. E. Bergin & S. L. Garfield (Eds.), *Handbook of psychotherapy and behavior change* (4th ed., pp. 19–71). New York: Wiley.

Kazdin, A. E., Kratochwill, T. R., & VandenBos, G. R. (1986). Beyond clinical trials: Generalizing from research to practice. *Professional Psychology: Research and Practice, 17,* 391–398.

Kendall, P. C., & Brady, E. U. (1995). Comorbidity in the anxiety disorders of childhood. In K. D. Craig & K. S. Dobson (Eds.), *Anxiety and depression in adults and children.* Newbury Park, CA: Sage.

Kenny, D. A. (1979). *Correlation and causality.* New York: Wiley.

Kiesler, D. (1973). *The process of psychotherapy: Empirical foundations and systems of analysis.* Chicago: Aldine.

Klerman, G. L., Weissman, M. M., Rounsaville, B. J., & Chevron, E. S. (1984). *Interpersonal psychotherapy of depression.* New York: Basic Books.

Knapp, M. (Ed.) (1995). *The economic evaluation of mental health care.* London: Arena, Aldershot.

Kopta, S. M., Howard, K. I., Lowry, J. L., & Beutler, L. E. (1994). Patterns of symptomatic recovery in psychotherapy. *Journal of Consulting and Clinical Psychology, 62,* 1009–1016.

Kraemer, H. C., & Telch, C. F. (1992). Selection and utilization of outcome measures in psychiatric clinical trials: Report on the 1988 MacArthur Foundation Network I Methodology Institute. *Neuropsychopharmacology, 7,* 85–94.

Kraemer, H. C., & Thiemann, S. (1987). *How many subjects? Statistical power analysis in research,* Newbury Park, CA: Sage.

Lambert, M. J., & Ogles, B. M. (1988). Treatment manuals: Problems and promise. *Journal of Integrative and Eclectic Psychotherapy, 7,* 187–204.

Leach, C. (1979). *Introduction to statistics: A nonparametric approach for the social sciences.* New York: Wiley.

Lebowitz, B. D., & Rudorfer, M. V. (1998). Treatment research at the millennium: From efficacy to effectiveness. *Journal of Clinical Psychopharmacology, 18,* 1.

Levenson, H. (1995). *Time-limited dynamic psychotherapy: A guide to clinical practice.* New York: Basic Books.

Lueger, R. J. (1998). Using feedback on patient progress to predict outcome of psychotherapy. *Journal of Clinical Psychology, 54,* 383–393.

Margraf, J., Ehlers, A., Roth, W. T., Clark, D. B., Sheikh, J., Agras, W. S., & Taylor, C. B. (1991). How "blind" are double-blind studies? *Journal of Consulting and Clinical Psychology, 59,* 184–187.

McGrew, J. H., Bond, G. R., Dietzen, L., & Salyers, M. (1994). Measuring the fidelity of implementation of a mental health program model. *Journal of Consulting and Clinical Psychology, 62,* 670–678.

Mintz, J., Drake, R. E., & Crits-Christoph, P. (1996). Efficacy and effectiveness of psychotherapy: Two paradigms, one science. *American Psychologist, 51,* 1084–1085.

Multiple Risk Factor Intervention Trial Group. (1977). Statistical design considerations in the NHLI multiple risk factor intervention trial (MRFIT). *Journal of Chronic Disease, 30,* 261–275.

Ney, P. G., Collins, C., & Spensor, C. (1986). Double blind: Double talk or are there ways to do better research. *Medical Hypotheses, 21,* 119–126.

Newman, F. L., & Tejeda, M. J. (1996). The need for research that is designed to support decisions in the delivery of mental health services. *American Psychologist, 51,* 1040–1049.

O'Leary, K. D., & Borkovec, T. D. (1978). Conceptual, methodological, and ethical problems of placebo groups in psychotherapy research. *American Psychologist, 33,* 821–830.

Orlinsky, D. E., Grawe, K., & Parks, B. K. (1994). Process and outcome in psychotherapy—Noch einmal. In A. E. Bergin & S. L. Garfield (Eds.), *Handbook of psychotherapy and behavior change* (pp. 270–376). New York: Wiley.

Orlinsky, D. E., & Howard, K. I. (1986). Process and outcome in psychotherapy. In S. L. Garfield & A. E. Bergin (Eds.), *Handbook of psychotherapy and behavior change* (3rd ed. pp. 311–381). New York: Wiley.

Parloff, M. B. (1986). Placebo controls in psychotherapy research: a sine qua non or a placebo for research problems? *Journal of Consulting and Clinical Psychology, 54,* 79–87.

Rabkin, J. G., Markowitz, J. S., Stewart, J., McGrath, P., Harrison, W., Quitkin, F. M., & Klein, D. F. (1986). How blind is blind? Assessment of patient and doctor medication guesses in a placebo-controlled trial of imipramine and phenelzine. *Psychiatry Research, 19,* 75–86.

Rice, L. N., & Greenberg, L. S. (1984). *Patterns of change: Intensive analysis of psychotherapy process.* New York: Guilford Press.

Rosenthal, R., & Rosnow, R. L. (1991). *Essentials of behavioral research: Methods and data analysis.* New York: McGraw-Hill.

Rosnow, R. L., & Rosenthal, R. (1989). Statistical procedures and the justification of knowledge in psychological science. *American Psychologist, 44,* 1276–1284.

Roth, A., & Fonagy, P. (1996). *What works for whom? A critical review of psychotherapy research.* New York: Guilford Press.

Russell, R. L. (Ed.) (1987). *Language in psychotherapy: Strategies of discovery.* New York: Plenum.

Seligman, M. (1995). The effectiveness of psychotherapy. The *Consumer Report* study. *American Psychologist, 50,* 965–974.

Seligman, M. (1996). Science as an ally of practice. *American Psychologist, 51,* 1072–1079.

Shadish, W. R. (1995). The logic of generalization: Five

priciples common to experiments and ethnographies. *American Journal of Community Psychology, 23,* 419–428.

Shadish, W. R., Matt, G. E., Navarro, A. N., Siegle, G., Crits-Christoph, P., Hazelrigg, M. D., Jorm, A. F., Lyons, L. C., Nietzel, M. T., Prout, H. T., Robinson, L., Smith, M. L., Svartberg, M., & Weiss, B. (1997). Evidence that therapy works in clinically representative conditions. *Journal of Consulting and Clinical Psychology, 65,* 355–365.

Shaw, B. F. (1984). Specification of the training and evaluation of cognitive therapists for outcome studies. In J. B. W. Williams & R. L. Spitzer (Eds.), *Psychotherapy research: Where are we and where should we go?* (pp. 173–189). New York: Guilford Press.

Schulberg, H. C., Block, M. R., Madonia, M. J., Scott, P., Rodriguez, E., Imber, S. D., Perel, J., Lave, J., Houck, P. R., & Coulehan, J. L. (1996). Treating major depression in primary care practice: Eight-month clinical outcomes. *Archives of General Psychiatry, 53,* 913–919.

Speer, D. C. (1994). Can treatment research inform decision makers? Nonexperimental method issues and examples among older outpatients. *Journal of Consulting and Clinical Psychology, 62,* 560–568.

Strupp, H. H., & Hadley, S. (1979) Specific vs. nonspecific factors in psychotherapy. *Archives of General Psychotherapy, 36,* 1125–1136.

Task Force on Promotion and Dissemination of Psychological Procedures (1995). Training in and dissemination of empirically-validated psychological treatments: Report and recommendations. *The Clinical Psychologist, 48,* 3–24.

Waltz, J., Addis, M. E., Koerner, K., & Jacobson, N. S. (1993). Testing the integrity of a psychotherapy protocol: Assessment of adherence and competence. *Journal of Consulting and Clinical Psychology, 61,* 620–630.

Wei, L. J. (1978). An application of an urn model to the design of sequential controlled trials. *Journal of the American Statistical Association, 73,* 559–563.

Wells, K. B., & Sturm, R. (1996). Informing the policy process: From efficacy to effectiveness data on pharmacotherapy. *Journal of Consulting and Clinical Psychology, 64,* 638–645.

Wilson, G. T. (1996). Manual-based treatments: The clinical application of research findings. *Behavior Research and Therapy, 34,* 295–314.

Wolff, N., Helminiak, T. W., & Tebes, J. K. (1997). Getting the cost right in cost-effectiveness analyses. *American Journal of Psychiatry, 154,* 736–743.

Woody, S. R., & Kihlstrom, L. C. (1997). Outcomes, quality, and cost: Integrating psychotherapy and mental health services research. *Psychotherapy Research, 7,* 365–381.

Yates, B. T. (1996). *Analyzing costs, procedures, process, and outcomes in human services.* Thousand Oaks, CA: Sage.

Yates, B. T. (1997). From psychotherapy research to cost–outcome research: What resources are necessary to implement which therapy procedures that change what processes to yield which outcomes? *Psychotherapy Research, 7,* 345–364.

3.11
Mental Health Services Research

WILLIAM A. HARGREAVES
University of California, San Francisco, CA, USA
RALPH A. CATALANO, TEH-WEI HU
University of California, Berkeley, CA, USA
and
BRIAN CUFFEL
United Behavioral Health, San Francisco, CA, USA

3.11.1 INTRODUCTION

The US National Institute of Mental Health blueprint for improving services (NIMH, 1991; Attkisson et al., 1992; Lalley et al., 1992; Mechanic et al., 1992; Steinwachs et al., 1992) broadened and clarified the scope of mental health services research. New and experienced investigators trying to understand mental health services research, however, may find it hard to comprehend the multiple perspectives on the field and how seemingly disparate research agendas contribute to a unified body of knowledge. Nevertheless, a unified view of the field can be gained by reflecting on key constructs and the causal paths that connect them.

Mental health services research is inherently multidisciplinary, drawing from clinical psychology, psychiatry, health economics, epidemiology, sociology, political science, social work, nursing, pharmacology, pharmacy, general medicine, and public health. This multidisciplinary character is reflected in the authorship of this article, including two clinical psychologists, an urban planner, and a health economist. Many clinical psychologists are contributing to mental health services research and more are needed.

In spite of great heterogeneity of methodology, all of services research can be viewed as examining some aspect of a nested system of causal processes that influence the mental health and well being of society. At the inner core are the effects of specific services on individual users of these services. These effects are contained within the broader effects of the way services are organized into local or other end-user service systems, how services are financed, and how these services systems impact relevant target populations. These effects of the organization and financing of services are in turn influenced by policy innovations of local, state, national, and international scope that influence the functioning of local service systems. These three domains of effects correspond to different types of services research: cost-outcome studies, service system studies, and policy studies.

The inner core of services research, cost-outcome studies, in turn grew out of an established tradition of clinical efficacy research utilizing the randomized clinical trial. The Agency for Health Care Policy Research of the US Government, in an attempt to foster services research, popularized a distinction between efficacy and effectiveness research in the evaluation of medical technologies (Salive, Mayfield, & Weissman, 1990). Efficacy studies evaluate the effect of an intervention under optimal conditions, when implemented by highly skilled clinicians using comprehensive treatment protocols under expert supervision, and where the intervention is usually delivered to patients with a single, well-defined disorder. Effectiveness studies complement the findings of efficacy studies by evaluating interventions in conditions, settings, and target populations that reflect the usual circumstances in the delivery of services, often giving attention to long-term effects of treatments on both costs and outcomes. The term "cost-outcome" is used to avoid confusion between "effectiveness" studies and "cost-effectiveness" studies, since the latter use a specific subset of cost-outcome methods.

Cost-outcome research remains conceptually and methodologically linked to efficacy research. The refinement of clinical trial methodology over several decades has established a useful state of the art that includes random assignment to treatment, appropriate blinding, complete follow-up with "intent-to-treat" analyses, and improved statistical handling of longitudinal data with missing or unevenly spaced measurement occasions, as discussed in Chapter 3, this volume. Cost-outcome studies involve the extension and improvement of clinical trials methodology necessary to address broader questions of generalizability, accessibility, acceptability, cost, and long-term outcome of interventions.

This chapter contrasts efficacy research and the three types of services research on several dimensions, and gives examples of each. These

research models differ on a number of features: (i) their typical unit of analysis; (ii) the outcomes of primary interest; (iii) their typical design strategies; (iv) the independent variables usually experimentally controlled or sampled by the investigator; and (v) the hypothesized causal variables of greatest interest. Table 1 summarizes these features for each of the four models. As each model is discussed it will illustrate the causal pathways of usual interest, as portrayed in Figures 1 to 4.

3.11.2 EFFICACY RESEARCH

Efficacy studies examine the effects of a well-defined treatment or other service on the clinical and rehabilitation outcomes of individual recipients of care. Figure 1 is familiar to clinical trials investigators and shows the key groups of variables and causal paths of primary interest. Fifteen causal paths, numbered A1 to A15, encompass the scientific focus of efficacy research.

The ultimate outcomes of efficacy studies are reductions in illness symptoms, changes in behavior, or improvements in skills. Outcomes are usually measured over weeks or months rather than years. The unit of analysis is the person who consumes services. The typical study will compare an innovative treatment to either a placebo, an accepted "standard" treatment, or some other control for attention and expectation effects. Double-blind controls are employed to minimize bias that might be caused by expectation effects on outcomes and on judgments of outcomes. When the blind is likely to "leak" or is otherwise impossible to maintain, blinding of interviewers and raters is sometimes attempted as a partial effort to reduce bias.

The causal chain of primary interest is usually causal path A10, the effect of the implemented service on ultimate outcomes. Investigators may also be interested in the mediation of this effect through the use and "receipt" of service and through proximal outcomes. Thus, several aspects of the whole cascade of effects A1 to A8 may be examined. Even more broadly, efficacy studies may take account of the characteristics of the person at baseline such as diagnosis, severity of disability, history of treatment compliance, and stage of illness in order to understand their modulation of intervention effects (A11 and A13). Similarly, the effects of the person's preservice life context (e.g., homelessness, poverty, social support system, entitlements, insurance coverage) may be examined, along with life context during and after service (A14 to A15). In efficacy studies,

Table 1 Typical features of different research models.

Feature	Research model			
	Efficacy	Cost-outcome	Service system	Policy
Unit of analysis	Individual representing a defined disorder group	Individual representing a system target population	Individuals in target population; Aggregate subgroup status, use, or change	Community service systems
Outcomes of primary interest	Symptom improvement; Rehabilitative outcome; Humanistic outcome; Public safety	Efficacy outcomes; Societal cost and payer mix; Preference-weighted outcomes or utilities	Service demand, access, and use; Service cost; Prevalence of psychiatric impairment	Local service policy adoption, innovation; Service cost; Prevalence of psychiatric impairment
Typical design strategies	Randomized clinical trial	Randomized trial with epidemiological specification of target population; Quasi-experiment	Policy experiment; Population survey; Org-network analysis; MIS analysis; Economic modeling and computer simulation	Policy experiment; Population survey; Org-network analysis; MIS analysis; Economic modeling and computer simulation
Variables experimentally controlled or set by investigator	Mental health system environment; Clinical environment and service context; Baseline characteristics of subjects; Amount, type and delivery of services to study subjects	Mental health system environment; Clinical environment and service context; Characteristics of available services	Mental health system environment; Policy innovation process	Population demographics; Government structure
Hypothesized causal variables of interest	Service delivery and receipt	Service delivery and receipt	Local system organization, financing, management, and innovation.	Policy innovation above the local level

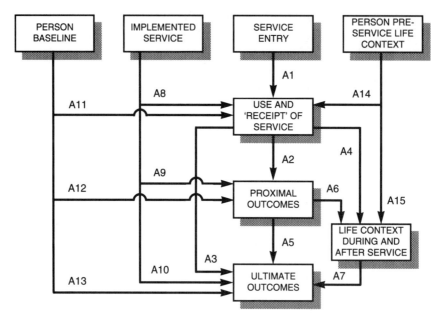

Figure 1   Efficacy studies.

however, the goal is usually focussed on causal path A10 while other causal paths are viewed as "nuisance" effects or "artifacts" that threaten a valid assessment of path A10.

The typical design strategy is the randomized trial. The design of efficacy studies typically emphasizes the "internal" validity of the estimate of the effect of a treatment, taking care to exclude alternative explanations for the observed effects, such as baseline or post-attrition differences in persons receiving different services.

Efficacy studies may focus on the mechanism of action of the intervention. Mechanism can often be inferred from analyses of "intermediate" variables that may account for the service effect, such as service use and "receipt" (e.g., medication or psychosocial treatment adherence, regularity of appointments, attitude toward the services), proximal outcomes (e.g., learning a communication skill, immediate symptomatic response to a medication), and changes in living setting or social support system resulting from the intervention.

The quest for internal validity and adequate statistical power often leads to considerable sacrifice of "external" validity, or generalizability. Service entry by study subjects is taken as a given, and usually little effort is made to relate the characteristics of the subject sample to those of the target population. Indeed, the usual efficacy study purposely employs narrow criteria to produce a homogeneous sample of subjects with few "distracting" sources of variance, such as comorbid illnesses, that may

be quite prevalent in the population likely to receive the innovative intervention. Subjects are recruited from some convenient source that can yield enough subjects who qualify and will consent, making the assumption (usually unstated and unexamined) that the clients entering screening represent the target population on the dimensions that matter for generalization.

3.11.2.1 Examples of Efficacy Research

The National Institute of Mental Health "Treatment Strategies in Schizophrenia" co-operative study is an example of a late-stage, complex efficacy study. Schooler, Keith, Severe, & Matthews (1989) and Schooler et al. (1997) compared maintenance treatment strategies for people with a recent schizophrenia relapse whose family is in the picture. The study assessed the impact of dose reduction of antipsychotic medication and family treatment on relapse and rehospitalization during maintenance treatment (paths A1 to A15 in Figure 1). Standard dose medication was compared to continuous low-dose or targeted treatment, in which active medication was used only upon incipient signs of relapse. A widely studied and effective type of family intervention was compared to a much less intensive family intervention in the context of assertive medication management and ongoing supportive assistance to patients and families. It was hypothesized that the more intensive family intervention would make the conservative low-dose and targeted medication strategies more effective, perhaps as effective as standard-dose but with less burden from medication side-effects. The three-by-two design thus produced six treatment combinations, and the interaction between dosing strategy and family intervention level was of primary interest. The investigators found that both continuous low-dose and targeted medication increased the use of "rescue" medication and the risk of symptomatic relapse, but only targeted treatment increased hospitalization compared to standard-dose medication. The two family interventions showed essentially no differences in effectiveness, and family intervention did not interact with dose effects. There were two important policy implications of the findings: (i) targeted treatment, which had been advocated by some investigators, should not be adopted as a standard maintenance strategy, and (ii) the intensive family interventions that had been shown in previous research to be effective compared to no family intervention are more intensive than needed when provided in the context of good continuity of maintenance treatment and initial education and support of family members.

Like most efficacy studies, however, the primary focus was on mechanism of action rather than policy generalization. All sites were university-affiliated clinics, not sites picked to represent the "usual" circumstances of schizophrenia treatment. The design limited the ability to generalize to patients who did not reconstitute within six months of their most recent psychotic episode.

Nevertheless this study also had some features of cost-outcome research. "Ordinary" clinicians were recruited and trained as family clinicians, the study was carried out in five sites allowing a test of whether the findings generalized across site, and costs were assessed, although cost analysis was not part of the original design.

The methodology for efficacy research is well developed and relies heavily on the randomized clinical trial. The field reached a reasonable consensus on efficacy methodology in clinical psychopharmacology in the 1970s, and in psychotherapy efficacy research since the mid-1980s.

3.11.3 COST-OUTCOME RESEARCH

Cost-outcome studies of mental health services expand the scope of efficacy research to address key questions related to the effects of mental health services delivered in typical care settings. Figure 2 illustrates the expanded causal paths examined in cost-outcome studies. These include the same causal paths (A1 to A15) from efficacy studies (Figure 1), but include additional factors not addressed in efficacy trials (B1 to B21). Access to services is often examined in cost-outcome trials (Paths B1 to B9), and cost-outcome studies always measure the use and cost of services, including services other than the experimental interventions themselves (B10, B14, and B15).

The ultimate outcomes of cost-outcome studies are broad, including clinical outcomes (illness symptoms, side effects), rehabilitative outcomes (productivity), humanistic outcomes (life satisfaction, family psychological burden), and public safety outcomes (disruptive behavior, assaultiveness, suicidality, criminal behavior). Cost-outcome studies also may consider determinants of outcomes resulting from a wider range of causes including program case mix, consumer life context, and service cost/payer mix (B3, B7 to B9).

More importantly, perhaps, there is a fundamental shift in the perspective on outcomes in cost-outcome studies (Hargreaves, Shumway, Hu, & Cuffel, 1997). The ubiquitous fact of multiple, poorly correlated outcomes in mental disorders creates a problem that cannot be ignored in cost-outcome studies, since policy conclusions regarding the choice of alternative interventions depend on the relation of overall cost to overall outcome.

Different approaches to integrating outcomes are reflected in four different types of cost-outcome studies Cost-minimization studies examine only costs, in situations in which outcomes are known or assumed to be equal (B10, B14, B15). Cost-benefit studies focus on outcomes that can be monetized, such as labor force productivity, and analyze either cost-benefit ratios or net benefits (benefits minus costs) (B11, B16, B17). Cost-effectiveness studies leave outcomes in their natural units, and cost-effectiveness ratios are computed either on single outcomes (e.g., cost per suicide prevented) or on a global or integrated outcome score (e.g., cost per one unit of level-of-functioning score gained) (B12, B18, B19). Cost-utility studies utilize cost-utility ratios, where utility is a preference-weighted unitary outcome (e.g., cost per quality-adjusted life year gained) (B13, B20, B21). All of these studies are comparative—no intervention is "cost-effective" by itself. The cost-outcome performance of an intervention is always judged against a policy-relevant standard, such as treatment as usual. Cost-outcome ratios are not needed to compare interventions when the less costly intervention produces better outcomes. When an innovation is both more expensive and more

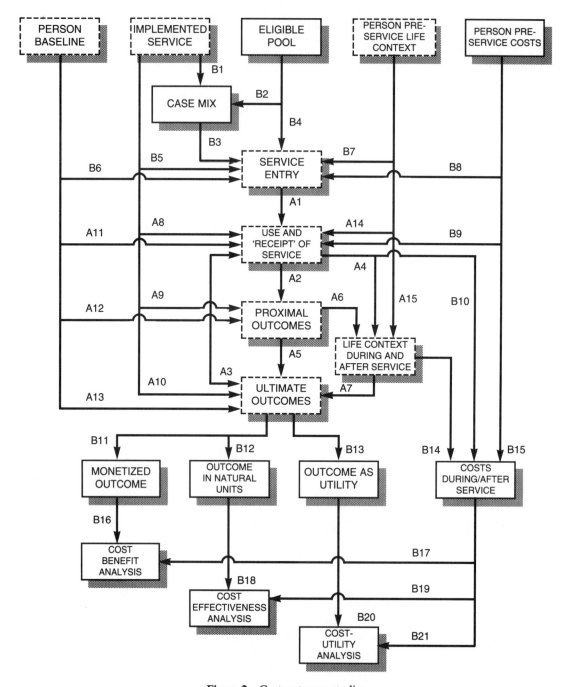

Figure 2 Cost-outcome studies.

effective than standard care, a common type of cost-outcome ratio compares the differential cost per differential outcome gained by the innovation compared to standard care.

Cost, as a consequence of an intervention, has its own measurement technology that has been carefully worked out in econometrics and health economics (Drummond, Brandt, Luce, & Rovira, 1993; Drummand, Stoddard, & Torrance, 1997; Sloan, 1995). Economic theory provides the conceptual underpinning of cost estimation methods. In a theoretically ideal competitive market, goods and services are exchanged at prices that reflect their true value. In the real world market quality varies, and in health care the operation of a free, competitive market is impaired because buyers and sellers have inadequate information, and because third-party payers and government regulation also introduce market distortions. The theory of welfare economics provides an alternative way to estimate the true value of goods and services when market pricing is not accurate. Under these circumstances the true value is estimated by considering the "opportunity cost" of resources. This value estimate, called a "shadow price," is the value of a resource were it to be used for its "next-best" purpose.

Economists also developed the concept of "societal" cost to describe a cost perspective of an entire economic system, without regard to who pays the cost. Societal cost is accepted widely as a standard reference method in cost-outcome research (Drummond et al., 1997). Most policy questions, however, also need to be informed by information about cost burdens to particular payers. For example, if a new intervention results in the same cost as usual care (from a societal perspective), but shifts the payment burden from the state and federal government to local government, or from government to the ill person's family, the payer information is important. Economists call shifts in payer burden a "distributional effect" of the innovative intervention, since it distributes the grief in a new way.

The difference in societal cost of two intervention strategies is the difference of the value of resources consumed or lost. Resources consumed (e.g., treatment activities) are called "direct" costs, while resources lost (e.g., time prevented from working, which produces resources) are called "indirect" costs. The amounts of resources are measured in natural units (hours of psychologist time, days of hospitalization), but values are assigned to these resource units by a separate process. In this way, questions about the accuracy of methods for measuring resource use can be examined separately from questions about the appropriateness of the values assigned to each type of resource.

Seven types of cost elements are often considered when planning mental health cost-outcome research: mental health treatment, physical health care, criminal justice procedures, social services, time and productivity of the patient and of family caregivers, other family costs, and sources and amounts of patient income. Different interventions and target populations vary greatly in the relative emphasis that needs to be given these seven types of cost. The most accurate measures of consumption and the most careful estimates of value are usually reserved for the most commonly used resources, especially the new activities introduced in the innovative intervention being studied.

Expert judgment is required to choose an appropriate balance of methods and to apply them skillfully. In most situations neither health economists nor clinical investigators can do it

alone, and effective collaboration is required. Hargreaves et al. (1997) provide an introduction to cost-outcome methods for mental health research, designed to prepare noneconomist investigators for this type of collaboration.

The unit of analysis in cost-outcome studies is still the person, but attention is given to the person as a member of a target population, the paths from target population membership to service, the generalization of the findings to this target population, and even the impact of service provision or access policies on the whole target population.

The typical design strategy is the randomized cost-effectiveness trial focused on both internal and external validity, comparing a service innovation to standard services, and estimating the impact on the total target population as well as individual members of that target population. Ideally the size and character of the target population is estimated, and a random sample is invited to participate in the study. More often, a series of analyses tracks the biases in selection from target population, to potential subject pool, to recruited subject sample, to analyzable subject sample.

In these decision-oriented studies, certain "standard" features of efficacy trials, such as double-blind conditions, may be avoided in order to enhance external validity. For example, an open study does not require sham procedures such as unnecessary blood samples, or active placebos that mimic side effects, both of which may obscure the relative acceptability of services being compared. This may increase risks to internal validity, as when an open study allows rater bias and alters client expectation effects. These problems should not be ignored, although they are less troublesome when conclusions hinge on long-term social and vocation functioning improvement rather than short-term symptom improvement.

Despite the broader scope of cost-outcome studies, several types of variables are taken as given or set by the investigator, including the service model, the character of the target population, the consumer's baseline clinical characteristics and life context, and preservice utilization and costs. In service system research, by contrast, it will be seen that investigators may view these variables as outcomes.

3.11.3.1 Examples of Cost-outcome Studies

A study of assertive community treatment was an exemplary cost-benefit study (Stein & Test, 1980; Test & Stein, 1980; Weisbrod, 1983; Weisbrod, Test, & Stein, 1980). In this study the experimental treatment was applied for 14 months. Subjects in the experimental program had less time in the hospital, more time in independent living situations, better employment records, increased life satisfaction, decreased symptoms, and improved treatment adherence. Family and community burden did not appear to increase (A1, A3, A4). Societal cost was found to be slightly lower in the experimental treatment when wages earned were considered monetary benefits and welfare support was considered a cost (B10, B11, B14 to B17). Thus, the innovative program showed both an economic advantage and a psychosocial advantage.

Research on assertive community treatment (ACT) for persons with severe mental illness is the strongest and most coherent body of cost-effectiveness investigation in mental health. More than a dozen additional randomized trials of ACT were published from 1986 to 1996 and the findings have been critiqued and summarized in many reviews (Bond, McGrew, & Fekete, 1995; Burns & Santos, 1995; Chamberlain & Rapp, 1991; Hargreaves & Shumway, 1989; Olfson, 1990; Rubin, 1992; Santos, Henggeler, Burns, Arana, & Meisler, 1995; Scott & Dixon, 1995; Solomon, 1992; Test, 1992). Studies in the 1990s utilize stronger usual care conditions, reflecting the widespread adoption of linkage case management in the USA (Burns & Santos, 1995; Randolph, 1992). These studies are refining understanding of the conditions and target groups in which assertive community treatment is cost-efficient or has such superior outcome in spite of increased cost that it can be considered cost-effective relative to available service alternatives.

A randomized cost-effectiveness study of the atypical antipsychotic clozapine for persons with schizophrenia was carried out by Essock; (Essock, Hargreaves, Covell, & Goethe, 1996a; Essock et al., 1996b). It featured a complete enumeration of clozapine-eligible patients in an entire state hospital system, and a mix of random and purposive selection of members of the eligible pool to be offered study entry during a time when clozapine was rationed by the state hospital system and study participation was essentially the only route of access to clozapine treatment (B1 to B9). Study subjects were randomized to clozapine or usual antipsychotic medication in an open study (A1 to A15). An effectiveness and cost evaluation was carried out over two years of treatment (B10, B12, B14, B15, B18, B19). Clozapine showed fewer side effects with some advantage in reduced restrictiveness of care and reduced assaultive or disruptive behavior. In this long-stay state hospital patient group (mean length of their hospital episode was over eight years) no effect was seen on time from study entry to hospital discharge. In contrast, once discharged, clozapine patients were much less likely to be readmitted, resulting in saved hospital days. Full cost analyses have not been completed, but saved hospital costs may fully offset the higher price of the novel antipsychotic medication plus the increased cost of community care when patients are out of the hospital. This study illustrates how the results of an effectiveness trial comparing a new treatment to usual practice can be more conservative than an efficacy trial comparing a novel medication to a single alternative. Previous efficacy trials had shown larger effects on symptom improvement, typically in patients who were in an acute illness exacerbation, not the relatively stable but still symptomatic long-stay state hospital patients who showed lower baseline scores on symptom scales.

A study by Henggeler, Melton, and Smith (1992) illustrates how research can have an intermediate position between efficacy and cost-outcome research. Henggeler studied "multi-systemic therapy" (MST) as an intervention for serious juvenile offenders and their multiproblem families. Yoked pairs of qualified subjects randomized to multisystemic therapy or usual services were referred by the South Carolina Department of Youth Services. Endpoints included family relations, peer relations, symptomatology, social competence, self-reported delinquency, number of arrests, and weeks of incarceration. Compared to youths who received usual services, youths who received MST had fewer arrests and self-reported offenses and spent an average of 10 fewer weeks incarcerated during a 59-week study period. Families assigned to MST reported increased family cohesion and decreased youth aggression in peer relations. Detailed cost analyses were not reported in this initial publication. This is one of the first controlled trials of interventions with this difficult target population to show significant beneficial outcomes and clinically important effects. The success of the intervention plausibly is related to its addressing each of the major factors found in multidimensional causal models of antisocial behavior in adolescents (Henggeler, 1991).

This study can be considered efficacy research in that it was delivered under close supervision of those who designed the intervention, and further evidence is needed that its effectiveness can be maintained when the intervention is taught and supervised by others. In addition, the statistical power of the initial study is limited, so while large and statistically significant effects were observed, effect size in the population still needs to be estimated more accurately before basic efficacy can be considered to be established. Features more like cost-outcome research include the construction of a subject pool that is plausibly representative of an important target population, and (except for service supervision) the intervention reflects much of the reality of providing such services in ordinary settings of care. The study can also provide preliminary information about the cost of the intervention and the cost savings that may result from its effective implementation.

The methodology for cost-outcome studies is a combination of cost-effectiveness methods from health economics, mental health epidemiology methods, and randomized controlled trial methods, applied to intervention processes that sometimes take place over several years. The merger seems to require ambitious and expensive multidisciplinary studies, but that conclusion is probably incorrect. The new investigator can work in this area by learning the methods and gathering appropriate consultants and collaborators. A workable state of the art is reasonably well advanced and accessible (Drummond et al., 1997; Hargreaves et al., 1997; Knapp, 1995; Sloan, 1995; Yates, 1995).

3.11.4 SERVICE SYSTEM RESEARCH

Research on local mental health service systems examines the effects of organization, financing, and service delivery mechanisms on utilization of services, costs, outcomes, cost-effectiveness, and community prevalence. The object of study, mental health service systems and community outcomes, are of broader scope than phenomena affecting the relative cost effectiveness of a circumscribed group of services for a specific problem or disorder. Therefore, cost-outcome research on mental health systems draws on economics, organizational sociology, epidemiology, and political science for explanatory theory and method. A mental health system serves an array of target populations whose service needs differ, yet these target populations also compete for many of the same services. Therefore it is reasonable to view system impact as its effect on a value-weighted sum of its impact on the prevalence of the array of mental disorders and their resulting impairments.

The ultimate outcomes in service system research are the prevalence and disability consequences of various mental disorders in the population. Intermediate outcomes include demand for mental health services, access and use of those services, and outcomes of those services. More broadly, the ultimate outcome is

seen as the quality of the life of all members of the community, to the extent that it is affected by psychiatric disorders. Mental health systems and system managers work within a political, fiscal, and organizational context to focus service resources on high priority target populations so that the overall cost-effectiveness or cost-utility of the system is maximized.

Service system utility implies value judgments not only about trade-offs in outcomes for a particular target population, but trade-offs in the value of higher levels of functioning in one target population as against another. For example, after many years during which community programs were focused on improving the level of functioning of clients and families with serious life problems but who were not severely and persistently mentally ill, these values were called into question, and service programs shifted their emphasis to the latter group. While many factors influenced this change (Mechanic, 1987), including a rise in the relative cost of hospital care, the change also reflected an implicit value judgment that serving the severely and persistently mentally ill in the community was of overriding importance to the overall utility of the mental health service system. This implicit utility judgement could never be examined explicitly, because the complexity of the problem exceeded capacity to study it. An effort to identify the parameters of this problem may clarify the advances in theory and method needed to address such issues.

The system dynamics of prevalence, demand, utilization, and outcome can be seen as interacting with the service process, which in turn interacts with the system structure. Process and structure subsystems may experience innovation or innovation may be introduced experimentally. In either case, innovation can give the investigator an opportunity to learn something about causal phenomena in the system.

A simplistic view of system dynamics (Figure 3) is that different levels of prevalence cause different levels of service seeking behavior, that service seeking leads to utilization, that utilization influences outcomes for individuals, and these outcomes change prevalence and disability. Some variables of interest in each of these subsystems can illustrate the possibility for more realistic models.

Prevalence is used here to include not only the local prevalence of persons with psychiatric disorders and subgroups of such persons, but the distribution within these populations of living independence/freedom, productivity, homelessness, life satisfaction, public safety, and the societal cost of illness. These valued

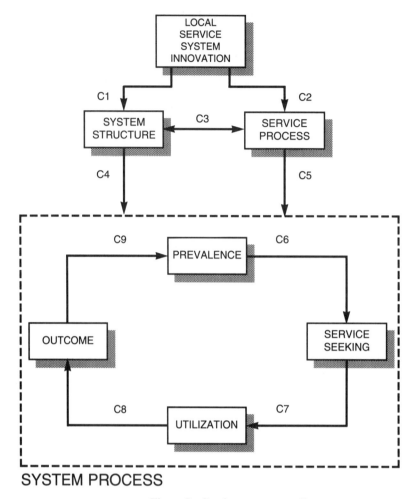

Figure 3 Service systems studies.

conditions and costs define the momentary utility of the human service system with regard to persons with psychiatric disorders. This utility can be influenced by effective human services. It can also be influenced by migration, system induced or otherwise. An innovation that incurs some marginal cost can be evaluated by comparing this cost to the change in utility that one is able to attribute to the innovation.

Priorities for various target populations and levels of disability are an unavoidable part of any definition of system utility. An egalitarian society aims to maximize cost utility without differential weighing of gender, age, socio-economic status, ethnic group, residence location, or reason for disability. While real-world policy is formulated from narrower perspectives, it is useful for science to identify the larger impact of narrow policies. In the short term more modest research goals should be sought. Practical compromises may include restricting study samples to persons known by the service system to be in the target population, and considering only expenditures within the mental

health system. This is a narrower perspective on target populations and cost than suggested for cost-outcome studies, in order to allow greater research investment to be focused on measuring a larger variety of intermediate effects and associated causes.

Service seeking results from experienced need and the lack of social supports (Alegria et al., 1991; Freeman et al., 1992), and is affected independently by economic conditions and job insecurity (Catalano, Rook, & Dooley, 1986). The need may be experienced by the ill person, by family members, or as a community response to illness-related disruptive behavior. Service seeking produces demand on each type of service provided in the system or seen as needed by each target population subgroup. There may be a pattern of over-capacity demand experienced by specific services, with demand-buffering patterns and consequent generation of secondary demand, that is, inappropriately high levels of care and lack of access to desired services. Cost-outcome and service system research should inform both providers and consumers about the relative value of alternative mental health services, enabling them to make informed choices about which services to supply or to consume.

Utilization is the actual amount of each type of service consumed by various subgroups of persons in the target population, and in some cases by other clients who compete for the same services. It is this consumption and its effects on outcome and cost compared to what would occur in the absence of service or with alternative services that are often the focus of research attention.

Outcome includes those changes in symptoms, functioning, life satisfaction, and public safety that result from the consumption of services. The strengthening of natural supports and the reduction of risk of relapse might be been as relevant outcomes. At the individual level these are the same variables as the prevalence conditions. Whether outcomes lead to changes in prevalence variables depends on the proportion of the target population that consumes appropriate and effective services, and the degree of offsetting changes that may occur in the rest of the target population.

The unit of analysis may be the individual for purposes of measurement although there is greater attention to the characteristics of the population from which samples are drawn. For example, service system research often attempts to make inferences about the effects of service system characteristics on mental health outcomes in the general population. In this regard, the unit of analysis can be the geographic area served by the local service system, particularly when the focus of study is aggregate statistics such as per capita rates of violence or suicide measured over time or across regions.

The causal chain of interest includes three broad aspects of local area service systems that are common sources of independent variables in service systems research. These are system structure, service process, and system innovation.

System structure includes a study of local system expenditures and expenditure decisions, the organization governance, networks, and environments, service system size, integration, and cohesiveness and local provider reimbursement policies, benefit eligibilities, risk-sharing incentives, and managed care strategies for monitoring and controlling the delivery of care.

Service process at the system level might be viewed as consisting of two types of variables: (i) service capacity mix (how many beds or slots of various types) and the unit costs of each type; and (ii) services integration methods such as linkage case management, assertive community treatment, entry and exit criteria, and treatment guidelines. For each service program or provider in the system one might examine management style, staff morale, and adherence to system-wide service delivery standards. Adequate measures of these aspects of the mental health delivery system need to be developed, especially such dynamic processes as eligibility criteria and service practices that shift in the demand-buffering process, or transient degradation of service capacity that may occur during rapid system change.

Local service system innovation can be viewed from a research perspective more as an event than a subsystem. Innovation, and indeed any change including financial disaster and dramatic downsizing, is of interest to the investigator because change offers the opportunity to study causal effects. This is particularly true when a similar change occurs or is introduced experimentally in a number of local mental health systems, allowing better strategies for distinguishing the effect of the change from other variations in system performance.

The typical design strategies that are employed in the study of local service systems draw from economics, organizational sociology, and epidemiology, in addition to traditional clinical research and cost-outcome research. Studies of the variability in local mental health policy often involve economic analysis of utilization and expenditure patterns across counties or other local geographical areas. Often system level changes resulting from imposed changes in conditions or local innovation facilitate naturalistic experiments, pre-post designs, or time series analyses that allow one to study the effects of these system changes on service seeking, use, and outcomes. States and the federal government in the USA are also seeking to learn from "pilot" innovation using experimental or quasi-experimental approaches, in collaboration with investigators.

The Substance Abuse and Mental Health Services Administration has sponsored a multi-state experiment comparing two experimentally introduced innovations in local systems of care focused on homeless persons with dual disorders (severe mental illness and a substance use disorder). State mental health authorities were invited to propose pairs of sites to undertake a program to reduce homelessness among substance abusing persons with mental illness by increasing case management and housing supports. Both sites in each applicant state were to propose two specific innovations appropriate for their site: (i) methods for delivering augmented case finding and case management services, and (ii) methods to achieve increased system integration to enhance services for homeless persons with dual disorders. Site pairs were evaluated for their suitability for the demonstration and selected by reviewers. Selected pairs of sites received funding for initial engagement, case management, and follow-up of a comparable cohort of clients, while one site of each pair was randomly selected to receive additional "services integration" funding. Thus, this design addresses causal paths C1 to C5 and C6 to C8 in Figure 3, although it does not examine changes in the prevalence of this homeless subpopulation (C9). Preliminary results have been reported showing that the additional services integration funding augmented the effectiveness of services for the target population over and above the provision of augmented engagement and case management services (CMHS, 1996; Robert Rosenheck, personal communication, November 20, 1996).

Not all service system research requires a large budget. Some dramatic system changes occur with little warning but can be investigated retrospectively using time series methods. For example, Fenton, Catalano, and Hargreaves (1996) studied the impact of passage of Proposition 187, a ballot initiative in California mandating that undocumented immigrants be ineligible for most state-funded health services and requiring health providers to report persons suspected of being undocumented to the Immigration and Naturalization Service. Hispanic-Americans widely felt this as a racist initiative specifically directed at them. Though quickly blocked in court, publicity about the initiative and its level of support (passing in 50 of 58 counties) was hypothesized by the investigators to cause young Hispanics to avoid preventive psychiatric services (outpatient mental health treatment) putting them at risk for increased use of emergency services at some subsequent time. This hypothesis could be seen as involving causal path C6 in Figure 3, though (to anticipate) it also reaches up to causal paths D5 and D7 in Figure 4, discussed in the Policy Studies section.

The investigators analyzed data on weekly initiation of public outpatient mental health episodes and psychiatric emergency service contacts in the City and County of San Francisco for 67 weeks before and 23 weeks after the date of the election. Young Hispanics were compared to young non-Hispanic whites using Box-Jenkins time series methods. Initiation of outpatient services by young Hispanics dropped significantly the week of the election and remained low compared to use by non-Hispanic whites.

To refine their hypothesis of a delayed effect on emergency services use, the investigators examined the "natural" variation in the initiation of outpatient mental health services and its relation to emergency service episodes. Low rates of outpatient initiations were correlated significantly with high levels of emergency service episodes six weeks later in the client population as a whole. Looking at emergency use by young Hispanics (controlling for use by young non-Hispanic whites), the investigators found significantly higher use of emergency services six weeks after the election. Analyses of older populations showed neither of these effects of the election. Thus, the effect was specific to the typical age range of undocumented Hispanic residents. For a relatively nontechnical introduction to time-series methods see Catalano and Serxner (1987), and for more detail see Box, Jenkins and Reinsel (1994).

Time-series analysis also can be used to test hypotheses about service system policies. In a provocative study, Catalano and McConnell (1996) tested the "quarantine" theory of involuntary commitment, which asserts that involuntary commitment of persons judged to be a danger to others reduces violent crime—a theory vigorously challenged by civil libertarians. This hypothesis could be seen as encompassing the entire causal loop in Figure 3 of paths C6 to C9.

No one has much enthusiasm for carrying out an experimental test of this theory. The investigators tested the specific hypothesis that the daily incidence of reported assaults and batteries by males is related negatively to the incidence of involuntary commitments of males as a danger to others during the preceding two days—the more men committed, the fewer the subsequent arrests. Involuntary commitments on the day of the reported assault were omitted because the direction of causality is ambiguous. Using data from the City and County of San Francisco for 303 days, the investigators carried out a time-series analysis that supported ($p < .05$) the conclusion that increased commitment of men judged a danger to others reduces the incidence of assault and battery offences. Score: paternalists, 1, civil libertarians, 0. The discussion continues.

These three examples illustrate that service system changes of interest may be introduced intentionally (a new intervention for homelessness), or arrive as unpredictable exogenous shocks (Proposition 187), or arise from endemic variations that all organizations exhibit by virtue of their inability to behave with perfect consistency over time (variation in the number of involuntary commitments). This third type of variation is of particular interest to managers of mental health systems. They manage organizations to minimize this inconsistency, but theories of rational management as well as common sense suggest that the effort to do so

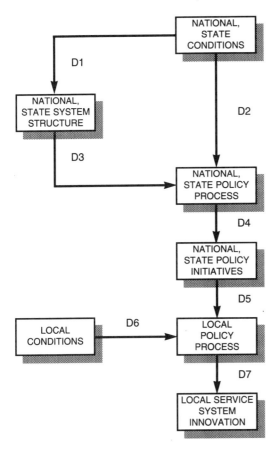

Figure 4 Policy studies.

should cost less than the benefit of greater standardization of output. Managed care is the health system's version of scientific management, and one of its consistency tools is the treatment guideline or algorithm.

Research on the impact of treatment guidelines and algorithms is an important and growing area of service systems research. Suppose an investigator wishes to test the hypothesis that new treatment guidelines improve outcomes while containing cost. The guidelines might be both restrictive (specifying when a procedure should not be provided even when sought by the client) and prescriptive (specifying when a procedure should be recommended proactively when the client fails to seek it). It is interesting to consider the design issues posed by this research goal.

To test the investigator's hypothesis for a particular disorder, the investigator needs to identify or articulate the relevant restrictive and prescriptive guidelines. Identifying potential health risks and benefits from these guidelines compared to usual practice will guide the choice of outcomes and the length of observation needed to detect each outcome.

In implementing the study the investigator needs to demonstrate that the implementation has induced optimal or near-optimal guideline adherence by health care providers, has induced it relatively rapidly, and has maintained adherence consistently over the long haul. This will usually require prompting and monitoring techniques, which are part of the cost of the intervention being tested. The investigator also will want to demonstrate that the usual-care control condition had not undergone similar practice changes. Another concern is that guidelines may alter the detection of the targeted health conditions. The investigator needs a way to determine whether detection of the target conditions is altered in either experimental or usual care. Given these possible diagnostic screening effects, the investigator has the problem of designing an unbiased way to select "tracer" patients to assay outcomes in both experimental and control conditions.

These competing threats to validity demand well-articulated hypotheses and carefully chosen design compromises. Rather than randomizing patients, an investigator may decide to randomize clinician practices or clinical sites to experimental and usual-care conditions. Cluster randomization often is used in educational research, where an innovative teaching method is randomized to teachers or classrooms (Murray et al., 1994). Thus, individual subjects are nested within the unit of randomization. This does not preclude examining individual baseline characteristics in the analysis, however.

Power is limited by the number of units randomized, but error variance is also reduced (and power increased) by increasing the number of subjects within each randomization unit. For each of the primary outcome measures, the power analysis informs the investigator about trade-offs between the number of randomization units and the number of subjects within each unit. The efficiency of the design will further depend on the cost of adding units versus the cost of adding subjects within units. Feasibility and cost constraints often limit the number of randomization units to a smaller than optimal number. Under these circumstances the investigator may be able to gain power if between-unit outcome variance can be reduced by using covariates (Raudenbush, 1997).

As these considerations illustrate, the important design issues in service systems research are the same as in efficacy and cost-outcome research. Intervention effects are most easily understood when interventions are introduced experimentally with some form of random assignment. Multistep causal processes can be studied most effectively with a clear theory about intermediate causal pathways and effects, and ways to demonstrate that expected intermediate effects are produced and potential confounding effects are avoided.

3.11.5 POLICY RESEARCH

National and state reform of the organization and finance of mental health systems is a major research issue in mental health economics. Financing processes and incentives are changing rapidly. Local government is being given increasing responsibility for providing mental health services for persons with severe mental illness, either through direct operation of the services or through contracting with the private sector. Mental health services research is examining the impact of these economic forces and changes at both the national and local levels. Figures 3 and 4 illustrate the linkage between national and state policy decisions and their effects on local service system innovation and adaptation. Research focuses on the impact of these changes on access to care, organiza-

tional adaptation, outcomes for the most vulnerable target populations, costs, and the changes in cost burden to various payers.

Figure 4 suggests that policy initiatives by national and state government agencies offer a useful research focus for the mental health services investigator. Examining the link between national/state initiatives and the cost-effectiveness of services at the client level involves "long-chain" causal paths in the extreme. Therefore, research designs need to be thoughtful and realistic. Some research questions may focus simply on the link from national/state policy initiatives to local service system innovation. This research strategy will be most defensible when a national policy aims to encourage specific types of local innovation and previous services research has demonstrated the value of those specific innovations in improving the cost effectiveness of services. Political scientists and organizational sociologists may also discover useful links among "national/state conditions," "national/state system structure," and the "national/state policy process" that generate policy initiatives. Such investigators may also fruitfully examine the comparable processes at the local level that influence local response to outside policy initiatives.

A third strategy is to take a national or state policy initiative, such as a state decision to enter into capitated contracts with local providers or managed care companies, and treat it as a case example in policy research, but to carry out an experimental or quasi-experimental study across local treatment systems of the impact on client access, client outcomes, and other endpoints. The evaluation of state adoption of managed care and capitation contracting in providing publicly funded mental health services in the USA is being evaluated in several states using this type of design.

Thus, the typical outcomes of national and state policy research are changes in local organization or financing of mental health services. It is also important, although more difficult, to determine the effect of national and state policy initiatives on the prevalence and consequences of mental disorder in the general population.

The causal chain of interest includes the effects of national and state conditions, system structure, and policy processes on those characteristics of local service systems thought to be related to their cost-effectiveness. The independent variables of causal interest to national and state policy research bear directly on local service systems as shown by the intersection of Figures 3 and 4 (C1 in Figure 3 and D5, D6, and D7 in Figure 4).

National/state conditions that influence the policy process include such variables as political stability, economic conditions, human resources mix, and cultural conditions such as family and community caretaking traditions. Corresponding factors presumably make up some of the relevant local conditions that influence local policy.

System structure at the national/state level includes such variables as centralization of control and funding, administrative standards, level of funding from sources above the local tax base, eligibility and benefit design, financing incentives for local innovation such as supply-side and demand-side payment incentives. In considering the economic concept of demand-side incentive as affecting local innovation behavior, copayment requirements imposed on persons with psychiatric illnesses and their families, might be included, and also copayment requirements that funding initiatives may impose on the local tax base.

Policy process at all levels includes such variables as leadership, research, and advocacy. Advocacy may come from research and service professionals, from industry, and from consumers and family members. Advocacy can be an important pathway from research findings to policy initiatives.

Mental health system reform in the USA, and specifically the introduction of capitated financing and competitive contracting for the provision of publicly funded mental health care for the severely and persistently mentally ill by many states, is of great interest (Brach, 1995). Several investigators are examining state policy initiatives such as carve-out capitation in mental health Medicaid, interventions related to causal paths D5 to D7 in Figure 4 (e.g., Christianson & Gray, 1994; Christianson & Osher, 1994; Dickey et al., 1996). Christianson, Gray, Kihlstrom, and Speckman (1995a) are studying Utah's prepaid mental health plan and have reported preliminary findings (Christianson et al., 1995b). There is also a study of Colorado's Medicaid carve-out capitated contracting for mental health services (Bloom et al., unpublished). Studies of state Medicaid innovations typically take advantage of a sequential conversion of different regions of a state from fee-for-service reimbursement to capitation contracts to study as a quasi-experiment.

In Colorado the state initially contracted with a for-profit contractor for coverage of a region of the state containing about one-third of the population, contracted with several existing community mental health centers to cover another third of the state's population, and delayed conversion in the rest of the state. Research assessments focus on organizational

innovation and adaptation, service utilization, access to services, and individual client outcomes using a pre-post design in each of the three regions. Studies are in progress in several other states. Studies like this of statewide mental health system reform are of necessity relatively large projects, but state mental health authorities, services research investigators, and research funding agencies have joined together to mount major research efforts. By the end of the twentieth century the field will have a set of findings about cost control and outcomes that will set the policy and research agenda for the decade that follows.

As in the other areas of services research, small studies also make important contributions. Cuffel, Wait, and Head (1994) studied a 1990 innovation in the state of Arkansas in which the state transferred hospital funding and admission authority to local mental health agencies, essentially putting state hospitals into a competitive market. The investigators found, as expected, that state hospital use was reduced significantly after decentralization, although the reduction in urban areas was proportionally greater than in rural areas. Contrary to expectation, admissions were not limited to the most severely ill, disruptive, or substance-abusing patients, nor were discharged patients more likely to be readmitted. For patients treated in the state hospitals, communication between the community and the state hospital increased after decentralization.

Studies of national and state innovations such as the examples above make this aspect of mental health services research both feasible and increasingly important in guiding the evolution of mental health care.

3.11.6 CONCLUSION

Mental health services research encompasses a broad range of mental health services research projects. No one project can ordinarily study the whole system of variables at any of the three levels discussed in this Chapter. The scope of mental health services research, however, invites construction of integrated theory, especially in service system and policy domains. Such theory can lay the groundwork for a coordinated approach to empirical research. Furthermore, in spite of its great diversity, mental health services research shares a common objective to understand and improve the effectiveness and efficiency of mental health services for individual consumers and for entire target populations.

3.11.7 REFERENCES

Alegria, M., Robles, R., Freeman, D. H., Vera, M., Jimenez, A. L., Rios, C., & Rios R. (1991). Patterns of mental health utilization among island Puerto Rican poor. *American Journal of Public Health, 81,* 875–879.

Attkisson, C., Cook, J., Karno, M., Lehman, A., McGlashan, T. H., Meltzer, H. Y., O'Connor, M., Richardson, D., Rosenblatt, A., Wells, K., Williams, J., & Hohmann, A. A. (1992). Clinical services research. *Schizophrenia Bulletin, 18,* 561–626.

Bloom, J., Hu, T., Cuffel, B., Hausman, J., Wallace, N., & Scheffler, R. (Unpublished). Mental health costs under alternative capitation systems in Colorado.

Bond, G. R., McGrew, J. H., & Fekete, D. M. (1995). Assertive outreach for frequent users of psychiatric hospitals: A meta-analysis. *Journal of Mental Health Administration, 22,* 4–16.

Box, G. E. P., Jenkins, G. M., & Reinsel, G. (1994). *Time series analysis: Forecasting and control,* (3rd ed.). Englewood Cliffs, NJ: Prentice Hall.

Brach, C. (1995). *Designing capitation projects for persons with severe mental illness: A policy guide for state and local officials.* Boston: Technical Assistance Collaborative.

Burns, B. J., & Santos, A. B. (1995). Assertive community treatment: An update of randomized trials. *Psychiatric Services, 46,* 669–675.

Catalano, R. A., & McConnell, W. (1996). A time-series test of the quarantine theory of involuntary commitment. *Journal of Health and Social Behavior, 37,* 381–387.

Catalano, R., Rook, K., & Dooley, D. (1986). Labor markets and help-seeking: A test of the employment security hypothesis. *Journal of Health and Social Behavior, 27,* 277–287.

Catalano, R., & Serxner, S. (1987). Time series designs of potential interest to epidemiologists, *American Journal of Epidemiology, 126,* 724–731.

Center for Mental Health Services. (1996). *Second year interim status report on the evaluation of the ACCESS demonstration program.* (Vol. I., Summary of Second year findings). Rockville, MD: Center for Mental Health Services.

Chamberlain, R., & Rapp, C. A. (1991). A decade of case management: A methodological review of outcome research. *Community Mental Health Journal, 27,* 171–188.

Christianson, J. B., & Gray, D. Z. (1994). What CMHCs can learn from two states' efforts to capitate Medicaid benefits. *Hospital and Community Psychiatry, 45,* 777–781.

Christianson, J. B., Gray, D. Z., Kihlstrom, L. C., & Speckman, Z. K. (1995a). Development of the Utah Prepaid Mental Health Plan. *Advances in Health Economics and Health Services Research, 15,* 117–135.

Christianson, J. B., Manning, W., Lurie, N., Stoner, T. J., Gray, D. Z., Popkin, M., & Marriott, S. (1995b). Utah's prepaid mental health plan: The first year. *Health Affairs, 14,* 160–172.

Christianson, J. B., & Osher, F. C. (1994). Health maintenance organizations, health care reform, and persons with serious mental illness. *Hospital and Community Psychiatry, 45,* 898–905.

Cuffel, B. J., Wait, D., & Head, T. (1994). Shifting the responsibility for payment for state hospital services to community mental health agencies. *Hospital and Community Psychiatry, 45,* 460–465.

Dickey, B., Normand, S. L., Norton, E. C., Azeni, H., Fisher, W., & Altaffer, F. (1996). Managing the care of schizophrenia: Lessons from a 4-year Massachusetts Medicaid study. *Archives of General Psychiatry, 53*(10), 945–952.

Drummond, M., Brandt, A., Luce, B., Rovira, J. (1993). Standardizing methodologies for economic evaluation in health care. *International Journal of Technology Assessment in Health Care, 9,* 26–36.

Drummond, M. F., Stoddard, G. L., & Torrance, G. W. (1997). *Methods for the economic evaluation of health care programmes* (2nd ed.). Oxford, UK: Oxford University Press.

Essock, S. M., Hargreaves, W. A., Covell, N. H., & Goethe, J. (1996a). Clozapine's effectiveness for patients in state hospitals: Results from a randomized trial. *Psychopharmacology Bulletin, 32,* 683–697.

Essock, S. M., Hargreaves, W. A., Dohm, F-A., Goethe, J., Carver, L., & Hipshman, L. (1996b). Clozapine eligibility among state hospital patients. *Schizophrenia Bulletin, 22,* 15–25.

Fenton, J., Catalano, R., & Hargreaves, W. A. (1996). Effect of Proposition 187 on mental health service use in California: A case study. *Health Affairs, 15,* 182–190.

Freeman, D. H., Alegria, M., Vera, M., Munoz, C. A., Robles, R. R., Jimenez, A. L., Calderon, J. M., & Pena, M. (1992). A receiver operating characteristic (ROC) curve analysis of a model of mental health services use by Puerto Rican poor. *Medical Care, 30,* 1142–1153.

Hargreaves, W. A., & Shumway, M. (1989). Effectiveness of mental health services for the severely mentally ill. In C. A. Taube, D. Mechanic, & A. A. Hohmann (Eds.), *The future of mental health services research.* Rockville, MD: National Institute of Mental Health.

Hargreaves, W. A., Shumway, M., Hu, T.-W., & Cuffel, B. (1997). *Cost-outcome methods for mental health.* San Diego, CA: Academic Press.

Henggeler, S. W. (1991). Multidimensional causal models of delinquent behavior. In R. Cohen & A. Siegel (Eds), *Context and development* (pp. 211–231). Hillsdale, NJ: Erlbaum.

Henggeler, S. W., Melton, G. B., & Smith, L. A. (1992). Family preservation using multisystem therapy: An effective alternative to incarcerating serious juvenile offenders. *Journal of Consulting and Clinical Psychology, 60,* 953–961.

Knapp, M. R. J. (Ed.) (1995). *The economic evaluation of mental health care.* Aldershot, UK: Ashgate.

Lalley, T. L., Hohmann, A. A., Windle, C. D., Norquist, G. S., Keith, S. J., & Burke, J. D. (1992). Caring for people with severe mental disorders: A national plan to improve services. *Schizophrenia Bulletin, 18,* 559–560.

Mechanic, D. (1987). Correcting misperceptions in mental health policy: Strategies for improved care of the seriously mentally ill. *Milbank Quarterly, 65,* 203–230.

Mechanic, D., Bevilacqua, J., Goldman, H., Hargreaves, W., Howe, J., Knisley, M., Scherl, D. J., Stuart, G., Unhjem, M. B., & Lalley, T. L. (1992). Research resources. *Schizophrenia Bulletin, 18,* 669–696.

Murray, D., McKinlay, S., Martin, D., Donner, A., Dwyer, J., Raudenbush, S., & Graubard, B. (1994). Design and analysis issues in community trials. *Evaluation Review, (August),* 493–514.

National Institute of Mental Health. (1991). *Caring for people with severe mental disorders: A national plan of research to improve services.* DHHS Pub. No. (ADM)91-1762. Washington, DC: US Government Printing Office.

Olfson, M. (1990). Assertive community treatment: An evaluation of the experimental evidence. *Hospital and Community Psychiatry, 41,* 634–641.

Randolph, F. L. (1992). NIMH funded research demonstration of (P/ACT) models. *Outlook, 2*(2), 9–12.

Raudenbush, S. W. (1997) Statistical analysis and optimal design for cluster randomization trials. *Psychological Methods, 2,* 173–185.

Rubin, A. (1992). Is case management effective for people with serious mental illness? A research review. *Health and Social Work, 17,* 138–150.

Salive, M. E., Mayfield, J. A., & Weissman, N. W. (1990). Patient outcomes research teams and the Agency for Health Care Policy Research. *Health Services Research, 25,* 697–708.

Santos, A. B., Henggeler, S. W., Burns, B. J., Arana, G. W., & Meisler, N. (1995). Research on field-based services: Models for reform in the delivery of mental health care to populations with complex clinical problems. *American Journal of Psychiatry, 152,* 1111–1123.

Schooler, N. R., Keith, S. J., Severe, J. B., & Matthews, S. (1989). Acute treatment response and short term outcome in shizophrenia: First results of the NIMH Treatment Strategies in Schizophrenia study. *Psychopharmacology Bulletin, 25,* 331–335.

Schooler, N. R., Keith, S. J., Severe, J. B., Matthews, S. M., Bellack, A. S., Glick, I. D., Hargreaves, W. A., Kane, J. M., Ninan, P. T., Frances, A., Jacobs, M., Lieberman, J. A., Mance. R., Simpson, G. M., & Woerner, M. (1997). Relapse and rehospitalization during maintenance treatment of schizophrenia: The effects of dose reduction and family treatment. *Archives of General Psychiatry, 54,* 453–463.

Scott, J. E., & Dixon, L. B. (1995). Assertive community treatment and case management for schizophrenia. *Schizophrenia Bulletin, 21,* 657–691.

Sloan, F. (Ed.) (1995). *Valuing health care: Costs, benefits, and effectiveness of pharmaceuticals and other medical technologies.* Cambridge, UK: Cambridge University Press.

Solomon, P. (1992). The efficacy of case management services for severely mentally disabled clients. *Community Mental Health Journal, 28,* 163–180.

Stein, L., & Test, M. A. (1980). Alternative to mental hospital treatment: I. Conceptual model, treatment program, and clinical evaluation. *Archives of General Psychiatry, 37,* 392–397.

Steinwachs, D. M., Cullum, H. M., Dorwart, R. A., Flynn, L., Frank, R., Friedman, M. B., Herz, M. I., Mulvey, E. P., Snowden, L., Test, M. A., Tremaine, L. S., & Windle, C. D. (1992). Service systems research. *Schizophrenia Bulletin, 18,* 627–668.

Test, M. A. (1992). Training in community living. In R. P. Liberman (Ed.). *Handbook of Psychiatric Rehabilitation.* Boston: Allyn and Bacon.

Test, M. A., & Stein, L. (1980). Alternative to mental hospital treatment: III. Social cost. *Archives of General Psychiatry, 37,* 409–412.

Weisbrod, B. A. (1983) A guide to benefit-cost analysis, as seen through a controlled experiment in treating the mentally ill. *Journal of Health Politics, Policy and Law, 7,* 808–845.

Weisbrod, B., Test, M. A., & Stein, L. (1980). Alternative to mental hospital treatment: II. Economic benefit cost analysis. *Archives of General Psychiatry, 37,* 400–405.

Yates, B. T. (1995). Cost-effectiveness analysis, cost-benefit analysis, and beyond: Evolving models for the scientist–manager–practitioner. *Clinical Psychology: Science and Practice, 2,* 385–398.

3.12
Descriptive and Inferential Statistics

ANDREW C. LEON
Cornell University Medical College, New York, NY, USA

3.12.1 INTRODUCTION

A fundamental motivation in science is to understand individual differences. It is *deviation* and *variability* that stimulate scientific curiosity. When do behavioral scientists study constants? One is not compelled to study differences in clinical psychology students who did and did not experience infancy. Instead a comparison of clinical psychology students who do and do not remember parental affect expression in infancy might be compelling. Similarly it is differences among scores on an achievement test that are exciting, not the proportion of psychology graduate students who took the Graduate Record Examination.

Psychological research is conducted to understand *individual differences*. In reporting research results, data are summarized with statistical analyses. In choosing among appropriate statistical procedures, several issues must be considered. First, are the results to be used strictly to describe one sample or will they also be used to draw inferences about the population from which the sample was drawn? *Descriptive statistics* are used for the former purpose, whereas *inferential statistics* are used for the latter. Here several of the more commonly used procedures are discussed. The choice among statistical procedures is also guided by the distribution, the sample size, and of course, the research question. This chapter gives an overview of those statistical procedures. It is not meant to provide a comprehensive explication of each technique, but instead provide a guide to the selection, implementation, and interpretation of appropriate procedures. References which provide comprehensive discussions of the procedures are cited in each section.

Descriptive statistics are used to summarize and describe data from a sample. Measures of *central tendency* and *variability* are fundamental. The former include quantities that represent the typical data from the sample, whereas the latter provide information on the *dispersion* of data within a sample. Data from a *hypothetical* clinical trial comparing the effects of two forms of psychotherapy for depression, interpersonal therapy (IPT) and cognitive-behavioral therapy (CBT), will be used repeatedly in this chapter. Table 1 presents only the data from the CBT group. Taking pedagogical license, the structure of the data will be changed to illustrate a variety of statistical procedures in this chapter. Throughout the chapter X_i will refer to an individual observation of the variable, X. For example, X_{17} represents the X value for subject number 17 (where i is each subject's arbitrarily assigned, unique identifying number, which ranges from 1 to N, in a study of N subjects).

3.12.2 TABULAR AND GRAPHIC DISPLAYS

There are a variety of tabular displays used to summarize data. Hamilton Rating Scale for Depression (HRSD) data will be used for illustration. Initially a *frequency distribution* is constructed by counting the number of occurrences, or frequency, of each value of the variable (X_i). In this case, X_i represents the HRSD rating for subject i, where i ranges from 1 to N. Five columns are included in the frequency distribution that is displayed in Table 2. The first column displays the values of X_i, in ascending order. The second column displays

Table 1 Hamilton Rating Scale for Depression (HRSD: X_i) for 20 patients (CBT group).

Subject number	X_i
1	12
2	12
3	13
4	14
5	15
6	17
7	18
8	19
9	21
10	21
11	21
12	22
13	24
14	25
15	26
16	27
17	27
18	28
19	29
20	29

Table 2 Frequency distribution of HRSD: CBT group.

X_i	f	cum(n)	%	cum (%)
12	2	2	10	10
13	1	3	5	15
14	1	4	5	20
15	1	5	5	25
17	1	6	5	30
18	1	7	5	35
19	1	8	5	40
21	3	11	15	55
22	1	12	5	60
24	1	13	5	65
25	1	14	5	70
26	1	15	5	75
27	2	17	10	85
28	1	18	5	90
29	2	20	10	100
Total	20		100	

the frequency for the value of X_i. The third column shows the number of subjects that have a value of X_i or lower, which is referred to as the *cumulative frequency*. In the fourth column the percentage of subjects with each value of X_i, or relative frequency, is displayed. In the fifth column, the cumulative percentage, or *cumulative relative frequency*, is shown, which is the percentage of subjects with a value less than or equal to X_i. Two column totals (sums, which are symbolized Σ) are presented. In the second column, the total of the frequencies is displayed, the value of which should be equal to the sample size (N). The total of the fourth column should equal 100%. Other cell entries worth noting include the final number in the column of cumulative frequencies which should equal N and the final entry in the cumulative relative frequencies column, which should be equal to 100%. Finally, the number of values of X_i provides an initial indication of its variability.

A graphic display of the contents of any of the last four columns can be informative. In these graphs, the x-axis of the graph represents the X_i values and the frequency data are represented on the y-axis. These graphs provide the reader with a sense of the distribution of the data at a glance. For instance, Figure 1 is a bar chart, or *histogram*, displaying the frequencies of each X value. (If there were no variability, only one bar would be displayed.) Figure 2 displays the *relative frequencies*. Figure 3 displays the *cumulative frequency* distribution. Finally, the *cumulative relative frequencies* of the HRSD ratings are displayed in Figure 4. Although Figures 1 and 3 display sample sizes,

the proportions presented in Figures 2 and 4 can be readily compared across samples of diverse sizes.

3.12.3 DESCRIPTIVE STATISTICS

Descriptive statistics are summary measures that describe characteristics of data. The two general areas of descriptive statistics that will be discussed here are measures of *central tendency* and measures of variability. The data that were originally shown in Table 1 are now displayed in Table 3, with additional information that will be used for calculations throughout this section.

3.12.3.1 Measures of Central Tendency

The arithmetic mean ($\bar{X}$) of a sample, commonly referred to as the average, is equal to the sum of all observations in the sample, $\sum_{1}^{n} X_i$, divided by the number of observations (N) in the sample.

$$\bar{X} = \frac{\left(\sum_{i=1}^{N} X_i \right)}{N} = \frac{420}{20} = 21$$

The *median*, *Md*, is the middle observation in a sample of ordered data (i.e., ranked from lowest to highest value of X_i). In the case of ordered data, the subscript represents the ascending rank, ranging from 1 to n. With an

Table 3 HRSD: CBT group ($N = 20$).

X_i	X_i^2	$X_i - \bar{X}$	$(X_i - \bar{X})^2$
12	144	−9	81
12	144	−9	81
13	169	−8	64
14	196	−7	49
15	225	−6	36
17	289	−4	16
18	324	−3	9
19	361	−2	4
21	441	0	0
21	441	0	0
21	441	0	0
22	484	1	1
24	576	3	9
25	625	4	16
26	676	5	25
27	729	6	36
27	729	6	36
28	784	7	49
29	841	8	64
29	841	8	64
Total 420	9460	0	640

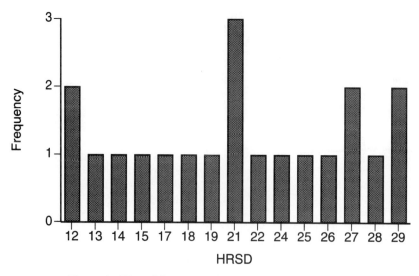

Figure 1 Plot of frequency distribution of HRSD: CBT group.

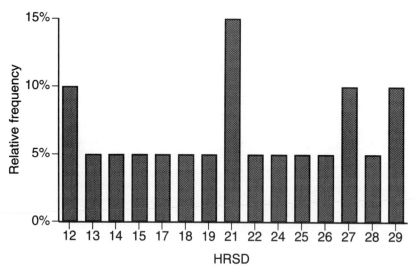

Figure 2 Plot of relative frequencies of HRSD: CBT group.

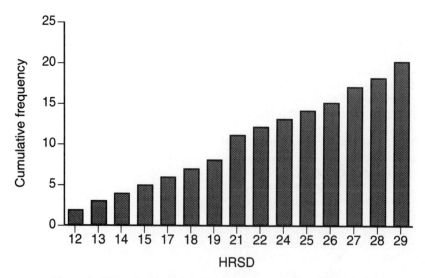

Figure 3 Plot of cumulative frequencies of HRSD: CBT group.

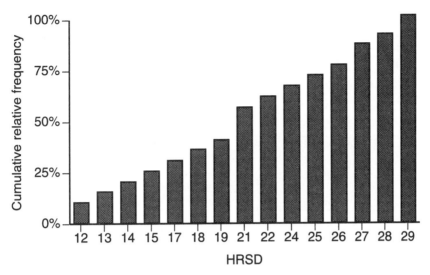

Figure 4 Plot of cumulative relative frequencies of HRSD: CBT group.

even number of observations, the median is the mean of the two middle observations. For instance, there are 20 observations in the sample presented in Table 1. Thus the median of the sample is the mean of the middle two values: 10 and 11:

$$Md = X_{(n+1)/2} = 21 \text{ (mean of 2 middle scores)}$$

The median represents the fiftieth percentile, the point below which half of the data fall. For example, in Table 1, a value of 21 is the median. When the data include a very small number of extreme values, the data set is referred to as skewed (discussed in greater detail below). With *skewed* data, the median is a more representative measure of central tendency than the mean because the mean is influenced by extreme values. For instance, the median is a more appropriate measure of central tendency of the US household income than the mean.

The mode, Mo, is the most frequently occurring value. The modal value can be determined by examining the frequency distribution which is presented in Table 1 and selecting the X_i with the largest value of f_i:

$$Mo = 21 (f = 3)$$

3.12.3.2 Measures of Variability

This chapter began by stating that it is an understanding of individual differences that motivates a great deal of behavioral research. A wide range of statistical procedures are used to analyze differences. Each of the procedures that is discussed in this chapter has to do with differences: individual or group; temporal or

conditional. Here the quantities used to assess differences, or *variability*, are discussed. The crudest measure of variability is the *range*, which is the difference between the maximum and minimum value in the data. For instance, in Table 1:

$$\text{Range} = \text{Maximum} - \text{Minimum}$$
$$= X_N - X_1 = 29 - 12 = 17$$

There are several quantities that provide a more comprehensive description of the variability in data. Most are derived from the *Sum of Squares (SS)*, which is the sum of squared deviations from the mean. The squared deviations are presented in the right-hand column of Table 3. Note that one of the properties of the mean is that the sum of the deviations from the mean is equal to zero:

$$\sum_{i=1}^{N}(X_i - \bar{X}) = 0$$

Notice that the sum of the deviations from the mean in Table 3 is equal to zero. However, the sum of squared deviations from the mean is a useful quantity:

$$SS = \sum_{i=1}^{N}(X_i - \bar{X}) = 640$$

The SS can be used for calculating the *variance* (s^2), which is approximately the mean of the squared deviations from the mean. The variance, a quantity that is commonly used to convey information regarding variability, is calculated as $\frac{SS}{n-1}$, and not $\frac{SS}{n}$, because it provides an unbiased estimator of the population variance. Further discussion of the reasons for this will not be discussed here. Note that, as the sample size increases the difference between $\frac{SS}{n-1}$ and $\frac{SS}{n}$ becomes trivial. The variance is calculated as follows:

$$s^2 = \frac{\sum_{i=1}^{N}(X_i - \bar{X})^2}{N-1} = \frac{640}{20-1} = 33.684$$

Or, if the *SS* is available:

$$s^2 = \frac{SS}{N-1} = \frac{640}{20-1} = 33.684$$

The *standard deviation* (*s*), a fundamental measure of variability, is equal to the square root of the variance. It is approximately equal to the average deviation from the mean. It is approximately equal because the deviations have been squared, summed, and divided by $N-1$, not by N, before the square root is computed. Note that by taking the square root, the original unit of measurement is restored.

$$s = \sqrt{s^2} = \sqrt{33.684} = 5.804$$

3.12.3.3 Describing a Frequency Distribution

Modality has to do with the number of modes contained within a frequency distribution. The HRSD data in Figure 1 has one mode and is thus referred to as unimodal. The most commonly occurring value in this sample is 21. There are three observations equal to 21 and there is no other value that is represented as often as 21. Because the *y*-axis represents the frequency, the mode is the highest point in the plot of the frequency distribution in Figure 1. In contrast to these data, some frequency distributions are bimodal, having two peaks, or multimodal, having more than two peaks.

3.12.3.3.1 Skewness

If one folds the distribution, vertically in the middle and one half can be superimposed on the other, the distribution is *symmetric*. The extent to which a frequency distribution diverges from symmetry is described as *skewness*. With help from Bill Gates and a few of his peers, incomes in the United States are positively skewed. The skewness, which is one aspect of the departure from symmetry, is described as either skewed to the right, positively skewed as shown in Figure 5, or skewed to the left, negatively skewed, as shown in Figure 6. For example, with a different set of HRSD data, a positively skewed distribution is one in which there are a very few severely depressed scores, whereas a distribution in which there are a very few number of euphoric scores might be negatively skewed.

3.12.3.3.2 Kurtosis

Kurtosis has to do with the extent to which a frequency distribution is peaked or flat. A normal bell-shaped distribution is referred to as a *mesokurtic* shape distribution. An example of this, a nicely rounded distribution, is shown in Figure 7. Many human traits are normally distributed including height and intelligence. A *platykurtic*, like a platypus, is a somewhat flat creature. For instance, as shown in Figure 8, this would describe data in which there are several modes, which cluster around, and include, the median. A *leptokurtic* distribution is more peaked. In Figure 9 hypothetical data show that such data would be characterized by a very high, unimodal peak, at the median.

3.12.3.4 Other Graphic Displays

Two other formats for graphic display are the *Stem and Leaf* and the *Box and Whisker* plots. These graphic displays, which are described in detail by Tukey (1977), each provide the researcher with a great deal of information about the distribution of the data. The importance of examining such plots cannot be overemphasized. One outlier (i.e., extreme score) in a data set can markedly alter the mean and exaggerate trivial group differences. The existence of outliers is most readily apparent in a good graph.

A *Stem and Leaf plot* is an efficient method of displaying a frequency distribution. In Figure 10, the vertical line, called the stem, displays the possible values, ranging from the minimum (at the top) to maximum value (at the bottom). Each leaf represents an individual with a particular value. A leaf could be an "*x*," an asterisk, or more commonly the value itself. A data value (on the stem) with several leaves is a frequently occurring value. Of course, the mode has the most leaves.

Box and Whisker plots are based on five points as shown in Figure 11. The first three of those have been discussed: the median, the minimum, and maximum. The final two points of the box and whisker plot are the values that fall midway between each extreme score and the median. These are the first and third *quartiles*. A long thin box is drawn with the latter two points serving as the *hinges*. A horizontal bar is drawn through the median. *Whiskers* are drawn at the two extreme values. The figure illustrates how easily outliers are detected in a Box and Whisker plot. In some situations, the plot is more informative when an identifier is used to label values such as an outlier.

When an outlier is identified, the researcher must determine if the value is real or if it is a keypunch error. The raw data forms will help

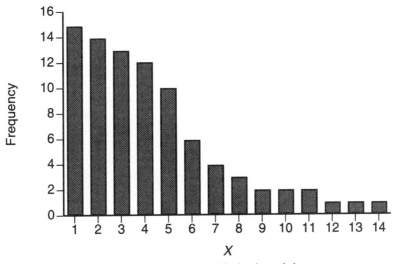

Figure 5 Example of positively skewed data.

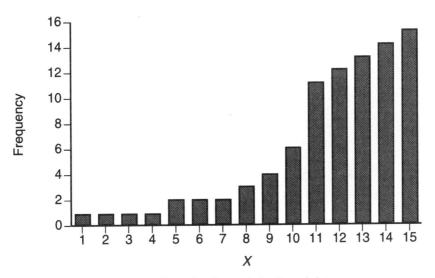

Figure 6 Example of negatively skewed data.

one correct keypunch errors. However, extreme scores are not necessarily incorrect values. In a study of depression, an HRSD score of 58 is possible, but extremely rare. In analyzing data in which valid extreme values have been identified, one has several strategies to choose from. First, a nonparametric procedure could be used in which the ranks of the raw data values are used. In such a case the minimum and maximum are equal to 1 and N, respectively. Second, a transformation of the data values using either the natural logarithm, where $y' = \ln(y)$, or square root of the original scale $y'' = \sqrt{y}$. Third, an extreme score might be *winsorized*, a process in which an outlier is simply recoded to the second highest value (see Tukey, 1977). Alternative strategies for outliers are discussed in detail by Wilcox (1996).

3.12.3.5 Statistical Software

Many of the statistical procedures that are described in this chapter involve tedious calculations. This leaves a great deal of room for computational errors. For all practical purposes, most statistical analyses in psychological research are conducted using a computer. There is a wide variety of statistical software that is commercially available for personal computers. Software that is commonly used in the social sciences includes SPSS, SAS, BMDP, and SYSTAT. Comprehensive reviews of statistical software are available (Lurie, 1995; Morgan, 1998). The choice among statistical software has to do with the statistical procedures that are included, the data management capabilities, and the ease of use. Nevertheless, a

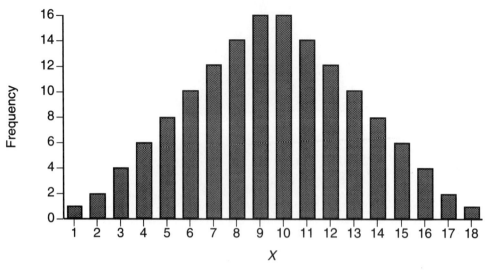

Figure 7   Example of normally distributed data.

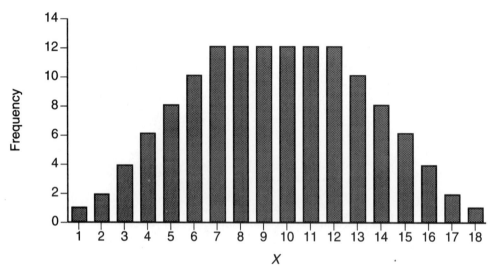

Figure 8   Example of data with a platykurtic distribution.

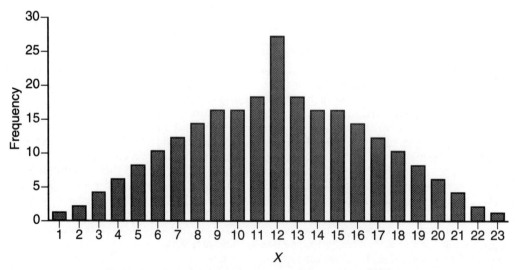

Figure 9   Example of data with a leptokurtic distribution.

Frequency	Stem and Leaf
4	1*2234
4	1.5789
5	2*11124
7	2.5677899

Stem width:	10.00
Each leaf:	1 case(s)

Figure 10 HRSD: Stem and Leaf Plot.

statistical procedure should only be used in appropriate situations. A thorough understanding of the statistical technique, the assumptions, and a familiarity with the estimation procedure is necessary. Furthermore, the user must have the background necessary to interpret the results that are generated by the software. One of the goals of this chapter is to provide the reader with such a background for a variety of descriptive and inferential procedures. In addition, the appendix of this chapter includes SPSS command lines for each of the analyses that is discussed (SPSS, 1997). SPSS is used for illustration here because it is accessible with minimal programming skills, it covers a wide array of statistical procedures, and it has excellent data management capacity.

3.12.4 INFERENTIAL STATISTICS

Once again, an *inferential* statistical test is used to make an inference about a population based on data from a sample. In choosing among inferential procedures, one must consider the nature of both the independent and dependent variable, whether a between-subject design or within-subject design is employed, and the sample size. The procedures that are presented below are organized to reflect such considerations. Initially statistical procedures for between-subject designs are discussed. This is followed by a discussion of procedures for within-subject designs. In each of those sections both parametric and nonparametric procedures are considered. The distinction between parametric and nonparametric procedures is discussed in detail in Section 3.12.4.2.

First a digression into general features regarding inferential tests. A statistical test is used to draw an inference about a population(s) based on sample data. The test is used to

examine the research question at hand. For instance, "Which of two forms of psychotherapy is more effective for the treatment of depression?" For purposes of hypothesis testing, the question is reframed into a null hypothesis (i.e., a hypothesis of *no difference*). For example, "There is no difference in the effects of CBT and IPT for the treatment of depression." In conducting such tests, the researcher might make a correct decision, but errors are certainly possible. Consider the correspondence between the *truth* and the research results (see Table 4). Assume that with omniscient (noninferential) ability, someone is able to describe the *truth* (e.g., population characteristics) without conducting a statistical test. Thus the omniscience. (Every department has at least one member with self-rated ability of that level.) For example, consider a clinical trial in which the post-treatment psychopathology of two groups (CBT and IPT) is being compared. Our colleague, Dr. Omniscient, could tell us whether or not the severity of psychopathology in the two groups differs. If there is no difference in the population, the correct decision would be to conclude that there is no difference (i.e., fail to reject the null hypothesis). In contrast, if there is no population difference, yet we find a difference, we would be in error. Specifically, rejecting a true null hypothesis is referred to as *Type I Error*. The probability of Type I Error is referred to as the alpha level (α).

On the other hand, if Dr. Omniscient tells us that there is, in fact, a treatment difference (i.e., population treatment differences), we would be correct if we detected the difference (rejected a false null hypothesis). The probability of such a rejection is referred to as *statistical power*. In contrast, we would be in error if we fail to detect the treatment difference (i.e., fail to reject a false null hypothesis). This is referred to as *Type II Error* and the p(Type II error) $= \beta$. In the absence of Dr. Omniscient's assistance, replication of results in subsequent studies provides convincing evidence that our inference was likely to be accurate.

One further general digression regarding inferential statistics. In general a test statistic

Table 4 Cross-classigication of the "truth" and research results.

Results of research	Placebo = Active (H_0 true)	Placebo ≠ Active (H_0 false)
No difference (CBT = IPT)	Correct decision	Type II error
Difference (CBT = IPT)	Type I error	Correct decision "Power"

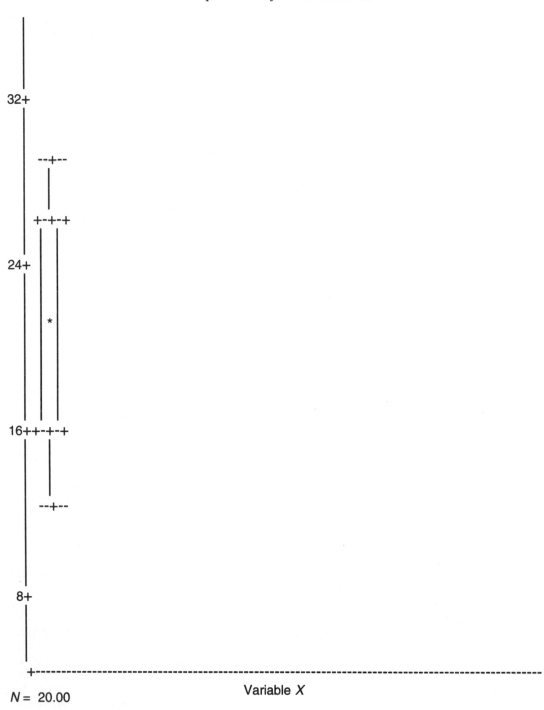

Symbol key: * - Median

Figure 11   HRSD: Box and Whisker Plot.

is a ratio of a statistic (e.g., difference in means) to its *standard error*. Loosely speaking, the standard error is an estimate of the variability of the statistic in the population. Stated differently, and hypothetically, if the experiment were conducted repeatedly, say 10 000 times (with the same sample size each time), and the quantity of interest (e.g., difference between two means)

were calculated in each of those experiments, the standard error would represent the standard deviation of that distribution (the sampling distribution) of that quantity (e.g., the standard deviation of the differences between two means).

As stated earlier, one component of each inferential statistical test is the null hypothesis,

Table 5 Hamilton Depression Ratings (X_i) for 20 patients (IPT group).

X_i	X_i^2	$X_i - \bar{X}$	$(X_i - \bar{X})^2$
6	36	−9	82
7	49	−8	65
8	64	−7	50
9	81	−6	37
12	144	−3	9
12	144	−3	9
12	144	−3	9
13	169	−2	4
17	289	2	4
17	289	2	4
18	324	3	9
18	324	3	9
19	361	4	16
19	361	4	16
19	361	4	16
19	361	4	16
19	361	4	16
19	361	4	16
19	361	4	16
19	361	4	16
Total 301	4945	0	414.95

$$\bar{X} = \frac{\sum_1^n X_i}{n} = \frac{301}{20} = 15.05$$

$$\text{SS} = \sum (X_i - \bar{X})^2 = 414.95$$

$$s^2 = \frac{\text{SS}}{n-1} = \frac{414.95}{20-1} = 21.839$$

$$s = \sqrt{s^2} = \sqrt{21.839} = 4.673$$

H_0. In fact that is one of the eight components of the hypothesis testing procedure which are listed below:

(i) State research question.

(ii) State two hypotheses which are mutually exclusive and exhaustive:

    (a) null hypothesis (e.g., $H_0 : \mu_1 = \mu_2$)

    (b) alternative hypothesis
    (e.g., $H_A : \mu_1 \neq \mu_2$).

(iii) Choose an appropriate statistical test

(iv) Specify the critical value for the statistical test and the alpha level (both of which are discussed below).

(v) Collect data.

(vi) Perform calculations.

(vii) Make decision regarding H_0.

(viii) Conclusion. The results are interpreted as an inference about the population (which the sample represents) based on the sample data. The *generalizability* of the findings should be discussed. Inferences about the results cannot be generalized beyond the scope of the data that was examined. For instance, results from a clinical trial for the treatment of patients with depression cannot be used to draw inferences about the treatment of patients with panic disorder.

3.12.4.1 One- vs. Two-tailed Tests

In some settings, the researcher might have preconceived expectations regarding the outcome of the experiment. For instance, it might be expected that a novel treatment is superior to the standard. The researcher can then choose to specify the null hypothesis as that of *no treatment difference* or *superiority of the novel treatment*. A two-tailed null hypothesis is designed to detect any difference, positive or negative, whereas a one-tailed null hypothesis is designed to detect a difference in the prespecified direction (e.g., efficacy) but it would fail to detect the opposite (e.g., detrimental) effects. It is often as important, and ethically compelling, to detect detrimental treatments as it is to detect efficacious treatments. A two-tailed test is used for a nondirectional null hypothesis and a one-tailed test is used for a directional null hypothesis. Although there is debate regarding the exclusive use of two-tailed tests, there is a consensus that the rationale for a one-tailed test must be stated *a priori*. That is, if a one-tailed test is to be used, it must be so stated prior to study implementation and data collection. There has been an extensive discussion in the literature of the costs and benefits of one and two-tailed tests (e.g., Fleiss, 1981, pp. 27–29; Hopkins, Glass, & Hopkins, 1987, pp. 164–165, 205–206). All examples in this chapter employ two-tailed, nondirectional tests.

3.12.4.2 Parametric vs. Nonparametric Tests

Technically speaking, one must not use parametric tests such as a *t*-test and an ANOVA unless assumptions such as normality are fulfilled. By normality, it is assumed that the sample come from a population with normally distributed data. Briefly, in a normal distribution, which is bell-shaped, the mean, median, and mode are equal. The distribution is symmetrical around these measures of central tendency. The shape of a normal distribution is determined by the population means and variance. The nonparametric alternatives to the *t*-test and the ANOVA are the Mann–Whitney test and Kruskal–Wallis test. Neither of these makes the normality assumptions. Many of the nonparametric procedures require a simple rank transformation of the data (Conover, 1980; Sprent, 1989). This involves pooling the data from all subjects, regardless of treatment group, and ranking in ascending order based on the value of the dependent variable. The subject with the lowest value is assigned the rank of 1. The subject with the next lowest is assigned the value of 2, and so on, until the subject with the highest value is assigned a rank of N. If all assumptions have been reasonably fulfilled and all other aspects of the analysis are equal, parametric tests generally have more statistical power than nonparametric tests. However, if the assumptions are not met, parametric tests could provide misleading results about the population which the sample represents.

3.12.4.3 Between-subject Designs: Dimensional and Ordinal Dependent Variables

3.12.4.3.1 t-*test*

The *t*-test is used to compare the means of two groups. For instance, in a clinical trial, the severity of depression of two treatment groups (IPT and CBT) can be compared with a *t*-test. The HRSD is the dependent variable. The *null hypothesis* is that the population means do not differ: $H_0 : \mu_1 = \mu_2$ and the alternative hypothesis is that population means are not the same: $H_A : \mu_1 \neq \mu_2$.

The test is simply a ratio of the *between-group* differences relative to the *within-group* differences. It is used to ask the question, "Is the mean difference *between groups* large relative to the fluctuation that is observed *within* each group?" To illustrate this, the data from the CBT group (presented in Table 3) are compared with data from the other group of subjects in the hypothetical clinical trial that was described earlier, those assigned to IPT (see Table 5).

The algorithm for the *t*-test is a ratio of *between-group* variability to *within-group* variability:

$$t = \frac{\bar{X}_1 - \bar{X}_2}{S_{\bar{X}_1 - \bar{X}_2}}$$

where the numerator represents the between-group variability (i.e., difference between the group means) and the denominator is derived from the pooled variance. The pooled variance is estimated as:

$$s_p^2 = \frac{(SS_1 + SS_2)}{(n_1 - 1) + (n_2 - 1)}$$

and

$$s_{(\bar{X}_1 - \bar{X}_2)} = \sqrt{\frac{s_p^2}{n_1} + \frac{s_p^2}{n_2}}$$

Applied to the CBT vs. IPT data set: the pooled variance estimate,

$$s_p^2 = \frac{(SS_1 + SS_2)}{(n_1 - 1) + (n_2 - 1)}$$

$$= \frac{640.0 + 414.95}{(20 - 1) + (20 - 1)} = 27.76$$

and

$$s_{(\bar{X}_1 - \bar{X}_2)} = \sqrt{\frac{s_p^2}{n_1} + \frac{s_p^2}{n_2}} = \sqrt{\frac{27.76}{20} + \frac{27.76}{20}} = 1.67$$

$$t = \frac{\bar{X}_1 - \bar{X}_2}{s_{(\bar{X}_1 - \bar{X}_2)}} = \frac{21.00 - 15.05}{1.67} = 3.56$$

This *t*-statistic is compared with a critical value from tabled values, which can be found in the appendix of any statistics book. To identify that critical value, one must determine the *degrees of freedom (df)*. Although a discussion of the meaning of degrees of freedom is beyond the scope of this chapter, a value for *df* is often needed to find the critical value of a test statistic. In the case of a two-group *t*-test, *df* is equal to the total number of subjects minus the number of groups:

$$df = n_1 + n_2 = 20 + 20 - 2 = 38$$

Using this value for *df*, and a two-tailed alpha level of 0.05, the *critical t*-statistic is 2.024. The *observed t* of 3.56 exceeds this critical value. Thus the null hypothesis is rejected and one can conclude that the population means are not identical. IPT treatment is superior to CBT. Without the *t*-test it was apparent that the IPT mean indicated lower symptom severity as measured by the HRSD than the CBT mean. To get a handle on the magnitude of that difference, it is compared with the within-group standard deviations. The IPT mean was over 6 HRSD points lower, which exceeds one within-group standard deviation (i.e., $s_{IPT} = 4.67$ and $s_{CBT} = 5.80$). Using the *t*-test, one can conclude that the difference in group means is greater than would be expected by chance.

The *assumptions* of the *t*-test include:

(i) Independence among observations. For example, one subject cannot re-enroll in the clinical trial to try another treatment if the initial treatment does not result in symptom remission. If that were permitted, some subjects would contribute multiple observations to the sample and those observations would not be independent.

(ii) The data are normally distributed in the population. Technically, this assumption has to do with the distribution of the *difference in means*, $\bar{X}_1 - \bar{X}_2$ or the population sampling distribution of $\mu_1 - \mu_2$. This assumption is generally met if the sample distributions of the raw data (i.e., the actual measurements), as opposed to the mean differences, are normal, or if the sample sizes are *reasonably* large.

(iii) Homogeneity of variance. The population variances are presumed to be equal. There are several tests of homogeneity of variance including Levene's (1960) test of equality of variances, Bartlett's test for homogeneity of variances, or Hartley's *F*-Max test (1950). These tests will not be discussed here. In calculating the *t*-test statistic, one generally uses a pooled variance estimate. However, when the assumption cannot be met, separate variance estimates can be incorporated into the *t*-test, or another procedure altogether, such as the Mann–Whitney test (discussed below), can be used. In the case of *heteroscedasticity* (unequal group variances), a different algorithm for the *t*-test is used which incorporates separate variance estimates in the denominator. In addition, an adjustment in degrees of freedom is necessary. This will not be discussed here, but is presented in a variety of other references (Armitage & Berry, 1987; Fleiss, 1986; Zar, 1996).

In summary, the hypothesis testing steps for the *t*-test are as follows:

(i) State research question. Do CBT and IPT have similar effects for the treatment of patients with depression?

(ii) State two mutually exclusive and exhaustive hypotheses:

(a) $H_0 : \mu_1 = \mu_2$
(b) $H_A : \mu_1 \neq \mu_2$

(iii) If the assumptions appear to be fulfilled, choose the *t*-test to evaluate the hypotheses.

(iv) The critical value for the *t*-test with $\alpha = 0.05$ and $df = 38$ is 2.024. If $|t_{observed}| > t_{crititcal}$, reject H_0.

(v) Data are displayed in Table 3 for the CBT group and Table 5 for the IPT group.

(vi) Calculations were described above.

(vii) Decision regarding H_0 Because $|t_{observed}| > t_{crititcal}$ (i.e., 3.56 > 2.024), reject H_o.

(viii) Conclusion. IPT is a more effective treatment of depressive symptoms in these patients with major depressive disorder.

3.12.4.3.2 Mann–Whitney test

If the assumptions of the *t*-test cannot be met, yet the observations are independent, the Mann–Whitney test, (also called the Wilcoxon test), may be an appropriate method for two group comparisons, if the data are at least ordinal in nature. An ordinal measurement need not have equal intervals between units, but must be ordered numbers (e.g., 1st, 2nd, 3rd, ...). The Mann–Whitney test can be used to compare two groups without making any distributional

assumptions. It is used when there is reason to believe that the data are not normally distributed, when the sample sizes are small, or when the variances are heterogeneous. It can be used for dimensional data (e.g., HRSD), as well as ordered categorical data [e.g., illness severity categories rated on a Likert scale from 0 (none) to 10 (severe)].

Analyses are not conducted on the raw data, but instead on rank transformed data, as described above. For instance, using the data from the clinical trial comparing IPT and CBT, the ranked data are displayed in Table 6. Instead of analyzing the actual Hamilton scores (the dependent variable), each of the scores is ranked, with the lowest rank assigned a rank of 1 and the highest assigned a rank of N. For purposes of ranking the data are pooled across groups. In the case of ties, the midpoint is used. Subsequent calculations are conducted with the ranks.

The rationale behind the Mann–Whitney test is that if the treatments are equally effective, one would expect about half of each group to be below the median rank for the pooled sample. Another way to think of it is to consider all possible pairs of data across groups: subject 1 from group 1 with subject 1 from group 2; then subject 1 with subject 2 from group 2; ... subject 20 from group 1 with subject 20 from group 2.

Table 6 Hamilton Rating Scale of Depression for patients in the IPT group ($N = 20$) and patients in the CBT group ($N = 20$): raw ratings (X_i) and rank-transformed ratings ($R(X_i)$).

	IPT		CBT	
X_{i1}	$R(X_{i1})$	X_{i2}	$R(X_{i2})$
12	7	13	10.5
12	7	12	7
17	15	14	12
18	18	15	13
19	24	17	15
19	24	18	18
19	24	21	30
19	24	21	30
19	24	21	30
12	7	22	32
13	10.5	12	7
17	15	25	34
18	18	24	33
19	24	19	24
19	24	28	38
19	24	27	36.5
6	1	26	35
7	2	29	39.5
8	3	29	39.5
9	4	27	36.5
Total 301	299.5	420	520.5

Examine whether or not in more than half of the ranked pairs the group 1 member is lower than its counterpart from group 2. That is, we would count the number of times that a subject in group 1 has a higher rank than a subject in group 2. Computationally, the tedious process of all $n_1 \cdot n_2$ comparisons need not be made.

The computations for the Mann–Whitney U test that are now described are based on the formula for the case where both n_is are less than or equal to 20. The total number of subjects across groups is $N = n_1 + n_2$ and $U = n_1 \cdot n_2 + \frac{n_1(n_1+1)}{2} - R_1$, where R_1 is the sum of the ranks for group 1. Note that, in general, the sum of N ranks $= \frac{N(N+1)}{2}$. More specifically, in this case, $\frac{40(40+1)}{2} = 820$, which is equal to the sum of the ranks: $299.5 + 520.5 = 820$.

The observed U statistic (U_{obs}) is compared with a critical range which is tabled in most introductory statistics texts (see for example, Fleiss, 1986; Zar, 1996). The critical range is a function of the sample size of each group.

$$U_{obs} = n_1 \cdot n_2 + \frac{n_1(n_1 + 1)}{2} - R_1$$

$$= 20 \cdot 20 + \frac{20 \cdot 21}{2} - 299.5 = 310.5$$

For the Mann–Whitney test, the hypothesis testing steps are as follows:

(i) State research question. Do CBT and IPT have similar effects for the treatment of patients with depression?

(ii) State two mutually exclusive and exhaustive hypotheses with respect to the population medians (M_k).

$H_0: M_1 = M_2$
$H_A: M_1 \neq M_2$

(iii) Choose the Mann–Whitney test to evaluate the hypotheses.

(iv) The critical values for the Mann–Whitney test, with $\alpha = 0.05$ and $n_1 = n_2 = 20$, are 127 and 273. Thus, if $U_{obs} \leq 127$ or $U_{obs} \geq 273$, reject H_0.

(v) The ranked data are displayed in Table 6 for the IPT and CBT groups.

(vi) Calculations were described above.

(vii) Make decision regarding H_0. $U_{obs} \geq U_{critical}$ (i.e., $310.5 \geq 273$), thus reject H_0.

(viii) Conclusion: IPT is a more effective treatment of depressive symptoms in patients with major depressive disorder.

The assumptions of the Mann–Whitney test include:

(i) The two samples have been independently and randomly sampled from their respective populations.

(ii) The groups are independent.

(iii) The scale of measurement is at least ordinal.

For larger samples (i.e., when n_1 or n_2 is greater than 20), a Normal Approximation can be used for the Mann–Whitney test (see Conover, 1980).

3.12.4.3.3 One-way analysis of variance

When more than two groups are compared on a dimensional dependent variable, a fixed effects analysis of variance (ANOVA) is used. As with the t-test, the test statistic is a ratio of between-group differences to within-group differences. In this case the sum of squares is the quantity representing variability. The sums of squares was introduced earlier as the sum of squared deviations from the mean. For example, consider the clinical trial that has been described above, with the addition of a placebo group. Say that patients are randomly assigned to one of *three* treatments: CBT, IPT, or a psychotherapy placebo. The psychotherapy placebo patients see their clinicians for medical management (MM)—a brief nondirective/reflective talk therapy. The data from the MM group are presented in Table 7. The efficacy of the three treatments for depression in this study can be compared using an ANOVA, once again with the HRSD as the dependent variable.

Initially, three different types of sums of squared deviations are computed. The total sum of squared deviations (SS_{Total}), sum of squared deviations accounted for by treatment group ($SS_{Treatment}$), and the residual sum of squared deviations, also referred to as "sum of squares error" ($SS_{Residual}$), are calculated as described below. There are several aspects about these three quantities that are worth noting at this point. First, the SS_{Total} is the sum of squared deviations from the grand mean (i.e., for all subjects pooled, without regard to treatment group). Second, $SS_{Treatment}$ is a measure of the squared deviations of the treatment group means from the grand mean. It can be thought of as the sum of squares that is *explained* (by knowing what treatment the subjects received). Third, the sum of squared differences between each observation and its sample mean is the $SS_{Residual}$. It represents the sum of squares that is not explained by treatment, and in this context, is the difference between SS_{Total} and $SS_{Treatment}$. These quantities are used in the F-test of the fixed effects ANOVA that is presented in Table 8 (the calculation of each quantity is also described in Table 8).

The assumptions of fixed effects ANOVA are:

(i) The samples are independent.

(ii) The populations from which the sample are drawn are normally distributed.

(iii) Each of the populations has the same variance.

For a fixed effects ANOVA, the hypothesis testing steps are as follows:

(i) State research question. Do CBT, IPT and MM have similar effects for the treatment of patients with depression?

(ii) State two mutually exclusive and exhaustive hypotheses:

$$H_0: \mu_1 = \mu_2 = \mu_3$$
$$H_{A_1}: \mu_1 \neq \mu_2 \text{ or } H_{A_2}: \mu_1 \neq \mu_3 \text{ or } H_{A_3}: \mu_2 \neq \mu_3$$

(iii) If assumptions are met, choose the fixed effects ANOVA to evaluate the hypotheses.

(iv) The critical value for the F-test with $\alpha = 0.05$ and $df = 2,57$ is 3.16 (df is defined in Table 8). If $F_{observed} > F_{critical}$, reject H_0.

(v) Data are displayed in Tables 3, 5, and 7 for the CBT, IPT, and MM groups, respectively.

(vi) Calculations are described above in text and in Table 8.

(vii) Make decision regarding H_0. Since $F_{observed} > F_{critical}$ (i.e., 10.966 > 3.16) reject H_0.

(viii) Conclusion: There is a significant difference in severity of depression among the treatments. And which is superior?

3.12.4.3.4 *ANOVA:* **Post hoc** *tests*

A significant omnibus F-test indicates that the null hypothesis is rejected: $H_0: \mu_1 = \mu_2 = \mu_3$. Nonetheless, further analyses are necessary to determine where the difference lies, that is, which groups are significantly different from each other. A variety of *post hoc* tests can be used for this purpose. A *post hoc* test is designed to be used *only* after an omnibus F-test is statistically significant. Each test incorporates the mean square within (MSW), which comes from the calculations that are presented in the ANOVA table (Table 8). The MSW is the denominator of the F-test. A nonsignificant omnibus F-test, however, indicates that there is not a difference in means among the groups. Of course, when there is no difference, there is no need to look for differences. Consequently, the use of a *post hoc* test after a nonsignificant omnibus F-test is inappropriate.

Post hoc procedures provide a strategy for multiple comparisons while at the same time maintaining the probability of Type I error (i.e., the probability of detecting differences that do not actually exist). This is in stark contrast with the inappropriate strategy of following a significant omnibus F-test with several t-tests, each used to compare a pair of groups. That approach fails to account for the multiple tests, and as a consequence, increases the probability of Type I error. Three *Post hoc* tests are

Table 7 Hamilton Depression Ratings (X_i) for 20 patients in the MM group.

X_i	X_i^2	$X_i - \bar{X}$	$(X_i - \bar{X})^2$
16	256	−6.25	39.0625
16	256	−6.25	39.0625
17	289	−5.25	27.5625
17	289	−5.25	27.5625
19	361	−3.25	10.5625
19	361	−3.25	10.5625
19	361	−3.25	10.5625
19	361	−3.25	10.5625
20	400	−2.25	5.0625
20	400	−2.25	5.0625
21	441	−1.25	1.5625
21	441	−1.25	1.5625
22	484	−0.25	0.0625
25	625	2.75	7.5625
27	729	4.75	22.5625
28	784	5.75	33.0625
28	784	5.75	33.0625
29	841	6.75	45.5625
31	961	8.75	76.5625
31	961	8.75	76.5625
Total 445	10385	0	483.75

$$\bar{X} = \frac{\sum_1^n X_i}{n} = \frac{445}{20} = 22.25$$

$$SS = \sum (X_i - \bar{X})^2 = 483.75$$

$$s^2 = \frac{SS}{n-1} = \frac{483.75}{20-1} = 25.46$$

$$s = \sqrt{s^2} = \sqrt{25.46} = 5.046$$

described below. The choice among these tests is based on the research question and the design of the study.

(i) *Tukey's Honestly Significant Difference*

Tukey's Honestly Significant Difference (HSD) test is used to compare all *pairs* of groups means. HSD can be applied when each of the pairwise comparisons is of interest to the researcher, or when the researcher does not have specific hypotheses about which group means will differ. Initially the groups means are calculated. In the hypothetical clinical trial example that has been discussed in this chapter, the groups are arranged in ascending order of their means: IPT ($\bar{X} = 15.05$), CBT ($\bar{X} = 21.00$), MM ($\bar{X} = 22.25$). Note that with k groups there are $\frac{k(k-1)}{2}$ pairwise comparisons. Thus, in this example, there are $\frac{k(k-1)}{2} = \frac{3(3-1)}{2} = 3$ comparisons: IPT vs. CBT, IPT vs. MM, and CBT vs. MM.

Table 8 ANOVA Table

Source	SS	df	MS	F
Treatment	592.033	2	296.017	10.966
Within	1538.697	57	26.995	
Total	2130.730	59		

$$SS_{Total} = \sum_{i=1}^{n}(X_i - \bar{X}_{..})^2$$

$$= (12 - 19.43)_2 + (12 - 19.43)^2$$

$$+ \cdots + (31 - 19.43)^2(31 - 19.43)^2$$

$$= 2130.733$$

$$SS_{Treatment} = \sum_{j=1}^{p} n_j(X_j - \bar{X}_{..})^2$$

$$= 20(21.00 - 19.43)^2$$

$$+ 20(15.05 - 19.43)^2$$

$$+ 20(22.25 - 19.43^2 = 592.033)$$

$$SS_{Within} = \sum_{i=1}^{N}(\bar{X}_{ij} - \bar{X}_j)^2$$

$$= (12 - 21)^2 + (12 - 21)^2$$

$$+ \cdots + (31 - 21)^2$$

$$+ (31 - 21)^2 = 1538.697$$

$$df_{Treatment} = k - 1, \text{where } k = \text{number of groups}$$

$$df_{Within} = N - k$$

$$df_{Total} = N - 1$$

$$MS_{Treatment} = \frac{SS_{Treatment}}{df_{Treatment}}$$

$$MS_{Within} = \frac{SS_{Within}}{df_{Within}}$$

$$F = \frac{MS_{Treatment}}{MS_{Within}}$$

The three pairwise mean differences are then calculated. The HSD test statistic, q, a ratio of the mean difference over the standard error, is computed for each pairwise comparison. For each comparison, if the observed $q >$ critical q (a tabled value), the null hypothesis of no difference between the pair of means is rejected. When there are an equal number of subjects per group, the standard error (se) is calculated as:

$$se = \frac{\sqrt{MSE}}{n_k} = \frac{\sqrt{26.995}}{20} = 1.16$$

where *MSE* comes from the ANOVA table (Table 8) and n_k is the number of subjects per group. The algorithm for unequal sample sizes

can be found in other texts (e.g., Zar, 1996). The results are presented in Table 9.

The hypothesis testing steps for Tukey's HSD are as follows:

(i) State research question. The ANOVA results indicated that the IPT, CBT, and MM do not have similar effects for the treatment of patients with depression. Which pairs of groups differ?

(ii) State two mutually exclusive and exhaustive hypotheses for each pairwise comparison:
    (a) $H_0 : \mu_{IPT} = \mu_{CBT}$
        $H_A : \mu_{IPT} \neq \mu_{CBT}$
    (b) $H_0 : \mu_{IPT} = \mu_{MM}$
        $H_A : \mu_{IPT} \neq \mu_{MM}$
    (c) $H_0 : \mu_{CBT} = \mu_{MM}$
        $H_A : \mu_{CBT} \neq \mu_{MM}$

(iii) Choose Tukey's HSD as a *post hoc* test to evaluate the hypotheses.

(iv) The critical value for the q-test with $\alpha = 0.05$ and df = 3,56 is 3.408. (Note that $df = k, v$, where $k =$ number of groups and $v = n - k - 1$.) Reject H_0 if $q > 3.408$.

(v) Data are displayed in Table 9 for the three pairwise comparisons.

(vi) Calculations were described above.

(vii) Decisions regarding H_0.
    IPT vs. CBT: $q_{observed} > q_{critical}$
    (i.e., 5.13 > 3.408), thus reject H_0.
    IPT vs. MM: $q_{observed} > q_{critical}$
    (i.e., 6.21 > 3.408), thus reject H_0.
    CBT vs. MM: $q_{observed} < q_{critical}$
    (i.e., 1.07 < 3.408), thus do not reject H_0.

(viii) Conclusion: IPT was more effective than either CBT or MM for the treatment of depressive symptoms in patients with major depressive disorder. There was no difference between CBT and MM for the treatment of depressive symptoms.

(ii) The Dunnett test

The Dunnett test is to be used when a control group is to be compared with each of several other treatments, and when no other comparisons are of interest. For instance, it could be used to demonstrate the efficacy of each treatment relative to placebo, but not to examine differences between active treatments. In the example that has been discussed, the

Table 9 Tukey HSD pairwise comparisons

Comparison	Mean difference	se	q
IPT vs. CBT	5.95	1.16	5.13
IPT vs. MM	7.20	1.16	6.21
CBT vs. MM	1.20	1.16	1.07

Dunnett test could be used for two comparisons: (i) CBT vs. MM, and (ii) IPT vs. MM. It could be used to show that IPT and CBT each have *active ingredients*; but the Dunnett test could not be used by members of the IPT and CBT camps to settle the score of whose method is superior. The Dunnett test, which will not be illustrated here, is described in detail in Fleiss (1986).

(iii) Scheffe Post Hoc Procedure

The Scheffe test is a more general procedure than those described above. It is not restricted to pairwise comparisons, but can evaluate comparisons of any linear combination of means. For instance, in the above example, one might have two comparisons of interest: (i) active (CBT and IPT) vs. placebo (MM), and (ii) CBT vs. IPT. The Scheffe procedure would be appropriate for those comparisons. The Scheffe test is somewhat more conservative than others in that it has less statistical power. For that reason some criticize the test for being more likely to miss true differences. Others consider the conservative nature of the test appealing. The Scheffe test will not be applied here. It is discussed in detail in Fleiss (1986).

3.12.4.3.5 Kruskal–Wallis test

The Kruskal–Wallis test (1952) is a nonparametric approach to the one-way ANOVA. The procedure is used to compare three or more groups on a dependent variable that is measured on at least an ordinal level. Ordinal data extends beyond rating scores such as the HRSD, and can include ordered categorical variables such as Hollingshead and Redlich's (1958) four broad categories of socioeconomic status. As with the Mann–Whitney test, which is a special two-group case of the Kruskal–Wallis test, the data are pooled (across groups) and ranked from *1* for the lowest value of the dependent variable to *N* for the highest value. In the case of ties, the midpoint is used. For example, if two subjects had the third lowest value, they would each be given a rank of 3.5, the midpoint of 3 and 4. The data from the hypothetical clinical trial comparing CBT, IPT, and MM (originally displayed in Tables 3, 5, and 7, respectively) have been ranked and are presented in Table 10.

After the data have been ranked, the sum of the ranks for each group is calculated:

$$R_j = \sum_{i=1}^{n_j} r_i$$

The mean rank for each of the three groups is then calculated:

$$\bar{r}_j = \frac{\sum_{i=1}^{n_j} r_i}{n_j}$$

The respective rank sums and means for each group are also presented in Table 10. Note that the IPT (18.075) group has a substantially lower mean rank than either the CBT (34.975) or MM (38.45) groups. The Kruskal–Wallis test can be used to determine whether that difference is larger than might be expected by chance. Stated differently, consider an experiment in which 20 numbers are randomly selected from a box that contains 60 balls, numbered 1 though 60. Would it be unlikely to randomly select a group of 20 balls whose sum is 361.5 or lower? Or whose mean is 18.075 or lower? In essence, the Kruskal–Wallis test addresses this question.

Once the ranking has been conducted and the sum of ranks for each group has been determined, the calculations for the Kruskal–Wallis test statistic, T, can proceed as follows:

$$T = \frac{(N-1)(S_t^2 - C)}{S_r^2 - C}$$

where

$$S_t^2 = \sum_{i=1}^{k} \frac{R_i^2}{n_i}$$

$$S_r^2 = \sum_{i=1}^{N} r_{ij}^2$$

$$C = \frac{N(N+1)^2}{4}$$

Applying these algorithms to the data that is presented in Table 10:

$$S_t^2 = \sum_{i=1}^{k} \frac{R_i^2}{n_i} = \frac{699.5^2}{20} + \frac{361.5^2}{20} + \frac{769^2}{20}$$
$$= 60567.175$$

$$S_r^2 = \sum_{i=1}^{N} r_{ij}^2$$
$$= 1^2 + 2^2 + 3^2 + \dots + 56^2 + 59^2 + 59^2$$
$$= 73587$$

$$C = \frac{N(N+1)^2}{4} = \frac{60(60+1)^2}{4} = 55815$$

$$T = \frac{(N-1)(S_t^2 - C)}{S_r^2 - C}$$
$$= \frac{(60-1)(60567.175 - 55815)}{73587 - 55815} = 15.776$$

Table 10   HRSD for 60 patients in the clinical trial of CBT, IPT, and MM: raw (X_{ij}) and ranked (R_{ij}) values.

	CBT		IPT		MM	
	X_{ij}	R_{ij}	X_{ij}	R_{ij}	X_{ij}	R_{ij}
	12	7	6	1	16	14.5
	12	7	7	2	16	14.5
	13	10.5	8	3	17	18
	14	12	9	4	17	18
	15	13	12	7	19	30
	17	18	12	7	19	30
	18	22	12	7	19	30
	19	30	13	10.5	19	30
	21	41	17	18	20	37.5
	21	41	17	18	20	37.5
	21	41	18	22	21	41
	22	44.5	18	22	21	41
	24	46	19	30	22	44.5
	25	47.5	19	30	25	47.5
	26	49	19	30	27	51
	27	51	19	30	28	54
	27	51	19	30	28	54
	28	54	19	30	29	57
	29	57	19	30	31	59.5
	29	57	19	30	31	59.5
Total	420	699.5	301	361.5	445	769
$\bar{R}$		34.975		18.075		38.45

Assumptions of the Kruskal–Wallis test include:

(i) The samples are independent random samples from their respective populations.

(ii) The scale of measurement (of the dependent variable) is at least ordinal.

The hypothesis testing steps for the Kruskal–Wallis test are as follows:

(i) State research question. Do CBT, IPT, and MM have similar effects for the treatment of patients with depression?

(ii) State two mutually exclusive and exhaustive hypotheses with regard to group medians:

    (a) $H_0:M_1 = M_2 = M_3$
    (b) $H_A:M_1 \neq M_2 \neq M_3$

(iii) Use the Kruskal–Wallis test to evaluate the hypotheses.

(iv) The critical value for the Kruskal–Wallis test comparing k groups comes from an χ^2 distribution, with $k-1$ degrees of freedom and $\alpha = 0.05$. In this case there are three groups ($k = 3$) and df $= 3-1 = 2$. Therefore, the critical $\chi^2_{(2,.05)} = 5.99$. If $T_{observed} > 5.99$, reject H_0

(v) Data are displayed in Table 10 for the three groups.

(vi) Calculations are described above.

(vii) Decision regarding H_0. $T_{observed} > \chi^2_{critical}$ (i.e., $15.77 > 5.99$), thus reject H_0.

(viii) Conclusion. There is a significant difference in severity of depression among the treatments. (Which groups actually differ can

only be determined using an appropriate *post hoc* test, as discussed below.)

This significant result in a Kruskal–Wallis test indicates that there are group differences, but does not indicate which groups differ. As with an ANOVA, a *post hoc* procedure that is analogous to the HSD for ANOVAs can be used to determine which groups are significantly different from each other. That procedure, which will not be discussed here, is described in detail by Conover (1980). Note that in this case, the Kruskal–Wallis results are similar to those of the ANOVA. This is not always the case. The choice between the two tests should be based on whether or not the assumptions of the test are fulfilled and *not* on a comparison of their results. When the results from an ANOVA and a Kruskal–Wallis test conflict, the degree of discrepancy between the two tests may, in part, reflect the extent to which the assumptions were fulfilled.

3.12.4.3.6 Factorial analysis of variance

The fixed effect ANOVA model that was just discussed can be extended to include more than one independent variable. Consider a clinical trial in which the two treatments (CBT and IPT) were compared among samples of two types of mood disorders (major depressive disorder and dysthymia). In such a design the two fixed *factors* (independent variables) are treatment and diagnosis, which each have two *levels*. The two-way ANOVA is used to test *main effects* of each independent variable and the *interaction* between the independent variables. The null hypotheses are:

Main effect of
treatment $\quad H_0: \mu_1. = \mu_2.$
Main effect of
diagnosis $\quad H_0: \mu._1 = \mu._2$
Treatment by diagnosis
interaction $\quad H_0: \mu_{11} - \mu_{12} = \mu_{21} - \mu_{22}$

Note that the first subscript represents treatment level (where 1 = CBT and 2 = IPT), the second subscript represents diagnosis (where 1 = dysthymia and 2 = MDD). In the null hypotheses for the main effects, a dot (.) in the subscript indicates that the corresponding particular variable is ignored. These three null hypotheses are tested with data from one experiment. The *two* main effects in this two-way ANOVA represent an extension of the one main effect that is tested in a one-way ANOVA model described earlier. What is more novel about a *factorial* ANOVA design is the interaction between the factors, which is used to examine the moderating effect one factor has on the effect that the other factor has on the dependent variable. In the hypothetical study presented here, an interaction is used to compare treatment differences (CBT vs. IPT) across diagnostic groups. Stated differently, it is used to examine whether there is a larger difference between IPT and CBT for subjects with MDD or for subjects with dysthymia.

The data from the clinical trial shown earlier in Tables 3 and 5 have been stratified by diagnosis and are presented in Table 11. In a simple comparison of the means, it is clear that the IPT group has a substantially lower mean than the CBT group. Likewise, the dysthymia group has a lower mean than the MDD group. In both cases, the differences are of the order of one standard deviation. The factorial ANOVA is used to evaluate whether or not these differences are larger than might be expected by chance. Furthermore, the ANOVA will be used to compare the treatment effects across diagnostic groups.

The calculations for a two-way factorial ANOVA involve partitioning the total sums of squares into four components: SS_{Tx}, SS_{Dx}, SS_{TxbyDx}, SS_{within}. The algorithms are described in Table 12 and illustrated in Table 13. Note that the subscript *g* represents treatment ($g = 1,2$), the subscript *h* represents diagnosis ($h = 1,2$), and the subscript *i* represents individual subject ($i = 1-N$; $N = 40$ in this case).

The formulae that are presented are applicable for designs with cells of equal size (n; $n = 10$ in this case) and are presented to illustrate the concept of the partitioning of sums of squares in a two-way ANOVA. Notice that each estimates a different form of sum of squared deviations (SS) from a mean that represents a component of the variability among the HRSD of all subjects in the clinical trial.

In order to conduct the *F*-tests of the ANOVA that correspond to the three null hypotheses, several additional calculations are required. The algorithms for these quantities are presented in Table 12. The first column of the table indicates the *source of variability*. The second column displays the SS (calculated above) that correspond to each of the four sources of variability. The third column of Table 12 presents the degrees of freedom that correspond to each source of variability. The calculation of degrees of freedom is described in Table 12. The fourth column in Table 12 presents the mean square (*MS*) for each source of variability which is equal to the sum of squares for that source divided by the corresponding degrees of freedom. In the final column of Table 12, the *F*-test for each effect is equal to the mean squares for that effect divided by the mean square within (MS_{within}). The results of the data from the example are shown in Table 13.

Assumptions of the factorial ANOVA are as follows:

(i) The observations in each of the cells are independent samples.

(ii) The population data are normally distributed.

(iii) The populations all have equal variances.

The hypothesis testing steps for the factorial ANOVA are as follows:

(i) State research questions.

(a) Do CBT and IPT have similar effects on depressive symptomatology for the treatment of patients with depression?

(b) Do patients with major depressive disorder and dysthymia have similar depressive symptomatology after the treatment of depression?

(c) Do CBT and IPT have similar effects on depressive symptomatology for patients with major depressive disorder and dysthymia?

(ii) State sets of mutually exclusive and exhaustive hypotheses:

(a) Main effect of treatment
$H_0: \mu_1. = \mu_2.$
$H_A: \mu_1. \neq \mu_2.$

(b) Main effect of diagnosis
$H_0: \mu._1 = \mu._2$
$H_A: \mu._1 \neq \mu._2$

(c) Interaction of treatment by diagnosis
$$H_0 : \mu_{11} - \mu_{21} = \mu_{12} - \mu_{22}$$
$$H_A : \mu_{11} - \mu_{21} = \mu_{12} - \mu_{22}$$
(iii) If assumptions have been fulfilled, use the two-way factorial ANOVA to evaluate the hypotheses.

(iv) The critical F-values are selected from an F-table based on the degrees of freedom numerator, degrees of freedom denominator, and alpha-level. The critical value for the F-test with $\alpha = 0.05$ and $df = 1,36$ is 5.47. Reject H_0 if $F_{observed} > F_{critical}$.

(v) Data are displayed in Table 11.

(vi) Calculations are described above.

(vii) Decisions regarding the three H_0s.

(a) Main effect of treatment
The main effect of treatment is statistically significant:
$F_{obs} > F_{critical(1,36;.05)}$ (i.e., 17.114 > 5.47).

(b) Main effect of diagnosis
The main effect of diagnosis is statistically significant:
$F_{obs} > F_{critical(1,36;.05)}$ (i.e., 14.359 > 5.47).

(c) Interaction of treatment by diagnosis
The treatment by diagnosis interaction is not statistically significant:
$F_{obs} < F_{critical(1,36;.05)}$ (i.e., 0.639 < 5.47).

(viii) Conclusion. IPT is a significantly more effective treatment than CBT for depressive symptoms. Patients with major depressive disorder have significantly more depressive symptomatology than those with dysthymia after treatment. The differential effects of IPT and CBT are similar for patients with major depressive disorder and patients with dysthymia.

In this case, *post hoc* tests such as those described earlier are not needed to interpret these results because there are only two levels of each significant factor and there is not a significant interaction. To determine which level of each factor had a better outcome in this clinical trial, simply compare the means of each level of the significant effects and determine which is lower (i.e., less depressed on the HRSD). For the treatment effect, the IPT group mean (sd) is substantially lower than that of the CBT group: 15.05 (4.67) vs. 21.00 (5.80). The two groups differ by more than one standard deviation, which is a very large difference. Similarly, the dysthymia group mean (sd) is substantially lower than that of the MDD group: 15.30 (5.57) vs. 20.75 (5.24). Here the groups differ by slightly less than one standard deviation, which is

Table 11   Hamilton Depression Ratings for 40 patients in the clinical trial of CBT and IPT stratified by diagnosis.

Treatment Diagnosis		CBT DYS	CBT MDD	IPT DYS	IPT MDD
		12	14	6	12
		12	19	7	13
		13	26	8	17
		15	27	9	17
		17	22	12	18
		18	24	12	19
		21	25	18	19
		21	28	19	19
		21	29	19	19
		27	29	19	19
Four cells	sum	177	243	129	172
	mean	17.70	24.30	12.90	17.20
	sd	4.88	4.81	5.38	2.62
	SS	3347	6113	1925	3020
Diagnosis		DYS	MDD		
	sum	306	415		
	mean	15.30	20.75		
	sd	5.57	5.24		
	SS	5272	9133		
Treatment		CBT	IPT		
	sum	420.00	301.00		
	mean	21.00	15.05		
	sd	5.80	4.67		
	SS	9460	4945		

Table 12 Two-way ANOVA table.

Source	SS	df	MS	F
Treatment	SS_{Tx}	$p-1$	$SS_{Tx}/(p-1)$	MS_{Tx}/MS_{within}
Diagnosis	SS_{Dx}	$q-1$	$SS_{Dx}/(q-1)$	MS_{Dx}/MS_{within}
Tx by dx	$SS_{Tx\ by\ Dx}$	$(p-1)(q-1)$	$SS_{Tx\ by\ dx}/(p-1)(q-1)$	$MS_{Tx\ by\ dx}/MS_{within}$
Within	SS_{within}	$pq(n-1)$	$SS_{within}/pq(n-1)$	
Total	SS_{Total}	$n-1$		

$$SS_{Total} = \sum_{i=1}^{N}(X_{ghi} - \bar{X}...)^2$$

$$SS_{Tx} = nq\sum_{j=1}^{p}(\bar{X}_{g..} - \bar{X}...)^2$$

$$SS_{Dx} = np\sum_{k=1}^{q}(\bar{X}_{.h.} - \bar{X}_{...})^2$$

$$SS_{TxbyDx} = n\sum_{g=1}^{p}\sum_{h=1}^{q}\left[(\bar{X}_{gh.} - \bar{X}_{...}) - (\bar{X}_{g..} - \bar{X}_{...}) - (\bar{X}_{.h.} - \bar{X}_{...})\right]^2$$

$$SS_{Within} = \sum_{g=1}^{p}\sum_{h=1}^{q}\sum_{i=1}^{n}(\bar{X}_{ghi} - \bar{X}_{gh.})^2$$

again a substantial difference. In contrast, the interaction was not significant. Consider the differences in treatment means across diagnoses:

$$\bar{X}_{CBT/DYS} - \bar{X}_{IPT/DYS} = 17.70 - 12.90 = 4.80$$

and

$$\bar{X}_{CBT/MDD} - \bar{X}_{IPT/MDD} = 24.30 - 17.20 = 7.10$$

Relative to the variation within treatment (marginal standard deviations range from 4.67 to 5.80), the difference in mean differences ($7.10 - 4.80 = 2.30$), is not substantial enough to consider it more than might be expected by chance.

The *two-way factorial ANOVA* example that was just discussed included two factors (i.e., independent variables: treatment and diagnosis), each of which had two levels. The factorial ANOVA can incorporate factors which have more than two levels each. This was shown in the earlier example of the one-way ANOVA in which there were three levels of treatment (CBT, IPT, and MM). In addition, the factorial design can be extended to include more than two factors. For instance, the clinical trial could have been conducted to test the effect of gender as well as treatment and diagnosis. Such a design is called a *three-way ANOVA*, which includes tests of three main effects (treatment,

diagnosis, and gender), three two-way interactions (treatment by diagnosis, treatment by gender, and diagnosis by gender), and one three-way interaction (treatment by diagnosis by gender). For an extensive discussion of ANOVA designs see Keppel (1991).

In this chapter, two multivariate statistical procedures will be introduced, but not discussed in depth. For a comprehensive discussion of these and other multivariate tests, see Bock (1985), Grimm and Yarnold (1995), Marcoulides and Hershberger (1997), or Stevens (1992). Here multivariate means that multiple dependent variables are being examined in one test. For instance, consider the comparison of affectively ill patients with schizophrenic patients on a battery of six personality scales. There are two schools of thought for use of a multivariate procedure such as this. One is that it should be used if there is a multivariate research question. For example, do the personalities of the two diagnostic groups differ as a whole? The researcher who asks this question, might be most interested in personality as a general construct, and less interested in the specific differences in ego resiliency, dependency and other personality characteristics. In contrast, others would argue that the multivariate procedures should be used to protect against Type I error whenever several dependent variables are examined.

Table 13 Hamilton depression ratings for clinical trial of CBT and IPT by diagnosis: ANOVA table.

Source	SS	df	MS	F
Treatment	354.025	1	354.025	17.114
Diagnosis	297.025	1	297.025	14.359
Tx by dx	13.225	1	13.225	0.639
Within	744.70	36	20.686	
Total	1408.975	39		

$$\mathrm{SS_{Total}} = \sum_{i=1}^{n}(X_{ghi} - \bar{X}_{...})^2$$

$$= (12 - 18.025)^2 + (12 - 18.025)^2$$
$$+ \cdots + (19 - 18.025)^2$$
$$+ (19 - 18.025)^2 = 1408.975$$

$$\mathrm{SS_{TX}} = nq\sum_{j=1}^{q}(\bar{X}_{g..} - \bar{X}_{...})^2$$

$$= 10 \cdot 2 \cdot \left[(21 - 18.025)^2\right.$$
$$\left. + (15.05 - 18.025)^2\right] = 354.025$$

$$\mathrm{SS_{DX}} = np\sum_{k=1}^{q}(\bar{X}_{.h.} - \bar{X}_{...})^2$$

$$= 10 \cdot 2 \cdot \left[(15.3 - 18.025)^2\right.$$
$$\left. + (20.75 - 18.025)^2\right] = 297.025$$

$$\mathrm{SS_{TxbyDx}} = n\sum_{g=1}^{p}\sum_{h=1}^{q}\left[(\bar{X}_{gh.} - \bar{X}_{...}) - (\bar{X}_{g..} - \bar{X}_{...})\right.$$
$$\left. - (\bar{X}_{.h.} - \bar{X}...)\right]^2$$

$$= 10 \cdot \left[(17.7 - 18.025) + (21.0 - 18.025)\right.$$
$$\left. + (15.3 - 18.025)\right]^2 + \cdots$$
$$\cdots + \left[(17.2 - 18.025) + (20.75 - 18.025)\right.$$
$$\left. + (15.05 - 18.025)\right]^2 = 13.225$$

$$\mathrm{SS_{Within}} = \sum_{g=1}^{p}\sum_{h=1}^{q}\sum_{i=1}^{n}(\bar{X}_{ghi} - \bar{X}_{gh})^2$$

$$= (12 - 17.7)^2 + (12 - 17.7)^2$$
$$+ \cdots + (19 - 17.2)^2 + (19 - 17.2)^2$$
$$= 744.70$$

3.12.4.3.7 Hotelling's T²

Hotelling's T^2 is used to compare two groups on multiple continuous dependent variables, simultaneously. Consider that if a series of six univariate *t*-tests were performed on these scales, the probability of a Type I error would be substantially elevated from the conventional 0.05 level. In general, the experimentwise alpha level for *c* comparisons is calculated as follows: $\alpha_{EW} = 1 - (1 - \alpha)^c$. Thus, in lieu of a multivariate procedure, the two groups might be compared using six univariate *t*-tests (one for each of the six dependent variables—the personality scales) and the resulting experimentwise alpha level would be $\alpha_{EW} = 1 - (1 - 0.05)^6 = 1 - 0.735 = 0.265$, which certainly exceeds the conventional Type I error level of 0.05.

Although the computational details of Hotelling's T^2 are beyond the scope of this chapter, some general issues regarding the procedure will be introduced. First, the null hypothesis is that the populations from which the two groups come do not differ on (a linear combination) of the scales (see below). Second, assumptions of Hotelling's T^2 include multivariate normality and independence of observations across subjects. Third, Hotelling's T^2 is an omnibus multivariate procedure. If, and only if, the multivariate null hypothesis is rejected, can subsequent *post hoc* univariate tests be used to identify the source of the difference (i.e., on which dependent variable(s) do the groups differ?). This is similar to the approach to the comparison of three or more groups in an ANOVA where, if the omnibus *F*-test is significant, a *post hoc* test must be used to determine which groups differ significantly. However, those *post hoc* tests cannot be used if the omnibus *F* of the univariate ANOVA is not significant. In the case of Hotelling's T^2, the *post hoc* tests would simply be a *t*-test for each dependent variable.

The hypothesis testing steps for Hotelling's T^2 are as follows:

(i) State research question. Are the personality profiles of affectively ill patients and schizophrenic patients similar (using a battery of six personality scales)?

(ii) State two mutually exclusive and exhaustive hypotheses:

$$H_0 : \begin{bmatrix} \mu_{11} \\ \mu_{21} \\ \mu_{31} \\ \mu_{41} \\ \mu_{51} \\ \mu_{61} \end{bmatrix} = \begin{bmatrix} \mu_{12} \\ \mu_{22} \\ \mu_{32} \\ \mu_{42} \\ \mu_{52} \\ \mu_{62} \end{bmatrix}$$

$$H_A : \begin{bmatrix} \mu_{11} \\ \mu_{21} \\ \mu_{31} \\ \mu_{41} \\ \mu_{51} \\ \mu_{61} \end{bmatrix} \neq \begin{bmatrix} \mu_{12} \\ \mu_{22} \\ \mu_{32} \\ \mu_{42} \\ \mu_{52} \\ \mu_{62} \end{bmatrix}$$

(iii) If the assumptions are met, use the Hotelling's T^2 evaluate the hypotheses.

(iv) The critical value, calculations, decision rules, and interpretation of Hotelling's T^2 are described elsewhere (e.g., Stevens (1992) or Marcoulides & Hershberger (1997)).

3.12.4.3.8 Multivariate analysis of variance

Multivariate analysis of variance (MANOVA) is an extension of the T^2 for the comparison of three or more groups. For example, three groups (e.g., mood disorders, schizophrenics, and no history of a mental disorder) can be compared on a battery of six personality scales using a MANOVA. Similar to the factorial ANOVA, MANOVA can also be extended to incorporate more than one factor. For instance, a two-way MANOVA could evaluate the main effects and interaction of gender and diagnosis (mood disorders vs. schizophrenics vs. no history of a mental disorder) in which the dependent variables are a battery of six personality scales. If any of those three omnibus multivariate tests (i.e, main effects of gender or diagnosis or the gender by diagnosis interaction) are statistically significant, subsequent *post hoc* tests must be conducted to determine the source of the group differences. The choice among multivariate test statistics (e.g., Pillais, Hotelling's, Wilks, or Roy) is considered by Olson (1976). *Post hoc* tests for MANOVA are described in detail by Stevens (1992).

Assumptions of MANOVA include:

(i) independence among observations (i.e., subjects)

(ii) a multivariate normal distribution among the dependent variables

(iii) equal population covariance matrices for the dependent variables.

The hypothesis testing steps for MANOVA are as follows:

(i) State research question. Are the personality profiles of affectively ill patients, schizophrenic patients, and those with no history of mental disorders similar (using a battery of six personality scales)?

(ii) State two mutually exclusive and exhaustive hypotheses:

$$H_0 : \begin{bmatrix} \mu_{11} \\ \mu_{21} \\ \mu_{31} \\ \mu_{41} \\ \mu_{51} \\ \mu_{61} \end{bmatrix} = \begin{bmatrix} \mu_{12} \\ \mu_{22} \\ \mu_{32} \\ \mu_{42} \\ \mu_{52} \\ \mu_{62} \end{bmatrix} = \begin{bmatrix} \mu_{13} \\ \mu_{23} \\ \mu_{33} \\ \mu_{43} \\ \mu_{53} \\ \mu_{63} \end{bmatrix}$$

$$H_A : \begin{bmatrix} \mu_{11} \\ \mu_{21} \\ \mu_{31} \\ \mu_{41} \\ \mu_{51} \\ \mu_{61} \end{bmatrix} \neq \begin{bmatrix} \mu_{12} \\ \mu_{22} \\ \mu_{32} \\ \mu_{42} \\ \mu_{52} \\ \mu_{62} \end{bmatrix} \neq \begin{bmatrix} \mu_{13} \\ \mu_{23} \\ \mu_{33} \\ \mu_{43} \\ \mu_{53} \\ \mu_{63} \end{bmatrix}$$

(iii) If the assumptions are met, use a MANOVA to evaluate the hypotheses.

(iv) The critical value, calculations, decision rules, and interpretation of MANOVA are described elsewhere (e.g., Marcoulides & Hershberger, 1997; Pedhazur, 1982; Stevens, 1992).

3.12.4.4 Linear Relations

3.12.4.4.1 Pearson correlation coefficient

The strength of the bivariate linear relation between variables can be examined with a correlation coefficient. The Pearson product moment correlation coefficient, r, is most often used for this purpose. In correlational analyses, a distinction need not be made between the independent and dependent variables. Unlike the univariate analyses that were discussed earlier, each subject contributes data in the form of paired coordinates (x, y) to the analysis.

Consider the data in Figure 12 which represents the relation between depression (on the x-axis) and functional impairment (on the y-axis). (These same data are presented in the first two columns of Table 14.) If there were even a modest linear relation between depression and functional impairment, one would expect minimal impairment in the mildly depressed and greater impairment in the severely depressed. It is a correlation coefficient that quantifies the strength of that linear relationship. (Once again, as a point of clarification, unlike much of the prior discussion in this chapter, here we consider two variables from one group of subjects.)

A brief digression may help with this explanation. It is quite likely that the two variables in a correlational analysis are measured on very different scales. For instance, in this sample, the impairment and depression means (21.00 and 14.45, respectively) and standard deviations (5.80 and 4.93, respectively) differ somewhat. For that reason, consider a scale-free metric, a standardized score, referred to as a "z-score," which has the property of a mean of zero and standard deviation of one. A transformation from the original scale (X_i) to the standardized scale (Z_i) is quite simple. The original variable (X_i) is transformed by subtracting the mean and dividing by the standard deviation:

Table 14 Hamilton depression ratings and Sheehan Disability Scale for CBT group.

X_i	Y_i	X_i^2	Y_i^2	X_iY_i	$X_i - \bar{X}$	$Y_i - \bar{Y}$	$(X_i - \bar{X})^2$	$(Y_i - \bar{Y})^2$	$x \cdot y$	z_x	z_y	$Z_x \cdot Z_y$
12	11	144	121	132	−9.00	−3.45	81.00	11.90	31.05	−1.55	−0.70	1.09
12	8	144	64	96	−9.00	−6.45	81.00	41.60	58.05	−1.55	−1.31	2.03
13	6	169	36	78	−8.00	−8.45	64.00	71.40	67.60	−1.38	−1.72	2.36
14	14	196	196	196	−7.00	−0.45	49.00	0.20	3.15	−1.21	−0.09	0.11
15	11	225	121	165	−6.00	−3.45	36.00	11.90	20.70	−1.03	−0.70	0.72
17	8	289	64	136	−4.00	−6.45	16.00	41.60	25.80	−0.69	−1.31	0.90
18	16	324	256	288	−3.00	1.55	9.00	2.40	−4.65	−0.52	0.31	−0.16
19	8	361	64	152	−2.00	−6.45	4.00	41.60	12.90	−0.34	−1.31	0.45
21	15	441	225	315	0.00	0.55	0.00	0.30	0.00	0.00	0.11	0.00
21	22	441	484	462	0.00	7.55	0.00	57.00	0.00	0.00	1.53	0.00
21	12	441	144	252	0.00	−2.45	0.00	6.00	0.00	0.00	−0.50	0.00
22	19	484	361	418	1.00	4.55	1.00	20.70	4.55	0.17	0.92	0.16
24	15	576	225	360	3.00	0.55	9.00	0.30	1.65	0.52	0.11	0.06
25	19	625	361	475	4.00	4.55	16.00	20.70	18.20	0.69	0.92	0.64
26	16	676	256	416	5.00	1.55	25.00	2.40	7.75	0.86	0.31	0.27
27	22	729	484	594	6.00	7.55	36.00	57.00	45.30	1.03	1.53	1.58
27	18	729	324	486	6.00	3.55	36.00	12.60	21.30	1.03	0.72	0.75
28	21	784	441	588	7.00	6.55	49.00	42.90	45.85	1.21	1.33	1.60
29	11	841	121	319	8.00	−3.45	64.00	11.90	−27.60	1.38	−0.70	−0.97
29	17	841	289	493	8.00	2.55	64.00	6.50	20.40	1.38	0.52	0.71
Total												
420	289	9460	4637	6421.00	0.00	0.00	640.00	460.95	352.00	0.00	0.00	12.31
Mean												
21.00	14.45	473.00	231.85	321.05	0.00	0.00	32.00	23.05	17.60	0.00	0.00	0.62
sd												
5.804	4.925	239.790	142.538	165.468	5.803	4.925	28.038	22.404	23.171	1	1	0.8106

$x_i = X_i - \bar{X}$; $y_i = Y_i - \bar{Y}$; $Z_{x_i} = \frac{X_i - \bar{X}}{s_x}$; $Z_{y_i} = \frac{Y_i - \bar{Y}}{s_y}$.

Relationship between depression and functional impairment

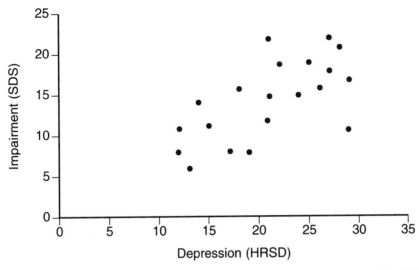

Figure 12 Plot of Hamilton Depression Ratings and Sheehan Disability Scale for CBT group.

$$Z_i = \frac{X_i - \bar{X}}{s_x}$$

The plot of standardized depression and functional impairment in Figure 13 looks identical to that of Figure 12, with the exception of the scale of the axes. (Note that in order to distinguish between the standardized X_is and standardized Y_is, Xs and Ys will be included in the subscript of the standardized scores: Z_{xi} and Z_{yi}.) As a consequence of the standardization, the Z_x-axis is plotted at $Y = 0$, which is the unstandardized y-mean, and the Z_y-axis is plotted at $X = 0$, the unstandardized x-mean.

As stated earlier, if there were a modest linear relation between depression and impairment, there would be minimal impairment in the mildly depressed and greater impairment in the severely depressed. Consider this positive linear relationship as presented in Figure 12. The points that are plotted tend to cluster either in quadrant I or in quadrant III. The latter fall in the upper-right quadrant, where subjects tend to have both relatively elevated depression and relatively elevated functional impairment. Stated differently, both the x-values and y-values are above the mean in Figure 12, and the standardized z_x and z_y scores are both positive in Figure 13. On the other hand, the subjects who have both relatively lower depression and relatively lower functional impairment are in the lower-left quadrant. That is, both the x-values and y-values are below the mean. In contrast, a negative linear relationship would characterize an association in which a high x-value tends to correspond with a low y-value,

and a low x-value corresponds with a high y-value (e.g., depression and work productivity). Nunnally (1978) shows that the Pearson r can be calculated as approximately the mean of the sum of the product of z-scores:

$$r_{xy} = \frac{\sum\limits_{i=1}^{N} Z_x Z_y}{N - 1}$$

With this algorithm it can be seen that if most subjects tend to have either high Z_xs and high Z_ys, or low Z_xs and low Z_ys, r will be larger and positive, approaching 1.0. In contrast, if most subjects tend to have either high Z_xs with low Z_ys, or low Z_xs with high Z_ys, r will have a large absolute value, but will be negative, approaching -1.0.

Using the data that are presented in Table 14:

$$r = \frac{\sum\limits_{i=1}^{N} z_x z_y}{N - 1} = \frac{12.31}{20 - 1} = 0.648$$

The presentation of the algorithm for the Pearson correlation coefficient (r) usually comes from a seemingly different perspective which will now be discussed. The correlation coefficient is derived from the covariance. First, consider that the sum of cross-products ($\sum xy$) is a sum of the product of both the x-deviations (x) and y-deviations (y) from their respective means: $\sum xy = \sum (X_i - \bar{X})(Y_i - \bar{Y})$.

For instance, the first subject in Table 14 has an X-value (HRSD) of 12 and a Y-value (SDS) of 11. The respective deviation scores are:

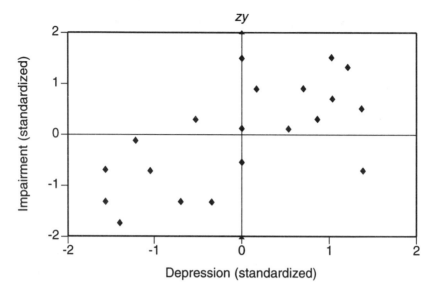

Figure 13 Plot of standardized Hamilton Depression Ratings and standardized Sheehan Disability Scale for subjects in the CBT group ($N = 20$).

$$x_1 = X_1 - \bar{X} = 12 - 21 = -9$$
$$y_1 = Y_1 - \bar{Y} = 11 - 14.45 = -3.45$$

The product of the deviation scores is called the cross-product. For the first subject, the cross-product is:

$$x_1 y_1 = -9 \cdot (-3.45) = 31.05$$

Once again, the sum of cross-products $\left(\sum_{i=1}^{N} x_i y_i\right)$ or $\left(\sum xy\right)$ is a sum of each subject's product of deviation scores. Notice that the sum of cross-products is a bivariate extension of the sum of squares that was described earlier, but the sum of cross-products incorporates two variables:

$$\sum x^2 = \sum (X_i - \bar{X})(X_i - \bar{X})$$

The covariance (s_{xy}), therefore, is a bivariate analogue of the variance. Consequently, the covariance is a function of the sum of cross-products:

$$s_{xy} = \frac{\sum xy}{n-1}$$

Using the equations above, the covariance (s_{xy}) can also be calculated:

$$s_{xy} = \frac{\sum (X_i - \bar{X})(Y_i - \bar{Y})}{n-1}$$

The covariance (s_{xy}) is a useful quantity that also measures the strength of the linear relationship between two variables. However,

its interpretability is somewhat limited because it is not scale-free. As a consequence, unlike the correlation coefficient (r), which ranges from negative to positive (i.e., $-1.0 \leqslant r \leqslant 1.0$), the covariance does not have a fixed range.

Notice that the variance of a variable can be thought of as a special case of the covariance of that variable with itself: $S_{xx} = \sum (X_i - \bar{X})(X_i - \bar{X})$. A variance–covariance matrix is a convenient format to display the variances and covariances among several variables:

	X	Y	Z
X	s_X^2	s_{XY}	s_{XZ}
Y	s_{YX}	s_Y^2	s_{YZ}
Z	s_{ZX}	s_{ZY}	s_Z^2

The variances are on the main diagonal and the covariances are the remaining elements of the matrix. The matrix is symmetrical about the main diagonal. That is, in general, $s_{ij} = s_{ji}$. Or in the case, $s_{XY} = s_{YX}$.

Using the data from Table 14, the covariance is:

$$S_{xy} = \frac{\sum xy}{n-1} = \frac{\sum_{i=1}^{n}(X_i - \bar{X})(Y_i - \bar{Y})}{n-1}$$
$$= \frac{352}{20-1} = 18.526$$

Turning back to the correlation coefficient, r can be calculated using these quantities. It is equal to the covariance (s_{xy}) of X_i and Y_i, divided by the product of their standard deviations:

$$r_{XY} = \frac{S_{XY}}{S_X S_Y} = \frac{18.526}{5.803 \cdot 4.925} = 0.648$$

As stated earlier, the correlation coefficient (r) can range from -1 to $+1$. The greater the absolute value of r, the greater the strength of the bivariate linear relationship.

The statistical significance of the population correlation coefficient, ρ, can be tested using the sample data. The null hypothesis, $H_0: \rho = 0$, is tested with the following ratio:

$$t = \frac{r}{s_r}$$

where s_r is the standard error of r,

$$s_r = \sqrt{\frac{1 - r^2}{n - 2}}$$

This t-ratio is tested with $n-2$ dfs. Applying this to the data from Table 14, the standard error of r is:

$$s_r = \sqrt{\frac{1 - r^2}{n - 2}} = \sqrt{\frac{1 - 0.648^2}{20 - 2}} = 0.1795$$

The t-ratio is:

$$t = \frac{r}{s_r} = \frac{0.648}{0.1795} = 3.61$$

The hypothesis testing steps for the Pearson correlation coefficient are as follows:

(i) State research question. Is there a linear relationship between depression and impairment?

(ii) State two mutually exclusive and exhaustive hypotheses:

    (a) $H_0: \rho_{XY} = 0$

    (b) $H_A: \rho_{XY} \neq 0$

(iii) Choose the t-ratio to evaluate the hypotheses about the Pearson correlation coefficient.

(iv) The critical value for the t-ratio with $\alpha = 0.05$ and df $= 18$ is 2.101. If $t_{observed} > t_{critical}$, reject H_0.

(v) Data regarding depression and impairment are displayed in Table 14.

(vi) Calculations were described above.

(vii) Decision regarding H_0. Since $t_{observed} > t_{critical}$ (i.e., $3.61 > 2.101$), reject H_0.

(viii) Conclusion. Based on data from this sample, we conclude that there is a statistically significant linear relationship between depression and impairment.

Although the null hypothesis, $H_0: \rho = 0$, was rejected, be cautious not to overinterpret the results of such a test. The hypothesis simply examines the likelihood of observing a correlation of the *magnitude* seen in the sample, when the population correlation is zero (i.e., $\rho = 0$).

Nevertheless, it ignores the meaningfulness of the magnitude of r. There is a disproportionate emphasis on the *statistical significance* of r while at the same time a tendency to ignore the *magnitude* of r in the research literature.

The magnitude of the correlation can be thought of as the proportion of variance in Y_i explained by X_i. In fact, because in correlational analyses a distinction between independent variable and dependent variable is unnecessary, the magnitude of the correlation can also be thought of as the proportion of variance in X_i explained by Y_i. In either case, the magnitude of the correlation coefficient r is calculated as the squared correlation coefficient, r^2, or, more commonly, R^2. Since the variability in human behavior and affect are not easily explained, meaningful R^2s in behavioral sciences can be quite small ($R^2 < 0.10$) and an $R^2 > 0.20$ may be considered substantial. Using the data from the *hypothetical* example in Table 14, 42% of the variance in functional impairment is explained by depression (i.e., $R^2 = r^2 = 0.648^2 = 0.420$).

3.12.4.4.2 Test for a difference between two independent correlation coefficients

The correlation coefficients of two groups can be compared by testing the following null hypothesis:

$$H_0: \rho_1 = \rho_2$$

The test is conducted in the following manner. First, each correlation coefficient (r_k) is transformed into a Z_k using a procedure called the r_k to Z_k transformation. Note that the subscript k represents group k. Unlike earlier notation, in this context the subscript is not used to differentiate among subjects.

$$Z_k = 0.5 \cdot \ln\left(\frac{1 + r_k}{1 - r_k}\right)$$

where $k = 1$ or 2 and ln represents the natural logarithm.

Next a standard error is calculated:

$$\rho_{z_1 - z_2} = \sqrt{\frac{1}{n_1 - 3} + \frac{1}{n_2 - 3}}$$

Finally, the Z-statistic is calculated:

$$Z = \frac{Z_1 - Z_2}{\sigma_{z_1 - z_2}}$$

For example, this could be used to address the question, "Is the strength of the linear relation between depression and functional impairment different in the subjects in the CBT and IPT groups?" Although IPT impairment data are not presented in a table, for illustration assume that for the IPT group $r = 0.41$. Comparison of the correlation coefficients for the CBT and IPT groups proceeds as follows:

$$Z_1 = 0.5 \cdot \ln\left(\frac{1 + r_1}{1 - r_1}\right) = 0.5 \cdot \ln\left(\frac{1 + .648}{1 - .648}\right)$$

$$= .772$$

$$Z_2 = 0.5 \cdot \ln\left(\frac{1 + r_2}{1 - r_2}\right) = 0.5 \cdot \ln\left(\frac{1 + .41}{1 - .41}\right)$$

$$= .436$$

$$\sigma_{z_1 - z_2} = \sqrt{\frac{1}{n_1 - 3} + \frac{1}{n_2 - 3}}$$

$$= \sqrt{\frac{1}{20 - 3} + \frac{1}{20 - 3}} = .343$$

$$Z = \frac{Z_1 - Z_2}{\sigma_{z_1 - z_2}} = \frac{.772 - .436}{.343} = .980$$

The assumptions of the Z-test of correlation coefficients across two groups is that X and Y come from a bivariate normal distribution. What this means is that, if X comes from a normal distribution, and Y is normally distributed at every value of X.

The hypothesis testing steps for the Z-test to compare correlation coefficients across two groups are as follows:

(i) State research question. Is the strength of the linear relation between depression and functional impairment different for subjects in the CBT and IPT groups?

(ii) State two mutually exclusive and exhaustive hypotheses:

    (a) $H_0 : \rho_1 = \rho_2$
    (b) $H_A : \rho_1 \neq \rho_2$

(iii) Choose the Z-test to evaluate the hypotheses.

(iv) The critical value for the Z-test with $\alpha = 0.05$ is 1.96. If $z_{observed} > z_{critical}$, reject H_0.

(v) Data are displayed in Table 14 for the CBT group. The correlation for the IPT group was specified in the text as $r = 0.41$.

(vi) Calculations were described above.

(vii) Decision regarding H_0. Since $z_{observed} < z_{critical}$ (i.e., $.980 < 1.96$), do not reject H_0.

(viii) Conclusion. There is not a statistically significant difference in the strength of the linear relationship between depression and impairment for those in the CBT and IPT groups in this study of treatment of depressive symptoms in patients with major depressive disorder.

There are several more points regarding the Pearson r that will be discussed briefly. First, the correlation of a *variable* with a *constant* is zero. One of the methods of calculating r that was described above includes the covariance (s_{xy}) in the numerator. Recall that the covar-

iance is equal to the sum of cross-products over $N - 1$. Also, recall that the sum of the cross-products: $\sum xy = \sum(X_i - \bar{X})(Y_i - \bar{Y})$. If Y_i is a constant, then for each subject $Y_i = \bar{Y}$ and thus the sum of cross-products is also equal to zero:

$$\sum xy = \sum(X_i - \bar{X})(Y_i - \bar{Y})$$
$$= \sum(X_i - \bar{X}) \cdot 0 = 0$$

If the covariance is equal to zero, $r = 0$.

There is another useful fact about how r is affected by a constant (c_i). If the correlation between depression (X_i) and impairment (Y_i) is r_{xy}, and a constant is added to either X_i or Y_i, the correlation is not affected. For instance, say that the 24-item HRSD ratings were to be collected for all acutely suicidal subjects in a study. However, in the interest of time the HRSD suicide item was not scored and not included in a modified HRSD 23-item total, call it Y_{M_i}. Technically, all of these subjects, being acutely suicidal would rate 2 on the HRSD suicide item. Thus a 24-item total, Y_i, could be calculated for each subject simply by adding 2 to the subject's 23-item total. The addition of a constant (c_i) to a variable (Y_i) increases the value of the y-mean by c_i (i.e., $\bar{Y}_M = \bar{Y} + c_i$) and it does not affect the standard deviation (i.e., $S_{Y_M} = S_Y$). As a consequence neither the covariance (s_{xy}) nor the sum of cross-products $\sum xy$ is changed, and thus the correlation coefficient is not affected:

$r_{xy} = r_{xy_M}$.

Finally, correlation coefficients for pairs of several variables (x, y, and z) can be conveniently presented in the form of a correlation matrix:

	X	Y	Z
X	1.0	r_{XY}	r_{XZ}
Y	r_{YX}	1.0	r_{YZ}
Z	r_{ZX}	r_{ZY}	1.0

Notice that the elements of the correlation matrix are symmetric. That is, the correlation of X_i with Y_i (r_{XY}) is equal to the correlation of Y_i with X_i (r_{YX}). Furthermore, the correlation of a variable (e.g., X_i) with itself is equal to unity. All elements of the main diagonal of a correlation matrix are 1.0: $r_{XX} = r_{YY} = r_{ZZ} = 1.0$.

3.12.4.4.3 Spearman rank correlation

The Spearman rank correlation is a non-parametric correlation coefficient, which is computed using the ranks of the raw data. This is appropriate when the population data are believed to be non-normal. The Spearman rank correlation is especially useful when data contain an outlier (i.e., an extreme value),

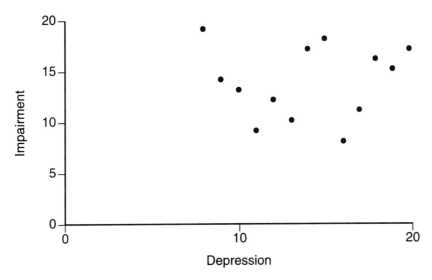

Figure 14 Plot of Hamilton Depression Ratings and Sheehan Disability Scores.

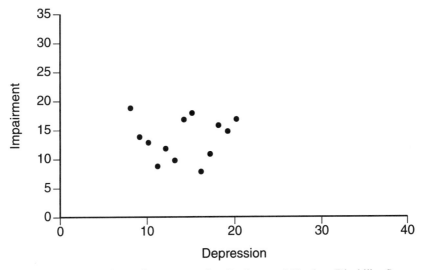

Figure 15 Plot of Hamilton Depression Ratings and Sheehan Disability Scores.

which can strongly, and inappropriately, increase the magnitude of the Pearson correlation coefficient. For instance, compare the plots presented in Figures 14 and 15. The only difference in these plots is that Figure 15 includes one additional case, which is an outlier. That is, the additional case has extreme values on both the x- and y-variables. In Figure 14 there is no linear relationship between depression (X) and impairment (Y). Stated differently, knowledge of the level of depression (X_i) will not help in "guessing" the level of impairment (Y_i). In fact, for the data in Figure 14, the Pearson correlation coefficient between depression and impairment is $r = 0.066$. In stark contrast, with the addition of one outlier, the Pearson correlation coefficient between depression and

impairment is $r = 0.697$ for the data in Figure 15. In Figure 15, which includes one outlier, knowledge of the severity of a subject's depression would not help in guessing the corresponding level of impairment.

The discrepancy between these two Pearson correlation coefficients illustrates that the Pearson correlation coefficient can be quite sensitive to an outlier. The influence of outliers on the correlation coefficient can be minimized by calculating the correlation on the rank-transformed data to examine the linear relationship between the ranks of X_i and Y_i. The Spearman rank correlation is used for that purpose.

For example, the data displayed in Figure 15 are presented in Table 15. In addition to the actual depression (X_i) and impairment (Y_i) ratings, the ascending ranks of those ratings are presented in Table 15. The rank transformation procedure was described earlier in this chapter (see discussion of the Mann–Whitney test). Although this is a bivariate analysis, the rankings of the depression (R_{X_i}) and impairment (R_Y) ratings are performed independently. (The upper-case R is used to represent a ranked variable and is not to be confused with lower-case r, which is generally used to represent a Pearson correlation coefficient.) To calculate the Spearman rank correlation coefficient r_s, the difference (d_i) between the paired ranks for each subject is calculated $(d_i = R_{X_i} - R_{Y_i})$ and squared (d_i^2). The sum of the squared differences in ranks $\sum(d_i^2)$ (is used in the calculations of r_s. In the case of no tied ranks, r_s is calculated:

$$r_s = 1 - \frac{6\sum\limits_{i=1}^{N} d_i^2}{n^3 - n} = 1 - \frac{6 \cdot 345}{14^3 - 14} = 0.242$$

Notice that the value of d_i is minimized, and consequently the quantity, $6\sum\limits_{i=1}^{N} d_i^2$ is minimized, as the pairs of ranks of X_i and Y_i for each subject correspond closely. Since the ratio in that equation is subtracted from unity, the value of r_s is closer to 1.0 when that ratio is small; and r_s is closer to zero when the ratio approaches 1.0. Thus, r_s is a quantity that reflects the strength of a linear relationship.

An r_s of .242 is certainly a more reasonable reflection of the strength of the linear relationship between X_i and Y_i in Table 15 than the Pearson r of .697.

The calculations for data involving tied data are more extensive (see, for example, Conover, 1980) and will not be discussed here. Incidentally, the data displayed in Figure 14 come from the first 13 of the 14 subjects that are presented in Table 15. The Pearson and Spearman rank correlation coefficients for the sample of 13 subjects are $r = 0.066$ and $r_s = 0.052$, respectively.

In using the Spearman rank correlation coefficient, it is assumed that the data are randomly sampled, that the subjects are independent, and that the scale of measurement is at least ordinal.

The hypothesis testing steps for the Spearman rank correlation coefficient are as follows:

(i) State research question. Is there a relationship between depression and impairment such that high values of depression tend to be associated with high values of impairment? Alternatively, one might hypothesize that there is a negative relationship between two variables X and Y (i.e., $r_s < 0$), such that high values of X tend to be associated with low values of Y.

(ii) State two mutually exclusive and exhaustive hypotheses:
    (a) $H_0 : \rho_{S_{XY}} = 0$
    (b) $H_A : \rho_{S_{XY}} \neq 0$

(iii) Use a table of critical values for the Spearman rank correlation coefficient (for example, see Conover, 1980, p. 456). The critical value with a two-tailed $\alpha = 0.05$ and $N = 14$ is 0.534. If $|r_{S_{observed}}| > r_{S_{critical}}$, reject H_0.

(iv) Data regarding depression and impairment are displayed in Table 15.

(v) Calculations were described above.

(vi) Decision regarding H_0. Since $|r_{S_{observed}}| < r_{S_{critical}}$ (i.e., $0.242 < 0.534$), do not reject H_0.

(viii) Conclusion. Based on data from this sample, we conclude that there is not a statistically significant correlation between depression and impairment.

3.12.4.4.4 Simple linear regression analysis

If a distinction between the independent and dependent variables is made, a correlational analysis can be extended to a *simple linear regression analysis*. In a regression analysis, the dependent variable (y) is regressed on the independent variable (x). Graphically, the x-axis represents the independent variable and the y-axis represents the dependent variable. As in a correlational analysis, each subject contributes data in the form of paired coordinates (x, y) to the regression analysis. The regression equation, $\hat{Y} = a + bX$, includes two variables, Y and X, and two constants, the y-intercept (a) and the slope (b). After the constants have been calculated, the equation can be used to estimate a conditional value of Y. That is, the equation is used to estimate a value of Y, *conditioned* on a value of X (i.e., $Y|X$). The algorithms which are used to estimate the regression constants, a and b, employ the *least-squares criterion*, which minimizes the sum of the squared distances from the observed data (Y_i) and those estimated with the regression equation $(\hat{Y}_i)$. $\hat{Y}$ is called *predicted Y* or *Y-hat*. The estimated values of $\hat{Y}$ are points along the regression line, which is defined by the regression equation.

For example, consider the relation between depression (X) and functional impairment (Y), where the latter is the dependent variable. The data from Table 14 are plotted in Figure 16 where depression is measured using the HRSD and functional impairment is measured with the Sheehan Disability Scale. The slope (b) represents the expected change in functional impairment that is associated with a one-unit change in depression. Stated differently, consider two subjects with depression ratings of X_i and $X_i + 1$, respectively. If the former subject has an impairment rating of Y_i, the latter will have

Table 15 Depression (X_i) and impairment (Y_i) ratings of 14 patients with affective symptomatology.

X_i	$Rank(X_i)$	Y_i	$Rank(Y_i)$	d_i	d_i^2
8	1	19	13	-12	144
9	2	14	7	-5	25
10	3	13	6	-3	9
11	4	9	2	2	4
12	5	12	5	0	0
13	6	10	3	3	9
14	7	17	10	-3	9
15	8	18	12	-4	16
16	9	8	1	8	64
17	10	11	4	6	36
18	11	16	9	2	4
19	12	15	8	4	16
20	13	17	10	3	9
36	14	31	14	0	0
218	105	210	104	1	345

an expected impairment rating of $Y_i + b$. The intercept (a) represents the functional impairment that is expected with a *hypothetical* depression rating of 0. Of course, an HRSD of 0 is not realistic in a clinical trial for subjects meeting criteria for major depressive disorder, but it represents the point along the y-axis where an extrapolated regression line would cross.

The two regression constants are estimated as follows (using the summary data that are presented in Table 14):

$$b = \frac{\sum_{i=1}^{N} xy}{\sum_{i=1}^{N} x^2} = \frac{352}{640} = 0.55$$

$$a = \bar{Y} - b\bar{X} = 14.45 - 0.55 \cdot 21.0 = 2.90$$

Thus, the regression equation is:

$$\hat{Y} = a + bX = 2.90 + 0.55X$$

This indicates that a one-unit increase on the HRSD is associated with a 0.55 unit increase on the Sheehan Disability Scale. A regression line can be graphed by plotting two paired coordinates, $(0,a)$ and $(\bar{X},\bar{Y})$, and drawing a line between the two points. Applying this to the data from Table 14, the regression line might be graphed by plotting: $(0,2.9)$ and $(21,14.45)$. However, it is inappropriate to extrapolate beyond the range of the sample data. This is because the relation between X and Y might look entirely different for values beyond the range of the data. In the example, the association between functional impairment and depression might be very different for those with minimal depressive

symptomatology than for those meeting criteria for major depressive disorder.

In lieu of extending the regression line beyond the range of the sample data, consider the minimum and maximum HRSD (X_i) ratings. In this sample, the HRSD ratings range from 12 to 29. The corresponding predicted functional impairment (i.e., $\hat{Y}_i$) for the lowest and highest HRSD ratings in this sample are estimated by substituting the respective HRSD values in the regression equation:

$$Y = 2.90 + 0.55X = 2.90 + 0.55(12) = 9.50$$

$$Y = 2.90 + 0.55X = 2.90 + 0.55(29) = 18.85$$

Consequently, the regression line, which is presented in Figure 16, will go from (12,9.50) for the least severely ill to (29,18.85) for the most severely ill. Note that the regression line passes through the intersection of the X and Y means, $(\bar{X},\bar{Y})$, which in this case is (21,14.45).

Recall that the proportion of variance in functional impairment that is explained by depression was presented above in the discussion of the correlation coefficient as: $R^2 = r^2 = 0.648^2 = 0.420$ These are the same data and thus the same value of R^2 applies. As with correlational analyses, R^2 is a measure of the magnitude of the association between Y_i and X_i in simple linear regression. One of the descriptive statistics that was discussed earlier in this chapter is a measure of variability called the sum of squared deviations, in this case, deviations from the Y-mean:

$$\sum y_i^2 = \sum_{i=1}^{N} \left(Y_i - \bar{Y} \right)^2$$

In the context of a regression analysis, this quantity can be partitioned into two components:

$$\sum y_i^2 = \sum \left(\hat{Y}_i - \bar{Y} \right) + \sum \left(Y_i - \hat{Y}_i \right)$$

or

$$\sum y_i^2 = SS_{reg} + SS_{res}$$

The former of the two components, the *sum of squares regression*, or SS_{reg}, represents the sum of squares in Y that is accounted for by X. If one were attempting to guess the level of impairment (Y_i), SS_{reg} can be thought of as the improvement over guessing the mean impairment $(\bar{Y})$ for each subject, and instead using the information known from the sample data about the $X_i - Y_i$ relation. SS_{reg} is estimated as follows (using the summary data from the total row in Table 14):

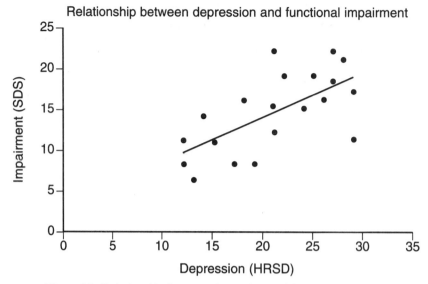

Figure 16   Relationship between depression and functional impairment.

$$SS_{reg} = \sum \left(\hat{Y} - \bar{Y} \right)^2 = \frac{\left(\sum xy \right)^2}{\sum x^2}$$

$$= \frac{352.00^2}{640.0} = 193.6$$

The sum of squares residual (SS_{res}) is the latter component of $\sum y^2$ and represents the sum of squared deviations of Y that is not accounted for by the $X_i - Y_i$ relation:

$$SS_{res} = \sum \left(Y_i - \hat{Y} \right)^2 = \sum y^2 - SS_{reg}$$

$$= 460.95 - 193.6 = 267.35$$

$R^2_{Y \cdot X}$ is the quantity that represents the magnitude of the association between Y and X. It represents the proportion of variance in Y that is accounted for by X:

$$R^2_{Y \cdot X} = \frac{SS_{reg}}{SS_{reg} + SS_{res}} = \frac{193.6}{193.6 + 267.35}$$

$$= 0.42$$

Being a proportion, $R^2_{Y \cdot X}$ can range from 0 to 1; $0 \leqslant R^2_{Y \cdot X} \leqslant 1$. $R^2_{Y \cdot X}$ can also be estimated as follows:

$$R^2_{Y \cdot X} = \frac{\left(\sum xy \right)^2}{\sum x^2} \cdot \frac{1}{\sum y^2} = \frac{352^2}{640} \cdot \frac{1}{460.95}$$

$$= 0.42$$

The first component is the numerator of the prior equation (SS_{reg}) and the second component is the denominator (SS_{res}) of that equation. Presented as one ratio, using the data from Table 14:

$$R^2_{Y \cdot X} = \frac{\left(\sum xy \right)^2}{\sum x^2 \sum y^2} = \frac{352^2}{640 \cdot 460.95} = 0.420$$

which is the square of the correlation between Y and X: $R^2_{Y \cdot X} = r^2_{YX} = 0.648^2 = 0.420$

Thus 42% of the variance in Y is accounted for by X. Although this seems to be a substantial proportion of variance, a statistical test is used to determine whether this is more than might be expected by chance. The null hypothesis, $H_0 : \rho^2 = 0$, is tested with an F-test:

$$F = \frac{R^2/k}{(1 - R^2)/(N - k - 1)}$$

where k is equal to the number of independent variables, $k = 1$ in this case:

$$F = \frac{R^2/k}{(1 - R^2)/(N - k - 1)}$$

$$= \frac{.402/1}{(1 - .420)/(20 - 1 - 1)} = 13.034$$

The degrees of freedom for the F-test are k and $(N - k - 1)$, or with these data, 1 and 18. The corresponding critical F, $F_{(1,18; \alpha = .05)} = 4.41$. The null hypothesis is rejected because 13.034 > 4.41. In other words, the amount of variance in functional impairment that is explained by depression is statistically significant.

The statistical significance of the regression coefficient b can also be tested using the null hypothesis as $H_0 : B = 0$. Consider that if the null hypothesis is not rejected, the regression coefficient could not be considered to be different than zero. Then if $b = 0$, the X-term would fall out of the regression equation, and $\hat{Y}$

would not be a function of X. The statistical significance of the regression coefficient b is tested with a t-ratio, which is equal to the regression coefficient divided by its standard error:

$$t = \frac{b}{s_b}$$

where the standard error of the regression coefficient s_b is estimated as:

$$s_b = \frac{\sqrt{SS_{res}/N - k - 1}}{\sqrt{\sum_{i=1}^{N} x^2}}$$

Notice that since s_b is in the denominator of the t-ratio, a larger value of s_b reduces the value of t. Holding other aspects of the analysis constant, if SS_{res} is large, which can result from a small $X-Y$ relation, then s_b will be large, and t will be small. In contrast, with a larger sample size (N), s_b will be smaller and, as a consequence, t will be larger.

$$SS_{res} = \sum_{i=1}^{N} \left(Y_i - \hat{Y}\right) \sum y^2$$

This quantity incorporates the differences between the observed (Y_i) and predicted ($\hat{Y}_i$) values of Y. In lieu of calculating each of the predicted values, SS_{res} can be calculated using quantities that have been calculated above:

$$SS_{res} = \left(1 - R_{Y \cdot X}^2\right) \sum y^2$$
$$= (1 - .420) \cdot 460.95 = 267.351$$

The standard error of the regression coefficient is given as: s_b

$$s_b = \frac{\sqrt{SS_{res}/N - k - 1}}{\sqrt{\sum_{i=1}^{N} x^2}}$$
$$= \frac{\sqrt{267.351/(20 - 1 - 1)}}{\sqrt{640}} = .152$$

and the t-ratio as:

$$t = \frac{b}{s_b} = \frac{0.55}{0.152} = 3.61$$

In a simple linear regression analysis there is one independent variable. Thus the tests of significance of $R_{Y \cdot X}^2$ and b are synonymous. In fact, the square root of F is equal to t: $\sqrt{13.034} = 3.61$

The assumptions of simple linear regression analysis include:

(i) independence across observations (i.e., subjects);
(ii) the independent variable is fixed;
(iii) the error term (e) is not correlated with the independent variable (X);
(iv) the variance of the error terms is constant across all values of X. This is referred to as homoscedasticity.

The hypothesis testing steps for a simple linear regression analysis are as follows:
(i) State research question. Is there a linear relationship between depression and impairment?
(ii) State two mutually exclusive and exhaustive hypotheses:
(a) Hypotheses about the regression coefficient (β):
$H_0: \rho_{XY} = 0$
$H_A: \rho_{XY} \neq 0$
(b) Hypotheses about the population R^2 (i.e., ρ_{XY}^2):
$H_0: \rho_{XY}^2 = 0$
$H_A: \rho_{XY}^2 \neq 0$
(iii) Choose the t-ratio to evaluate the hypotheses about the regression coefficient (β). Use an F-test to test hypotheses about R^2.
(iv) The critical value for the t-ratio with two-tailed $\alpha = 0.05$ and df $= 18$ is 2.101. If $t_{observed} > t_{critical}$, reject $H_0: \beta_{XY} = 0$. The critical value for the F-test with $\alpha = 0.05$ and df $= 1,18$ is 4.41. If $F_{observed} > F_{critical}$, reject $H_0: \rho_{XY}^2 = 0$.
(v) Data regarding depression and impairment are given in Table 14.
(vi) Calculations were described above.
(vii) Decision regarding H_0 about (β). Observed $t >$ critical t, thus reject H_0 (i.e., 3.61 > 2.101). Decision regarding H_0 about R^2. Observed $F >$ critical F (i.e., 13.064 > 4.41), thus reject H_0.
(vii) Conclusion. Based on data from this sample, we conclude that there is a statistically significant linear relationship between depression and impairment.

Linear regression is a useful statistical procedure for examining a bivariate relation. Unlike a correlational analysis in which $r_{yx} = r_{xy}$, linear regression is *not* a symmetric procedure. That is, the regression of Y_i on X_i will not result in the same regression constants (a and b) as the regression of Y_i on Y_i.

3.12.4.4.5 Multiple linear regression analysis

A *simple* linear regression analysis involves the regression of a dependent variable on one independent variable. *Multiple* linear regression analysis extends the statistical model such that one dependent variable is regressed on multiple independent variables. Multiple linear regression analysis is a general statistical model that can evaluate both dimensional and categorical independent variables. In fact it can test main effects and interactions of the ANOVA model and can be used to control for variables (i.e., covariates) if certain assumptions are fulfilled (see Pedhazur, 1982, Chap. 12).

Pedhazur (1982) distinguishes between the use of regression for prediction and explanation. The former has to do with estimating the dependent variable given a value of the independent variable (i.e., Y_i given X_i), whereas the latter focuses on the proportion of variance in the dependent variable that is explained by the independent variables (R^2). Although this chapter will not discuss multiple linear regression analysis in detail, several comprehensive examinations of multiple linear regression analysis are available (Aiken & West, 1991; Cohen & Cohen, 1983; Cook & Weisberg, 1982; Neter, Wasserman, & Kutner, 1989; Pedhazur, 1982; Pedhazur & Schmelkin, 1991).

3.12.4.5 Between-subject Designs: Categorical Dependent Variables

The statistical procedures that have been discussed until this point in the chapter are appropriate for continuous or ordinal dependent variables. Nevertheless, it is not unusual for the dependent variable to be categorical. There are a multitude of examples: pass or fail, sick or well, and live or die. There are many statistical procedures for categorical data and comprehensive texts devoted exclusively to categorical data analysis (see for example Agresti, 1996; Bishop, Feinberg, & Holland, 1975; Fleiss, 1981).

Consider the data from the hypothetical clinical trial that have been used throughout this chapter (originally presented in Tables 3 and 5). The HRSD is a continuous dependent variable

that could be dichotomized such that the subjects with an HRSD rating of 14 or less are classified as "responders" and all other subjects are classified as "nonresponders." (For readers familiar with the HRSD, this is a rather crude and quite unconventional threshold, used only as an example for data analysis and not for the study of psychopathology.) Both the independent variable (treatment CBT vs. IPT) and the dependent variable (response: yes vs. no) are categorical variables. Although there is some literature discouraging categorization of continuous measures because of the loss of precision and statistical power, in the clinical setting decisions often must be dichotomous.

3.12.4.5.1 Chi-square test

The chi-square (χ^2) test is generally used to compare rates or proportions across groups (Fleiss, 1981). In the example presented in Table 16, the χ^2 test is used to compare the response rates, and determine if rates as diverse as 20% and 40% can be expected by chance. This format of data display is referred to as a *contingency table*. Initially, notice that the IPT group had twice the response rate as the CBT group (40% vs. 20%). Also note the degree to which the rate for each group differs from that of the marginal (30%), which is presented in the margins of Table 16, and represents the response rate of the sample as a whole ($N = 40$).

The null hypothesis is that the population rates do not differ, $H_A : \pi_1 = \pi_2$. That hypothesis is tested by comparing the *observed* cell frequencies with those *expected* if treatment and response were independent. It is tested in the following manner:

$$\chi^2 = n.. \sum_{i=1}^{2} \sum_{j=1}^{2} \frac{(|p_{ij} - p_i p_j| - 1/(2n..))^2}{p_{i.} p_{.j}}$$

where p_{ij} is the proportion of the entire sample that is in row i and column j (i.e., $cell_{ij}$). Note that a dot (.) in the subscript represents a dimension (row or column) that is ignored. For example, the marginal value $p_{i.}$ represents the proportion of subjects in row i and $p_{.j}$ represents the proportion of subjects in column j. The product of those marginal proportions is the proportion of subjects that would be expected in the cell if the row and column variables were independent of each other. This product is referred to as the *expected value*. The χ^2 test essentially compares the *observed* and *expected* values. Applied to the data from Table 16:

Table 16 Treatment response status of subjects in CBT and IPT groups

	Nonresponse	Response	Total
CBT	16 (a)	4 (b)	20
[row %]	[80%]	[20%]	[100%]
{column %}	{57.1%}	{33.3%}	{50%}
IPT	12 (c)	8 (d)	20
[row %]	[60%]	[40%]	[100%]
{column %}	{42.9%}	{66.7%}	{50%}
Total	28	12	40
[row %]	[70%]	[30%]	[100%]
{column %}	{100%}	{100%}	{100%}

$$\chi^2 = \frac{(|.10 - .50 \cdot .70| - 1/(2 \cdot 40))^2}{.50 \cdot .70}$$
$$+ \frac{(|.40 - .50 \cdot .30| - 1/(2 \cdot 40))^2}{.50 \cdot .30}$$
$$+ \frac{(|.3 - .50 \cdot .70| - 1/(2 \cdot 40))^2}{.50 \cdot .70}$$
$$+ \frac{(|20 - .50 \cdot .30| - 1/(2 \cdot 40))^2}{.50 \cdot .30} = 1.07$$

Another algorithm for a *fourfold table* (i.e., a two by two contingency table) is somewhat simpler, using cell and marginal frequencies, but no proportions:

$$\chi^2 = \frac{n_{..}(|n_{11}n_{22} - n_{12}n_{21}| - \frac{1}{2}n_{..})^2}{n_{1.}n_{2.}n_{.1}n_{.2}}$$

With the data presented in Table 16:

$$\chi^2 = \frac{40(|16 \cdot 8 - 4 \cdot 12| - \frac{1}{2}40)^2}{20 \cdot 20 \cdot 28 \cdot 12} = 1.07$$

Assumptions of the χ^2 test include:
(i) The samples are independent of each other.
(ii) The subjects within each group are independent of each other.
(iii) No subject can be classified in more than one category.
(iv) No cell has an expected value less than five.
The hypothesis testing steps for the χ^2 test are as follows:
(i) State research question. Do CBT and IPT have similar effects for the treatment of patients with depression?
(ii) State two mutually exclusive and exhaustive hypotheses:
    (a) $H_0 : \pi_1 = \pi_2$
    (b) $H_A : \pi_1 \neq \pi_2$
(iii) If the assumptions are met, use the χ^2 test to evaluate the hypotheses.
(iv) The critical value for the χ^2 test with two-tailed $\alpha = 0.05$ and df = 1 is 3.84. (Note that df is equal to the product of # rows and # columns.) If $\chi^2_{observed} > \chi^2_{critical}$, reject H_0.
(v) Data are displayed in Table 16.
(vi) Calculations were described above.
(vii) Decision regarding H_0: $\chi^2_{observed} < \chi^2_{critical}$ (i.e., $1.07 < 3.84$), thus do not reject H_0.
(viii) Conclusion. In this sample of patients with major depressive disorder, those who were treated with IPT did not have different response rates than those who were treated with CBT.
The null hypothesis is not rejected because the difference in response rates across treatment groups (20% vs. 40%) is not more than is expected by chance. The chi square test can also be used for two-way contingency tables that have more than two rows and two columns.

3.12.4.5.2 Fisher's Exact test

When at least one expected frequency in a fourfold table is less than five, the Fisher's Exact test is more appropriate than the χ^2 test. The test assesses the probability of the cell frequencies, given the marginal frequencies. Stated differently, given the respective sample sizes and the response rates of the sample as a whole, the Fisher's Exact test evaluates the probability of the four cell frequencies. The algorithm, which is based on the hypergeometric probability distribution, is:

$$p = \frac{n_{1.}!n_{2.}!n_{.1}!n_{.2}!}{n_{..}!n_{11}!n_{12}!n_{21}!n_{22}!}$$

Where "n-factorial" ($n!$),

$$n! = n \cdot (n-1) \cdot (n-2) \cdot \ldots \cdot 1$$

and, by definition, $0! = 1$.
The algorithm for p calculates the probability of getting precisely the observed configuration of frequencies. There were no expected frequencies that were less than five in Table 16. For that reason, the data in Panel A of Table 17 will be used to illustrate the calculations involved in a Fisher's Exact test. These data, which will be referred to as the *observed* data, come from a *hypothetical pilot* study comparing electroconvulsive therapy (ECT) and psychodynamic psychotherapy (PP) for the treatment of dysthymia. The response rates were 93.33% for ECT and 85.0% for PP.
Applying the above algorithm:

$$p = \frac{15! \cdot 20! \cdot 4! \cdot 31!}{35! \cdot 1! \cdot 14! \cdot 3! \cdot 17} = 0.3266$$

That is, given the observed marginals, about one of every three *random* configurations will be that which is contained in Table 17. Consider that there are only four other configurations of cell frequencies that conform to the marginals of this contingency table, which are also presented in Table 17, Panels B–E. Fisher's Exact test involves calculating the probability of each configuration that conforms to the marginals. Applying the equation that was presented above, the respective probabilities of those tables are presented in the final column of Table 17. (Note that the sum of these four probabilities, and that of the *observed* table, 0.3266, is 1.00. That is, the probability of *any* of the possible outcomes is 1.00.)
For the Fisher's Exact test, one determines which of the configurations have a probability that is less than or equal to the probability

Table 17 Treatment by responder status.

Configuration		Treatment	Nonresponder	Responder	Total	p
Panel A	#1	ECT	1	14	15	0.3266
		PP	3	17	20	
		Total	4	31	35	
Panel B	#2	ECT	0	15	15	0.0925
		PP	4	16	20	
		Total	4	31	35	
Panel C	#3	ECT	2	13	15	0.3810
		PP	2	18	20	
		Total	4	31	35	
Panel D	#4	ECT	3	12	15	0.1738
		PP	1	19	20	
		Total	4	31	35	
Panel E	#5	ECT	4	11	15	0.0261
		PP	0	20	20	
		Total	4	31	35	

associated with the *observed* contingency table, configuration #1. In this case, the probabilities of configurations #2 ($p = 0.0925$), #4 ($p = 0.1738$), and #5 ($p = 0.0261$) are all less than the observed configuration #1 ($p = 0.3266$). These probabilities, and that of the observed, are summed and compared to the alpha level:

$$p^* = 0.0925 + 0.1738 + 0.0261 + 0.3266 = 0.6190$$

Assumptions of the Fisher's Exact test are as follows:

(i) The data are in a contingency table with two rows and two columns.

(ii) The samples are independent of each other.

(iii) The subjects within each group are independent of each other.

(iv) No subject can be classified in more than one category.

(v) The row and column totals are given. They are not random.

The hypothesis testing steps for the Fisher's Exact test are as follows:

(i) State research question. Do ECT and PP have similar effects on *response*?

(ii) State two mutually exclusive and exhaustive hypotheses:

  (a) $H_0 : \pi_1 = \pi_2$

  (b) $H_A : \pi_1 \neq \pi_2$

(iii) If assumptions are fulfilled, use Fisher's Exact test to evaluate the hypotheses.

(iv) The critical value for the Fisher's Exact test with two-tailed $\alpha = 0.05$ is 0.05. If $p^* \leqslant 0.05$, reject H_0.

(v) Data are displayed in Table 17.

(vi) Calculations were described above.

(vii) Decision regarding H_0: $p_{observed} > p^*_{critical}$ (i.e., $0.619 > 0.05$), thus do not reject H_0.

(viii) Conclusion. Dysthymic subjects treated with ECT and PP do not have differential response rates.

There is a growing body of literature on the use of *exact tests*, such as that just described, in other contexts (e.g., Agresti, 1992; Mehta & Patel, 1997). These procedures are based on minimal distributional assumptions. As a consequence they can be applied in situations when the use of other procedures is more tenuous, particularly with small data sets. Because exact procedures are often computationally extensive, their use was rare until software that implemented the exact algorithms were available. StatXact software (Mehta & Patel, 1997) is designed to conduct exact tests for a wide variety of types of data. It is available as a stand-alone package and also as an add-on module with statistical software such as SPSS and SAS.

3.12.4.5.3 Logistic regression

Logistic regression analysis is used to examine the association of (categorical or continuous) independent variable(s) with one *dichotomous* dependent variable. This is in contrast to *linear* regression analysis in which the dependent variable is a continuous variable. The discussion of logistic regression in this chapter is brief. Hosmer and Lemeshow (1989) provide a comprehensive introduction to logistic regression analysis.

Consider an example in which logistic regression could be used to examine the research question, "Is a history of suicide attempts associated with the risk of a subsequent (i.e., prospectively observed) attempt?" The logistic regression model compares the odds of a prospective attempt in those with and without prior attempts. The ratio of those odds is called the *odds ratio*. A logistic regression does not analyze the odds, but a natural logarithmic transformation of the odds, the log odds. Although the calculations are more complicated when there are multiple independent variables, computer programs can be used to perform the analyses. However, because of the logarithmic transformation of the odds ratio, the interpretation of results from the computer output is not necessarily straightforward. Interpretation requires a transformation back to the original scale by taking the inverse of the natural log of the regression coefficient, which is called *exponentiation*. The exponentiated regression coefficient represents the strength of the association of the independent variable with the outcome. More specifically, it represents the increase (or decrease) in risk of the outcome that is associated with the independent variable. The exponentiated regression coefficient represents the difference in risk of the outcome (e.g., suicide attempt) for two subjects who differ by one point on the independent variable. In this case, that is the difference between those with and without history of attempts (i.e., when history of attempts is coded: $0 =$ no and $1 =$ yes).

The logistic regression model can be extended to include several independent variables (i.e., hypothesized risk factors). For instance, are history of attempts, severity of depression, and employment status risk factors for suicidal behavior, controlling for diagnosis, age, and gender? Each odds ratio from such a model represents the change in risk of the outcome (i.e., a suicide attempt) that is associated with the independent variable, controlling for the other independent variables.

3.12.4.5.4 Survival analysis

In a study such as the example used above, the probability of the event is somewhat constrained by the follow-up time of the study. That is, the number of subjects with a suicide attempt will very likely be much smaller in a six-week study than in a six-year study. Survival analysis is a statistical technique that is used to examine the risk of an event *over time*. As with logistic regression analysis, this technique is appropriate for a dichotomous dependent variable. For example, survival analyses can

be used to examine the risk of a suicide attempt over the course of a follow-up study. The survival model incorporates the differential risk period of the subjects. For that reason, it makes use of the available data in a follow-up study.

For example, in a 15-year follow-up study of subjects with affective disorders, some of the subjects will be followed for the entire study. Yet others will be followed for as short as a few weeks and others for several years, but not the duration of the entire 15-year study. The Kaplan–Meier product limit estimate (Kaplan & Meier, 1958) is used to estimate the proportion of subjects who have not had a postbaseline suicide attempt (i.e., the proportion *surviving* without a suicide attempt). Patients who do not attempt suicide by the end of follow-up, or who drop out of the follow-up study, are classified as *censored*. The Kaplan-Meier (1958) estimate is calculated as the probability of the event up to a given point in the follow-up. In this example, say that there are monthly assessments in which the investigators ask about psychopathology, suicide attempts, and treatment during the preceding month. The researcher could estimate the proportion of subjects who remained *suicide-free* after one month, two months, and so on to the end of follow-up.

There are several survival analytic procedures. For instance, the cumulative probability of an event (i.e., a suicide attempt) can be compared across groups using a logrank test (Peto & Peto, 1972). The survival model can be further extended to incorporate many independent variables that are hypothesized to be associated with risk of the event using a Cox proportional hazards regression model (Cox, 1972). There are several comprehensive texts on survival analytic techniques (e.g., Collett, 1994; Kalbfleisch & Prentice, 1980; Lawless, 1982; Lee, 1980; Parmar & Machin, 1995).

3.12.4.6 Within-subject Designs: Dimensional and Ordinal Dependent Variables

Subjects can serve as their own controls by being successively exposed to each treatment condition. The major advantage is that a design such as this reduces the between-subject variability that is inherent in a between-subjects design. As a consequence, a smaller number of subjects is needed in such a study. However, this design is inappropriate for many types of experimental intervention. For instance, the approach cannot be used in most studies of learning, unless it is feasible to get subjects to *unlearn* a task that has been mastered. The same holds true for acute treatment of psychopathology. Once a subject is well, the efficacy of subsequent treatments cannot be evaluated.

3.12.4.6.1 Paired t-test

The paired t-test is used for a within-subject comparison of dimensional dependent variables. For example, in a one-group design, the pretreatment HRSD scores could be compared with the post-treatment HRSD scores. (Note that there are many reasons that a multigroup design is preferable, but that is beyond the scope of this presentation. See Campbell & Stanley, 1963, for a comprehensive discussion of this.) The null hypothesis is $H_0: \mu_{pre} = \mu_{post}$, whereas the alternative hypothesis is $H_A: \mu_{pre} \neq \mu_{post}$. Stated differently, the data that are examined are the paired differences $(d_i = X_i - Y_i)$ between prereatment (X_i) and post-treatment (Y_i) for each subject. A mean difference $(\bar{d})$ and standard deviation of *differences* (s_d) are calculated.

For illustration, Table 18 presents HRSD scores for a group of 20 subjects before and after CBT treatment of depression. (At this point, focus only on the first three columns of Table 18.) Prior to treatment, the mean HRSD rating was 21.0 (sd = 5.8). After treatment, the mean HRSD rating was reduced to 15.95 (sd = 5.8). The paired t-test, which can generally be thought of as a test of whether the mean *difference* is equal to zero, is calculated as follows:

$$t = \bar{d}/s_{\bar{d}} \quad \text{where}$$

$$s_{\bar{d}} = \sqrt{\frac{s_d^2}{n}}$$

and s_d^2 is the variance of the *differences* (i.e., the square of the standard deviation of the *differences*):

$$s_d^2 = 5.46^2 = 29.84$$

$$s_{\bar{d}} = \sqrt{\frac{s_d^2}{n}} = \sqrt{\frac{29.84}{20}} = 1.22$$

$$t = \frac{\bar{d}}{s_{\bar{d}}} = \frac{5.10}{1.22} = 4.13$$

In a paired t-test, it is assumed that
(i) the data consist of correlated pairs of observations (i.e., paired data);
(ii) the subjects are randomly sampled;
(iii) the differences between each pair of observations are from a normally distributed population of differences.

The hypothesis testing steps for the paired t-test are as follows:
(i) State research question. Is there a difference in depression severity from pre- to post-CBT treatment?
(ii) State two mutually exclusive and exhaustive hypotheses:
   (a) $H_0: \mu_d = 0$
   (b) $H_A: \mu_d \neq 0$
(iii) If assumptions are met, use the paired t-test.
(vi) The critical value for the paired t-test with a two-tailed $\alpha = 0.05$ and $df = 19$, $t_{critical} = 2.093$ (Note that for a paired t-test, df is equal to one less than the number of pairs.) If $t_{observed} > t_{critical}$, reject H_0.
(v) Data are displayed in Table 18.
(vi) Calculations were described above.
(vii) Decision regarding H_0: $t_{observed} > t_{critical}$ (i.e., $4.13 > 2.093$), thus reject H_0.
(viii) Conclusion. There is a statistically significant reduction in severity of depression, as measured by the HRSD, from pre- to post-CBT treatment.

3.12.4.6.2 Wilcoxon signed-rank test

The Wilcoxon signed-rank test is used to test differences of paired data without the normal distribution assumption of the differences that is required for the paired t-test. The procedure is as follows. First, the difference between each pair of data is calculated. The differences are then ranked. Next, the ranks are assigned the sign ($\pm$) of the corresponding difference. Then two sums are computed: the sum of the positive signed ranks (T_+) and the sum of the absolute values of the negative signed ranks (T_-). (The differences of zero are ignored in these calculations.) Note that the sum of the totals should be: $T_+ + T_- = n(n+1)/2$, where n is the number of nonzero differences. If H_0 were true, one would expect about half of the differences to be positive and about half of the differences to be negative. If so, the sum of positive ranks would be approximately equal to the sum of the negative ranks: $T_+ \approx T_- \approx 1/2 \cdot n(n+1)/2$. The test statistic (W_{obs}) is used to examine this. W_{obs} is equal to the smaller of the two signed rank totals.

For example, see Table 18 which displays the pre- and post-HRSD scores and the difference scores. The median pretreatment rating (21.0) and the median post-treatment rating (15.0) appear to be quite different. The Wilcoxon Rank Sum test examines the magnitude of the difference. Separate columns display the ranks of the positive differences and the ranks of the absolute values of the

Table 18 HRSD scores: pre-(X) and post-(Y) CBT treatment ($N = 20$).

X	Y	Difference	Ranked |Difference|	Signed rank	Positive ranks	Negative ranks
12	11	1	5	5	5	
12	4	8	15.5	15.5	15.5	
13	15	−2	3	−3		3
14	8	6	11	11	11	
15	9	6	11	11	11	
17	8	9	17	17	17	
18	11	7	14	14	14	
19	13	6	11	11	11	
21	5	16	20	20	20	
21	22	−1	4	−4		4
21	28	−7	1	−1		1
22	25	−3	2	−2		2
24	21	3	6	6	6	
25	15	10	18	18	18	
26	22	4	7	7	7	
27	22	5	8	8	8	
27	14	13	19	19	19	
28	22	6	11	11	11	
29	23	6	11	11	11	
29	21	8	15.5	15.5	15.5	
Total 420.00	319.00	101.00	210.00	190.00	200.00	10.00
Mean 21.00	15.95	5.05				
sd 5.80	7.16	5.46				

$d = X - Y$.

negative differences. The sums of those columns are:

$$T_+ = 200$$

$$T_+ = 10$$

$$W_{observed} = T_- = 10$$

Check the calculations the sum of the positive signed ranks and absolute values of the negative signed ranks:

$$T_+ + T_- = \frac{n(n+1)}{2}$$

$$T_+ + T_- = 200 + 10 = 210$$

and $$\frac{n(n+1)}{2} = \frac{20(20+1)}{2} = 210$$

The assumptions of the Wilcoxon Signed Rank Sum test include:

(i) the data consist of correlated observations (i.e., paired data);

(ii) subjects with paired data are randomly and independently sampled;

(iii) The differences are measured on at least an ordinal scale.

The hypothesis testing steps for the Wilcoxon Signed Rank Sum test are as follows:

(i) State research question. Is there a difference in depression severity from pre- to post-CBT treatment?

(ii) State two mutually exclusive and exhaustive hypotheses with regard to location (e.g., median):

(a) H_0: Median$_{Time1}$ = Median$_{Time2}$

(b) H_A: Median$_{Time1}$ ≠ Median$_{Time2}$

(iii) If the assumptions are fulfilled, use the Wilcoxon Signed Rank Sum test to evaluate the hypotheses.

(iv) The critical value for the Wilcoxon Signed Rank Sum test, with two-tailed $\alpha = 0.05$ and $N = 20$, is $W_{observed} < W_{critical}$, reject H_0.

(v) Data are displayed in Table 18.

(vi) Calculations were described above.

(vii) Decision regarding H_0: $W_{observed} < W_{critical}$ (i.e., 22.5 < 52), thus reject H_0.

(viii) Conclusion. There is a significant reduction in depressive severity from pre- to post-CBT treatment.

3.12.4.6.3 *Repeated measures ANOVA*

The repeated measures ANOVA is a statistical procedure that can include both *within*-subject and *between*-subject factors. Initially the former will be considered. Most simply, it can be an extension of the paired *t*-test, used to compare subjects over time. Consider three HRSD assessments during the course of 12 weeks of CBT (e.g., weeks 0, 6, and 12). The null hypothesis is that there is no change in depression over the three assessments: $H_0: \mu_1 = \mu_2 = \mu_3$. The alternative hypothesis is that the null hypothesis is false. The F-test of the repeated measures ANOVA tests whether that difference is more than can be expected by chance. If H_0 is rejected, the source of the difference must be examined more closely in a *post hoc* test. This is discussed in detail elsewhere (e.g., Keppel, 1991; Winer, 1971).

3.12.4.7 Within-subject Designs: Categorical Dependent Variables

The repeated measures design can be extended to include *between*-subject factors as well as *within*-subject factors. Such a design is referred to as a *split plot design*. There are two types of within- and between-subject factors: *fixed* and *random* effects. The specific levels of fixed variables are determined by the experimenter, whereas the levels of a random effect are randomly selected from a larger population of levels. Results of fixed effects cannot be generalized beyond the levels of the factors that are tested. In contrast, results of random effects can be generalized to the population from which the levels were selected. The within-subject factor that was discussed in the repeated measures model above, was a fixed effect. Random effects are discussed in detail elsewhere (e.g., Keppel, 1991; Winer, 1971). An extension of the previous example that includes two independent treatment groups (e.g., IPT vs. CBT) illustrates a design in which a repeated measures ANOVA with both within-subject and between-subject factors would be applied. Treatment would be the between-subjects factor, whereas time would be the within-subjects factor. Subjects are treated with only one modality, but have all levels of the within-subject factor (i.e., assessments at weeks 0, 6, and 12). This ANOVA includes three F-tests: the main effect of treatment, the main effect of time, and the interaction of treatment by time.

3.12.4.7.1 McNemar test

The McNemar test is used to examine paired dichotomous data. For example, one might compare the symptomatology pretreatment and post-treatment. Specifically, one might hypothesize that the sleep disturbance is neither developed nor overcome during the course of treatment with IPT for depression as presented in Table 19. The McNemar test is calculated as

follows: $\chi^2 = (|b - c| - 1)^2/b + c$. (The algorithm, as presented with the term outside of the absolute value, incorporates a continuity correction in the numerator.) Note that the calculations focus on the *discordant* pairs and ignore the *concordant* pairs. More specifically, the test is a ratio of the squared difference in discordant frequencies relative to the total discordant frequencies. In the example above, the test would detect a disproportionate representation of an emergent sleep disturbance among those who had a change in sleep disturbance. This is illustrated with data in Table 19, where 11 of the 13 (84.5%) with changes in sleep disturbance developed the symptom during the course of treatment: $\chi^2 = (|11 - 2| - 1)^2/(11 + 2) = 4.92$. The McNemar χ^2 of 4.92 exceeds the critical χ_2 with 1 *df*, 3.84, and is thus statistically significant at the 0.05 level.

3.12.5 SUMMARY

There are several components of the analysis one must consider when choosing among statistical procedures. Is there a dependent variable? If so, is it dimensional, ordinal, or categorical? What are the comparisons that will answer the research question? Are there group comparisons? If so, how many groups are being compared? If not, is it bivariate linear relations that are of interest? In addition, the assumptions of the statistical procedures should be carefully considered before the procedure is applied. Figure 17 is a flow chart that is designed to facilitate selection of the appropriate inferential statistical procedure.

Finally, the value of descriptive statistical procedures must not be minimized. They are used not only to summarize data and describe a sample, but also to help a researcher become familiar with the data. The initial examination of descriptive statistics provides information that is useful when choosing among inferential statistical procedures.

In summary, this chapter began by stating that a fundamental motivation in science is to understand individual differences. A variety of

Table 19 Cross-classification of presence of symptoms before and after treatment.

	Post absent	Post present
Pre absent	76 (a)	11 (b)
Pre present	2 (c)	47 (d)

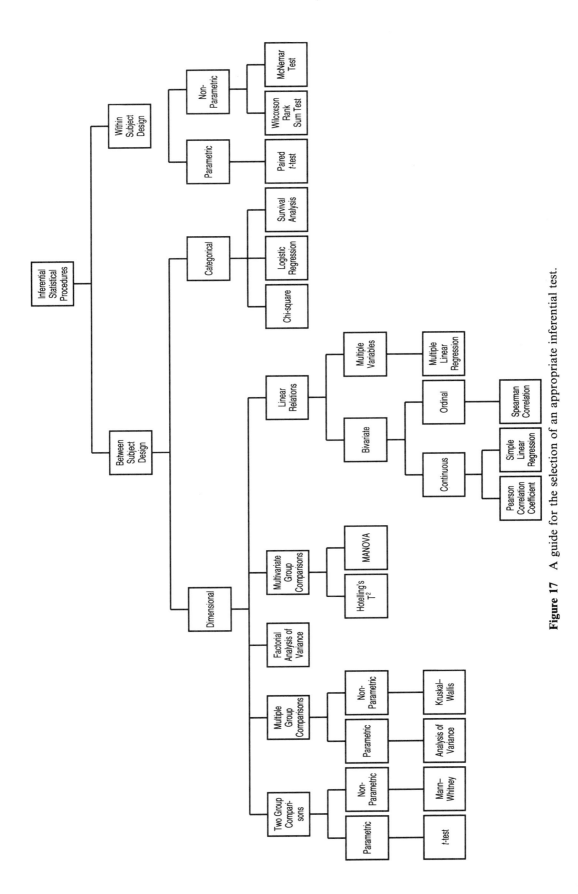

Figure 17 A guide for the selection of an appropriate inferential test.

statistical procedures that are used to examine *deviation* and *variability* have been outlined. The decision rules to choose among them has been discussed. Reference citations have been provided for a more comprehensive discussion of each technique. In closing, the reader is encouraged to consider not only the test statistic and corresponding *statistical significance* of research results, but also focus on the *clinical meaningfulness* of the findings. If a result cannot be replicated because it is trivial or if a finding has no practical value, it will serve no useful scientific or clinical purpose.

ACKNOWLEDGMENTS

The author is grateful to Laura Portera, M.S., who provided valuable feedback regarding the structure and content of earlier versions of this manuscript, and to Kira Lowell, M.A., who provided editorial assistance.

3.12.6 APPENDIX: SPSS COMMAND LINES

3.12.6.1 Descriptive Statistics

Descriptive variables = hrsd /statistics = all.
Frequency variables = hrsd
/histogram = normal /statistics = all.
Examine variables = hrsd by tx /plot = boxplot stemleaf histogram /statistics = all.

3.12.6.2 Inferential Statistics

3.12.6.2.1 Between-subject analyses

Dimensional/Ordina Dependent Variables
Two-group Comparisons
t-test
t-test group = tx (1,2) /variables = hrsd.
Mann–Whitney
Npar tests m–w = hrsd by tx (1,2)
Multiple-group Comparisons
Analysis of Variance (One-Way ANOVA)
Oneway hrsd by tx (1,3)
/posthoc = tukey, scheffe, dunnett
/statistics = descriptives,homogeneity.
Kruskal–Wallis
Npar tests k–w = hrsd by tx (1,3)
Factorial Analysis of Variance
(Two-Way ANOVA)
Anova variables = hrsd by tx (1,2)
diagnosis (1,2)
/maxorders = all.
Bivariate Linear Relations
Pearson Correlation Coefficient
Correlations variables = depression with impairment.

Spearman Rank
Nonpar corr variables = depression with impairment
/print = spearman.
Simple Linear Regression
Regression variables = impairment depression
/descriptives = default
/statistics = default
/dependent = impairment
/method = enter depression.
Categorical Dependent Variables
Chi-square
Crosstab tx by response /cell = count row column /sta = chisq.

3.12.6.2.2 Within-group analyses

Dimensional Ordinal Dependent Variables
Paired t-test
t-test pair = prehrsd with posthrsd.
Wilcoxon
Npar test wilcoxon = prehrsd with posthrsd
/statistics = descriptives.
Categorical Dependent Variables
McNemar test
Npar test mcnemar = presx with postsx.

3.12.7 REFERENCES

Agresti, A. (1992). A survey of exact inference for contingency tables. *Statistical Science, 7,* 131–177.
Agresti, A. (1996). *An introduction to categorical data analysis.* New York: Wiley.
Aiken L. S., & West S. G. (1991) *Multiple regression: testing and interpreting interactions.* Newbury Park, CA: Sage.
Armitage, P., & Berry, G. (1987). *Statistical methods in medical research* (2nd ed.). Oxford, UK: Blackwell Science.
Bishop, Y. M. M., Feinberg, S. E., & Holland, P. W. (1975). *Discrete multivariate analysis: Theory and practice.* Cambridge, MA: MIT Press.
Bock, R. D. (1985). *Multivariate statistical procedures for behavioral research.* Chicago: Scientific Software Inc.
Campbell, D. T., & Stanley, J. (1963). *Experimental and quasi-experimental designs for research.* Chicago: Rand McNally.
Cohen, J., & Cohen, P. (1983). *Applied multiple regression/ correlation analysis for the behavioral sciences* (2nd ed.). Hillsdale, NJ: Erlbaum.
Collett, D. (1994). *Modelling survival data in medical research.* London: Chapman and Hall.
Conover, W. J. (1980). *Practical nonparametric statistics* (2nd. ed.). New York: Wiley.
Cook, R. D., & Weisberg, S. (1982). *Residuals and influence in regression.* New York: Chapman and Hall.
Cox, D. R.(1972). Regression models and life tables (with discussion). *Journal of Royal Statistical Society, B34,* 187–220.
Fleiss, J. F. (1981). *Statistical methods for rates and proportions* (2nd. ed.). New York: Wiley.
Fleiss, J. F. (1986). *The design and analysis of clinical experiments.* New York: Wiley.

Grimm, L. G., & Yarnold, P. R. (Eds.) (1995). *Reading and understanding multivariate statistics*. Washington, DC: American Psychological Association.

Hartley, H. O. (1950). The maximum *F*-ratio as a short cut test for heterogeneity of variances. *Biometrika 37*, 308–312.

Hollingshead, A. B., & Redlich, F. C. (1958). *Social class and mental illness*. New York: Wiley.

Hopkins, K. D., Glass, G. V., & Hopkins, B. R. (1987). *Basic statistics for the behavioral sciences* (2nd ed.). Englewood Cliffs, NJ: Prentice-Hall.

Hosmer, D. W., & Lemeshow, S. (1989). *Applied logistic regression*. New York: Wiley.

Kalbfleisch, J. D., & Prentice, R. L. (1980). *The statistical analysis of failure time data*. New York: Wiley.

Kaplan, E. L., & Meier, P. (1958). Nonparametric estimation from incomplete observations. *Journal of the American Statistical Association, 53*, 457–481.

Keppel, G. (1991). *Design and analysis: A researcher's handbook* (3rd ed.). Englewood Cliffs, NJ: Prentice-Hall.

Lawless, J. F. (1982). *Statistical models and methods for lifetime data*. New York: Wiley.

Lee, E. T. (1980). *Statistical methods for survival data methods*. Belmont, CA: Wadsworth Inc.

Levene, H. (1960). Robust tests for equality of variances. In I. Olkin (Ed.), *Contributions to probability and statistics*. Palo Alto, CA: Stanford University Press.

Lurie, P. M. (1995). A review of five statistical packages for Windows. *The American Statistician, 49*, 99–107.

Marcoulides, G. A., & Hershberger, S. L. (1997) *Multivariate statistical methods: A first course*. Hillsdale, NJ: Erlbaum.

Mehta, C., & Patel, N. (1997). *StatXact 3.1 for Windows: Statistical software for exact nonparametric inference: User manual*. Cambridge, MA: CYTEL Software Corporation.

Morgan, W. T. (1998). A review of eight statistics software packages for general use. *The American Statistician, 52*, 70–82.

Neter, J., Wasserman, W., & Kutner, M. H. (1989). *Applied linear regression models* (2nd ed.). Homewood, IL: Richard D. Irwin Inc.

Nunnally, J. C. (1978). *Psychometric theory* (2nd ed.). New York: McGraw-Hill.

Olson, C. L. (1976). On choosing a test statistic in multivariate analysis of variance. *Psychological Bulletin, 83*, 579–586.

Parmar, M. K. B., & Machin, D. (1995). *Survival analysis: A practical approach*. New York: Wiley.

Pedhazur, E. J. (1982). *Multiple regression in behavioral research: Explanation and prediction*. New York: Holt, Rinehart and Winston.

Pedhazur, E. J., Schmelkin, L. P. (1991). *Measurement design and analysis: An integrated approach*. Hillsdale, NJ: Erlbaum.

Peto, R., & Peto, J. (1972). Asymptotically efficient rank invariant procedures (with discussion). *Journal of the Royal Statistical Society, Series A, 135*, 185–206

Sokal, R. R., & Rohlf, F. J. (1995) *Biometry* (3rd. ed.). New York: W. H. Freeman.

Sprent, P. (1989). *Applied nonparametric statistical methods*. London: Chapman and Hall.

SPSS (1997) *SPSS Base 7.5 Syntax reference guide*. Chicago: SPSS Inc

Stevens, J. (1992). *Applied multivariate statistics for the social sciences* (2nd ed.). Hillsdale, NJ: Erlbaum.

Tukey, J. W. (1977). *Exploratory data analysis*. Reading, MA: Addison-Wesley.

Wilcox, R. R. (1996). *Statistics for the social sciences*. San Diego, CA: Academic Press.

Winer, B. J. (1971) *Statistical principles in experimental design* (2nd. ed.). New York: McGraw-Hill.

Zar, J. H. (1996). *Biostatistical analysis* (3rd. ed.). Upper Saddle River, NJ: Prentice-Hall.

3.13
Latent Variables, Factor Analysis, and Causal Modeling

BRIAN S. EVERITT

Institute of Psychiatry, London, UK

3.13.1 INTRODUCTION

Many psychological investigations involve the collection of multivariate data, a term used when more than a single variable value is observed on each subject in a study. Table 1, for example, shows a set of data giving the examination scores obtained in four subjects by 15 students. For many such data sets the question of most interest is how the variables are related, and the first step in answering this question usually involves the calculation of the covariance or more commonly the correlation between each pair of variables (Table 2).

The techniques discussed in this chapter are aimed primarily at explaining and describing as concisely as possible the relationships between the variables in a set of multivariate data. Some of the methods are most applicable when the investigator has only limited expectation of what patterns to expect, and wishes to explore the covariance or correlation matrix in an effort to uncover hopefully some psychologically meaningful structure. Other methods are designed to test specific

Table 1 Examination scores for four subjects.

Student	English	French	Algebra	Statistics
1	77	82	67	67
2	63	78	80	70
3	75	73	71	66
4	55	72	63	70
5	63	63	65	70
6	53	61	72	64
7	51	67	65	65
8	59	70	68	62
9	62	60	58	62
10	64	72	60	62
11	52	64	60	63
12	55	67	59	62
13	50	50	64	55
14	65	63	58	56
15	31	55	60	57

theories or hypotheses as to why the variables have their observed relationships. Both approaches rely heavily on the concept of a latent variable, a topic discussed in the next section.

3.13.2 LATENT VARIABLES, OR, HOW LONG IS A PIECE OF STRING?

Table 3 shows the lengths of 15 pieces of string as measured by a ruler (R) and as estimated (guessed) by three different people (G, B, and D). Corresponding to each piece of string is a true but unknown length. The four observed measurements all give the true length plus some amount of measurement error, although R is likely to be considerably more accurate than the others. The four measurements are said to be fallible indicators of length.

Fascinating though the data in Table 3 may be (at least to the author), many readers of this article may quite reasonably ask what they have to do with psychology in general, and factor analysis in particular? To answer such questions consider again the data shown in Table 1, consisting of the examination scores of 15 individuals in four subjects. Analogous to the true string length of each of the 15 observations in Table 3, each individual in Table 1 might be assumed to have a particular, but unknown, level of cognitive ability (which some bolder psychologists might label "intelligence"), of which the four observed examinations scores are again fallible indicators.

And so in the data sets in both Tables 1 and 3, it can be assumed that the observed or manifest variables are fallible indicators of an underlying variable that cannot be measured directly—a so-called latent variable. Length is, of course, a far more straightforward latent variable than

intelligence and one which most people would find little difficulty in accepting; its direct measurement is prevented simply by measurement error. Many of the latent variables postulated in psychology and related disciplines, however, are often more problematical and even in some cases controversial. Certainly there has been considerable debate about the nature of intelligence. The reason that such variables cannot be measured directly is often more complex than simple measurement error.

The question of how seriously latent variables should be taken in general is discussed in Section 3.13.5 but, as will be seen in later examples, invoking the concept of a latent variable is frequently extremely useful when exploring the relationships between manifest variables. In an exploratory analysis the aim will be to assess whether there is any evidence that the structure in an observed correlation matrix is due to a number of underlying latent variables and, if so, to describe and possibly label these variables.

When testing a specific hypothesis or model for the data, the relationships between the observed and latent variables will be specified *a priori,* and the investigator will be primarily interested in assessing the fit of the suggested model for the observed correlations or covariances. In addition to specifying how observed and latent variables are related, more complex models might also specify relationships between the latent variables themselves; examples are given later.

3.13.3 FACTOR ANALYSIS

Factor analysis is a generic term given to a class of multivariate statistical methods whose primary purpose is data reduction and summarization. In general terms factor analysis

Table 2 Covariances and correlations.

(i) A set of multivariate data is generally represented by a matrix $\mathbf{X}$ where

$$\mathbf{X} = \begin{bmatrix} x_{11} & x_{12} & \cdots & x_{1p} \\ x_{21} & x_{22} & \cdots & x_{2p} \\ \cdot & \cdot & \cdot & \cdot \\ \cdot & \cdot & \cdot & \cdot \\ \cdot & \cdot & \cdot & \cdot \\ x_{n1} & x_{n2} & \cdots & x_{np} \end{bmatrix}$$

where n is the number of observations in the data, p is the number of variables, and x_{ij} represents the value of variable j for observation i

(ii) The sample covariance s_{ij} of variables i and j is given by

$$s_{ij} = \frac{1}{n-1} \sum_{k=1}^{n} (x_{ki} - \bar{x}_i)(x_{kj} - \bar{x}_j)$$

where $\bar{x}_i$ and $\bar{x}_j$ are the sample means of the two variables

(iii) A covariance can take any value from $-\infty$ to ∞. A value of zero indicates that there is no association (strictly, no linear association) between the variables. A positive value occurs when, as one of the variables increases in value then, on average, so does the other. A negative covariance indicates that as one variable increases, the other decreases, and vice versa

(iv) The sample covariance matrix is a matrix with the variances of each variable on the main diagonal and the covariances of each pair of variables as off-diagonal elements

(v) The sample correlation coefficient, r_{ij} between variables i and j is given by

$$r_{ij} = \frac{s_{ij}}{(s_{ii} s_{jj})^{\frac{1}{2}}}$$

where s_{ii} and s_{jj} are used to denote the variances of the two variables

(vi) A correlation takes values between -1 and 1, with the two extremes indicating that the two variables are perfectly linearly related

(vii) The sample correlation matrix is

$$\mathbf{R} = \begin{bmatrix} 1 & r_{12} & \cdots & r_{1p} \\ r_{21} & 1 & \cdots & r_{2p} \\ \cdot & \cdot & \cdot & \cdot \\ \cdot & \cdot & \cdot & \cdot \\ r_{p1} & r_{p2} & \cdots & 1 \end{bmatrix}$$

techniques address themselves to the problem of analyzing the interrelationships amongst a possibly large set of observed variables and explaining these relationships in terms of a (hopefully) small number of underlying latent variables. By using factor analysis, the investigator should be able to identify the separate dimensions being measured by the manifest variables. When used in an exploratory mode, factor analysis methods place no constraints on the possible relationships between observed and latent variables. When used in a confirmatory manner, however, these relationships will be constrained in particular ways specified by the hypothesized model. The next section deals with exploratory factor analysis and Section 3.13.3.2 with confirmatory factor analysis.

Table 3 How long is a piece of string? Measurement by ruler (R) and guesses by three observers (G, B, and D) are given.

Piece	R	G	B	D
1	6.3	5.0	4.8	6.0
2	4.1	3.2	3.1	3.5
3	5.1	3.6	3.8	4.5
4	5.0	4.5	4.1	4.3
5	5.7	4.0	5.2	5.0
6	3.3	2.5	2.8	2.6
7	1.3	1.7	1.4	1.6
8	5.8	4.8	4.2	5.5
9	2.8	2.4	2.0	2.1
10	6.7	5.2	5.3	6.0
11	1.5	1.2	1.1	1.2
12	2.1	1.8	1.6	1.8
13	4.6	3.4	4.1	3.9
14	7.6	6.0	6.3	6.5
15	2.5	2.2	1.6	2.0

3.13.3.1 Exploratory Factor Analysis

The mathematical details of the factor analysis model are listed in Table 4, and the essential features of the technique are now demonstrated by considering an application.

3.13.3.1.1 Statements about pain

This illustration is based on a subset of the data reported in Skevington (1990). The study was concerned with beliefs about controlling pain and 123 individuals suffering from severe pain were presented with nine statements about pain. Each statement was scored on a scale from 1 to 6, ranging from disagreement to agreement. The nine statements and the observed correlations between them are shown in Table 5. One of the aims of the study was to ascertain whether the responses reflected the existence of subscales or groups of attitudes.

In an attempt to identify the latent variables that might account for the observed pattern of correlations between the pain statements, a particular form of factor analysis, maximum likelihood factor analysis was applied (described by Everitt & Dunn, 1991). The results from a factor analysis consist of the estimated regression coefficients of each observed variable on each latent variable (also known in this context as common factors). When the factor analysis has been carried out on the observed correlation matrix rather than the covariance matrix, the estimated regression coefficients are simply the correlations between each manifest variable and each latent variable. (In an exploratory factor analysis the choice of covariance or correlation matrix is not critical

since there is a simple relationship between the solutions derived from each.) Table 6 shows these estimated correlations for both the two- and three-factor solutions. (Methods for deciding on the appropriate number of common factors are discussed later.)

How are the results given by a factor analysis interpreted? First, the estimated correlations (more commonly known as factor loadings) can be used to identify and perhaps name the underlying latent variables, although this is often more straightforward after the process of rotation, which is discussed in Section 3.13.3.1.3. But for now, examining the unrotated results in Table 6 it is seen that for both solutions the second factor is positively correlated, to a greater or lesser extent, with all nine statements. It would not require a great leap of imagination to suggest that this factor might be labeled "general pain level." The first factor is negatively correlated with statements taking personal responsibility for one's pain and positively correlated with statements in which the control of, and reasons for, pain are attributed elsewhere. Factors with a mixture of positive and negative loadings (often referred to as bipolar factors), usually become easier to understand after rotation and so further interpretation of the results is left until Section 3.13.3.1.3.

Apart from the factor loadings, a number of other quantities which need explanation are given in Table 6. First, the sum of squares of the factor loadings of a particular observed variable gives what is known as the communality of that variable, that is, the variance shared with the other manifest variables via their relationships with the common factors. Subtracting the communality of a variable

Table 4 The factor analysis model.

(i) In general terms factor analysis is concerned with whether the covariance, or correlations between a set of observed variables, $x_1, x_2, \ldots, x_p$ can be explained in terms of a smaller number of unobservable latent variables (common factors), $f_1, f_2, \ldots f_k$ where $k < p$ (hopefully k, the number of common factors, will be much less than the number of original variables p)

(ii) The factor analysis model is essentially a regression-type model in which the observed variables are regressed on the assumed common factors. In mathematical terms the factor analysis model can be written as

$$x_1 = \lambda_{11}f_1 + \lambda_{12}f_2 + \ldots + \lambda_{ik}f_k + e_1$$
$$x_2 = \lambda_{21}f_1 + \lambda_{22}f_2 + \ldots + \lambda_{2k}f_k + e_2$$
$$\vdots$$
$$x_p = \lambda_{p1}f_1 + \lambda_{p2}f_2 + \ldots + \lambda_{pk}f_k + e_p$$

The λs are factor loadings and the terms $e_1, e_2, \ldots, e_p$ are known as specific variates—they represent that part of an observed variable not accounted for by the common factors

(iii) The following assumptions are made:
  (a) The common factors are in standardized form and have variance one
  (b) The common factors are uncorrelated
  (c) The specific variates are uncorrelated
  (d) The common factors are uncorrelated with the specific variates

(iv) With these assumptions the factor analysis model implies that the population variances ($\sigma_i^2, j = 1, 2, \ldots, p$) and covariances ($\sigma_{ij}$) of the observed variables can be written as

$$\sigma_i^2 = \sum_{j=1}^{k} \lambda_{ij}^2 + \psi_i$$

$$\sigma_i^2 = \sum_{l=1}^{k} \lambda_{il}\lambda_{jl}$$

where ψ_i is the variance of specific variate e_i, i.e., the specific variance of variable x_i

(v) The model implies that the variance of an observed variable can be split into two parts $\sum_{j=1}^{k} \lambda_{ij}^2$ and ψ_i. The first of those is known as the communality of the variable x_i; it is the variance in the variable shared with the other observed variables via their relationships with the common factors

(vi) Note that the covariances of the observed variables are generated solely from their relationships with the common factors. The specific variates play no part in determining the covariances of the observed variables; they contribute only to the variances of those variables

(vii) There are a number of different methods for fitting the factor analysis model. The two most commonly used are principal factor analysis and maximum likelihood factor analysis—both are described in Everitt and Dunn (1991)

(viii) A method of factor analysis commonly used in practice is principal components analysis (Everitt & Dunn, 1991). Although this is an extremely useful technique for the summarization of multivariate data, it is not discussed in detail here because it is not a natural precursor to the confirmatory and causal models to be discussed later. It may, however, be worthwhile listing the main differences between the two approaches:

  (a) Factor analysis (FA) and principal components analysis (PCA) each attempt to describe a set of multivariate data in a smaller number of dimensions than one starts with, but the procedures used to achieve this goal are essentially quite different in the two approaches

  (b) FA, unlike PCA, begins with a hypothesis about the covariance (or correlational) structure of the variables, namely that there exists a set of k latent variables ($k < p$) and these are adequate to account for the interrelationships of the variables though not for their full variances

  (c) PCA, however, is merely a transformation of the data and no assumptions are made about the form of the covariance matrix of the data. In particular PCA has no part corresponding to the specific variates of FA. Consequently, if the FA model holds and the specific variances are small, both forms of analysis would be expected to give similar results

  (d) A clear advantage of FA over PCA is that there is a simple relationship between the solutions obtained from the covariance and correlation matrices

  (e) It should be remembered that PCA and FA are both pointless if the observed variables are uncorrelated—FA because it has nothing to explain and PCA because it would lead to components which are essentially identical to the original variables

(ix) In many (perhaps most) examples the results from a principal components analysis and an exploratory factor analysis will be similar, with any differences not usually affecting the substantive interpretation

Table 5 Pain statements and their correlations.

Pain statements

(1) Whether or not I am in pain in the future depends on the skills of the doctors
(2) Whenever I am in pain, it is usually because of something I have done or not done
(3) Whether or not I am in pain depends on what the doctors do for me
(4) I cannot get any help for my pain unless I go to seek medical advice
(5) When I am in pain I know that it is because I have not been taking proper exercise or eating the right food
(6) People's pain results from their own carelessness
(7) I am directly responsible for my pain
(8) Relief from pain is chiefly controlled by the doctors
(9) People who are never in pain are just plain lucky

Correlations

	1	2	3	4	5	6	7	8	9
1	1.0000								
2	−0.0385	1.0000							
3	0.6066	−0.0693	1.0000						
4	0.4507	−0.1167	0.5916	1.000					
5	0.0320	0.4881	0.0317	−0.082	1.0000				
6	−0.2877	0.4271	−0.1336	−0.2073	0.4731	1.0000			
7	−0.2974	0.3045	−0.2404	−0.1850	0.4138	0.6346	1.0000		
8	0.4526	−0.3090	0.5886	0.6286	−0.1397	−0.1329	−0.2599	1.0000	
9	0.2952	−0.1704	0.3165	0.3680	−0.2367	0.1541	−0.2893	0.4047	1.000

Table 6 Maximum likelihood factor analysis solutions for pain statement correlations.

(i) Two-factor solution

Statement	Factor 1	Factor 2	Communality	Specific variance
1	0.643	0.211	0.458	0.542
2	−0.361	0.413	0.301	0.699
3	0.718	0.401	0.676	0.324
4	0.687	0.288	0.555	0.445
5	−0.311	0.569	0.420	0.580
6	−0.521	0.614	0.448	0.352
7	−0.563	0.477	0.544	0.456
8	0.709	0.254	0.567	0.433
9	0.482	0.004	0.233	0.767
Variance	2.950	1.451		

(ii) Three-factor solution

Statement	Factor 1	Factor 2	Factor 3	Communality	Specific variance
1	0.605	0.295	0.372	0.592	0.408
2	−0.455	0.291	0.431	0.477	0.523
3	0.613	0.498	0.192	0.641	0.339
4	0.621	0.399	0.000	0.545	0.455
5	−0.407	0.450	0.372	0.506	0.494
6	−0.671	0.594	−0.149	0.825	0.175
7	−0.625	0.342	−0.060	0.512	0.488
8	0.681	0.475	−0.273	0.253	0.237
9	0.449	0.162	−0.138	0.247	0.753
Variance	3.007	1.502	0.619		

from the value one gives the specific variance of a variable, that is, the variation in the variable *not* shared with the other variables. So, for example, in the two factor solution the communality of the statement "people who are never in pain are just plain lucky," is rather low at 0.23 and its specific variance consequently relatively high at 0.77. Variation in the response to this statement is largely unrelated to the two common factors.

The sum of squares of the loadings on a common factor gives the variation in the manifest variables accounted for by that factor. This is to be compared with the total variation in the observed variables, which since this example uses a correlation matrix and hence relates to variables standardized to have variance one, is simply equal to the number of variables, that is, nine. So, in the two-factor solution, the first factor has variance 2.95 and accounts for 33% of the variation in the observed variables. Both factors together in the two-factor solution account for 49% of the variance. The factors in the three-factor solution together account for 57% of the variance.

Note that factors are extracted in order of their variance, and are so constructed that they are uncorrelated, that is, independent—an alternative technical term that is sometimes encountered is "orthogonal."

3.13.3.1.2 Determining the number of factors

Before rotating and interpreting a factor solution the investigator needs to answer the important question, "How many factors?" A variety of informal and formal methods have been suggested. The former include, taking as many factors as account for an adequate amount of the variation in the observed variables (where "adequate" is usually interpreted as roughly around 60% or above), and plotting factor variances against factor number (a so-called scree plot) and identifying the point where the curve flattens out. When applying the maximum likelihood method of factor analysis a more formal significance testing procedure is available based on what is known as the likelihood function, which is essentially, a measure of how well the estimated factor solution fits the observed correlations. Everitt and Dunn (1991) give a specific definition. With this approach a sequential procedure is used to determine k, the number of common factors. Starting with some small value of k (usually one), the test for number of factors is applied and, if the test is nonsignificant, the current value of k is deemed acceptable; otherwise k is increased by one and the process repeated until an acceptable solution is found.

Each of the procedures described above can be applied to the pain statements data, and the results are shown in Table 7 and Figure 1. It is clear from these results that the three-factor solution is the one to choose and is consequently subjected to the process of rotation described in the next section.

3.13.3.1.3 Factor rotation

The initial factors extracted from a factor analysis are often difficult to interpret and

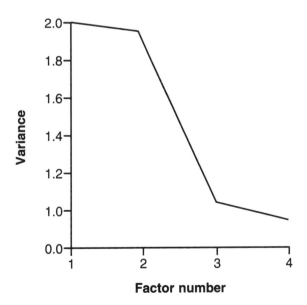

Figure 1 Scree plot.

Table 7　Determining number of factors for pain statement data.

(i) Percentage variance accounted for in a five-factor solution

Number of factors	Percentage variance accounted for
1	22
2	44
3	55
4	65
5	70

(ii) Significance test for number of factors

Model	Test statistic	Degrees of freedom	P-value
One-factor	172.34	27	< 0.001
Two-factor	58.95	19	< 0.001
Three-factor	18.19	12	0.11
Four-factor	10.01	6	0.124
Five-factor	0.85	1	0.356

name. A process which can frequently aid in these tasks is factor rotation whereby the initial solution is described in a different and, in many cases, a simpler fashion. A rotated and unrotated factor analysis solution are mathematically equivalent, but the former usually leads to a clearer picture of the nature of the underlying latent variables. The rotation methods usually employed are designed to lead to a factor solution with the properties that Thurstone (1947) referred to as a simple structure. In very general terms such a structure results when the common factors involve subsets of the original variables with as little overlap as possible, i.e., variables have high loadings on a particular factor and negligible loadings on the others. In this way the original variables are divided into groups relatively independent of each other. Methods of rotation operate by seeking, essentially, to make large loadings larger and small loadings smaller. This rather vague aim is translated into more specific mathematical terms by selecting a rotated solution so that the loadings optimize some suitable numerical criterion. For example, a well known method of rotation known as varimax attempts to maximize the within-factor variance of the squared loadings. Other methods (of which there are several) choose to optimize somewhat different criteria in their aim to achieve simple structure. In many examples the solutions given by the competing methods of rotation will be very similar.

To illustrate the application of rotation, Table 8 shows the varimax-rotated, three-factor solution for the pain statement data. Note that although the factor loadings have changed, the communalities of the variables are unaltered, as is the total variance accounted for by the solution. The variance attributable to each common factor, *has* however, changed.

A possible interpretation of the rotated three-factor solution is in terms of different aspects of the control of, and responsibility for, one's pain. The first factor attributes both to others, particularly doctors. The second factor, with high loadings on statements 6 and 7, involves complete personal responsibilty for one's pain and the third factor, having its highest loadings on statements 2 and 5, might be seen as attributing pain to deficiencies in one's lifestyle.

The possibility of rotating factor solutions arises because of the lack of uniqueness of the factor loadings in the basic factor analysis model described in Table 5 (Everitt, 1996). This property once caused many statisticians to view factor analysis with grave suspicion, since apparently it allows investigators licence to consider a large number of solutions (each corresponding to a different rotation of the factors) and to select the one closest to their *a priori* expectations (or prejudices) about the factor structure of the data. In general, however, such suspicion is misplaced and factor rotation can be a useful procedure for simplifying an exploratory factor analysis solution. Factor rotation merely allows the fitted factor analysis model to be described as simply as possible. Rotation does not alter the overall structure of a solution, but only how the

Table 8 Rotated three-factor solution for pain statement data.

Statement	Factor 1	Factor 2	Factor 3	Communality
1	0.654	−0.358	0.188	0.591
2	−0.121	0.200	0.650	0.478
3	0.793	−0.138	0.112	0.661
4	0.726	−0.10	−0.09	0.545
5	0.02	0.305	0.642	0.506
6	−0.09	0.827	0.365	0.825
7	−0.226	0.598	0.323	0.512
8	0.813	0.06	−0.312	0.763
9	0.435	−0.08	−0.229	0.247
Variances	2.509	1.340	1.279	

solution is described; rotation of factors is a process by which a solution is made more interpretable without changing its underlying mathematical properties.

It should be noted that there are two distinct types of rotation, orthogonal and oblique. With the former, the factors in the rotated solution remain independent of one another as they were in the initial solution but, with the latter, correlated factors are allowed. The consequence of allowing correlations between factors is that the sum of squares of a factor's loadings can no longer be used to determine the amount of variance attributable to a factor. Additionally, the sums of squares of factor loadings for each variable no longer give the communality of the variable. In practice, in an exploratory factor analysis, orthogonal rotation is far more commonly used than oblique rotation since the solutions are often satisfactory without introducing the complication of factor correlations.

3.13.3.2 Confirmatory Factor Analysis

In a confirmatory factor analysis, particular parameters of the model, for example, some of the factor loadings, are specified *a priori* to be fixed at some specified value, usually zero or one, whilst other parameters are free to be estimated from the data. The model considered may have arisen from theoretical considerations, or perhaps on the basis of the results of earlier exploratory factor analyses in the same area.

How is such a model fitted to an observed correlation or covariance matrix? The simple answer is by using the appropriate software as described in the Appendix. The essentials of the fitting process are, however, also given in Table 9. Once again, however, much can be learnt from examining a series of examples.

3.13.3.2.1 Confirmatory factor analysis models for length and intelligence

Consider once again the string data given in Table 3. The model suggested previously for these data is that the four observed measurements of string length are fallible estimates of the latent variable true string length. This model can be represented more specifically in mathematical terms as shown in Table 10, and in the form of a diagram as shown in Figure 2. The model is a very simple example of a confirmatory factor analysis model, and differs from the exploratory models considered in the previous section in two ways: (i) the number of factors, one, is specified *a priori*; and (ii) the loadings of the observed variables on the postulated latent variable are all fixed to be one.

The correlations between the four measurements are given in Table 11. Applying the procedure outlined in Table 9 to these correlations using the EQS package (Bentler, 1995), gives the results shown in Table 12.

Judged by the chi-squared statistic the model fits very well. As was to be expected, measurement by ruler is the most accurate; observer B appears to be the marginally less successful than G and D in guessing the string lengths. The residuals are all very small.

In the same way, the model detailed in Table 9 can be fitted to the examination scores data in Table 1. Details of the results are shown in Table 13. Here the model again fits reasonably well as judged simply by the chi-squared statistic, but rather less satisfactorily than for the string data, reflecting the less certain nature of intelligence as compared to length. In fact, the residuals in Table 13 indicate that the predicted and observed correlations differ quite considerably and that the model cannot really be considered adequate for these data despite the nonsignificant chi-squared value. The latter may be misleading here since it is not strictly

Table 9 Estimation and goodness of fit in confirmatory factor analysis models.

(i) Suppose that **S** is the observed covariance (or correlation) matrix with elements s_{ij}. Corresponding to **S** will be a matrix $\hat{\mathbf{S}}$ giving the correlations as predicted by the assumed model

(ii) The elements of the matrix $\hat{\mathbf{S}}$ will be functions of the parameters of the confirmatory factor analysis model, for example, factor loadings, specific variances, and factor correlations

(iii) Estimation of a confirmatory factor analysis (CFA) model involves finding values for the model's parameters (parameter estimates) so that the corresponding predicted and observed covariances and variances are as close as possible to one another

(iv) More specifically, a function of the differences between s_{ij} and $\hat{s}_{ij}$ is minimized with respect to the parameters

(v) One such function would be the sum of squares of the differences; this corresponds to least-squares estimation

(vi) Other estimation criteria are discussed in Everitt (1984)

(v) Having decided on a measure of closeness, some type of mathematical optimization algorithm (Everitt, 1987) is applied to find the parameter values that minimize the measure

(viii) The fitting procedure leads not only to parameter estimates but also to the standard errors of the estimates

(ix) A chi-squared statistic measuring the discrepancies between the observed variances and covariances and those predicted by the model is one of the methods that can be used to assess the fit of the model. The degrees of freedom are

$$\nu = p(p + 1)/2 - t$$

where p is the number of observed variables and t is the number of free parameters in the model

(x) Fit can (and should) also be assessed by examining the differences between the corresponding elements of the observed and predicted covariance or correlation matrix. Any differences (residuals) which are unacceptably large, or a pattern of moderately sized residuals sheds some doubt on the acceptability of the model

---

valid for samples as small as 15. Questions of the appropriate sample size necessary to achieve an adequate statistical power are as relevant when fitting confirmatory factor analysis as when applying a simple t-test (examples of how to determine sample size for the former are given in Dunn, Everitt, & Pickles, 1993).

A natural question that arises therefore is how the model might be amended to improve its fit. Some general points about how poorly fitting models might be amended are made later, but one relatively minor change that might be considered here is to allow the loading on each examination score to be a free parameter to be estimated rather than having a fixed value of one. Such a model is again easily fitted using the EQS software and the results are given in Table 14. Now the residuals are much more acceptable with only the correlation between algebra and statistics scores being poorly predicted. The estimated factor loadings show that the algebra scores are least related to the postulated latent variable.

3.13.3.2.2 Ability and aspiration

As a further example of fitting a confirmatory factor analysis model, the study of ability and aspiration described in Caslyn and Kenny (1977) is used. In this study the investigators

observed the values of the following six variables for 556 white eighth-grade students: (1) self-concept of ability, (2) perceived parental evaluation, (3) perceived teacher evaluation, (4) perceived friend's evaluation, (5) educational aspiration, and (6) college plans.

The correlations between the six variables are given in Table 15. The model postulated to explain these correlations involves two latent variables, named by the authors as ability and aspiration. The first four observed variables are assumed to be indicators of ability and the last two observed variables are assumed to be indicators of aspiration. In addition the two latent variables are assumed to be correlated. Consequently the model is known as a correlated two-factor model. It may be represented in a diagram (a so-called path diagram (Everitt, 1996)) as shown in Figure 3. The mathematical form of the model appears in Table 16. Note again the differences between this model and the exploratory models of Section 3.13.3.1; here, each observed variable is constrained to have fixed zero loadings on one of the latent variables, and on the other, a free loading to be estimated from the data. The results of fitting the model to the observed correlations, using once again the EQS package, are shown in Table 17. Of particular note among these results is the estimate of the correlation between the two postulated latent variables. This estimate

Table 10 Mathematical specification of one-factor model for string data.

The factor analysis model for the string length data is

$$R = f + e_1$$
$$G = f + e_2$$
$$B = f + e_3$$
$$D = f + e_4$$

where f represents the true length and e_1, e_2, e_3, and e_4 are the errors in the four observed length measurements. These errors are assumed to have zero mean and their estimated variances will reflect the accuracy of R, G, B, and D

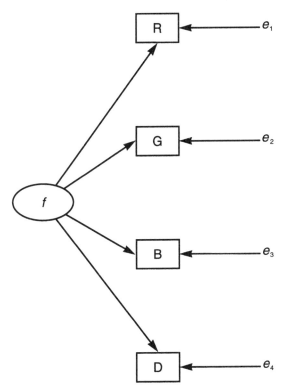

Figure 2 Single-factor model for string lengths.

(0.666 with a standard error of 0.03) is the disattenuated correlation, which represents the correlation between true ability and true aspiration, uncontaminated by measurement error in the observed indicators of these concepts. Note that the value of the disattenuated correlation is higher than any of the observed correlations.

3.13.3.2.3 *Drug usage among American students*

As a final example of fitting a confirmatory factor analysis model, an investigation of drug usage among American college students reported by Huba, Wingard, and Bentler (1981) is considered.

The majority of adult and adolescent Americans use psychoactive substances during an increasing proportion of their lifetime. Various forms of licit and illicit psychoactive substance use are prevalent, suggesting that patterns of psychoactive substance taking are major components of the individual's behavioral repertoire and have pervasive implications for the performance of other behaviors. In an investigation of these phenomena, Huba et al. (1981) collected data on drug usage rates for 1634 students in the seventh to ninth grades in 11 schools in the greater metropolitan area of Los Angeles. Each participant completed a questionnaire about the number of times he or she had ever used a particular substance.

Table 11   Correlation matrix for the four measurements of string length.

$$
\begin{array}{cccc}
 & R & G & B & D \\
\mathbf{R} = \begin{array}{c} R \\ G \\ B \\ D \end{array} &
\left[\begin{array}{cccc}
1.0000 & & & \\
0.9802 & 1.0000 & & \\
0.9811 & 0.9553 & 1.0000 & \\
0.9899 & 0.9807 & 0.9684 & 1.0000
\end{array}\right]
\end{array}
$$

Table 12   Results from fitting one-factor model with equal loadings for each variable to string data.

(i) Residuals (differences between observed and predicted correlations)

$$
\begin{array}{cccc}
 & R & G & B & D \\
\mathbf{R} = \begin{array}{c} R \\ G \\ B \\ D \end{array} &
\left[\begin{array}{cccc}
0.007 & & & \\
-0.010 & -0.025 & & \\
-0.009 & -0.035 & -0.028 & \\
0.000 & -0.009 & -0.022 & -0.007
\end{array}\right]
\end{array}
$$

(ii) Variances of error terms for each observed variable and their standard errors (SE)

R: variance = 0.003, SE = 0.005
G: variance = 0.035, SE = 0.014
B: variance = 0.038, SE = 0.016
D: variance = 0.017, SE = 0.008

(iii) Chi-squared goodness of fit statistic = 2.575, degrees of freedom = 5, P-value = 0.765

The substances for which data were collected were as follows: (1) cigarettes, (2) beer, (3) wine, (4) spirits, (5) cocaine, (6) tranquilizers, (7) drugstore medications used to get high, (8) heroin and other opiates. (9) marijuana, (10) hashish, (11) inhalents (glue, petrol, etc.), (12) hallucinogenics (LSD, mescalin, etc.), and (13) amphetamine stimulants.

Responses were recorded on a five-point scale which ranged from "never tried" to "used regularly." The correlations between the usage rates of the 13 substances are shown in Table 18. The model proposed by Huba et al. (1981) for these data arose from considering previously reported research in the area, and postulated the following three latent variables:

(i) Alcohol use (f_1) with nonzero loadings on beer, wine, spirits, and cigarettes.

(ii) Cannabis use (f_2) with nonzero loadings on marijuana, hashish, cigarettes, and wine. The cigarette variable is assumed to load on both the first and second latent variable because it sometimes occurs with both alcohol and marijuana and at other times does not. The nonzero loading on wine was allowed because of reports that wine is frequently used with marijuana and that consequently some of the use of wine may be an indicator of tendencies towards cannabis.

(iii) Hard drug use (f_3) with nonzero loadings on amphetamines, tranquilizers, hallucinogenics, hashish, cocaine, heroin, drugstore medication, inhalants, and spirits. The use of

Table 13 Results of fitting the one-factor model to examination scores, with loadings
fixed at one.

(ii) Correlations

	English	French	Algebra	Statistics
English	1.000			
French	0.683	1.000		
Algebra	0.286	0.451	1.000	
Statistics	0.431	0.690	0.544	1.000

(ii) Residuals

	English	French	Algebra	Statistics
English	−0.113			
French	0.104	0.147		
Algebra	−0.293	−0.128	−0.265	
Statistics	−0.148	0.111	−0.035	0.025

(iii) Variances of error terms for each observed variable and their standard errors

English: variance = 0.534, SE = 0.244
French: variance = 0.274, SE = 0.156
Algebra: variance = 0.686, SE = 0.299
Statistics: variance = 0.396, SE = 0.196

(iv) Chi-squared goodness-of-fit statistic = 4.136, degrees of freedom = 5, P-value = 0.530.

each of these substances was considered to suggest a strong commitment to the notion of psychoactive drug use.

The path diagram of the proposed model is shown in Figure 4, and Table 19 shows the equivalent mathematical structure of the model. Note that each pair of the postulated variables is allowed to have a nonzero correlation. The results of fitting the model are detailed in Table 20. The chi-squared goodness-of-fit statistic takes a value 323.96 with 58 degrees of freedom and has a very small associated P-value. It appears that the proposed model does *not* provide an adequate explanation for the correlations between the recorded usage rates of the 13 substances, although the large sample size ($n = 1634$) may lead to even relatively trivial discrepancies between observed and predicted correlations being declared significant. In practice the chi-squared statistic is only one of the pieces of evidence that should be used when judging the fit of a model; other measures of fit are discussed in Dunn et al. (1993).

Amending a model that is considered not to provide an adequate fit will generally involve a mixture of the theoretical and empirical. Information from the data about possibly better fitting models is provided by two types of tests, the Lagrange multiplier test and Wald's test, both of which are described in detail in the EQS manual (Bentler, 1995). Essentially, however, the former evaluates whether, from a statistical viewpoint at least, the model could be improved by freeing a previously fixed parameter. The latter is designed to determine whether sets of parameters that were treated as free in the model could in fact be simultaneously set to zero without substantial loss in model fit. Examples of the use of the two test procedures are given in Dunn et al. (1993). In

Table 14   Results of fitting further single-factor model to examination scores; loadings now free parameters to be estimated.

(i) Residuals

	English	French	Algebra	Statistics
English	0.000			
French	0.010	0.000		
Algebra	−0.052	−0.016	0.000	
Statistics	−0.070	−0.002	0.197	0.000

(ii) Variances of error terms for each observed variable and their standard errors

English: variance = 0.513, SE = 0.226
French: variance = 0.069, SE = 0.217
Algebra: variance = 0.766, SE = 0.298
Statistics: variance = 0.485, SE = 0.221

(iii) Estimated factor loadings and their standard errors

English: loading = 0.698, SE = 0.247
French: loading = 0.965, SE = 0.225
Algebra: loading = 0.484, SE = 0.262
Statistics: loading = 0.718, SE = 0.246

(iv) Chi-squared goodness-of-fit statistic = 1.940, degrees of freedom = 2, P-value = 0.379

the original analysis of the drug usage data given in Huba et al. (1981) various amendments to the correlated three-factor model were tried in order to improve fit; for example, a number of error terms were allowed to be correlated. However, making such amendments to gain small improvements in fit is not always satisfactory and it should perhaps be pointed out that, in most cases, a theoretically justifiable model that provides a less adequate fit than a model adjusted on an *ad hoc* basis, is likely to be preferred.

Recent examples of the application of confirmatory factor analysis in clinical psychology are given in Osman et al. (1995) and Hittner (1995).

3.13.4 CAUSAL MODELS AND STRUCTURAL EQUATION MODELING

The confirmatory factor analysis models described in the previous section are a subset of the models for correlational data that can now be fitted routinely using software such as EQS or LISREL (see Appendix). More complex models that specify regression-type relationships between latent variables, as well as how the manifest and latent variables are linked, have now been used in many areas from models of the female orgasm (Newcomb & Bentler, 1983) to models to represent both psychological and physical processess in cognitive functioning (Hines, Chiu, McAdams, Bentler, & Lipcamon, 1992).

Such models are most generally (and most suitably) referred to as structural equation models. However, since they are often used as a means of describing some prespecified causal theory of the structure of a set of variables of interest, they are also often labeled causal models where "causal" implies that a change in one variable is assumed to result in the change of another variable. No matter how convincing, respectable, and reasonable a path diagram and its associated model may appear, it is important to recognize that seldom do structural equation models provide any direct test of the causal

Table 15 Observed correlations for ability and aspiration example.

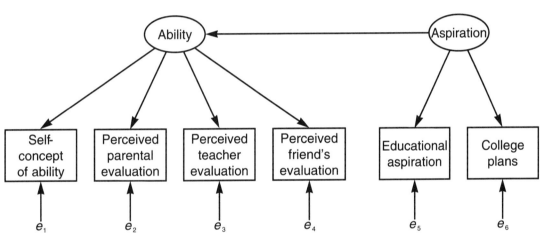

	1	2	3	4	5	6
1	1.00					
2	0.73	1.00				
3	0.70	0.68	1.00			
4	0.58	0.61	0.57	1.00		
5	0.46	0.43	0.40	0.37	1.00	
6	0.56	0.52	0.48	0.41	0.72	1.00

Figure 3 Path diagram for ability and aspiration.

assumptions on which these models are based. This is generally true simply because, in most cases, an investigator's belief about the causal structures which underlie a set of observed variables are based on little more than common sense and intuition; it is only rarely that there is strong evidence (such as that provided by controlled experimentation) about the causal structure involved, and the only satisfactory way to demonstrate causality is through the active control of variables. As pointed out by Cliff (1983) it is simply not possible, with correlational data, to isolate the empirical system sufficiently so that the nature of the relationships among variables can be unambiguously ascertained. It seems that the old aphorism much stressed in introductory statistics courses, "correlation does not imply causation" is still apposite even in the sophisticated world of structural equation modeling.

Many investigators proposing causal models might, of course, argue that they are using the term causal in a purely metaphorical fashion. As pointed out by deLeeuw (1985), however, such a cavalier attitude towards terminology becomes hard to defend if, for example, educational programs are based on the metaphors, such as "intelligence is largely genetically determined" or "allocation of resources to schools has only very minor impact on the careers of students."

Many of the problems of so called causal modeling mentioned above arise largely because of the relative lack of well specified causal theories in the social sciences. However, not all is doom and gloom for an investigator eager to try out such models. Although it may be the case

Table 16   Mathematical structure of correlated two-factor model for ability and aspiration.

(i) The two common factors or latent variables are ability (f_1) and aspiration (f_2) Both are assumed to have variance of one (this is necessary since they are unobserved and their scale needs to be set in some arbitrary way)

(ii) The proposed model postulates that the relationships between the observed variables and the latent variables are as follows:

$$x_1 = \lambda_1 f_1 + 0f_2 + e_1$$
$$x_2 = \lambda_2 f_1 + 0f_2 + e_2$$
$$x_3 = \lambda_3 f_1 + 0f_2 + e_3$$
$$x_4 = \lambda_4 f_1 + 0f_2 + e_4$$
$$x_5 = 0f_1 + \lambda_5 f_2 + e_5$$
$$x_6 = 0f_1 + \lambda_6 f_2 + e_6$$

(iii) This may be rewritten as

$$x_1 = \lambda_1 f_1 + e_1$$
$$x_2 = \lambda_2 f_1 + e_2$$
$$x_3 = \lambda_3 f_1 + e_3$$
$$x_4 = \lambda_4 f_1 + e_4$$
$$x_5 = \lambda_5 f_2 + e_5$$
$$x_6 = \lambda_6 f_2 + e_6$$

(iv) Note that, unlike an exploratory factor analysis, a number of loadings are fixed *a priori* at zero, that is, they play no part in the estimation process

(v) The model also allows for f_1 and f_2 to be correlated

(vi) The model has a total of 13 free parameters (six loadings, six error variances and one correlation). The observed correlation matrix has six variances and 15 correlations, a total of 21 terms. Consequently the postulated model has $21-13 = 8$ degrees of freedom

Table 17   Results from fitting the correlated two-factor model to correlations in Table 15.

Parameter	Estimates	Standard error	Estimate/standard
λ_1	0.863	0.035	24.558
λ_2	0.849	0.035	23.961
λ_3	0.805	0.035	22.115
λ_4	0.695	0.039	18.000
λ_5	0.775	0.040	19.206
λ_6	0.929	0.039	23.569
var(e_1)	0.255	0.023	19.911
var(e_2)	0.279	0.024	11.546
var(e_3)	0.352	0.027	13.070
var(e_4)	0.516	0.035	14.876
var(e_5)	0.399	0.038	10.450
var(e_6)	0.137	0.044	3.152
corr(f_1, f_2)	0.667	0.031	21.521

The chi-square test of the fit of the model takes the value 9.26 with 8 degrees of freedom. The associated *P*-value is 0.321. The model provides a very adequate fit for the data.

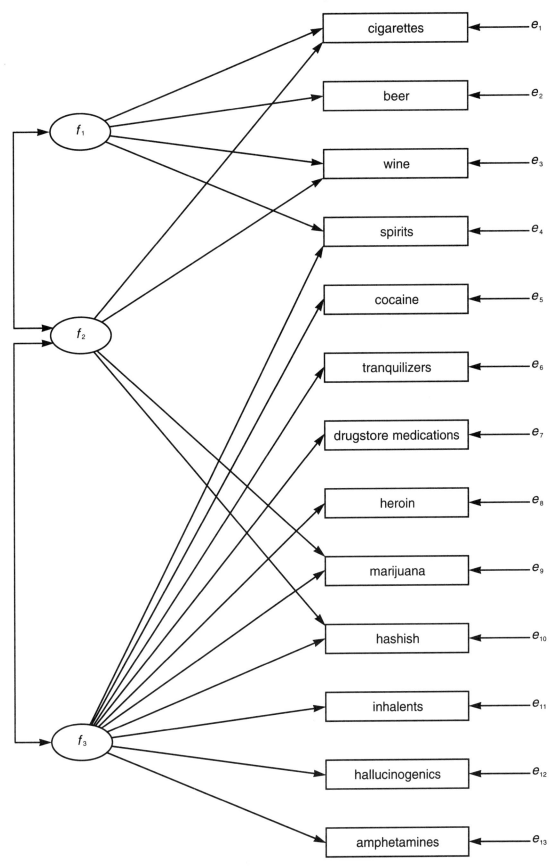

Figure 4 Path diagram for three-factor model for drug usage example.

Table 18 Correlations between usage rates for 13 substances (key to substances is given in text).

	1	2	3	4	5	6	7	8	9	10	11	12	13
1	1.000												
2	0.447	1.000											
3	0.422	0.619	1.000										
4	0.436	0.604	0.585	1.000									
5	0.114	0.068	0.053	0.115	1.000								
6	0.203	0.146	0.139	0.258	0.349	1.000							
7	0.091	0.103	0.110	0.122	0.209	0.221	1.000						
8	0.082	0.063	0.066	0.097	0.321	0.355	0.201	1.000					
9	0.513	0.445	0.365	0.482	0.186	0.316	0.150	0.154	1.000				
10	0.304	0.318	0.240	0.368	0.303	0.377	0.163	0.219	0.534	1.000			
11	0.245	0.203	0.183	0.255	0.272	0.323	0.310	0.288	0.301	0.302	1.000		
12	0.100	0.088	0.074	0.139	0.279	0.367	0.232	0.320	0.204	0.368	0.340	1.000	
13	0.245	0.199	0.184	0.293	0.278	0.545	0.232	0.314	0.394	0.467	0.392	0.511	1.000

Table 19 Mathematical structure of the correlated three-factor model for the drug usage data.

(i) Three latent variables, alcohol use (f_1), cannabis use (f_2), and hard drug use (f_3) are postulated. All are assumed to have variance unity

(ii) The proposed model postulates the following relationship between the observed and latent variables:

$$\text{cigarettes} = \lambda_1 f_1 + \lambda_2 f_2 + e_1$$
$$\text{beer} = \lambda_3 f_1 + e_2$$
$$\text{wine} = \lambda_4 f_1 + \lambda_5 f_2 + e_3$$
$$\text{spirits} = \lambda_6 f_1 + \lambda_7 f_3 + e_4$$
$$\text{cocaine} = \lambda_8 f_3 + e_5$$
$$\text{tranquilizers} = \lambda_9 f_3 + e_6$$
$$\text{drugstore} = \lambda_{10} f_3 + e_7$$
$$\text{heroin} = \lambda_{11} f_3 + e_8$$
$$\text{marjuanna} = \lambda_{12} f_2 + e_9$$
$$\text{hashish} = \lambda_{13} f_2 + \lambda_{14} f_3 + e_{10}$$
$$\text{inhalants} = \lambda_{15} f_3 + e_{11}$$
$$\text{hallucinogenics} = \lambda_{16} f_3 + e_{12}$$
$$\text{amphetamines} = \lambda_{17} f_3 + e_{13}$$

(iii) The proposed model also allows for nonzero correlations between each pair of latent variables. The proposed model has a total of 33 parameters to estimate (17 loadings, 13 error variances, and 3 between-factor correlations). Consequently, the model has $13 \times 14/2 - 33 = 58$ degrees of freedom

that correlation does not imply causation, it is equally true that a well specified causal model implies testable propositions about the structure of observed correlations, and so is amenable to falsification in the same way as is any other scientific theory. At the very least, such a model may provide a convenient and parsimonious description of a set of correlations and serve to rule out many alternative hypotheses about the structure of the data.

3.13.4.1 Examples of Causal Models

After the rather lengthy discussion of their merits or otherwise given above, it is now time to look at some examples of the application of structural equation/causal modeling.

3.13.4.1.1 Ability scores over time

Table 21 gives, for a group of children, the means, standard deviations, correlations and covariances for four measures of ability (percentage of test questions correct) made at the ages of 6, 7, 9, and 11 (Osbourne & Suddick, 1972). As one would expect, the means increase progressively over time, as do the standard deviations. The correlation matrix shows higher correlations between adjacent measures than between those further apart in time.

The simplest model that might be considered for these data is that specified by the path diagram shown in Figure 5; here, ability is assumed to be a fixed trait and that variation over time arises solely from measurement error. Fitting such a model to the covariance matrix in

Table 20 Results of fitting the correlated three-factor model to the drug usage data.

Parameter	Estimates	Standard error	Estimate/standard error
λ_1	0.358	0.035	10.371
λ_2	0.332	0.035	9.401
λ_3	0.792	0.023	35.021
λ_4	0.875	0.038	23.285
λ_5	−0.152	0.037	−4.158
λ_6	0.722	0.024	30.673
λ_7	0.123	0.023	5.439
λ_8	0.465	0.026	18.079
λ_9	0.676	0.024	28.182
λ_{10}	0.359	0.025	13.602
λ_{11}	0.476	0.026	18.571
λ_{12}	0.912	0.030	29.958
λ_{13}	0.396	0.030	13.379
λ_{14}	0.381	0.029	13.050
λ_{15}	0.543	0.025	21.602
λ_{16}	0.618	0.025	25.233
λ_{17}	0.763	0.023	32.980
var(e_1)	0.611	0.024	25.823
var(e_2)	0.374	0.020	18.743
var(e_3)	0.379	0.024	16.052
var(e_4)	0.408	0.019	21.337
var(e_5)	0.784	0.029	26.845
var(e_6)	0.544	0.023	23.222
var(e_7)	0.871	0.032	27.653
var(e_8)	0.773	0.029	26.735
var(e_9)	0.169	0.044	3.846
var(e_{10})	0.547	0.022	24.593
var(e_{11})	0.705	0.027	25.941
var(e_{12})	0.618	0.025	24.655
var(e_{13})	0.418	0.021	19.713
corr(f_1,f_2)	0.634	0.027	23.369
corr(f_1,f_3)	0.313	0.029	10.674
corr(f_2,f_3)	0.499	0.027	18.412

Table 21 gives the results shown in Table 22. The chi-squared goodness-of-fit statistic is significant at the 5% level, suggesting that the simple single factor model does not provide an adequate fit for the covariance matrix.

In this example, the observed covariance matrix has been used as the basis for fitting the model of interest. In general the question of whether the covariance or correlation matrix should be used as the basis for structural equation modeling is probably not of great importance, although there are some situations where the covariance matrix is definitely to be preferred (Cudeck, 1989).

A path diagram for a more plausible model for the ability data is shown in Figure 6; this model postulates causal effects between one latent variable and another and the presence of the disturbances terms on f_2, f_3, and f_4 (terms d_2, d_3, and d_4) means that latent ability is not regarded as an entirely fixed and stable trait, but may vary, increasing or decreasing relative to other children, from one time to the next. The results of fitting this model are shown in Table 23. The chi-squared test statistic now indicates that the model fits satisfactorily. The regression coefficients of each latent variable on the one preceding it in time are all highly significant (see Dunn et al., 1993, for a detailed accident).

3.13.4.1.2 Stability of alienation

As a further example of structural equation modeling a study reported by Wheaton, Muthen, Alwin, and Summers (1977) is used. The study was concerned with the stability over time of attitudes such as alienation and their relationships to background variables such as

Table 21 Ability scores over time.

Statistic	Age 6	Age 7	Age 9	Age 11
Mean	18.034	25.819	35.255	46.593
Standard deviation	6.374	7.319	7.796	10.386

(i) Correlation matrix

	Age 6	Age 7	Age 9	Age 11
Age 6	1.000			
Age 7	0.809	1.000		
Age 9	0.806	0.850	1.000	
Age 11	0.765	0.831	0.867	1.000

(ii) Covariance matrix

	Age 6	Age 7	Age 9	Age 11
Age 6	40.628			
Age 7	37.741	53.568		
Age 9	40.052	48.500	60.778	
Age 11	50.643	63.169	70.200	107.869

education and occupation. Data were collected on attitude scales from 932 people in two rural regions in Illinois at three points in time (1966, 1967, and 1971). Only that part of the data collected in 1967 and 1971 will be of concern here and Table 24 shows the covariances between six observed variables. The anomia and powerlessness subscales are taken to be indicators of a latent variable, alienation, and the two background variables, education (years of schooling completed) and Duncan's socio-economic index (SEI) are assumed to relate to a respondent's socioeconomic status. The path diagram for the model postulated to explain the covariances between the observed variables is shown in Figure 7. The model involves a combination of a confirmatory factor analysis model with a regression model for the latent

variables. One of the important questions here involves the size of the regression coefficient of alienation in 1971 on alienation in 1967, since this reflects the stability of the attitude over time. Note that the error terms of anomia and powerlessness are allowed to be correlated over time to account for possible memory or other retest effects. Some of the results of fitting the proposed model are shown in Table 25.

The chi-squared goodness-of-fit statistic takes a value of 4.73 with four degrees of freedom and suggests that the proposed model fits the observed covariances extremely well. The estimated regression coefficient of aliena-tion on socioeconomic status in both 1967 and 1971 is negative, as might have been expected since higher socioeconomic status is likely to result in lower alienation and vice versa. The

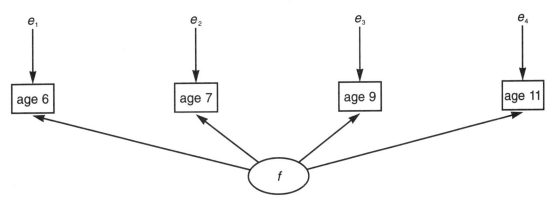

Figure 5 Single-factor model for ability data.

Table 22 Simple single-factor model—results for ability data.

Parameter	Estimates	Standard error	Estimate/standard error
λ_1	5.84	0.360	15.244
λ_2	6.684	0.397	16.842
λ_3	7.326	0.414	17.705
λ_4	9.476	0.564	16.813
$var(e_1)$	10.555	1.225	8.617
$var(e_2)$	8.89	1.197	7.427
$var(e_3)$	7.113	1.163	6.133
$var(e_4)$	18.084	2.424	7.460

(i)   Chi-squared goodness-of-fit statistic 6.085, degrees of freedom = 2, *P*-value = 0.048.
(ii)   Note that these estimates are obtained from the covariance matrix so that the factor loadings are no longer correlations between observed and latent variables. They now represent regression coefficients.
(iii)   The statistical significance of each parameter can be judged by the *z*-statistics given in the final column. Values outside (–2,2) are roughly significant at the 5% level.

estimated regression coefficient for alienation in 1971 on alienation in 1967 is positive and highly significant. Clearly the attitude remains relatively stable over the time period.

An example of the application of structural equation modeling in clinical psychology is given in Taylor and Rachman (1994).

3.13.5 LATENT VARIABLES—MYTHS AND REALITIES

Having already commented in Section 3.13.4 that the "causal" in causal modeling is usually a misnomer, what can be said about the concept of a latent variable, central to the methods described in this chapter? In one sense, latent variables can never be anything more than is contained in the observed variables and never anything beyond what has been specified in the model. For example, in the statement that verbal ability is whatever certain tests have in common, the empirical meaning is nothing more than a shorthand for the observation of the correlations. It does not mean that verbal ability is a variable that is measurable in any manifest sense. In fact latent variables are essentially hypothetical constructs invented by a scientist for the purpose of understanding some research area of interest, and for which there exists no operational method for direct measurement. Consequently, a question that needs to be asked is "Can science advance by inferences based upon hypothetical constructs that cannot be measured or empirically tested?" According to Lenk (1986) the answer is a resounding "sometimes." For example, atoms in the eighteenth and nineteenth centuries were hypothetical constructs which allowed the foundation of thermodynamics; gravity and the electromagnetic field are further examples from physics. Clearly a science can advance using the concept of a latent variable, but their importance is not their reality or otherwise, but rather to what extent the models of which they are a part are able to describe and predict

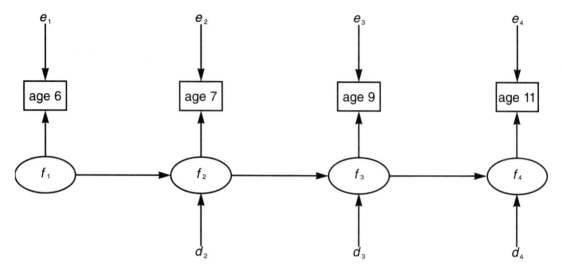

Figure 6 Causal model for ability data.

Table 23 Results from fitting causal model for ability data.

(i) Regression coefficients of latent variables on preceding latent variables

f_2 on f_1: 1.120, SE = 0.064
f_3 on f_2: 1.044, SE = 0.046
f_4 on f_3: 1.296, SE = 0.054

(ii) Chi-squared goodness-of-fit statistic = 1.433, degrees of freedom = 2, *P*-value = 0.489

phenomena (Lakatos, 1977). This point is nicely summarized by D. M. Fergusson and L. J. Horwood (personal communication, 1986):

> Scientific theories describe the properties of observed variables in terms of abstractions which summarize and make coherent the properties of observed variables. Latent variables, are, in fact, one of this class of abstract statements and the justification for the use of these variables lies not in an appeal to their "reality" or otherwise but rather to the fact that these variables serve to synthesize and summarize the properties of observed variables.

This point was also made by the participants in the Conference on Systems under Indirect Observation who concluded, after some debate (Bookstein, 1982) that latent variables are "as real as their predictive consequences are valid." Such a comment implies that the justification for postulating latent variables is their theoretical utility rather than their reality.

3.13.6 SUMMARY

The possibility of making causal inferences about latent variables has great appeal for the social and behavioural scientist, simply because many of the concepts in which they are most interested are not directly measurable. Many of the statistical and technical problems in applying the appropriate models to empirical data have largely been solved, and sophisticated software such as EQS means that researchers can investigate and fit extremely complex models routinely. Unfortunately, in their rush not to be left behind in the causal modeling stakes, many investigators appear to have abandoned completely their proper scientific skepticism, and accepted models as reasonable, simply because it has been possible to fit them to data. This would not be so important if it were not the case that much of the research involved is in areas where action, perhaps far-reaching action, taken on the basis of the findings of the research can have enormous implications, for example, in resources for education and

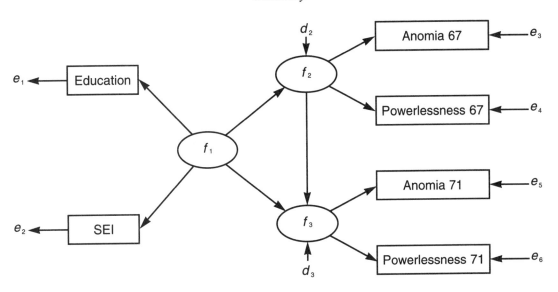

Figure 7 Causal model for stability of alienation.

Table 24 Covariance of manifest variables in the stability of alienation example.

	1	2	3	4	5	6
1	11.834					
2	6.947	9.364				
3	6.819	5.09	12.532			
4	4.783	5.028	7.495	9.986		
5	−3.839	−3.889	−3.841	−3.625	9.610	
6	−2.190	−1.883	−2.175	−1.878	3.552	4.503

Note. 1 = Anomia 67, 2 = Powerlessness 67, 3 = Anomia 71, 4 = Powerlessness 71, 5 = Education, 6 = Duncan's Socioeconomic Index.

Table 25 Regression coefficients for stability of the alienation model in Figure 5.

Alienation 67 on socioeconomic status: −1.500, SE = 0.124

Alienation 71 on alienation 67: 0.607, SE = 0.051

Alienation 71 on socioeconomic status: −0.592, SE = 0.131

legislation on racial inequality. Consequently, both producers of such research and audiences or consumers of it need to be particularly concerned that the conclusions reached are valid ones. With this in mind I would like to end with the caveat issued by Cliff (1983, p.125):

beautiful computer programs do not really change anything fundamental. Correlational data are still correlational, and no computer program can take account of variables that are not in the analysis.

Causal relations can only be established through patient, painstaking attention to all the relevant variables, and should involve active manipulation as a final confirmation

ACKNOWLEDGMENT

I would like to thank Dr. Nina Schooler for many helpful suggestions which substantially improved this chapter.

Table 26 Identification examples.

(i) Consider three variables, x_1, x_2, and x_3, with correlation matrix R given by

$$\mathbf{R} = \begin{array}{c} \\ x_1 \\ x_2 \\ x_3 \end{array} \begin{array}{ccc} x_1 & x_2 & x_3 \\ \left[\begin{array}{ccc} 1.00 & & \\ 0.83 & 1.00 & \\ 0.78 & 0.67 & 1.00 \end{array}\right] \end{array}$$

(ii) Suppose we are interested in fitting a single-factor model, that is

$$x_1 = \lambda_1 f + e_1$$
$$x_2 = \lambda_2 f + e_2$$
$$x_3 = \lambda_3 f + e_3$$

(iii) There are seven parameters to be estimated, namely

$$\lambda_1, \lambda_2, \lambda_3, \text{var}(f), \text{var}(e_1), \text{var}(e_2), \text{var}(e_3)$$

(iv) There are, however, only six statistics for use in parameter estimation:

$$\text{var}(x_1), \text{var}(x_2), \text{var}(x_3), \text{corr}(x_1, x_2), \text{corr}(x_1, x_3), \text{corr}(x_2, x_3)$$

(v) Consequently, the model is underidentified

(vi) If var(f) is set equal to one then the model is just identified—there are exactly the same number of parameters to estimate as there are informative sample statistics

(vii) Equating observed and expected variances and correlations will give the required estimates:

$$\hat{\lambda}_1 \hat{\lambda}_2 = 0.83$$
$$\hat{\lambda}_1 \hat{\lambda}_3 = 0.78$$
$$\hat{\lambda}_2 \hat{\lambda}_3 = 0.67$$
$$\hat{\text{var}}(e_1) = 1.0 - \hat{\lambda}_1^2$$
$$\hat{\text{var}}(e_2) = 1.0 - \hat{\lambda}_2^2$$
$$\hat{\text{var}}(e_3) = 1.0 - \hat{\lambda}_3^2$$

(where "hats" indicate estimates)

(ix) Solving these equations leads to the estimates

$$\hat{\lambda}_1 = 0.99, \hat{\lambda}_2 = 0.84, \hat{\lambda}_3 = 0.79, \text{var}(e_1) = 0.02, \text{var}(e_2) = 0.30, \text{var}(e_3) = 0.38$$

(x) Now consider an analogous measurement model with four observed variables and again set var(f) = 1 (this model is now the one used on the string data and the examination scores data)

(xi) Equating observed and expected variances and correlations in this case will lead to more than a single unique estimate for some of the parameters. The model is overidentified and represents a genuinely more parsimonious description of the structure of the data. Here a better strategy for estimation is clearly needed (see Table 9)

3.13.7 APPENDIX

Explanatory factor analysis methods such as principal factor analysis and maximum likelihood factor analysis are available in all major packages, for example, SPSS, SAS, MINITAB, and SYSSTAT. Options that need to be selected include (i) method of factor analysis, (ii) method of estimating initial communalities, and (iii) method of rotation.

For many examples the solutions given by a different combination of the available options will be very similar. In most cases the available software makes the derivation of the results of a factor analysis very simple; interpretation of these results is often, however, a different matter.

Confirmatory factor analysis and structural equation modeling are generally undertaken using either the LISREL or EQS package. The former is described in Jöreskog and Sörborm (1993) and the latter in Dunn et al. (1993). Using either piece of software requires some degree of understanding of how to translate proposed models into equations that specify the model explicitly (see Tables 10 and 19). One of the problems of structural equation modeling conveniently ignored in the text is that of model identification which refers to the degree to which there is a sufficient number of equations to solve for each of the parameters to be estimated. Models can be (i) underidentified (too few equations), (ii) just identified (no degrees of freedom remain for testing the fit of the model—the model will fit perfectly but will not give a more parsimonious description of the data than is provided by the observed correlations or covariances), or (iii) overidentified (more equations than parameters—the fit of model can be tested). Table 26 illustrates these different situations with a number of simple models, and a full discussion of identification is given in Dunn et al. (1993). In many cases the identification status of a complex model (and, at times, relatively simple models) is very difficult to ascertain *a priori*. Nonidentified models will cause problems for both EQS and LISREL and users need to be very wary of results which are accompanied by messages that point out that a parameter is, for example, at its lower or upper bound (i.e., a variance is zero or a correlation is one) or that some parameters are linearly dependent on others.

3.13.8 REFERENCES

Bentler, P. M. (1995). *EQS Structural Equations Program Manual*. Encino, CA: Multivariate Software.
Bookstein, F. L. (1982). Panel discussion—modeling method. In K. Jöreskog & H. Wold (Eds.), *Systems under indirect observation: Causality, structure and prediction*, (pp. 317–322). Amsterdam: North-Holland.
Caslyn, R. J. & Kenny, D. A. (1977). Self-concept of ability and perceived evaluation of others. Cause or effect of academic achievement? *Journal of Educational Psychology, 69*, 136–145.
Cliff, N. (1983). Some cautions concerning the application of causal modeling methods. *Multivariate Behavioral Research, 18*, 115–126.
Cudeck, R. (1989). Analysis of correlation matrices using covariance structure models. *Psychological Bulletin, 105*, 317–327.
deLeeuw, J. (1985). Book review. *Psychometrika, 50*, 371–375.
Dunn, G., Everitt, B. S., & Pickles, A. (1993). *Modelling covariances and latent variables using EQS*. London: Chapman and Hall.
Everitt, B. S. (1984). *An introduction to latent variable models*. London: Chapman and Hall.
Everitt, B. S. (1987). *An introduction to optimization methods and their application in statistics*. London: Chapman and Hall.
Everitt, B. S. (1996). *Making sense of statistics in psychology*. Oxford: Oxford University Press.
Everitt, B. S. & Dunn, G. (1991). *Applied multivariate data analysis*. London: Arnold.
Hines, M., Chiu, L., McAdams, L. A., Bentler, P. A., & Lipcamon, J. (1992). Cognition and the corpus callosum: Verbal fluency, visuospatial ability and language lateralization related to midsagittal surface areas of callosal subregions. *Behavioral Neuroscience, 106*, 3–14.
Huba, G. J., Wingard, J. A., & Bentler, P. M. (1981). A comparison of two latent variable causal models for adolescent drug use. *Journal of Personality and Social Psychology, 40*, 180–193.
Hittner, J. B. (1995). Factorial validity and equivalence of the alcohol expectancy questionnaire tension-reduction subscale across gender and drinking frequency. *Journal of Clinical Psychology, 51*, 563–576.
Jöreskog, K. & Sörbom, D. (1993). *Lisrel 8 structural equation modeling with the simplis command language*. Hillsdale, NJ: Erlbaum.
Lakatos, I. (1977). *The methodology of scientific research programmes*. Cambridge, UK: Cambridge University Press.
Lenk, P. J. (1986). Book review. *Journal of the American Statistical Association, 81*, 1123–1124.
Newcomb, M. D. & Bentler, P. M. (1983). Dimensions of subjective female orgasmic responsiveness. *Journal of Personality and Social Psychology, 44*, 862–873.
Osborne, R. T. & Suddick, D. E. (1972). A longitudinal investigation of the intellectual differentiation hypothesis. *Journal of Genetic Psychology, 121*, 83–89.
Osman, A., Barrios, F. X., Kopper, B., Osman, J. R., Grittman, L., Troutman, J. A., & Panak, W. J. (1995). The pain behavior check list (PBCL); psychometric properties in a college sample. *Journal of Clinical Psychology, 51*, 775–782.
Skevington, S. M. (1990). A standardised scale to measure beliefs about controlling pain: A preliminary study. *Psychology and Health, 4*, 221–232.
Taylor, S. & Rachman, S. J. (1994). Stimulus estimation and the overprediction of fear. *British Journal of Clinical Psychology, 33*, 173–181.
Thurstone, L. L. (1947). *Multiple factor analysis*. Chicago: University of Chicago Press.
Wheaton, B., Muthen, B., Alwin, D., & Summers, G. (1977). Assessing reliability and stability in panel models. In D. R. Heise (Ed.), *Sociological methodology* (pp. 84–136). San Francisco: Jossey-Bass.

3.14

The Shift from Significance Testing to Effect Size Estimation

MICHAEL BORENSTEIN
Hillside Hospital, Glen Oaks, NY, USA

3.14.1 INTRODUCTION

A statistical wit once remarked that researchers often pose the wrong question and then proceed to answer that question incorrectly. Statistical analyses in psychological research traditionally have taken the form of significance tests. The near-universal use of significance tests has made them the *de facto* standard of proof in research and the logic that underlies significance tests has played an important role in shaping the development of psychological theory. In fact, though, significance tests are generally not appropriate for the kinds of questions that are addressed in psychological research. First, significance tests address the wrong question. Researchers are concerned with clinical significance (i.e., the magnitude of the effect) but significance tests address only statistical significance (whether or not the effect is zero). Second, the significance test, by focusing attention on the *p*-value, lends itself to mistakes of interpretation. Significant *p*-values are assumed to reflect clinically important effect sizes, while in fact a significant *p*-value may reflect a large sample size rather than a large effect size. Similarly, nonsignificant *p*-values are taken as evidence that the treatment has no impact, though this conclusion is almost always incorrect.

To address these issues researchers have been moving away from significance tests and toward effect size estimation. Rather than report that "$p = 0.01$," the researcher would report that "the treatment improved the response rate by 20 percentage points (95% confidence interval of 0.15–0.25)." While there is widespread consensus that the shift toward effect size estimation is appropriate, there is considerable disagreement over the nature of the proposed shift. Some feel that the logic of the significance test should be retained, with the shift to the use of confidence intervals being one of format rather than substance. From this perspective, the confidence intervals serve as a surrogate for the significance test. Others argue that we need

to rethink the role of the single study as an element in the research process, and that any vestige of the significance test should be excluded. From this perspective, confidence intervals serve as an index of precision only.

We also consider the implications of this paradigm for study planning. The discussion of significance tests is followed by a section on power analysis, which is used in study planning to ensure that the study will yield a statistically significant result. The discussion of effect size estimation is followed by a discussion of precision analysis, which may be used in study planning to ensure that the study will yield a precise estimate of the treatment effect.

3.14.2 THE SIGNIFICANCE TEST

3.14.2.1 The Logic of the Significance Test

Research trials are always carried out on a sample of finite size. The results obtained in the sample are assumed to be representative of the larger population but because of random sampling error will rarely, if ever, mirror that population exactly.

For example, consider a study whose goal is to determine whether or not a new drug being tested with acute schizophrenics yields a higher response rate than the current treatment. Assume that the drug really is effective, and (in the population) increases the response rate by 20 percentage points. The mean effect over an infinite number of samples would be 20 points, but the effect observed in any single sample would almost invariably fall somewhat below or above 20 points. Similarly, if the drug really has zero effect in the population then the mean effect over an infinite number of samples would be zero points, but the effect observed in any single sample would likely fall somewhat below zero (the response rate being lower for new drug), or above zero.

Therefore, if we run a study and observe a difference in response rates for the two groups, we need to determine whether or not the sample may have been drawn from the second population above (where the treatment effect is zero). To this end we pose the null hypothesis that the two treatments are equally effective. If the null hypothesis is true, then the effect observed in our sample, if not zero, should fall within a "reasonable" distance of zero. If our sample were to yield a rate difference that was "compelling," in the sense that it was not "reasonably close to zero," we would conclude that the assumption of equal response rates is not viable.

Our ability to conclude that the observed effect is "compelling" will depend on three factors, each of them intuitive. The first is the size of the effect. An observed difference of 40 points in response rates is more compelling than an observed difference of 20 points. The second is the size of the sample. An observed difference of 20 points may be discounted if based on a sample of 10 cases per group since a single aberrantly responding patient could pull the response rate by 10 percentage points in either direction. The same size effect would be more convincing in a sample of 40 patients per group, and would probably be seen as definitive in a study that employed 100 patients per group. The third element is the stringency of the criteria we require as evidence that a difference exists. If the treatment carried little risk of harm and was inexpensive, we might be willing to declare it "effective" even if the evidence was relatively weak. On the other hand, if it carried a nontrivial risk of harm or a high cost we might require that it meet a more stringent criterion.

This logic (how large is the effect, how large is the sample, how certain do I want to be) is formalized in the test of significance that is routinely applied to studies. Significance tests vary from one statistical procedure to the next but are all variations on the theme

$$\text{Test statistic} = \frac{\text{Observed difference}}{\text{Dispersion of the difference}}$$

The numerator in this equation is the observed difference, for example, a rate difference of 10 points or 20 points between groups. The denominator reflects the sample-to-sample dispersion expected in the numerator, and incorporates information about the sample size (when the sample is large, the expected dispersion is small). The test statistic is computed as the ratio of these two values. As such, it will be high when the observed effect is large and/or the sample size is large. In a sense, the test statistic serves as a kind of signal-to-noise ratio: if the population effect is zero we expect the sample effect to vary within some range of zero. The numerator in the equation reflects the observed effect and the denominator defines the expected range in which sample effects will normally fall. The test statistic tells us whether or not the sample effect falls outside the normal range.

The test statistic is compared with a table of values showing the expected range of the test statistic under the assumption that the null hypothesis is true. If our test statistic falls within this range, we cannot reject the null. If our test statistic falls outside this range, however, we would conclude that the null hypothesis is most likely false, and the treatment does have an effect. We need to decide what level of evidence we will require prior to rejecting the null, and this threshold is known as alpha. For example, if alpha is set at 0.05, then the study result will be deemed significant if, on the assumption that the null is true, the study effect (or larger) would be observed in only 5% of cases.

3.14.2.2 Errors of Inference

The significance test carries the potential for two types of error: We may reject as false a null hypothesis that in fact is true (type I error), or we may accept as true a null hypothesis that in fact is false (type II error).

3.14.2.2.1 Type I error

As noted earlier, study results would be declared "significant" if the sample effect was "compelling." The type I error rate is denoted by alpha. With alpha set at 0.05, over an infinite number of studies where the null is true, our sample will nevertheless meet the criterion and be declared significant in 5% of the studies. This situation—where the null is true but we decide in error that the treatment is effective—is referred to as a type I error.

This point is repeated for emphasis. There is a general perception that 5% of studies will result in a type I error, but this is not correct. When the null hypothesis is true 5% of studies will result in a type I error. However, if the treatment really is effective, then by definition a type I error is not possible and the type I error rate is zero.

3.14.2.2.2 Type II error

To meet the criterion for statistical significance a study must yield an effect size that is large enough to establish significance, given the sample size and the criterion alpha. Even if the treatment is effective, and even if the size of the effect is substantial (in the population and/or in the sample), there is no guarantee that the study will yield a statistically significant result. The effect observed in the sample may be smaller than the population effect (in half of all unbiased studies, it will be), which may yield a nonsignificant result. Indeed, even if the sample effect is as large (or larger) than the population effect, unless the sample size is adequate the results may not meet the criterion for statistical significance. The type II error rate is denoted by beta. If the treatment really is effective and beta is 0.20, then 20% of all studies will yield nonsignificant results.

3.14.3 POWER ANALYSIS

The likelihood that a study will yield a statistically significant effect is the study's power and the process of designing a study to ensure an appropriate level of power is referred to as a power analysis. If the purpose of the study is to test the null hypothesis, then a power analysis is a critical element in study planning, to ensure that the study will be able to meet this goal.

The statistical significance computed subsequent to the study is a function of three elements—effect size, sample size, and alpha. It follows that power, which reflects the likelihood that the study will yield statistical significance, is determined by the same three elements. Specifically, the larger the effect size used in the power analysis, the larger the sample size, and/or the more liberal the criterion required for significance (alpha), the higher the expectation that the study will yield a statistically significant effect. These three factors, together with power, form a closed system—once any three are established, the fourth is completely determined. The goal of a power analysis is to find an appropriate balance among these factors by taking into account the substantive goals of the study and the resources available to the researcher.

3.14.3.1 Role of Effect Size in Power Analysis

Power analysis gives power for a specific effect size. For example, the researcher might report "If the treatment increases the response rate by 20 percentage points the study will have power of 80% to yield a significant effect." For the same sample size and alpha, if the treatment effect is less than 20 points then power will be less than 80%. If the treatment effect exceeds 20 points, then power will exceed 80%.

Since our computation of power ensures, to some likelihood, that the study will succeed in rejecting the null given a specific effect size, it follows that the effect size used in the power analysis should represent the smallest effect that would be of clinical or substantive significance. In clinical trials, for example, the selection of an effect size might take account of the following factors:

(i) The severity of the illness being treated. If we are testing a treatment that will reduce the likelihood of relapse among schizophrenics, we might decide that a reduction of as little as 10% is clinically important since the implications of a relapse can be relatively severe. By contrast, if we are testing a treatment that was expected to reduce the likelihood of an anxiety attack, a 10% reduction might be of little clinical import since the attacks are transitory. In this case, we might decide that only a reduction of 20% or more is clinically important.

(ii) The availability of alternate treatments. If no treatments exist for a particular condition, then a treatment that was effective in even a small proportion of patients might be clinically important. By contrast, if treatments already exist for the condition, then a new treatment might need to surpass these to be considered clinically important. This might mean that the new treatment was effective in a larger proportion of affected persons, or had a larger impact for individual patients.

(iii) Treatment cost and side effects. In deciding what constitutes a clinically important effect we might want to take account of such issues as treatment costs and side effects. A drug that carried a risk of serious side effects or that carried a high price might be considered clinically useful only if it was effective in a substantially higher proportion of cases than available treatments, or was being used to treat a severe condition.

The factors that are taken into account for identifying a clinically important effect will of course vary from one study to the next and the three items mentioned above are intended only as examples. The general point is that the selection of an effect size should be made on the basis of substantive issues and that these will vary from one study to the next.

A study that has adequate power to detect a relatively large effect will not have adequate power to detect a small effect. By contrast, a study that has adequate power to detect a relatively small effect will, of course, have more than enough power to detect moderate or large effects. While one might therefore be tempted to set the "clinically important effect" at a small value to ensure high power for even a small effect, this determination cannot be made in isolation. Small effects will require a larger investment of resources than large effects. The selection of an effect size reflects the need for balance between the size of the effect that we can detect, and the resources available for the study. Figure 1 shows power as a function of sample size for three levels of effect size (assuming alpha, two-tailed, is set at 0.05). For the smallest effect (30% vs. 40%), we would need a sample of 376 per group to yield power of 80%. For the intermediate effect (30% vs. 50%), we would need a sample of 103 per group to yield this level of power. For the highest effect size (30% vs. 60%), we would need a sample of 49 per group to yield power of 80%. In this example we may decide that it would make sense to enroll 103 patients per group to detect the intermediate effect but inappropriate to enroll 376 patients per group to detect the smallest effect.

3.14.3.1.1 The effect size used in power analysis is not necessarily the population effect size

Researchers often assume that the effect size used in a power analysis is the "true" (population) effect size. In fact, though, the "true" effect size is not known. While the effect size in the power analysis is assumed to reflect the population effect size for the purpose of calculations, the power analysis is more appropriately expressed as "If the true effect is 20 percentage points power would be ... " rather than "The true effect is 20 percentage points, and therefore power is ... "

This distinction is an important one. Researchers sometimes assume that a power analysis cannot be performed in the absence of pilot data. In fact, it is usually possible to perform a power analysis based entirely on a logical assessment of what constitutes a clinically (or theoretically) important effect. Indeed, while the effect observed in prior studies might help to provide an estimate of the true effect it is not likely to be the true effect in the population—if we knew that the effect size in these studies was accurate, there would be no need to run the new study.

Since the effect size used in power analysis is not the "true" population value, the researcher may elect to present a range of power estimates. For example (assuming $N = 103$ per group and alpha $= 0.05$, two-tailed), "The study will have power of 80% to detect a treatment effect of 20 points (30% vs. 50%), and power of 99% to detect a treatment effect of 30 points (30% vs. 60%)."

The nature of the effect size will vary from one statistical procedure to the next. In all cases, however, it serves the same function of providing a pure index of the effect, that is, an index that focuses exclusively on the effect, independent of the sample size, and that is not affected by the metric in which the effect is measured.

3.14.3.1.2 Conventions for effect size

Cohen (1988, 1992) has suggested conventional values for "small," "medium," and "large" effects in the social sciences. For tests of a mean difference between two groups the effect size index is *d*, the standardized mean difference (i.e., mean difference divided by the

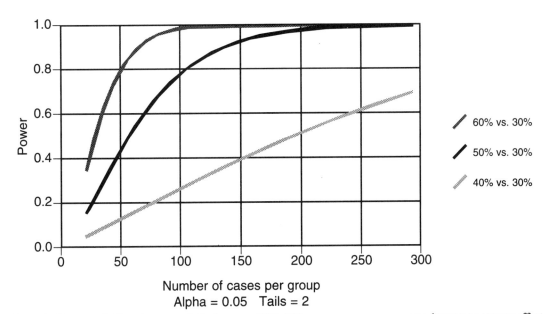

**Power as a function of effect size and N:
two sample proportions**

Number of cases per group
Alpha = 0.05   Tails = 2

Figure 1   Impact of effect size on statistical power. With 100 cases per group, power to detect a treatment effect of 10 percentage points (response rates of 40% vs. 30%) is about 0.25, power to detect a treatment effect of 20 points is about 0.80, and power to detect a treatment effect of 30 points is about 0.99.

318   *The Shift from Significance Testing to Effect Size Estimation*

common within-group standard deviation). A "small" effect is given as $d = 0.20$ (i.e., 20% of the common within-group standard deviation); a medium effect as $d = 0.50$; and a large effect as $d = 0.80$. For tests of a difference between proportions a small effect is given as proportions of 40% vs. 50%; a medium effect corresponds to proportions of 40% vs. 65%; and a large effect corresponds to proportions of 40% vs. 78%. Note that the effect size for proportions cannot be specified simply by giving the difference between the two proportions, but requires that the absolute proportions be specified. For example, the effect size of 10% vs. 20% is larger than the effect size of 40% vs. 50%, despite the fact that the difference is 10 points in either case. For tests of a single correlation, the effect size is the correlation itself. A small effect is given as a correlation of 0.10, a medium effect is a correlation of 0.30, and a large effect is a correlation of 0.50. Cohen also provides conventions for other tests including analysis of variance and multiple regression. These conventions are also included in some computer programs (Borenstein & Cohen, 1988; Borenstein, Cohen, Rothstein, Pollack, & Kane, 1990, 1992; Borenstein, Rothstein, & Cohen, 1997; Rothstein, Borenstein, Cohen, & Pollack, 1990).

Cohen himself cautions that these conventions should not be used routinely, since it is preferable to select an effect size based on the substantive issues involved in the specific study (as above). Nevertheless, these conventions do serve two functions. In all cases the researcher may want to use these values as a kind of reality-check, to ensure that the values specified make sense relative to these anchors. Additionally, in cases where the researcher has difficulty deriving any kind of effect size index, they may elect to fall back on these conventions (see also Kraemer & Thiemann, 1987).

3.14.3.2 Role of Alpha in Power Analysis

The significance test yields a *p*-value that reflects the likelihood of obtaining an effect as large (or larger) than the observed effect, under the assumption that the null hypothesis is true. For example, a *p*-value of 0.02 means that, assuming that the treatment has no effect, and given the sample size, an effect as large as the observed effect would be seen in only 2% of studies. The *p*-value obtained in the study is evaluated against the criterion alpha. If alpha is set at 0.05, then a *p*-value of 0.05 or lower is required to reject the null hypothesis and establish statistical significance.

If our only concern in study design were to prevent a type I error, it would make sense to set alpha as conservatively as possible (e.g., at 0.001). However, alpha does not operate in isolation. If we select a more stringent criterion for alpha, then our ability to meet this criterion

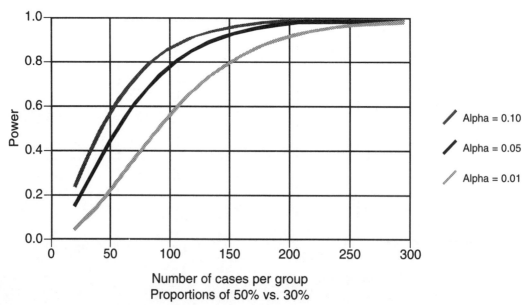

Figure 2   Impact of alpha on statistical power. With 100 cases per group and alpha set at 0.01, power is less than 0.60; with alpha at 0.05, power is about 0.80; and with alpha at 0.10, power is about 0.85. These computations are based on response rates of 50% vs. 30%, corresponding to the center line in Figure 1.

is reduced. By moving alpha from (say) 0.10 toward 0.01, we reduce the likelihood of a type I error but increase the likelihood of a type II error. (More accurately, and to emphasize a point made earlier: We reduce the likelihood of a type I error if the null is true, but increase the likelihood of a type II error if the null is false.)

Figure 2 shows power as a function of sample size for three levels of alpha (assuming an effect size of 30% vs. 50%, which is the intermediate effect size in the previous figure). With a sample size of 100 per group, with alpha set at 0.10 power exceeds 85%; with alpha set at 0.05 power is about 80%; and with alpha set at 0.01, power is under 60%.

Traditionally, researchers in some fields have accepted the notion that alpha should be set at 0.05 and power at 80% (corresponding to a beta of 0.20). This notion is implicitly based on the assumption that a type I error is four times as harmful as a type II error (the ratio of alpha to beta is 0.05–0.20), which notion has no basis in fact. Rather, it should fall to the researcher to strike a balance between alpha and beta as befits the issues at hand. For example, if the study will be used to screen a new drug for further testing we might want to set alpha at 0.20 and power at 95%, to ensure that a potentially useful drug is not overlooked. On the other hand, if we were working with a drug that carried the risk of side effects and the study goal was to obtain Federal Drug Administration (FDA) approval for use, we might want to set alpha at 0.05 while keeping power at 95%.

3.14.3.3 Role of Tails in Power Analysis

The significance test is always defined as either one- or two-tailed. A two-tailed test is a test that will be interpreted if the effect meets the criterion for significance and falls in either direction. As such, it is appropriate for the vast majority of research studies. A one-tailed test is a test that will be interpreted only if the effect meets the criterion for significance and falls in the expected direction (i.e., the treatment improves the cure rate).

A one-tailed test is appropriate only if an effect in the unexpected direction would be functionally equivalent to no effect. For example, assume that the treatment we are using for depression is relatively inexpensive and carries a minimal risk of side effects. We will be testing a new treatment which is more expensive but carries the potential for a greater effect. The possible conclusions are that (i) the old treatment is better, (ii) there is no difference, or (iii) the new treatment is better. For our purposes, however, conclusions (i) and (ii) are

functionally equivalent since either would lead us to retain the standard treatment. In this case, a one-tailed test, whose only goal is to test whether or not conclusion (iii) is true, might be an appropriate choice.

Note that a one-tailed test should be used only in a study in which, as in this example, an effect in the reverse direction is, for all intents and purposes, identical to "no effect." It is not appropriate to use a one-tailed test merely because one is able to specify the expected direction of the effect prior to running the study. In psychological research, for example, we typically expect that the new procedure will increase, rather than decrease, the cure rate. Nevertheless, a finding that it decreases the cure rate would be important, since it would demonstrate a possible flaw in the underlying theory. Even in the example cited, one would want to be certain that a profound effect in the reverse direction could safely be ignored— under a one-tailed test, it cannot be interpreted. In behavioral research, the use of a one-tailed test can be justified only rarely.

For a given effect size, sample size, and alpha, a one-tailed test is more powerful than a two-tailed test (a one-tailed test with alpha set at 0.05 has the same power as a two-tailed test with alpha set at 0.10). However, the number of tails should be set based on the substantive issue ("Will an effect in the reverse direction be meaningful?"). In general, it would not be appropriate to run a test as one-tailed rather than two-tailed as a means of increasing power. (Note also that power is higher for the one-tailed test only under the assumption that the observed effect falls in the expected direction. When the test is one-tailed, the power for an effect in the reverse direction is zero by definition).

3.14.3.4 Role of Sample Size in Power Analysis

For any given effect size and alpha, increasing the sample size will increase the power. As is true of effect size and alpha, sample size cannot be viewed in isolation but rather as one element in a complex balancing act. In some studies it might be important to detect even a small effect while maintaining high power. In this case it might be appropriate to enroll many thousands of patients (as was done in the "Physicians" study that found a relationship between aspirin use and cardiovascular events).

Typically, though, the number of available cases is limited. The researcher might need to find the largest N that can be enrolled, and work backwards from there to find an appropriate balance between alpha and beta. They may need to forgo the possibility of finding a small effect, and acknowledge that power will be adequate for a large effect only.

For studies that involve two groups, power is generally maximized when the subjects are divided evenly between the two groups. When the number of cases in the two groups is uneven the "effective N" for computing power falls much closer to the smaller sample size than the larger one.

There is one exception to the rule that an increase in sample size will always yield an increase in power. When we are working with exact formulas for discrete distributions, such as the binomial test for a single proportion or the Fisher exact test for a crosstabulation, it is possible that a modest increase in sample size will serve to lower power (Borenstein et al., 1997).

3.14.3.5 Computing Power in Power Analysis

Power is the fourth element in this closed system—for given effect size, alpha, and sample size, power is completely determined. A convention exists that power should be set at 80% but this convention has no clear *a priori* basis. The appropriate level of power should be decided on a case-by-case basis, taking into account the potential harm attendant on a type I error, the determination of a clinically important effect, the available sample size, as well as the importance of identifying a small, medium, or large effect.

While power is a function of three elements (effect size, sample size, and alpha), as a practical matter the effect size tends to dominate the calculation of power. Sample size plays a secondary role, and the impact of alpha is relatively modest. For example, with response rates of 30% vs. 50%, a sample size of 100 per group, and alpha (two-tailed) set at 0.05, power would be 83%. Consider, then, the impact of changes to these factors. If we elect to work with an effect size of 25 percentage points rather than 20 percentage points (i.e., 55% vs. 30% rather than 50% vs. 30%) power would be increased from 83% to 95%. To achieve the same 12-point increase in power by manipulating the sample size we would have to increase the sample size from the initial value of 100 per group to 160 per group. To achieve the same increase in power by selecting a more liberal value for alpha we would need to move alpha from 0.05 to 0.20.

Because the effect size plays such an important role in the computation of power, it is imperative for the researcher to use an appropriate effect size in the computations. If we use an effect size that is too large, then the study will not have adequate power to detect a more modest effect. If we use an effect size that

is too low, then we might increase the sample size in an effort to reach acceptable levels of power, thus inappropriately putting patients at risk. Rather, the effect size used in the power analysis should be selected carefully, based on the kinds of substantive issues outlined earlier.

3.14.3.6 The Null Hypothesis vs. the Nil Hypothesis

Power analysis focuses on the study's potential for rejecting the null hypothesis. In most cases the null hypothesis is the null hypothesis of no effect, or the "nil" hypothesis. In some studies, however, the researcher might want to test another null hypothesis. For example, rather than testing the null hypothesis that a correlation coefficient is zero, a researcher might want to test the null hypothesis than the correlation is 0.80 (i.e., to demonstrate that the correlation exceeds this value). Intuitively, it is easier to show that an observed correlation exceeds zero than to show that it exceeds 0.80. In the latter case the effect size is smaller and a substantially larger sample would be required to ensure adequate power.

3.14.3.7 Retrospective Power Analysis

One occasionally sees a retrospective power analysis of the following form. A researcher completes a study, and reports that the effect size in the study was, for example, a standardized mean difference of $d = 0.2$. The researcher then goes on to report that, based on this effect size, the study actually had power of only, for example, 40%. However well intentioned, this type of retrospective power analysis is generally misguided for several reasons. First, as noted earlier, the role of effect size in a power analysis is not "The effect size is $d = 0.4$ and therefore power is 80%" but rather "If the effect size is $d = 0.4$, then power would be 80%." The effect size $d = 0.4$ is supposed to represent the smallest effect that would be important to detect. As such, it is not affected by evidence that the actual size of the effect might be larger or smaller than this value. Second, even if one wanted to base power on the "true" effect, the fact remains that the value observed in any single study is not likely to be the true effect. Indeed, if we had confidence that observed effect size was the true effect we would have no need to run another study to pinpoint the effect size, much less to test the hypothesis that it was zero.

While this application of a retrospective power analysis is inappropriate, there are two related applications where it may be useful. One is the use of study data to identify a base rate.

Assume, for example, that our goal is to reduce by 20% the proportion of patients having a panic attack within two days of treatment. Initially, we assume that the base rate for these attacks is 30%, compute power for a difference of 30% vs. 24% (corresponding to a 20% decrease), and set the sample size on this basis. It emerges in the study that the base rate is 20%, which means that we should have computed power for a difference of 20% vs. 16% (corresponding also to a 20% decrease). In this case, one could argue that the original power calculations were based on incorrect assumptions, and that for the *a priori* effect size the study was underpowered. Similarly, if the effect size was computed as a mean difference in raw units (such as SAT [Scholastic Achievement Test] scores) but we underestimated the standard deviation of the scores, one could argue that our initial computations had been in error and that power for the desired effect was too low. A second logical application along these lines is to use the study data to obtain a more informed estimate of the likely effect size by computing the confidence intervals based on the sample. This information could prove useful in the design of a subsequent study.

Retrospective power analyses are usually reported subsequent to a study that failed to yield a significant effect. Occasionally, though, researchers who have obtained a significant result may discover that their study had been under-powered and then wonder if the study results are still valid. Of course, this is a nonissue. Power tells us the likelihood is that the study will yield a significant effect and is used for purposes of planning. If the study is completed, then we know the outcome—either the effect was significant, or it was not. To worry in retrospect that the chances of success were small is akin to the parent whose teenager has taken the car for a ride during a bad rain but returned home safely. There might have been reason for worry while the teenager was still out (and the parent might want to be more careful the next time) but it makes no sense to worry about the outcome of this particular trip after the fact.

3.14.3.8 Ethical Issues in Power Analysis

Some studies involve putting patients at risk. At one extreme, the risk might involve a loss of time spent completing a questionnaire. At the other extreme, the risk might involve the use of an ineffective treatment for a potentially fatal disease. While an extensive discussion of research ethics is outside the scope of this chapter, it must be emphasized that ethical issues should play a central role in power

analysis. If a study to test a new drug will have adequate power with a sample of 100 patients, then it would be inappropriate to use a sample of 200 patients since the second 100 are being put at risk unnecessarily. At the same time, if the study requires 200 patients to yield adequate power, it would be inappropriate to use only 100. These 100 patients consent to take part in the study on the assumption that the study is likely to yield useful information. If the study is underpowered, then the 100 patients will have been put at risk for no reason.

Of course, the actual decision-making process is complex. One can argue about whether "adequate" power for the study is 80%, or 90%, or 99%. One can argue about whether power should be set based on an improvement of 10 points, or 20 points, or 30 points. One can argue about the appropriate balance between alpha and beta. The point being made here is that these kinds of issues need to be addressed explicitly as part of the decision making process.

3.14.3.9 Power Analysis in Perspective

To this point we have focused on the details of a power analysis, but it is important also that the entire procedure be seen in an appropriate context. The use of a power analysis in study planning is appropriate only when the study goal is to test the null hypothesis. By contrast, if the study goal is to estimate the magnitude of a treatment effect, then statistical power has no bearing on sample size. Later in this chapter it is argued that most studies should focus on effect size estimation rather than power analysis, and so this becomes a critical point.

More generally, before performing a power analysis or any other procedure to set sample size, it behooves the researcher to ensure that the study should be conducted at all. Chalmers and co-workers have shown that many studies have put patients at risk in attempts to test treatments when, in fact, the data required to answer the question already existed from prior studies. In one famous example (Lau et al., 1992), a series of 33 randomized trials were carried out between 1959 and 1988 to assess the impact of intravenous (iv) streptokinase in preventing mortality subsequent to a myocardial infarction. In fact, the life-saving power of these drugs could have been proven as early as 1973, if the data available at that time had been subjected to a meta-analysis. At that time, a total of eight studies had been completed using a total of 2432 patients. The p-value for a test of the nil was <0.01 and the effect size (odds ratio) 0.74 with a 95% confidence interval of

0.59–0.92. Subsequent to 1973, researchers ran an additional 25 studies which employed a total of 34 542 additional patients, with approximately half of these assigned to placebo and denied the potential benfits of the treatment. In fairness, it must be noted that meta-analysis was not widely accepted in 1973, and even if the researchers had access to meta-analytic methods, results based on a these procedures might not have been accepted by the medical community. Our intention is not to argue that this specific set of studies was not needed, but to make the point that the study must hold the potential to provide useful information and that power analysis is only one element in this process.

3.14.3.10 Some Real World Issues in Power Analysis

In some ways, the funding process and other constraints ensure that studies will continue to be run with low power. Feinstein (1975) may have identified one part of the problem with his straightforward account of how studies are designed in real life. The statistician (i) computes the maximum number of patients for which funding can be obtained, (ii) finds the effect size required to yield power of 80%, given the sample size, and (iii) develops a rationale to present to the finding agency to show that the effect size is the smallest effect size that would be clinically important to detect. The process identified by Feinstein leads to grant applicants asserting that a clinically important effect would be one that improves the response rate by precisely "22 percentage points."

In fact, the thrust of this approach is not necessarily inappropriate. The selection of an effect size should take into account any number of factors, and it might be appropriate to allocate resources to detect a large effect but not a small one. However, the grant application would be more credible if the applicant acknowledged that the effect size was set in this way, rather than arguing that the smallest effect of clinical importance would be a rate difference of precisely 22 percentage points.

3.14.3.11 Computer Programs for Power Analysis

Power is defined as the proportion of samples that will yield a statistically significant effect, given a specific set of assumptions. The computation of this value is a two-step process. First, we compute the effect size required to yield a significant effect, for the given alpha and

sample size. Second, we compute the proportion of samples that will yield an effect this large (or larger), given the effect size in the population.

As a practical matter, computation of power is performed by means of computer programs designed for this purpose. The example that follows is taken from *Power and Precision*, a program developed by Borenstein et al. (1997). The example is for a study in which patients will be assigned at random to either a new treatment or the standard treatment, and we will compare the proportion responding in the two groups.

Computation of power proceeds as follows (Figure 3):

(i) Optionally, enter names for the two groups: "New treatment" and "Standard treatment."

(ii) Enter the proportion responding in either group: 40% for the standard group and 60% for the new treatment.

(iii) Click "Find N." The program shows that a sample of 107 per group will yield power of 80%.

(iv) At this point the researcher may elect to vary the study parameters, for example, to modify the effect size or sample size and see the impact on power. This may be done interactively. Alternatively, the program will automatically generate a table and graph that allows the researcher to simultaneously take account of several factors.

One possible graph is shown in Figure 4. The three lines in the graph represent treatment effects of 25 points, 20 points, and 15 points (specifically, response rates of 65% vs. 40%, 60% vs. 40%, and 55% vs. 40% for the new treatment vs. the standard treatments). The sample size required to yield power of 80% is 70 patients per group for the largest effect, 107 per group for the second effect, and 186 per group for the third.

In this example, taking account of substantive issues and available resources, we decide that we will base the study on the center line. In other words, we decide that a 20-point improvement in response rates is important enough to justify a trial with 107 patients per group. By following the trajectory of the center line we see that 139 patients per group would yield power of 90% for this effect, but decide that we cannot commit the additional resources. By comparing the position of the three lines at "107 per group" we note that if the treatment effect is actually 25 points (65% vs. 40%) rather than 20 points, then the study's power is actually 95% rather than 80%. If the true effect is actually 15 points (55% vs. 40%) then power is actually 54%.

The program will also generate a text report of the computation which serves as an educational tool and may also be copied into

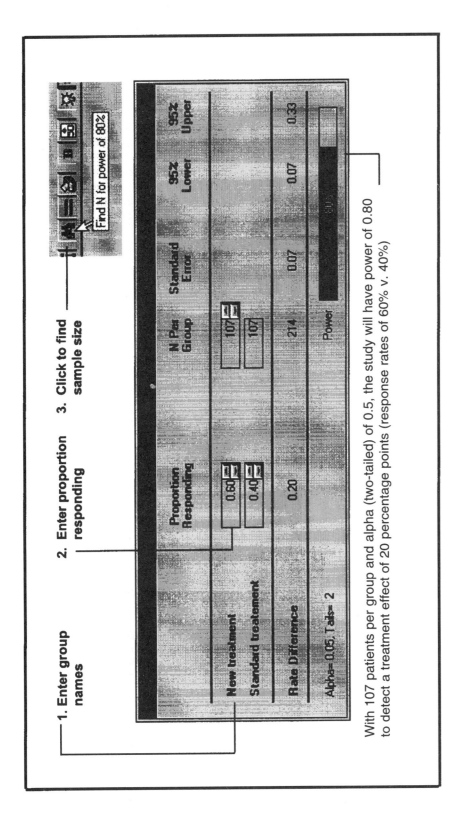

1. Enter group names
2. Enter proportion responding
3. Click to find sample size

Find N for power of 80%

	Proportion Responding	N Per Group	Standard Error	95% Lower	95% Upper
New treatment	0.60	107			
Standard treatment	0.40	107			
Rate Difference	0.20	214	0.07	0.07	0.33
Alpha=0.05, Tails= 2		Power		80%	

With 107 patients per group and alpha (two-tailed) of 0.5, the study will have power of 0.80 to detect a treatment effect of 20 percentage points (response rates of 60% v. 40%)

Figure 3 Screen from *Power and Precision* showing computation of power. The researcher enters an effect size (response rates of 60% vs. 40%), alpha (0.05, two-tailed) and clicks "Find N" on the toolbar. The program shows that a sample size of 107 per group will yield a power of 80%. The researcher may modify any of the study parameters, and the program will update power automatically in response.

**Power as a function of effect size and N:
two sample proportions**

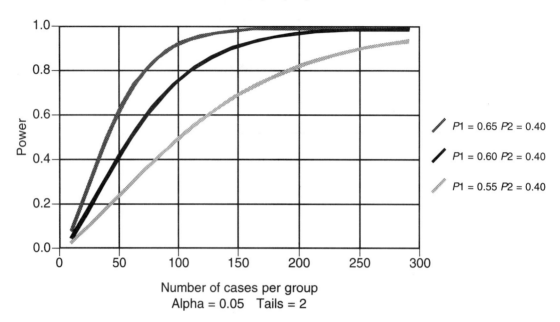

Number of cases per group
Alpha = 0.05   Tails = 2

Figure 4   Power as a function of effect size and sample size. This graph, which is an extension of Figure 3, allows the researcher to take account of multiple factors simultaneously while planning the study. We can design the study to detect the largest effect (top line) which would require only about 70 cases per group but would result in low power to detect the more modest effects. We can design the study to detect the middle effect, which would require 107 cases per group but would result in low power to detect the smallest effect. To ensure power for the smallest effect (with the least potential benefit) we would need to enroll some 180 cases per group.

a word-processing program. In this example the text of the report reads (in part) as follows: "One goal of the proposed study is to test the null hypothesis that the proportion responding is identical in the two populations. The criterion for significance (alpha) has been set at 0.05. The test is two-tailed, which means that an effect in either direction will be interpreted. With the proposed sample size of 107 and 107 for the two groups, the study will have power of 80.1% to yield a statistically significant result. This computation assumes that the difference in proportions is 0.20 (specifically, 0.60 vs. 0.40). This effect was selected as the smallest effect that would be important to detect, in the sense that any smaller effect would not be of clinical or substantive significance. It is also assumed that this effect size is reasonable, in the sense that an effect of this magnitude could be anticipated in this field of research."

The software available for power analysis is constantly changing but up-to-date information is available on the Internet. Information on the program used in this example is available at http://www.PowerAndPrecision.com. Thomas and Krebbs (1997) maintain a site with links to any number of programs for power analysis at http://www.Interchg.ubc.ca/cacb/power.

3.14.4 PROBLEMS WITH THE SIGNIFICANCE TEST

To this point we have highlighted the key features of significance testing and power analysis. The vast majority of statistical analyses in psychological research take the form of significance tests and an understanding of the process is essential to an understanding of the research literature.

However, this was intended primarily as an introduction. The thesis of this chapter is that while the significance test is ubiquitous in the literature of psychological and medical research, its use in these fields is inappropriate for a number of reasons. In this section we will make the following points:

(i) The significance test addresses the wrong question. Researchers are concerned with clinical significance (i.e., the magnitude of the treatment effect), but significance tests address statistical significance (whether or not the effect is zero).

(ii) The question that is addressed by significance tests (whether or not the null hypothesis is true) is inappropriate not only because it is tangential to clinical significance but also because it is almost always false in psychological research.

Additional problems derive from the fact that significance tests lend themselves to mistakes of interpretation. In particular:

(i) A significant *p*-value is assumed to reflect a clinically important effect, and the level of significance is assumed to reflect the magnitude of the effect. In fact, though, the *p*-value incorporates information about the size of the sample as well as the size of the effect. Therefore, the use of the *p*-value for this purpose results in confusion and errors of interpretation.

(ii) Historically, a majority of studies have been run with low power, which means that even moderate or large treatment effects may go undetected. Additionally, the absence of significance is often interpreted, inappropriately, as evidence that the treatment effect is zero. The combination of these two types of error has seriously impeded research in psychology.

3.14.4.1 Significance Tests Address the Wrong Question

The key problem with significance testing is that it addresses the wrong question. The question that researchers want to ask is "How large is the treatment effect?" By contrast, the question actually addressed by the significance test is "Can we conclude that the treatment effect is not zero?"

Researchers typically assume that reports of "significance" or "nonsignificance" refer to clinical significance. This assumption follows from the fact that clinical significance is the question of interest, and also from the fact that "significance" refers to substantive (or clinical) significance in common parlance. Nevertheless, this assumption is incorrect. A significant *p*-value tells us only that the treatment (probably) increases the response rate by some amount. It does not provide information about the size of the effect.

The clinician, of course, needs information about the magnitude of the treatment effect— Does the treatment increase the likelihood of response by five percentage points, or 10 points, or 50 points?—since this is the kind of information required to balance the treatment's potential benefits against the costs and potential side effects. It is also the kind of information required to allow for an informed choice between the treatment in question and other possible treatments. The only information that the significance test can provide—that the treatment effect exceeds zero—is at best of tangential interest.

The same point being made here about implications for clinical practice applies also to the development of psychological theory. For example, Tukey (1969) points out that if the nature of elasticity had been defined as "when you pull it, it gets longer" the science of elasticity would have progressed very slowly. In psychological research as well, we need to address the size of the effect in order for theory to develop, and this is not addressed by the significance test.

3.14.4.2 The Null Hypothesis is not a Viable Hypothesis

There is a second problem with the use of the null hypothesis in psychological research. In addition to being irrelevant, it is also not a viable hypothesis, in the sense that it is known to be false in the overwhelming majority of psychological research.

For example, consider studies that compare the impact of two treatments. Hunter (1997) points to a survey conducted by Lipsey and Wilson (1993) which reviewed 302 meta-analyses of treatment studies in psychology and education. The average number of studies in each meta-analysis is 60, and the total number of studies included is 18 120. The treatment effect was zero (the null hypothesis was true) in less than 1% of the domains studied. Similarly, studies that look at the relationship between behaviors or traits are designed to test the null hypothesis that the correlation between traits is zero. In fact, though, it would be difficult to name two human characteristics whose correlation with each other is 0.0000000. In this kind of study the null hypothesis is always false.

The typical retort to the argument that the null is always false is that we do not intend to test whether or not the response rates are identical—rather, we intend to test whether or not they differ by some important amount. But this is exactly the problem. What we care about is whether or not the difference is clinically important, but what we are testing is whether or not the difference is exactly zero (Cohen, 1990).

This fact, followed to its logical conclusion, leads to an interesting paradox. Given that the effect is not zero, and since the *p*-value is a function of both effect size and sample size, it follows that with a large enough sample size, any effect will meet the criterion for significance. One can extend this argument in several ways:

(i) With a large enough sample size we know the study will yield a significant effect, so there is no need to run the study (Cohen, 1994).

(ii) With a large enough sample size we know the study will yield a significant effect, so if our result is not significant, then by definition we are committing a type II error (Schmidt, 1992).

(iii) With a large enough sample size the study will yield a significant effect, so what we are really testing is not whether the effect is large, but whether or not we have run enough subjects. Thompson (1992) suggests that instead of testing for significance we can assess how tired the researchers are. If they are tired, then we probably ran a lot of subjects and have a "significant" effect. If they are very tired, then we probably ran even more subjects and have a "very significant" effect.

There are exceptions to this point, which are discussed later, but these are rarely encountered in psychological research.

3.14.4.3 The Gratuitous Use of Significance Tests

Even those who argue that significance tests can serve an important role in psychological research recognize that the tests are almost invariably abused. Abelson (1997a) wrote a chapter in which he argues that the null hypothesis should not be banned, but includes a section entitled "The Null Hypothesis: Merely Misused, or Really Idiotic?" He uses the term "gratuitous" to describe the ritualistic application of significance tests to all kinds of data where the test could not possibly provide any useful information.

Indeed, significance tests are sometimes applied in ways that defy common sense. Abelson (1997a) cites the example of a researcher who divided a cohort of subjects at the group median into "low" and "high" groups and then performed a significance test to find out whether or not the groups were, in fact, different. In doing so the researcher missed the point that we use significance tests to make inferences about whether or not the groups differ in some systematic way, but in this case we know that they differ systematically because we created them that way. Simply put, one is high and one is low. In fact, this is the archetypical case of the situation cited earlier, where the groups clearly differ, and the only thing being tested is whether or not we have a large enough sample. What if the test had failed to yield a significant effect? Would the researcher have concluded that he had assigned persons to the two groups at random?

Cohen (1994) cites the case of a researcher who wanted to test the hypothesis that a particular ailment would never exist in a specific population. He tested 30 patients and found the ailment in only one. He wanted to know whether or not this (one case in 30) was "significant." In doing so, he missed the point that the theory required that there be no cases in the population, and if he found any then the theory was clearly false.

Papers are often seen in which persons report significance tests for reliability coefficients, in effect making the point that the scale's reliability is not zero. To show that the test has reliability better than zero is hardly reassuring to potential users of the test. Surely, the relevant question is whether or not the reliability exceeds 0.70 or 0.80. Abelson (1997b) suggests that "... declaring a reliability coefficient to be nonzero constitutes the ultimate in stupefyingly vacuous information" (p. 13).

Cohen (1994) traces the history of harangues against null hypothesis significance testing (NHST) and some of his quotes are reproduced here. Rozeboom (1960) wrote "The statistical folkways of a more primitive past continue to dominate the local scene" (p. 417). Bakan (1966), writing that "a great deal of mischief has been associated [with the significance test]" noted that the idea was hardly original with him and that "to say it 'out loud' is ... to assume the role of the child who pointed out that the emperor was really outfitted in his underwear" (p. 423). Meehl (1967) likened NHST to "a potent but sterile intellectual rake who leaves in his merry path a long train of ravished maidens but no viable scientific offspring." Rothstein (personal communication) noted that "... researchers [using NHST] often pose the wrong question and then proceed to answer that question incorrectly."

Cohen (1994) goes on to say that " ... we, as teachers, consultants, authors, and otherwise perpetrators of quantitative methods, are responsible for the ritualization of null hypothesis significance testing ... to the point of meaninglessness and beyond ... NHST has not only failed to support the advance of psychology as a science but also has seriously impeded it" (p. 997) (see also Cohen, 1990).

Rothman (1986b) writes "Testing for statistical significance today continues not on its own merits as a methodological tool but on the momentum of tradition. Rather than serving as a thinker's tool, it has become for some a clumsy substitute for thought, subverting what should be a contemplative exercise into an algorithm prone to error" (p. 447).

Additional citations on this topic include Abelson (1995, 1997a, 1997b); Borenstein (1994b); Carver (1978); Dar (1987); Estes (1997); Fisher (1959); Gonzalez (1994); Hagen (1997); Harlow, Mulaik, and Steiger (1997); Harris (1997a, 1997b); Hunter (1997); Loftus (1991); Lykken (1968); Meehl (1967, 1978, 1990); Murphy (1990); Neyman and Pearson (1932a, 1932b); Oakes (1986); Peto and Doll (1977); Scarr (1997); Schmidt (1992, 1996); Schmidt and Hunter (1996); Shaver (1993), and Shrout (1997).

3.14.4.4 *p*-Values: Responding with a Misdirected Answer

To this point we have shown that significance tests address a question that is at best tangential to the question of interest and at often entirely irrelevant. The use of significance tests carries with it an additional problem: Significance tests produce *p*-values that lend themselves to mistakes of interpretation.

The "*p*-value" highlighted by the significance test is a function of two elements—the size of the effect, and the precision of the estimate. When we consider the logic of the significance test, that is, to determine whether or not the population effect is zero, we can appreciate the simple elegance of the *p*-value. Either a large effect, or a large sample (yielding a precise estimate of the effect), or some appropriate combination of the two, provides evidence that the effect is not zero. By the same logic, however, it would not be appropriate to press the *p*-value into service as an indicator of effect size. Since the *p*-value incorporates information about both the size of the effect and the size of the sample, it does not allow us to distinguish between the two.

3.14.4.4.1 Misinterpreting the significant p-value

Statistical significance is often assumed to reflect substantive significance. Almost invariably, the first question asked by the reader, and the first point made by the researcher, is that the results were "significant." This is the point highlighted at meetings, in abstracts, and in the results section of publications. Often, the discussion of effect does not proceed beyond the question of significance at all. Even when it does, the issue of significance, that is, statistical significance, is emphasized over clinical significance or effect size. In fact, though, the only information imparted by a statistically significant *p*-value is that the true effect is (probably) not nil. A significant *p*-value could reflect a clinically meaningful effect. It could also reflect a clinically trivial effect that had been found in a large sample (because of the large sample the effect size is reported precisely, and though small is known to be non-nil).

Cohen (1965) writes "Again and again, the results section of an article describing an effect as significant or highly significant is followed by a discussion section which (usually implicitly) proceeds to treat the effect as if it had been found to be large or very large" (p. 102). The same point has been documented repeatedly in the field of psychology and medicine (Feinstein, 1975, 1976, 1977; Friedman & Phillips, 1981; Mainland, 1982; Nelson, Rosenthal, & Rosnow, 1986; Rothman, 1986b; Tversky & Kahneman, 1971; Wonnacott, 1985).

A review of a manuscript is recalled that purported to show a substantial advantage for a novel antipsychotic drug. The basis for this claim was a difference between treatment groups on a critical variable, with $p < 0.001$. As it happens, the sample size was of the order of 2000 patients, and a *p*-value < 0.001 could reflect a difference that was so small as to be trivial. In fact, some of the baseline differences between the groups (which had, appropriately, been dismissed as negligible in size) were larger (and more significant!) than the post-treatment differences being submitted as evidence of the drug effect.

It gets worse. If the confusion of statistical significance with clinical significance is a problem in the interpretation of single studies, the situation is even worse when researchers use *p*-values to compare the results in different studies. This type of comparison is common when we want to know if the treatment is more effective in men than it is for women, or if one treatment is more effective than another.

Since the *p*-value incorporates information about both the sample size and effect size, a *p*-value of 0.05 could represent response rates in two groups of 50% vs. 70% (a 20-point effect) with a sample size of 50 cases per group. It could also represent response rates of 50% vs. 90% (a 40-point effect) with a sample size of 10 cases per group. In the second case the effect size is substantially larger than it is in the first case, but this fact is lost in the *p*-values, which are identical. Similarly, a *p*-value of 0.01 could represent response rates of 40% vs. 65% (25 points) with 50 cases per group, or 40% vs. 95% (55 points) with 10 cases per group. Again, the difference in effect sizes is not evident from the *p*-value.

In fact, Tversky and Kahneman (1971) found that students presented with information about *p*-values and sample sizes tend to make exactly the wrong conclusions about the effect size. Students were presented with two studies where the *p*-value was 0.05, and told that the sample size was 10 per group in one and 50 per group in the other. Invariably, students assumed that the effect size in the second case was more impressive, while exactly the reverse is true (see also Berkson, 1938, 1942; Friedman & Phillips, 1981; Rosenthal & Gaito, 1963, 1964; Rozeboom, 1960).

The possibilities for mistakes expand when we consider the possibility of comparing results between studies when both the *p*-value and the sample size differ. If one study yielded a *p*-value of 0.05 and another yielded a *p*-value of 0.01, then in the absence of any additional information a reader might assume that the effect size was stronger in the latter case. In fact, though, if the first study ($p = 0.05$) used a sample of 10 per group and the second ($p = 0.01$) used 50 per group, then the effect size would have been substantially larger in the study with the modest p-value (a 40-point effect as compared with a 25-point effect).

3.14.4.4.2 *Misinterpreting the nonsignificant* p-value

The complement to misinterpreting the significant p-value is to misinterpret the nonsignificant p-value. The only information imparted by a nonsignificant p-value is that we have failed to reject the null. Assume, for example, that refractory schizophrenic patients currently in relapse are assigned to be treated either with clozapine or with haldol. In this hypothetical example we find that the proportion meeting a remission criterion within six weeks is not significantly different in the two groups. The nonsignificant p-value could reflect a finding in a large sample that the proportion remitting was virtually identical in the two groups (the large sample ensuring to a high degree of certainty that the same would hold true in the population). Or, it could reflect a finding in a small sample that the remission rate was twice as high (or more) for the patients treated with clozapine (the finding failing to prove significant in part because of the low sample size). The first scenario would justify a conclusion that clozapine does not substantively increase the likelihood of remission and the second scenario would not justify this conclusion. However, researchers and readers almost invariably fail to make this distinction, and routinely interpret the absence of significance to mean that an effect does not exist. A related problem is the fact that many studies in psychological research suffer from low statistical power. In this section we will make four points.

(i) Power for research in psychology is abysmally low;

(ii) Rule (i) appears to be impervious to change;

(iii) The absence of significance should be interpreted as "more information is required" but is interpreted in error as meaning "no effect exists"; and

(iv) Rule (iii) appears to be impervious to change.

While Cohen has often made the point that he discovered, rather than invented, power analysis, the fact is that Cohen's papers over a series of decades have played a key part in making researchers aware of the power issue, and providing them with the mechanisms for computing power. At present, Cohen's papers and texts (Cohen, 1962, 1965, 1969, 1977, 1988, 1990, 1994) also serve as a kind of historical map that traces the role of power analysis since the 1960s.

Cohen (1962) surveyed papers published in the *Journal of Abnormal and Social Psychology* in 1960. Mean power to detect a small, medium, or large effect, respectively, was 0.18, 0.48, and 0.83. (Definitions of small, medium, and large were developed by Cohen with reference to the effect sizes typically found in social science research; the definitions were modified slightly subsequent to the 1962 paper.) The implications of this were spelled out clearly in the paper. At a minimum, a great deal of time and effort is being wasted on studies that have little chance of meeting their goals. Worse, when the studies with "negative" results are published, readers tend to interpret the absence of statistical significance as evidence that the treatment has been proven ineffective.

What was the response to this paper? Woody Allen has spoken of the time that he was kidnapped as a child. It took his father a while to catch on ("He had bad reading habits—he started reading the ransom note, but in the middle he fell asleep") but eventually he "sprang into action and rented out my room." In that vein, it took the scientific community a while to appreciate the implications of Cohen's paper but eventually it sprang into action also. First one, then another researcher found that what Cohen had done for the field of psychology could be done equally as well for any field of research, and in the years that followed a kind of cottage industry developed of papers that documented the fact of low power in any number of journals in the area of behavioral research. Many of these are cited in Sedlmeier and Gigerenzer (1989) and Rossi (1990). Similar papers were published to document the same problem in the field of medicine (Borenstein, 1994b; Hartung, Cottrell & Giffen, 1983; Phillips, Scott, & Blaszczynski, 1983; Reed & Slaichert, 1981; Reynolds, 1980) and psychiatry (Kane & Borenstein, 1985).

One oft-cited paper by Frelman, Chalmers, Smith and Kuebler (1978) surveyed reports of controlled clinical trials that had been published in a number of medical journals (primarily the *Lancet*, the *New England Journal of Medicine*, and the *Journal of the American Medical Association* during the period 1960–1977), and selected 71 that had reported negative results. The authors found that if the true drug effect had been on the order of 50% (e.g., a mortality rate of 30% for placebo vs. 15% for drug), median power would have been 60%. In other words, even if the drug cut the mortality rate in half there was still a 40% probability that the study would have failed to obtain a significant result.

How does the story end? In Woody Allen's tale the FBI surrounded the kidnappers. They wanted to "toss in the tear gas," but they had no tear gas so instead they put on the death scene from Camille. The kidnappers were overcome. The FBI and the kidnappers bargained with each other and eventually reached an agreement that the kidnappers would "throw out their guns and keep the kid."

The power analysis story has a similar ending. In keeping with the general move away from isolated studies and toward meta-analysis, papers that document low power in specific journals are now being replaced by meta-analysis of these papers. Now, researchers have been able to document the fact that low power exists not only in specific journals, but also in every field of research.

Sedlmeier and Gigerenzer (1989) published a paper entitled "Do studies of statistical power have an effect on the power of statistical studies?" They found that in the 25 years since Cohen's initial survey power had not changed in any substantive way. Specifically, they reported that in the 1984 volume of the *Journal of Abnormal Psychology*, mean power to detect small, medium, and large effects was 0.21, 0.50, and 0.84, which are essentially similar to the values reported by Cohen for the 1960 volume (in 1960, for the *Journal of Abnormal and Social Psychology*). Similarly, Rossi (1990) reviewed papers published in 1982 in the *Journals of Abnormal Psychology, Consulting and Clinical Psychology*, and *Personality and Social Psychology*. Mean power to detect small, medium, and large effects, respectively, was 0.17, 0.57, and 0.83. In fact, since papers with higher power are more likely to yield significant results and be published, the mean power reported by these surveys is almost certainly higher than the mean power for all studies in the field.

Given that the fact of low power is well documented, one would hope that researchers would adapt their thinking to accommodate to this state of affairs. In fact, though, the mistake of interpreting nonsignificant results as implying the absence of an effect runs through the psychological and medical literature. One could say that it practically gallops.

Cohen (1990) relates the story of a doctoral candidate who completed a study with 20 cases per group, and power of 0.33 to detect a medium sized effect. As Cohen recalls "He ended up with non-significant results—with which he proceeded to demolish an important branch of psychoanalytic theory" (p. 1304).

Earlier, the paper by Freiman et al. (1978) was cited, showing that power for papers published in some of the most prestigious medical journals was clearly at unacceptable levels. The authors went on to make a second point: Despite the fact that power was terribly low, in most cases the absence of significance was interpreted as meaning that the drug was not effective. The authors wrote: "The conclusion is inescapable that many of the therapies discarded as ineffective after inconclusive 'negative' trials may still have a clinically meaningful effect" (p. 694). In fact, it is possible (or likely) that some of the therapies discarded on this basis might well have had very substantial therapeutic effects.

In fact, Sedlmeier and Gigerenzer reported that power had actually dropped slightly over the 25 years subsequent to Cohen's initial survey. The magnitude of the drop is of little consequence, but the reason for the drop is interesting—researchers in 1990 were more likely to be making adjustments to alpha when running multiple tests (e.g., using alpha of 0.025 rather than 0.05) to ensure that the type I error rate was kept at 0.05. Schmidt (1996) points to the irony that researchers were protecting themselves against an error that could not occur (since the null hypothesis was false) while oblivious to the type II error rate, which exceeds 50%.

As was the case for misinterpretation of significant results, the misinterpretation of nonsignificant results becomes even more complicated when researchers try to compare results across studies. One would hope that the error of interpretation would be obvious when there are a series of studies, with some yielding a significant effect and others failing to do so. In some such series the effect size is remarkably consistent from one study to the next—the studies with a large sample size met the criteria for significance and those with a smaller sample size did not. Even in these cases, however, there is usually a perception that "the studies yield conflicting results."

Even in 1998 a cardiologist remarked that thrombiolytics are incredibly effective in reducing mortality for patients suffering a myocardial infarction, and that he sees clearly that they save lives, but that the studies of effect "flip back and forth." In fact, thrombiolytics represent the textbook case (literally) cited earlier (Lau et al., 1992), where the treatment effect is consistent from one study to the next, and the presence or absence of statistical significance varies with sample size.

Even worse, when the significant study was performed in one type of sample and the nonsignificant study was performed in another type of sample, researchers sometimes try to interpret this difference as meaning that the effect exists in one population only (e.g., males but not females). Abelson (1997a) notes that if a treatment effect yields a *p*-value of 0.07 for wombats and 0.05 for dingbats we are likely to see a discussion explaining why the treatment is effective only in the latter group—completely missing the point that the treatment effect may have been virtually identical in the two. The treatment effect may have even been larger in the nonsignificant group, if the sample size was smaller.

A more serious example of this is cited by Poole (1987a). Selikoff, Hammond, and Churg (1968) found a statistically significant association between asbestos exposure and lung cancer among cigarette smokers (the risk of death from lung cancer was 90 times as high as that for nonsmokers in the general population), but failed to find this same association among nonsmokers (no deaths were reported in this group during the observation period). The authors, taking into account the low statistical power for detecting this effect, drew no conclusions about the nonsmoking group. Others, however, were less cautious and proceeded to (mis)interpret this negative finding. Hoffman and Wynder (1976) wrote: "We conclude from [this study] that asbestos induces mesothelioma of the pleura and peritoneum, but not by itself [cancer] of the bronchus." Similarly, Cole and Goldman (1975) interpreted the study to mean that "[A]pparently, asbestos will produce lung cancer only in smokers." Poole reports that this finding was eventually summarized in a pamphlet distributed to workers in the asbestos industry: "Studies show that if you don't smoke cigarettes, asbestos does not increase your risk of lung cancer." Poole used the data reported in the original study to compute confidence intervals for the risk of cancer associated with asbestos exposure for the nonsmokers, and found the odds ratio to fall in the range of zero to 46.1.

We have shown that power for many studies is low, which leads to nonsignificant results even when treatments are actually effective. And, we have shown that the nonsignificant results are often taken as evidence that the treatment is not effective. Either of these two issues would be problematic by itself, and together these items seriously impede research in psychology.

Schmidt (1996) outlines the impact of this practice on research and policy: an idea is proposed (school integration will result in better test scores for African-American children). A number of studies are run. All of the studies show that scores are increased and the magnitude of the increase is consistent from one study to the next, but the sample sizes are small and, in some of the studies, not significant. Researchers report that the evidence is "conflicting." A series of studies are funded to determine why the integration had a positive effect in some studies but not others (is it the teacher's attitude? Is it the students' socioeconomic status; is it the students' age?), entirely missing the point that the effect was actually consistent from one study to the next. No pattern can be found (since none exists). Eventually, researchers decide that the issue cannot be understood. A promising idea is lost, and a perception builds that research is not to be trusted. A similar point is made by Meehl (1978, 1990).

Rossi (1997) gives an example of this same phenomenon from the field of memory research. The issue of whether or not researchers could demonstrate the spontaneous recovery of previously extinguished associations had a bearing on a number of important learning theories, and some 40 studies on the topic were published between 1948 and 1969. Evidence of the effect (i.e., significant findings) was obtained in only about half the studies which led most texts and reviews to conclude that the effect was ephemeral and "the issue was not so much resolved as it was abandoned" (page 179). Recently, Rossi returned to these studies and found that the average effect size (d) for the studies was 0.39. If we assume that this is the population effect size then, given the sample size in the various studies, the mean power for these studies would have been slightly under 50%. On this basis we would expect about half the studies to yield a significant effect, which is exactly what happened.

It seems unlikely that these errors of interpretation will change as long as researchers continue to work under the current system of significance testing. These types of problems have continued despite educational efforts such as those of Cohen (1962, 1990). They have continued despite the development of simple techniques for computing power, including rule-of-thumb tables (Cohen, 1988; Kraemer & Thiemann, 1987) and computer programs (Borenstein & Cohen, 1988; Borenstein et al., 1990, 1992, 1997; Goldstein, 1989; Rothstein et al., 1990). They have continued despite research that has addressed the kinds of thought processes on the part of researchers that appears to drive these kinds of errors (Tversky & Kahneman, 1971). There are many researchers who are very cognizant of power issues and insist that their studies be properly powered. Most large-scale and multicenter studies are also designed to ensure adequate power for important tests. In this sense, there has been some very substantial progress since the late

1960s. Still, it is clear from Sedlmeier and Gigerenzer, and Rossi, that low power continues to be a problem.

3.14.4.5 Summary

Significance tests are not the appropriate vehicle for the vast majority of psychological research, both because they are inherently inappropriate for this role and additionally because they foster mistakes of interpretation. Specifically:

(i) Significance tests focus attention on statistical significance (whether or not we can reject the nil) rather than clinical significance (which is the question of interest). The test can tell us about the direction of the effect, but in virtually all cases we want also to address the size of the effect.

(ii) There is a general perception that significance tests allow us to distinguish between effects that are "real" and those that are not. In fact, though, virtually all effects we test are nonzero, so the only question resolved by the significance test is whether or not we used a large enough sample.

(iii) The significance test yields *p*-values that lend themselves to misinterpretation. A significant *p*-value is assumed to reflect a clinically important effect, but it may not. A nonsignificant *p*-value is taken to reflect a zero effect, but it does not. These problems are compounded when a series of studies are seen as yielding "conflicting results" for one population, or are seen as evidence that the effect exists in one population but not another.

3.14.5 FOCUSED SIGNIFICANCE TESTS—A DIGRESSION

To this point we have used the term significance test to refer to the null hypothesis of no effect. Overwhelmingly, this is the manner in which statistical tests are applied in the literature. For example, the null hypothesis being tested is that the mean in two groups is identical (i.e., the intervention had no effect), or the response rates in two groups are identical, or the correlation between two variables is zero.

In fact, though, we can adopt a more focused approach by formulating and testing a hypothesis that predicts the magnitude of an effect. This would be appropriate if a theory had developed to the point that questions of effect size would bear on the validity of the theory. It would also be appropriate if we were working with a prospective treatment and the question of interest was whether or not the treatment was clinically useful.

For example, assume that we are planning to test a new drug as a maintenance medication for schizophrenic patients. The drug is known to increase the level of negative symptoms slightly, but would nevertheless be considered useful if it increased the response rate (defined by control of positive symptoms) by 20 percentage points. The hypothesis to be tested is not "Does it increase the response rate at all" but rather "Does it increase the response rate by 20 points *or more.*"

The same logic can be extended to a test of means. Assume, for example, that we want to evaluate a new teaching strategy that is expected to yield an improvement in SAT scores. The strategy will be expensive to implement, and a decision is made that it would be adopted on a wide scale only if it increased the mean score by at least 50 points. The hypothesis to be tested is obvious.

The idea of using significance testing in this way is not new. In the psychological literature the null hypothesis tested is almost invariably the null hypothesis of no effect and it is commonly assumed that the word "null" in "null hypothesis" refers to the size of the effect. In fact, though, it is a reference to the hypothesis to be tested, or "nullified" (Cohen, 1997). While the hypothesis to be nullified is usually the hypothesis that two response rates are identical it could also be the hypothesis that, for example, the response rates differ by 20 percentage points. To avoid confusion, Cohen suggests that the term "null hypothesis" be used to refer to any hypothesis to be tested, while the term "nil hypothesis" be used to refer to the null hypothesis of no effect.

Similarly, in the clinical literature the term "significance test" is almost invariably used to refer to a test of the nil hypothesis, but it can refer to any null hypothesis. Cohen suggests that the term "significance test" be used to refer to a test of the nil, while the term "hypothesis test" be used to refer to other tests (such as the 20 point difference). These conventions will be followed here to avoid confusion. The reader should note, however, that these terms are used interchangeably elsewhere.

The use of hypothesis testing rather than significance testing would provide some obvious benefits. For one thing, it would force researchers to think about the meaning of the null hypothesis. Earlier, the example of researchers testing the null hypothesis that a reliability coefficient is zero was cited. With a focused test the researcher could test the hypothesis that the reliability was significantly better than, for example, 0.80. If these kinds of tests were in common use, researchers would have an incentive to formulate the hypotheses more clearly. Additionally, in those cases where the null hypothesis was rejected, one could assert that the effect size fell in a clinically important range ("the relapse rate is reduced by at least 20%").

However, many of the problems described for the use of significance tests with the nil hypothesis would apply also to the use of hypothesis tests for other null hypotheses.

First, the problems in logic that were identified for significance tests apply also, albeit in modified form, to hypothesis tests. It was argued earlier that the significance test addresses the question of whether or not the effect is precisely nil, which is of little import. Similarly, the focused hypothesis test might address the question of whether or not the effect is precisely 20 points. A 20-point difference might be of more interest than a nil effect but is still an arbitrary value. In practice, what we would like to do is to get a feel for the size of the effect as being trivial, or moderate, or substantial, rather than to rule out any specific value. Similarly, it was argued earlier that the nil hypothesis was rarely true, and that with a large enough sample it would almost always be disproved. Similarly, the null hypothesis that the rate difference is *precisely* 20 points is virtually certain to be false and with a large enough sample will almost always be rejected. Under the system of hypothesis testing, with a large enough sample, an observed rate difference of 21 points, or even 20.1 points, will require us to reject the null of 20 points. Of course, this is not the intention in running the test, but it serves as a stark example of why the test is not the appropriate vehicle for this kind of application.

Second, the mistakes of interpretation that were identified for significance tests apply, again in modified form, to focused hypothesis tests. One problem with the significance test is that researchers use p-values (improperly) as surrogates for effect size indices. A p-value of 0.05 was assumed to reflect a modest effect and a p-value of 0.01 was assumed to reflect a strong effect. While the focused hypothesis test does introduce the concept of effect size (a 20-point effect in this example) the key index continues to be the p-value. A p-value of 0.05 is likely to be seen as reflecting a modest departure from 20 points, and a p-value of 0.01 as reflecting a substantial departure from 20 points. Similarly, the absence of significance has traditionally been mistaken as evidence that the effect is zero. With the focused hypothesis test it would be mistaken as evidence that the effect is precisely 20 points.

Additionally, if a move was made to focused hypothesis tests, low power would become even more of a problem than it is now. For example, with a sample of 70 per group using a 50-point

difference as the effect size (and $SD = 100$), power to show that one educational method is superior to another is 84%. With the same assumptions, power to show that it is superior by at least 20 points is only 42%. Logically, in fact, we might want to use 50 points as the effect size and also test the hypothesis that the effect is 50 points. When the effect size and the effect being tested are identical to each other, then no sample size will yield power greater than alpha (e.g., 5%).

In sum, the adoption of hypothesis tests would be appropriate for some studies but would not address the key problems outlined above for significance tests, and would additionally introduce some new problems. In any event, the possibility of working with hypothesis tests rather than significance tests is something of an academic point, since the field has bypassed this approach in favor of a more comprehensive approach—the report of effect size with confidence intervals, and it is to this approach that we turn now.

3.14.6 EFFECT SIZE AND CONFIDENCE INTERVALS

For the reasons outlined above researchers and journals are now moving away from significance tests and toward a focus on effect size estimation. Rather than report that an effect is (or is not) significantly different from zero, we report the size of the effect, and specify additionally a confidence interval, the range of treatment effects in the population that are likely to have given rise to the observed data.

In the example cited earlier, assume that we had completed the study and obtained response rates of 30% on drug A vs. 50% for drug B, with a sample size of 100 patients per group. We would report that drug B increased the response rate by 20 percentage points, with a 95% confidence interval of 7–33. The effect size observed in the sample (a rate difference of 20 points) is our best guess about the size of the effect in the population. The confidence interval (seven points to 33 points) reflects the likely upper and lower bounds of the effect in the population (Altman, Gore, Gardner, & Pocock, 1983; Borenstein, 1994a, 1994b; Gardner & Altman, 1986, 1989a, 1989b; Morgan, 1989; Simon, 1986, 1987).

3.14.6.1 The Key Advantage of this Approach

If the key problem with significance tests is that they address the wrong question, then the key advantage of effect size estimation is that it addresses the right question. Working with significance tests we defined an effect and asked whether or not that effect was probably true. It was problematic that the effect was typically of little interest (the nil effect) or selected arbitrarily (the focused hypothesis test). Working with effect size and confidence intervals, rather than report on what the effect is not we report on what the effect is. By doing so we focus on the question of interest. Additionally, we bypass the need to specify an arbitrary null hypothesis.

The effect size with its corresponding confidence interval provides three key pieces of information:

(i) An estimate of effect size that is separate and distinct from the precision of this estimate. Because this is a pure measure of effect, it focuses our attention on the substantive impact. For example, the treatment increases the response rate by 25 percentage points.

(ii) A value for the lower bound of this value in the population (for a given confidence level). With the traditional test we know only that the response rate is increased by some amount exceeding zero. By contrast, with the confidence interval we may be able to report that it is increased by at least 20 percentage points.

(iii) A value for the upper bound of this value in the population. The traditional test provides no estimate at all of the upper bound. By contrast, with the confidence interval we might report that the upper bound for the treatment's impact is 10 percentage points (in which case we know that the impact is of limited substantive value) or that the upper bound is 50 percentage points.

miology, are the relative risk and the odds ratio, either of which is often presented in log units. For studies that deal with correlations, the correlation itself serves as an index of effect size. For studies that focus on time to an event, or survival, the effect size reported is often the hazard ratio, that is, the relative risk per unit time in one group vs. the other. Computational details for any of these computations are readily available (see, for example, Harris & Albert, 1991; Kleinbaum, Kupper, & Morgenstein, 1982; Lawless, 1982; Rosner, 1990; Selvin, 1991). The goal here is to point out that these exist, and that the effect size can be presented for any type of study.

The effect size is reported with a corresponding confidence interval. The computation of confidence intervals is always some variation on the theme

Lower Limit = Observed effect minus
(Standard Error* 1.96)
Upper Limit = Observed effect plus
(Standard Error* 1.96)

At the core of either equation is the observed effect, about which the confidence interval is constructed. The lower and upper limits represent the lower and upper bounds for the effect size in the population from which the sample was drawn. Computation of confidence intervals for proportions, correlations, or survival times is more complicated than suggested by this summary, and is discussed in more detail below. These computational details aside, the formula shown here offers a straightforward conceptual overview.

3.14.6.2 Effect Size and Confidence Intervals can be Computed for Any Type of Study

Any study that may be used to compute a *p*-value may also be used to generate an effect size with confidence intervals. This follows from the fact that the *p*-value includes both components (the effect size and the precision). The *p*-value combines the two to yield a single value, but each value can be presented separately. As was the case with significance tests, the exact form of the report will vary with the nature of the data, but the differences are minor.

For studies that focus on the mean difference between groups a natural index of effect is the mean difference itself (either in the original metric, such as SAT points, or standardized to a common metric with a standard deviation of 1.0). For studies that focus on the proportion of cases responding to a treatment, one index of effect is the rate difference, that is, the difference in the proportion responding in either group. Other indices, common in medicine and epide-

3.14.6.3 Factors Affecting the Confidence Interval Width

The width of the confidence interval is based on two factors. The first of these is the sample-to-sample dispersion of the effect size: The higher the dispersion within a sample, and/or the lower the sample size, the more the effect size will vary from one sample to the next. When working with means the dispersion within a sample is indexed by the standard deviation of the scores. Intuitively, if working with a select group of students and the SAT scores cluster in the range of 600–750, sample-to-sample dispersion will be modest. By contrast, if we are working with a broader population, in which the scores cover the full range of 200–800, sample-to-sample dispersion will be wider. The impact of sample size on the standard error of the effect size is also intuitive. If the sample size is small the group mean might be affected substantially by a few outliers. By contrast, if the sample size is large the impact of outliers will be dissipated. It should be noted that when working with proportions or correlations, the first of these elements, the within-sample dispersion, is a function of the index itself. In the case of proportions, when the population proportion is close to 50% the standard deviation is relatively high, and it declines as the proportions approach either zero or unity. Intuitively, one can imagine that samples drawn from a population where the proportion of responders is 99% will yield values close to 99%—it would be difficult to draw many nonresponders since they do exist. By contrast, if the proportion of responders is 50% it would not be hard to draw one sample with a 40% response rate and another with a 60% response rate. Similarly, for correlations, the standard deviation is highest when the correlation is zero, and it declines as the correlation approaches minus one or plus one.

The second factor controlling the width of the confidence interval is the level of confidence desired. For example, one could choose to present the effect size plus/minus one standard error. In approximately 68% of all studies where the confidence intervals are reported in this manner, the interval will include the population effect size. One could also choose to present the effect size ± 1.96 standard errors (assume for this example that the variance is known). On the normal curve, 95% of all observations will fall inside the interval of -1.96 to $+1.96$. Therefore, if the effect size is presented as ± 1.96 standard error units, over an infinite number of studies 95% of the intervals will include the population effect.

The researcher may elect to compute two-tailed or one-tailed bounds for the confidence interval. A two-tailed confidence interval extends from some finite value below the observed effect to another finite value above the observed effect. A one-tailed confidence interval extends from minus infinity to some value above the observed effect, or from some value below the observed effect to plus infinity (the term "interval" is a misnomer in the one-tailed case but is used to maintain readability).

3.14.6.4 Information Conveyed by the Effect Size and Confidence Interval

Figure 5 shows the results of six fictional studies. For each study, the effect (the difference in response rates between placebo and drug) is depicted as a vertical line, bounded on either side by the 95% confidence interval. A solid line from the top to the bottom of the graph marks the null effect of no difference. An effect to the left of this line indicates that the drug group was inferior to placebo, while an effect to the right indicates that the drug group was superior. The studies with narrow confidence intervals are based on a sample of 700 patients per group. Those with wide confidence intervals are based on a sample of between 10 and 15 patients per group. All examples assume that the response rate on placebo is 30%. We can visualize a hierarchy of possible study results, some of which are depicted on this schematic.

Study A: Zero difference (-30 to $+30$). We cannot rule out the possibility that the effect is nil. Nor, however, can we rule out the possibility that the effect is large enough to be clinically useful or clinically harmful.

Study B: Zero difference (-4 to $+4$). We cannot rule out the possibility that the effect is nil. More to the point, however, it is clear that the effect is trivial, at best.

Study C: Twenty-five point difference (-10 to $+54$). The effect size in the sample (and our best estimate of the population effect) is 25 points. We cannot rule out the possibility that the effect is nil (nor can we rule out the possibility that it is quite potent).

Study D: Five-point difference (1–9). The effect is probably not nil. More to the point, however, we can assert with a high level of certainty that the effect is not clinically important (at best, a nine-point advantage in favor of the drug).

Study E: 40-point difference (10–63). The effect is probably not nil. The possible magnitude of the effect ranges from small to extremely potent (the interval is intentionally asymmetric).

Study F: 40-point difference (36–44). The drug is quite potent. The likely range of effects falls entirely within the "very potent" range.

3.14.7 THE RELATIONSHIP BETWEEN SIGNIFICANCE TESTING AND EFFECT SIZE ESTIMATION

The formulas for significance tests and for confidence intervals are mathematically congruent. The standard error of the effect size in confidence intervals is identical to the standard error used in significance testing. The confidence level used for confidence intervals can be complementary to the significance level used in significance tests (with the 95% confidence level corresponding to alpha of 5%).

Given the correspondence between the two methods, any significance test of the form "the difference is zero" and tested with alpha of 0.05 may also be tested by computing the 95% confidence interval and determining whether or

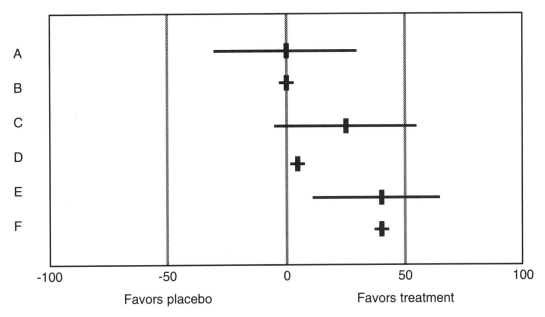

Figure 5 Data for six fictional studies. The effect size for each study is depicted by a vertical line bounded by the corresponding 95% confidence interval. The effect size highlights the magnitude of the effect while the interval width provides information about the precision with which the effect is estimated. This schematic also provides information about the significance test—if the 95% confidence interval excludes zero, the study is significant at the 0.05 level.

not this interval includes zero. More generally, any hypothesis test of the form "the difference is 20 points" and tested with alpha of 0.05 may also be tested by computing the 95% confidence interval and determining whether or not the difference includes 20 points. If the confidence interval includes the null, then we do not reject the possibility that the true effect is the null. If the confidence interval does not include the null, then we conclude that the effect is (probably) not the null. The same holds true, of course, for a significance test with alpha set at 0.01, and a report of the 99% confidence interval.

When we report a confidence interval and then focus on the question of whether or not the interval includes zero, the distinction between confidence intervals and significance tests is one of format rather than substance. However, as suggested by Figure 6, this shift in format is critically important. Working within the traditional framework of significance testing (shown by the columns in this figure) the key distinction is between studies A, B, C (nonsignificant) on the one hand, as opposed to D, E, F (significant) on the other. By contrast, working within the framework of effect size estimation (shown by the rows) we would group studies B and D (not clinically important), then A, C, E (possibly clinically important), while study F (clinically important) would be classified by itself. (A 20-point difference in response rates would be clinically important in the context of this study.)

3.14.7.1 Confidence Intervals as a Surrogate for the Significance Test

Mathematically, then, confidence intervals can serve as a surrogate for the significance test. Should they be used in this way? Researchers have staked out three positions:

(i) Confidence intervals should be used only as a surrogate for the significance test. Otherwise the results are entirely subjective, and we have no basis to make a decision about whether or not the treatment is effective.

(ii) Confidence intervals can serve as a surrogate for the significance test but they can also stand on their own. Some studies will serve best if used to provide an estimate of effect size, accompanied by an estimate of precision. Others would additionally take note of whether or not the confidence interval included specific values.

(iii) Confidence intervals should never serve as a surrogate for the significance test. The significance test has no role in psychological research, and any vestige of the significance test should be removed.

There is a substantial literature developing on these points of view. In general, the debate in the medical literature is between the first two options while the debate in the psychological literature is between the first and the third. The rationale for each of the positions is outlined here.

| | | Statistically significant | |
		No	Yes
Clinically important	No	B	D
	Possibly	A,C	E
	Yes		F

Figure 6 Effect size estimation vs. significance testing. The columns correspond to significance tests—Studies A, B, C are not significant while studies D, E, F are significant. The rows correspond to effect size estimation—Studies B and D show that the treatment is not clinically important, studies A, C, E show that the treatment may be clinically important, and study F shows that the treatment is clinically important.

3.14.7.1.1 Confidence intervals should serve only as a surrogate for the significance test

Some researchers have taken the position that the basic idea of significance testing is a good one, and that the problems outlined above stem from the misuse of these tests rather than from any flaw inherent in the method. They argue that it is critical to retain the logic of the significance test since the researcher and the reader need to make a decision at the end of the study about whether or not the treatment effect was probably "real." By using confidence intervals as a surrogate for the significance test these decision rules are maintained while gaining the following critical advantages over the traditional significance test.

First, attention is focused on the magnitude of the treatment effect. By doing so the tendency is avoided to press the *p*-value into service as an indicator of effect size. A rate difference of five percentage points is seen as being a small effect (in most contexts), even if the sample is so large that the confidence interval does not include zero (and the test is statistically significant). By the same logic an effect of 50 percentage points is large, even if the sample size is so small that the confidence interval does include zero (and the test is not statistically significant).

Second, unambiguous information is provided about the precision of the effect. An effect reported with a precision of ± 5 percentage points is definitive—the effect is known to be useless if small, or is known to be useful if large. An effect reported with a precision of ± 30 percentage points is likely to leave open the question of clinical utility, but this point will be obvious to the researcher and the reader. Mistakes of interpretation will be less likely than they are with significance tests.

At the same time, this approach preserves the protective mechanisms that are incorporated in the significance test. Specifically, if the confidence interval excludes zero then it is assumed that the effect is not nil; if it includes zero then it is acknowledged that the true effect may in fact be zero (see, for example, Chow, 1988, 1989; Walker, 1986a, 1986b).

3.14.7.1.2 Confidence intervals can optionally be used as a surrogate for the significance test

Others have taken the position that confidence intervals can be used as a surrogate for the significance test, but that it is not necessary to focus on significance when interpreting the results. In the running example one could articulate a series of goals, including the following:

(i) We would like to be certain (where "certain" corresponds to a given level of certainty) that the treatment is not actually harmful.

(ii) We would like to be certain that the treatment effect exceeds zero.

(iii) We would like to be certain that the treatment effect is large enough to be clinically important.

As suggested by Figure 5, the 95% confidence interval might or might not exclude effects that are clinically harmful, that are zero, or that are clinically trivial. More generally, the effect size and confidence intervals might allow us to draw a conclusion about some of these points but not others. Or, they might allow us to answer some questions with one level of certainty, and others at another level of certainty.

In fact, rather than focus on the issue of whether or not the interval includes any single value we can consider the full range of population parameters that are consistent with the study results, recognizing the fact that those falling closer to the observed effect are more probable than those closer to the extremes. This approach was suggested by Birnbaum, (1961). More recently, it has been popularized by Miettenan and by Poole (1987a) who suggests that this is displayed most effectively as a graph of confidence interval by confidence level (see also Foster & Sullivan, 1987; Poole, 1987b, 1987c; Sheehe, 1993; Smith & Bates, 1993; Sullivan & Foster, 1990).

In the running example, assume that 20 patients were followed under each treatment condition and the proportion responding was 25% in one treatment group as compared with 50% in the other. The continuous confidence interval for this data is shown in Figure 7. This graph highlights the fact that the most likely impact of the new treatment mode is to increase the response rate by about 25 percentage points. The 60% confidence interval includes a benefit of between 12 and 37 percentage points for the new treatment; the 80% confidence interval extends from five percentage points to 42 percentage points; the 90% confidence interval extends from zero to 46 percentage points; and the 95% confidence interval extends from minus five (a five-point advantage for the standard treatment) to plus 49 (a 49 percentage point advantage for the new treatment).

While it might seem at first glance that this approach introduces an element of subjectivity into the analysis, the fact is that any test of significance involves an element of subjectivity since the decision to set alpha at a particular level is a subjective one, based (at least in theory) on the researcher's need to balance type-I error against type-II error. Additionally, the decision to focus on whether or not the interval includes the nil effect, rather than (say) an effect of five points or 10 points, is also arbitrary. Therefore, the use of confidence intervals in the manner being discussed here, rather than introducing an element of subjectivity into the analysis, merely shifts the subjectivity that is already there from the researcher and on to the reader (Fleiss, 1986a, 1986b; Thompson, 1987a, 1987b, 1987c, 1987d. See also Cohen, 1962; Derouen, 1987; Lachenbruch et al., 1987; Rosnow & Rosenthal, 1989, Rothman, 1986b; Savitz, 1987).

Perhaps more to the point, the reader may not feel a need to frame the answer as a dichotomy, and to conclude that the treatment does (or does not) have any impact on recurrence rates. Rather, the take-home message might be the more comprehensive picture, that is, (in Figure 7 and introducing subjective judgments) "the 40% confidence interval falls entirely in the range of substantial effects; the 80% interval falls in the range of substantial or moderate effects; and the 95% interval includes effects that are trivial" with the entire gamut of possibilities being

factored into a decision about the utility of this treatment (see also Burnand, Kernan & Feinstein, 1990; Poole, 1987a, 1987b, 1987c; Rothman, 1986a, p. 119; Walker, 1986a, 1986b; Walter, 1991).

3.14.7.1.3 Confidence intervals should never be used as a surrogate for the significance test

Others have taken the position that even if the abuse associated with the significance test could be avoided, there is a fatal flaw inherent in this approach. The argument cited above in favor of the first position is also the key argument cited for this position: "If we use confidence intervals as surrogates for the significance test, then we retain the basic protective mechanisms of the significance test. Specifically, if the confidence interval excludes zero then we assume that the effect is not nil; if it includes zero then we explicitly acknowledge that the true effect may in fact be zero." Proponents of the third position would add "And therein lies the problem."

It was argued earlier that the null hypothesis is of little interest. If this is true, then when reporting an effect size we should care about the precision of the estimate, but not about whether or not the confidence interval (CI) includes zero. Put another way, an effect of 30 points with CI of 20–40 is informative; with CI of 10–50 is less informative; with CI of 0–60 is less informative, still. But there is no reason that we should be more concerned about "ruling out zero" than about "ruling out" a five-point effect or a 10-point effect. Knowing that the effect is probably not zero does not tell us that the effect is probably clinically important.

Similarly, it was argued that significance tests are misleading since they allow us to confuse effect size with precision. Studies meet the criterion for significance in part because the sample size is large; studies fail to meet the criterion for significance in part because the sample size is not large enough. By exactly the same logic, if the confidence interval includes zero it is in part because the sample size is too small. If the key issue being addressed by the significance test is whether or not there was a large enough sample, then it makes no sense to perform a significance test, in any format. To do so is to propagate and codify exactly the same error that attempts are being made to avoid (see Schmidt, 1992; Schmidt & Hunter, 1996, 1997).

3.14.7.2 Should the Significance Test be Banned?

In 1998 the significance test continues to serve as the *de facto* standard of proof in most research

**Confidence interval function
for difference in proportions**

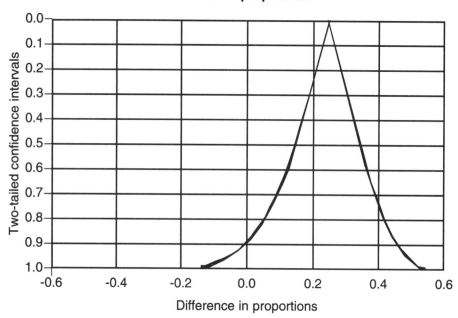

Figure 7 Continuous confidence intervals. Rather than focus on whether or not we can exclude a specific effect size with an arbitrary level of confidence, we can consider the full range of population parameters that are consistent with the study results, recognizing that those falling closer to the observed effect are more probable than those falling closer to the extremes.

studies. As a practical matter, the grant applicant who proposes to skip the significance test is not likely to be taken seriously by the funding agency; drug manufacturers are not likely to submit studies for FDA approval without data on statistical significance; and papers submitted for publication without tests of significance will face a serious obstacle in most journals. In the context of the three positions outlined above, the current state is somewhere prior to the first position. Nevertheless, recent debate has focused on the proposition that the significance test should be banned, which falls at or beyond the third position.

The most vocal proponents in favor of a ban are Schmidt and Hunter (1997) who attack the null hypothesis test on three fronts. First, they note that the null hypothesis is almost always false. Rather than thinking of studies as "significant" or "not significant" we would do well to think of them as "correct" and "incorrect." As long as researchers are permitted to report significance tests, type-II error will continue to run rampant in psychological research. Second, they argue that the role of the single study should be to accumulate data which can later be incorporated in a meta-analysis, and so there is no need to perform a significance test for the single study. As long as significance tests are permitted, the significant

studies will be accepted for publication at a higher rate than non-significant studies, which will introduce a bias into the research literature and impair ability to conduct a meta-analysis at a later point. Finally, they contend that the significance test serves no useful function at all. In support of this latter point they proposed a ban on significance tests and then systematically collected objections to this proposal. They summarize these objections by reporting that "Each of these objections is intuitively appealing and plausible but is easily shown to be logically and intellectually bankrupt" (p. 37). Some of the objections to a ban follow, together with comments.

Some have taken issue with the contention that the nil hypothesis is always false. For example, if using a randomized trial to test an entirely new class of drug that actually has zero effect, then the null hypothesis would be true. This is a valid point but largely irrelevant, since it applies to only a trivial number of studies.

Some have argued that significance tests assure objectivity. In fact, one could argue that the hypothesis test is not objective since the selection of a criterion alpha, and also the selection of a specific null to be tested, are made subjectively. Even if one accepts the idea that confidence intervals are less objective, the fact remains that this objectivity leads to ubiquitous errors of interpretation. To paraphrase Tukey, "Be approximately right rather than exactly wrong."

Others have taken issue with Schmidt and Hunter's contention that a single study cannot provide definitive evidence to support or refute a theory. Abelson, for example, cites the classic Festinger experiment, which raised questions about the prevailing theory and set the stage for the studies that followed. (In this study one theory predicted that one group would score higher and the competing theory predicted that the second group would score higher. Ratings were conducted on an arbitrary scale, and the only issue to be resolved was the direction of the effect). This is a single study that had a substantial impact on the direction of the field, inasmuch as it set the direction for numerous confirmatory studies that followed. Again, these arguments are valid but they apply in only a small fraction of studies.

Perhaps the key point of Schmidt and Hunter is not that any single objection to the of banning significance tests is or is not valid, but the fact that researchers cling so hard to their beliefs about significance tests. For example, researchers keep coming back to the idea that we need the tests to distinguish between "real" effects and "chance effects," thereby missing the key point: All effects are real. The tests distinguish between studies that showed this and those that (in error) did not. Schmidt and Hunter write "We attribute this psychologically interesting fact to the virtual brainwashing in significance testing that all of us have undergone, beginning with our first undergraduate course in psychological statistics."

Should significance tests be banned, then? Abelson (1997a) wrote that the idea of such a ban is appealing "In the words of a famous empathizer 'I feel your pain'" (p. 118). The abuse of significance tests is so pervasive that it is likely to require some kind of absolute ban to prevent the continued abuse of this tool. If significance tests are allowed to continue, they will continue to be abused, and if the confidence interval is allowed to serve as a surrogate for the significance test, then the door to abuse will be wide open. He notes that abuse would be not only possible, but inevitable: "Indeed, under the Law of Diffusion of Idiocy, every foolish application of significance testing will beget a corresponding foolish practice for confidence limits." Despite these concerns, Abelson concludes that the tests should not be banned. He writes, "Create a list of things that people misuse—for example, oboes, ice skates, band saws, skis, and college educations. Would you be inclined to ban them because people make errors with them? Will we want to ban effect sizes, too, when their misuse escalates?" (p. 13).

While Abelson is correct that the idea of imposing a ban is unappealing, it is also clear that some kind of decisive action is required. Without some concrete and clear action on the part of educators, funding agencies, and journal editors, the shift away from significance tests will drag out over an indeterminate period of time. During this period a great deal of effort will be spent in repeatedly making the case for the shift, harm will be caused, and a great deal of potentially important work will go undone.

It is submit that the appropriate course of action would be not to ban the significance test but rather to require that researchers report effect size indices and confidence intervals. Scientifically, this is more defensible. Pragmatically, this can take effect immediately without further debate. In fact, this requirement is implicit in guidelines now, in the sense that analyses are expected to address the research question and conclusions are expected to follow logically from the analyses. Only rarely do we care about excluding a specific value, and even more rarely do we care about excluding the nil. In virtually all studies, the requirement that analyses address the research question will require that the report highlight the effect size and the precision with which this is reported.

While researchers would be free to report *p*-values in addition to the effect size and confidence interval, it is likely that this practice would disappear because it would become evident that the significance test is of tangential interest, at best. The experience of Rothman is informative in this regard. As an editor at the *American Journal of Public Health*, he took a firm stance against the inappropriate use of significance tests, and in doing so both educated and empowered researchers to focus on effect size in their analyses. More recently, as the editor of *Epidemiology*, Rothman has established a policy that prohibits references to significance testing, but reports that "Interestingly, few readers seem to be aware of this policy, which tells me that they don't miss the absence of claims regarding statistical significance. As you urge, we emphasize the measurement of effect size, and this gets a clear message across to readers."

3.14.7.3 Should the Analysis of the Single Study be Banned?

Similarly, while one can empathize with the desire to ban the analysis of single studies, Schmidt and Hunter overstate their case when they argue that no single study can provide definitive information on its own. Abelson writes, "Indeed, one might say that Hunter and Schmidt use the 'Brooklyn' method of argumentation: The Brooklynite asks you a question, tells you his answer, and then says that you are wrong." The fact is that some studies are well designed, with adequate power and appropriate controls. In fact, some single studies contain more subjects and better designed controls than some meta-analyses. To balance Hunter and Schmidt's point that no substantive issue in psychology has ever been resolved by a single study and that all testing should be deferred to the meta-analysis, we cite a recent editorial in the *New England Journal of Medicine*. Bailar (1997, 1998) noted that no substantive issue in medicine has ever been resolved by a meta-analysis, and that the randomized clinical trial is still considered to be the gold standard. (Bailar acknowledges that meta-analysis hold great potential but objects to the improper use of this procedure. Recall Abelson's prediction, cited earlier.) Additionally, even when the single study cannot yield adequate precision there is a need to provide advice about treatment options based on the evidence at hand, or to use this evidence to help design subsequent research. In such cases the analysis of a single study may be required.

Schmidt and Hunter highlight an important problem when they note that the practice of allowing significance testing for individual studies contributes to the problem of publication bias, but this problem exists, in large part, because researchers and editors focus on the *p*-value. Abelson wrote that in deciding whether or not a study should be published he takes into account five components, including such issues as the role of the study in the context of other research and theory. The *p*-value is a subset of the fifth component, and the least interesting one, at that. If the recommendations outlined above for focusing on effect size are followed, the illogic of basing a publication decision on the significance test should become clear, and the publication bias minimized.

3.14.7.4 Looking Ahead

It seems likely that the shift from significance tests to effect size estimation with confidence intervals is likely to take place over the next several years. Earlier, the history of researchers railing against the null hypothesis tests was outlined, beginning in the 1950s and proceeding to the present. The impact of these writings has been modest. Nevertheless, whether or not significance tests are banned, it is likely that the next few years will be marked by a shift away from significance tests and toward effect size estimation with confidence intervals. This prediction is based on the convergence of several factors (Schmidt, 1996).

The first is a shift in educational resources. Some statistics texts now place more of an emphasis on confidence intervals than they had in the past. Computer programs used for analysis are more likely now than in the past to present confidence intervals as well as tests of significance. Some programs for study planning now incorporate the ability to plan for confidence intervals as well as statistical significance (see, for example, Borenstein et al., 1997 or Elashoff, 1997).

The second is the acceptance of effect size estimation by important segments of the mainstream research community. Journal editors in some fields now encourage or require the use of confidence intervals in research reports (Altman, 1991; Altman et al., 1983; Rothman, 1978, 1986b; Rothman & Yankauer, 1986). The use of confidence intervals is also encouraged in the *Uniform Requirements for Manuscripts Submitted to Biomedical Journals* (International Committee of Medical Journal Editors (International Committee of Medical Journal Editors, 1991) [p. 425]). There is now a task force working on behalf of the American Psychological Association, charged with the goal of studying the issues raised in this paper and making recommendations. Harlow et al. (1997) edited a book entitled "*What if there were no significance tests*" and discuss eight points that are endorsed by some or all of the chapter contributors. There is unanimous rejection of the traditional use of significance tests—specifically the exclusive focus on the nil hypothesis and *p*-values. There is unanimous agreement that researchers should present effect size estimates with confidence intervals, should be cognizant of power issues, and should evaluate the results in the context of a theory rather than in isolation. There is strong support, with a few dissenters, for the use of tests that are designed to confirm or refute specific, hypothesis-based theories other than the nil hypothesis.

The third, and most important, factor in this move away from significance tests is the increasingly common application of meta-analyses. Meta-analyses serve both to highlight the flaws in significance tests and to provide a realistic mechanism for the application of effect size estimation. Meta-analysis is the next logical step in the research process and we return to this point at the conclusion of this chapter.

3.14.8 USE OF CONFIDENCE INTERVALS IN STUDIES WHOSE PURPOSE IS TO PROVE THE NULL

Some studies are conducted for the express purpose of showing that the null is true—for example, that two drugs are bioequivalent or that two treatments are equally effective. These studies are framed along the following lines: A study compares the mortality rates in patients treated with either of two drugs. The study has power of 95% to detect a difference of, say, five percentage points in mortality rates and so if the study fails to yield a significant effect we can conclude (with 95% certainty) that the groups do not differ by five percentage points.

The same logic is sometimes applied after the fact to a study which was initially run in hopes of finding a significant group effect. It was shown earlier that the absence of an effect is often interpreted without justification as meaning that the groups are identical. While a conclusion that the treatments are equivalent cannot be justified, one can make the argument that the study had power to detect a difference of some magnitude, and the absence of significance indicates that the groups do not differ by this much. While this approach is technically correct it suffers from two basic flaws.

First, it involves the loss of useful information. Assume, for example, that a study is planned in which schizophrenic patients currently in remission are assigned to treatment with either a low dose or a standard dose of neuroleptic treatment ($N = 40$ per group) and followed for a year. The study has power of 95% to detect a difference of 38 percentage points in recurrence rates (specifically, rates of 0.80 vs. 0.42). Therefore, if the study failed to yield significance it would be fair to conclude that the impact of treatment on recurrence rates, if any, is less than 38 percentage points.

However, the study that fails to yield significance could yield a rate difference of 18 percentage points (0.80 vs. 0.62) with $p = 0.08$ and a 95% confidence interval of -0.02 to 0.35. Or, it could yield a rate difference of two percentage points (0.80 vs. 0.78) with $p = 0.83$ and a confidence interval of -0.15 to 0.18. Once the study is completed it would be inappropriate to fall back on the original computations and report that the rate difference in the population is less than 38 percentage points. Rather, we could report (in the first example) that the rate difference could be as much as 35 points and (in the second) that it is at most 18 percentage points.

Second, the logic of using a power analysis to argue that two groups are comparable is muddled and often misunderstood. We are arguing that if the effect had been of a certain size we would have found it, and we did not, so we can assert that the effect is not that large. Consider, by contrast, the elegant simplicity by which the same information is conveyed in the context of confidence intervals. In the examples cited above we would report that the rate difference falls in the range of -0.02 to 0.35, or the rate difference falls in the range of -0.15 to 0.18. In other words, confidence intervals allow us to report what the effect is rather than what the effect is not (Blackwelder, 1982; Detsky & Sackett, 1985, 1986; Makuch & Johnson, 1986).

The response which had been framed in terms of significance tests and *p*-values is confusing because the sole function of the significance test is to evaluate the null hypothesis. If we try to reframe the null to mean almost null because we are trying to estimate the magnitude of an effect, then we are using the technique in a manner for which it was not intended and the results are awkward.

3.14.9 COMPUTATIONAL ISSUES IN CONFIDENCE INTERVALS

Earlier, it was noted that a confidence interval could be approximated as the observed effect plus/minus a specified distance. This is a shortcut that yields approximate results, and two caveats are in order. First, even for this approximation the computation is somewhat more complex than suggested here. If the index is based on a mean difference, then to compute the 95% interval we would multiply not by 1.96 but by a factor, based on the *t*-distribution, that takes sample size into account. Additionally, for most indices, including those based on proportions or correlations, we would transform the data prior to computing the confidence interval and then convert back to the original metric prior to reporting the results. Formulas for these transformations are widely available (Fleiss, 1981; Kleinbaum et al., 1982; Rothman, 1986a; Selvin, 1991) and are applied as a matter of course by computer programs. Second, even when these transformation are applied, for most indices the result is still approximate. While the approximation yields an interval that is accurate enough for most purposes, it is not identical to the interval obtained by more sophisticated procedures (see, for example, Cornfield, 1956; Fleiss, 1979, 1981). The assertion that the 95% confidence interval will exclude the null if and only if the significance test is significant at 0.05 assumes that exact formulas (or the identical approximation) are used for computing the *p*-value and the confidence interval.

3.14.10 STUDY PLANNING: PRECISION ANALYSIS VS. POWER ANALYSIS

If the goal of a study is to yield a test of significance, it follows that the study should have adequate power to yield a significant effect. By the same logic, if the goal of a study is to provide an estimate of effect size, it follows that the study should be able to provide this estimate with an acceptable degree of precision. While the research community is clearly moving toward effect size estimation for data analysis, relatively little has been said about the need for a corresponding shift in the mechanisms used for study planning. In fact, it is not unusual to see a paper that focuses on effect size in the analysis but whose sample size was set on the basis of a power analysis. There is neither a mathematical nor a logical basis for this mixture of apples and estimates. The two goals, significance tests and effect size estimation, have in common that they are both things we can do with data. Beyond this, however, the two criteria are quite different.

Power addresses the likelihood that a study will yield a significant effect. As such, it is controlled by effect size, sample size, and alpha—the same elements that control statistical significance. Precision addresses the width of the confidence interval surrounding the effect size estimate. As such, it is controlled by the confidence level and the sample size—the same elements that control the confidence interval width. Of particular note, effect size is the dominant factor in computation of power but plays little (if any) role in the computation of precision. The sample size required to yield adequate power and the sample size required to yield adequate precision will differ from each other in almost all cases, and often by very substantial amounts.

3.14.10.1 Planning for Precision

To determine the study's precision during the process of study planning, we may "plug in" the sample size and confidence level, and compute the confidence interval width that will result. As was the case for power analysis, this process is facilitated by computer programs designed for this purpose.

Figure 8 is an example of this process using the program cited earlier for power analysis. On this panel the researcher has entered response rates of 60% and 40% for the new treatment and the standard treatment, respectively, and a sample size of 190 patients per group. The program displays the effect size as a rate difference of 20 points. This effect will be reported with a 95% confidence interval of plus/minus 10 points (0.10–0.30).

The researcher may modify the sample size—increases to sample size will yield a more precise estimate. The researcher may modify the confidence level—setting the level at 90% rather

than 95% will yield a narrower interval. If the study index is a mean difference, the researcher may modify the standard deviation (SD) within groups—a smaller SD will yield a narrower interval. The researcher may also modify the effect size but, as noted earlier, the confidence interval width will be affected only slightly, if at all.

It should be noted that Figure 8 is an extension of the example cited earlier for power (Figure 3). In that case the researcher had determined that a sample of 107 patients per group would yield power of 80%, and the confidence interval is shown as 0.07–0.33. When planning for precision the researcher has increased the sample size to 190 to yield a more precise estimate of the effect size, and power has increased as well, from 80% to 97%.

As it did for power, the program will generate a table or graph of precision that allows us to quickly take account of the larger picture (Figure 9). With 50 patients per group we will be able to report the rate difference with a precision (95% confidence interval) $\pm$ 20 percentage points. With 100 patients per group we will report the rate difference with a precision of $\pm$ 13 percentage points. With 200 patients per group we will report the rate difference with a precision of $\pm$ 10 percentage points.

The program will also generate a summary of the analysis. This report reads (in part) "A second goal of this study is to estimate the difference between the two populations ... The study will enable us to report the difference in proportions with a precision (95.0% confidence level) of approximately $\pm$ 0.098 points. Specifically, an observed difference of 0.200 would be reported with a 95.0% confidence interval of 0.100–0.296. The precision estimated here is the approximate expected precision. Precision will vary as a function of the observed proportions (as well as sample size), and in any single study will be narrower or wider than this estimate."

In this example the power analysis led to a sample size requirement of 107 per group while the precision analysis led to a sample size of 190 per group. In other studies the relationship between the two sample sizes will be different, and could even be reversed (with the sample for power being larger than the sample for precision). The key point is that the two goals of significance testing and effect size estimation are distinct. Precision analysis focuses on the precision of the estimate rather than the power to test the null hypothesis, and as such is the appropriate method to use when the study goal is to estimate the magnitude of the treatment effect (Bristol, 1989; Burnand et al., 1990; Cobb, 1985; Feinstein, 1990; Gordon, 1987;

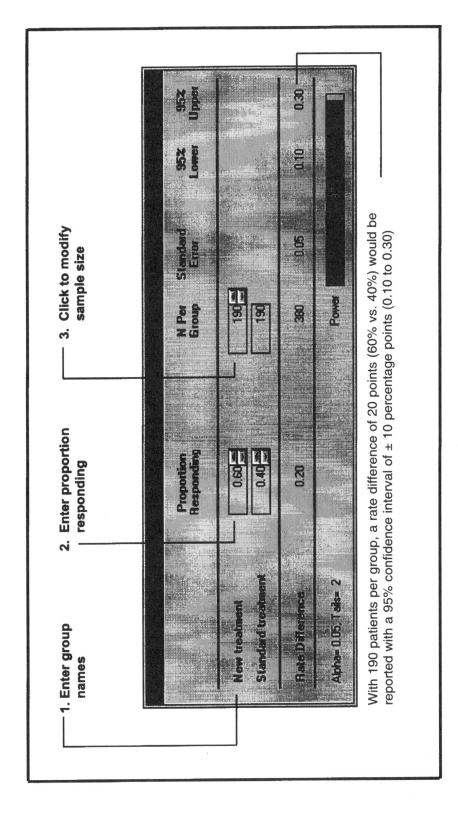

1. Enter group names

2. Enter proportion responding

3. Click to modify sample size

	Proportion Responding	N Per Group	Standard Error	95% Lower	95% Upper
New treatment	0.60	190			
Standard treatment	0.40	190			
Rate Difference	0.20	380	0.05	0.10	0.30
Alpha= 0.05 Tails= 2		Power			

With 190 patients per group, a rate difference of 20 points (60% vs. 40%) would be reported with a 95% confidence interval of ± 10 percentage points (0.10 to 0.30)

Figure 8 Screen from power and precision showing computation of precision. The effect size is shown as a rate difference of 20 points with a 95% confidence interval of 0.10–0.30. The researcher may modify any of the study parameters such as sample size and confidence level and immediately see the impact on the confidence interval width.

**95% confidence interval for rate difference:
two sample proportions**

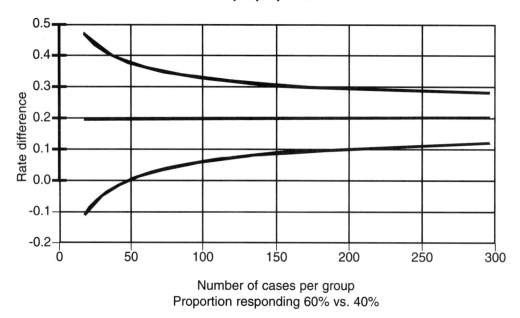

Number of cases per group
Proportion responding 60% vs. 40%

Figure 9   Planning for precision. With a sample of 50 cases per group the treatment effect will be reported with a 95% confidence interval some 40 percentage points wide. With 100 cases per group the interval will narrow to 30 points, and with 200 per group the interval will narrow to 20 points.

Greenland, 1988; Oakes, 1986; Smith & Bates, 1992; Walter, 1991).

Of course, even a fairly narrow interval may include some effects that are clinically meaningful and others that are not, but as the interval narrows in width it becomes increasingly likely that the study results will provide the information required for an informed clinical decision. In many cases, the sample size required for a precise estimate will exceed the available resources. For example, if only 50 cases per group are available, then the 95% interval will be nearly 40 points wide. In this case the study could still provide data that would be pooled with data from other studies, in a meta-analysis.

The method presented here for planning for precision shows provides an estimate of the confidence interval width, but the actual confidence interval in any given study will almost always be narrower or wider than the width estimated in this way. When working with means, for example, the confidence intervals are based in part on the sample standard deviation, which will vary from one sample to the next. When working with proportions, correlations, or survival data the confidence intervals are based in part on the absolute effect size obtained which will vary from one sample to the next. The procedure outlined here is based on the assumption that the sample effect will mirror the population effect precisely. As such, it yields

the median confidence interval width for some procedures and the expected (mean) width for others. Computer programs use more complex formulas that take account of the sampling distribution of the confidence intervals. As such they may allow us to report, for example, that "With a sample of 50 cases per group and a standard deviation of 10 rating points within groups, the median width of the confidence interval will be 7.9 points. In 80% of studies, the confidence interval will be no wider than 8.4 points." If the researcher needs to ensure that the confidence interval width will fall within a specific range, then these formulas should be employed (Borenstein et al., 1997; Elashoff, 1997; Hahn & Meeker, 1991).

3.14.11 META-ANALYSIS

Meta-analysis is the process of developing a comprehensive picture of a field of research by performing analyses on summary data from individual studies, and as such is the next logical step in the research process. The thesis of this chapter has been that the goal of research should be to identify the size of a treatment effect. The single study, because it includes a limited number of subjects, typically yields an imprecise estimate. By combining data from multiple studies we effectively increase the sample size and yield a more precise estimate of the effect. Additionally, the single study typically includes one treatment and one treatment population. The meta-analysis, by contrast, may synthesize data from multiple treatments or multiple populations, and as such may be used to identify the type of treatment that will work best for a specific type of patient. Meta-analyses are being used to provide treatment recommendations based on the results of completed studies. They are also being used to identify areas where the questions of interest have not yet been answered, and to help shape the development of new studies.

The relatively widespread acceptance of meta-analysis since the late 1980s has important implications for the topic of this chapter in a more direct sense as well. The thesis of this chapter is that in psychological research the null hypothesis is rarely true, and what appear to be "conflicting results" (one study is statistically significant while another is not) often reflects normal sample-to-sample variation in effect size coupled with variations in sample size. In past decades this argument had been made in the abstract. With the advent of meta-analysis it is possible to actually "see" the bigger picture. Almost invariably, it becomes clear that the null hypothesis is false, and the study-to-study variations can be seen in context. This has been a critical factor in the shift toward effect size estimation (Cook et al., 1992; Cooper, 1989; Cooper & Hedges, 1994; Eagly & Wood, 1994; Hedges, 1990; Hedges & Olkin, 1985; Schmidt & Hunter 1997; Shadish, 1992).

3.14.12 CONCLUSIONS

Researchers typically want to know whether or not a treatment has any impact, and also what the size of this impact might be. Researchers working exclusively with significance tests are able to address only the first of these issues, and leave the second unanswered. Worse, because the issue of effect magnitude is such a compelling one, the significance tests are often pressed into service to address this issue as well, which often leads to study results—whether statistically significant or not—being misinterpreted. Statistical significance is equated with clinical significance, though this interpretation may not be warranted. Absence of statistical significance is taken as evidence that a treatment is not effective, though this interpretation is rarely justified.

By contrast, estimates of effect size bounded by confidence intervals provide the kind of information that researchers and clinicians require. The report of effect size focuses attention on the magnitude of the effect, and the confidence intervals tell us how much confidence we can have that the population effect lies within a given range. The data may allow us to conclude that the treatment is clearly not effective, or that it clearly is effective, or that additional information is required. Critically, though, this type of report focuses attention on the relevant issues. If and when we elect to make a dichotomous decision, the format of the presentation helps to ensure that the meaning of this decision is clearly understood.

There is an ongoing debate about the role of the single study as part of the research process. Some take the position that any single study should allow researchers to conclude that a specific effect size is or is not tenable. Others have argued that the single study cannot provide this kind of information reliably, and that hypothesis testing should be deferred to the time that the data from many studies can be synthesized in a meta-analysis.

This debate has carried over to the role of confidence intervals. There is complete agreement that researchers should present the effect size bounded by confidence intervals since this will focus attention of the issue of interest and will help to prevent mistakes of interpretation. However, there is sharp disagreement over how the confidence interval should be interpreted. Some take the position that confidence intervals should serve as a surrogate for the significance test, and the focus should be in the question of whether or not the interval includes a specific value. When used in this way the shift from significance tests to confidence intervals is one of format rather than substance—it helps to focus attention on the proper issue and to avoid mistakes of interpretation. Others feel that this approach will merely codify the kinds of errors inherent in significance tests. They argue that the key element in a shift to confidence intervals should be the abandonment of significance testing, and that one should refrain from any discussion of whether or not specific points fall within the interval.

The issues addressed in study planning should correspond to the issues that will be addressed in the data analyses. If the goal of a study is to yield a test of significance, the study should have adequate power to yield a significant effect. Similarly, if the goal of a study is to provide an estimate of effect size that can stand on its own, the study should be able to provide this estimate with an acceptable degree of precision. Prior to ensuring that the power analysis is performed properly it behooves the researcher to ensure that it makes sense to test the null, and indeed that the study should be carried out at all.

The argument that effect size estimation and confidence intervals should replace significance testing in behavioral research is not new but the research community is beginning to take concrete steps in this direction. This shift has been driven by the advent of meta-analysis. Meta-analyses have served to highlight the kinds of errors that are fostered by the use of significance tests, and at the same time provide a vehicle for estimating treatment effects precisely. Additionally, they provide a vehicle for moving beyond the single study and for synthesizing data from multiple sources, which is the next logical step in the research process.

ACKNOWLEDGMENTS

This work was supported in part by the following grants: NIMH/SBIR MH-43083, NIMH/SBIR MH-52969, NIMH/SBIR MH 558483, and NIMH 41960. I am grateful for their comments to Hannah Rothstein, Nina Schooler, Kenneth Rothman, and the late Jacob Cohen, to whom this chapter is dedicated.

3.14.13 REFERENCES

Abelson, R. P. (1995). *Statistics as principled argument.* Mahwah, NJ: Erlbaum.
Abelson, R. P. (1997a). A retrospective on the significance test ban of 1999 (if there were no significance tests, they would be invented). In L. L. Harlow, S. A. Mulaik, & J. H. Steiger (Eds.), *What if there were no significance tests?* (pp. 117–144). Mahwah, NJ: Erlbaum.
Abelson, R. P. (1997b). On the surprising longevity of flogged horses: Why there is a case for the significance test. *Psychological Science, 8*(1), 12–15.
Altman, D. G. (1991). Statistics in medical journals: Developments in the 1980s. *Statistics in Medicine, 10,* 1897–1913.
Altman, D. G., Gore, S. M., Gardner, M. J., & Pocock, S. J. (1983). Statistical guidelines for contributors to medical journals. *British Medical Journal, 286,* 1489–1493.
Bailar, J. C. (1997). The promise and problems of meta analysis. *New England Journal of Medicine, 337,* 559–561.
Bailar, J. C. (1998). Letter. *New England Journal of Medicine, 338,* 62.
Bakan, D. (1966). The test of significance in psychological research. *Psychological Bulletin, 66,* 423–437.
Berkson, J. (1938). Some difficulties of interpretation encountered in the application of the chi-square test. *Journal of the American Statistical Association, 33,* 526–542.
Berkson, J. (1942). Tests of significance considered as evidence. *Journal of the American Statistical Association, 37,* 325–335.
Birnbaum, A. (1961). Confidence curves: An omnibus technique for estimation and testing statistical hypotheses. *Journal of the American Statistical Association, 56,* 246–249.
Blackwelder, W. C. (1982). "Proving the null hypothesis" in clinical trials. *Controlled Clinical Trials, 3,* 345–353.
Borenstein, M. (1994a). Planning for precision in survival studies. *Journal of Clinical Epidemiology, 47*(11), 1277–1285.

Borenstein, M. (1994b). The case for confidence intervals in controlled clinical trials. *Controlled Clinical Trials, 15,* 411–428.
Borenstein, M., & Cohen, J. (1988). *Statistical power analysis: A computer program.* Hillsdale, NJ: Erlbaum.
Borenstein, M., Cohen, J., Rothstein, H., Pollack, S., & Kane, J. (1990). Statistical power analysis for one-way analysis of variance: A computer program. *Behavior Research Methods, Instruments, and Computers, 22,* 271–282.
Borenstein, M., Cohen, J., Rothstein, H., Pollack, S., & Kane, J. (1992). A visual approach to statistical power analysis on the microcomputer. *Behavior Research Methods, Instruments & Computers, 24,* 565–572.
Borenstein, M., Rothstein, H., & Cohen, J. (1997). *Power and precision.* Teaneck, NJ: Biostat. http://www. PowerAndPrecision.com
Bristol, D. R. (1989). Sample sizes for constructing confidence intervals and testing hypotheses. *Statistics in Medicine, 8,* 803–811.
Burnand, B., Kernan, W. N., & Feinstein, A. R. (1990). Indexes and boundaries for "quantitative significance" in statistical decisions. *Journal of Clinical Epidemiology, 43,* 1273–1284.
Carver, R. P. (1978). The case against statistical significance testing. *Harvard Educational Review, 48,* 378–399.
Chow, S. L. (1988). Significance test or effect size? *Psychology Bulletin, 103,* 105–110.
Chow, S. L. (1989). Significance tests and deduction: Reply to Folger (1989). *Psychological Bulletin, 106,* 161–165.
Cobb, E. B. (1985). Planning research studies: An alternative to power analysis. *Nursing Research, 34,* 386–388.
Cohen, J. (1962). The statistical power of abnormal–social psychological research: A review. *Journal of Abnormal and Social Psychology, 65*(3), 145–153.
Cohen, J. (1965). Some statistical issues in psychological research. In B. B. Wolman (Ed.), *Handbook of clinical psychology* (pp. 95–121). New York: McGraw-Hill.
Cohen, J. (1969). *Statistical power analysis for the behavioral sciences.* New York: Academic Press.
Cohen, J. (1977). *Statistical power analysis for the behavioral sciences* (Rev. ed.). New York: Academic Press.
Cohen, J. (1988). *Statistical power analysis for the behavioral sciences* (2nd ed.). Hillsdale, NJ: Erlbaum.
Cohen, J. (1990). Things I have learned (so far). *American Psychologist, 45,* 1304–1312.
Cohen, J. (1992). A power primer. *Psychology Bulletin, 112,* 155–159.
Cohen, J. (1994). The Earth is round ($p < 0.05$). *American Psychologist, 49,* 997–1003.
Cohen, J. (1997). The earth is round ($p < .05$). In L. L. Harlow, S. A. Mulaik, & J. H. Steiger (Eds.), *What if there were no significance tests?* (pp. 21–36). Mahwah, NH: Erlbaum.
Cole, P., & Goldman, M. B. (1975). Occupation. In J. F. J. Fraumeni (Ed.), *Persons at high risk of cancer: An approach to cancer etiology and control* (pp. 167–183). New York: Academic Press.
Cook, T. D., Cooper, H., Cordray, D. S., Hartman, H., Hedges, L. V., Light, L. V., Louis, T. A., & Mosteller, F. (1992). *Meta-analysis for explanation.* New York: Russell Sage Foundation.
Cooper, H. (1989). *Integrating research: A guide for literature reviews* (2nd ed.). Newbury Park, CA: Sage.
Cooper, H., & Hedges, L. V. (1994). Research synthesis as a scientific enterprise. In H. Cooper & L. V. Hedges (Eds.), *The handbook of research synthesis* (pp. 3–14). New York: Russell Sage Foundation.
Cornfield, J. (1956). A statistical problem arising from retrospective studies. In J. Neyman (Ed.), *Proceedings of the Third Berkeley Symposium on Mathematical Statistics and Probability* (pp. 135–148). Berkeley, CA: University of California Press.

Dar, R. (1987). Another look at Meehl, Lakatos, and the scientific practices of psychologists. *American Psychologist, 42,* 145–151.

Derouen, T. A. (1987). Letter. *American Journal of Public Health, 77,* 237.

Detsky, A. S., & Sackett, D. L. (1985). When was a "negative" clinical trial big enough? How many patients you need depends on what you found. *Archives of International Medicine, 145,* 709–712.

Detsky, A. S., & Sackett, D. L. (1986). Establishing therapeutic equivalency: What is clinically significant difference? *Archives of International Medicine, 146,* 861–862.

Eagly, A. H., & Wood, W. (1994). Using research synthesis to plan future research. In H. Cooper & L. V. Hedges (Eds.), *The handbook of research synthesis* (pp. 485–500). New York: Russell Sage Foundation.

Elashoff, J. (1997). *nQuery.* Cork, Ireland: Statistical Solutions.

Estes, W. K. (1997). Significance testing in psychological research: Some persisting issues. *Psychological Science, 8*(1), 18–20.

Feinstein, A. R. (1975). Clinical biostatistics XXXIV: The other side of "statistical significance": Alpha, beta, delta, and the calculation of sample size. *Clinical Pharmacology and Therapeutics, 18,* 491–505.

Feinstein, A. R. (1976). Clinical biostatistics XXXVII. Demeaned errors, confidence games, nonplussed minuses, inefficient coefficients, and other statistical disruptions of scientific communication. *Clinical Pharmacology and Therapeutics, 20,* 617–631.

Feinstein, A. R. (1977). Clinical biostatistics XL: Stochastic significance, consistency, apposite data, and some other remedies for the intellectual pollutants of statistical vocabulary. *Clinical Pharmacology and Therapeutics, 22,* 113–123.

Feinstein, A. R. (1990). The unit fragility index: An additional appraisal of "statistical significance" for a contrast of two proportions. *Journal Clinical Epidemiology, 43,* 201–209.

Fisher, R. A. (1959). *Statistical methods and scientific inference* (2nd ed.). Edinburgh, UK: Oliver & Boyd.

Fleiss, J. (1979). Confidence intervals for the odds ratio in case-control studies: The state of the art. *Journal of Chronic Diseases, 32,* 69–77.

Fleiss, J. (1981). *Statistical methods for rates and proportions* (2nd ed.). New York: Wiley.

Fleiss, J. L. (1986a). Confidence intervals vs. significance tests: Quantitative interpretation (letter). *American Journal Public Health, 76,* 587.

Fleiss, J. L. (1986b). Significance tests have a role in epidemiologic research: Reactions to A. M. Walker. *American Journal Public Health, 76,* 559–560.

Foster, D. A., & Sullivan, K. M. (1987). Computer program produces *p*-value graphics (letter). *American Journal Public Health, 77,* 880–881.

Freiman, J. A., Chalmers, T. C., Smith, H., Jr., & Kuebler, R. R. (1978). The importance of beta, the type-II error, and sample size in the design and interpretation of the randomized control trial. Survey of 71 "negative" trials. *New England Journal Medicine, 299,* 690–694.

Friedman, S. B., & Phillips, S. (1981). What's the difference? Pediatric residents and their inaccurate concepts regarding statistics. *Pediatrics, 68,* 644–646.

Gardner, M. J., & Altman, D. G. (1986). Confidence intervals rather than *P* values: Estimation rather than hypothesis testing. *British Medical Journal, 292,* 746–750.

Gardner, M. J., & Altman, D. G. (1989a). *Confidence intervals analysis.* London: British Medical Journal.

Gardner, M. J., & Altman, D. G. (1989b). *Statistics with confidence—confidence intervals and statistical guidelines.* London: British Medical Journal.

Goldstein, R. (1989). Power and sample size via MS/ PC–DOS computers. *American Statistician, 43,* 253–260.

Gonzalez, R. (1994). The statistics ritual in psychological research. *Psychological Science, 5,* 321–328.

Gordon, I. (1987). Sample size estimation in occupational mortality studies with use of confidence interval theory (see comments). *American Journal of Epidemiology, 125,* 158–162.

Greenland, S. (1988). On sample-size and power calculations for studies using confidence intervals. *American Journal of Epidemiology, 128,* 231–237.

Hagen, R. L. (1997). In praise of the null hypothesis significance test. *American Psychologist, 52,* 15–24.

Hahn, G. J., & Meeker, W. Q. (1991). *Statistical intervals.* New York: Wiley.

Harlow, L. L., Mulaik, S. A., & Steiger, J. H. (1997). *What if there were no significance tests?* Mahwah, NJ: Erlbaum.

Harris, E. K., & Albert, A. (1991). *Survivorship analysis for clinical studies.* New York: Marcel Dekker.

Harris, R. J. (1997a). Reforming significance testing via three-valued logic. In L. L. Harlow, S. A. Mulaik, & J. H. Steiger (Eds.), *What if there were no significance tests?* (pp. 145–174). Mahwah, NJ: Erlbaum.

Harris, R. J. (1997b). Significance tests have their place. *Psychological Science, 8*(1), 8–11.

Hartung, J., Cottrell, J. E., & Giffen, J. P. (1983). Absence of evidence is not evidence of absence. *Anesthesiology, 58,* 298–300.

Hedges, L. V. (1990). Directions for future methodology. In K. W. Wachter & M. L. Straf (Eds.), *The future of meta-analysis* (pp. 11–26). New York: Russell Sage Foundation.

Hedges, L. V., & Olkin, I. (1985). *Statistical methods for meta-analysis.* Boston: Academic Press.

Hoffman, D., & Wynder, E. L. (1976). Smoking and occupational cancers. *Preventative Medicine, 5,* 245–261.

Hunter, J. E. (1997). Needed: A ban on the significance test. *Psychological Science, 8*(1), 3–7.

International Committee of Medical Journal Editors (1991). Uniform requirements for manuscripts submitted to biomedical journals. *New England Journal of Medicine, 324,* 424–428.

Kane, J. M., & Borenstein, M. (1985). Compliance in the long-term treatment of schizophrenia. *Psychopharmacology Bulletin, 21,* 23–27.

Kleinbaum, D. G., Kupper, L. L., & Morgenstern, H. (1982). *Epidemiologic research: Principles and quantitative methods.* Belmont, CA: Lifetime Learning Publications.

Kraemer, H. C., & Thiemann, S. (1987). *How many subjects? Statistical power analysis in research.* Newbury Park, CA: Sage.

Lachenbruch, P. A., Clark, V. A., Cumberland, W. G., Chang, P. C., Afifi, A. A., Flack, V. F., & Elashoff, R. M. (1987). Letter. *American Journal of Public Health, 77,* 237.

Lau, J., Antman, E. M., Jimenez Silva, J., Kupelnick, B., Mosteller, F., & Chalmers, T. C. (1992). Cumulative meta-analysis of therapeutic trials for myocardial infarction. *New England Journal of Medicine, 327,* 248–254.

Lawless, J. F. (1982). *Statistical models and methods for lifetime data.* New York: Wiley.

Lipsey, M. W., & Wilson, D. B. (1993). The efficacy of psychological, educational, and behavioral treatment. Confirmation from meta-analysis. *American Psychologist, 48,* 1181–1209.

Loftus, G. R. (1991). On the tyranny of hypothesis testing in the social sciences. *Contemporary Psychology, 36,* 102–105.

Lykken, D. T. (1968). Statistical significance in psychological research. *Psychology Bulletin, 70,* 151–159.

Mainland, D. (1982). Medical statistics—thinking vs. arithmetic. *Journal of Chronic Diseases, 35,* 413–417.

Makuch, R. W., & Johnson, M. F. (1986). Some issues in

348   *The Shift from Significance Testing to Effect Size Estimation*

the design and interpretation of "negative" clinical studies. *Archives of Internal Medicine, 146*, 986–989.

Meehl, P. E. (1967). Theory-testing in psychology and physics: A methodological paradox. *Philosophy of Science, 34*, 103–115.

Meehl, P. E. (1978). Theoretical risks and tabular asterisks: Sir Karl, Sir Ronald, and the slow progress in soft psychology. *Journal of Consulting and Clinical Psychology, 46*, 806–834.

Meehl, P. E. (1990). Why summaries of research on psychological theories are often uninterpretable. *Psychological Reports, 66*, 195–244.

Morgan, P. P. (1989). Confidence intervals: From statistical significance to clinical significance. *Canadian Medical Association Journal, 141*, 881–883.

Murphy, K. R. (1990). If the null hypothesis is impossible, why test it? *American Psychology, 45*, 403–404.

Nelson, N., Rosenthal, R., & Rosnow, R. L. (1986). Interpretation of significance levels and effect sizes by psychological researchers. *American Psychologist, 41*, 1299–1301.

Neyman, J., & Pearson, E. S. (1932a). On the use and interpretation of certain test criteria for purposes of statistical inference: Part II. *Biometrika, 20A*, 263–294.

Neyman, J., & Pearson, E. S. (1932b). On the use and interpretation of certain test criteria for purposes of statistical inference: Part 1. *Biometrika, 20A*, 175–240.

Oakes, M. (1986). *Statistical inference: A commentary for the social and behavioral sciences.* New York: Wiley.

Peto, R., & Doll, R. (1977). When is significant not significant. *British Medical Journal, 2*, 259.

Phillips, W. C., Scott, J. A., & Blasczcynski, G. (1983). The significance of "No significance": What a negative statistical test really means. *American Journal of Roentgenology, 41*, 203–206.

Poole, C. (1987a). Beyond the confidence interval. *American Journal of Public Health, 77*, 195–199.

Poole, C. (1987b). Confidence intervals exclude nothing. *American Journal of Public Health, 77*, 492–493.

Poole, C. (1987c). Mr. Poole's response (letter). *American Journal of Public Health, 77*, 880.

Reed, J. F., & Slaichert, W. (1981). Statistical proof in inconclusive "Negative" trials *Archives of Internal Medicine, 141*, 1307–1310.

Reynolds, T. B. (1980). Type II error in clinical trials (Editor's reply to letter). *Gastroenterology, 79*, 180.

Rosenthal, R., & Gaito, J. (1963). The interpretation of levels of significance by psychological researchers. *Journal of Psychology, 55*, 33–38.

Rosenthal, R., & Gaito, J. (1964). Further evidence for the cliff effect in the interpretation of levels of significance. *Psychological Reports, 15*, 570.

Rosner, B. (1990). *Fundamentals of biostatistics* (3rd ed.). Boston: PWS-Kent Publishing.

Rosnow, R. L., & Rosenthal, R. (1989). Statistical procedures and the justification of knowledge in psychological science. *American Psychology, 44*, 1276–1284.

Rossi, J. (1990). Statistical power of psychological research: What have we gained in 20 years? *Journal of Consulting and Clinical Psychology, 58*, 646–656.

Rossi, J. (1997). A case study in the failure of psychology as a cumulative science: The spontaneous recovery of verbal learning. In L. L. Harlow, S. A. Mulaik, & J. H. Steiger (Eds.), *What if there were no significance tests?* (pp. 175–198). Mahwah, NJ: Erlbaum.

Rothman, K. J. (1978). A show of confidence (letter). *New England Journal of Medicine, 299*, 1362–1363.

Rothman, K. J. (1986a). *Modern epidemiology.* Boston: Little, Brown and Company.

Rothman, K. J. (1986b). Significance questing (editorial). *Annals of Internal Medicine, 105*, 445–447.

Rothman, K. J., & Yankauer, A. (1986). Editors' note. *American Journal of Public Health, 76*, 587–588.

Rothstein, H., Borenstein, M., Cohen, J., & Pollack, S. (1990). Statistical power analysis for multiple regression/correlation: A computer program. *Educational and Psychological Measurement, 50*, 819–830.

Rozeboom, W. W. (1960). The fallacy of the null hypothesis significance test. *Psychological Bulletin, 57*, 416–428.

Savitz, D. (1987). Letter. *American Journal of Public Health, 77*, 237–238.

Scarr, S. (1997). Rules of evidence: A larger context for the statistical debate. *Psychological Science, 8*(1), 16–17.

Schmidt, F. L. (1992). What do data really mean? Research findings, meta-analysis, and cumulative knowledge in psychology. *American Psychologist, 47*, 1173–1181.

Schmidt, F. L. (1996). Statistical significance testing and cumulative knowledge in psychology: Implications for training of researchers. *Psychological Methods, 1*, 115–129.

Schmidt, F. L., & Hunter, J. E. (1996). Measurement error in psychological research: Lessons from 26 research scenarios. *Psychological Methods, 1*, 199–223.

Schmidt, F. L., & Hunter, J. E. (1997). Eight common but false objections to the discontinuation of significance testing in the analysis of research data. In L. L. Harlow, S. A. Mulaik, & J. H. Steiger (Eds.), *What if there were no significance tests?* (pp. 37–64). Mahwah, NJ: Erlbaum.

Sedlmeier, P., & Gigerenzer, G. (1989). Do studies of statistical power have an effect on the power of studies? *Psychological Bulletin, 105*, 309–316.

Selikoff, I. J., Hammond, E. C., & Churg, J. (1968). Asbestos exposure, smoking and neoplasia. *Journal of the American Medical Association, 204*, 106–112.

Selvin, S. (1991). *Statistical analysis of epidemiologic data.* New York: Oxford University Press.

Shadish, W. R. (1992). Do family and marital psychotherapies change what people do? A meta-analysis of behavioral outcomes. In T. D. Cook & H. Cooper (Eds.), *Meta-analysis for explanation* (pp. 129–208). New York: Russell Sage.

Shaver, J. P. (1993). What statistical significance testing is, and what it is not. *Journal of Experimental Education, 61*, 293–316.

Sheehe, P. R. (1993). A variation on a confidence interval theme (letter). *Epidemiology, 4*, 185–186.

Shrout, P. E. (1997). Should significance tests be banned? Introduction to a special section exploring the pros and cons. *Psychological Science, 8*, 1–2.

Simon, R. (1986). Confidence intervals for reporting results of clinical trials. *Annals of Internal Medicine, 105*, 429–435.

Simon, R. (1987). The role of overviews in cancer therapeutics. *Statistics in Medicine, 6*, 389–396.

Smith, A. H., & Bates, M. N. (1992). Confidence limit analyses should replace power calculations in the interpretation of epidemiologic studies. *Epidemiology, 3*, 449–452.

Smith, A. H., & Bates, M. N. (1993). A variation on a confidence interval theme (Reply to letter). *Epidemiology, 4*, 186–187.

Sullivan, K. M., & Foster, D. A. (1990). Use of the confidence interval function. *Epidemiology, 1*, 39–42.

Thomas, L., & Krebs, C. (1997). A comprehensive list of power analysis software for microcomputers. http://www.Interchg.ubc.ca/cacb/power.

Thompson, B. (1992). Two and one-half decades of leadership in measurement and evaluation. *Journal of Counseling and Development, 70*, 434–438.

Thompson, W. D. (1987a). Exclusion and uncertainty (letter). *American Journal of Public Health, 77*, 879–880.

Thompson, W. D. (1987b). Letter. *American Journal of Public Health, 77*, 238.

Thompson, W. D. (1987c). On the comparison of effects. *American Journal of Public Health, 77*, 491–492.

Thompson, W. D. (1987d). Statistical criteria in the interpretation of epidemiologic data (published erratum appears in *American Journal of Public Health*, 1987(Apr), 77(4), 515). *American Journal of Public Health, 77,* 191–194.

Tukey, J. W. (1969). Analyzing data: Sanctification or detective work? *American Psychologist, 24,* 83–91.

Tversky, A., & Kahneman, D. (1971). Belief in the law of small numbers. *Psychological Bulletin, 76,* 105–110.

Walker, A. M. (1986a). Reporting the results of epidemio-logic studies. *American Journal of Public Health, 76,* 556–558.

Walker, A. M. (1986b). Significance tests represent consensus and standard practice (letter). *American Journal of Public Health, 76,* 1033.

Walter, S. D. (1991). Statistical significance and fragility criteria for assessing a difference of two proportions. *Journal of Clinical Epidemiology, 44,* 1373–1378.

Wonnacott, T. (1985). "Statistically significant." *Canadian Medical Association Journal, 133,* 843.

3.15
Meta-analytic Research Synthesis

SHARON H. KRAMER and ROBERT ROSENTHAL
Harvard University, Cambridge, MA, USA

3.15.1 INTRODUCTION

3.15.1.1 A Brief History

A little over 20 years ago, educational researcher, Gene V. Glass was interested in the question of the whether psychotherapy works. In other words, does it help patients any more than would a placebo treatment? Further-more, if in fact psychotherapy overall is effective, can it be determined whether one form is more effective than another? Glass was not the first researcher interested in this question. Hundreds of studies had previously been conducted in this area. Yet the results from these studies, and even from reviews which summarized the studies, had reached contra-dictory conclusions. What was unique about Glass' attempt to answer this question was that he was the first to conduct a quantitative synthesis of the research, a procedure which he called a "meta-analysis" (Glass, 1976; Smith, Glass, & Miller, 1980). In conducting the meta-analysis, Glass first located studies which asked this question of whether psychotherapy works and then he quantitatively characterized the outcomes and features of the studies and statistically described his findings. Glass ulti-mately found that psychotherapy shows posi-tive results and that there is little difference between the different types of therapy.

While Glass is responsible for coining the term and for carrying out the first large-scale meta-analysis, meta-analytic enterprises had previously been undertaken. For example, in 1904, Karl Pearson, the inventor of the Pearson product moment correlation coefficient, had been investigating the degree to which inocula-tion against smallpox saved lives. He collected the following six correlation coefficients (r's) which measured the relationship of inoculation to survival: 0.58, 0.58, 0.60, 0.63, 0.66, and 0.77, and averaged them, finding a mean correlation of 0.6. Thus, his "meta-analysis" or synthesis of these six studies found a rather large effect of inoculation on survival.

In the 1930s, Ronald Fisher was experiment-ing with combining significance levels of independent studies (Fisher, 1938) as were Frederick Mosteller and Robert Bush in the 1950s (Mosteller & Bush, 1954). Mosteller and Bush also showed the usefulness of combining effect sizes as well as significance levels. Even in George Snedecor's 1946 statistics textbook is included an example drawn from agriculture of combining correlation coefficients measuring

the relationship between the initial weight of steers and their subsequent gain in weight. Finally, back to the field of psychology, in early work on experimenter expectancy effects in the 1960s, there is an example of combining three probability levels to give an overall test of significance of three experiments (Rosenthal, 1966).

Since Glass' use of the term, meta-analyses have become widely used for research in the behavioral and physical sciences and in applied situations, such as for policy making. By one estimate, nearly 2000 meta-analytic reviews have been conducted in the social and health sciences between 1980 and 1994 (Bausell, Li, Gau, & Soeken, 1995). In addition to the growing numbers of meta-analyses that have been conducted, a number of different proce-dures for conducting meta-analyses have also been described. Indeed, whole books, not to mention numerous individual papers and chapters, have addressed the issue of conducting meta-analyses (e.g., Cooper, 1989; Cooper & Hedges, 1994; Glass, McGaw, & Smith, 1981; Hedges & Olkin, 1985; Hunter & Schmidt, 1990; Light & Pillemer, 1984; Rosenthal, 1991). This chapter will illustrate the basic quantitative procedures for conducting a meta-analysis. This chapter draws on material presented in Ro-senthal, (1984, 1991, 1993, 1995a, 1995b, 1998) and in Rosenthal and Rosnow (1991). For more detailed information about the procedures discussed here, the reader may wish to consult these sources. As the chapter will demonstrate, the level of quantitative skill and training required to employ basic meta-analytic proce-dures is so modest that any researchers capable of analyzing the results of their own research will be capable of learning the small number of calculations required to conduct a first-rate meta-analysis.

3.15.2 WHY DO A META-ANALYSIS?

3.15.2.1 The Problem of Poor Cumulation

A meta-analysis is literally an analysis of analyses or a procedure for quantitatively cumulating research results addressing specific research questions. Unlike a typical literature review, a meta-analysis addresses the problem of "poor cumulation" in the social sciences. It is quite common to find a literature review in which dozens of studies are discussed but which ends with a call for more research. When these studies are discussed within the review, only the statistical significance or nonsignificance of the results, without any information about the size of the effects, are presented. Until somewhat recently, when there existed only a small number of studies in any given research area, it was easier to form conclusions about a body of research, but now, as hundreds of studies have been conducted in many fields in the social sciences, the problem of. poor cumulation continues to grow.

Unlike the physical sciences in which newer work builds directly upon the older work, in the social sciences each succeeding volume of our scientific journals almost seems to be starting anew, posing the same research questions time and again. The common explanation for this problem is that there is more variability or less agreement in our field which prevents the kind of building seen in other fields. Yet, this commonly held belief has not been supported. A recent comparison of 13 research areas in particle physics with 13 areas in psychology did not actually find more conflicting results in our field (Hedges, 1987). For the researcher trying to develop theory, for the practitioner trying to decide on treatment, for the policy maker trying to change policy, and for the funding agency trying to allocate research money, meta-analysis holds great promise.

3.15.2.2 Primary Purposes of Meta-analyses

The first primary purpose of a meta-analysis is to summarize for a set of studies the overall relationship between the two variables that had been investigated in each study. It can be used, as with the Glass psychotherapy meta-analysis, for pulling together hundreds of studies, or it can also be used simply by an investigator asking whether a study and its replication produce similar or different results and what the net results of these two studies might be. By quantitatively summarizing the existing research, a meta-analysis is able to discover what has so far been learned and help to discover what has not yet been learned.

Another equally important purpose of meta-analytic work is to learn from comparisons between studies. By comparing the studies in a meta-analysis, the researcher hopes to determine factors that are associated with variations in the magnitudes of the relationships between two variables. These factors are known as moderator variables because they moderate or alter the magnitude of a relationship. For example, a meta-analysis might suggest that the effectiveness of a given type of therapy is moderated by the age of the patient, such that it is more effective with adolescents but less so with adults. By comparing studies, the meta-analysis uncovers new relationships or provides support for suspected relationships, thus paving the way for future research.

3.15.2.3 Pooling Pilots

While meta-analysis is potentially valuable in all fields, it can be particularly helpful for clinical research. Often in clinical research, the number of patients available is so small that all the researcher is able to do is to conduct pilot studies, none of which will ever reach a significance level of $p < 0.05$. However, the researcher is able to combine these individual studies meta-analytically. A recent example of this appeared in an issue of *Science* (Cohen, 1993) which described two pilot studies in which experimental monkeys were vaccinated using SIV (akin to HIV), while control monkeys were not. In the first pilot, six monkeys were available, three vaccinated and three controls. The results showed two of the three vaccinated monkeys and none of the three controls in better health ($p = 0.20$, one-tailed). In the second pilot, 11 animals were available and two of five of the experimentals and none of six of the controls wound up in better health ($p = 0.18$, one-tailed). While the results of neither one of these tiny pilot studies was significant, if treated meta-analytically, they show dramatic benefits of vaccination.

3.15.3 CONDUCTING A META-ANALYSIS

3.15.3.1 Formulating the Question

The first step in conducting a meta-analysis, as with any research enterprise, is a clear formulation of the question being examined. The only constraint on the question is that primary research on the topic must have already been conducted. The specificity and clarity of the question is especially important in a meta-analysis in that it will help the researcher define the criteria for inclusion (see below). The primary question the meta-analysis seeks to answer is: what is the relationship between any variable X and any variable Y? In order to answer this question, we need to have

(i) an estimate of the level of significance of the difference between the obtained effect size and the effect size expected under the null hypothesis (usually an effect size of 0). Estimates of levels of significance are expressed by p values associated with the given significance test, such as t, F, chi-square or Z;

(ii) an estimate of the magnitude of the relationship between X and Y (an effect size). An effect size commonly used by Glass and his colleagues is the number of standard deviation units that separate outcome scores of experimental and control group, expressed as *d*.

According to Cohen (1977), *d*'s around 0.2 are considered small, around 0.5 are considered medium, and around 0.8 are large. A concrete example of the meaning of an effect size which is drawn from educational research is that a *d* of 0.2 would raise a student's performance from the 50th percentile to the 58th percentile, a 0.5 would raise it to the 69th, and a 0.8 would raise it to the 79th percentile (Cohen, 1977). Another common effect size estimate is given by *r*. The relationship between *r* and *d* is $r = d / [(d^2 + 4)^{12}]$.

The relationship between an effect size and a significance test is given by:

$$\text{test of significance} = \text{size of effect} \times \text{size of study} \quad (1)$$

Table 1 provides several examples of this relationship.

As this basic equation illustrates, as a study increases its sample size, it will obtain more significant results (except in the unusual case where an effect size is truly zero in which case a larger study will not produce a result any more significant than a smaller study). An effect size, however, would not be affected by the size of the sample used in the study.

3.15.3.2 Defining Criteria for Inclusion

Once the research question has been formulated, the next step in the meta-analysis is a careful consideration of what criteria must be met in order for a study to be included in the synthesis. For example, a study comparing individual to group therapy would need to define what constitutes group therapy. Would

couples therapy meet these criteria; would therapy which combines group meetings with individual sessions meet these criteria? Deciding on the criteria should be theory or hypothesis driven. For example, if previous research had found that couples therapy is fundamentally different from group therapy, then studies with couples should be excluded from the meta-analysis.

Regardless of the specific question being examined, a basic criterion for inclusion in the meta-analysis is that the studies have reported, or have provided the necessary information for us to obtain, an estimate of an effect size and a significance level for each study. Studies which do not provide this information or a way for the reader to derive this information are not ordinarily included in the analysis.

3.15.3.3 Searching the Literature

There are four basic types of documents from which studies may be retrieved: (i) published books or book chapters; (ii) published journal articles, magazines, newsletters, and newspapers; (iii) bachelor's, master's, and doctoral theses; (iv) unpublished works such as technical reports, convention papers, or raw data. There are a number of computer databases available to help with the retrieval process, such as PsycLit or PsycInfo (see Dickersin, 1994; Reed & Baxter, 1994; Rosenthal, 1994; White, 1994 for specific details on helpful retrieval techniques). Because successful retrieval from these databases is dependent on identifying the right keyword or key subject, the searcher may occasionally miss some references. Therefore, retrieval should also rely on the "ancestry approach," also known as "footnote chasing" (White, 1994), which involves searching reference lists of relevant articles and books. Past issues of relevant

Table 1 Examples of the relationship between tests of significance and effect size: chi-square, *Z*, *t*, and *F*.

Test of significance	=	Size of effect	x	Size of study
$\chi^2_{(1)}$	=	ϕ^2	x	N
Z	=	ϕ	x	$\sqrt{N}$
t	=	$\frac{r}{\sqrt{1-r^2}}$	x	$\sqrt{df}$
t	=	d	x	$\frac{\sqrt{df}}{2}$
F	=	$\frac{r^2}{1-r^2}$	x	df
t^a	=	d	x	$\sqrt{df}$

[a]Correlated observtions.

journals should also be hand searched. Finally, if primary researchers in the field can be contacted, they should be consulted for their knowledge of any unpublished work in the field by themselves or by their colleagues. This last method has been referred to as using the "invisible college" grapevine (Crane, 1972).

A comprehensive search for all the research on the given topic is necessary in order to avoid conducting a biased retrieval of only the major journals which may selectively publish results characterized by lower p values. If the field we are searching is too vast for us to analyze every study, it is better to sample randomly from this complete selection than to analyze only the more readily retrievable results.

3.15.3.4 Recording Study Characteristics and Identifying Moderators

In addition to an estimate of effect size and a level of significance, there are always other features of the retrieved studies that will be of interest both for purely descriptive purposes and for analysis as potential moderating variables. For example, the meta-analyst should always record and report the following study characteristics: (i) descriptions of the participant population, such as number, age, sex, education, and volunteer status; (ii) descriptions of how the study was conducted, such as whether it was conducted in a laboratory or in the field, whether it was observational or randomized; and (iii) year and form of publication of the study. In addition to listing each study and its relevant characteristics, it is also good meta-analytic practice to provide the range and median of these features, such as the range and median of dates of the studies and ages of the participants.

All of the study characteristics recorded can also be employed as moderator variables, that is, variables correlated with the magnitude of the effect size obtained for the different studies. For example, a meta-analysis conducted by social psychologist Alice Eagly on sex differences in influenceability found that the time when a study was published was strongly related to the study's results. Studies published before 1970 were somewhat more likely to show greater influenceability among females, while studies published during the period of the women's movement in the 1970s were less likely to find differences between sexes (Eagly & Carli, 1981).

In addition to these general characteristics, each area of research will also have its own specific moderator variables which are of particular interest or meaning. For example, a meta-analysis in the field of the effects of teachers' expectations on pupils' IQ gains specifically looked at the possible moderator variable of how long teachers had known their pupils before the expectations were assigned (Raudenbush, 1994). This analysis found that the longer teachers had known their pupils before the experiment began, the smaller were the effects of experimentally-induced teacher expectations. One method of organizing the various relevant variables that has often proven helpful is to break down the variables into substantive and methodological variables. Substantive variables are those relating to the phenomenon under investigation while methodological variables are those that relate to the procedural aspect of the study (Lipsey, 1994). Some examples of substantive features might be type of treatment administered or characteristics of the subject population. Some methodological variables of interest might be variations in the research design or procedure or internal validity of the study (e.g., random assignment of participants to conditions or use of a control group).

An example of a methodological variable from the study of female influenceability mentioned above that was found to play a large role was the sex of the researcher (Eagly & Carli, 1981). In this meta-analysis, male researchers were more likely to find female influenceability in their studies than female researchers. An explanation for this finding may be that if a difference was found between the sexes, it was equally as likely to be reported by male and female researchers. However, if no difference was found, a male researcher would tend to report the results less often than a female researcher who would be more likely to see the absence of an effect as important in that it disputes the stereotype of females being more conforming and persuasible. After forming a preliminary list of moderators which have been identified, this form should be discussed with colleagues, advisors, and other workers in the field for suggestions of other moderators that should be coded.

3.15.3.5 Coding

Once relevant features have been identified, they need to be coded and entered into a database type of system. Some variables, such as subject sex or number of subjects in the study, can be easily coded (e.g., a 1 for female subjects or a 0 for males). Others, such as an assessment of the quality of the study, will require more sophisticated coding. For these types of codings, each study should be coded by several knowledgeable methodologists who are not necessarily specialists in the field being examined. The agreement or reliability of the judges can then be assessed (for details on how to compute reliability, see Rosenthal, 1991 or Rosenthal & Rosnow, 1991) and when agreement is satisfactory the feature is coded. Table 2 provides an example of a partial database of relevant variables which were coded from a recent meta-analysis examining individual vs. group problem-solving performance (Kramer & Rosenthal, 1997).

3.15.3.6 Descriptive Data Displays

Once all the studies have been collected and the relevant information extracted and recorded from each, the next step is to display what has been found. One of the most important parts of a meta-analysis is a graphic display of the effect sizes and the summary of their distribution and central tendency. We will describe two visual displays that may be used, but there are a great many more to choose from (e.g., Cooper, 1989; Glass et al., 1981; Greenhouse & Iyengar, 1994; Hedges & Olkin, 1985; Light & Pillemer, 1984; Light, Singer, & Willett, 1994; Rosenthal & Rosnow, 1991; Tukey, 1977).

3.15.3.6.1 Stem and leaf

Table 3 is a stem and leaf display (Tukey, 1977) from a recent meta-analysis of the effects of gender on judgments of sexual harassment (Blumenthal, 1997). Each of the 83 effect sizes is recorded with the first digit found in the column labeled "stem" and the second digit found in the column labeled "leaf." The top two entries of Table 3, therefore, are read as two *r*'s of 0.65, and 0.43. The stem and leaf display provides a clear overall impression of all of the results; in this particular case, the display quickly and easily demonstrates that most of the effects of gender differences found in these studies tend to be small. It can also point out when there is an unusual distribution of effect sizes, for example, a bimodal distribution may suggest that a certain innovation works well for one group but not for another.

3.15.3.6.2 Box plot and summary table

The box plot or box graph, originally called a box-and-whisker plot (Tukey, 1977), provides a pictorial summary of five descriptive statistics from the distribution of effect sizes: the maximum, the minimum, the median, the 75th percentile, and the 25th percentile. Figure 1 displays a box plot of the data in Table 3. The top and bottom dots represent the maximum and minimum scores, the top and bottom of the rectangle represent the 75th and 25th percentile

and the line dividing the rectangle represents the median. The box plot is especially useful when there are data to display from several subsamples.

In addition to the graphic display, it is also instructive to provide a summary table of these measures of central tendency and variability. Several indices of central tendency should be reported: the unweighted mean effect size, the weighted mean effect size, (see below for more details on weighting), and the median. The number of independent effect sizes on which these indices are based should be reported. The standard deviation, the maximum and minimum effect size, and the effect sizes found at the 75th percentile (Q3) and the 25th percentile (Q1) should also be given. The following may also be reported: the proportion of studies showing effect sizes in the predicted direction; the total number of subjects on which the weighted mean is based; and the median number of subjects per obtained effect size. Table 4 provides a summary of the data displayed in the box plot in Figure 1.

3.15.4 QUANTITATIVELY ANALYZING THE STUDIES

In addition to the descriptive techniques just discussed, there are also procedures for inferential analysis of the retrieved data. As Table 5 shows, there are two major ways to evaluate the results of research studies: (i) terms of their statistical significance (e.g., *p* levels); and (ii) in terms of their effect sizes (e.g., *r*). When evaluating, there are two major analytic processes that can be applied to the set of studies: comparing and combining. Because there are some especially convenient computational procedures for the two-study situation, Table 5 separates the procedures applicable to the case of combining and comparing two studies from three or more studies. In cases of three or more studies being represented, we are able to compare studies on two levels: with diffuse tests and with focused tests. When diffuse tests are used to show whether significance levels or effect sizes differ, the researcher may learn that they differ but not how they differ. By using focused tests, or contrasts, we are able to expand on the knowledge of the diffuse tests by learning whether the studies differ in a theoretically predictable or meaningful way.

3.15.4.1 Comparing Two Studies

3.15.4.1.1 Significance testing

Although we are generally more interested in comparing the results of the effect sizes of the

Table 2 An example of a partial coding database of four studies from a meta-analysis of individual vs. group problem-solving performance.

Author	Year	Type of publication	N	Subject occupation	Size of group	Type of task	Signifi-cance level	Effect size estimate
Barnlund	1959	Journal article	143	Students	5	Logic problem	Z = 6.3	r = 0.88
Campbell	1968	Journal article	48	Managers	4	Human relations problem	Z = −1.4	r = −0.43
Kanekar	1982	Journal article	36	Students	2	Anagrams	Z = 6.9	r = 0.80
Knight	1921	Master's thesis	35	Students	6	Judgment task	Z = 5.2	r = 0.74

Table 3 A stem and leaf display of 83 effect sizes of the effect of gender on judgments of sexual harassment.

Stem	Leaf
0.6	5
0.6	
0.5	
0.5	
0.4	
0.4	3,3
0.3	7,7,9,9
0.3	0,0,2,3
0.2	5,5,5,5,5,6,7
0.2	2,2,3,3,4,4
0.1	5,5,5,5,5,6,6,6,7,7,7,8,8,8,8,9,9,9
0.1	0,1,1,1,2,2,2,3,3,3,3,4,4,4
0.0	5,6,6,6,7,7,8,8,8,8,8,8,9,9,9,9,9
0.0	0,0,0,0,0,0,0,0,0,3

two studies, sometimes this information is not available and all we are able to compare is p values. The following is the procedure for comparing the significance levels of two studies (Rosenthal & Rubin, 1979); all p levels are one-tailed. First, for each of the studies, we obtain as exact a p level as possible. For example, if we obtain $t(150) = 2.32$, our $p = 0.011$ not < 0.05. Extended tables of the t distribution are helpful here (e.g., Federighi, 1959; Rosenthal & Rosnow, 1991) or calculators and software packages with built-in distributions of Z, t, F, and chi-square that will provide exact p values for the various statistical tests. Second, for each p, we find Z, the standard normal deviate corresponding to the p value (using a Z table or calculator or statistical software that converts from p to Z). Since only one-tailed p's were used,

if both Z results are in the same direction, they will both have positive signs; if the results are in the opposite direction, one of the two Z's will be negatively signed. The two Z's are then compared by the following formula:

$$Z = \frac{Z_1 - Z_2}{\sqrt{2}} \qquad (2)$$

Example 1

Studies A and B yield results in the same direction; one is significant at the 0.05 level, the other is not. The p level of Study A is 0.04, the p level of Study B is 0.30. The Z's corresponding to these p's are found in a table of the normal curve to be 1.75 and 0.52 respectively. Using Equation (2), we find that:

$$\frac{Z_1 - Z_2}{\sqrt{2}} = \frac{1.75 - 0.52}{\sqrt{2}} = 0.87$$

The p value associated with this Z is 0.19 one-tailed. Thus, when comparing these two studies, one of which reaches "significance," while the other does not, we find that the difference between them does not come close to the conventional levels of significance. The examples in the chapter are hypothetical in order to keep the computational examples small and manageable. For illustrations of various meta-analytic procedures with real-life examples, see the final chapter in Rosenthal (1991).

Example 2

Studies A and B yield results in different directions and both are significant. One p is 0.001, the other is 0.03. The Z's corresponding to these p's are 3.09 and -1.88 (note the opposite signs to indicate results in opposite directions). From Equation (2), we have:

$$\frac{(3.09) - (-1.88)}{\sqrt{2}} = 3.51$$

which has a corresponding p of 0.0002, which indicates that the two p values differ significantly.

3.15.4.1.2 *Effect size estimation*

When comparing studies, we are usually more interested in looking at the consistency or heterogeneity of the effect sizes than of the significance levels since a difference in Z's might simply be due to the difference in the size of the studies but not truly reflective of whether the two studies differ in effect size.

Researchers do not routinely report an effect size estimate together with their test of significance. Yet, in most cases, by rearranging the formulas in Table 1 into the following formulas, the meta-analyst can compute the

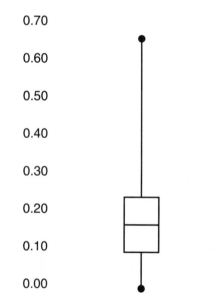

Figure 1 A box plot of the data displayed in Table 3.

Table 4 A summary table of the measures of central tendency and variability of the distribution of effect sizes in Table 3.

Central tendency		Variability	
Unweighted mean	0.17	Maximum	0.65
Weighted mean	n.a.	Q3	0.23
Median	0.15	Median	0.15
Proportion of studies greater than 0.00	0.89	Q1	0.09
Median number of subjects per effect size	n.a.	Minimum	0.00
		Q3–Q1	0.14
Total number of independent effect sizes	83	Standard deviation	0.13
Total number of subjects	34 350		

n.a. = information not available

necessary effect size from the information that has been reported. There are several ways of computing effect sizes (r) from significance test results (t, Z, chi-square, and F) as shown below.

$$r = \sqrt{\frac{t^2}{t^2 + df}}$$

$$r = \sqrt{\frac{x^2(1)}{N}}$$

$$r = \frac{Z}{N}$$

$$r = \sqrt{\frac{F(1, _{-})}{F(1, _{-}) + df_{error}}}$$

The effect size emphasized in this chapter will be r but analogous procedures are available for comparing other effect size indicators such as Hedge's g or d' (Hedges, 1982; Hsu, 1980; Rosenthal, 1991; Rosenthal & Rubin, 1982a; Rosenthal, Rosnow, & Rubin, 1997).

As the population value of r gets further and further from zero, the distribution of r's sampled from that population becomes more and more skewed. To adjust for this skew, it is recommended that all r's first be transformed to Fisher z_rs (Fisher, 1928), which are distributed nearly normally, before further computations are carried out. The relationship between r and z is given by $1/2 \log_e [(1 + r)/(1 - r)]$. There are handy tables available which convert r to z_r and z_r to r (e.g., Rosenthal & Rosnow, 1991) and most statistical software packages will easily perform this transformation as well. After converting obtained r's to z_r's, the following formula may be used:

$$\frac{z_{r_1} - z_{r_2}}{\sqrt{\frac{1}{n_1-3} + \frac{1}{n_2-3}}} \qquad (3)$$

which is distributed as Z (Snedecor & Cochran, 1989).

Example 3

Studies A and B yield results in the same direction with effect sizes of $r = 0.70$ ($n = 25$) and $r = 0.25$ ($n = 100$), respectively. The Fisher z_r's corresponding to these r's are 0.87 and 0.26, respectively. From Equation (3), we have

$$Z = \frac{z_{r_1} - z_{r_2}}{\sqrt{\frac{1}{n_1-3} + \frac{1}{n_2-3}}} = \frac{0.87 - 0.26}{\sqrt{\frac{1}{22} + \frac{1}{97}}} = 2.58$$

Table 5 An overview of 10 meta-analytic procedures.

	Significance testing	*Effect size estimation*
Comparing		
Two studies		
Three or more studies: diffuse tests		
Three or more studies: focused tests		
Combining:		
Two studies		
Three or more studies		

which has an associated p of 0.005, one-tailed. Thus, these two studies agree on a significant positive relationship between variables X and Y but disagree significantly in their estimates of the size of that relationship.

3.15.4.2 Combining Two Studies

3.15.4.2.1 Significance testing

While comparisons of two studies allow us to ask whether our studies differ in some way, it is also of interest to combine the two studies. By combining the significance levels of two studies, we are able to obtain an overall estimate of the probability that the two p levels might have been obtained if there truly were no relationship between the variables X and Y. We will present here the simplest and most versatile procedure combining probability levels, the method of adding Z's called the Stouffer method (Mosteller & Bush, 1954); other methods are summarized elsewhere (Rosenthal, 1978, 1991).

Like the method for comparing p values, the first step is to obtain accurate p levels for each of the two studies and then to find the Z's corresponding to those p's. The following equation is then applied:

$$\frac{Z_1 + Z_2}{\sqrt{2}} = Z \qquad (4)$$

Example 4
Studies A and B yield results in the same direction but neither are significant. One p value is 0.10, the other is 0.15, with corresponding Z's of 1.28 and 1.04. From Equation (4), we have

$$\frac{Z_1 + Z_2}{\sqrt{2}} = \frac{1.28 + 1.04}{\sqrt{2}} = 1.65$$

the p associated with this Z is 0.05. Thus, we have an example of two studies, neither of which yielded significant results when considered individually but which were significant when meta-analytically combined.
Example 5
The results of Studies A and B are in opposite directions and are both significant. One p is 0.00001, one-tailed, and the other is 0.03, one-tailed, but in the opposite direction. The Z's corresponding to these p's are 4.26 and -1.88 (note the opposite signs indicate results in opposite directions). Using Equation (4), we have

$$\frac{(4.26) + (-1.88)}{\sqrt{2}} = 1.68$$

with an associated p of 0.046. Thus, the combined p supports the finding of the more significant of the two results. However, since the two p's were so significantly different, we should

be cautious in our interpretation and should search for that factors may have led Studies A and B to have obtained such different results.

3.15.4.2.2 Effect size estimation

Once we have computed the associated Fisher z_r's for each r, the combined effect size estimate is simply

$$\frac{z_{r_1} - z_{r_2}}{2} = \bar{z}_{r_1} \qquad (5)$$

or the Fisher z_r corresponding to our mean r. We can then look up the r associated with this mean z_r (using an r to z_r or z_r to r table or statistical software).
Example 6
Studies A and B yield results in the same direction, one $r = 0.95$, the other $r = 0.25$. The Fisher z_r's corresponding to these r's are 1.83 and 0.26, respectively. Applying Equation 5, we have

$$\frac{z_{r_1} + z_{r_2}}{2} = \frac{1.83 + 0.26}{2} = 1.045$$

which is our mean Fisher z_r. This value can then be converted back to an r of 0.78 which can be interpreted as showing a rather large combined mean effect (Cohen, 1977, 1988) from these two studies.
Example 7
Study A and B yield effect sizes of $r = 0.30$ and 0.00 respectively. The Fisher z_r's corresponding to these two effect sizes are 0.31 and 0.00. Again applying Equation (5) we have

$$\frac{0.31 + 0.00}{2} = 0.155$$

as our mean z_r which is associated with a mean r of 0.15.

These last two examples also illustrate that the use of Fisher's z_r gives heavier weight to r's that are further from zero in either direction but makes little difference when working with very small r's. If we had averaged the two r's from Example 6 without first transforming them to Fisher z_r's, we would have found a mean r of $(0.95 + 0.25)/2 = 0.60$, substantially smaller than the 0.78 which we found using the Fisher z_r's. However, if we recompute Example 7 using r's instead of Fisher z_r's, we would obtain the same result: $(0.30 + 0.00)/2 = 0.15$.

3.15.4.3 Comparing Three or More Studies: Diffuse Test

The following procedures are generalizations of the procedures just described which can be used to compare more than two studies. As mentioned earlier, when dealing with three or more studies, we are able to conduct both diffuse comparisons as well as focused comparisons. We will begin with the procedures for diffuse tests.

3.15.4.3.1 Significance testing

As with two studies, the first step is to find the Z associated with each p level. The studies can then be compared using the following equation:

$$\sum (Z_j - \bar{Z})^2 = \chi^2 \qquad (6)$$

which is distributed as chi-square with $K - 1$ df. In this equation, Z_j is the Z for any one study, $\bar{Z}$ is the mean of all the Z's obtained, and K is the number of studies being compared. A significant chi-square tells us that the p's associated with our studies differ significantly among themselves.

Example 8

Studies A, B, C, and D yield one-tailed p values of 0.05, 0.001, 0.17, and 0.01, respectively. However, Study C shows results in the opposite direction from Studies A, B, and D. We find the Z's corresponding to these p's to be 1.64, 3.09, −0.95, and 2.33 (note the negative sign for Study C whose results were in the opposite direction). Using Equation (6) we find a chi-square value of

$$\sum (Z_j - \bar{Z})^2 = [(1.64) - (1.53)]^2 +$$
$$[(3.09) - (1.53)]^2 + [(-0.95) - (1.53)]^2 +$$
$$[(2.33) - (1.53)]^2 = 9.24$$

which for $K - 1 = 3$ df is significant at $p = 0.03$. The p values from these four studies, then, are significantly heterogeneous.

3.15.4.3.2 Effect size estimation

The statistical significance of the heterogeneity of the effect sizes of three or more studies is also obtained from a chi-square using the following equation

$$\sum (n_j - 3)(z_{r_1} - \bar{z}_r)^2 = \chi^2 \qquad (7)$$

where n is the number of sampling units on which each r is based, z_{rj} is the Fisher z_r corresponding to each r, and $\bar{z}_r$ is the weighted mean z_r, that is

$$\bar{z}_r = \frac{\sum (n_j - 3)z_{r_j}}{\sum (n_j - 3)} \qquad (8)$$

Example 9

Studies A, B, C, and D yield effect sizes of $r = 0.70$ $(n = 30)$, $r = 0.45$ $(n = 45)$, $r = 0.10$ $(n = 20)$, and $r = -0.15$ $(n = 25)$, respectively.

The Fisher z_r's corresponding to these r's are 0.87, 0.48, 0.10, −0.15. First, using Equation (8), the weighted mean, z_r, is

$$\frac{[27(0.87) + 42(0.48) + 17(0.10) + 27(-0.15)]}{27 + 42 + 17 + 22}$$

$$= 0.39$$

Then, applying Equation (7), we find that

$$27(0.87 - 0.39)_2 + 42(0.48 - 0.39)_2 +$$
$$17(0.10 - 0.39)_2 + 22(-0.15 - 0.39)^2 = 14.4$$

which for $K - 1 = 3$ df is significant at $p = 0.0024$. These four effect sizes, then, are significantly heterogeneous.

3.15.4.3.3 Comparing three or more studies: focused tests

While the two examples above showed us that the set of four studies were found to be significantly heterogeneous both in terms of their significance levels and effect sizes, they merely told us that overall the four studies differed. It is generally more useful to have more focused information about how the four studies differed. For example, did the prescribed treatment differ when given to women vs. men? Or, for example, did the studies in which the subjects lived in nursing homes differ from those studies in which the subjects lived with their families? In order to answer this question, it is necessary to conduct focused tests, also known as contrasts.

3.15.4.3.4 Significance levels

As with the diffuse comparisons, we first find the Z's that correspond to the p level of each study. We then compute a Z from the following equation

$$\frac{\sum \lambda_j Z_j}{\sqrt{\sum \lambda_j^2}} = Z \qquad (9)$$

In this equation λ_j is the theoretically derived prediction or contrast weight for any one study, chosen such that the sum of the λ_j's will be zero. Z_j is the Z for any one study.

Example 10

Studies A, B, C, and D were conducted to examine the efficacy of a new type of behavioral therapy. They yielded the following one-tailed p values: 0.0001, 0.03, 0.15, and 0.10, all in the same direction. We calculate the Z's corresponding to these p's to be 3.72, 1.88, 1.04, and 1.28, respectively. We also know that the amount of therapy given in each of the studies differed such that Studies A, B, C, and D involved 8, 6, 4, and 2 h of therapy per month, respectively. A focused question that would be of interest to us in this example might be whether there was a significant linear relationship between the number of hours of therapy and the statistical significance of the result. The weights of a linear contrast involving four studies are 3, 1, − 1, − 3, as obtained from a table of orthogonal polynomials (e.g., Rosenthal & Rosnow, 1991). Therefore, from Equation (9) we have

$$\frac{\sum \lambda_j Z_j}{\sqrt{\sum \lambda_j^2}}$$

$$= \frac{(3)3.72 + (1)1.88 + (-1)1.04 + (-3)1.28}{\sqrt{(3)^2 + (1)^2 + (-1)^2 + (-3)^2}}$$

$$= 1.82$$

as our Z value which is significant at $p = 0.03$. Thus, the four p values tend to grow more significant as more hours of therapy are received per month.

3.15.4.3.5 Effect size estimation

It is almost always quite valuable to the researcher to compute a focused comparison on a series of effect sizes. For example, given a set of effect sizes for studies of a new behavioral therapy, we might want to know whether these effects are increasing or decreasing linearly with the number of hours of therapy received per month. It is from the focused comparison of effects that we are able to test moderator variables and often form new theories.

As was the case for diffuse tests, we begin by computing the effect size r, its associated Fisher z_r and $n - 3$ where n is the number of sampling units on which each r is based. The statistical significance of the focused test or contrast then is obtained from a Z computed as follows (Rosenthal & Rubin, 1982a):

$$\frac{\sum \lambda_j z_{r_j}}{\sqrt{\sum \frac{\lambda_j^2}{W_j}}} = Z \qquad (10)$$

Once again, λ_j is the theoretically derived prediction or contrast weight for any one study, chosen such that the sum of the λ_j's will be zero. The z_{rj} is the Fisher z_r for any one study and w_j is the inverse of the variance of the effect size for each study. When using Fisher z_r transformations of the effect size r, the variance is $1/(n_j - 3)$, so for the present example, $w_j = n_j - 3$.

Example 11

Studies A, B, C, and D yield effect sizes of 0.89, 0.76, 0.23, and 0.59, respectively, all with n

= 12. The Fisher z_r's corresponding to these r's are found to be 1.42, 1.00, 0.23, and 0.68, respectively. We also know that Studies A, B, C, and D involved 8, 6, 4, and 2 h of therapy per month, respectively. We are interested in whether there is a relationship between number of hours of therapy received and size of observed effect favoring the new therapy. As in Example 10, the appropriate λ's are 3, 1, − 1, and − 3. Therefore, applying Equation (10) we find

$$\frac{\sum \lambda_j z_{r_j}}{\sqrt{\sum \frac{\lambda_j^2}{W_j}}}$$

$$= \frac{(3)1.42 + (1)1.00 + (-1)0.23 + (-3)0.68}{\sqrt{\frac{(3)^2}{9} + \frac{(1)^2}{9} + \frac{(-1)^2}{9} + \frac{(-3)^2}{9}}}$$

$$= 2.01$$

as our Z value which is significant at $p = 0.22$. Thus, the four effect sizes tend to grow larger as the number of hours of therapy increases.

(i) Interpretation of moderator variables

Examples 10 and 11 seem to show that number of hours of therapy is linked linearly to effectiveness of the therapy. Yet, in these hypothetical examples, subjects were not assigned at random to the four studies, each of which studied the effects of treatment employing a different number of hours per week of therapy. Therefore, our interpretation of this finding must be cautious. We cannot be sure that differences between the four studies are due to the different number of therapy hours and not to some other variable that is also correlated with this moderator. The finding should not be taken as evidence for a causal relationship, rather as being suggestive of the possibility of a causal relationship, a possibility which can then be studied experimental in future research (Hall, Tickle-Degnen, Rosenthal, & Mosteller, 1994).

3.15.4.4 Combining Three or More Studies

3.15.4.4.1 Significance testing

By combining the p levels of a set of studies, we are able to obtain an overall estimate of the probability that the set of p levels might have been obtained if the null hypothesis of no relationship between X and Y were true. The method presented here is the generalized version of the method presented earlier as applying to the results of two studies; other methods are described in detail elsewhere (e.g., Rosenthal, 1991).

As before, we first obtain the Z's corresponding to our p levels (with Z's disagreeing in direction given negative signs). The sum of the Z's is then divided by the square root of the number of studies (K) yielding a new statistic which is distributed as Z, as follows:

$$\frac{\sum Z_j}{\sqrt{k}} = Z \qquad (11)$$

Example 12

Studies A, B, C, and D yield one-tailed p values of 0.05, 0.001, 0.17, and 0.01, respectively. However, Study C shows results in the opposite direction from Studies A, B, and D. We find the Z's corresponding to these p's to be 1.64, 3.09, -0.95, and 2.33 (note the negative sign for Study C whose results were in the opposite direction). Applying Equation (11) we then find:

$$\frac{\sum Z_j}{\sqrt{k}} = \frac{(1.64) + (3.09) + (-0.95) + (2.33)}{\sqrt{4}}$$

$$= 3.06$$

as our new Z value which is associated with a p of 0.001, one-tailed. (We would normally use a one-tailed p if we had correctly predicted the bulk of the findings but would use a two-tailed p value if we had not.) Thus, we find a combined p level for the four studies that would be highly unlikely if the null hypothesis were true. Yet, we should be very cautious about drawing any simple overall conclusion from this combined significance level because of the heterogeneity of these four p levels. Example 8 employed the same p values and found that they were significantly different at $p = 0.03$. This heterogeneity, however, could be due to heterogeneity of effect sizes, of sample sizes, or both. We should always look carefully at the effect sizes and sample sizes of the studies before drawing any conclusions based on the significance levels above.

3.15.4.4.2 *Effect size estimation*

When combining the results of three or more studies, we are at least as interested in the combined effect size estimate as in the combined probability discussed above. In computing this value, we once again convert our r's to the associated Fisher z_r's and simply find the mean Fisher z_r as follows:

$$\frac{\sum z_r}{k} = \bar{z}_r \qquad (12)$$

where K refers to the number of studies being combined. We then find the r associated with this mean z_r.

Example 13

Studies A, B, and C yield effect sizes of $r = 0.70$, 0.45, and 0.10, respectively, all in the same direction. The Fisher z_r values associated with these r's are 0.87, 0.48, and 0.10, respectively. Applying Equation (12), we find

$$\frac{\sum z_r}{k} = \frac{0.87 + 0.48 + 0.10}{3} = 0.48$$

as our mean Fisher z_r, which corresponds to an r of 0.45, a rather strong combined effect of the three studies. In this example, all the effect sizes were in the same direction; however, if we had a case of three studies where effect sizes seemed to be substantially heterogeneous, we would be cautious in our interpretation of the combined effect size, just as we were in our treatment of the combined probabilities in Example (12).

3.15.4.5 Weighting Studies

When combining two or more studies, the meta-analyst may choose to weight each study by size of study (df), estimated quality of study, or any other desired weights (Mosteller & Bush, 1954; Rosenthal, 1978, 1980, 1984). The general procedure for weighting Z's is to (i) first assign to each study a given weight (symbolized by w and which is assigned before inspection of the data); (ii) multiply each Z by the desired weight, w; (iii) add the weighted Z's and; (iv) divide this sum by the square root of the sum of the squared weights, as follows:

$$\frac{\sum w_j Z_j}{\sqrt{\sum w_j^2}} = Z_w \qquad (13)$$

Example 14

We are interested in finding the combined Z from the four studies discussed in Example 12 and now we want to weight them each by their degrees of freedom which are 24, 75, 4, and 50, respectively. From Example 12, we found Z's for the four studies to be 1.64, 3.09, -0.95, and 2.33. Applying Equation (13) we now find:

$$\frac{\sum w_j z_j}{\sqrt{\sum w_j^2}}$$

$$= \frac{24(1.64) + 75(3.09) + 4(-0.95) + 50(2.33)}{\sqrt{(24)^2 + (75)^2 + (4)^2 + (50)^2}}$$

$$= 4.11$$

as our combined Z which is associated with a p of 0.00002. We should keep in mind that when weighting Z's by df, the size of the study is actually playing a doubly large role since it has already been entered into the determination of each Z initially.

We can similarly weight effect sizes by df or any other desired weight using the following equation:

$$\bar{z}_{r_{weighted}} = \frac{\sum w_j z_{r_j}}{\sqrt{\sum w_j}} \quad (14)$$

Example 15

From Example 13, we found that Studies A, B, and C yield Fisher z_r values of 0.87, 0.48, and 0.10, respectively. The df's for each study are 56, 120, and 24, respectively. Applying Equation (14), we find:

$$\begin{aligned} \bar{z}_{r_{weighted}} &= \frac{\sum w_j z_{r_j}}{\sqrt{\sum w_j}} \\ &= \frac{56(0.87) + 120(0.48) + 24(0.10)}{56 + 120 + 24} \\ &= 0.54 \end{aligned}$$

as our mean weighted Fisher z_r which corresponds to an r of 0.49, slightly larger than the unweighted mean effect size r of 0.45 which we found above.

3.15.5 SPECIAL CASES

3.15.5.1 Imprecisely Reported *p*'s

The meta-analytic procedures discussed above for combining and comparing significance levels require the meta-analyst to find the Z associated with the given p from each study. Unfortunately, it is quite common for p's to be reported imprecisely as $p < 0.05$ or < 0.01 so that p might be 0.001 or 0.0001 or even 0.00001. When this is the case, the researcher needs to go back to the original test statistic employed, for example, t, F, Z, or chi-square, which many journals require their contributors to report. The df for the t and for the denominator of the F test tell us about the size of the study. The df for chi-square is analogous to the df for the numerator of the F test and so tells us about the number of conditions, not the number of sampling units. Fortunately, the 1983 edition of the Publication Manual of the American Psychological Association has added the requirement that the total N be reported together with the df for conditions for chi-square tests. Using the reported test statistic and the information about the size of the study, we should be able to obtain the exact p value for the given test statistic and the Z associated with that p.

Occasionally, we may have information about an effect size estimator (such as r, d, or g) but not a test statistic. Using the equations in

section 3.15.4.1.2 we can often derive the associated test statistic, its exact p value, and the associated Z.

If a result is simply reported as "nonsignificant," and if no further information is available, we have little choice but to treat the result as a p of 0.50, which corresponds to a Z of 0.00. Although this procedure is ordinarily conservative leading to effect size estimates that are too small, the alternative of not using those studies is likely to lead to effect size estimates that are too large and almost surely to p values that are too significant. The recommended approach is to conduct the analysis both ways—with the studies and without the studies and to see how much of a difference it will make to the overall view of the data.

3.15.5.2 Repeated Measures Designs

A recent meta-analysis (Kramer & Rosenthal, 1997) introduced the concept of the repeated measures meta-analysis. In this situation, the question of interest concerns the difference between two or more effect sizes for each study. The meta-analysis compared the improvement in problem-solving performance when individuals were formed into noninteracting groups vs. their performance when they actually interacted as a group. A similar situation where one may be interested in a repeated measures question might be where patients' improvement is first measured one month after receiving a new treatment and this improvement is then compared to their improvement a year after receiving the treatment. One useful way to approach this type of meta-analysis is to treat it as if it were two meta-analyses whose results are then compared. In the first example above, a meta-analysis was conducted of the effect sizes associated with improvement from the individual to the non-interacting group condition. The results from this meta-analysis were then compared with the meta-analytic results of the size of the effect associated with improvement due to interaction.

3.15.5.3 Random vs. Fixed Effects

A common area of confusion is the distinction between random and fixed effects models of analysis. The fixed effects model is in the same spirit as a regression model or a fixed analysis of variance in which the treatment levels are considered fixed and the random variation is from the sample of individuals within treatment levels. With a fixed effects analysis, we are able to generalize to participants of the type found in the studies we included in the meta-analysis but we are not able to generalize to other studies.

This is because the source of sampling error in the fixed model is the variation among the people in the studies. Although our generalizability is somewhat restricted by using a fixed effects model, we gain in statistical power because our *df* are drawn from the total *N* of all the studies.

With a random effects model, our generalizability increases to all studies of the type from which our sample of studies was drawn. However, by employing a random effects model, we lose in statistical power compared to the fixed effects analysis. A simple one-sample *t*-test on the mean effect size (Mosteller & Bush, 1954) is often an appropriate random effects analysis. It will typically be more conservative than the results of the Stouffer method, but would allow for more generalizability. It is highly recommended to conduct an analysis both with a random and a fixed effects model and to compare the two methods. (For more detailed discussion of these issues, see Hedges, 1994; Raudenbush, 1994; Rosenthal, 1995a; Shadish & Haddock, 1994).

3.15.6 CRITICISMS OF META-ANALYSIS

3.15.6.1 Sampling Bias and the File Drawer Problem

One of the most frequent criticisms leveled against meta-analyses is that they are inherently biased because there is a greater likelihood that published studies will have significant results and thus might not be representative of the population of studies which have been conducted. This criticism, while well taken, could equally well be applied to narrative reviews of the literature. However, with a meta-analysis, there are now certain computational procedures that can be employed to address this problem. One visual way of examining the issue of publication bias is through the use of a Funnel Plot (Light & Pillemer, 1984), a scatterplot of sample size vs. estimated effect sizes. Another method is to compute a "file drawer analysis" (Rosenthal, 1991; Rosenthal & Rubin, 1988) as follows.

To find the number (*X*) of new, filed, or unretrieved studies averaging null results required to bring the new overall *p* to any desired level of significance (e.g., *p* = 0.05, *Z* = 1.645), the following equation may be used:

$$X = \frac{(\sum Z)^2}{2.706} - k \qquad (15)$$

where *K* is the number of studies combined and ΣZ is the sum of the *Z*'s obtained for the *K* studies.

Example 16

57 experiments have been conducted examining the effect of a new treatment for alcoholism. The ΣZ of these 57 studies was 98.6. How many new, filed, or unretrieved studies (*X*) would be required to bring this *Z* down to a barely significant level (*Z* = 1.645)? From Equation (15) we have

$$X = \frac{(98.6)^2}{2.706} - 57 = 3535$$

Thus, there would need to be over 3000 studies averaging null results tucked away in file drawers before one could conclude that the overall results of the 57 experiments were due to sampling bias.

3.15.6.2 Combining Apples and Oranges: Problems of Heterogeneity

Meta-analysis has been criticized for combining apples and oranges, in other words, for combining studies with different operationalizations of independent and dependent variables and different sampling units. This is in fact true, and a good meta-analysis will examine these differing factors as potential moderating variables as was discussed above.

Critics of meta-analysis have also pointed out the dangers of combining studies of different quality and treating them all as equal. This is an issue which can be dealt with by weighting studies according to their quality using the same procedures illustrated in Examples 14 and 15 where studies were weighted by study size. Consider the following example.

Example 17

Studies A, B, and C yield effect sizes of Fisher z_r = 0.70, 0.23, and 0.37. A group of judges rated these three studies for their internal validity and found mean ratings of 1.5, 3.4, and 4.0. Using these mean ratings as weights, the weighted combined effect size can be calculated using Equation (14):

$$\frac{\sum w_j z_{r_j}}{\sum w_j} = \frac{1.5(0.70) + 3.4(0.23) + 4.0(3.7)}{1.5 + 3.4 + 4.0}$$
$$= 0.37$$

We can conclude that weighting by quality of research in this case led to a somewhat different result than not weighting in that it lowered the perhaps somewhat elevated effect size of the poorer quality study.

Coding of studies for their quality involves having raters check each study for the presence of certain aspects, such as random assignment, experimenter blind to hypothesis, presence of demand characteristics, etc. and then adding the number of desirable features present for each study. Ratings of studies involves having raters make a more global, overall assessment of the methodological quality of a study. When establishing weightings of quality, the coding or rating should be done, as in hypothetical Example 17, by a group of disinterested judges, rather than by the researchers conducting the meta-analysis. This will safeguard against the understandable tendency to think of our own studies, of those of our students and our friends, and of those who successfully replicate our work as good studies while thinking of those studies conducted by our enemies and by those who failed to replicate our work as bad studies. Reliability of coding or rating should also be reported.

3.15.6.3 Problems of Independence

3.15.6.3.1 Nonindependence of subjects

It would not be unusual for the meta-analyst to discover multiple studies in which the same subjects have participated or that within one study subjects have contributed to more than one dependent variable. For example, a study may present the assessments of a group of subjects on a number of different measures of sensitivity to nonverbal cues. In this situation, the results generated by each dependent variable (each measure of nonverbal sensitivity) cannot be considered independent of each other since the same subjects contributed toward each one. Although it would be an error to treat multiple results from one study as though they were independent for significance testing, there is nothing wrong in doing so for the purposes of effect size estimation. By doing so, the researcher weights each study in proportion to the number of different effect sizes it generates, a procedure which meta-analysts might not choose to do but one which would not be unjustifiably wrong. Our recommendation is to use any of the procedures mentioned in order to produce only one effect size estimate and significance level for each study for the overall analysis. One option for combining the various significance levels and effect sizes would simply be to take the mean or the median Z or z_r of all the dependent variables. (The mean Z could be computed by averaging the Z's or by first averaging the z_r's and then getting the Z associated with the mean z_r; the mean z_r could also be computed by averaging the p levels and then computing the effect size that corresponds to that mean p level. These different procedures can yield different results, none of which is intrinsically more correct, but one should be chosen beforehand and used consistently through out the meta-analysis.)

However, unless the dependent variables are perfectly correlated, using the mean or the median estimates is likely to be somewhat conservative. If the meta-analyst has available the degrees of freedom and typical intercorrelation among the dependent variables, another approach, described in more detail elsewhere (Rosenthal & Rubin, 1986), can provide a more accurate combination of the effect sizes which can then be entered into the meta-analysis. This approach also allows the meta-analyst to compute contrasts among the effect sizes for the multiple dependent variables.

3.15.6.3.2 Nonindependence of experimenters

Given that researchers within the same laboratory or who once worked within the same laboratory group may have similar interests, it quite frequently occurs that several of the studies in the meta-analysis have been conducted by the same experimenter or experimental team. This may be problematic in that the results of researcher A may be correlated with those of researcher B despite the fact that they used different participants. It would be sound practice to analyze the studies by laboratory as well as by study. For example, a recent meta-analysis of the predictive power of short samples of nonverbal behavior (Ambady & Rosenthal, 1992) compared studies authored by either of the two meta-analysts to studies conducted by other researchers. The comparison showed all the effect sizes to be quite homogenous with a mean effect size of studies by the two researchers of $r = 0.38$ compared to a mean r of 0.39 by the others.

3.15.6.4 Exaggerated Significance Levels

The "criticism" that meta-analyses yield more significant results is to a great extent true. As we saw with Equation(1) (Significance Test = Size of Effect × Size of Study), as more subjects are added, either to a single study or to a meta-analysis of many studies, the results will become more significant. In fact, this is one of the benefits of conducting meta-analyses in that it allows for the cumulation of knowledge that was discussed above so that we no longer dismiss studies which have not found p's < 0.05 but rather cumulate them so that the body of work may show its overall significance level and effect size.

3.15.6.5 Too Small Effects

In contrast to the argument above, another criticism of meta-analysis is that the results of

Table 6 A binomial effect size display (BESD) of the relationship between aspirin usage and heart attacks.

	Heart attack	*No heart attack*	*Total*
Aspirin	48.3	51.7	100
Placebo	51.7	48.3	100
Total	100	100	200

some meta-analyses really only show "small effects" because the obtained *r*'s and subsequent *r*'s are small. While this may be true, it is also true that small effects can have great importance. A classic example of this is the Physician's Aspirin Study (see Rosenthal, 1995b). In 1988, a study of the effects of aspirin on reducing heart attacks was prematurely terminated. It had become clear to the physicians involved that it would be unethical to continue to give half of the subjects a placebo, since aspirin clearly prevented heart attacks. What was the *r* of this study? The *r* was 0.034, with an r^2 of 0.0011.

Table 6 presents the results of the aspirin study as a Binomial Effect Size Display (BESD), a display which allows us to see the practical importance of the effect (Rosenthal & Rubin, 1982b). The correlation is shown as the difference in outcome rates between the experimental and the control group. As the BESD shows, aspririn lead to a 4% decrease in heart attacks, a small but rather important, effect.

3.15.6.6 Abandonment of Primary Studies

Finally, critics have claimed that the growing use of meta-analysis has destroyed the motivation (or even the need) to conduct primary research studies. Certainly not: first of all, the primary studies are needed in order to do a meta-analysis. Second, the research suggested by meta-analyses can only be addressed by newly designed primary studies employing randomization. A great benefit of meta-analysis is that it will prevent unnecessary duplication, replication, and the wasting of scientifically and socially valuable resources. Conducting more meta-analyses may very well reduce the number of primary studies conducted, but it should increase the potential value of those that are conducted.

3.15.7 REFERENCES

Ambady, N., & Rosenthal, R. (1992). Thin slices of expressive behavior as predictors of interpersonal consequences: A meta-analysis. *Psychological Bulletin, 111*, 256–274.

Bausell, R. B., Li, Y., Gau, M., & Soeken, K. L. (1995). The growth of meta-analytic literature from 1980 to 1993. *Evaluation and the Health Professions, 18*, 238–251.

Blumenthal, J. A. (1998). The reasonable woman standard: A meta-analytic review of gender differences in perceptions of sexual harassment. *Law and Human Behavior, 22*, 33–57.

Cohen, J. (1977). *Statistical power analysis for the behavioral sciences* (Rev. ed.). New York: Academic Press.

Cohen, Jon (1993). A new goal: Preventing disease, not infection. *Science, 262*, 1820–1821.

Cooper, H. M. (1989). *Integrating research: A guide for literature reviews* (2nd ed.). Newbury Park, CA: Sage.

Cooper, H. M., & Hedges, L. V. (Eds.) (1994). *The handbook of research synthesis*. New York: Sage.

Crane, D. (1972). *Invisible colleges: Diffusion of knowledge in scientific communities*. Chicago: University of Chicago Press.

Dickersin, K. (1994). Research registers. In H. M. Cooper & L. V. Hedges (Eds.), *The handbook of research synthesis* (pp. 71–83). New York: Sage.

Eagly, A. H., & Carli, L. L. (1981). Sex of researchers and sex-typed communications as determinants of sex differences in influenceability: A meta-analysis of social influence studies. *Psychological Bulletin, 90*, 1–20.

Federighi, E. T. (1959). Extended tables of the percentage points of Student's t-distribution. *Journal of the American Statistical Association, 54*, 683–688.

Fisher, R. A. (1928). *Statistical methods for research workers* (4th ed.). London: Oliver & Boyd.

Fisher, R. A. (1938). *Statistical methods for research workers* (7th ed.). London: Oliver & Boyd.

Glass, G. V. (1976). Primary, secondary, and meta-analysis of research. *Educational Researcher, 5*(10), 3–8.

Glass, G. V., McGaw, B., & Smith, M. L. (1981). *Meta-analysis in social research*. Beverly Hills, CA: Sage.

Greenhouse, J. B., & Iyengar, S. (1994). Sensitivity analysis and diagnostics. In H. M. Cooper & L. V. Hedges (Eds.), *The handbook of research synthesis* (pp. 383–398). New York: Sage.

Hall, J. A., Tickle-Degnen, L., Rosenthal, R., & Mosteller, F. (1994). Hypotheses and Problems in Research Synthesis. In H. M. Copper & L. V. Hedges (Eds.), *The handbook of research synthesis* (pp. 17–28). New York: Sage.

Hedges, L. V. (1982). Fitting categorical models to effect sizes from a series of experiments. *Journal of Educational Statistics, 7*, 119–137.

Hedges, L. V. (1987). How hard is hard science, how soft is soft science? *American Psychologist, 42*, 443–455.

Hedges, L. V. (1994). Fixed effects models. In H. M. Cooper & L. V. Hedges (Eds.), *The handbook of research synthesis* (pp. 285–299). New York: Sage.

Hedges, L. V., & Olkin, I. (1985). *Statistical methods for meta-analysis*. Orlando, FL: Academic Press.

Hsu, L. M. (1980). Tests of differences in p levels as tests of differences in effect sizes. *Psychological Bulletin, 88*, 705–708.

Hunter, J. E., & Schmidt, F. L. (1990). *Methods of meta-analysis: Correcting error and bias in research findings*. Newbury Park, CA: Sage.

Kramer, S. H., & Rosenthal, R. *Why are two heads better than one: A meta-analytic comparison of individual, statistical, and interacting group problem solving.* Manuscript submitted for publication.

Light, R. J., & Pillemer, D. B. (1984). *Summing up: The science of reviewing research*. Cambridge, MA: Harvard University Press.

Light, R. J., Singer, J. D., & Willett, J. B. (1994). The visual presentation and interpretation of meta-analyses. In H. M. Cooper & L. V. Hedges (Eds.), *The handbook of research synthesis* (pp. 439–453). New York: Sage.

Lipsey, M. W. (1994). Identifying potentially interesting variables and analysis opportunities. In H. M. Cooper & L. V. Hedges (Eds.), *The handbook of research synthesis* (pp. 111–124). New York: Sage.

Mosteller, F. M., & Bush, R. R. (1954). Selected quantitative techniques. In G. Lindzey (Ed.), *Handbook of social psychology: Vol. 1. Theory and method* (pp. 289–334). Cambridge, MA: Addison-Wesley.

Raudenbush, S. W. (1994). Random effects models. In H. M. Cooper & L. V. Hedges (Eds.), *The handbook of research synthesis* (pp. 301–322). New York: Sage.

Reed, J. G., & Baxter, P. M. (1994). Using reference databases. In H. M. Cooper & L. V. Hedges (Eds.), *The handbook of research synthesis* (pp. 57–70). New York: Sage.

Rosenthal, R. (1966). *Experimenter effects in behavioral research.* New York: Appleton-Century-Crofts.

Rosenthal, R. (1978). Combining results of independent studies. *Psychological Bulletin, 85,* 185–193.

Rosenthal, R. (Ed.) (1980). *New directions for methodology of social and behavioral science: Quantitative assessment of research domains* (No. 5). San Francisco: Jossey-Bass.

Rosenthal, R. (1984). *Meta-analytic procedures for social research.* Beverly Hills, CA: Sage.

Rosenthal, R. (1991). *Meta-analytic procedures for social research.* Newbury Park, CA: Sage.

Rosenthal, R. (1993). Cumulating evidence. In G. Keren & C. Lewis (Eds.), *A handbook for data analysis in the behavioral sciences: Methodological issues* (pp. 519–559). Hillsdale, NJ: Erlbaum.

Rosenthal, M. C. (1994). The fugitive literature. In H. M. Cooper & L. V. Hedges (Eds.), *The handbook of research synthesis* (pp. 85–95). New York: Sage.

Rosenthal, R. (1995a). Writing meta-analytic reviews. *Psychological Bulletin, 118*(2), 183–192.

Rosenthal, R. (1995b). Progress in clinical psychology: Is there any? *Clinical Psychology: Science and Practice, 2,* 133–50.

Rosenthal, R. (1998). Meta-analysis: Concepts, corollaries and controversies. In J. G. Adair D. Bellanger, & K. L. Dion (Eds.), *Advances in psychological science. Vol. 1: Social personal and cultural aspects* (pp. 371–384). Hove, UK: Psychology Press.

Rosenthal, R., & Rosnow, R. L. (1991). *Essentials of behavioral research: Methods and data analysis* (2nd ed.). New York: McGraw-Hill.

Rosenthal, R., Rosnow, R. L., & Rubin, D. B. *Contrasts and effect sizes in behavioral research: A correlational approach.* Unpublished Volume.

Rosenthal, R., & Rubin, D. B. (1979). Comparing significance levels of independent studies. *Psychological Bulletin, 86,* 1165–1168.

Rosenthal, R., & Rubin, D. B. (1982a). Comparing effect sizes of independent studies. *Psychological Bulletin, 92,* 500–504.

Rosenthal, R., & Rubin, D. B. (1982b). A simple, general purpose display of magnitude of experimental effect. *Journal of Educational Psychology, 74,* 166–169.

Rosenthal, R., & Rubin, D. B. (1986). Meta-analytic procedures for combining studies with multiple effect sizes. *Psychological Bulletin, 99*(3), 400–406.

Rosenthal, R., & Rubin, D. B. (1988). Comment: Assumptions and procedures in the file drawer problem. *Statistical Science, 3,* 120–125.

Shadish, W. R., & Haddock, C. K. (1994). Combining estimates of effect size. In H. M. Cooper & L. V. Hedges (Eds.), *The handbook of research synthesis* (pp. 261–281). New York: Sage.

Smith, M. L., Glass, G. V., & Miller, T. I. (1980). *The benefits of psychotherapy.* Baltimore, MD: Johns Hopkins University Press.

Snedecor, G. W. (1946). *Statistical methods applied to experiments in agriculture* (4th ed.). Ames, IA: Iowa State University Press.

Snedecor, G. W., & Cochran, W. G. (1967). *Statistical methods* (6th ed.). Ames, IA: Iowa State University Press.

Tukey, J. W. (1977). *Exploratory data analysis.* Reading, MA: Addison-Wesley.

White, H. D. (1994). Scientific communication and literature retrieval. In H. M. Cooper & L. V. Hedges (Eds.), *The handbook of research synthesis* (pp. 41–55). New York: Sage.

Subject Index

Every effort has been made to index as comprehensively as possible, and to standardize the terms used in the index in line with the following standards:

Thesaurus of Psychological Index Terms, APA, Eighth Edition, for the selection of psychological terms.

Thesaurus of ERIC Descriptors, ERIC, Twelfth Edition, for the selection of education terms not covered by the above.

EMTREE Thesaurus for the selection of medical terms not covered by the above.

IUPAC Recommendations for the nomenclature of chemical terms, with trivial names being employed where normal usage dictates.

In general, the index follows the recommendations laid down in BS ISO 999:1996.

In view of the diverse nature of the terminology employed by the different authors, the reader is advised to search for related entries under the appropriate headings.

The index entries are presented in word-by-word alphabetical sequence. Chemical terms are filed under substituent prefixes, where appropriate, rather than under the parent compound name; this is in line with the presentation given in the *Thesaurus of Psychological Index Terms*.

The index is arranged in set-out style, with a maximum of three levels of heading. Location references refer to page number; major coverage of a subject is indicated by bold, elided page numbers; for example,

> professional licensing, oral examinations **1234–55**
> and public accountability 266

See cross-references direct the user to the preferred term; for example, character *see* personality
See also cross-references provide the user with guideposts to terms of related interest, from the broader term to the narrower term, and appear at the end of the main heading to which they refer; for example

> credentialing
> *see also* professional certification; professional licensing; recredentialing